MATTHEW ARNOLD: PROSE WRITINGS

THE CRITICAL HERITAGE

THE CRITICAL HERITAGE SERIES

GENERAL EDITOR: B. C. SOUTHAM, M.A., B.LITT. (OXON.)
Formerly Department of English, Westfield College, University of London

For a list of books in the series see the back end paper

MATTHEW ARNOLD

Prose Writings

THE CRITICAL HERITAGE

Edited by
CARL DAWSON
University of New Hampshire

and

JOHN PFORDRESHER
Georgetown University

ROUTLEDGE & KEGAN PAUL
LONDON, BOSTON AND HENLEY

First published in 1979
by Routledge & Kegan Paul Ltd
39 Store Street,
London WC1E 7DD,
Broadway House,
Newtown Road,
Henley-on-Thames,
Oxon RG9 1EN and
9 Park Street,
Boston, Mass. 02108, USA

Printed in Great Britain by
Redwood Burn Ltd
Trowbridge & Esher

British Library Cataloguing in Publication Data
Matthew Arnold, prose writings.
(The critical heritage series).
1. Arnold, Matthew - Criticism and interpretation
- Addresses, essays, lectures
I. Title. II. Dawson, Carl
III. Pfordresher, John. IV. Series
828'.8'08   PR4024   79-40780
ISBN 0 7100 0244 0

For our children
Geoffrey and Sarah Dawson
and
Peter and Rebecca Pfordresher

Contents

Matthew Arnold is of all the Victorians most to my taste: a great poet, a civilized citizen, and a prophet who has managed to project himself into our present troubles, so that when we read him now, he seems to be in the room.

E. M. Forster, 'Two Cheers for Democracy'

If Arnold is not one of the great critics, who are they?

F. R. Leavis, Matthew Arnold

Acknowledgments

Our debt to other students of Arnold and to editors of his
works should be evident from the notes and bibliography.
But our reliance on R. H. Super's magnificent edition of
Arnold's prose exceeds all that references can show. We
have also made use of editions by Frasei Neiman, Sister
Thomas Marion Hoctor, and Ian Gregor, and we have found
particularly helpful the studies of Arnold by David J.
DeLaura, Marion Mainwaring, John Henry Raleigh, Lionel
Trilling, and Sidney M. B. Coulling. Professor Coulling's
'Matthew Arnold and His Critics' (1974) reached us when
this book was essentially complete. The work of Walter
Houghton and the Wellesley Index staff has been invaluable
to this as to almost any project involving nineteenth-
century British periodicals. Professor Houghton kindly
pointed to an error of ascription in 'Matthew Arnold, The
Poetry' (Critical Heritage Series, 1973). Further corrections and suggestions have come from Professor Robert
Tener and from Dr Park Honan, who is writing a long-needed
biography of Arnold.

At various times we have had generous help from John
Rouman and W. H. Owen, from Hugh Pritchard and the University of New Hampshire library, and from Deborah Lam-
bert, Patricia Rooney, and Mary Dargon. We would like to
express thanks to the libraries of Georgetown University
and Harvard University, and to the Library of Congress,
the Huntington Library, and the British Library.

A Central University Research Council grant from the
University of New Hampshire and a fellowship from the
American Council of Learned Societies have made some of
the work on this volume possible.

The editors and publishers gratefully acknowledge per-
mission to reproduce copyright material, as follows:
George Allen & Unwin (Publishers) Ltd for an extract from
John Mackinnon Robertson's 'Modern Humanists' (No. 60);

the Estate of George Saintsbury for Nos 43 and 63; and The
Society of Authors as the literary representative of the
Estate of A. E. Housman for No. 58.

Durham, New Hampshire
Washington, DC

Note on the Text

In nearly all cases, the texts reproduced are those of the
original magazine article or the first printed version.
We have indicated deletions by spaces and have tried to
account for missing material in the appropriate headnotes
or, occasionally, in square brackets within the text. For
the most part our cuts - though more extensive than we had
hoped - still allow the intent of the original article.
We have not, however, retained many of the original foot-
notes, since these are largely page references to contemporary editions. Those few we have included are marked by
asterisks and daggers. The numbered notes are our own.
Where we reproduce a very short passage, we have deleted
material not pertaining to Arnold and have sought to avoid
what Walter Bagehot called 'the slow torture of tedious
extracts'. Whenever possible, however, we have included
pieces whole or nearly whole.

Introduction

In an age receptive to prophets, and self-admittedly in
need of them, Matthew Arnold was something of an 'anomaly'.
He would have objected to the word, but it is not inaccu-
rate. Unlike Carlyle, Ruskin, or Newman, Arnold attracted
few zealous disciples, and the few he did attract appeared
mainly towards the end of the century and in the USA. (1)
The range of his studies and his imperturbable irony no
doubt determined the response of his contemporaries, for
the critical and disinterested search for truth that he
advocated invited a sceptical reading of his own pronouncements. Though seen to be of enormous significance,
he was seldom received uncritically. When Henry Sidgwick
called him 'the Prophet of Culture' (in 1867), (2) the
phrase was clearly ironical. For what indeed was culture?
What needs did it answer? To whom would it apply? And
who was Arnold to set himself up as its apostle? Sidgwick's shrewd and representative assessment, written while
Arnold worked at 'Culture and Anarchy', remains pertinent.
Its questions still matter. But the questions matter because Arnold's views on literature and society have themselves endured.

Not many people perhaps would think of themselves as
Arnoldian. We are most of us sure of what we think to be
Arnold's limits or of where and how he failed. Yet, well
over a century after publication of 'Culture and Anarchy'
(1869), Arnold expresses important positions about literature, politics, and religion, both for people who never
consider their relationship with their society and for
those who do. Possibly because he has not had many disciples, because he has stimulated thought rather than
adulation, Arnold has influenced our thinking and our
institutions as much as any of his contemporaries. This
is not simply because he has emerged as the pre-eminent
Victorian, or the best guide to the times. The 'poet of

1

our modernity' (3) is also a prose writer who can speak to
us. If his contemporaries rightly called him illogical,
or at least unsystematic, and if he addressed his public,
in G. K. Chesterton's words, like 'the teacher in an idiot
school', (4) still the mind proved extraordinary in its
flexibility and its effect.

Arnold recognized his power. He quotes Bulwer-Lytton,
who says 'that it is no inconsiderable advantage to me
that all the writing world have a kind of weakness for me,
even at the time they are attacking me'. (5) 'However
much I may be attacked,' he writes elsewhere, 'my manner
of writing is certainly one that takes hold of people and
proves effective' (ii, 5). He was aware, sometimes overly
aware, of his critics, and probably right about his reception. In our own day, when attacks on Arnold have diminished, they have not disappeared. And as long as critics
make him an antagonist, they acknowledge the effectiveness
of his writing. The effectiveness means more than that
Arnold represents certain attackable positions or that --
on the positive side -- journals such as 'Scrutiny' and
'Essays in Criticism' or individual critics such as T. S.
Eliot, Irving Babbitt, Lionel Trilling, and F. R. Leavis
owe many of their assumptions to Arnold. It means that
Arnold informs both our critical dialogues and our notions
of liberal education. Professor Leavis has spoken about
Arnold's influence and appeal. In a comparison of Arnold
and John Stuart Mill, he writes: 'Because of the peculiar
quality of his intelligence and the peculiar nature of his
relation to his time, [Arnold] will repay special study
in a way no others will.' (6) To show the 'peculiar
nature' of Arnold's relation to Victorian England and to
hint at the 'peculiar quality of his intelligence' is the
aim of this book.

The first volume of 'Matthew Arnold: The Critical
Heritage' was concerned with the responses of Arnold's
contemporaries to his poetry; (7) this volume is concerned
with the responses to his prose. And here looms an immediate problem. The writings about Arnold in the late
nineteenth century were, as in our own day, voluminous.
His ideals of culture, perfection, style, and urbanity
were commonplaces in the writings of his countrymen, to
whom he became the foremost man of letters. In England
and the USA (though scarcely at all on the Continent), (8)
he elicited hundreds of commentaries and innumerable
incidental remarks. The mass of material has persuaded us
to several courses. First, we have grouped reviews and
essays around Arnold's principal works, sometimes to the
minor expense of chronology or to the loss of criticisms
about individual pamphlets and essays. Second, we have

excised more than we might have wished in order to offer a
wide variety of critical responses. Since 'Matthew Arnold,
The Poetry' included commentaries on the 1853 preface and
the preface to 'Merope', we have excluded responses to
these works, seminal as they are. We have also excluded
responses to 'England and the Italian Question' (1859),
both because there was little notice of this early pamphlet and because its best critic, James Fitzjames Stephen,
more than acquits himself in reviews of Arnold's later
writings.
     Some of the later writings raise a question of balance.
For nearly a decade in the 1870s, and while at the height
of his powers, Arnold devoted himself to books on theology. These studies were not a sudden aberration.
Arnold's early poetry is preoccupied with religious doubt,
and in the early 1860s, when he wrote the essays later
collected into 'Essays in Criticism, First Series', he was
involved with ideas that anticipated 'St. Paul and Protestantism' (1870) and 'Literature and Dogma' (1873).
     But from the time of their first publication, critics
have disagreed about the value and significance of
Arnold's theological books. In the 1870s, F. H. Bradley
dismissed them as nonsense (No. 42); half a century later,
T. S. Eliot called them the work of an amateur and Philistine. (9) However, the guarded approval of some contemporaries finds modern support. For Basil Willey, Arnold's
theological writings are 'the corner-stone' of his work,
(10) and Douglas Bush says that to dismiss them out of
hand 'would leave us with a very imperfect understanding
of Arnold'. (11) Many readers come to Arnold with such a
pronounced interest in his literary or social criticism
that they find the theology irritating or irrelevant.
Yet even the sympathetic reader finds problems. As David
DeLaura says: (12)

     The difficulty, first, of describing Arnold's religious
     position accurately and second, of assigning him a
     place in the history of religious speculation is com-
     pounded by the discontinuities of modern theological
     traditions and by the fact that ... the issues raised
     by Arnold are again the subject of vigorous debate.

Unfortunately, Arnold's theology is not always at the
centre of the debate. When Elliott-Binns and other historians of nineteenth-century religion discuss Arnold they
are usually less interested in 'St. Paul and Protestantism' than in 'Stanzas From the Grande Chartreuse' or
'Dover Beach'. (13) And in spite of Arnold's vigorous
quarrel with Dissenters, modern accounts of English

Protestant Dissent often fail to mention.his writings altogether. Faced with the controversial stature of Arnold's theology and with the author's own high estimate of its importance, we have chosen to include a substantial number of commentaries devoted to the religious books.

Another question of balance arises when we address Arnold's writings on education. Pervasive as his influence on educational theory and on institutions has been, (14) his professional reports and related topical pieces are understandably dated. Nor did they elicit the most thoughtful of contemporary responses. Typically, a review of The Popular Education of France (1861) for the 'Edinburgh Review' contained only a brief paragraph about Arnold in a long, tendentious argument. The 'Edinburgh's' was in fact one of few reviews of Arnold's book, and there were comparably few reviews of 'A French Eton' (1864). Arnold's next book on education fared better. 'Schools and Universities on the Continent' (1868), which proffers European models for middle-class education, appeared between 'On the Study of Celtic Literature' (1867) and 'Culture and Anarchy' (1869). Hoping to place our selections in the context of Arnold's developing positions, we have used 'Schools and Universities' to draw together a decade of criticisms about the educational writings. However, we have held to few examples, on the assumption that the issues raised in these works are manifest -- and were manifest to Arnold's contemporaries -- in the better-known books.

With the education books, as with 'Culture and Anarchy' or 'Literature and Dogma', choosing one review has meant rejecting many more. Arnold wrote, after all, in an age of prolific journalism. Despite his unrelenting censure of the 'Daily Telegraph', the 'Morning Star', the 'Nonconformist', 'The Times', and 'my kind monitor', the 'Guardian' -- and despite their healthy rejoinders -- we have chosen sparingly from these papers. The better journalism lay elsewhere: in the still respectable, if long-winded, quarterlies; in the new monthlies, like the 'Cornhill'; in the 'Academy' (founded on Arnold's principles); and in the excellent 'Fortnightly', which, along with the 'Contemporary Review', led the way towards signed instead of anonymous reviews. Among the most vigorous of the periodicals were the weeklies: the 'Athenaeum', the 'Saturday Review', and the 'Spectator'. We have included a variety of reviews from the weeklies, some by R. H. Hutton (for the 'Spectator') and Fitzjames Stephen (for the 'Saturday'), to illustrate the continuing reactions of specific periodicals and critics. (15)

Almost unavoidably, consideration of the response to

Arnold's works centres on the public reaction, which means
the reaction of periodicals. And if eminent writers no
longer hesitated to publish in magazines, clearly not all
eminent writers could address a given topic. We would want
Henry James's opinion about 'Essays in Criticism' whether
or not he reviewed the book for the 'North American
Review' (No. 9). But we might rather have what is unavailable, Newman's or Ruskin's opinion, than the opinions
of, say, S. H. Reynolds (No. 5) or E. S. Dallas (No. 10),
however acute these men may have been. 'Culture and
Anarchy' had, like 'Essays in Criticism', a number of distinguished critics, among them Sidgwick and Frederic Harrison. What is missing and can be found only in brief,
private remarks, are the views of other important contemporaries. We know that Dickens paid tribute to Arnold
when sailing from the USA; (16) that Tennyson sent a message suggesting Arnold give up his reforming and get back
to poetry; (17) that George Eliot quietly disagreed with
Frederic Harrison, telling him that Arnold's definition of
culture, if admittedly broad, was rightly broad; (18) we
know, too, that John Stuart Mill wondered why Arnold insisted on placing him among the enemies of culture, indeed as
an example of both Hellenism and Hebraism gone astray. (19)
George Eliot had written a short review of Arnold's early
poems. Otherwise, we have no substantial comment from
her, and none from Dickens, Tennyson, or Mill.

There were, nevertheless, many eminent Victorians who
wrote about Arnold. The private comments and tacit bor-
rowings of William Morris, Walter Pater, and Thomas Hardy,
for example, had their counterparts in the public assessments of Harrison, Swinburne, Leslie Stephen, George
Saintsbury, Henry James. And even the commentaries of
forgotten men and women show much about the climate of
criticism and of social and religious thought through the
last decades of the century. When, in the 1860s, Fitzjames Stephen opposed Mr. Matthew Arnold and His Countrymen (No. 6), he anticipated the scope of Arnold's debate
with his contemporaries, rightly foreseeing his singular
role. Criticism of Matthew Arnold in the nineteenth century can be read as England's comments on its own cultural
life.

'ON TRANSLATING HOMER' (1861); 'HOMER: LAST WORDS' (1862)

Arnold had, in his own words, 'inaugurated' his five-year
term as Professor of Poetry with the admirable but dull
'Merope' (the contemporary assessment still holds) and its
long, explanatory preface. The Oxford chair gave him the

opportunity to lecture on a variety of topics, more or less
when it suited him, and he chose -- no doubt to the relief
of his listeners -- to present his lectures in English
rather than in the traditional Latin. In most of the early
lectures Arnold elaborated the classical principles of
'Merope' and the 1853 preface. 'On Translating Homer',
the first published book to come from the Oxford lectures,
was in a sense the culmination of what the 1853 preface
had begun. The four Homer lectures deal, of course, with
Homer and with translation, but Arnold takes the opportunity to speak broadly about tastes and standards, about
the uses of the classics for English literature and English life.
     Writing towards the end of the century, George Saints-
bury wondered whether any of Arnold's works could have had
such 'a stimulating effect upon English men of letters' as
the Homer lectures. The lectures, he said, offered a
dramatic alternative to what had come before: (20)

> To read even the best of that immediately preceding
> criticism ... - nay, even to return to Coleridge and
> Hazlitt and Lamb -- and then to take up 'On Translating
> Homer', is to pass to a critic with a far fuller
> equipment, with a new method, with a style of his own.

Arnold alone could provide a 'synoptic' view of ancient
and modern letters.
     Such an estimate of the Homer lectures is unlikely to
be shared today, not perhaps because Saintsbury overestimated their importance, but because Homer has lost some of
his pre-eminence in the general decline of classical studies. Several of Arnold's contemporaries chided him for
anticipating a waning interest in Homer, and, in 1861,
their objection would have seemed reasonable. Arnold knew
better. The man who admitted to excessive 'Bibliolatry'
in the Homer lectures had the foresight about the Homeric
poems that he had about the Bible. 'On Translating Homer'
attempts a defence of Homer and of classical tradition in
English literature much as 'Literature and Dogma' attempts
a defence of the Bible and of its significance in English
thought. Arnold recognized the enemy of these two monumental works in the shape of future neglect.
     It was, however, timely and appropriate for Arnold to
lecture on Homer, partly because he had been criticized at
Oxford for slighting poetry, partly because Homer enjoyed
an academic vogue. There was 'a great run upon Homer',
with men as diverse as W. E. Gladstone (then Chancellor of
the Exchequer) and Professor Francis Newman adding translations to an already burgeoning list and offering commen-

taries to justify their work. As Henry Lancaster pointed
out, four new translations of Homer appeared in the
months following publication of Arnold's book. (21) And
Arnold himself, a bit coyly, included in his discussions
what amounted to brief model translations. These were
appreciated no more than the lengthy model of 'Merope'.
   On his immediate audience, those who heard him lecture
at Oxford, Arnold apparently made a strong impression. He
speaks of being 'cheered, which is very uncommon at
Oxford', and he felt, as he said, that the lectures 'were
very well received' (i, 129-30). Arnold's occasional
sallies notwithstanding, Oxford provided a sympathetic
audience. (22) But the tone of a lecture, so much a
matter of the speaker's presence, rarely carries over to
the printed page. Almost immediately after publication
the lectures drew mixed and sometimes contradictory reactions. Reviewers chastized Arnold for his 'sublime dogmatism' and complimented him for taking discussions of
Homer out of the realm of pedantry (Nos 2 and 3).
   Arnold's partly ironic but none the less merciless
whipping of Francis Newman led to a famous if dreary mid-
century controversy. For Newman, baffled and hurt,
replied to Arnold's first three lectures in a lengthy
pamphlet (No. 1), while other critics ran to his aid.
Arnold called his own 'Last Words' an attempt 'to set
things straight, at the same time soothing Newman's
feelings' (i, 139). Newman's pamphlet which appeared
before Arnold's moderate reply, is the best-known of the
contemporary responses, and it has won, as R. H. Super
remarks, a fame out of proportion to its value. (23) A
number of critics quickly pointed out that Newman's pamphlet was more erudite, in detail more correct, than
Arnold's lectures. But they admitted Newman to be a
clumsy antagonist. Insensitive to Arnold's real arguments, he makes angry lunges at dozens of points, losing
any sort of perspective. His essay is included in our
text -- in a much abbreviated form -- mainly because of
Arnold's repeated allusions.
   Arnold's contempt for Newman began in the late 1840s,
when Newman published 'The Soul' and other religious
works that Arnold thought fatuous. Newman was an 'hass',
the very opposite of his brother, John Henry Newman, for
whom Arnold always had the highest regard. Arnold no
doubt treated Francis unfairly, mocking his scholarship
and tacitly disregarding his scrupulous honesty. (24)
Francis Newman suited his purposes too well. 'Here was a
man of intellectual position, of learning and pretension,
living in a topsy-turvy world in which tobacco and religion, the Bactrian camel and democracy received almost

equal emphasis.' (25) Newman's indiscriminate enthusiasms
led him to translate 'Hiawatha' into Latin and 'Robinson
Crusoe' into Arabic. Although Arnold mentions other
translators, Chapman and Cowper, Pope and Wright, it is
mainly Newman's 'Iliad' that disturbs him. When Newman
'Newmanises', he does not merely pervert Homer; his version typifies the eccentric and the arbitrary, all that is
'ignoble' in English literature and English life.

Newman derived the basic idea for his translation from
the still debated theories of the eighteenth-century
German scholar Friedrich Wolf, who argued the oral genesis
of the Homeric poems. The assumed lack of sophistication
in the 'Iliad' involved for Newman the corollary notion
that Homer must have seemed 'quaint' to readers in the
Greek classical age. An English translation should
approximate Homer's quaintness and garrulity for ordinary
readers. In short, Newman differed with Arnold on almost
every issue, for he conceived of Homer as anything but
'plain', 'rapid', and 'noble', and his ideal judges came
from the broad public. Newman made Homer quaint by introducing terms such as 'bulkin' (meaning a calf) and 'brag-
ley' (proudly fine), concocting a vocabulary drawn from
his sense of medieval and Renaissance English. He also
argued that the nearest Homeric equivalent for English
readers was the English ballad; yet Newman's own translation so little approximated the ballad that his friend
Professor J. S. Blackie could review his 'Iliad' without
recognizing the intent -- and then in turn propose the
ballad as a suitable model. (26) As Noel Annan writes,
(27) Newman

> chose a metre which had the disquieting effect for
> American readers of being identical with that of
> Yankee Doodle --
>
>   Oh, brother, thou of me who am a mischief making
>   vixen,
>   A numbing horror....
>
> The creator of such lines was unlikely to comprehend
> a single phrase of his sardonic, well-balanced critic.

Metre emerged as a central issue for most reviewers,
just as for Arnold himself. His experimental hexameters
pleased hardly anyone, and they afforded Newman a telling
argument, since he could show that hexameters no more
suited an English version of Homer than did his own odd
verse. On this point he had the best of the debate.
'Now, to my ear', wrote James Spedding in 'Fraser's'

(No. 2),

> the movement of the best English hexameters ... is so
> very unlike the movement of any Greek or Latin hexa-
> meters ... that unless Mr. Arnold either reads Homer
> very oddly, or means by English hexameter a measure
> constructed upon a principle totally and essentially
> different from any that I have seen attempted, his ear
> is surely under some strange delusion.

Even 'The Times', which stood almost alone in approving
Arnold's theory, dismissed his examples out of hand. (28)
Most reviewers considered neither Arnold nor Newman competent to translate Homer, and several wished that Tennyson would try -- as, in a limited way, he would shortly do.
(29)
    It was easy enough to disagree with Arnold. What con-
fused critics of the Homer books was Arnold's mixing of
urbanity and cleverness with a stinging irony. If Newman
seemed dumbfounded by the Oxford professor, other critics
wondered about his manners. Should a man in his public
capacity become so personal, so apparently vindictive?
('Sometimes,' Arnold wrote, '... turning oneself one way
after another, one must make unsuccessful and unwise hits'
(i, 310). Later in the century Leslie Stephen would say,
rather archly, that he wished he had Arnold's gift for
making nasty remarks in such a pleasant manner (No. 59).
His brother Fitzjames Stephen, may have implied the same
thing when he said that Arnold refused to fight. This
utilitarian, John Bull journalist (uncle of Virginia
Woolf) had already attacked 'England and the Italian Question' and was emerging as one of Arnold's most determined
opponents. (30) In his review of the Homer lectures for
the 'Saturday' (No. 3), Stephen spoke of Arnold's 'contemptuous language' and his 'outrageous self-conceit'.
'Das grosse Ich' and 'I -- I -- I', carry-overs in part from
the rhetoric of the lectures, could offend readers, who
pointed as proof of Arnold's egotism to the first sentence
of the book: 'It has more than once been suggested to me
that I should translate Homer.' (31)
    Arnold responded to complaints about his egotism and
his acerbity by modifying the tone of the later writings
and by revising lectures before they were published. To
some extent, his ironic mannerisms, his sometimes exces-
sively patronizing repetitions, his 'quite inexhaustible
mildness', (32) in the later works are attempts to mask
the absoluteness of his judgments. Arnold perfected, as
Kathleen Tillotson says, the technique in which 'he became
regrettably expert, which might be called presenting a

bunch of snakes tied up with flowers'. (33)

Dissatisfaction with the tone of 'On Translating Homer' did not hide from all reviewers the strengths of Arnold's criticism. Henry Lancaster wrote what was at once a representative and a prophetic assessment: 'He is not a very close reasoner, but his criticism, though dogmatic, is refined and subtle, as if instinctively true'. (34) Thirty years later, A. E. Housman came to a comparable judgment. Complaining that 'On Translating Homer' was out of print, Housman had this to say (No. 58):

Who are the great critics of the classical literatures, the critics who teach with authority and not as the scribes? They are such men as Lessing or Goethe or Matthew Arnold, scholars no doubt, but not scholars of minute or profound learning.

'ESSAYS IN CRITICISM, FIRST SERIES' (1865)

'Essays in Criticism' established Arnold as the foremost English critic. Here finally, was a dominant figure in what contemporaries saw as the wilderness of English criticism. Essentially, Arnold had no rival. Ruskin's major efforts lay elsewhere; Carlyle was old and had turned away from imaginative literature. Astute critics like George Henry Lewes and Richard Simpson, writing much that was ordinary, never established clear or arresting positions. A lesser man like E. S. Dallas, who thought of himself as a new Aristotle, and whose ambition had manifested itself in a 'Poetics' (1853), lacked what Johnson, say, or Coleridge, or Arnold conspicuously offered: a powerful personal voice. Arnold himself was no Aristotle, but he was something of a Longinus, the apologist for a new sublimity, tailored to meet the needs of the age.

Like Dallas, Arnold argued for critical ideals that seemed antiromantic, at least to the extent that they proposed classical models for English poetry and found modern English literature inadequate. But Arnold's criticism, which emphasized affective rather than structural principles, fell into no simple category. Arnold espoused a new cosmopolitanism, both with the urbanity of his manner and with the European models he introduced to his readers. Understandably, but oddly, he begged off the criticism of many prominent countrymen, suggesting that such discussions would fetter him.

I am much tempted [he wrote in 1864] to say something about the Enoch Arden volume. I agree with you

[J. Dykes Campbell] in thinking 'Enoch Arden' itself
very good indeed -- perhaps the best thing Tennyson has
done.... But is it possible for one who has himself
published verses to print a criticism on Tennyson in
which perfect freedom shall be used? And without perfect freedom, what is criticism worth? I do not think
Tennyson a great and powerful spirit in any line....

Disregarding his own temptation and his readers' express
desire that he comment on modern English writers, he would
'say nothing' (i, 239). Since Arnold showed little hesitation about discussing contemporaries in other fields,
and since his hesitation extended to fiction as well as
poetry, his position remains somewhat puzzling. It is the
more puzzling when we remember his categorical statement
(in The Bishop and the Philosopher): 'Literary criticism's
most important function is to try books as to the influence which they are calculated to have upon the general
culture of single nations or of the world at large'
(Super, iii, 41).

Although Arnold maintained his reluctance to 'try' the
contemporary literature of England, his countrymen found
in his writings what they thought they needed. They found,
indeed, many of their own tacit assumptions. Arnold
shared with the bulk of his readers a distrust of frivo-
lity, of dilettantism. He followed tradition in accepting
a hierarchy of literary genres, in which the novel ranked
low. He also expressed, by his interest in the personal
genesis of literature, an implicit agreement with the contemporary faith in 'genius'. On the other hand, Arnold
emphasized -- persuasively and originally -- technical
aspects of poetry in an age that tended to think of art
primarily as inspired utterance. He had, however, drawn
back from the absolute positions of the 1853 preface --
that, for example, the business of poets 'is not to praise
their age, but to afford to the men who live in it the
highest pleasure' (Super, i. 13) -- to positions that were
scarcely less socially directed than those of his opponents. At a time when criticism was as chaotic as it was
prolific, Arnold offered an elevated and 'lucid' version
of what many writers had been aiming towards.

If Arnold's readers could agree with F. D. Maurice, the
influential Christian Socialist -- and a man whom Arnold
thought 'dim in his own mind' (i, 179) -- that Arnold's
'consciousness of possessing' 'high culture' betrayed him
into errors of dogmatism and pride (No. 4); and if 'the
Philistine portion of the English press', as Henry James
put it, often received Arnold with 'uncomprehending dis-
approbation' (No. 9), the overall response to 'Essays in

Criticism' must have pleased Arnold. In fact, he spoke of
the book (in March 1865) as 'doing better than anything of
mine has yet done' (i, 252). His comment on James's
review was: 'The "North American Review" for July had an
article on me which I like as well as anything I have
seen' (i, 309).
    James responded to Arnold's finished book. But because
reviewers had commented on the separate periodical essays
when they appeared, the reactions to Arnold's work had
continued steadily since the Homer controversy. As the
remark on James suggests, Arnold listened and replied to
his critics. 'How attentive Mr. Arnold has been to discussions raised by his opponents,' said a reviewer for the
'Athenaeum', 'and how he accepts criticism with a prudent
and graceful readiness to modify [excessive] statements.'
(35) Although Arnold's modifications were usually restate-
ments of his own positions, he was and remained 'attentive'
to critics, as page after page of his letters make clear.
In one less than elegant comment -- and after insisting as
ever that he will not 'argue' -- he writes:

> My sinuous, easy, unpolemical mode of proceeding has
> been adopted by me, first, because I really think it
> the best way of proceeding if one wants to get at, and
> keep with, truth; secondly, because I am convinced only
> by a literary form of this kind being given to them can
> ideas such as mine ever gain any access in a country
> such as ours. (i, 243)

    The implication of self-control is obvious here, even
in the contorted syntax. Elsewhere he writes: 'The great
thing is to speak without a particle of vice, malice, or
rancour' (i, 194). Such comments indicate the importance
for Arnold of 'conduct', the virtue he defined and re-
defined through the writings on culture and religion.
They indicate too, the constant tension in his prose between the polemicist or literary fighter, the man tempted
by the 'fascinating and exciting' attractions of 'newspaper writing' (i, 315), and the literary aesthete, the
man who himself would be called, as he was to call
Shelley, an ineffectual angel.
    This inner conflict in Arnold's writings raises ano-
ther, related issue. It is often assumed that Arnold's
'easy, unpolemical' style, his 'positively unscrupulous'
politeness, as G. K. Chesterton put it, (36) prompted
his critics either to devoted adulation or, especially in
the early years, to outraged dislike. And certainly
periodicals of the day were given to excesses of praise
and censure, often based on political or religious

assumptions. Recently, Sister Thomas Marion Hoctor has
written: 'From the outset, the response to Arnold as a
critic was divided. On one count only there was a kind of
unanimity: whether they enjoyed him or despised him,
Arnold's public received him with vehemence.' (37) A man
like Francis Newman was seldom less than vehement, be the
subject Homer, God, or himself; and James's characteriza-
tion of the Philistine press was also partly accurate: the
Dissenters were often angry when replying to Arnold. But
vehemence was not usually characteristic of Arnold's
critics. Rather, most, though strong in their disagreement with Arnold's ideas, strove for a measured tone in
stating their objections. Carlyle's remark on Arnold's
Heine essay, that its subject was 'a filthy, foetid sau-
sage', (38) is mercifully untypical.
    In the USA the response to Arnold tended more towards
extremes. It was in the USA that Arnold won, conspicuously
in W. C. Brownell and Melville Anderson, men who best
approximated disciples, who took his writings, critical,
social, or religious, as a kind of gospel (see, for
example, No. 46). It was also in the USA that Arnold found
some of his most aggressive antagonists. Walt Whitman, who
could admire other English writers, thought Arnold inimical
to the 'distinctive genius of our new world'. (39)

> My own criticism of Arnold -- the worst I could say of
> him -- the severest ... would be that Arnold brings coals
> to Newcastle -- that he brings to the world what the
> world has a surfeit of: is rich, hefted, lousy, reeking,
> with delicacy, refinement, elegance, prettiness, propri-
> ety, criticism, analysis: all of the things which
> threaten to overwhelm us.

There were, of course, many Americans, like Charles Eliot
Norton, who considered Arnold important but were not ready
to battle either for or against him.
    Although Arnold had, as Sister Hoctor points out, (40)
made certain enemies for life with the publication of the
Homer lectures, the ensuing controversies in England were
curiously tempered. Two good examples of this, an attack
and an endorsement, can be seen in essays by S. H. Reynolds (No. 5) and Fitzjames Stephen (No. 6).
    Like his earlier criticisms, Stephen's piece appeared
in the 'Saturday Review'. Founded in 1855, the year the
newspaper stamp was repealed, the 'Saturday' soon emerged
as the pre-eminent weekly, outstripping the older 'Athenaeum' and 'Spectator', and winning grudging respect, as
'my old adversary', from Arnold himself. Arnold might
have equated the influence of the 'Saturday' in his own

time with that of the 'Edinburgh' in the early years of
the century. 'The chief sources of intellectual influence
in England during [the last century and a half] have been
its chief organs of criticism -- Addison, Johnson, the first
Edinburgh Reviewers' (Super, iii, 41). Fitzjames Stephen
wrote regularly for the 'Saturday'. In his reviews -- anonymous, but easily identifiable for Arnold -- his position is
really that of the utilitarians, whose quantitative assessments of life could hardly be expected to welcome Arnold's
humanism. Mr. Matthew Arnold and His Countrymen (No. 6),
which prompted Arnold's My Countrymen, was published in
December 1864 in response to The Function of Criticism at
the Present Time. Stephen offers here what might have been
expected from his Homer review and what came to be a standard defence of the English intellect and character against
Arnold's subversions. He derides Arnold as a 'transcenden-
talist', who is irritatingly unaware of practical considerations.

Almost boastfully Philistine, Stephen is nevertheless
more than the 'bear in a china-shop' (i, 141) of Arnold's
description. He joins F. D. Maurice and many later critics in a basic and partly unanswerable charge: that the
risk in Arnold's criticism is its elitism. On the one
hand Arnold makes a sweeping indictment of his countrymen;
on the other hand he seems to uphold what is foreign or
past -- what in any event is unavailable for the people
whose cultural plight he laments. For how, ultimately,
will the spiritual beauties of Eugénie de Guérin or the
liberal spirit of Heine ever bear on poor Wragg in custody? Arnold seemed to Stephen to propose a way for the
already enlightened or privileged few. Wragg, he writes,
'is still in custody in Nottingham Gaol, and will be tried
at the assizes ... next month'. Like William Morris
later on, Stephen wonders whether Arnold really cares. (41)
In charging Arnold with a kind of intellectual parochial-
ism, Stephen fundamentally rejects his arguments. 'Vehement' may characterize the energy of his review, but even
at his most energetic, or most categorical, Stephen tries
to match Arnold in a show of urbanity.

The antithesis of Stephen's point of view can be seen
in an early defence of Arnold by S. H. Reynolds, The Critical Character (October 1863; No. 5). 'It contains so
much praise', Arnold wrote to Lady de Rothschild, 'that
you must have thought I wrote it myself, except that I
should hardly have called myself by the hideous title of
"Professor"' (i, 199). Written a year before The Function
of Criticism, Reynolds's review is remarkable for its sympathetic identification with Arnold's thought. Reynolds
draws inferences startlingly like Arnold's own. Arnold

could have written it himself. Did Reynolds's essay possibly help him to his conclusions, the positions in The
Function of Criticism? In any case, though Reynolds finds
minor faults in Arnold, he agrees with Arnold about the
powers of criticism, the deficiency of criticism in England, its strengths across the Channel; and he argues that,
given the intellectual chaos in English letters, 'we may
be content at present that the modern spirit in literature
should display itself as chiefly critical'. If this sounds
absurd in the age of Tennyson, Browning, Dickens, Trollope,
and George Eliot, it nevertheless approximated Arnold's own
position. Reynolds assumes Arnold's ideas; more obviously,
he uses Arnold's terms. He savours 'the grand style',
'adequacy', and 'Philistinism', repeating them as Arnold
himself and as future generations of writers were to do.
     Most of the critics of 'Essays in Criticism' were given
to less praise than Reynolds, less censure than Stephen.
They acknowledged the importance of Arnold's statements,
and they respected his ambition, although they found much
to differ with. R. H. Hutton spoke for many when he wrote
in the 'Spectator' (No. 7): 'Mr. Arnold has few equals
amongst the living masters of English prose; -- perhaps but
one....' The one is the man whom Arnold himself praises
for urbanity: John Henry Newman. Arnold has learned,
Hutton implies, from Newman's work. He shares with his
master 'the happy power of striking a clear key-note for
every separate essay or lecture in which there is neither
obscurity nor exaggeration ...' Obviously Hutton has great
admiration for Arnold, who has written 'essays that will
live'. He borrows from Arnold, modelling his prose on the
very essays under review. Yet Hutton finds in the essays
crippling limitations. If Arnold loves 'measure' in
literature, he is also too 'fastidious' (a common charge).
Worse, he is insensitive to writers like Shelley, who for
one reason or another do not fit his ideal. An able
critic, and also a magazine editor, Hutton was long to
remain a generous reader of Arnold. It may be a mark of
Arnold's contempt for even the best periodical writers
that he described Hutton as able to 'see very far -- into a
millstone' (i, 249).
     Notwithstanding his contempt for most of the journalism
and most of what stood for criticism in his time, Arnold's
own choice of medium, along with public lectures, was the
periodical press, especially the 'Cornhill' and the 'Pall
Mall Gazette'. His attacks on periodical literature
therefore coincided with his tacit admission of its importance. Henry Lancaster, in a strong endorsement of
'Essays in Criticism' (and one that Arnold appreciated,
though its author was a 'Scotchman' (i, 249)), pointed out

that 'men of the greatest ability ... do not now think it
unworthy of them to write ... in magazines'. Lancaster
allows himself the truism to make an important clarifica-
tion. For while an apologist for periodicals, he sub-
scribes entirely to Arnold's charges against bad criticism.
'The vagaries of half-educated readers have had', he says,
'no direction.' 'The virtue of [Arnold's] teaching consists in the excellence of the standards he sets up, and
in the soundness of the principles he applies.' As a
model as well as a guide, Arnold is what English periodical
criticism manifestly needs. When he 'passes from confut-
ing Mr. Adderley and Mr. Roebuck to analyze the beauties
of Maurice de Guérin, he carries his readers into a new
atmosphere of warmth and light'. (42)

The allusion to Adderley and Roebuck points once more
to an issue raised by Fitzjames Stephen. Nearly all the
reviewers of 'Essays in Criticism' admired Arnold on Joubert or the Guérins, and some readers, including Benjamin
Disraeli, even liked the notion of an English academy.
(43) Whatever their arguments they were pleased to honour
writers in foreign literatures and to respond to the framing of new and important questions. At the same time,
they were almost unanimous in their displeasure with
Arnold the social prophet, with the 'elegant Jeremiah', as
the young lions of the 'Daily Telegraph' were to call him.
Arnold's response typifies his career. For while he returned to literary criticism and soon published 'On the
Study of Celtic Literature', he answered the critiques of
'Essays in Criticism' with another kind of book, with
'Culture and Anarchy', which carried him headlong after
the Adderleys and Roebucks. To most of his readers Arnold
seemed to be compounding a mistake. Why, they wondered,
was the perfect critic to write so little *literary* criticism?

A brief, final point about the response to 'Essays in
Criticism' concerns the unity of the essays. Critics of
Arnold still argue the question, probably beyond its intrinsic importance. (44) His contemporary public acknowledged the piecemeal composition of the book and its reflection of Arnold's developing positions. But Lancaster's
sense of Arnold's setting standards and James's sense of
his taking 'high ground' imply an agreement about unity of
purpose. Hutton remarked on the 'key-note' in each essay
that at once distinguished and united disparate topics.
J. M. Ludlow, writing in the 'Reader' (No. 8), described
the unity in diversity of the collection: 'Each one ...
helps to interpret the rest; the greater the diversity of
topics, the more they conduce to the general object.'
What was the general object? Ludlow and other sympathetic

readers understood it as the improvement of taste.   'The
best that has been thought and said' points towards a principle of culture rather than a programme for or a synthesis
of poetry.   Reviewers also recognized the modifications in
Arnold's views from the 1853 preface.   In fact, they interpreted Arnold's critical ideals in relation to his
career, seeing a link between the writer of profoundly personal verse and the powerful and no less personal literary
advocate.   James's understanding of Arnold is of a finely
honed aesthetic temperament merely shifting its literary
mode.   He was as grateful for the essayist as for the poet.
'The effect of Mr. Arnold's writings', he said in 1884,
(45)

> is of course difficult to gauge; but it seems evident
> that the thoughts and judgments of Englishmen about
> a good many matters have been quickened and colored by
> them.   All criticism is better, lighter, more sym-
> pathetic, more informed, in consequence of certain
> things he has said....

'ON THE STUDY OF CELTIC LITERATURE' (1867)

'It is very difficult to satisfy oneself', Arnold wrote,
'when one has to treat a subtle matter such as I have been
treating now, the marks of a Celtic leaven subsisting in
the English spirit and its productions ...' (i, 316).
Arnold was finally satisfied with the whole of 'On the
Study of Celtic Literature', if not with each of his four
lectures.   When preparing the lectures and later when revising them for the 'Cornhill' (they appeared in the
March, April, May, and July numbers, 1866), he had doubts
about his subject, or his treatment of the subject, and
about his possible effect.   He wrote in May 1866: 'I have
... to give a lecture on Celtic poetry, of which, as the
"Saturday Review" truly says, I know nothing ...' (i, 328).
Even allowing for the humour, Arnold intimates less confidence than he felt, for example, while working at the
Homer lectures.   Here was new ground for himself as well
as for the university and the larger public.
    Still, the Celtic lectures seem naturally to grow from
the earlier lectures and to take a logical part in the
development of Arnold's critical positions. (46) They
reflect, too, what Arnold called his 'great penchant for
the Celtic races, with their melancholy and unprogressive-
ness' (i, 240).   The Celts are, in a sense, analogous to
Oxford itself, that idyllic home of lost causes.   They are
also representative of a strain in English culture, as

well as a sign of English failings. 'I hate all over-
preponderance of single elements,' Arnold wrote in a private letter: 'and all my efforts are directed to enlarge
and complete us by bringing in as much as possible of
Greek, Latin, Celtic authors' (i, 247). Hence the Celtic
lectures were to complement the Homer lectures and the
'Essays in Criticism', with the relationship clear in his
mind. In the same letter in which he deplored his countrymen's 'over-preponderance of single elements', he spoke of
what for him seemed the affective unity of 'Essays in Criticism'. The book offers a 'sort of unity' since in parts
and as a whole 'it stimulates the better humanity in us'
(i, 247).

The lectures that materialized as 'On the Study of
Celtic Literature' may have lost some of their appeal because of Arnold's immediate cultural or educational
intent, but they remain as important historically as they
are dated. They led, as Arnold hoped they might, to the
founding of a Celtic chair at Oxford (the first holder
being John Rhys, who as a young man heard Arnold's first
Celtic lecture); more seminally, they anticipated and
served the apologists of the Celtic Revival, a quarter of
a century later. As Frederic Faverty says, Arnold became
'a patron saint of the Celtic Renaissance'. (47) Even
Yeats drew much of his information from Arnold, at the
same time 'correcting' his errors of fact or interpretation. (48) Fiona McLeod (in 1899) identified Arnold along
with the man who prompted Arnold's own studies as the
forces behind the Celtic Revival: (49)

Renan's essay in France and Arnold's in this country
and America, were the torches that lit so many brands,
or, let us say, were the two winds which fanned the
Celtic flame which is now one of the most potent influences in contemporary literature.

Arnold may, however, have been put to uses of which he
would not have approved. John Kelleher suggests that
minor Celtic apologists of the 1890s were to reproduce
'element for element Arnold's picture of Celtic literature, with the difference that every weakness Arnold
deplored in the Celt and his works has now become a
characteristic strength'. (50)

The contemporary response to the Celtic papers began in
the 'Philistine' press, which saw in them yet another
broadside aimed at the middle class, possibly even as an
attack upon England itself. 'The Times', for example,
responded vigorously to Arnold, although not immediately
to 'Celtic Literature' (No. 12). Arnold's letter to

Sir Hugh Owen, declining an invitation to speak at the
annual Eisteddfod (the revived Congress of the Welsh
Bards), appeared in 'The Times' for 6 September 1866.
A few days later 'The Times' editorialized:

> Mr. Matthew Arnold himself, who appears more Welsh than
> the Welsh, professes a desire 'to avoid the danger of
> giving offense to practical men by retarding the spread
> of the English language in the Principality.' But he
> believes that 'to preserve and honour the Welsh lan-
> guage and literature is quite compatible with not
> thwarting for a single hour the introduction ... of a
> knowledge of English throughout all classes in Wales.'
> We must be permitted to say plainly that this is arrant
> nonsense.

Evidently Arnold's work with Celtic studies did not
'stimulate the better humanity' of 'The Times'. Their
article serves to illustrate all that Arnold found smug,
mean-spirited, and narrow in English journalism. For 'The
Times' the issues are simply not those of Celtic literature, which is beneath contempt: they are, first, issues
of taste and, second, issues of nationality and power.
   The 'Daily Telegraph', also pouncing on Arnold's letter
to Owen, found what 'The Times' found and more. 'Mr.
Arnold has done it at last.' This 'elegant Jeremiah', this
'high priest of the kid-glove persuasion', has proved himself an arrogant coxcomb. 'The time has not come for recognising as a Jeremiah the man who can pen pretty verses,
turn pretty sentences, and express pretty sentiments.
There is no analogy ... between a prophet and a fop' (No.
13). 'I take the "Star" for wisdom and charity,' Arnold
wrote in 'Friendship's Garland', 'and the "Telegraph" for
taste and style' (Super, v, 48). James Macdonell, a young
Scot who had been hired by the 'Telegraph' for his pungent
writing, admitted privately that he had delivered the
attack on Arnold: (51)

> In a savage article, written by way of retort to
> Arnold's fling at 'the magnificent roaring of the young
> lions of the "Daily Telegraph"' ... I called him 'an
> elegant Jeremiah.' He didn't like the phrase; but it's
> true for all that, and he was never more emphatically
> an elegant Jeremiah than in the present volume ['St.
> Paul and Protestantism']. Still, Arnold is the most
> delicate of living English critics....

Macdonell's unexpected praise emphasizes the astuteness
of Bulwer's remark: that even Arnold's enemies were

attracted to him. Macdonell's public statement, on the
other hand, represents the 'Daily Telegraph's' hammering
at Arnold through most of the decade. After 1867, the
'Telegraph' roared a little less, softening critiques and
evidently making gestures of conciliation. Arnold's strictures on the paper continued for several years, stopping --
it has been suggested -- only at the threat of a law suit
from G. A. Sala, the paper's energetic editor. (52). This
leader of the young lions wrote in a memoir, and without
mention of the law suit: (53)

> How little people know about one another, to be sure!
> There was brilliant, whole-souled Matthew Arnold, who
> was so fond of snarling and sneering at the journalists
> whom he called 'the young lions of the "Daily Tele-
> graph."' Bless and save us! When he was jibing, some
> of the writers whom he assailed were growing middle-
> aged lions; and three of us ... [were] rather ancient
> lions.

In spite of unpleasant remarks from 'The Times' and the
'Telegraph', Arnold had reason to say (in May 1866): 'The
Celtic papers are certainly producing an effect beyond
what I had ventured to hope' (i, 329). He had worried
about the lectures proving too 'scientific' for the
'Cornhill', and he was convinced that 'a more hopeless
subject in itself to approach the British public with one
could hardly imagine' (i, 329). But if 'The Times' and
the 'Telegraph' represented common attitudes towards John
Bull's other territories, in fact, as the 'Athenaeum'
pointed out the following year, Arnold was having an
effect: 'The Celt begins to attract his full share of
the public attention'. (54)
The response of newspapers to the Celtic pieces was
straightforward enough; that of qualified judges is more
difficult to define. There were, of course, many people
competent to assess Arnold's explorations into the Celtic
twilight. Interest in Celtic studies had continued, with
fluctuations, since the eighteenth century, as amateurs
like T. L. Peacock, poets like Tennyson, and scholars like
D. W. Nash would illustrate. Professor Kelleher has
argued that 'until 1892 or after, nobody in Ireland paid
any serious attention to what Arnold had to say on any
Celtic or Irish subject' and that no contemporaries
offered 'competent rebuttals' to Celtic literature. (55)
A political change would be necesary before any Englishman, frankly addressing his own countrymen, might be
acceptable to nationalist Irishmen. But well-grounded
opposition to Arnold's work appeared early, and some of
the best came from sympathetic Celts.

Robert Giffen, the Scottish economist (writing in July 1867, No. 14), recognized Arnold's desire to stimulate a wide audience in a non-partisan way about essential and overlooked issues. 'The chief value of the book will consist in its tendency to produce [a public reaction] by popularizing the Celtic case.' Giffen, who ran counter to the 'Fortnightly's' inclination to disparage Arnold's prose, did however point to flaws in Arnold's assumptions while praising the intent and the methods of the book. Mainly, Giffen accuses Arnold of pseudo-science. Instead of elaborating mistakes about language and race, he should have concentrated on what he knew. 'Mr. Arnold [ought to have] devoted even more space to the latter questions -- the originality and value of Celtic literature -- instead of entering on the more doubtful question as to what Celtic fibre there is in Englishmen.'

Giffen's arguments were amplified in Henry Stuart Fagan's review in the 'Contemporary' (for October 1867). Like Giffen, Fagan emphasizes the absurdity of Arnold's ethnological pronouncements:

> Now, a Philo-Celt's first impulse on looking through Mr. Arnold's book is to thank Nemesis for having brought the son of such a Celt-despising father to write as he has written. His next is to ask himself whether all this talk about Celtic extravagance and 'sentimental reaction against the despotism of fact,' is wholly true to the national character.

He finds that Arnold's 'very suggestive' book includes too many 'wild assertions' about racial and nationalistic character. (56) At a time of proliferating racial theories, both Fagan's and Giffen's reviews were more than commentaries on Arnold's inadequate notions. They were acute assessments of scholarly as well as popular myths.

When Arnold came to publish the 'Cornhill' pieces in book form, he spoke of doing 'penance in a little preface' -- after the 'inhuman attacks of which I have been made the victim in "The Times" and "Daily Telegraph"' (i, 338). As usual, he employed a preface to reply to critics of the work in its periodical format, blending the polemical with the intrinsic issues of the book. He used the preface to 'Celtic Literature' for another, less 'ignoble', penance, an acknowledgment of his debt to Lord Strangford, 'a savant of the very first force on these subjects' (i, 323). In March 1866 (No. 11) and again in September, Strangford, a friend of Arnold and a noted linguist, wrote shrewd little assessments of Arnold's essays. Strangford questions Arnold's etymologies, his premises as to the origins

of languages, his facts about modern Irish. Acknowledging
Arnold as a useful cultural middle man with a sympathetic
intelligence, Strangford leaves no doubt that his friend,
for all his wide reading, remains an amateur student of
Celtic literature. A sign of Arnold's own candour and
modesty was his welcoming Strangford's corrections. When
writing the preface he awaited Strangford's information
about 'one or two points', 'points where I have no doubt I
am fearfully shaky'. (57) He then included the corrections in his book, though they tended to be, as Robert
Giffen pointed out, 'destructive of a good deal of the
philological matter he had originally ventured to use'.
It is characteristic of Arnold that he would put together
the bullying remarks of the daily papers with the astute
and scholarly remarks of Strangford when he offered his
book to the public.

   Arnold's explorations of Celtic literature were short-
lived and were only to have their full effect in later
years. But while the public soon forgot his little book,
Edward Burne-Jones indicated that some people continued to
read it. (58)

   There was a brilliant and really fine set of essays by
   Matthew Arnold on the study of Celtic Literature,
   based entirely on guesses, but demonstrably right
   guesses. He knew absolutely nothing about the subject,
   but he scented the truth from afar. Besides that poor,
   thin little volume there is not a line that I know of
   in English to hint that anyone knows or cares for it.
   Even [William] Morris doesn't, who knows about everything.

Burne-Jones's comment anticipates the opinions Yeats would
express in The Celtic Element in Literature, and Yeats,
writing near the turn of the century, still draws on
Arnold's 'poor, thin little volume' more than he cares to
admit.

'SCHOOLS AND UNIVERSITIES ON THE CONTINENT' (1868)

Speaking of himself as a 'sincere but ineffectual liberal',
Arnold reminded his readers, in Porro Unum Est Necessarium,
of the inadequacy of English schools: 'For some twenty
years I have been full of this thought, and have striven
to make the British public share it with me; but quite
vainly' (Super, viii, 348). His comment, with its rueful
modesty, was partly true. Arnold never did convince the
British public that they had failed to educate themselves

and were, because of their insular smugness, systematically depriving their children. Throughout his career
Arnold remained something of an ineffectual liberal: an
idealist, who seemed to be addressing future generations
and to be thinking -- despite his protestations -- about the
salvation of a few. The irony of Arnold's position, as
Raymond Williams has shown, is that his vision of culture,
though intended to be broad and pervasive, appeared to his
contemporaries as narrow and privileged. (59) There is a
further irony when we consider his writings on education,
because, from the outset, Arnold addressed himself to the
question of education for all. And precisely where there
should have been no misunderstanding, his readers did con-
trive to misunderstand.

At the same time, Arnold's efforts proved far from
vain. His effect as an educational theorist should be
measured not in terms of contemporary reviews but in terms
of results, and his own dissatisfaction with his influence
may reflect a tendency to overvalue the reactions of the
press. Yet Arnold did have cause for impatience. He
spent much of his career opposed to Robert Lowe's Revised
Code (of 1862), which instituted the dubious principle of
'payment by results', and by the time of his death Lowe's
system had still not been displaced. Nor was there, in
1888, a Minister of Education, overseeing the entire educational situation of the country. Arnold had urged such
a reform for almost forty years. It is evident, nevertheless, that Arnold, along with Kay-Shuttleworth, helped
to modify Lowe's proposal, so that not all payments to
schools hinged on examination results, and also that
subsequent education acts reflected his efforts. Arnold
may not have been happy with Forster's Education Act of
1870 (Forster was his brother-in-law), but that act and
any number to follow (including the reform of 1944) are
partly attributable to what he told his countrymen. (60)

Arnold's views on education had been developing at
least since 1851, when, through the influence of Lord
Lansdowne, he became an inspector of schools. He accepted
the position with reluctance and often complained about
the amount of work, but it was as an inspector, as a man
immersed in the practical questions of education, that he
spent most of his career. His professional reports, which
show his ability to make specific suggestions and to theo-
rize about large problems, won the recognition of superiors. In 1859 (for the Newcastle Commission) and in 1865
(for the Taunton Commission) he supplemented his experience in English schools with observations of schools on
the Continent. In the 1880s, a few years before his
death, he served as an authority for the Cross Commission

and as a direct source for many of its recommendations.

Arnold's writings on education include his reports as inspector (these were first published in 1889) (6) and the books which grew from his observations of foreign schools. In 1861 he published 'The Popular Education of France'; this was followed by 'A French Eton' (1864), 'Schools and Universities on the Continent' (1868), 'A Bible-Reading for Schools' (1872), some of the pieces in 'Mixed Essays' (1879), and A Special Report on ... Elementary Education in Germany, Switzerland, and France (1886). But with little or no distortion, nearly all Arnold's prose may be considered to be educational. In 'Culture and Anarchy' Arnold speaks of the *social idea* of the men of culture, of their 'passion for diffusing culture'. The many discussions of 'equality', of the functions of criticism, of the reason for Celtic studies, presuppose Arnold's conviction that the English of all classes need education. He said in Porro Unum:

> If there is one need more crying than another, it is the need of the English middle class to be rescued from a defective type of religion, a narrow range of intellect and knowledge, a stunted sense of beauty, a low standard of manners. (Super, viii, 369)

The alternative to the civilizing force of education is anarchy. And to forestall anarchy the *state* (itself a kind of literary academy writ benevolent and large) must assume the burden of education.

Because Arnold's views on education mix inextricably with his views about literature and society, much of the contemporary criticism of his writings overlaps. A critique of 'Popular Education of France' (which includes the seminal Democracy, later republished in 'Mixed Essays') is likely to contain the same charges as a critique of 'Culture and Anarchy', though the one predates the other by eight years. To take an example, Henry Reeve, the distinguished editor of the 'Edinburgh Review', wrote a piece for the 'Edinburgh' called Popular Education in England (1861). Reeve was, in his upbringing and schooling, more cosmopolitan than Arnold himself, and far more familiar with Continental education. But his omnibus piece for the 'Edinburgh' typifies the insularity of a generation of Arnold's critics, who found it hard to admit that institutions might be better abroad. What Reeve says anticipates any number of later critiques. He equates state control with a threat to liberty, and, in short, prefers English muddle to French order: (62)

We are unwilling to speak with any harshness of the
opinions of Mr. Matthew Arnold, whose name, whose
talents, and whose character entitle him to our regard
and respect. But we must say that the whole tone of
his Report on the popular education of France betokens
a propensity to adopt the bureaucratic spirit of continental administration to a degree which is painful and
repugnant to the mind of every liberal Englishman.
God forbid that public spirit in this country should be
so dead ... that we should consign our first social
concerns to the paid officials of the State, and make
State administration the panacea of social evils!

Reeve's judgment clarifies an essential difference between
Arnold's positions and those of his countrymen. For
Arnold, democracy must be predicated on equality; for most
of his countrymen, democracy meant liberty. On this question Reeve was at one with Stephen and Macdonell, with
Edward Miall and the Dissenters (No. 20), and of course
with John Stuart Mill.

There was, as we have said, relatively sparse notice
of Arnold's educational writings, and though Arnold himself considered 'A French Eton' among the best of his
books (i, 231), the few reviews of the work worried the
same issues that Reeve had worried and let the work lie.
(63)

Our selections from the criticisms of Arnold's educational books are reviews of 'Schools and Universities on
the Continent' (1869). Several distinguished writers commented on this work. F. W. Farrar, later Dean of Canterbury, recognized the justice in Arnold's strictures of
English education, and in his sympathetic assessment (for
the 'Fortnightly', No. 15), he supported Arnold's call for
reform. On the other side, Thomas Markby (in the 'Contemporary') defended whatever Arnold attacked and, by over-
looking Arnold's irony and missing his key arguments,
showed his inability to understand. (64) Not so Oscar
Browning, who disagreed with Arnold but who spoke with
authority (No. 17). A master at Eton and a Cambridge
fellow, Browning questioned Arnold's capacities as an
observer -- a fair criticism, since Arnold's poor planning
caused him to arrive at several institutions when they
were closed for vacation. Browning rightly accuses Arnold
of drawing inferences from inadequate observation. He is
even more concerned about Arnold's exaggeration of European virtues and English shortcomings. Ironically,
Arnold's own letters from abroad consistently praise
England and belittle Prussian Philistinism or Belgian incompetence. Yet in his public writings he habitually

points to a foreign excellence in order to find fault with
England.
   A further critique of 'Schools and Universities' came
from the recent author of 'The English Constitution'. In
the 'Fortnightly' (No. 16) Walter Bagehot called Arnold
to task for criticizing London University without knowing
the institution. His essay is a rare consideration of
Arnold on higher education (see also Thomas Huxley, No.
48). For although Arnold anticipated and to a great
extent helped to determine university curricula in England
and the USA, his main writings on education were directed
elsewhere. Bagehot's review expresses great respect, but
Bagehot doubts that Arnold, bred to the seclusive retreat
of Oxford, can understand the needs of a university in an
urban society. Implicitly, he accuses Arnold of an ideal
too close to that of John Henry Newman. Since 'there
never was a time in English history when there was such an
appetite for knowledge', the university must be open,
diverse, and able to bear directly on its society.
   In spite of profound disagreement as to means, Bagehot
shares with Arnold a hope for the improvement of society
by its educational institutions. But it is typical of
Arnold's opponents that even Bagehot overlooks the intensity of his convictions. Like Stephen, Bagehot applauds
Arnold for style and brilliance. 'In the long-run',
Arnold had written, 'one makes enemies by having one's
brilliance and ability praised' (i, 219). Arnold always
thought of his rhetoric as a means to an end. He speaks
in 'A French Eton' about man 'climbing upwards to his perfection' (Super ii, 325). The desired effect of criticism
as of education is culture, and for Arnold culture involves 'the humanization of man in society' (Super, viii,
370). 'Culture and Anarchy', his next book, addresses
itself to the practical and theoretical problems of the
humanizing process.

'CULTURE AND ANARCHY' (1869) and 'FRIENDSHIP'S GARLAND'
(1871)

Towards the end of the 1860s Arnold said, as though it
surprised him, that he was coming to have 'a considerable
effect' (ii, 11). At the least he had become a common
topic of debate. The 'Saturday', the 'Spectator', 'The
Times', the 'Fortnightly', 'Macmillan's', the 'Edinburgh',
the 'Quarterly', as well as the 'Daily Telegraph', the
'Daily News', and other papers, had all discussed his
writings, argued with them, made their judgments. 'Mr.
Matthew Arnold has a claim to be heard,' wrote a reviewer

for the 'Nonconformist' in 1866. (65) Without question,
Arnold did make himself heard in these active years. He
wrote prolifically, published his last important edition
of poems (1867), and, whether as a professional addressing
European education or as an amateur discounting the
Deceased Wife's Sister's Bill, contributed steadily to
periodicals. Yet while it was 'considerable', his influence was somewhat different from what he hoped it would
be. The 'Saturday' could write (in 1869) that Arnold was
already 'in the ranks of the played-out' as an English
Socrates, though as a poet and critic he had still to be
reckoned with. (66) Long before the end of the decade,
Arnold had established himself as the 'Apostle of Culture',
the arch-foe of Philistinism, and to some of his critics
he had become more a symbol of a point of view than a
reforming teacher.

His odd position bears on the response to 'Culture and
Anarchy' and 'Friendship's Garland', since neither of
these books as books received many reviews. The lack of
critical interest may have reflected the fact that,
excepting the preface to 'Culture and Anarchy' and the
short Dedicatory Letter to 'Friendship's Garland', the
materials of both volumes had long been known to Arnold's
readers. According to the 'Saturday', people not only
knew Arnold's writings, they had also made up their minds
about them. The important response to the two Anarchy and
Authority books is the response to Arnold's individual
essays as they appeared in the periodical press. So, for
instance, the first appearance of My Countrymen in the
'Cornhill Magazine' for February 1866 caused a stir that
delighted Arnold. He wrote to his mother that 'most of
the ... weekly newspapers mention it as the event of the
"Cornhill", very witty and suggestive ...' and reported
that, from the gossip he had heard, 'Carlyle almost wholly
approves ...' (i, 316-17). For each of the following
essays, Arnold could count on prompt and extensive commentary from a range of attentive critics.

In a sense, the critics became a part of 'Culture and
Anarchy' and 'Friendship's Garland'. As the individual
essays appeared, and as critics reacted, Arnold continually reconsidered his ideas along with the form in which
he expressed them. In the preface to 'Culture and
Anarchy' Arnold quotes himself, not untypically, addressing an eminent Nonconformist manufacturer: '"Ah, but, my
dear friend," I answered, "only think of all the nonsense
which you now hold quite firmly, which you never would
have held if you had not been contradicting your adversary
in it all these years!"' (Super, v, 244). The comment
could be justly applied to Arnold himself. When he

gathered his assorted pieces into book form, he revised
them, once again deleting the unkindest of his remarks,
remarks which might offend or might lose currency in a
finished book. In their final versions, nevertheless,
both 'Culture and Anarchy' and 'Friendship's Garland'
remain records of controversy -- whole books to be sure,
but local, specific, and dynamic, in that they grew with
Arnold's responses to his critics.

A record of the criticisms of 'Culture and Anarchy', as
R. H. Super has said, 'is almost a history of criticism of
Arnold in general' (Super, v, 416). This long and complex
history is beyond the scope of an introduction. Moreover,
the record is now fairly complete, as presented by Professor Super himself, by Martha Vogeler and Ian Gregor,
and especially by Sidney M. B. Coulling. (67) Here we
need only add a few notes about the dominant contemporary
issues and about some of the readers who most influenced
Arnold.

There were, essentially, two kinds of readers who influenced Arnold during these years. In addition to the
public press, he cared a great deal about his private audience. His sister, Mrs Forster, one of his favourite
readers for his poems, became also a valued reader of his
prose. So, too, did Lady de Rothschild, a frequent correspondent and sympathetic listener. The reader Arnold
most cared for, in this private circle, would seem to have
been his mother, partly because of her own insights,
partly because she represented the continuation of his
father's ideals. References to Thomas Arnold recur with
intriguing frequency through the correspondence of these
years, and Arnold often asks himself whether his father
would have been pleased with his books and to what extent
he was completing his father's work. (68) In short, the
dead father is very much in Arnold's mind as he writes,
possibly more in his mind than the antagonists of the
press. A letter of 1868 serves to illustrate Thomas
Arnold's importance:

> The nearer I get to accomplishing the term of years
> which was papa's [he writes to his mother], the more I
> am struck with admiration at what he did in them. It
> is impossible to conceive him exactly as living now,
> amidst our present ideas, because those ideas he him-
> self would have so much influenced.... Still, on the
> whole, I think of the main part of what I have done,
> and am doing, as work which he would have approved and
> seen to be indispensable. (i, 391-2)

But Thomas Arnold's response to his son's writings was a

matter of speculation, even for Arnold himself. What concerns us here is the public response, and that was articulate enough.

The articles that became 'Culture and Anarchy' and
'Friendship's Garland' were more harshly received than
'Essays in Criticism'. For although Arnold's conception of
criticism went beyond the specifically literary, readers of
'Essays in Criticism' could focus on the discussions of
Maurice de Guérin or Heine while objecting to the socially
pointed arguments of The Function of Criticism. Even more
than the Celtic lectures, the Anarchy and Authority essays
invited readers to take positions. Edward Miall and the
Dissenters rejected the interpretations of puritanism in
English life, just as they dismissed Arnold's call for
national education. Liberals (who might be Dissenters)
scorned Arnold's ineffectuality, his 'really effeminate
horror', as the 'London Illustrated News' put it, 'of
simple, practical, common-sense reforms'. (69) Critics of
various persuasions objected to Arnold's concept of the
State, since most were confirmed believers in 'doing as one
likes'. There was also fairly unanimous agreement about
the intangibility of words like 'Geist'. C. S. M. Phillips
complained about Arnold's 'invincible reluctance to take the
trouble of explaining and defining'. (70) The reluctance
implied more than manipulation of terms: here again Arnold
seemed to be tilting at English character and English life.

To sketch the nature of Arnold's opposition, we might
look at two of his most prominent critics. Henry Sidgwick
and Frederic Harrison were not typical in their intellectual powers, but they were typical in the objections they
made to Arnold's work -- and in the way Arnold made them a
part of his work.

Sidgwick, a Cambridge philosopher who had been influenced by John Stuart Mill, was beginning his career when he
published The Prophet of Culture in 'Macmillan's' (August
1867; No. 21). He opens his article by speculating about
the changes in periodicals occasioned by the shift from
anonymous to signed essays, and he sees one of the profoundest developments as being the advent of one writer. 'We
did not, in short, foresee a Matthew Arnold.' Sidgwick's
acknowledgment is of Arnold's stature as well as his fame,
and it indicates the degree of attention Arnold's writings
had won. Sidgwick is, however, troubled rather than elated
by Arnold's success. 'The Prophet of Culture' masks with
his 'airy dogmatism' shallow religious thinking and vague
analysis of social forces. With his sweeping distinctions,
categories, and assessments, Arnold reminds Sidgwick of
Hegel's interpretation of history. The difficulty is that
Arnold lacks a philosophic mind. He 'skims over' ideas

'with a lightly-won tranquillity', whereas 'a man ought
not to touch cursorily upon [a subject] without showing he
has mastered the elements of the problem'. His sallies at
the Nonconformists are petty in themselves and illustrat-
ive of large misunderstandings about history and about
culture. Even as he defines culture, Sidgwick thinks,
Arnold remains inadequately 'curious'. 'The root of
[Arnold's] culture, when examined critically, is found to
be a refined eudaemonism....' So Arnold reveals himself
as a hedonist who fails to examine his own positions. He
is also something of a hypocrite. With an Arnoldian turn
of phrase, Sidgwick says: 'I cannot see that intellectual
Pharisaism is any less injurious to true culture than
religious Pharisaism to true worship....' Finally Sidgwick compares the serious philosopher, Plato, with 'the
cheerful modern [Arnold], tempered by renouncement, shuddering aloof from the rank exhalations of vulgar enthusiasms, and holding up the pouncet box of culture betwixt
the wind and his nobility'.

Just as Sidgwick may be thought to represent Cambridge
and the basically liberal assumptions of John Stuart Mill,
Frederic Harrison (No. 22) represents English Positivism.
Harrison became indeed one of the foremost exponents of
Comtian philosophy in England. At the time he published
Culture: A Dialogue (in the 'Fortnightly', November 1867),
he was a young Oxford scholar. As Arnold knew and had
made use of in his final Oxford lecture, Harrison had
become unpopular in the university because of his defence
of working-class movements and his radical religious positions. One irony in Arnold's repeated allusions to the
Oxford Positivist is his tacit agreement with Harrison on
a number of issues. Martha Vogeler has shown that Harrison's Positivism often coincided with Arnold's understanding of culture. (71) Although the two men differed on
matters of education and the Church (Harrison opposed
national education and considered Arnold a friend of and
to the church establishment), Harrison's later observation
makes sense: Arnold had in part been 'talking Comte without knowing it' (No. 61). Already in 1867 an anonymous
writer in the 'Daily News' (No. 23) compared Arnold and
Harrison and pointed out that Arnold came very close to the
Comtian positions he attacked.

At various times in his career Harrison opposed Arnold.
He spoke, for example, in Our Venetian Constitution about
'the very silliest cant of the day ... , the cant of culture'. (72) Yet he respected his antagonist and ultimately
praised him as a thinker as well as a poet (No. 61). In
Culture: A Dialogue (No. 22), Harrison turns Arnold upon
himself in a witty and astute critique of Arnold's social

philosophy. Culture: A Dialogue *is* a dialogue, a form
that Arnold himself used with difficulty, in spite of his
reputation as a self-styled Socrates. Several of Arnold's
critics accused him of writing prose effusions, meditations without discipline or logic, and if they overlooked
the rhetorical strengths of his essays, they indicate why
Harrison's zany conversations would be seen as implicit
criticism of Arnold's style. Arnold as usual read the
article immediately and later addressed himself to its
charges. He found it 'so amusing that I laughed till I
cried' (i, 372).

Introducing Arnold's own Arminius, Harrison pretends to
have encountered the opinionated Prussian and to have
spoken with him about his compatriot. Arminius criticizes
Arnold directly, while Harrison acts as a tongue-in-cheek
innocent. In defence of Arnold's definitions of culture,
Harrison says to Arminius: 'A master of style like our
teacher may put his own sense on the word, I suppose?'
Harrison's substantive points are familiar and close to
those of Sidgwick: Arnold is all very well, but what does
he mean? And why does he toy with matters beyond his
grasp? Harrison's deepest irritation -- and it was perhaps
the basic objection to 'Culture and Anarchy' -- comes in
this outburst from the irascible Arminius: 'In the name of
human woe, what Gospel does this offer to poor stricken
men?' Harrison shared with the entire liberal press the
conviction that the 'liberal of the future' was elitist as
well as self-contradictory. If culture does remain disinterested, seeking out the best, holding to sweetness and
light, how can Arnold concern himself with opposing the
meagre reforms of divorce, or the Deceased Wife's Sister's
Bill? To delay reform in the name of future culture is to
betray humanity for false, because vague and unrealizable,
ideals. Harrison might have pointed out that, in matters
of education, Arnold had no compunctions about supporting
limited reforms.

Both Harrison and Sidgwick were writing long before
publication of 'Friendship's Garland' and well over a
year before the appearance of 'Culture and Anarchy' in its
final form. Yet their responses to Arnold, extending and
refining the objections of earlier critics, characterize
the public reaction to Arnold's social and political works
from the time of The Function of Criticism. 'Tell him',
says Harrison's Arminius of the social prophet, 'to do
more in literature -- he has the talent for it; and to
avoid Carlylese as he would the devil.'

Harrison's dialogue points to an anomalous aspect of
Arnold's reputation in the 1860s. Professor Coulling
describes Arnold's efforts to show the practical values of

culture and the necessity for individual perfection if
general improvement was to follow, and -- in the later
stages of debate -- to moderate some of his comments on the
Dissenters and to prove himself a bit more systematic than
he had pretended to be. (73) But the point is that the
charges raised against him remained unchanged, even when
he had directly replied. In this sense, Professor Super
is only partly right when he speaks of a history of Arnold
criticism in these years providing an emblem for the overall response to Arnold's career. For in the late 1860s
the elegant Jeremiah, the pseudo-Carlyle, *was* Arnold in
the eyes of many of his countrymen. His critics lamented
the wasting of a career, the perverting of poetical and
critical talents in a weary political campaign. To understand the blindness in these reactions to Arnold's assessments of English culture, we should recall the sense of
crisis, of urgency, in so many writers -- including, for
example, Marx, who was commenting on some of the same
events and the same political figures. (74) That Arnold
perhaps appreciated the relationship between specific
issues and a general cultural malaise or came the closest
of his contemporaries to a sane overview, can be argued
from our vantage point. On the other hand, Harrison,
Sidgwick, Morris, Mill, and Stephen lived in a world they
thought was crying for change; and they did not see how
Arnold's 'eudaemonism', however cleverly expressed, could
help. Hence the common charge: 'Culture in the next generation, anarchy meanwhile' (see, for example, No. 25).

If the ultimate impact of Arnold's social writings
proved less than he hoped it would when he spoke of 'Hellenism and Hebraism' forming 'a kind of centre for English
thought', there can be no question about his power to
create the terms of later discussion. It seems likely,
for example, that E. B. Tylor's seminal work, 'Primitive
Culture' (1871), owes its title to the Apostle of Culture.
(75) After a meeting with Disraeli, in 1881, Arnold speculated as to why Disraeli 'read me with delight' and said
'that I was doing very great good'. 'The fact is that
what I have done in establishing a number of current
phrases -- such as Philistinism, sweetness and light, and
all that -- is just the sort of thing to strike him' (ii,
188-9). But Disraeli notwithstanding, the terms caught on
because they seemed appropriate, because Arnold expressed
an ideal of a stable and ordered society when he -- no less
than his critics -- feared social chaos. 'I do hope that
what influence I have may be of use in the troubled times
I see are before us as a healing and reconciling influence' (ii, 36). His own ambivalence about his social
writings, which he put aside with relief in 1869, found an

echo in Charles Kingsley, who sent an astute if belated
letter about 'Culture and Anarchy'. 'I have at last', he
wrote,

> had time to read carefully your 'Culture and Anarchy',
> and here is my verdict, if you care for it: That it is
> an exceeding wise and true book, and likely, as such,
> to be little listened to this autumn, but to sink into
> the ground and die, and bear fruit next spring -- when
> the spring comes. (Quoted in ii, 43)

'ST. PAUL AND PROTESTANTISM' (1870)

'St Paul and Protestantism', which appeared between 'Culture and Anarchy' and 'Friendship's Garland', addresses
largely theological issues. But it is in no way discon-
tinuous with Arnold's general intellectual development or
with the arguments of the social books. Nor was 'St.
Paul' the first of Arnold's ventures into theology. One
of the earliest essays he wrote for periodical publication, The Bishop and the Philosopher (1862), grew from an
attack on Bishop Colenso into both a summary of the radical ideas of Spinoza and an estimate of what Arnold took
to be the religious crisis of his era. Colenso's book
called into question the historical accuracy of the Pentateuch; it was a searching but isolated and amateurish
study. While asserting the insubstantial nature of the
bishop's arguments, Arnold acknowledged graver challenges
to the authority of Scripture being made by Continental
critics. He knew the theoretical directions of the Higher
Criticism and the practical questions to which it could
lead:

> If the old theory of Scriptural Inspiration is to be
> abandoned, what place is the Bible henceforth to hold
> among books? What is the new Christianity to be like?
> How are governments to deal with national churches
> founded to maintain a very different conception of
> Christianity? (Super, iii, 49)

In this early essay Arnold articulates two major problems
that his future studies of theology and society explore;
the status of Christian religion in an age of scientific
scepticism, and its future relationship with English
society.
From the outset, Arnold thought himself qualified to
deal with such complex issues. When he insisted in The
Bishop and the Philosopher that 'literary criticism's most

important function is to try books as to the influence
they are likely to have' (Super, iii, 41), he specifically
included theological studies under the books that criticism must judge. Arnold's theological books of the 1870s
involve, however, far more than simple reviewing. Beyond
even the Celtic materials of a decade before, they invited
the objection that he toyed with issues he could not fully
comprehend. Arnold was ready for the objection, having
long ago implied what his role in the religious crises of
his times might be. In Dr. Stanley's Lectures on the
Jewish Church (1863), he says that the age lacks a true
religious reformer and must therefore rely on a religious
teacher, a person who,

> not yet reconciling all things, at least esteems things
> still in their due order, and makes his hearers so
> esteem them; who, shutting his mind against no ideas
> brought by the spirit of his time, sets these ideas, in
> the sphere of religious life, in their right promin-
> ence ... (Super, iii, 69-70)

This remark anticipates both the definition of the critic
in The Function of Criticism at the Present Time (1864)
and Arnold's strategy in the theological books.

If the essays from the early 1860s lay the groundwork
for the theological writings of the 1870s, Arnold's return
to theology emerged directly from his social and political
criticism. In My Countrymen (1866), the essay which
begins the campaign against Protestant Dissenters, Arnold
confronts one of his most formidable obstacles: the fact
that the Philistines see nothing wrong with their lives
or with the culture they create. He argues that their two
primary sources of pleasure are commerce and religion, 'a
religion narrow, unintelligent, repulsive' (Super, v, 19).
Since Arnold never directly attacks dedication to either
work or wealth, he turns his scrutiny on Philistine religion. During the summer of 1869, a time when, with
'Culture and Anarchy' published, he started to think about
'St. Paul and Protestantism', he wrote to his mother:

> I am doing what will sap [the Dissenters] intellect-
> ually, and what will also sap the House of Commons
> intellectually, so far as it is ruled by the Protestant
> Dissenters; and more and more I am convinced that this
> is my true business at present. (ii, 17-18)

In chapter V of 'Culture and Anarchy' (first published
June and July 1868) Arnold turned to St Paul to show that
poverty of culture had rendered Dissenters incapable of

understanding Paul's epistles.   On a far broader scale
his argument forms the basis of 'St. Paul and Protestantism'.   In fact, as Leslie Stephen immediately recognized,
'Culture and Anarchy' and 'St. Paul and Protestantism'
form complementary parts in the battle with the Philistines. (76) Arnold's interpretation of St Paul rested on
his method of reading the Bible, a method he drew from
Coleridge, Spinoza, and his father, as well as from his
father's friends, the so-called 'Oriel Noetics'. The
method was not new, but the energy of its application was.
For Arnold's struggle with the Dissenters became a kind of
intellectual crusade. His purpose in writing the book, he
says in the first chapter, is 'to rescue St. Paul and the
Bible from the perversions of them by mistaken men' (Super,
vi, 7).

     As with most of his prose works, Arnold published parts
of the book serially, the two chapters on Pauline theology
appearing in October and November 1869, the chapter on the
relationship between Dissenting sects and the Church of
England in February 1870 -- all three in the 'Cornhill'.
By the time he finished the book Arnold had, in David
DeLaura's words, 'undercut all historic Christian positions, Protestant and Catholic, and made the Church of
England a nondoctrinal mediatorial Church of the Future
beyond the dreams of all but the most aggressive Latitu-
dinarians'. (78) To some extent, Arnold's vision of the
mediatorial Church had been anticipated by John Stuart
Mill, in his 1850 'Westminster' essay, The Church of England, but Arnold went beyond Mill in establishing the
Church on a reading of St Paul and in arguing the responsibility of Dissenters to re-enter the Church. Merely
being raised in the national Church, as Arnold had said
in the preface to 'Culture and Anarchy', affords 'a lesson
of religious moderation, and a help towards culture and
harmonious perfection' (Super, v, 239).

     Important as Arnold's theological stand was, the first
reviewers of 'St. Paul and Protestantism' cared more about
its practical implications. The Dissenters themselves
loudly rejected Arnold's call for unity. The 'British
Quarterly Review', which Arnold had labelled the organ of
'political Dissenters' (Super, iii, 270), and which he
conceded to have 'a distinct and important part to fill'
in English intellectual life, (79) devoted two long
articles to the refutation of his positions (No. 30). The
reviewer argues that 'the schism and sectarianism of English Protestantism' is not the fault of those who left,
but of 'the Church which has ... intruded into the sacred
domain of conscience, [and] which has ... sought by sta-
tute law to frame their creeds and regulate their worship'.

Far from apologizing for the history of Nonconformity, the
reviewer pictures its leaders as 'heroic old Puritans'
with 'battle-stained' doublets. The fight, he says, has
nearly been won.

So strong were Arnold's views on Dissent that the
'British Quarterly' found an unlikely ally in Leslie
Stephen, an avowed agnostic. Stephen agreed with the
'British Quarterly' on universal disestablishment: 'The
Church, as at present constituted, is, like so many other
English institutions, the relic of an exploded order of
things, and can by no means survive those ideas from which
it once received its vitality'. (80) The Church remains
as a hindrance to the State and therefore to national progress. Stephen will have nothing to do with Arnold's
recommendation that the sects ignore doctrinal differences
for the sake of organizational unity. For if differences
separate Christian from Christian, the fault lies no less
with the Church than with the Dissenters. Stephen con-
curred with the 'British Quarterly' on another point. The
'British Quarterly' roared when Arnold rubbed in his 'preparation of Hellenic sulfur, ecclesiastical nitre, and
anti-dogmatic charcoal', while Stephen, less immediately
touched, began to 'fancy that one great advantage of
possessing "sweetness and light" is the power of calling
names without being quite as annoying [as the users of]
ordinary Billingsgate'. (81) No one liked Arnold's
'manner of writing', which seemed to exclude rather than
persuade. This is, implicitly, John Morley's point in his
terse notice of 'St. Paul' for the 'Fortnightly' (No. 29).
'The Dissenters would be more likely to be impressed by
the exhortation [to "submit" to the Anglican Church] if it
had shown any faintest appreciation of the ignoble attitude, morally, intellectually, socially, of the other
side.'

Arnold did not stand alone on the issue of church unity
and disestablishment. Writing in the conservative 'Quarterly', Richard Church, soon to be appointed Dean of St
Paul's, found Arnold's view of the situation to be accurate (No. 32). He suggests that the established Church has
had a long and fruitful union with the State, which the
Dissenters cannot have, and which it would be foolish to
give up. Like Arnold, Church characterizes the Church of
England as possessing an 'uncontroversial religion, and a
not too definite theology'. But while he agrees with
Arnold in finding theological diversity conducive to unity,
Church becomes alarmed at the extent to which Arnold has
refashioned the teachings of St Paul. Church is one of
the first to appreciate the radical perspectives in
Arnold's theology: 'Mr. Arnold's interpretation of St. Paul

makes a clean sweep of a good deal more than Puritan divinity and tradition....' Arnold has in essence denied what
Church calls the 'real outward facts of history' on which
the Church is based, and which, 'if they fall, must bring
down Christianity with them....' Since the observation
raises a crucial question about modern belief, it is
surprising that Church leaves it undeveloped. But increasingly, later Anglican apologists complained how little
Christianity Arnold seemed to have left them. Conservative
churchmen found themselves, in relation to Arnold, a little
like the liberals: Arnold defended the right principles but
chose the wrong reasons or fought the wrong battles. As
late as 1895, W. E. Gladstone could write to a correspondent: 'It is very difficult to keep one's temper in dealing
with M. Arnold when he touches on religious matters. His
patronage of Christianity fashioned by himself is to me
more offensive than rank unbelief.' (82)
     Contemporary reviewers of 'St. Paul' were not altogether
sure that Arnold avoided 'rank unbelief'. One element of
his reading of St Paul that reviewers singled out time and
again was his account of the relationship between the individual Christian and Christ. Eliminating traditional notions of Christ's active love for an individual, Arnold
argues that the soul itself effects spiritual progress
because of its sympathy with Christ. If faith and love
spring from human need, then religion must be independent
of supernatural machinery. Predictably, most reviewers
worried about this inversion of accepted theological positions. 'The deeper and truer conception of religious life
which ... Mr. Arnold uniformly misses, is, that it is the
spiritual union with God of the religious man' (No. 31).
They might applaud Arnold's emphasis on righteousness,
even his insistence on righteousness as the centre of
Pauline religion, but when they faced his attempt to make
St Paul amenable to the modern, 'scientific' mind, they
baulked.
     Following the first reviews of 'St. Paul' came a small
book of lectures called 'Culture and Religion', written by
an old acquaintance of Arnold, J. C. Shairp, now Principal
of United College, St Andrews (No. 33). Shairp's general
argument reasserts conventional Christian values while
faulting Arnold for subordinating religion to culture.
Arnold's dream of harmonious perfection can never be clear
'of the taint of self-reverence' and of 'a principle of
exclusion' at odds with the universalism of Christianity.
Underlying his ideal of culture is 'a very inadequate
notion of the evil of the human heart'. This last point,
an acute insight into Arnold's work, bears on matters of
social progress and individual perfection as well as on

belief. Although Arnold never gave Shairp's criticisms
an adequate reply, he had responded in a private letter
several years before to comparable charges by R. H. Hutton.
'No one has a stronger and more abiding sense of the "daemonic" element ... ,' he wrote in 1865, 'but I think, as
Goethe thought, that the right thing is ... to keep pushing on one's posts into the darkness, and to establish no
post that is not perfectly in light ...' (i, 249). Even
if Shairp could have read this disclaimer, he could have
argued, first, that the question of evil remained central
to religious speculation, and, second, that Arnold had
established quite a number of dimly lit posts.

It is characteristic of Arnold's intellectual courage
that he persevered in his views, stating and restating
them for over a decade; it is somewhat less characteristic
that he applied his Biblical studies to a specific peda-
gogical project. In May of 1872 Macmillan's published a
small volume, edited and with a preface by Arnold, containing parts of the Prophecies of Isaiah adapted from the
Authoriz.d Version. 'A Bible Reading for Schools' exemplifies Arnold's lasting concern with education and with
the role literature should play in the curriculum. He
speaks in the preface about his 'conviction of the immense
importance in education of what is called *letters*', and he
says that 'on our *schools for the people* ... the power of
letters has hardly been brought to bear at all' (Super,
vii, 499-500). Arnold hopes that his little volume will
make an essential literary document available to the
young.

Unfortunately, the response to Arnold's edition was
much the same as the response to his translations of Homer,
over a decade earlier. Even when his critics agreed with
his theory, they questioned his practice. Sidney Colvin
wondered whether Arnold's book could at all serve its purpose. Children of the poor live, he wrote, in conditions
where the Bible cannot be read as literature. Despite his
experience in the schools, Arnold deceives himself when he
expects students to look at the Bible as a literary document, for he assumes both leisure and taste. (83)

Arnold sent a copy of his book to John Henry Newman,
doubtless realizing that Newman would disapprove. Newman
did disapprove. Like Colvin, he thought Arnold had overlooked practical problems; but he was more concerned with
Arnold's emphasis on Isaiah as literature rather than as a
sacred text. Although fundamentally objecting to Arnold's
positions, Newman's letter to Arnold is kind to the point
of indirection. Newman says that Arnold's text is too
good for children; he means that they have neither the
time nor the capacity to understand it. He wonders

politely whether other texts might not better suit the educational purpose. Arnold's reply to Newman indicates his
way of absorbing criticism. On the one hand, he praises
Newman as one of his four teachers (with Goethe, Wordsworth, and Sainte-Beuve); on the other hand, he calmly
ignores Newman's objections. (84) This studied courtesy
marked much of Arnold's reaction, public as well as private, to those who challenged his work.

'LITERATURE AND DOGMA' (1873)

The muted response, amounting almost to indifference, which
greeted the book versions of 'Culture and Anarchy' and
'Friendship's Garland' gave way, as we have seen, to considerable interest and controversy over 'St. Paul and Protestantism'. But with publication of 'Literature and
Dogma: An Essay Towards a Better Appreciation of the Bible'
Arnold became, for the first time, a 'best-selling' author
and the subject of an enormous amount of attention. The
book sold very well for several years and made Arnold's
name current in sections of the reading public which had
never heard of him before. Further, 'Literature and
Dogma' was the first of Arnold's books to be translated,
as 'La Crise Religieuse' (1876). By this time there had
been five English editions. (85)
    Arnold thought the book of sufficient significance to
merit wide attention. On its publication he wrote to his
publisher, Macmillan: (86)

    the book is sure to be much attacked and blamed. No
    one should suffer himself to exaggerate what can be
    done at one moment by one individual and one book:
    all I venture to say is that the so-called orthodox
    position cannot, I think, ever again be precisely the
    same in England after the publication of this book,
    than it hitherto has been.

There is more than a trace of hubris here, and Arnold
clearly overestimated his ultimate effect. For contrast,
we might think of George Saintsbury's retrospective comment on the same book: 'Much of it must have been written
amid the excitement of the French-Prussian War, when the
English public was athirst for "skits" of all sorts....'
(87) Whatever the actual worth of 'Literature and Dogma',
Arnold's contemporaries took it seriously, attacking and
blaming as the author foresaw. After the first onslaught
Arnold wrote to Charles Appleton, editor of the 'Academy':
'The English notices have for the most part been wholly

unprofitable, concerning themselves with the mere fringes
and externals of the book only.' (88)   This was unfair.
As in the past, he proved fortunate in his reviewers, and
'Literature and Dogma' received a thorough and sometimes
generous treatment at the hands of critics.

A few even praised it.   Albert Réville, a French Protestant theologian writing in the 'Academy', called it
'one of the most interesting documents for the contemporary history of ideas', a book 'of European interest' -- an
assessment which Arnold, more than any other Victorian,
must have appreciated.   Arnold's intent in writing the
book had been essentially conservative, to prove, as he
wrote to his sister, 'that everything essential to [the
"progress" of Christianity] stands firm and unchanged'
(ii, 120).   Réville understands this; he describes 'Literature and Dogma' as a book 'penetrated with the great need
which the present age feels for a religious renovation
that, without breaking with the past, will do justice to
the progress accomplished by the general intelligence'.
(89)   An American critic, H. W. Preston, writing in the
'Atlantic' (No. 36), went so far as to say that Arnold's
work made a 'clean sweep' of 'the tenets of orthodoxy'
while anticipating the shape of future belief.   'Literature and Dogma', she added, gave a consistency and completeness to Arnold's prose works and showed them to be
part of a great plan.   Such enthusiasm and such sensiti-
vity to Arnold's own valuation of his work were, however,
more the exception than the rule.

Arnold's attempt to revise Christianity, in itself a
bold undertaking, seemed especially bold coming from a
poet, critic, and school inspector.   When Arnold renewed
his claim to competence in the preface to 'Literature and
Dogma', many readers were sceptical.   John Tulloch, Professor of Theology at St Mary's College, St Andrews,
entitled his review in 'Blackwood's' Amateur Theology
(No. 35) and began with a survey of what he took to be a
trend towards theologizing by writers of dubious competence.   Tulloch's piece is careful, informed, and conservative.   As if ignoring Arnold's thesis, he recommends to
him 'the study of dogma' as 'the best corrective of extravagant theory and self-confidence'.   The 'Saturday
Review', though less damning, also needled the amateur
theologian (No. 34).   Misrepresenting Arnold's criticism
as a theory which holds that 'if we are to discover the
truth on any subject, we have more need to know a good
deal about many things than to be thoroughly acquainted
with the subject at hand', the 'Saturday' reviewer concludes that Arnold's criticism is liable to a sprightly
dilettantism and a 'frequent and tempting abuse'.

Doubts about Arnold's critical posture led most reviewers to disagree with his re-reading of the Bible. In a
thorough but inconsistent review for the 'Contemporary',
J. L. Davies began by calling 'Literature and Dogma' 'a
book of rare moral and intellectual force, original in the
greatness and directness of its aim' and a possible 'promise of certainty' to 'the much shaken mind of this generation'. Yet Davies soon found so many grounds for disagreeing with Arnold that he wondered whether 'there is a
conscious wilfulness in these individualistic interpretations of the New Testament'.(90) Even the generally favourable Réville insisted that 'it is only by doing great
and constant violence to the gospel history' that Arnold
can reach his theoretical goal.

The most important issue for reviewers was not, how-
ever, what Arnold called his 'method', but his concept of
God. Although this had already been articulated in 'St.
Paul', some readers found it stated fully for the first
time in 'Literature and Dogma'. For example, the 'British
Quarterly' announced that 'here formally [Arnold] renoun-
ces all belief in a Personal God ... and practically
plunges into the melancholy Styx of Atheism', (91) and the
'Theological Review' demanded to know, '... does Mr.
Arnold conform ...?' (92) and of course concluded that he
no longer did. For most reviewers this renunciation of a
personal God was frightening. Not even the radical 'Westminster' openly applauded it. Conventional theologians
spent much of their efforts trying to prove that the personal dimension alone gives significance to the deity and
meaning to human worship. 'By insisting on a religion
that is verifiable ... [Arnold] simply excludes religion,
and puts in its place something else', (93) to wit, a
theory of ethics as religion.

There were, as well, repeated and sound objections to
Arnold's definition of religion as 'binding to Righteousness'. The 'Westminster' reviewer, possibly a non-
believer, gave a definition of religion as 'a system of
belief and worship, not necessarily including morality'
and went on to argue that while this definition fits the
religion of the Hebrews, Arnold's kind of religion does
not. Arnold's assertion of the righteousness of the
Jewish nation later disturbed Samuel Butler. The theory
'sounds well', Butler writes (No. 44), 'but can we think
the Jews ... were really more righteous than the Greeks
and Romans?' Reminding Arnold of his own Hellenic positions, Butler says that the major traits of Jewish conduct are intolerance and Pharisaism and that Greco-Roman
civilization has actually generated our sense of the ideal
person. 'Righteousness' is a dubious good, since it

involves 'the general reference of our lives to the supposed will of an unseen but supreme power'.

By educating religious and intellectual leaders, Arnold
hoped to return belief to 'the majority of souls', whom he
thought deprived by modern scepticism. His implicit assumption is that the working classes have uncritically
accepted rationalism. However, John Tulloch was sure that
(94)

> the mass of people are alienated from the Bible, not
> because it is supposed to declare a personal God, but
> because they have an instinctive feeling of a personal
> God, and the Bible is offered to them in connection
> with views of His character and dealings with men which
> come into no real relations with their experiences....

The 'British Quarterly' was even sanguine about the current situation. 'After some thirty years of pretty extensive knowledge of the lower classes in London and elsewhere ... [we are sure that] there is far less speculative
infidelity among the lower classes than there was a quarter of a century ago....' (95) (The reference may have
been to the 1851 census, with its startling figures of low
church attendance.) One of the sharpest critiques of
Arnold's hopes for the conversion of the masses came from
F. W. Newman. If, Newman argued, the Bible is so complex
a document that only a few men of culture have been able
to read it properly, then it will never be readily accessible to the common people, and the 'High Churchmen and
the Romanists are right, who deprecate putting it into the
hands of the laity'. (96) Newman's comments offer an
ironic contrast to his brother's criticism of 'A Bible
Reading for Schools', since both Newmans disagreed with
Arnold -- for totally different reasons.

Another of Newman's old charges came back to haunt
Arnold. As with 'St. Paul', there was one question on
which, no matter how diverse their other views, nearly
every critic agreed: they objected to Arnold's literary
mannerisms. It is in 'Literature and Dogma' that Arnold
makes his notorious comparison of the Holy Trinity to the
three, superhuman Lord Shaftsburys and continually ridicules the Bishops of Winchester and Gloucester for their
belief in a personal God. Tulloch, irritated by Arnold's
'dreary' reiteration of his jokes and finding the jokes
themselves in bad taste, summed up the view of many critics: 'No Philistine who had never heard of "sweetness
and light" could have further transgressed.'

The reminder to Arnold that he had betrayed his own
ideals of sweet reasonableness or at least of impartiality

prompted him, in the Popular Edition of 'Literature and Dogma', to cut many of the offending passages. When contemplating his revisions, he wrote to his sister in justification of the original version and its pointed remarks.

> I write in the manner which is natural to me; the manner has, no doubt, its weak points. But ponderous works produce no effect; the religious world which complains of me would not read me if I treated my subject as they say it ought to be treated ... (ii, 120)

This could of course be a humourless apology for the sort of yellow journalism that Arnold had long attacked, but in spite of his protestations, he did make the revised text less offensive.

Probably the keenest and the harshest commentary on Arnold's religious positions treats Arnold as Arnold had treated the hapless bishops. In the conclusion to his 'Ethical Studies' (No. 42), F. H. Bradley scornfully assesses Arnold's theological notions and finds them to be -- using Arnold's own term -- 'clap-trap'. Defining religion as 'morality touched by emotion' is, according to Bradley, to 'say nothing'. For the definition simply means that 'it is religion when with morality you have -- religion'. The objection deftly reduces Arnold's proposition to a tautology. Another of Arnold's basic premises is that virtue leads to happiness. With ironic detail Bradley points out that happiness frequently does not come with virtue -- indeed quite the opposite is possible. Bradley also scoffs at Arnold's phrase 'the Eternal not ourselves'. He says that to speak of God as 'the Eternal not ourselves which makes for righteousness' makes no more sense than to call the habit of going 'Early to Bed "the Eternal not ourselves that makes for longevity"'. Since Arnold insisted in 'St. Paul' and 'Literature and Dogma' upon 'scientific' verification, Bradley casts doubt on his entire theological undertaking.

'GOD AND THE BIBLE' (1875) and 'LAST ESSAYS ON CHURCH AND RELIGION' (1877)

So extensive and detailed was the criticism of 'Literature and Dogma' that Arnold decided, soon after its publication, to write a response defending his views. At first he considered just an additional chapter to the book itself. But that proved far too small a canvas, and he arranged with Knowles, editor of the 'Contemporary Review', to publish a series of articles called Review of

Objections to 'Literature and Dogma' which were, upon their
completion, to be gathered into a book with a new preface.

The first of the 'Contemporary' articles revealed
clearly Arnold's intent. Forgetting his ideal of a thinker as one capable of turning back on what he has thought
and written in order to see it afresh, Arnold announces
that all the critical 'outcry does not make us go back one
inch' (Super, vii, 142) and goes on to defend, not only
his ideas, but even his mode of writing, with its banter
and attacks on personalities. He reassures his audience
that his purpose is to quash any doubts about the validity
of his ideas which critics may have stirred in the minds
of intelligent and approving readers. Needless to say,
the critics found his tone 'aggravating to a high degree'.
Leslie Stephen, having read the first essay, described it
as 'Mat in excelsis -- the very cheekiest production I have
yet seen of his'. (97)

The articles themselves, upon their first appearance,
stirred some interest. R. H. Hutton replied almost immediately to the first of them, in an essay which appeared in
the 'Spectator' the same month. Recognizing Arnold's in-
transigence and sensing that the new series of essays would
simply enlarge upon the earlier books, Hutton insisted that
Arnold had read the Bible selectively and therefore arbitrarily. (98) Arnold's response, in his January 1875 article (which was to become Chapter III of the book), is
inadequate, because it ignores Hutton's central objection.

Arnold continued his piecemeal composition through
1875, the whole finally appearing as a book in November.
He hoped for the same kind of popular interest 'Literature
and Dogma' had enjoyed, but was disappointed. The reviews
were fewer in number, smaller in size, more tepid in response. Readers considered the book a rehash of old ideas.
What was new was technical, complex, and yet open to
simple objections. For instance, the 'Westminster' (No.
39) could praise Arnold for doing his homework this time,
while concluding that his new ideas, such as his conten-
tions about the authorship of the Fourth Gospel, want
intellectual seriousness. Réville, writing in the 'Academy' (No. 38), sums up the response: '" God and the
Bible" leaves matters in statu quo.... Apart from the
very real pleasure of having read a work of high merit in
point of form and originality, we are no farther forward
than before.'

The scholarly distrust and popular failure of 'God and
the Bible' carried over to the reception of 'Last Essays
on Church and Religion' (1877). 'Last Essays' is a far
looser collection of religious pieces than the previous
books, and despite Arnold's efforts in the preface to tie

together his ideas, it remains casual in format. As with
'God and the Bible', the book contained few surprises, and
the press responded with short notices or with silence.
Sales were even worse than for 'God and the Bible', and
'Last Essays' never entered a second edition during
Arnold's lifetime.

It must have been painful for Arnold to note that the
reviews concentrated on his valedictory to theology, and
that most welcomed it. The 'Saturday' found Arnold im-
modest in announcing his departure from the arena. But
the announcement pleased Edward Dowden, who mused on the
potential tendencies in Arnold's writing (No. 40). Now
that he has attained a greater intellectual serenity,
through the construction of a pattern of religious convictions, Dowden hopes that Arnold's future literary criticism will have 'a harmony, a continuity, a sane energy,
and adult power', fulfilling the promise of the early
works.

ARNOLD IN THE 1870S

Arnold's excursions in the Biblical wilderness led critics
to conclude that the balance in Arnold between Hellene and
Hebrew had shifted: he was David, son of Goliath (as Swinburne put it), hurling stones against his enemies; and he
had abandoned Athens for Palestine. *Et in Philistia ego.*
Henry Hewlett was one of the first to describe the change,
which he considered implicit self-betrayal. (91) Hewlett
and others could acknowledge that 'Literature and Dogma'
had won for Arnold a wide audience, but they could not
acknowledge the authority of the religious works or think
them comparable in quality to Arnold's literary criticism
and verse. The contemporary judgment anticipated that of
William Madden, who argues the intrinsically aesthetic
nature of Arnold's temperament, (100) and though such an
argument overlooks a large tendency in Arnold's work, it
has a useful application to his nineteenth-century reputation. Arnold's contemporaries wanted the Arnold who had
never entirely existed, the sensitive, incisive literary
critic who limited himself to aesthetic questions; they
would not accept Arnold's broad definition of criticism,
which seemed to include religious and social writings at
the expense of literary studies.

What happened, then, to Arnold's aesthetic ideas while
he devoted himself to political and theological works?
They were left for others to develop. Walter Pater, the
most significant critic of the 1870s, drew heavily from
Arnold, whose work he knew intimately. (101) Perhaps the

most striking example of Arnold's influence on Pater is
the way Pater's essay Wordsworth (1874) anticipates
Arnold on the same subject. Pater himself said that
Arnold 'has exercised the most potent influence in intellectual matters' among the half dozen 'famous' Englishmen
of the 1870s who are certain to be remembered. (102) At
the same time, Pater's extension of Arnold's ideas often
leads him to positions far from Arnold's own. In the preface to 'The Renaissance: Studies in Art and Poetry',
Pater begins by paying homage to his mentor, quoting the
famous statement from The Function of Criticism at the
Present Time. Pater agrees that the purpose of criticism
is 'to see the object as in itself it really is', but he
immediately goes on to argue that 'in aesthetic criticism
the first step towards seeing one's object as it really is,
is to know one's own impression as it really is ...'. (103)
In a stroke Pater reverses Arnold's attempts to instate an
Aristotelian objectivity, proposing instead a subjective
theory of critical analysis. Since Pater, though deeply
involved with Arnold's methods and principles, avoided
writing about Arnold himself, he cannot be represented in
this book. But the discussions of Arnold in the 1870s
should be read with Pater in mind.

Pater must have felt that Arnold, by straining in Philistia, had bequeathed aesthetic criticism to a younger
generation. In a related way, William Morris might have
agreed. Because Morris's aesthetics depended on his social
philosophy, he could be expected to share Arnold's concern
for the interrelationship of art and the commonweal. And
to an extent he did. He spoke in 1878 in praise of Arnold:
'Under his name and example ... , I will shelter myself'.
(104) Yet, as Raymond Williams has shown, Arnold became
the 'principal opponent' for Morris, who associated 'culture' with things effete and -- worse -- with a subtle defence of the status quo. (105) In a private letter of
March 1878, Morris responded to a friend who had sent him
a copy of Arnold's Equality (delivered in February): (106)

> Thanks for sending me Arnold's lecture ... with the
> main part of which of course I heartily agree: the
> only thing is that if he has any idea of a remedy he
> dursn't mention it. I think myself that no rose-water
> will cure us: disaster and misfortune of all kinds, I
> think, will be the only things that will breed a
> remedy: in short, nothing can be done till all rich men
> are made poor by common consent. I suppose he dimly
> sees this, but is afraid to say it, being, though
> naturally a courageous man, somewhat infected with the
> great vice of that cultivated class he was praising so
> much -- cowardice, to wit.

For Morris, too, Arnold does not go far enough. His position is conservative, his motives ultimately selfish or
fearful. Arnold was not, in fact, a coward, but Morris is
right about his basic apprehension as to the stability of
the State and about his developing conservatism.
   Pater and Morris show, in their different ways, how
Arnold was having his 'effect'. Another sign is the
increased number of parodies. Little jokes in 'Punch',
for example, become common, as do take-offs on Arnold's
poems. The best-known satire in the 1870s is W. H.
Mallock's 'New Republic' (1877), a conspicuously non-
Socratic book, in which Arnold, as 'Mr. Luke', tests his
wit against parodic versions of Ruskin, Benjamin Jowett,
Huxley, and other recognizable members of the intellectual
establishment. As the name implies, Mr. Luke in his own
estimate has effected the marriage of culture and religion.
   Related to Mallock's satire are common distortions or
overstatements in polemical treatises, for which Arnold
serves as an easily identifiable straw man. Herbert
Spencer, working throughout the 1870s on his 'Principles
of Sociology', concluded that, because of his desire for
centralized institutions and his criticism of Dissenters,
Arnold had proved himself an example of 'anti-patriotism'.
Typical of his progressive bias and his careless reading,
Spencer constructed a long list of British scientific
achievements to demonstrate that England was full of
'ideas'. (107)
   Beginning from entirely different assumptions, J. W.
Courthope also used Arnold for a target. In Modern Culture (No. 41), Courthope seeks to undercut the bases of
Arnold's liberalism. He says that Arnold's intellectual
position resembles that of the Girondins during the French
Revolution. Given to abstract philosophizing, modern
Girondins (who include Goethe and Carlyle) seek an imagin-
ary perfection. While their destructive criticism may be
apt, they offer no useful remedies and lack any kind of
practical sense. Like Harrison, Sidgwick, and Morris,
with whom he would normally disagree, Courthope accuses
Arnold of hedonism, of advocating criticism based on
'taste' and 'tact', and of indulging in a prose style that
approximates poetry. Where nothing is proven but everything suggested, he says, criticism becomes romance. In
Courthope's essay we have one of the strongest and one of
the sharpest attacks on Arnold from a political conservative. In effect, Courthope denies Arnold's concern for
the State, dismisses his approaches to politics and art,
worries about the aestheticism lurking in his theories,
and generally finds him a dangerous influence. Courthope

may be biased and ungenerous, but his essay raises fundamental questions about the shape and the tendencies of
Arnold's thought.

After the efforts of the late 1860s and early to mid
1870s, when he produced five books of considerable length
and complexity, Arnold never again undertook a major project. The title of his next book offers an apt emblem for
his last decade of work. But the title 'Mixed Essays'
(1879), and even a glance at its contents, can be misleading. Although the book is strictly a collection of
essays written between January 1877 and November 1878
(along with Democracy, reprinted from 'The Popular Education of France', 1861), the consistency of Arnold's ideas
was now such that when he turned to different topics, he
naturally linked the work at hand with what he had written
through the years.

The matter of unity had for Arnold a commercial aspect.
Since the sales of 'Last Essays' had been so poor, Arnold
had fears about a book that drew together pieces on education and equality with studies of Falkland and George
Sand. He even suggested the title 'Literature and Civilization -- Mixed Essays', arguing that 'half will be on
literary topics, which will be in the book's favour'.
(108) In fact, only the essay on Goethe keeps within
reasonable limits of literary criticism. His final defence for the collection, in the preface, is that it possesses a 'unity of tendency' (Super, viii, 370), a statement that drew immediate fire. In a characteristically
testy note in 'Blackwood's', Margaret Oliphant found no
unity whatever in 'Mixed Essays'. She suggested that
Arnold either lacked 'discrimination' or suffered from an
'exaggerated self-importance' in collecting 'criticisms
of a critic, reviews of a review'. (109)

But other critics agreed with Arnold's defence. The
'Athenaeum' reviewer, initially confused -- because 'the
unity, though announced, is not defined' -- realized that
the unifying principle is Arnold himself. Through his
own example, Arnold 'has continually reminded us ... of
the supreme value of noble conduct and high demeanour'.
(110) Arnold welcomed this comment, as he had welcomed
comparable statements about 'Essays in Criticism'. In a
delighted letter to the editor of the 'Athenaeum' he wrote:
'Nothing ... could be more serviceable to the book than
the line followed in the article' (Super, viii, 418). A
few months later, Mark Pattison emphasized this same,
personal unity of the book in a review for the 'Academy'
(No. 45). Pattison questions Arnold's plans for deliver-
ing his prosperous countrymen 'out of the slough of materialism'. As an Oxford tutor and administrator, he knew

about problems of education first hand, and he thought the
dream of Equality a distant one. But if he is not sanguine about Arnold's remedies, especially State-sponsored
schools, Pattison nevertheless credits him with improving
the tone of English criticism. 'There is an urbane quality, a play of the mind for the mind's sake', qualities he
sees only in Athenian and French prose, which give
Arnold's writing a special kind of educational value.

THE LAST DECADE

Despite his advancing years and the distractions of a long
lecture tour in America, Arnold continued, during the
1880s, to write regularly for the periodical press. He
published a number of essays on British politics, three
pieces on American civilization (for Arnold, almost a
contradiction in terms), discussions of theology, and
several of his well-known essays on literature and literary criticism. In addition, he edited selections from the
poems of Wordsworth and Byron.

Perhaps because of their scattered and varied character, none of Arnold's late writings received the attention
that followed the religious works. What criticism there
was tended to cluster around the appearance of the book
versions of his essays. So there is a response to the
editions of Wordsworth and Byron (in 1879 and 1881) and to
the collections of miscellaneous pieces entitled 'Irish
Essays and Others' (1882) and 'Discourses in America'
(1885). Less frequently there is an immediate rebuttal to
a periodical article, such as Alfred Austin's Loves of the
Poets, a stinging attack on Arnold's Shelley.

Austin's review points to one of Arnold's critical
tasks in this last decade. A glance at what he was writing between 1879 and 1881 shows a revival in his concern
with literary criticism and a focus within the criticism.
Framing that period are the Wordsworth and Byron editions.
In the middle are the essays Arnold contributed to Ward's
'The English Poets', including The Study of Poetry,
Thomas Gray, and John Keats. Clearly, Arnold was evaluat-
ing the Romantic heritage, about which he had long been
ambivalent, and which was now three-quarters of a century
old.

An important part of his evaluation, perhaps the most
important part, involves the relative merit of the Romantic poets. In general, as John Holloway has said, 'the
crucial operation, for Arnold, is to distinguish the major
work from the minor', (111) and in Wordsworth, Arnold
spends a great deal of time recounting the history of

Wordsworth's reputation, then insisting that Wordsworth
deserves international respect. At issue here is more
than the question of reputation. For a thinker like
Arnold who has placed such stress upon the useful qualities of great art, it is imperative to be able to separate
first-rate from second-rate work. Arnold wants a reliable
order in his overview of English literature. Looking back
- like Samuel Johnson, in the 'Lives' - he needs principles of evaluation, principles which can isolate 'the
best'. It was towards such principles, almost twenty
years earlier, that James, Lancaster, and Reynolds supposed him to be moving.

   In Wordsworth, Arnold settles on the principle of
'criticism of life'. The phrase by itself has been
unfortunate, since it omits the qualification that Arnold
attached to it: 'the application of these ideas under the
conditions fixed for us by the laws of poetic beauty and
poetic truth' (Super, ix, 45). Throughout the essay
Arnold insists upon this modification, deprecating poetry
that is merely didactic. Yet from the first, Arnold's
critics understood him to be requiring an explicit, moral
purpose in poetry, and from the first they tried to correct him.

   In an early review of the 'Wordsworth' edition, (No.
47) J. A. Symonds worried about Arnold's position: 'While
substantially agreeing with Mr. Arnold, it may be possible
to take exception to the form of his definition. He lays
too great stress, perhaps, on the phrases, *application* of
ideas, and *criticism*', when 'the prime aim of all art is
at bottom only presentation'. Now this is just what
Arnold had argued when he refused to philosophize Wordsworth and argued that Wordsworth's true power comes from
his ability to show the reader his joy in nature and 'to
make us share it' (Super, ix, 51). By ignoring Arnold's
distinction, Symonds struggles against a phantom. Two
years later Alfred Austin in his Old and New Canons of
Poetical Criticism was even less fair. Accusing Arnold of
writing intentionally deceptive prose, 'concealing his own
[ideas] behind a fascinating veil', Austin tries to reduce
Arnold's new canon of judgment to essentials and concludes
that, for Arnold, 'those poets are the greatest whose criticism of life is most healthy and most true'. He acknowledges the possibility that Arnold might dislike this way
of putting his ideas, but insists that it is correct.
(112) Yet Austin does have a point. Arnold's tacit
assumption is that reasonable men can agree on what is
moral and right and can seek those qualities in poetry.
Taking a relativistic position, Austin argues that there
will be no agreement about such matters, even among poets.

    Arnold's desire to establish a new, ranked order of the
Romantic poets prompted critics to reject his means of
selection or to proffer their own. Among the most force-
ful rebuttals of his views is A. C. Swinburne's Wordsworth and Byron (No. 51). An early apologist for Arnold,
Swinburne had written an enthusiastic review of the 1867
'Poems'. But he became increasingly hostile to Arnold's
criticism. Arnold, in slighting Shelley, suggested that
Shelley's essays and letters might last longer than his
verse. To Swinburne this was 'erratic and eccentric' -
words to make Arnold squirm. Yet Swinburne makes much the
same argument for Byron, indulges in uncritical praise of
Shelley, and seems satisfied that justice has been done.
W. E. Henley's earlier review of the Byron volume (No. 49)
is a saner piece of writing, but proceeds on similar lines.
Arnold fails because he is 'not altogether in sympathy
with his subject'. Henley is, and he praises Byron the
rebel, who was 'not interested in words and phrases, but
in the greater truths of destiny and emotion'. Once
Arnold's effort to establish 'objective' standards failed,
this sort of contrary assertion was inevitable. It has
continued, for both Shelley and Byron, to our own time.
    If Arnold could not institute criteria for ranking
earlier poets, he stimulated interest in them, becoming
himself - like T. S. Eliot in this century - the critic
to contend with. We have already suggested that by the
1870s Arnold had emerged as a major figure, a 'Victorian
sage'. In the 1880s the tendency to assess his overall
effect naturally increased. So, for instance, in a review
of 'Irish Essays and Others' (1882), the 'Athenaeum'
begins by noting the 'multifarious' nature of the collection and enters on a long summary of Arnold's criticism.
The reviewer sees Arnold as a corrective influence on his
time, whose function is to upbraid his contemporaries and
'call them to order'. (113) This is close to Arnold's own
sense of the critical function. His letters frequently
mention his intent, when lecturing, to touch on a central
weakness of his listeners. Joseph Jacobs recognized his
intent and called his lecture-essays 'lay sermons' (No.
52), in which Arnold 'invariably picks out the favourite
sin of his audience'. Jacobs's commentary also reflects
the growing acknowledgment - on both sides of the Atlantic
- of Arnold's deeply serious purpose. Sensing that
Arnold's role has not been easy, Jacobs says that 'he
alone possesses the lightness of touch, width of view,
sanity of criticism, and individuality of style which are
needed to give permanent value to what seems at first
sight to be merely a form of higher journalism'.
    By the 1880s there is widespread recognition that a

part of Arnold's success arises from the cosmopolitan
nature of his mind. Comments like that in the 'Saturday'
accusing him of a lack of 'catholicity of appreciation',
though defensible, have become rare. (114) More common is
the 'Athenaeum's' description of him as '"the most un-
English of Britons," the most cosmopolitan of islanders'.
(115) Andrew Lang, in an article that reviews Arnold's
career to 1882, credits Arnold with widening 'the scope of
contemporary English literature' through his 'large familiarity with foreign literature and Continental criticism'
(No. 50).

   Arnold himself had not stood still as the years passed,
and if Lang's testimony reflected a widespread admiration
for Arnold's criticism, reviewers became increasingly
interested in the ways his late work differed from the
early critical prefaces reprinted in 'Irish Essays'.
Like Hewlett in the 1870s, they assessed Arnold's career
in his own terms. Jacobs summarized his development in
this way: 'He began life as an Hellene of the Hellenes,
and was as one of those who are at ease in Zion. He has
gradually become more Hebraic than the Hebrews, but yet
retains the easy manner of the sons of light.' Again,
this is a complex question. To what extent had Arnold
shifted his aesthetic values from form towards content?
Is Lewis Gates right in saying that 'the emphasis in the
discussions of Wordsworth, Shelley, Byron, Keats, Gray,
and Milton is primarily on the ethical characteristics of
each poet'? (116) There were critics, men of a new generation, who thought this was so, and who perceived Arnold
as an aging representative of mid-Victorian earnestness
and frumpery. This perhaps helps to explain J. A.
Symonds's and Alfred Austin's misreadings of Arnold.
While Symonds agrees with Arnold that the greatest poets
must excel in both form and content he insists that formal
qualities can redeem poetry of negligible or even negative
moral impact. Austin argues analogously. He disclaims
any intent to 'extend the borders of morality in order to
suit the disposition of men of genius', but in fact this
is just what he does (No. 53). In his apology for moral
licence among artists and in Symonds's praise of formal
elements, we see again the movement towards aestheticism,
towards Wilde and the 'Yellow Book'. (117) But here it is
not a matter of men like Pater extending Arnold's earlier
aesthetic positions; it is a matter of unsympathetic
critics using Arnold as a Philistine straw man.

THE MAN OF LETTERS

In January 1888, an editor with Macmillan's wrote to
Arnold: 'Is it not time for you to make a volume of collected papers? You must have a great many Magazine articles that ought to be reprinted & we should much like to
publish them.'(118) Arnold replied, in a letter now evidently lost, with a list substantially the same as the
table of contents to 'Essays in Criticism, Second Series'.
But before he could superintend the publication of the
book, he died, suddenly, on 15 April 1888.

The first of the obituary notices, particularly those
from the USA, mix remarks on Arnold's death with critiques
of some of his last published essays about American society. These appeared posthumously in book form, entitled
'Civilization in the United States' (a volume published in
Boston and never widely available in England). In the
later, more considered obituaries, the 'Essays in Criticism, Second Series' receive passing notice in surveys of
Arnold's work, with the result that this final and important book missed the exclusive attention it would undoubtedly have won had Arnold still been alive.

Arnold's death tended to mitigate certain kinds of criticism while it invited general estimates about the significance and the problematic nature of his career. A major
question, already touched on in 'Matthew Arnold, The
Poetry', concerned Arnold's stature as a poet. The influential critic F. W. H. Myers wrote: 'As a poet, he will
... be the longest remembered' (No. 54). Other critics
took a different point of view. H. D. Traill and Arnold's
old friend - now Lord Chief Justice - Coleridge both
thought it nonsense to rate the poetry higher than the
criticism. Scoffing at the high obituary estimates of the
poetry, Traill wrote: 'He will be remembered, it seems,
for those achievements which have failed to attract the
attention of the public which is to remember him.' (119)

Traill was objecting a little perversely to what had
been a growing interest in Arnold's poetry, and he made,
in fact, the same sort of error he derided in others.
Just as praise of the poetry need not rule out admiration
for the prose, so respect for the prose hardly demanded
dismissal of the poetry. Arnold had written both. This
was George Saintsbury's basic position in his 'Matthew
Arnold' (No. 62). Saintsbury would have agreed with
Coleridge's estimate of the prose, that 'there was not to
be found in modern times such a body of literary criticism', (120) but Saintsbury wants to assess the entire
career. Like Leslie Stephen (No. 59), he echoes earlier
judgments of Arnold by acknowledging the power of Arnold's

criticism to be an extension of his poetic sensibility.
But where Saintsbury (and Henry James before him) found
the criticism strengthened by the poetic gifts, John
Robertson (No. 60) and Frederic Harrison (No. 61) could
argue just the opposite. Robertson's 'Modern Humanists'
includes an attack on Arnold as a critic who is too
'arbitrary', too reliant on taste. Harrison, though he
looks back with a surprising admiration and respect for
his old adversary, praising him as a critic with 'no superior, indeed no rival', shares Robertson's distrust of
the unsystematic mind.

     In Harrison's view, Arnold's theological works had
given an odd 'vogue' to his writings. The vogue has
passed, and Harrison agrees with most readers of the time
in his low opinion of Arnold's theology. Mowbray Morris's
judgment is extreme, but it is typical: he says that 'had
every line of those theological writings remained unwritten, their author's claim on the gratitude of our generation and the regard of the next would have stood far
higher than it now stands or is likely to stand' (No. 57).
For Traill, Arnold's theological efforts had been 'hopelessly unpractical and almost visionary', an instance of
'monumental self-deception'. Traill thinks that Arnold's
prime error lay in writing radical theology for simple
believers. Like Coleridge, he forgets Arnold's careful
description of his audience: those like himself for whom
modern scepticism has eroded the supports of traditional
belief. In any case, by the century's end Arnold's
'dreary apologetics for undogmatism', as Saintsbury called
them, continued to be viewed as a waste of time.

     Arnold's political writings received a more mixed
assessment. Coleridge refers ruefully to the Irish
essays, written about a country Arnold had never seen.
Lack of practical experience was of course a charge that
early raised its head; it provided Fitzjames Stephen's
basic objection to the essays of the 1860s. Ironically,
Leslie Stephen protested the charge (No. 59). Arnold's
task, he argued, was not practical reform but the modification of ruling ideas, with which he had had obvious
success. Here in Stephen's and other late evaluations of
Arnold - evaluations written, often enough, by men who had
once been hostile - Kingsley's prediction about 'Culture
and Anarchy' came true. The 'wise and true' book could
finally be read for what it was.

     As a writer who spent so much of his life immersed in
polemics, Arnold received after his death a remarkably
tender farewell. His old opponents Stephen and Harrison
speak about him with admiration for his ideas and a kind
of subdued fondness for the man himself. John Morley, who

wrote such a harsh notice of 'St. Paul' (No. 29), also
wrote a generous farewell, in a review of G. W. Russell's
collection of Arnold's letters. Morley glances back at
Arnold's writings, which may have 'wearied some, vexed
some, and shocked others'. For all his faults, Arnold's
lifelong purpose has been 'to make for wider circles of
the community, the springs and the rules of their action
and judgment more free, more true, more sound'. (121)
Morley's estimate is, however, blurry. Like most writers
he felt that Arnold's writings would live, that they were
destined for some sort of immortality, but when he came to
sum up Arnold's achievement, he was unsure what to say.
Probably nothing definitive could be said. A few years
ago, David DeLaura reviewed some books about Arnold that
began with entirely different assumptions and worked towards predictably different conclusions. DeLaura took for
his title Kingsley's famous line and inserted Arnold's
name: 'What, then, does Matthew Arnold mean?' (122) What
indeed? And the difficulties were compounded for Arnold's
contemporaries, who had argued with him, or known him personally, or were still too close to the writings. Some
readers thought of him as 'a great spiritual emancipator';
others hedged on his significance, like Stephen, who spoke
of him as 'a skirmisher who did more than most heavily-
armed warriors, against the vast oppressive reign of stupidity and prejudice'.

    As a matter of history, Arnold's skirmishes are intri-
guing, and they had their effect. But what remains of
lasting value in his work goes beyond immediate controversy, however compelling Arnold himself may have found
that controversy. It was not only later generations who
realized this. When Robert Bridges called Arnold 'Mr.
Kidglove Cocksure', Gerard Manley Hopkins replied: 'I have
more reason than you for disagreeing with him and thinking
him very wrong, but nevertheless I am sure he is a rare
genius and a great critic'. (123) Thomas Hardy, who also
had his reasons for disagreeing with Arnold, could applaud
the obituary in 'The Times', which 'speaks quite truly of
[Arnold's] "enthusiasm for the nobler and detestation for
the meaner elements in humanity"'. (124) And, to cite a
different sort of man again, George Meredith told G. M.
Trevelyan 'that he thought Matthew Arnold, if we take his
poetry and prose together, was the most considerable
writer of his age'. (125)

A NOTE ON THE LATER REPUTATION

It is not with the unqualified praise of late

contemporaries that notes on Arnold's twentieth-century
reputation should begin. George Saintsbury's study (1899),
the first book-length evaluation of Arnold, includes fine
tributes, but Saintsbury allows himself a wide range for
analysis and even censure. His book indicates the new
fashion around the turn of the century for long critical
studies, independent of magazine articles. Herbert Paul,
for example, soon included Arnold in the English Men of
Letters series (1902). Arnold's works were reprinted in
collected editions (1892 and 1903-4), for which Thomas
Smart compiled the first substantial bibliography.
Naturally the scope of longer studies along with their
increasing distance from Arnold's lifetime changed the
nature of critical dialogue. One of the best turn-of-the-
century discussions, Lewis Gates's 'Three Studies in
Literature', appeared in 1899. It is a long essay and
difficult to cut; otherwise it would be included in this
book. Gates helped to take consideration of Arnold out of
the largely evaluative stage and to begin the inquiries
that have interested later critics. He picks up Hutton's
and other readers' comparisons of Newman and Arnold; he
considers Arnold's response to Goethe; he points to connections with Pater; and he writes the first significant
appraisal of Arnold's prose styles. With Saintsbury and
Herbert Paul, he brings Arnold into the new century.

The history of Arnold's twentieth-century reputation
remains to be written. Whether it could be written in a
single volume is another matter. W. F. Connell has studied Arnold's educational influence. Vincent Buckley has
shown the historical connections between Arnold, T. S.
Eliot, and F. R. Leavis. (126) Raymond Williams has pursued theories of culture from Arnold's time (and before)
to our own. (127) Yet as these studies indicate, the
areas in which Arnold figures, and prominently figures,
are many. They are also complex. In spite of widespread
criticism, for example, a number of English churchmen have
drawn from Arnold's theology. (128) Arnold has had a profound effect on literary figures and literary movements.
Max Weber evidently learned from him, and R. H. Tawney
quotes him with approval in political discussions. (129)
George Stocking has argued his importance for anthropology. (130) Frederic Faverty has examined his impact on
Celtic studies and Celtic national movements.

Quite apart from the question of field or area, there
is a question of nationality: just where, that is, Arnold
has been influential. If Saintsbury's ranking him 'for
the world' seems excessive, there can be no doubt about
Arnold's widespread effect on English-speaking countries.
John Henry Raleigh and others have explored Arnold's

legacy to American writers and American universities. But
in the USA as in Britain, the extent and the implications
of his influence still deserve scrutiny.

There is no need here to duplicate David DeLaura's
authoritative bibliographical survey of Arnold criticism
in 'Victorian Prose: A Guide to Research' (1973). Along
with Faverty's earlier survey (1968), (131) DeLaura's
work offers a nearly complete guide to Arnold studies.
DeLaura also points to possible future directions and
areas for research. On the negative side, his account
illustrates what the 'Times Literary Supplement' reviewer
mentioned in a notice of 'Matthew Arnold, The Poetry': the
evident glut of works about Arnold. (132) Clearly, the
industry of his nineteenth-century commentators has been
more than matched by those in our own century. And the
reasons are easy to find. In the first place, as we have
suggested, Arnold has become a part of our thinking, of
our ideological inheritance. Then, too, he stands almost
alone in his attempt at a comprehensive vision and in his
proposing a tentative hope for civilization. That hope may
may well be unfounded; we may mouth Arnold's terms in a
world ill-suited to hear them. Arnold may be less the
'aesthetic' than the 'anaesthetic' escapist he has been
called in recent years, merely an urbane compromiser,
a spokesman for what Ezra Pound long ago dismissed as
Kulchur.

But however we may want to evaluate Arnold, he has
still to be reckoned with. Lionel Trilling records a
conversation with Edmund Wilson, who urged him to continue
work on Arnold at a time (in the 1930s) when ideals of
culture and disinterested criticism might have seemed, at
best, effete. (133) Trilling did continue, and he wrote
what is in effect a study of our own as well as of
Arnold's culture. Some years later, during the Second
World War, E. M. Forster was also to find uses for Arnold.
He could write, without qualification or irony: (134)

> Matthew Arnold is of all the Victorians most to my
> taste: a great poet, a civilised citizen, and a prophet
> who has managed to project himself into our present
> troubles, so that when we read him now, he seems to be
> in the room.

NOTES

1 See John Henry Raleigh, 'Matthew Arnold and American
   Culture' (1957).
2 Henry Sidgwick, The Prophet of Culture, 'Macmillan's

Magazine' (August 1867), xvi, 271-80. No. 21 in this
volume. Future references to articles included in
this volume will be cited in the text by number.
3 See Henry James, Matthew Arnold, 'English Illustrated
Magazine' (January 1884), i, 241-6.
4 G. K. Chesterton, 'The Victorian Age in Literature'
(1913), 13.
5 'The Letters of Matthew Arnold, 1848-1888', ed.
G. W. E. Russell (1895), i, 385. References to the
'Letters' will be cited by volume and page in the
text.
6 F. R. Leavis, Matthew Arnold, 'Scrutiny' (1938), in
'The Importance of Scrutiny', ed. Eric Bentley (1948),
88-9.
7 Carl Dawson, ed., 'Matthew Arnold, The Poetry: The
Critical Heritage' (1973).
8 For Arnold's reputation in France, see, for example,
E. K. Brown, The French Reputation of Matthew Arnold,
'Studies in English by Members of University College,
Toronto' (1931). Arnold met and established a relationship with Sainte-Beuve, who responded favourably
to several of his writings - much to Arnold's delight.
See R. H. Super, Documents in the Arnold Sainte-Beuve
Relationship, 'Modern Philology' (1963), and Arnold
Whitridge, Matthew Arnold and Sainte-Beuve, 'PMLA'
(1938).
9 T. S. Eliot, Matthew Arnold, 'The Use of Poetry and
the Use of Criticism' (1933), 105.
10 Basil Willey, 'Nineteenth-Century Studies' (1949),
253.
11 Douglas Bush, 'Matthew Arnold' (1971), 172.
12 David J. DeLaura, 'Victorian Prose: A Guide to
Research' (1973), 312-13.
13 See L. E. Elliott-Binns, 'English Thought, 1860-1900:
The Theological Aspect' (1956), 300 f.
14 See, for example, W. F. Connell, 'The Educational
Thought and Influence of Matthew Arnold' (1950).
15 Robert Tener has identified many of Hutton's contributions to the 'Spectator' (and to other periodicals)
in 'Victorian Periodicals Newsletter' (1972), xvii,
1-46, and (1973), xx, 14-31.
16 Edgar Johnson, 'Charles Dickens: His Triumph and
Tragedy' (1952), ii, 1132.
17 'Alfred Lord Tennyson, A Memoir by His Son' (1898),
ii, 225.
18 'The George Eliot Letters', ed. Gordon Haight (1955),
iv, 395.
19 'The Letters of John Stuart Mill', ed. H. S. R.
Elliott (1910), ii, 93. See 'Edward Alexander's
study, 'Matthew Arnold and John Stuart Mill' (1965).

20 George Saintsbury, 'Matthew Arnold' (1899), 66-7.
21 [Henry Hill Lancaster,] Recent Homeric Critics and Translators, 'North British Review' (May 1862), xxxvi, 345.
22 Arnold did, of course, needle Oxford and took pleasure in doing so; his final lecture was to be something of an apology for earlier 'liberties' (i, 364).
23 R. H. Super, ed., 'The Complete Prose Works of Matthew Arnold' (1960-77), i, 249.
24 Basil Willey offers stout defence of Newman in Chapter I of 'More Nineteenth-Century Studies' (1956), although he is more concerned with Newman's religious books.
25 Lionel Trilling, 'Matthew Arnold' (1949 ed.), 158.
26 [J. S. Blackie,] Homer and His Translators, 'Macmillan's Magazine' (August 1861), iv, 268-80.
27 Noel Annan, Books in General, 'New Statesman' (18 March 1944), 191.
28 'On Translating Homer', 'The Times' (28 October 1861), 8.
29 See, for example, On Translating Homer: Hexameters and Pentameters (1863) in 'The Poems of Tennyson', ed. Christopher Ricks (1969), 1153-4.
30 See Merle M. Bevington's edition of 'England and the Italian Question' (1953), which includes Stephen's review. Bevington has also written a useful study of the 'Saturday Review' (1941).
31 Super, 'Complete Prose Works', i, 97. Future references to Super's edition will be cited in the text.
32 G. K. Chesterton, Matthew Arnold, 'Bookman' (October 1902), 118.
33 Kathleen Tillotson, Matthew Arnold and Carlyle, 'Mid-Victorian Studies' (1965), 231.
34 Henry Lancaster, Recent Homeric Critics, 347.
35 'Athenaeum' (30 June 1864), no. 1918, 137-8.
36 Chesterton, Matthew Arnold, 119.
37 Sister Thomas Marion Hoctor, ed., 'Essays in Criticism, First Series' (1968), xxxiii.
38 David A. Wilson and David A. MacArthur, 'Carlyle in Old Age' (1934), 23.
39 Quoted in Raleigh, 60. See also Mark Twain's satiric commentary in 'A Connecticut Yankee in King Arthur's Court'.
40 Hoctor, viii.
41 For Morris's complicated response to Arnold, see pp. 46-7 below. Perhaps Arnold's main flaw as critic was a failure of generosity with regard to his English contemporaries.
42 [Henry Hill Lancaster,] 'Essays in Criticism', 'North British Review' (March 1865), iii, n.s., 81.

43 Disraeli often praised Arnold and went out of his way,
    when the two met, to say something complimentary.
    'Letters', ii, 188-9 includes Arnold's account of
    'Dizzie' 'declaring that I was the only living
    Englishman who had become a classic in his own life-
    time'.
44 See, for example, Robert Donovan, The Method of
    Arnold's 'Essays in Criticism', 'PMLA' (1956), lxxi,
    922-31.
45 Henry James, Matthew Arnold (1884). In 'Matthew
    Arnold, The Poetry', 283.
46 See Trilling, The Failure of the Middle Class, in
    'Matthew Arnold'; also Rachel Bromwich, 'Matthew
    Arnold and Celtic Literature' (1965).
47 Frederic E. Faverty, 'Matthew Arnold the Ethnologist'
    (1951), 111.
48 W. B. Yeats, The Celtic Element in Literature (1897),
    'Essays and Introductions' (1961).
49 Quoted in Faverty, 155.
50 John V. Kelleher, Matthew Arnold and the Celtic
    Revival, 'Perspectives in Criticism', ed. Harry Levin
    (1950), 204-5.
51 Quoted in Super, v, 394.
52 S. M. B. Coulling, Matthew Arnold and the 'Daily
    Telegraph', 'Review of English Studies' (1961), xii,
    n. s., 179.
53 G. A. Sala, 'Life and Adventures' (1895), i, 18-19.
54 On the Study of Celtic Literature, 'Athenaeum' (31
    August 1867), 265.
55 Kelleher, 200.
56 H. S. Fagan 'On the Study of Celtic Literature',
    'Contemporary Review' (October 1867), vi, 258-9.
57 William Buckler, 'Matthew Arnold's Books: Towards a
    Publishing Diary' (1958), 83.
58 Quoted in Lloyd W. Eshleman, 'A Victorian Rebel: The
    Life of William Morris' (1940), 157.
59 Raymond Williams, 'Culture and Society' (1958), 116.
    Williams says that Arnold 'brought down' on culture
    the charges of 'priggishness and spiritual pride'.
60 For a lucid and informative survey of Arnold's influ-
    ence, see Connell, 'The Educational Thought and Influ-
    ence of Matthew Arnold', passim.
61 'Reports on Elementary Schools', ed. Sir Francis
    Sandford (1889). A recent selection may be found in
    Peter Smith and Geoffrey Summerfield, eds, 'Matthew
    Arnold and the Education of the New Order' (1969),
    which includes a valuable introduction.
62 Henry Reeve, Popular Education in England, 'Edinburgh
    Review' (July 1861), cxlv, 11.

63 'Athenaeum' (6 July 1861), 15-16; (30 July 1864),
    137-8; 'North American Review' (October 1861), 581-2;
    'Macmillan's Magazine' (June 1864), 175-6; 'Cornhill
    Magazine' (October 1864), 409-26.
64 'T.M.' [Thomas Markby], Schools and Universities on
    the Continent, 'Contemporary Review' (September 1868),
    ix, 144-9.
65 'Nonconformist' (7 February 1866), 119.
66 Mr. Matthew Arnold on Culture and Anarchy, 'Saturday
    Review' (6 March 1869), xvii, 318.
67 Martha S. Vogeler, Matthew Arnold and Frederic Harri-
    son: The Prophet of Culture and the Prophet of
    Positivism, 'Studies in English Literature' (1962),
    ii, 441-62; S. M. B. Coulling, The Evolution of
    'Culture and Anarchy', 'Studies in Philology' (1963),
    lx, 637-68. See also Ian Gregor, ed., 'Culture and
    Anarchy' (1971), with an excellent chronology.
68 W. H. Auden's surprisingly crude estimate of Arnold's
    relationship with his father distorts Thomas Arnold's
    influence to the point of parody ('The Collected
    Poetry' (1945), 54);
        But all his homeless reverence, revolted, cried:
        'I am my father's forum and he shall be heard,
        Nothing shall contradict his holy final word....'
69 'Illustrated London News' (10 February 1866), 90.
70 [C. S. M. Phillipps,] Matthew Arnold's Critical Works,
    'Edinburgh Review' (April 1869), cxxix, 486-503.
71 Martha Vogeler, Matthew Arnold and Frederic Harrison,
    passim.
72 Frederic Harrison, Our Venetian Constitution, 'Fort-
    nightly Review' (March 1867), n.s., i, 276.
73 S. M. B. Coulling, The Evolution of 'Culture and
    Anarchy', 650 f.
74 See, for example, Marx on the death of Palmerston, in
    'Marx and Engels on Britain' (1962).
75 See George W. Stocking, Matthew Arnold, E. B. Tylor,
    and the Uses of Invention, 'American Anthropologist'
    (1963), lxvi, 783-99.
76 Leslie Stephen, Mr. Matthew Arnold and the Church of
    England, 'Fraser's Magazine' (October 1870), ii, n.s.,
    414.
77 See, for example, H. P. Owen, The Theology of Coler-
    idge, 'Critical Quarterly' (Spring 1972), 59-67;
    Eugene L. Williamson, 'The Liberalism of Thomas
    Arnold' (1964); William Blackburn, Matthew Arnold and
    the Oriel Noetics, 'Philological Quarterly' (January
    1946), 70-8; and Basil Willey, 'Nineteenth-Century
    Studies' (1949), 51-69; 251-83.
78 David J. DeLaura, Matthew Arnold and J. H. Newman,
    'Texas Studies in Literature' (1965), 643.

79 R. V. Osborne, 'The British Quarterly Review', 'Review of English Studies' (April 1950), 151.
80 Stephen, Mr. Matthew Arnold and the Church of England, 414.
81 Stephen, 414.
82 Quoted by John Morley, 'The Life of W. E. Gladstone' (1903), iii, 520.
83 Sidney Colvin, 'A Bible-Reading for Schools', 'Fortnightly Review' (1 August 1872), 240-1.
84 Newman's letter and Arnold's reply are printed in 'Unpublished Letters of Matthew Arnold', ed. Arnold Whitridge (1923), 62-5.
85 See E. K. Brown, The French Reputation of Matthew Arnold, 232-7.
86 William Buckler, 'Matthew Arnold's Books', 96.
87 George Saintsbury, 'Matthew Arnold', 131-2.
88 Diderik Roll-Hansen, Matthew Arnold and the 'Academy', 'PMLA' (1953), lxviii, 388-9.
89 Albert Réville, 'Literature and Dogma', 'Academy' (1 September 1873), iv, 327-30.
90 [J. L. Davies,] Mr. Matthew Arnold's New Religion of the Bible, 'Contemporary Review' (May 1873), xxi, 842.
91 'Literature and Dogma', 'British Quarterly Review' (April 1873), lvi, 579.
92 Religion in the Hands of Literary Laymen, 'Theological Review' (July 1873), x, 378.
93 Tulloch, 'Theological Review', 388.
94 Tulloch, 'Theological Review', 388.
95 'British Quarterly Review', 579.
96 F. W. Newman, 'Literature and Dogma', 'Fraser's Magazine' (July 1873), viii, n.s., 120.
97 Letter to C. E. Norton of 12 October 1874, in Frederic William Maitland, 'The Life and Letters of Leslie Stephen' (1906), 245.
98 R. H. Hutton, Mr. Arnold's Sublimated Bible, 'Spectator' (10 October 1874), xlvii, 1256-8).
99 Henry Hewlett, The Poems of Matthew Arnold, 'Contemporary Review' (September 1874), xxiv, 559-67. In 'Matthew Arnold, The Poetry', 233-54.
100 William Madden, 'Matthew Arnold: A Study of the Aesthetic Temperament' (1967).
101 See David DeLaura, 'Hebrew and Hellene in Victorian England' (1969), 192-3. There are many discussions of Arnold and Pater. See, for example, Kenneth Allott, Pater and Arnold, 'Essays in Criticism' (1952).
102 Thomas Wright, 'The Life of Walter Pater', i, 173. Quoted in DeLaura, 'Hebrew and Hellene', 193.
103 Walter Pater, 'Studies in the History of the Renaissance' (1873) v.

104 Lloyd W. Eshleman, 'A Victorian Rebel', 157.
105 Raymond Williams, 'Culture and Society' (1950), 145.
106 'Letters of William Morris', ed. Philip Henderson (1950), 113.
107 Herbert Spencer, The Study of Sociology. Part IX, 'Contemporary Review' (March 1873), xxi, 475-502.
108 Buckler, 159-60.
109 [Margaret Oliphant,] New Books, 'Blackwood's Magazine' (July 1879), cxxvi, 90-1.
110 Mixed Essays. By Matthew Arnold, 'Athenaeum' (8 March 1879), no. 2680, 303.
111 John Holloway, 'The Chartered Mirror' (1960), 154.
112 Alfred Austin, Old and New Canons of Poetical Criticism, 'Contemporary Review' (December 1881), 885.
113 'Athenaeum' (18 March 1882), no. 2838, 339-40.
114 'Saturday Review' (March 1882), 334.
115 'Athenaeum', 339.
116 Lewis Gates, 'Selections from the Prose Works of Matthew Arnold' (1898), xxxvii-xxxviii.
117 See Clyde L. Ryals, The Nineteenth-Century Cult of Inaction, 'Tennessee Studies in Literature' (1959), for a discussion of Arnold's influence on Wilde; also Leonard Brown, Matthew Arnold's Succession, 1850-1914, 'Sewanee Review' (1934).
118 Buckler, 75.
119 Henry Duff Traill, Matthew Arnold, 'Contemporary Review' (June 1888), 870. This section of Traill's essay can be found in 'Matthew Arnold, The Poetry: The Critical Heritage', 316.
120 Lord Coleridge, Matthew Arnold, Part II, 'New Review' (August 1889), i, 218.
121 John Morley, Matthew Arnold, 'Nineteenth Century' (December 1895), xxxviii, 1054.
122 David J. DeLaura, What, Then, Does Matthew Arnold Mean?, 'Modern Philology' (May 1969), lxvi, 345-55.
123 'The Letters of Gerard Manley Hopkins to Robert Bridges', ed. C. C. Abbott (1935), i, 172.
124 Quoted in Florence Hardy, 'The Early Life of Thomas Hardy, 1840-1891' (1928), 271. The book is almost entirely by Hardy himself.
125 G. M. Trevelyan, 'A Layman's Love of Letters' (1954), 22.
126 Vincent Buckley, 'Poetry and Morality: Studies on the Criticism of Matthew Arnold, T. S. Eliot, and F. R. Leavis' (1959).
127 Williams, 'Culture and Society', passim.
128 See DeLaura, 'Victorian Prose', 313-14.
129 See R. H. Tawney, 'Equality' (1931), especially Chapter I; also Reinhard Bendix, The Protestant Ethic -

Revisited, 'Comparative Studies in Society and History' (1967).
130   Stocking, Matthew Arnold and E. B. Tylor, passim.
131   Frederic Faverty, 'The Victorian Poets: A Guide to Research' (1968).
132   The Poet of Our Modernity, 'Times Literary Supplement' (4 January 1974), 11.
133   Lionel Trilling, Edmund Wilson: A Backward Glance, 'A Gathering of Fugitives' (1956), 50-1.
134   E. M. Forster, 'Two Cheers for Democracy' (1951), 202.

Chronology

1822   Born 24 December, the eldest son of Thomas and Mary
Arnold, at Laleham-on-Thames.
1828   Father, Dr Thomas Arnold, is appointed headmaster of
Rugby School.
1831   Visits the Lake District with family.
1836   Attends Winchester College, his father's old school.
First attempts at writing verse.
1837   Wins a prize at Winchester with a speech from
Byron's 'Marino Faliero'.
1838   Wins fifth form prize for Latin verse.
1840   Publishes prize-poem 'Alaric at Rome', Rugby.
Wins school prizes for Latin essay and Latin verse.
Enters Balliol College, Oxford, elected to an open
classical scholarship.
1842   Sudden death of Thomas Arnold.
1843   Publishes the Newdigate prize-poem, 'Cromwell'.
1844   Takes A.B. degree in *Literae Humaniores* (second-
class honours).
1845   Elected a fellow of Oriel College, Oxford.
1846   Visits France.
1847   Appointed private secretary to the Lord President of
the Council and Whig elder statesman, the Marquis of
Lansdowne.
1849   Publishes 'The Strayed Reveller, and Other Poems',
' by A.'. Visits Switzerland.
1850   Publishes 'Memorial Verses' in 'Fraser's Magazine'.
1851   Appointed inspector of schools by Lord Lansdowne.
Marries Frances Lucy, daughter of Sir William Wight-
man.
Begins work as inspector of schools.
1852   Publishes 'Empedocles on Etna, and Other Poems',
'by A.'.
1853   Publishes 'Poems. A New Edition'.
1854   Publishes 'Poems, Second Series' (dated 1855; a
further selection).

65

1855   Publishes 'Stanzas from the Grand Chartreuse' in
       'Fraser's Magazine'.
       Publishes 'Haworth Churchyard' in 'Fraser's Maga-
       zine'.
1856   First American edition of 'Poems. A New and Com-
       plete Edition'.
1857   Elected Professor of Poetry at Oxford.
       Visits Switzerland with his wife.
       14 November. Inaugural lecture at Oxford, On the
       Modern Element in Literature.
       Publishes 'Merope: A Tragedy' (dated 1858).
1858   Settles in London.
       Walking tour in Switzerland.
1859   Study of schools in France, Holland, and Switzer-
       land.
       Publishes 'England and the Italian Question'.
1860   Publishes Report to the Education Commission - Confi-
       dential Edition.
1861   Publishes 'On Translating Homer'.
       Publishes 'The Popular Education of France'.
       Death of A. H. Clough.
1862   Publishes 'On Translating Homer: Last Words'.
       Re-elected to Poetry Chair at Oxford.
1864   Publishes 'A French Eton; or, Middle Class Education
       and the State'. Publishes The Literary Influence of
       Academies in 'Cornhill Magazine' and The Function of
       Criticism at the Present Time in the 'National
       Review'.
1865   Publishes 'Essays in Criticism, First Series'.
       Travels in France, Italy, Germany, and Switzerland.
1866   Publishes his elegy on Clough, 'Thyrsis', in
       'Macmillan's Magazine'.
1867   Publishes 'On the Study of Celtic Literature'.
       Publishes 'New Poems' (this is the last major edi-
       tion with new poems).
1868   Publishes 'Schools and Universities on the Conti-
       nent'.
       Moves to Harrow.
       Death of sons Basil and Thomas.
1869   Publishes 'Culture and Anarchy'.
       Publishes 'Poems', the first collected edition (two
       volumes).
       Publishes essay on 'Obermann' in the 'Academy'.
       Publishes essay Sainte-Beuve in the 'Academy'.
1870   Publishes 'St. Paul and Protestantism'.
       Receives honorary degree from Oxford.
1871   Publishes 'Friendship's Garland', a series of
       letters originally published in the 'Pall Mall
       Gazette' (1866-7, 1869-70).

Visits France and Switzerland.

1872   Death of son, William.
Publishes 'A Bible Reading for Schools'.

1873   Publishes 'Literature and Dogma'.
Moves to Pains Hill Cottage, Cobham, Surrey.

1874   Publishes 'Higher Schools and Universities in Germany'.

1875   Publishes 'God and the Bible'.

1876   Reprints 'The New Sirens' in 'Macmillan's Magazine'.
'La Crise religieuse', a translation of 'Literature and Dogma', is published in Paris.

1877   Publishes 'Poems', the second collected edition (reissued, 1881).
Publishes 'Last Essays on Church and Religion'.
Publishes essay, George Sand, in the 'Fortnightly Review'.

1878   Publishes 'Selected Poems of Matthew Arnold' (Golden Treasury Series).

1879   Publishes 'Mixed Essays'.
Publishes the 'Poems of Wordsworth' (a selection).

1880   Visits Switzerland and Italy.
Contributes Introduction (later called On the Study of Poetry), Thomas Gray, and John Keats to T. H. Ward's 'The English Poets'.

1881   Publishes the 'Poetry of Byron' (a selection).

1882   Publishes 'Westminster Abbey', his elegy on A. P. Stanley, in the 'Nineteenth Century'.
Publishes 'Irish Essays'.

1883   Lecture-tour in America (to March 1884).

1884   Appointed Chief Inspector of Schools.

1885   Publishes 'Discourses in America'.
Publishes the collected Library Edition of 'Poems' (three volumes).

1886   On the Continent.
Retires from inspectorship of schools.
Second visit to America.

1888   Dies 15 April of heart failure.
Posthumous publications of 'Essays in Criticism, Second Series'.
'Civilization in the United States: First and Last Impressions of America' is published in Boston.

1889   'Reports on Elementary Schools, 1852-1882' is published.

1890   'Poetical Works of Matthew Arnold', the Popular Edition, is published.

On Translating Homer (1861)
and Homer: Last Words (1862)

1. FRANCIS NEWMAN, HOMERIC TRANSLATION IN THEORY AND
PRACTICE, A REPLY TO MATTHEW ARNOLD

1861

Francis W. Newman (1805-97), Professor of Latin at London
University, was for a time as well known as his brother,
John Henry Newman. He was an incredibly learned, eccentric man who wrote on theology, vegetarianism, political
economy - on almost any topic. For Arnold, Newman represented undisciplined learning and inadequate literary
sense. He coined from Newman the derisive verb 'to New-
manise'. Most of the contemporary reviewers seem to have
agreed with Arnold's estimate of Newman, but they thought
Arnold too harsh in his attack. Newman's self-defence
is a long, windy rebuttal, another example of all that
Arnold had censured in the translation itself. The following cut version omits much of Newman's elaborate
defence, but it retains his essential argument. Arnold
replied to Newman in 'On Translating Homer: Last Words'.

It is so difficult, amid the press of literature, for a
mere versifier and translator to gain notice at all, that
an assailant may even do one a service, if he so conduct
his assault as to enable the reader to sit in intelligent
judgment on the merits of the book assailed. But when the
critic deals out to the readers only so much knowledge as
may propagate his own contempt of the book, he has
undoubtedly immense power to dissuade them from wishing
to open it. Mr Arnold writes as openly aiming at this

end. He begins by complimenting me, as 'a man of great
ability and genuine learning'; but on questions of learning, as well as of taste, he puts me down as bluntly, as
if he had meant, 'a man totally void both of learning and
of sagacity.' He again and again takes for granted that
he has 'the scholar' on his side, 'the living scholar,'
the man who has learning and taste without pedantry. He
bids me please 'the scholars,' and go to 'the scholars'
tribunal'; and does not know that I did this, to the extent of my opportunity, before committing myself to a
laborious, expensive and perhaps thankless task. Of
course he cannot guess, what is the fact, that scholars
of fastidious refinement, but of a judgment which I think
far more masculine than Mr Arnold's, have passed a most
encouraging sentence on large specimens of my translations. I at this moment count eight such names, though of
course I must not here adduce them: nor will I further
allude to it, than to say, that I have no such sense
either of pride or of despondency, as those are liable to,
who are consciously isolated in their taste.
   Scholars are the tribunal of Erudition, but of Taste
the educated but unlearned public is the only rightful
judge; and to it I wish to appeal. Even scholars collect-
ively have no right, and much less have single scholars,
to pronounce a final sentence on questions of taste in
their court. Where I differ in Taste from Mr Arnold, it
is very difficult to find 'the scholars' tribunal,'
even if I acknowledged its absolute jurisdiction: but as
regards Erudition, this difficulty does not occur, and I
shall fully reply to the numerous dogmatisms by which he
settles the case against me.
   But I must first avow to the reader my own moderate
pretensions. Mr Arnold begins by instilling two errors
which he does not commit himself to assert. He says that
my work will *not* take rank as *the* standard translation of
Homer, but *other translations will be made*: as if I thought
otherwise! If I have set the example of the right direction in which translators ought to aim, of course those
who follow me will improve upon me and supersede me. A
man would be rash indeed to withhold his version of a poem
of fifteen thousand lines, until he had, to his best ability, imparted to them all their final perfection. He
might spend the leisure of his life upon it. He would
possibly be in his grave before it could see the light.
If it then were published, and it was founded on any new
principle, there would be no one to defend it from the
attacks of ignorance and prejudice. In the nature of the
case, his wisdom is to elaborate in the first instance
all the high and noble parts *carefully*, and get through

the inferior parts *somehow;* leaving of necessity very much
to be done in successive editions, if possibly it please
general taste sufficiently to reach them. A generous and
intelligent critic will test such a work mainly or solely
by the most noble parts, and as to the rest, will consider
whether the metre and style adapts itself naturally to
them also.

Next, Mr Arnold asks, 'Who is to assure Mr Newman, that
when he has tried to retain every peculiarity of his original, he has done that for which Mr Newman enjoins this
to be done – adhered closely to Homer's manner and habit
of thought? Evidently the translator needs more practical
directions than these.' The tendency of this is, to suggest to the reader that I am not aware of the difficulty
of rightly applying good principles; whereas I have in
this very connection said expressly, that even when a
translator has got right principles, he is liable to go
wrong in the detail of their application. This is as true
of all the principles which Mr Arnold can possibly give,
as of those which I have given; nor do I for a moment
assume, that in writing fifteen thousand lines of verse I
have not made hundreds of blots.

At the same time Mr Arnold has overlooked the point of
my remark. Nearly every translator before me has *knowingly, purposely, habitually* shrunk from Homer's thoughts
and Homer's manner. The reader will afterwards see
whether Mr Arnold does not justify them in their course.
It is not for those who are purposely unfaithful to taunt
me with the difficulty of being truly faithful.

I have alleged, and, against Mr Arnold's flat denial, I
deliberately repeat, that Homer rises and sinks with his
subject, and is often homely or prosaic. I have professed
as my principle, to follow my original in this matter. It
is unfair to expect of me grandeur in trivial passages.
If in any place where Homer is *confessedly* grand and
noble, I have marred and ruined his greatness, let me be
reproved. But I shall have occasion to protest, that
Stateliness is not Grandeur, Picturesqueness is not
Stately, Wild Beauty is not to be confounded with Elegance: a Forest has its swamps and brushwood, as well as
its tall trees.

The duty of one who *publishes* his censures on me is, to
select noble, greatly admired passages, and confront me
both with a prose translation of the original (for the
public cannot go to the Greek) and also with that which he
judges to be a more successful version than mine. Translation being matter of compromise, and being certain to
fall below the original, when this is of the highest type
of grandeur; the question is not, What translator is

perfect? but, Who is least imperfect? Hence the only fair
test is by comparison, when comparison is possible. But
Mr Arnold has not put me to this test. He has quoted two
very short passages, and various single lines, half lines
and single words, from me; and chooses to *tell* his readers
that I ruin Homer's nobleness, when (if his censure is
just) he might make them *feel* it by quoting me upon the
most admired pieces. Now with the warmest sincerity I
say: If any English reader, after perusing my version of
four or five eminently noble passages of sufficient length,
side by side with those of other translators, and (better
still) with a prose version also, finds in them high qualities which I have destroyed; I am foremost to advise him
to shut my book, or to consult it only (as Mr Arnold suggests) as a schoolboy's 'help to construe,' if such it can
be. My sole object is, to bring Homer before the unlearned public: I seek no self-glorification: the sooner I am
superseded by a really better translation, the greater
will be my pleasure.

It was not until I more closely read Mr Arnold's own
versions, that I understood how necessary is his repugnance to mine. I am unwilling to speak of his metrical
efforts. I shall not say more than my argument strictly
demands. It here suffices to state the simple fact, that
for a while I seriously doubted whether he meant his first
specimen for metre at all. He seems distinctly to say, he
is going to give us English Hexameters; but it was long
before I could believe that he had written the following
for that metre:

> So shone forth, in front of Troy, by the bed of
>   Xanthus,
> Between that and the ships, the Trojans' numerous
>   fires.
> In the plain there were kindled a thousand fires: by
>   each one
> There sate fifty men, in the ruddy light of the fire.
> By their chariots stood the steeds, and champ'd the
>   white barley,
> While their masters sate by the fire, and waited for
>   Morning.

I sincerely thought, this was meant for prose; at
length the two last lines opened my eyes. He *does* mean
them for Hexameters! 'Fire' (=feuer) with him is a spon-
dee or trochee. The first line, I now see, begins with
three (quantitative) spondees, and is meant to be spondaic
in the fifth foot. 'Bed of, Between, In the,' - are meant
for spondees! So are 'There sate,' '*By* their'; though

'Troy *by* the' was a dactyl. 'Champ'd the white' is a
dactyl. My 'metrical exploits' amaze Mr Arnold; but my
courage is timidity itself compared to his.

To avoid a needlessly personal argument, I enlarge on the
general question of hexameters. Others, scholars of
repute, have given example and authority to English hexameters. As matter of curiosity, as erudite sport, such
experiments may have their value. I do not mean to
express indiscriminate disapproval, much less contempt.
I have myself privately tried the same in Alcaics; and
find the chief objection to be, not that the task is impossible, but that to execute it *well* is too difficult
for a language like ours, overladen with consonants, and
abounding with syllables neither distinctly long nor distinctly short, but of every intermediate length. Singing
to a tune was essential to keep even Greek or Roman poetry
to true *time;* to the English language it is of tenfold
necessity. But if *time* is abandoned (as in fact it always
is), and the prose accent has to do duty for the ictus
metricus, the moral genius of the metre is fundamentally
subverted.

If by happy combination any scholar could compose fifty
such English hexameters, as would convey a living likeness of the Virgilian metre, I should applaud it as valuable for initiating schoolboys into that metre: but there
its utility would end. The method could not be profit-
ably used for translating Homer or Virgil, plainly because it is impossible to say for whose service such a
translation would be executed. Those who can read the
original will never care to read *through* any translation;
and the unlearned look on all, even the best hexameters,
whether from Southey, Lockhart or Longfellow, as odd and
disagreeable prose. Mr Arnold deprecates appeal to popular taste: well he may! yet if the unlearned are to be
our audience, we cannot defy them. I myself, before venturing to print, sought to ascertain how unlearned women
and children would accept my verses. I could boast how
children and half-educated women have extolled them; how
greedily a working man has inquired for them, without
knowing who was the translator; but I well know that this
is quite insufficient to establish the merits of a translation. It is nevertheless *one* point. 'Homer is popular,' is one of the very few matters of fact in this controversy on which Mr Arnold and I are agreed. 'English
hexameters are not popular,' is a truth so obvious, that

I do not yet believe he will deny it. Therefore, 'Hexameters are not the metre for translating Homer.' Q. E. D.

I think it fortunate for Mr Arnold, that he had *not* 'courage to translate Homer'; for he must have failed to make
it acceptable to the unlearned. But if the public ear
prefers ballad metres, still (Mr Arnold assumes) 'the
scholar' is with him in this whole controversy. Nevertheless it gradually comes out that neither is this the case,
but he himself is in the minority. He writes: 'When one
observes the boistering, rollicking way in which Homer's
English admirers - even men of genius, like the late Professor Wilson - love to talk of Homer and his poetry, one
cannot help feeling that there is no very deep community
of nature between them and the object of their enthusiasm.'
It does not occur to Mr Arnold that the defect of perception lies with himself, and that Homer has more sides than
he has discovered.

But I claim Mr Arnold himself as confessing that our
ballad *metre* is epical, when he says that Scott is
'*bastard*-epic.' I do not admit that his quotations from
Scott are all Scott's best, nor anything like it; but if
they were, it would only prove something against Scott's
genius or talent, nothing about his metre. The Κύπρια
ἔπη (1) or Ἰλίου πέρσις (2) were probably very inferior to
the 'Iliad'; but no one would on that account call them or
the Frogs and Mice bastard-epic. No one would call a bad
tale of Dryden or of Crabbe bastard-epic. The application of the word to Scott virtually concedes what I
assert. Mr Arnold also calls Macaulay's ballads 'pinchbeck'; but a man needs to produce something very noble
himself, before he can afford thus to sneer at Macauley's
'Lars Porsena.'

I do not say that any measure is faultless. Every measure
has its foible: mine has that fault which every uniform
line must have; it is liable to monotony. This is evaded
of course, as in the hexameter or rather as in Milton's
line, first, by varying the caesura, secondly, by varying
certain feet, within narrow and well understood limits,
thirdly, by irregularity in the strength of accents,
fourthly, by varying the weight of the unaccented syllables also. All these things are needed, *for the mere
sake of breaking uniformity*. I will not here assert that
Homer's many marvellous freedoms, such as ἐχηβολου

'Απόλλωνος, (3) were dictated by this aim, like those in
the 'Paradise Lost'; but I do say, that it is most unjust,
most unintelligent, in critics to produce *single* lines from
me, and criticise them as rough or weak, instead of examining them and presenting them as part of *a mass*. How would
Shakespeare stand this sort of test? nay, or Milton? The
metrical laws of a long poem cannot be the same as of a
sonnet: single verses are organic elements of a great
whole. A crag must not be cut like a gem. Mr Arnold
should remember Aristotle's maxim, that popular eloquence
(and such is Homer's) should be broad, rough and highly
coloured, like scene painting, not polished into delicacy
like miniature. But I speak now of metre, not yet of diction. In *any* long and popular poem it is a mistake to wish
every line to conform severely to a few types; but to claim
this of a translator of *Homer* is a doubly unintelligent ex-
action, when Homer's own liberties transgress all bounds...

So much of metre. At length I come to the topic of Diction, where Mr Arnold and I are at variance not only as to
taste, but as to the main facts of Greek literature. I had
called Homer's style quaint and garrulous; and said that he
rises and falls with his subject, being prosaic when it is
tame, and low when it is mean. I added no proof; for I did
not dream that it was needed. Mr Arnold not only absolutely denies all this, and denies it without proof; but
adds, that these assertions prove my incompetence, and
account for my total and conspicuous failure.

The young men who read Homer and Sophocles and Thucydides,
nay, the boys who read Homer and Xenophon, would know his
statements to be against the most notorious and elementary
fact: and the professors, whom he quotes, would only lose
credit, if they sanctioned the use he makes of their names.
But when he publishes the book for the unlearned in Greek,
among whom I must include a great number of editors of
magazines, I find Mr Arnold to do a public wrong to literature, and a private wrong to my book. If I am silent, such
editors may easily believe that I have made an enormous
blunder in treating the dialect of Homer as antiquated. If
those who are ostensibly scholars, thus assail my version,
and the great majority of magazines and reviews ignore it,
its existence can never become known to the public; or it
will exist not to be read, but to be despised without
being opened; and it must perish as many meritorious books
perish.

However, just because I address myself to the public
unlearned in Greek, and because Mr Arnold lays before *them*
a new, paradoxical, monstrously erroneous representation
of facts, with the avowed object of staying the plague of
my Homer; I am forced to reply to him.

Knowingly or unknowingly, he leads his readers to con-
fuse four different questions: 1. whether Homer is thoroughly intelligible to modern scholars; 2. whether Homer
was antiquated to the Athenians of Themistocles and Pericles; 3. whether he was thoroughly understood by them;
4. whether he is, absolutely, an antique poet.

I feel it rather odd, that Mr Arnold begins by complimenting me with 'genuine learning,' and proceeds to appeal
from me to the 'living scholar.' (What if I were bluntly
to reply: 'Well! I am the living scholar'?) After starting the question, how Homer's style appeared to Sophocles,
he suddenly enters a plea, under form of a concession
['I confess'!], as a pretence for carrying the cause into
a new court, that of the Provost of Eton and two Professors, into which court I have no admission; and then, of
his own will, pronounces a sentence in the name of these
learned men. Whether they are pleased with this parading
of their name in behalf of paradoxical error, I may well
doubt: and until they indorse it themselves, I shall treat
Mr Arnold's process as a piece of forgery. But, be this
as it may, I cannot allow him to 'confess' for me against
me: let him confess for himself that he does not know,
and not for me, who know perfectly well, whether Homer
seemed quaint or antiquated to Sophocles. Of course he
did, as every beginner must know. Why, if I were to
write *mon* for *man, londis* for *lands, nesties* for *nests,
libbard* for *leopard, muchel* for *much, nap* for *snap,
green-wood shaw* for *green-wood shade,* Mr Arnold would call
me antiquated, although every word would be intelligible.
Can he possibly be ignorant, that this exhibits but the
smallest part of the chasm which separates the Homeric
dialect not merely from the Attic prose, but from Aeschylus when he borrows most from Homer? Every sentence of
Homer was more or less antiquated to Sophocles, who could
no more help feeling at every instant the foreign and
antiquated character of the poetry, than an Englishman
can help feeling the same in reading Burns' poems.

Mr Arnold (as I understand him) blames Shakespeare for
being sometimes antiquated: I do not blame him, nor yet
Homer for the same; but neither can I admit the contrast
which he asserts. He says: 'Shakespeare can compose, when
he is at his best, in a language perectly intelligible, in

spite of the two centuries and a half which part him from
us. *Homer has not Shakespeare's variations:* he is never
antiquated, as Shakespeare is sometimes.' I certainly
find the very same variations in Homer, as Mr Arnold finds
in Shakespeare. My reader unlearned in Greek might hastily infer from the facts just laid before him, that Homer
is always equally strange to a purely Attic ear: but is
not so. The dialects of Greece did indeed differ strongly,
as broad Scotch from English; yet as we know, Burns is
sometimes perfectly intelligible to an Englishman, sometimes quite unintelligible. In spite of Homer's occasional wide receding from Attic speech, he as often comes
close to it.

Mr Arnold plays fallaciously on the words familiar and
unfamiliar. Homer's words may have been *familiar* to the
Athenians (*i.e.* often heard), even when they were *not*
understood, but, at most, were guessed at; or when, being
understood, they were still felt and.known to be utterly
foreign. Of course, when thus 'familiar,' they could not
'surprise' the Athenians, as Mr Arnold complains that my
renderings surprise the English. Let mine be heard as
Pope or even Cowper has been heard, and no one will be
'surprised.'
    Antiquated words are understood well by some, ill by
others, not at all by a third class; hence it is difficult
to decide the limits of a glossary. Mr Arnold speaks
scornfully of me (he wonders *with whom Mr Newman can have
lived*), that I use the words which I use, and explain
those which I explain. He censures my little Glossary,
for containing three words which he did not know, and
some others, which, he says, are 'familiar to all the
world.' It is clear, he will never want a stone to throw
at me. I suppose I am often guilty of keeping low company. I have found ladies whom no one would guess to be
so ill-educated, who yet do not distinctly know what *lusty*
means; but have an uncomfortable feeling that it is very
near to *lustful;* and understand *grisly* only in the sense
of *grizzled, grey.* Great numbers mistake the sense of
Buxom, Imp, Dapper, deplorably. I no more wrote my Glossary than my translation for persons so highly educated as
Mr Arnold.
    But I must proceed to remark: Homer might have been as
unintelligible to Pericles, as was the court poet of king
Croesus, and yet it might be highly improper to translate
him into an old English dialect; namely, if he had been
the typical poet of a logical and refined age. *Here is
the real question; -* is he absolutely antique, or only

antiquated relatively, as Euripides is now antiquated?

I say, that he *not only was* antiquated, relatively to
Pericles, but *is also* absolutely antique, being the poet
of a barbarian age. Antiquity in poets is not (as Horace
stupidly imagines in the argument of the horse's tail) a
question of years, but of intrinsic quality. Homer sang
to a wholly unfastidious audience, very susceptible to the
marvellous, very unalive to the ridiculous, capable of
swallowing with reverence the most grotesque conceptions.
Hence nothing is easier than to turn Homer to ridicule.
The fun which Lucian made of his mythology, a rhetorical
critic like Mr Arnold could make of his diction, if he
understood it as he understands mine. He takes credit to
himself for *not* ridiculing me; and is not aware, that I
could not be like Homer without being easy to ridicule.
An intelligent child is the second-best reader of Homer.
The best of all is a scholar of highly masculine taste;
the worst of all is a fastidious and refined man, to whom
everything quaint seems ignoble and contemptible.
    I might have supposed that Mr Arnold thinks Homer to be
a polished drawing-room poet, like Pope, when I read in
him this astonishing sentence. 'Search the English language for a word which does *not* apply to Homer, and you
could not fix on a better word than *quaint*.' But I am
taken aback at finding him praise the diction of Chapman's
translation in contrast to mine. Now I never open Chapman, without being offended at his pushing Homer's quaintness most unnecessarily into the grotesque.

But, while thus vindicating *Quaintness* as an essential
quality of Homer, do I regard it as a weakness to be apo-
logised for? Certainly not; for it is a condition of his
cardinal excellences. He could not otherwise be *Picturesque* as he is. So volatile is his mind, that what would
be a Metaphor in a more logical and cultivated age, with
him riots in Simile which overflows its banks. His sim-
iles not merely go beyond the mark of likeness; in extreme
cases they even turn into contrariety. If he were not so
carried away by his illustration, as to forget what he is
illustrating (which belongs to a quaint mind), he would
never paint for us such full and splendid pictures.
Where a logical later poet would have said that Menelaus

    With *eagle-eye* survey'd the field,

the mere metaphor contenting him; Homer says:

Gazing around on every side, in fashion of an eagle,
Which, of all heaven's fowl, they say, to scan the
   earth is keenest:
Whose eye, when loftiest he hangs, not the swift hare
   escapeth,
Lurking amid a leaf clad bush: but straight at it he
   souseth.
Unerring; and with crooked gripe doth quickly rieve its
   spirit.

I feel this long simile to be a disturbance of the
logical balance, such as belongs to the lively eye of the
savage, whose observation is intense, his concentration
of reasoning powers feeble. Without this, we should never
have got anything so picturesque.
    Homer never sees things *in the same proportions* as we
see them. To omit his digressions, and what I may call
his 'impertinences,' in order to give to his argument that
which Mr Arnold is pleased to call the proper 'balance,'
is to value our own logical minds, more than his picturesque but illogical mind.

In short, how *can* an Englishman read any Greek composition
and be affected by it as Greeks were? In a piece of
Euripides my imagination is caught by many things, which
he never intended or calculated for the prominence which
they actually get in my mind. This or that absurdity in
mythology, which passed with him as matter of course, may
monopolise my main attention. Our minds are not passive
recipients of this or that poet's influence; but the poet
is the material on which our minds actively work. If an
unlearned reader thinks it very 'odd' of Homer (the first
time he hears it) to call Aurora 'fair-thron'd,' so does
a boy learning Greek think it odd to call her εὔθρονος.
(4) Mr Arnold ought to blot every odd Homeric
out of his *Greek* Homer (or never lend the copy to a
youthful learner) if he desires me to expunge 'fair-
thron'd' from the translation. Nay, I think he should
conceal that the Morning was esteemed as a goddess,
though she had no altars or sacrifice. It is *all* odd.
But that is just why people want to read an English Homer,
- to know all his oddities, exactly as learned men do.
He is the phenomenon to be studied. His peculiarities,
pleasant or unpleasant, are to be made known, precisely
because of his great eminence and his substantial deeply
seated worth. Mr Arnold writes like a timid biographer,
fearful to let too much of his friend come out. So much
as to the substance. As to mere words, here also I hold

the very reverse of Mr Arnold's doctrine.

The Homeric style (whether it be that of an individual or
of an age) is peculiar, is 'odd,' if Mr Arnold like the
word, to the very core. Its eccentricities in epithet are
mere efflorescences of its essential eccentricity. If
Homer could cry out to us, I doubt not he would say, as
Oliver Cromwell to the painter, 'Paint me just as I am,
wart and all:' but if the true Homer could reappear, I am
sure Mr Arnold would start from him just as a bishop of
Rome from a fisherman apostle. If a translator of the
Bible honours the book by his close rendering of its
characteristics, however 'odd,' so do I honour Homer by
the same. Those characteristics, the moment I produce
them, Mr Arnold calls *ignoble*. Well: be it so; but I am
not to blame for them. They exist whether Mr Arnold likes
them or not.

From such a Homer as Mr Arnold's specimens and principles
would give us, no one could *learn* anything; no one could
have any motive for reading the translation. He smooths
down the stamp of Homer's coin, till nothing is left even
for miscroscopic examination. When he forbids me to let
my reader know that Homer calls horses 'single hoofed,'
of course he would suppress also the epithets 'white
milk,' 'dusky blood,' 'dear knees,' 'dear life,' etc. His
process obliterates everything characteristic, great or
small.

Mr Arnold further asserts, that Homer is never 'garrulous.' Allowing that too many others agree with me, he
attributes our error to giving too much weight to a sentence in Horace! I admire Horace as an ode-writer, but
I do not revere him as a critic, any more than as a moral
philosopher. I say that Homer is garrulous, because I
see and feel it. Mr Arnold puts me into a most unwelcome
position. I have a right to say, I have some enthusiasm
for Homer. In the midst of numerous urgent calls of duty
and taste, I devoted every possible quarter of an hour for
two years and a half to translate the 'Iliad,' toiled un-
remittingly in my vacations and in my walks, and going to
large expenses of money, in order to put the book before
the unlearned; and this, though I am not a professor of
Poetry nor even of Greek. Yet now I am forced to appear
as Homer's disparager and accuser! But if Homer were
always a poet, he could not be, what he is, so many other

things beside poet. As the Egyptians paint in their tombs
processes of art, not because they are beautiful or grand,
but from a mere love of imitating; so Homer narrates perpetually from a mere love of chatting. In how thoroughly
Egyptian a way does he tell the process of cutting up an
ox, and making *kebāb*; the process of bringing a boat to
anchor and carefully putting by the tackle; the process of
taking out a shawl from a chest, where it lies at the very
bottom!

But this is connected with another subject. I called
Homer's manner 'direct': Mr Arnold (if I understand) would
supersede this by his own epithet 'rapid.' But I cannot
admit the exchange: Homer is often the opposite of rapid.
Amplification is his characteristic, as it must be of every
improvisatore, every popular orator: condensation indeed is
improper for anything but written style; written to be read
privately. But I regard as Homer's worse defect, his lin-
gering over scenes of endless carnage and painful wounds.
He knows to half an inch where one hero hits another and
how deep. They arm: they approach: they encounter: we
have to listen to stereotype details again and again.
Such a style is anything but 'rapid.' Homer's garrulity
often leads him into it; yet he can do far better, as in
a part of the fight over Patroclus's body, and other splendid passages.
    Garrulity often vents itself in expletives.

When Mr Arnold denies that Homer is ever prosaic or homely,
his own specimens of translation put me into despair of
convincing him; for they seem to me a very anthology of
prosaic flatness. Phrases, which are not in themselves
bad, if they were elevated by something in the syntax or
rhythm distinguishing them from prose, become in him prose
out-and-out. 'To Peleus why did we give you, to a mortal?'
'In the plain *there* were kindled a thousand fires; by each
one *there* sate fifty men.' [At least he might have left
out the expletive.]

But I see something more in this phenomenon. Mr Arnold is
an original poet; and, as such, certainly uses a diction
far more elevated than he here puts forward to represent
Homer. He calls his Homeric diction *plain* and *simple*.
Interpreting these words from the contrast of Mr Arnold's
own poems, I claim his suffrage as on my side that Homer is
often in a style much lower than what the moderns esteem to

be poetical. But I protest, that he carries it *very much*
too far, and levels the noblest down to the most negligent
style of Homer. The poet is *not* always so 'ignoble,' as
the unlearned might infer from my critic'c specimens. He
never drops so low as Shakspeare; yet if he were as sustained as Virgil or Milton, he would with it lose his vast
superiority over these, his rich variety.

If Shakspeare introduces coarse wrangling, buffoonery, or
mean superstition, no one claims or wishes this to be in a
high diction or tragic rhythm; and why should anyone wish
such a thing from Homer or Homer's translator? I find
nothing here in the poet to apologise for; but much cause
for indignation, when the unlearned public is misled by
translators or by critics to expect delicacy and elegance
out of place.

The Homer of the 'Iliad' is morally pure and often very
tender; but to expect refinement and universal delicacy of
expression in that stage of civilisation is quite anachro-
nistic and unreasonable. As in earlier England, so in
Homeric Greece, even high poetry partook of the coarseness
of society. This was probably inevitable, precisely because Greek epic poetry was so *natural*.

Hitherto I have been unwillingly thrown into nothing but
antagonism to Mr Arnold, who thereby at least adds tenfold
value to his praise, and makes me proud when he declares
that the *structure* of my sentences is good and Homeric.
For this I give the credit to my metre, which alone confers on me this cardinal advantage. But in turn I will
compliment Mr Arnold at the expense of some other critics.
He does know, and they do not, the difference of *flowing*
and *smooth*. A mountain torrent is flowing, but often very
rough; such is Homer. The 'staircases of Neptune' on the
canal of Languedoc are smooth, but do not flow: you have
to descend abruptly from each level to the next. It would
be unjust to say absolutely, that such is Pope's smoothness; yet often, I feel, this censure would not be too
severe.

I shall now speak of the peculiarities of my diction,
under three heads: 1. old or antiquated words; 2. coarse
words expressive of outward actions, but having no moral
colour; 3. words of which the sense has degenerated in

modern days.
  1. Mr Arnold appears to regard what is *antiquated* as
ignoble. I think him, as usual, in fundamental error.
In general the nobler words come from ancient style, and
in no case can it be said that old words (as such) are
ignoble.   To introduce such terms as *whereat, therefrom,
quoth, beholden, steed, erst, anon, anent,* into the midst
of style which in all other respects is modern and prosaic,
would be like to that which we often hear from half-
educated people. The want of harmony makes us regard it
as low-minded and uncouth. From this cause (as I suspect)
has stolen into Mr Arnold's mind the fallacy, that the
words themselves are uncouth. But the words are excellent,
if only they are in proper keeping with the general style.
- Now it is very possible, that in some passages, few or
many, I am open to the charge of having mixed old and new
style unskilfully; but I cannot admit that the old words
(as such) are ignoble.

From an Oxford Professor I should have expected the very
opposite spirit to that which Mr Arnold shows. He ought
to know and feel that one glory of Greek poetry is its
great internal variety. He admits the principle that old
words are a source of ennoblement for diction, when he
extols the Bible as his standard: for surely he claims no
rhetorical inspiration for the translators. Words which
have come to us in a sacred connection, no doubt, gain a
sacred hue, but they must not be allowed to desecrate
other old and excellent words. Mr Arnold informs his
Oxford hearers that 'his Bibliolatry is perhaps excessive.'
So the public will judge, if he say that *wench, whore,
pate, pot, gin, damn, busybody, audience, principality,
generation,* are epical noble words because they are in the
Bible, and that *lief, ken, in sooth, grim, stalwart, gait,
guise, eld, hie, erst,* are bad, because they are not there.
Nine times out of ten, what are called 'poetical' words,
are nothing but antique words, and are made ignoble by Mr
Arnold's doctrine. His very arbitrary condemnation of
eld, lief, in sooth, gait, gentle friend in one passage of
mine as 'bad words,' is probably due to his monomaniac
fancy that there is nothing quaint and nothing antique in
Homer. Excellent and noble as are these words which he
rebukes, excellent even for Aeschylus, I should doubt the
propriety of using them in the dialogue of Euripides; on
the level of which he seems to think Homer to be.
  2. Our language, especially the Saxon part of it,
abounds with vigorous monosyllabic verbs, and dissyllabic
frequentatives derived from them, indicative of strong

physical action. For these words (which, I make no doubt,
Mr Arnold regards as ignoble plebeians), I claim Quiritar-
ian rights: but I do not wish them to displace patricians
from high service. Such verbs as *sweat, haul, plump,
maul, yell, bang, splash, smash, thump, tug, scud, sprawl,
spank,* etc., I hold (in their purely physical sense) to be
eminently epical: for the epic revels in descriptions of
violent action to which they are suited. Intense muscular
exertion in every form, intense physical action of the
surrounding elements, with intense ascription or description of size or colour: - together make up an immense
fraction of the poem. To cut out these words is to emas-
culate the epic. Even Pope admits such words. My eye in
turning his pages was just now caught by: 'They tug, they
sweat.' Who will say that 'tug,' 'sweat' are admissible,
but 'bang,' 'smash,' 'sputter' are inadmissible? Mr
Arnold resents my saying that Homer is often homely. He
is homely expressly because he is natural. The epical
diction admits both the gigantesque and the homely: it
inexorably refuses the conventional, under which is com-
prised a vast mass of what some wrongly call elegant.
But while I justify the use of homely words in a primary
physical, I depreciate them in a secondary moral sense.
Mr Arnold clearly is dull to this distinction, or he would
not utter against me the following taunt:

> *To grunt and sweat under a weary load* does perfectly
> well where it comes in Shakspeare: but if the trans-
> lator of Homer, who will hardly have wound up our minds
> to the pitch at which these words of Hamlet find them,
> were to employ, when he has to speak of Homer's heroes
> under the load of calamity, this figure of 'grunting'
> and 'sweating,' we should say, *He Newmanises.*

Mr Arnold here not only makes a mistake, he propagates
a slander; as if I had ever used such words as *grunt* and
sweat morally. If Homer in the 'Iliad' spoke of grunting
swine, as he does of sweating steeds, so should I. As the
coarse metaphors here quoted from Shakspeare are utterly
opposed to Homer's style, to obtrude them on him would be
a gross offence. Mr Arnold sends his readers away with
the belief that this is my practice, though he has not
dared to assert it. I *bear* such coarseness in Shakespeare, not because I am 'wound up to a high pitch' by
him, 'borne away by a mighty current' (which Mr Arnold,
with ingenious unfairness to me, assumes to be certain in
a reader of Shakspeare and all but impossible in a reader
of Homer), but because I know, that in Shakspeare's time
all literature was coarse, as was the speech of courtiers

and of the queen herself. Mr Arnold imputes to me Shakespeare's coarseness, from which I instinctively shrink;
and when his logic leads to the conclusion, 'he Shake-
spearises,' he with gratuitous rancour turns it into 'he
Newmanises.'

3. There is a small number of words not natural plebeians, but patricians on which a most unjust bill of attain-
der has been passed, which I seek to reverse. On the
first which I name, Mr Arnold will side with me, because
it is a Biblical word, *wench*. In Lancashire I believe
that at the age of about sixteen a 'girl' turns into 'a
wench,' or as we say 'a young woman.' In Homer, 'girl'
and 'young woman' are alike inadmissible; 'maid' or
'maiden' will not always suit, and 'wench' is the natural
word. I do not know that I have used it three times, but
I claim a right of using it, and protest against allowing
the heroes of slang to deprive us of excellent words by
their perverse misuse. If the imaginations of some men
are always in satire and in low slang, so much the worse
for them: but the more we yield to such demands, the
more will be exacted. I expect, before long, to be told
that *brick* is an ignoble word, meaning a jolly fellow, and
that *sell, cut* are out of place in Homer. My metre, it
seems, is inadmissible with some, because it is the metre
of Yankee Doodle! as if Homer's metre were not that of the
Margites. Every noble poem is liable to be travestied, as
the Iliad and Aeschylus and Shakspeare have been. Every
burlesque writer uses the noble metre, and caricatures the
noble style. Mr Arnold says, I must not render τανύπεπλος
'trailing-rob'd,' because it reminds him of 'long petti-
coats sweeping a dirty pavement.' What a confession as to
the state of his imagination!

Much perhaps remains to be learnt concerning Homer's perpetual epithets. My very learned colleague Goldstücke,
Professor of Sanscrit, is convinced that the epithet *cow-
eyed* of the Homeric Juno is an echo of the notion of
Hindoo poets, that (if I remember his statement) 'the
sunbeams are the *cows* of heaven.' The sacred qualities
of the Hindoo cow are perhaps not to be forgotten. I have
myself been struck by the phrase δϊιπετέοσ ποτάμοιο (5) as
akin to the idea that the Ganges falls from Mount Meru,
the Hindoo Olympus. Also the meaning of two other epithets has been revealed to me from the pictures of Hindoo
ladies. First, *curl-eyed,* to which I have referred above,
secondly, *rosy-fingered Aurora*. For Aurora is an 'Eastern
lady'; and, as such, has the tips of her fingers dyed

rosy-red, whether by henna or by some more brilliant drug.
Who shall say that the kings and warriors of Homer do not
derive from the East their epithet 'Jove-nurtured'? or
that this or that goddess is not called 'golden-throned'
or 'fair-throned' in allusion to Assyrian sculptures or
painting, as Rivers probably drew their later poetical
attribute 'bull-headed' from the sculpture of fountains?
It is a familiar remark, that Homer's poetry presupposes
a vast pre-existing art and material. Much in him was
traditional. Many of his wild legends came from Asia.
He is to us much beside a poet; and that a translator
should assume to cut him down to the standard of modern
taste, is a thought which all the higher minds of this age
have outgrown. How much better is that reverential Docility, which with simple and innocent wonder, receives the
oddest notions of antiquity as material of instruction yet
to be revealed, than the self-complacent Criticism, which
pronouncing everything against modern taste to be grotesque and contemptible, squares the facts to its own
'Axioms'! *Homer is noble: but this or that epithet is not
noble: therefore we must explode it from Homer!* I value,
I maintain, I struggle for the 'high a priori road' in its
own place; but certainly not in historical literature.
To read Homer's own thoughts is to wander in a world
abounding with freshness: but if we insist on treading
round and round in our own footsteps, we shall never
ascend those heights whence the strange region is to be
seen. Surely an intelligent learned critic ought to inculcate on the unlearned, that if they would get instruction from Homer, they must not expect to have their ears
tickled by a musical sound as of a namby-pamby poetaster;
but must look on a metre as doing its duty, when it
'strings the mind up to the necessary pitch' in elevated
passages; and that instead of demanding of a translator
everywhere a rhythmical perfection which perhaps can only
be attained by a great sacrifice of higher qualities, they
should be willing to submit to a small part of that rug-
gedness, which Mr Arnold cheerfully bears in Homer himself
through the loss of the Digamma. And now, for a final
protest. To be *stately* is not to be *grand*. Nicolas of
Russia may have been stately like Cowper, Garibaldi is
grand like the true Homer. A diplomatic address is
stately; it is not grand, nor often noble. To expect a
translation of Homer to be *pervadingly elegant,* is absurd;
Homer is not such, any more than is the side of an Alpine
mountain. The elegant and the picturesque are seldom
identical, however much of delicate beauty may be inter-
studded in the picturesque; but this has always got plenty
of what is shaggy and uncouth without which contrast the

full delight of beauty would not be attained.   I think
Moore in his characteristic way tells of a beauty

  Shining on, shining on, by no shadow made tender,
  Till love falls asleep in the sameness of splendour.

Such certainly is not Homer's. His beauty, when at its
height, is *wild* beauty: it smells of the mountain and of
the sea. If he be compared to a noble animal, it is not
to such a spruce rubbed-down Newmarket racer as our smooth
translators would pretend, but to a wild horse of the Don
Cossacks: and if I, instead of this, present to the reader
nothing but a Dandie Dinmont's pony, this, as a first
approximation, is a valuable step towards the true solution.
  Before the best translation of the 'Iliad' of which our
language is capable can be produced, the English public
has to unlearn the false notion of Homer which his *deliberately faithless* versifiers have infused. Chapman's con-
ceits unfit his translation for instructing the public,
even if his rhythm 'jolted' less, if his structure were
simpler, and his dialect more intelligible. My version, if
allowed to be read, will prepare the public to receive a
version better than mine. I regard it as a question about
to open hereafter, whether a translator of Homer ought not
to adopt the old dissyllabic *landis, houndis, hartis,* etc.,
instead of our modern unmelodious *lands, hounds, harts;*
whether the *ye* or *y* before the past participle may not be
restored; the want of which confounds that participle with
the past tense. Even the final -en of the plural of verbs
(we dancen, they singen, etc.) still subsists in Lancashire. It deserves consideration whether by a *few* such
slight grammatical retrogressions into antiquity a translator of Homer might not add much melody to his poem and
do good service to the language.

Notes

1 'The Epic Cypria'.
2 'The Fall of Troy'.
3 'of the far-shooting Apollo'.
4 'well-throned'.
5 'as a river fallen from Zeus' (swollen by rain).

2.   JAMES SPEDDING IN 'FRASER'S MAGAZINE'

June 1861, lxii, 703-14

James Spedding (1808-81) was known in his time for his
careful and conscientious edition of Francis Bacon, which
he published between 1857 and 1859. At the time of this
review, Spedding was working on his life of Bacon. While
not a prolific writer, he was intelligent and sensitive:
Tennyson called him 'the wisest man I know'. In this
passage from his review of 'On Translating Homer',
Spedding addresses himself to the question of hexameters -
that is, into which English verse form Homer should be
translated. He makes a good case against Arnold's metrical
suggestions, and he argues, like Newman, that the 'tribunal' for judging translation must be broad. Homer should
be, like the 'Arabian Nights', 'an English book' for a
large audience.

'The object of these Lectures (says 'Notes on Books'), 'is
to determine the most essential characteristics of Homer's
poetry; to point out how, from failing to preserve faithfully one or other of them, every English translation of
the "Iliad" up to the present time has been a false rendering of Homer; and to give advice to the future translator as to the best means for retaining these characteristics in his own version.'
     Upon the two first branches of the inquiry I have
little to say, except to express my admiration of Mr.
Arnold's criticism. But in his practical advice there is
one point which seems to me to require reconsideration.
I agree that a translation of the 'Iliad' should be 'rapid
in movement, plain in words and style, simple in ideas,
and noble in manner;' but I cannot think that it should be
in English hexameter; and since the recommendation comes
from a scholar and a poet, as the result of an inquiry
showing a very remarkable combination of scholar-like
taste with poetic sensibility, it deserves a fuller and
graver answer than I should otherwise have thought necessary. If indeed the practical question at issue were one
in which scholars only are interested, I would leave them
to settle it among themselves. But if another attempt is
to be made to produce a translation of the 'Iliad' for the
benefit of those who cannot read the original, the feelings of the patient should be taken into consideration;

and one whose Greek has long been at grass is in some respects better qualified to understand the case of the
'English reader' than those who have kept it in daily
exercise.
  According to Mr. Arnold, indeed, the appeal in this
case lies to scholars, and scholars only: for 'they alone
can say whether the translation produces, more or less,
the same effect upon them as the original.' But this is
not exactly the question, though it comes very near it.
The true question, in my opinion, is this - Does the
translation produce upon one who cannot read the original
the same effect, more or less, which the original produces
upon one who can? Now, the innumerable associations of
which the practised scholar cannot divest himself make it
very hard for him to judge what the effect will be upon
those whose associations are quite different. To him the
original shows through the translation, and gives it new
colours and qualities. In reading the English he feels
the Greek within it; and the illusion thereby produced is
seen in no more conspicuous example than that of a scholar
reading a page of English hexameters, and fancying that
the 'movement' of them is like that of the Greek or Latin.
'Applied to Homer,' says Mr. Arnold, 'this metre affords
to the translator the immense support of *keeping him more
nearly than any other metre to Homer's movement;* and since
a poet's movement makes so large a part of his general
effect, and to reproduce this general effect is at once
the translator's indispensable business, and so difficult
for him, it is a great thing *to have this part of your
model's general effect already given you in your metre,*
instead of having to get it entirely for yourself.'
  Now, to my ear the *movement* of the best English hexameters which I have seen is so very unlike the movement
of any Greek or Latin hexameters that I remember, since
the days when I had to *scan* the verse in order to understand the measure, counting the feet with my voice by
throwing a strong accent upon the first syllable of each;
and the movement produced by the scanning process was so
very unlike that with which even then I *read* them when I
was called up to construe; that unless Mr. Arnold either
reads Homer very oddly, or means by English hexameter a
measure constructed upon a principle totally and essentially different from any that I have seen attempted, his
ear is surely under some strange delusion.

I meant to confine myself to a protest against English
hexameters, which I hold to be admirably adapted for a
translation of *Propria quae maribus* (1) and *As in*

praesenti, (2) and for nothing else. But I will take the
opportunity of adding a few words in favour of an entirely
different way of dealing with the 'Iliad' - a way which
nobody seems to have thought of, though it offers a great
field for an enterprising genius.

To scholars 'who possess at the same time with knowledge
of Greek adequate poetical taste and feeling,' Mr. Arnold
tells us 'no translation will seem of much worth compared
with the original.' If this be so, is it judicious to
attempt a translation which shall aspire to present itself
for comparison with the original before that tribunal?
If the true effect of Homer cannot be reproduced in a
translation, is it well that any one should take upon him
a task which makes such reproduction 'his indispensable
business?' Is it not better that those who wish to know
what Homer is really like should be recommended, as the
shortest way, to learn Greek and read him?

But though we cannot have Homer himself in English,
there is no reason why we should not have in English the
story which Homer told. Why should not the 'Iliad' be
made an English book, like the 'Arabian Nights'? I want
somebody to invite the men and women, the boys and girls,
now living in England, to listen to an old story: and to
tell them all about the quarrel between Agamemnon and
Achilles, and what came of it.

Notes

1 'things more appropriate to the seas'.
2 'in the present'.

3.   FITZJAMES STEPHEN, UNSIGNED REVIEW, 'SATURDAY REVIEW'

27 July 1861, xii, 95-6

James Fitzjames Stephen (1829-94), brother of Leslie
Stephen (and Virginia Woolf's uncle), was known at Cambridge as 'the British Lion', a powerful debator and a
determined opponent. When Arnold later referred to the
'Saturday' as 'my old adversary', he must have had Stephen
in mind, for Stephen wrote a long series of vigorous, and
often acute, critiques. He had already argued with
Arnold's 'England and the Italian Question' two years

earlier. Arnold did not yet know Stephen as the 'Saturday's' adversary when he wrote: 'You will have seen the amenities of the "Saturday Review". It seems affected to say one does not care for such things, but I really do think my spirits rebound sooner than most people's. The fault of the reviewer, as of English criticism in general, is that ... he goes to work in such a desperate heavy-handed manner, like a bear in a china-shop - if a bear can be supposed to have hands.'

Here is a good stand-up fight which we have stood by and looked at with no common liking. Certainly scholars and professors can pitch into one another with a good will when they take it into their heads. Mr. Arnold can deal hearty blows, and Mr. Newman can deal them back in kind - we might almost say, with interest. In looking on, one almost forgets the cause in the mere excitement of the battle. If one does stop to think about the points at issue, one has a certain satisfaction in thinking that neither disputant is so clearly right that anybody can have the least objection to his being well mauled by the other. We would not stir a finger to save Mr. Newman from Mr. Arnold, or to save Mr. Arnold from Mr. Newman. If anything, we should like a little more fighting. We have not the least doubt that Mr. Arnold could put forth a rejoinder to Mr. Newman, and Mr. Newman put forth a further rejoinder to Mr. Arnold; and that, when they had done so, each would be as far from convincing the other as when he began. And we are quite certain that, in so doing, they would give us a great deal of fresh amusement. It gives one rather a feeling like Zeus himself, when Hera, and Poseidon, and Aphrodite and the rest of them, were all busy fighting: -

ἐγέλασσε δέ οἱ φίλον ἦτορ
γηθοσύνη, ὅθ' ὁρᾶτο θεοὺς ἔριδι ξυνιόντας. (1)

But, when looking at the matter more seriously, we cannot help expostulating with Mr. Arnold on the tone of his lectures. Right or wrong, they are intensely amusing, and some things in them are certainly very clever. But we are quite sure that they are not the sort of things which an Oxford Professor ought to deliver officially before the University. If Mr. Arnold chooses to write an article or a pamphlet against Mr. Newman, by all means let him, and let him be as severe as he pleases - Mr. Newman is quite able to defend himself. But we cannot think that it is at all a Professor's business to stand up before his

University and elaborately to ridicule, with every kind of
contemptuous and insulting language, a living scholar, and
one who, whatever may be his aberrations in other ways,
has certainly, as a scholar, a very much higher reputation
than Mr. Arnold himself. Mr. Arnold asks in one place
'with whom Mr. Newman can have lived.' It is easy to
answer that, at one time at least of his life, he 'lived
with' the other Fellows of Balliol, and that his academi-
cal honours were considerably higher than those of the
present Poetry Professor. All this is of course no reason
why Mr. Newman's errors should not be pointed out, but it
does suggest some questions as to the time, the place, and
the person. We do not say that a Professor ought not to
point out error, even living error. When a Thor's hammer
is raised to dash in pieces a Froude or a Buckle, it is a
good service to sound morals and to historic truth; and we
have not the slightest wish to stay the arm of the aven-
ger. But the bitterly contemptuous language of Mr. Arnold,
verging sometimes on personal abuse, sometimes on low buffoonery - and all about matters which are, after all,
mainly questions of taste - does seem to us utterly out of
place. And certainly Mr. Arnold is hardly so free from
glass windows as to be entitled to throw many stones at
Mr. Newman. Mr. Newman's translation seems to us, as it
does to Mr. Arnold, very bad; but we really think Mr.
Arnold's specimens are still worse. Mr. Newman is very
queer, but he is at least faithful. Mr. Arnold is almost
as queer, and is very far from being as faithful. - Mr.
Newman has chosen a very odd metre, but his lines will
scan according to his own system. Mr. Arnold has chosen
what is no English metre at all, and many of his lines,
even according to his own scheme, have no scansion whatever. We hold it to be an utter mistake to try to reproduce the Greek hexameter, which depends wholly upon quantity, in a language like English, whose metres depend
wholly upon accent. But if we are to have hexameters,
let them scan as hexameters. The apostolic precept -

    Hūsbānds | lŏve yoūr | wivēs, ānd | bē nōt | bĭttĕr
       ă | gainst thēm

is a perfect hexameter, and, as being full of spondees, it
ought to be one after Mr. Arnold's own heart. But Mr.
Arnold, who professes 'excessive Bibliolatry' - who makes,
wisely enough, the English Bible his standard of the English language - certainly has not caught the Biblical
rhythm. To our ears, the following lines sound like mere
prose, and mighty awkward prose too:-

So shone forth, in front of Troy, by the bed of
    Xanthus,
Between that and the ships, the Trojans' numerous
    fires....

On the point of diction the two professors dispute as
fiercely as on the point of metre. We really cannot profess to follow them into such deep questions as why 'spit'
should be forbidden and 'sputter' allowed. We grant that
Mr. Newman's language is very odd, and that some of Mr.
Arnold's criticisms on it are quite well founded. In
short, wherever it is purely a question of taste - except
as to the goodness of Mr. Arnold's own translations - Mr.
Arnold has the best of it; but whenever it becomes a question either of reasoning or of scholarship, the London
Professor of Latin makes very short work of the Oxford
Professor of Poetry. Even in the matter of diction, Mr.
Newman goes on a consistent, though we think a mistaken
theory - namely, to make his language as unusual and
antiquated as he can, consistently with its being, in the
main, intelligible. But Mr. Arnold's theory is beyond us.
He is always telling us - often several times in the same
page - that Homer is, and that translations of Homer ought
to be, in 'the grand style,' 'the grand manner.' But what
'the grand style' is Mr. Arnold never explains. We only
learn that Dante and Milton are the only modern poets who
have reached it; that Shakespeare has it not, and yet that
Shakespeare has the 'supremacy' over Milton; from which we
infer that, after all, there is some other style grander,
or at least, so to speak, supremer, than 'the grand style'
itself. Besides being in the 'grand style,' Homer also
is, and his translator should be, 'noble,' 'pre-eminently
noble' - 'noble' being used over and over again as a sort
of technical term, and poor Mr. Newman being pronounced to
be very 'ignoble.' What 'noble' means Mr. Arnold no more
tells us than he tells us what 'the grand style' is. We
fancy he got the word from Mr. Ruskin, who gives us a
recipe for a 'noble tower,' which is to have 'wrathful
crest,' 'vizor up,' and 'rent battlements.' Architectural
critics have asked what might be meant by the 'vizor' of a
tower, and whether no tower could pretend to nobility till
its parapet had been half broken down by a thunder-storm.
Poetical critics may really be quite as much in the dark
as to Mr. Arnold's notion of nobility in poetry. We only
know that Sir Walter Scott is not 'noble' - still less
Lord Macaulay, who is set aside very quickly as 'falsetto'
and 'pinchbeck.'
    The two Professors meet in fierce battle on the quest-
ion whether Homer seemed 'quaint and antiquated' to a

literary Athenian. Mr. Arnold, looking at it as a mere
poet, is shocked at the idea. Mr. Newman, taking a far
broader historical and philological view, stoutly maintains that he did seem thus quaint and antiquated. Mr.
Arnold seems to confound the two notions of 'antiquated'
and 'unintelligible.' Every educated Athenian could under-
understand Homer, because the study of Homer formed a
necessary part of his education; but nothing is plainer
than that Homer's Greek is something totally different
from what such an Athenian would naturally speak and
write. Not only are the grammatical forms widely unlike,
but Homer is full of words which a young Athenian would
never hear in conversation or see in contemporary writings, and of which, on his first reading of Homer, he
would certainly have to ask the meaning. Homer's Greek
was certainly 'antiquated' Greek in the historical times
of Greece. It was such Greek as nobody spoke, and such as
nobody wrote who was not designedly imitating Homer.
Whether it is 'quaint' is to a great extent a matter of
taste; but we cannot help asking Mr. Arnold whether he can
construe νυκτὸς ἀμολγῷ, (2) and whether he does not think
both that and ἕρκος ὀδόντων (3) very odd expressions. On
the score of history and philology Mr. Newman certainly
pounds Mr. Arnold to pieces. But as to Mr. Newman's inference from his facts - namely, that it is the duty of a
translator of Homer to turn him into such strange English
as Mr. Newman himself does - there we should have said
that Mr. Arnold had equally the advantage of Mr. Newman,
only that when Mr. Arnold comes to give us his own specimens of Homeric translation, they prove to be every whit
as bad as Mr. Newman's. In fact, Mr. Arnold has a good
deal of intuitive taste; but he seems incapable of reasoning. For instance, he argues, against Lord Macaulay and
others, that the Homeric poems have nothing in common with
ballads; and when one comes to dissect his arguments, they
merely come to this - that the Homeric poems are much
better than any other ballads. Mr. Arnold admires Homer
so much that he does not like to put him in the same class
with 'Adam Bell,' or even with the 'Nibelungen Lied.' But
he forgets that the merits of particular specimens have
nothing to do with the classes under which they are to be
arranged. A good comedy has points of affinity with a
good sermon, which it has not with a bad comedy; still, in
classifying, we put good and bad comedies together, and not
not good comedies and good sermons. That the Homeric
poems are incomparably superior to all other ballads Lord
Macaulay asserts as vigorously as Mr. Arnold; but that
does not prove the least in the world that they are not
ballads. Homer, we are told, is in 'the grand style,' and

ballads are not in 'the grand style:' but till we are
told what 'the grand style' is, this makes us no wiser
than we were before.

Mr. Arnold's notion that a translation of Homer ought
to produce the same effect as Homer himself, seems to us
to be grounded on complete misconception. A translation
cannot produce the same effect as the original, simply
because it is not the same thing as the original. No man
can make a translation of Homer which shall produce the
same effect on us as Homer did on his own contemporaries,
or as he did on an educated Athenian, or as he does on a
scholar now. Translations serve different purposes. A
translation of a common prose book is simply intended to
make the author's matter available to those who do not
understand the language in which he writes. Such a translation is best done when, supposing it to be perfectly
faithful to the matter of the original, the reader does
not feel it to be a translation. But in a translation of
a poet, in some degree of an orator, generally of any old
writer, or of a specimen of some very out-of-the-way
language - where distance of place does the same as distance of time - in all these cases we want to preserve the
manner of the author as well as his matter. In a prose
writer, you have nothing to do but to translate as literally as you can, consistently with the grammar of your
own language. In a poet, you have the constantly recurring difficulty, how to be at once literal, and to preserve the rules of metre and rhyme. And here the ancient
poets divide themselves into two classes. In some cases
it would be quite possible to produce something which
should have very much the same effect now, which the
author had on his contemporaries. But this will be done
rather by imitation than by direct translation. This is
what Johnson at least attempted in his imitations of Juve-
nal. He translated, not the words, but the persons, the
manners, the allusions of all kinds. So a clever man might
write an Aristophanic comedy on some point in modern politics or modern society, which might have much the same
effect as a comedy of Aristophanes had at Athens. But of
course this is not translation; it is not what Mr. Arnold
means; and of course it can only be done with authors
belonging to ages which have some analogy with our own.
Homer might have been imitated in this way in the time of
the Crusaders. He cannot be so imitated now, except in
the form of a burlesque. A translation of Homer is, we
suppose, meant to serve a practical purpose. It is not
merely meant, we will believe, to excite a sort of languid interest in those who are pleased or amused by comparing the translation with the original. We will suppose

it is meant to give some idea of the Greek poet to - we
will not use the old formula of 'ladies and country
gentlemen,' but to - the women and children and working-
men whom Mr. Newman describes as taking such an interest
in his performance. Neither Mr. Newman nor Mr. Arnold
seems to have thought of the alternative of prose - not
flowing newspaper prose, but such prose as our translators
have put the poems of David and Isaiah into. Here you may
show very fairly what the Homeric diction is, but you lose
the Homeric metre. If the translator chooses to translate
into verse, he must surely choose between blank verse and
fourteen-syllable verse, that is, between the metre - not
necessarily the manner - of Cowper and that of Chapman.
In blank verse he may retain much more of the diction. In
Chapman's metre he will give something like the general
effect of the Greek hexameter - something, we think, at
least more like it than the unnatural sound of hexameters
in English. But certainly any sort of verse, any sort of
prose, is better than such stuff as -

So shone forth in front of Troy, by the bed of Xanthus,
Between that and the ships, the Trojans' numerous fires.

Mr. Arnold is undoubtedly a clever man, and he sometimes shows signs not only of cleverness, but of good
sense; but all is spoilt, and much greater gifts might be
spoiled, by his outrageous self-conceit. The whole of the
lectures are one constant I - I - I - *Das grosse ich* (4)
reigns from one end to the other. The very first sentence is - 'It has more than once been suggested to me that
I should translate Homer.' Who suggested it we know not -
if he was a wise man, he has by this time withdrawn his
suggestion. And so it goes on throughout. 'I advise,'
'I shall not concern myself,' 'there are certain negative
counsels which I will give him,' 'I say the translator
should *penetrate* himself with a sense,' 'I say' this, 'I
say' that, to the end of the lectures. We are far from
admiring the mock-modesty of those authors who conceal
themselves in the third person or in the plural number,
and a Professor addressing a class will naturally be more
direct and personal, and will very properly say 'I' much
oftener than an author writing a book. But it is not the
mere number of I's in Mr. Arnold's lectures, it is the way
in which 'I' always comes in - an authoritative, oracular
way, something akin, we venture to guess, to 'the grand
style,' something reminding us of what, many years ago,
was known in the Oxford Union as the White pocket-
handkerchief style of oratory. Mr. Newman gives you
plenty of I's too, but his egotism is harmless and amusing.

Mr. Arnold is amusing also, but in a very different way. He has yet to learn that it is possible to be earnest without being offensively self-sufficient, and possible to point out errors of taste without such monstrous personal insolence as asking 'with whom' a man 'can have lived,' who, with all his defects and eccentricities, still remains in most respects so much Mr. Arnold's superior as is Mr. Francis Newman.

Notes

1 'And his dear heart laughed with amusement when he saw the Gods coming together in strife.'
2 'in the milking time' (twilight).
3 'the ramparts of the teeth'.
4 'the great I'.

Essays in Criticism, First Series (1865)

4. F. D. MAURICE, SPINOZA AND PROFESSOR ARNOLD,'SPECTATOR'

3 January 1863, xxxvl, 1472-4.

John Frederick Denison Maurice (1805-72), the influential
'Christian Socialist', had been Professor of English Literature and History at King's College, London, before
being dismissed for unorthodoxy. He was to return in
1866 to Cambridge as Professor of Moral Philosophy.
Maurice's review of the English version of Spinoza's
'Tractatus' is very much a comment on Arnold's own
review. He admires that review, but he argues that some
of Arnold's inferences are dangerous. 'Our young gentlemen' run the risk of reading Spinoza 'because they are
told that he speaks to persons of high culture, not to the
vulgar'. In a remark that might well have come from
Thomas Arnold and that seems to anticipate Arnold himself,
Maurice says: 'Remember, politics and theology *cannot* be
severed for us Englishmen.... In losing the connection
between them we lose both equally. We become mere slaves
of floating opinions....'

Sir, - You asked me to notice in the 'Spectator' the new
translation of Spinoza's 'Tractatus Theologico-Politicus',
which Mr. Trübner has put forth. My only qualification
for such a task would be that I have given some study, not
to this treatise only, but to the metaphysics and ethics
of its author, without which I conceive it must be unintelligible; that I have discovered in all his works profound instruction and profound reasons for personal

humiliation; that I have honoured and loved the man far
more than any of his speculations. I could not, however,
in virtue of these merits, put forth any claim to be a
reviewer of the 'Tractate,' seeing that they all appear to
be possessed in a much higher measure by Professor Arnold,
who has given an account of the book in 'Macmillan's Magazine'; and seeing that he combines with them other gifts
to which I can make no pretension – an exquisite clearness
of style, and that high culture to which he refers so
often in his article. How great my envy is of these endowments I shall perhaps show, while I notice one or two
faults into which, I think, the accomplished writer has
been betrayed by his consciousness of possessing them.
    1. Nothing can be more skilful and brilliant than Mr.
Arnold's summary of the contents of this treatise. All
its rough edges are rounded off with a cleverness which
only those who are tolerably well acquainted with it can
appreciate. Above all, any allusion is carefully suppressed to those parts of Spinoza's ethics which might
lead the reader to question the statement that his object
was, in the ordinary as well as in the highest sense, a
moral one – that the love of God was the basis of his
teaching and the end of his life. Being satisfied that
this was Spinoza's fundamental idea, Mr. Arnold deems
that nothing should be introduced into a sketch of him
which does not serve for the illustration of it. I submit
that this course, however tempting, is a dangerous one.
I do not deny – I fully believe – that Spinoza's aim *was* a
moral one. I know, however, also, that he used language,
not carelessly (when did he ever write carelessly?) but
with the fullest deliberation – as a necessary development and outcome of his system – which led one of his
correspondents to charge him with a tendency to the lowest
epicurism, which in our own day has induced a man so
little infected with any orthodox prejudices as Michelet,
to affirm that all morality and all freedom are lost in
the unfathomable abyss which Spinoza opened. Suppose the
readers of Mr. Arnold's article should give no heed to
these extravagant and unfair declamations, is it not possible that some of them may fall in with M. Saisset's
elaborate introduction to the French translation of Spinoza's books? That writer is as honest and impartial as a
critic can be; he has the personal respect for Spinoza
which every one acquainted with his life must have; he is
instructed in the history of European philosophy before
the time of the great Jew, and in his time; yet he is
fairly puzzled by what appears to him the enormous contra-
dictions in Spinoza's ethical creed. He treats that maxim
from which Mr. Arnold so naturally and gracefully deduces

the theologico-political treatise, not as a dishonest one,
or as one merely introduced for effect - he is far from
any such injustice - but certainly as one which it is
exceedingly hard to reconcile with other statements
equally Spinozistic, as little to be overlooked by any
careful student.

Those who read the sketch of this able Frenchman, having
previously accepted Mr. Arnold's statements will be sorely
puzzled. They will suspect their countryman of a pious
fraud, of which I am sure he is incapable - which he would
look upon as fit only for us priests. They will experience a vehement reaction against the man whose errors had
been hidden from them - a reaction which those who consider the circumstances of his life - the terrible isolation
of it from all ties of kindred and of nation - must deem
uncharitable and unreasonable. I find enough in his history to make me marvel that he could grasp so much of the
truth, in which the Rabbins who excommunicated him and
the Christian who stood aloof from him, thought he had no
share. I cannot feel the least surprise that he should
ignore the relation of politics to theology; that his
great labour should be to separate them; that in doing so
he should explain away the divine history of his race;
that he should turn its prophets into a set of highly
imaginative men, who were exceedingly good, but yet told
a great many shocking lies. One is infinitely thankful
for what he has held fast and taught us of the blessings
which were bestowed on the sons of Abraham. One is grateful also for the metaphysical truths which he seized and
appropriated from Descartes. That he should not have been
able to bring the two lessons into harmony, that his metaphysics should always have stood apart from his politics,
and that his theology, which could not unite them, alter-
nately took its shape and colour from each - this was a
calamity which we may lament for him, and which, if we
weigh it well, may impart the greatest 'information,' as
well as 'edification' to us.

2. Mr. Arnold has drawn the line between these two
words very sharply. *Edification* is for the herd. *Information* for the men of literary culture. To inflict information upon the first is often to do them harm. Edification the last value chiefly for the sake of their neighbours; they have no special need of it. Some of Mr.
Arnold's inferences from these maxims appear to me true as
well as beautiful; some of his applications of them useful
as well as humorous. And there is in the maxims themselves an appropriateness to the subject. He has a right
to claim Spinoza's own authority for them. He unquestionably held that the mass of men must be taught obedience,

that only the few could have knowledge. That belief was
no new one. He had borrowed it from priests to use it
against them. It was the explanation to him of the old
polity of his country; by help of it he could account for
the notion of a divine law; he could interpret the
glimpses of something diviner than law, which one so well
read as he was in the Old Testament could not fail to
detect in every part of it; he could see these glimpses
developed and assuming a substance and a mighty force in
the New.

I can find no *experimentum crucis* (1) of this distinction which is so valuable and complete as that furnished
by Spinoza. To complain of a man cut off from the synagogue, not admitted into the Church, for seeking such a
home as he could find in what is called the republic of
letters, would be monstrous. But that a republic of
letters had none of the patriotism which was the old
inheritance of the synagogue, little of the humanity which
is the true characteristic of the Church; that it is
nearly as exclusive and contemptuous as any sect of
Pharisees or Sadducees, almost as damnatory as any council
of ecclesiastical dogmatists, I cannot but gather from the
lessons of the man who was the best, because the most
involuntary, representative of his guild. I am sure Spinoza had a longing to be one of a kind. I see in him the
most pathetic struggles to assert for himself a human
position. He would give up his own individuality, his own
will, his own conscience, to obtain it. But all he gets
by that sacrifice is an idea of a Being in which the race
is lost, as well as each particular member of it. He
would fain glorify God at the expense of man and of nature
both. He ends with identifying all three. And this metaphysical universality becomes connected with the greatest
exclusiveness. For to know the divine nature is the
blessedness and perfection of the creature. And knowledge
is for the elect few. That there is a sort of salvation
for the many, provided they can be kept in obedience to
these elect few, Mr. Arnold has been careful to tell us.
There has been the dim hope of *such* a salvation held out
by all priests and doctors, who have regarded the high
culture of the universe, the true divine knowledge, as
intended for themselves. It has not satisfied men. It
has been scorned in every great moral and spiritual reformation. Mr. Arnold is right that the sixteenth-century
reformation did not derive its strength from its denial of
Purgatory or Virgin Worship. It derived its strength from
its assertion that God had made Himself *known* in the
person of One who was called a carpenter's son, that
through Him men might *know* their Father. Mr. Arnold

interprets the words of Christ, that it was given to His
disciples to know the mysteries of the Kingdom of Heaven,
precisely in the sense in which they were interpreted by
those who resisted the Reformation, by those who thought
they held the keys of the Kingdom of Heaven. The Reformers remembered that those words were spoken to fishermen
who were to preach a gospel to all nations, whose foes
were then, and would always be, the wise and prudent, who
were to proclaim the highest mysteries as meant for little
children.

There is a passage, I am satisfied, from the faith
which Spinoza cherished in his heart of hearts, to that
faith of little children. He had a sense of a mystery
surrounding us all into which the humblest may enter -
nay, into which only the humble can enter. I should not
despair of showing any affectionate admirer of his that
it is impossible to do him justice, impossible to vindi-
cate that principle which Mr. Arnold proclaims as the key-
note of his works and his life, except by taking the history of his fathers in a much more simple sense than he
took it, as an honest and divine history; except by seeing
the fulfilment of it in the divine life which he deeply
reverenced, which he would have contemplated as a fact,
not as a mere idea, if he could have reverenced anything
but ideas. Hereafter such effects may follow from the
publication of this translation. I do not, I own, anticipate any such effects from it at present. It may
possibly shake - as any the dreariest arithmetical calculations may shake - such opinions as those of Mr. Burgon
and the preacher at St. Mary's, whom Mr. Arnold quotes.
God may shatter idols and restore the faith in Himself by
ways that we cannot devise. But those who believe that
the Second Commandment proceeded from His mouth, those who
hold that Christ took our nature to reveal His Father,
have a better protection against the worshippers of letters, or of wood and stone, than any theologico-political
tractates can afford them. If, by rendering that tractate
into English, the knowledge of Spinoza himself were pro-
moted, it would be something. I fear it will rather
hinder any real knowledge of him. It is offered to us as
a popular work, which may be understood by those who do
not care to investigate his metaphysical doctrines. There
cannot be a greater delusion. 'Hamlet' cannot be played
with Hamlet's part omitted. Many a Polonius may have
crossed Spinoza's path, many a ghost. There is even a
glimpse of a pretty Ophelia throwing a shadow across his
boyhood. But these are scarcely persons in his drama;
they merely pass over the stage. The one figure to be
observed of all observers is the man engaged in the

soliloquy, '*To be or not to be.*' Those who do not attend
to that soliloquy of Spinoza's on Being will know nothing
of him as a commentator on Scripture, or in any other
character. Our young gentlemen will read him because they
are told that he speaks to persons of high culture, not to
the vulgar. They will carry away a vague notion that he
has somehow upset the ordinary faith in the Jewish Scriptures, has somehow substituted a very wise explanation of
his own. They will bow with as much implicit faith, with
as little of actual intelligence, to this new teacher, as
to any of those whom they threw aside. And if it is so
with the intellectual, many a poor Caliban will worship
the Trinculo who has brought him strange liquor, as a god,
and will become not less, but more brutal, from the taste
of it. 'What a good man that Spinoza is whom the priests
denounced. He held the love of God to be the beginning
and end of all his thoughts,' many an illuminated youth
and emancipated lady will exclaim. 'True, but has he
taught you how you may do the same?' Remember, politics
and theology *cannot* be severed for us Englishmen, as they
may be for a Dutch Jew, as they may be for a German. In
losing the connection between them we lose both equally.
We become mere slaves of floating opinions and superstitions in our public life - atheists in our hearts.

I have one word more to say. Mr. Arnold has dwelt
eloquently upon the influence which Spinoza has exerted
over some men of the highest culture, especially in
Germany. Two of his instances, at least, are most striking; the third, being himself of Jewish descent, may be
less happily chosen. That Lessing, that Goethe - men so
intensely Hellenic in their tastes, only combining their
Hellenism with a certain reverence for Christian art and
mediaeval romance - should have bowed before a Hebrew
maker of spectacles, indifferent to Greek lore, to Italian
Painting, to mere beauty of any kind, sternly mathematical
in his forms of expression, purely metaphysical, or, as
some would say, theological, in that which he had to express - this is a marvel on which men of high culture may
well meditate. There was nothing in the character of his
philosophy to attract them. His master, Descartes, had
been denounced in England by Locke and his disciples,
mocked in France by Voltaire and the Encyclopaedists,
superseded in Germany by Leibnitz and Wolff. What had he
to recommend him? He spoke of God as an actual being, as
near, as filling all things, to those who had fancied Him
a name in a book, at a distance, only speaking at rare
intervals. There lay his power. Where did he learn his
lesson? If he had been merely a pantheist - merely a
nature worshipper, - he would have had nothing to teach

those who were already so well trained in the schools of
pagan thought and life. The child of the circumcision
had a message to them, which these schools could not bring.
The Rabbins, Jewish and Christian, had misunderstood or
forgotten the message. Descartes could only conceive it
as a deep necessity of our nature. The Old Testament declared that God had Himself proclaimed it; that the law
and history of a nation stood upon it. Lessing and Goethe
might welcome Spinoza as a philosophical deliverer from
the yoke of old traditions. He really gave them an assurance of something which had not been dreamt of, or had
only been dreamt of, in their philosophy. There was a
breath of divinity in what he taught, a witness of something which is not only found by man, but discovered to
him. But Lessing and Goethe grew up - one died - in the
eighteenth century. The French Revolution had not come.
Its mighty demand for a humanity - a universal humanity -
had not been heard. That demand makes, it seems to me,
the negations of Spinoza obsolete, his naked absolution
incredible. It makes the cry for a God who speaks to man,
speaks through man, speaks through a human polity, more
vehement and irresistible. It may make us feel at last
that a theologico-political tractate is no substitute for
a revelation of God.

Note

1 'crucial test'.

5. S. H. REYNOLDS, UNSIGNED REVIEW, 'WESTMINSTER REVIEW'

October 1863, lxxx, 215-22

Samuel Harvey Reynolds (1831-97) was a clergyman, scholar,
and journalist. For much of his life he was associated
with Brasenose College, Oxford, where he was a lecturer
and a tutor. He edited several classical works, including
the 'Iliad'. In this sympathetic review of Arnold's
Oxford lectures, The Critical Character, Reynolds discusses Arnold in relation to Ruskin's 'Seven Lamps of
Architecture' and 'Modern Painters'. He thinks Arnold the
superior critic. But what is noteworthy about his review
is Reynolds's understanding of Arnold's positions and his

projections about them, since he seems to anticipate The
Function of Criticism at the Present Time. Omitted here
are his discussions of Ruskin.

'La Critique' (1) says M. Renan (the phrase is one for
which we have no precise English equivalent), 'has been
the growth of the present century;' and, if we are to
accept the term in its widest sense, the remark is no
doubt true. We must understand it, then, as the art or
science which judges not only of aesthetics but of the
entire range of literature; and brings to its task a
temper or habit of mind which is well-nigh peculiar to
our own age and circumstances. The growth and development
of this habit is certainly one of the most remarkable
'signs of the times.' We must admit, it is true, that to
create is in itself a work higher and nobler than passing
judgment upon the creations of others; but this is only so
if we suppose both powers to exist in a somewhat equal
degree of excellence. When our choice lies between third-
rate creation and first-rate criticism, we must be
excused if we prefer the latter.

In speaking of the present age as pre-eminently the age
of criticism, we must be understood as speaking with what
must appear to the English reader very considerable allow-
ance. England is not the land of criticism. It is not
of native growth with us, but has been introduced from
without - an exotic, which has taken root indeed among us,
but does not yet thrive as in the countries which can most
properly claim it as their own. Our faults and virtues as
a nation seem, at present, essentially opposed to it. It
demands especially perfect freedom of thought, or rather,
perhaps, perfect obedience to a law which we have not
learned; while our 'intellectual deliverance' is too incomplete for such freedom or such obedience to be possible
for us. It demands the truest and widest sympathy with
the past, and still more with the present; the wisest
foresight of the future; the most certain discrimination
between what is real and abiding, and what is provisional,
and therefore only transitory. These qualities are the
common conditions of all present greatness in thought or
action. We cannot do without them, whether it be our mission to create or to destroy. The special taste and knowledge which the critic requires in addition to them may be
the possession of the English critic as well as of any
other; but if he possess, besides these, those other and
higher faculties, he does so not by virtue of his place of
birth, but in spite of it - not as an Englishman, but

rather as a member of the family of Western Europe.

We have chosen for very different reasons the two names
which stand at the head of the present article. Professor
Arnold's, because, in spite of some faults, he is the
very best critic we possess; Mr. Ruskin's, because, in
spite of many great and noble qualities, he is one of the
most deficient in the true critical temper.

Professor Arnold['s] ... avowed office is that of a literary critic, - an office whose requirements are indeed
many, - but whose most proper duty appears to be to pass
judgment upon the literature of each age, viewed in its
relation to its own time and circumstances, and to pronounce accordingly upon its 'adequacy.' There is a vast
body of writing too, in almost every age, not adequate
indeed, but still with a certain value of its own; expressing something, but not all, of the life which sur-
rounds it, or has preceded it; and here it becomes the
critic's duty to discriminate between the better and the
worse; to assign each to its own place; and to explain, if
need be, its author's position and function.

Professor Arnold is not less bold [than Ruskin] or less
confident in his criticisms; but he is confident without
being self-willed, and bold without being paradoxical.
Never does he fail to bear in mind that golden rule of
moderation, the observance of which is not less necessary
for the critic than it is for the artist whom he criticizes. Deeply imbued himself with the spirit of modern
thought - a true child of the great nineteenth century, he
he is yet ever anxious not to do less than justice to
those who differ from himself so widely as to demand the
exercise of the keenest insight and the highest power of
sympathy on his part if he is to appreciate them as they
deserve indeed to be appreciated. In his later pieces it
appears to have been his especial aim to teach us that
there is a vast body of modern literature of the highest
order about which Englishmen know nothing. If the single
names of Maurice and Eugénie de Guérin were the only ones
he had revealed to us, we should owe him, even so, no
common debt of gratitude. But he has done more than this.
He has dared to tell us the unpopular truth that our own
literature stands only in the third rank; that our deficiency, as a nation, in the genuine critical spirit has
rendered unavailing alike our genius and our industry; and
that France and Germany must both be placed above us. To
work out steadily the proofs of this assertion; to show

the kind of excellence which is possible in the present
age; and to show how far we are from having attained to
it, and why it is that we have failed, is a task of no
little labour, and we may add, of no little odium. How
true are Professor Arnold's own words, which he does not
indeed apply to himself, but which some of his readers
will not fail so to apply. The quality, perhaps rather
the sum of qualities, which 'at last inexorably corrects
the world's blunders and fixes the world's ideals' is not
one whose possession is likely to make a critic very popular. No. Of 'this quality,' says the Professor, 'the
world is impatient; it chafes against it, rails at it,
insults it, hates it: it ends by receiving its influence,
and by undergoing its law.' Posthumous fame may not seem
a very cheering reward to look forward to; but the consciousness of deserving such fame - of toiling at a work,
which as far as it is achieved at all, will be enduring -
may well support a man when he is misunderstood or misrepresented by his contemporaries. He may despise neglect, and scorn, and hatred; for he knows that it is none
of it deserved, and that it cannot last for ever. There
is a reward, even now, not very different from the crown
of martyrdom, which may be earned in the world of letters,
and amid the bustle of the nineteenth century.
    There are several words and phrases, which Professor
Arnold has introduced into his criticisms, which are
either new, or at least new to the English reader, and
the meaning of which it may be worth while for us to en-
deavor to determine. 'The grand style' we have spoken of
already. The phrase has been accepted; and has won its
way to a place in our common vocabularies. There are
some others which are yet as it were, upon their trial;
they express something for which we had no previous name;
but they have not been adopted as 'the grand style' has,
and their acceptance is still uncertain. There is one
word especially, the need of which perhaps is not much
felt, and yet it would seem an immense gain to us if we
were at length prevailed upon to adopt it. The term is
'Philistine,' or 'Philistinism,' one of the happiest
sobriquets devised by the spirit of modern Germany.
'Philistine,' says Professor Arnold, 'must have originally
meant in the mind of those who invented the nickname, a
strong, dogged, unenlightened opponent of the chosen
people, of the children of the light. The party of
change, the would-be remodellers of the old traditional
European order, the invokers of reason against custom,
the representatives of the modern spirit in every sphere
to which it is applicable, regarded themselves, with the
robust self-confidence natural to reformers, as a chosen

people, as children of the light. They regarded their
adversaries as humdrum people, slaves to routine, enemies
to the light; stupid and oppressive, but at the same time
very strong. Philistinism - we have not the expression in
English. Perhaps we have not the word, because we have so
much of the thing. At Soli, I imagine, they did not talk
of solecisms; and here, at the very head-quarters of
Goliath, nobody talks of Philistinism.' The word is then
contrasted with the French *épicier,*(2) and with the use,
or rather abuse, by Mr. Carlyle, of the term 'respectable,'
and 'respectability.' These are rejected, the former because it seems to cast an undeserved sneer upon living men;
the latter because it is really a word of value, and means
something higher and better than Mr. Carlyle would have us
understand by it. If we are to have a word at all for the
thing signified (and such a word would be itself a weapon
of no little power), we may see reason perhaps to follow
the Professor's advice: - 'I think we had much better take
the term *Philistine* itself.'
     There is another word, too, not the watchword of any
party, the great value of which is that it indicates a
quality whose presence or absence we have either never
felt or at least never consciously expressed, - a new
virtue which we may learn to seek for and to discover in
works of the highest artists. We are told of some poets
that they have given adequately an expression of their own
times, or, in a single word, that they are 'adequate.'
Now this is an epithet which is not used to imply that
they have set before us in detail a complete picture of
the world around them. They may be adequate without hav-
having written a line about the present; and if so their
adequacy must be found in the fact that they have best
understood the past in its relations to (then) modern
life; not that they have worked in the spirit either of a
Dutch painter or of an antiquarian. Let us see, however,
from a few instances, the class of writers to whom the
term can be applied. We may begin with three or four
names whose claim to rank among the greatest has been
established beyond all discussion. Let us take Homer and
Pindar; and from our own poets, Milton and Shakspeare.
Now what have these in common, apart from their greatness
as mere artists? Why should we give them the praise of
adequacy and refuse it to Euripides, and Scott, and Wordsworth? Not merely from a comparison of their excellence
as poets, although indeed no one could venture now to
place the last three names on the same level as the
others. Euripides, and Scott, and Wordsworth, had each of
them genius sufficient to have enabled them to write
adequately; the reason that they have not done so must be

sought in some other deficiency. Homer and Pindar, and
Milton and Shakspeare, all felt and expressed the grandest
views that were possible in their own age concerning man
and his destiny, concerning his relations to the world
about him, and to the unseen world above him. They are
therefore adequate; for they have given us a noble reflex-
ion of the noblest features of their time, and have so
given us much that must remain true in all time, however
much we may need now to adapt their thoughts, and to translate them as it were into another language. A child
indeed among ourselves can correct their more superficial
errors: Bishop Colenso can prove to us with an abundance of
demonstration that some matters of fact to Milton are not
to be deemed historically true; and we make no question
that he might have proved the same about the gods and god-
desses of the 'Iliad.' But this sort of criticism leaves
subjects that are worth discussing at all pretty nearly
where it finds them. It is enough for us if each poet has
worked with the best materials that his age afforded him;
or, rather, if the construction is noble, we need not
attend much to the form and value of the scaffolding.

Again, we find in Professor Arnold's writings an
'intellectual deliverance' and a 'moral deliverance'
spoken of. The terms are new ones, and their meaning is
important enough to justify us in dwelling a little upon
them. The latter is perhaps the easier, easier, that is,
to apprehend, though certainly not the easier to attain.
The phrase has apparently been formed by working out an old
simile from the figure of speech by which a man's passions
and impulses are said to be in subjection to him, or, if
the case be so, to be his masters. He is 'delivered'
morally as far as he is freed from such mastery, as far as
he can regulate his life upon the principle that reason
shall govern, and that his lower nature shall submit, and
without a murmur. The passions are not to be extinguished:
reason might govern then, but it would be in a city of the
dead: they are only to be so far restrained that their
spontaneous action shall accord with the deliberate moral
judgment; so that a man's personal unity shall be complete
by the perfect accordance of his impulses with his higher
will. This is no other than the old virtue of σωφροσύνη.
(3) We need the same moral deliverance now that men did
two thousand years ago.

The 'intellectual deliverance' is something quite apart
from this, not inconsistent with it, but merely distinct
from it. 'Modern times,' says Professor Arnold, 'find
themselves with an immense system of institutions,
established facts, accredited dogmas, customs, rules which
have come to them from times not modern. In this system

their life has to be carried forward, yet they have a
sense that this system is not of their own creation, that
it by no means corresponds exactly with the wants of their
actual life, that, for them, it is customary, not rational. The awakening of this sense is the awakening of the
modern spirit. To remove this want of correspondence is
beginning to be the settled endeavour of most persons of
good sense.' The intellectual deliverance then is that
which fits us, as far as we have any power of working, to
become 'dissolvents of the old European system of dominant
ideas and facts;' and which so fits us because those facts
have first ceased to satisfy us, because those ideas have
first ceased to be our own. Free thought has come so
nearly to be another expression for an immoral and flippant atheism, that we gladly welcome a new phrase which
will express as great a fulness of liberty, yet without
the associations which have made free thought almost
necessarily a bye-word of reproach and censure.

   It is a great thing, this intellectual deliverance,
even if imply no more than the above, no more than what
we believe Professor Arnold intends to imply by it. The
absence of it must certainly injure or destroy the exercise of our active powers. We must work in the modern
spirit, if the work that we do is to endure, or to give
any lasting satisfaction even to ourselves. And yet we
think that a true deliverance should imply something more
than this; that, just as a man's moral deliverance does
not consist in the mere absence of restraint, so too his
intellectual deliverance cannot be perfected merely by
his casting away from him the chains of custom and tradition. For any real results we must seek something more
than merely negative antecedents. A man may have ceased
to be a Philistine, and yet be as little qualified to do
any good in his generation as the veriest Philistine of
us all. Truth has its claim upon our obedience when we
have rejected the claims of custom. The true land of
promise must be now, as of old, the inheritance of faith,
and not merely of disbelief in error.

   These were some of the considerations which suggested
themselves to us as we read Professor Arnold's brief
sketch of Heine's life and writings. Most of our readers
will no doubt have seen it. Few can have failed to read
it with the intensest interest. It needs no tribute of
praise on our part; but we are unwilling to pass it by
without at least an expression of gratitude to its
author. It shows us Heine in his weakness and in his
noble strength; 'without moral balance,' 'deficient in
self-respect, in true dignity of character,' and yet an
earnest 'soldier in the war of liberation of humanity.'

We know that Heine laboured long, unceasingly, unselfishly,
for this one object, the liberation of humanity; and more,
that he has done very much towards its accomplishment, in
the sense, that is, in which he aimed at it. If it were
enough to throw scorn on the unreasonableness of old
rules, or on the absurdity of old dogmas, if it were
enough to free men from the fetters of old systems, partly
intellectual, partly customary, and to upset, in the name
of the unknown future, the existing guarantees for order
and therefore for progress, if this could be done safely,
and nothing remained to be done but to await the further
progress of emancipation, and to make merry over the down-
fall of kingdoms and religions, as though these were mankind's worst enemies, and our only business with them could
be to get rid of them as fast as possible, - we could not
then doubt that it was indeed a holy war in which Heinrich
Heine was engaged, and that he has earned our gratitude by
the services he has done to the cause of enslaved humanity.
But we know, alas! that a service such as this is useful
only on the condition that it be on the whole a failure.
Intellectual emancipation is of necessity the privilege of
the few, and it is a perilous privilege even for those
most fitted to enjoy it. What real message had Heine for
the German people - for the peoples of modern Europe?
what message that they could listen to, or whose contents
could help them if they heard it? It is a strange idea of
human society to suppose that we can serve it best by most
effectually knocking it to pieces. Such a process of
demolition may indeed become necessary, but it is at best
a necessary evil. Our truest thanks are due not to those
who teach us how to destroy, but to those who can discharge the higher task of teaching us to repair our losses.
'The ideas of 1789,' however wittily applied, will
scarcely furnish us with what we require. The modern
spirit has failed hitherto to accomplish the task it set
itself; and it has failed no doubt because it has been
too exclusively critical in its method, and only negative
in its results. Far be it from us to say one word in
opposition to those ideas or to that spirit. We desire
only that their work should be completed; not merely that
old things should pass away, but, further, that all things
should become new. But we desire too that the older institutions and ideas 'which have come down to us from
times not modern' should not only be regarded as present
obstacles to the liberation of humanity. It would be
narrow liberalism indeed to deny their services in the
past; and those alone who are prepared to supply their
place have any right to lift one finger to destroy them.
These are the grounds, then, on which we doubt whether
Heinrich Heine can be said to have attained truly, in the

highest sense, even an intellectual deliverance. It was
his mission to destroy. The war he waged was a war of
extermination. We do not think he had either the temper
or the knowledge that could have enabled him to recreate.

We have said already that we believe Professor Arnold to
be a genuine critic. He is, above all, always fair,
always ready to see the utmost possible good in that with
which his nature does not lead him to sympathize. German
dulness does not weary him out, he can discern genius in
Scotchmen, and can hold the balance even, when he is
weighing the merits of his own countrymen against those of
foreigners. We must add to this, that he is a genuine
artist too. Seldom does he misplace a sentence, or throw
away even a single adjective. A biography from his pen is
indeed delightful reading. His men and women preserve all
their individual features, and yet become, to use an
expression of Emerson's 'representative.' Little gems of
biography are scattered indeed all over his writings, for
he can make a sentence do as much work as many men can get
out of a chapter. But we need only refer now to his sketches of Heinrich Heine and Mademoiselle Eugénie de Guérin
for an abundant confirmation of what we say. It is
scarcely possible for us to conceive two beings more different than these: Heine, the child of the Revolution, a
thorough modern, whose special mission it was to introduce
the French spirit into the thought and literature of Germany, and yet with every moral fault but just those which
would have unfitted him to be 'a brilliant soldier of the
war of the liberation of humanity.' And Eugénie de Guérin,
French, and yet a Catholic of Catholics, to whom religion
and love were the mainstay of her soul and being. She
cared little for ideas, her attachments were essentially
personal, and above all, to one person, her brother. With
an exquisite love of beauty in art and nature, with an
infinite sense of true grandeur in art and life, it is by
the rare qualities of her *soul* that she has obtained (if
indeed, as Professor Arnold tells us, she has obtained)
an imperishable name in literature. It is no little proof
of the biographer's own width of sympathy, that he has
been able to throw himself so completely into these so
opposite characters; to feel with them as far as he might,
to think their thoughts, and, when that was possible no
longer, to feel for them, and bear as it were their
sorrows.
     'It may be predicted,' says Professor Arnold, 'that in
the literature of other countries, too, the French spirit
is destined to make its influence felt as an element, in

alliance with the native spirit, of novelty and movement,
as it has made its influence felt in German literature.'
We are content to accept the prediction, but we wish to
lay down clearly within what limits we accept it. Now the
French spirit is essentially critical. As applied to
literature proper, it is scientific rather than imaginative; it is distinguished by precision and concentration
of thought; it is sensible rather than inspired. We shall
not need to look to France for models of creative genius.
Such models, indeed, the French certainly possess; but it
is not the characteristic of the French spirit to produce
them, and we have no occasion to borrow in a matter in
which our wants are already so amply supplied. But the
French are, as they have ever been, better critics than
ourselves. They have swept away for themselves, more
effectually than we have, the cobwebs of thought and language in which the unwary are so readily entangled. They
may err, as they often have erred, through an excess of
national vanity, but at least their process of thought
does not rest essentially upon a system of elaborate
error. They are not learned pedants, as the Germans are;
nor unlearned pedants, like some among the English. The
nets of metaphysics for them are spread in vain. They are
too clear, as their enemies would say, too shallow, thinkers to be subject to such delusions. Our literature will
feel their influence as far as we find ourselves, as a
nation, compelled to admit their ideas. The process must
be, as such a process always is, a slow one. Individuals,
here and there, will be first influenced, and the mass in
due time will follow. It is something that they are consistently held before us as models by some of our best, if
not our most popular writers; and the change, when it has
once really commenced, is likely to go forward rapidly.
But men do not gather grapes of thorns, or figs of
thistles; and we may hope to imitate them as critics only
when we have consented to make their forms of thought our
own. Those who are best acquainted with those forms will
best appreciate the vastness of the change which such
consent on our part would imply, and will be content to
wait patiently for a result which they will know is certain.
    'But,' the reader may ask, 'is it not a better thing
to create than to criticize the creations of others?
Shall we need to borrow anything from the spirit of modern
France, if we possess already a higher and more noble
spirit?' The objection is a plausible one; but, in the
first place, it seems to deal with the question as if it
could be a matter of choice whether we would follow along
with the tendencies of modern Europe. We may hang back,

it is true, for awhile, and permit the great drama of the Revolution to be played on without us. Our insular position and our antecedents, although in both these respects we are less favoured than Japan, may continue to delay a change which is yet inevitable. But there is too close an union between the nations of Western Europe, too constant an interchange of thoughts and sympathies, for it to be possible for one of them to take a step in advance, without sooner or later affecting all the others. We may choose to relinquish to others the dangerous honour of leading the vanguard, but the spoils of the victory will none the less be ours, even though we have declined to bear our share in the day's burden. There is no playing with the modern spirit, no accepting it in part, and as far only as we choose to accept it. We must be content that it shall possess us, and govern us; and that government and possession we must accept frankly, with all its consequences. The modern spirit must pervade our literature, as well as our politics and our religion. We shall have no power to choose for ourselves at what precise point its influence shall cease.

Again, what is this creative power on which we pride ourselves? What masterpieces has it produced of late? what permanent additions has it made to our higher literature? Let us quote from Professor Arnold a brief but discriminating sketch of the kind of work which has been done by our greatest recent poets. It may serve to show us in some degree the losses which we have sustained by our national waywardness; it may serve to teach us how great has been our wasteful misapplication of the highest creative genius.

'We in England,' says the Professor, 'in our great burst of literature during the first early years of the present century, had no manifestation of the modern spirit, as this spirit manifests itself in Goethe's works or Heine's. And the reason is not far to seek. We had neither the German wealth of ideas nor the French enthusiasm for applying ideas. There reigned in the mass of the nation that inveterate inaccessibility to ideas, that Philistinism - to use the German nickname - which reacts even on the individual genius that is exempt from it.' And then, after speaking of the work done by Shakspeare and Spenser, who applied to literature, as far as the advance of thought had permitted, the then modern spirit, and after telling us how the great English middle class, whose intelligent sympathy had upheld Shakspeare and Shakspeare's contemporaries, a few years afterwards entered the prison of Puritanism, and had the key turned on it there for two hundred years, he goes on to describe

the attempt made by two Englishmen to create a properly
modern literature, and their failure.

In the literary movement of the beginning of the nineteenth century the signal attempt to apply freely the
modern spirit was made in England by two members of the
aristocratic class, Byron and Shelley. But Byron and
Shelley did not succeed in their attempt freely to
apply the modern spirit in English literature; they
could not succeed in it; the resistance to baffle them,
the want of intelligent sympathy to guide and uphold
them, were too great. Their literary creation, compared with the literary creation of Shakspeare and
Spenser, compared with the literary creation of Goethe
and Heine, is a failure. The best literary creation
of that time in England proceeded from men who did not
make the same bold attempt as Byron and Shelley. - What
in fact was the career of the chief English men of
letters, their contemporaries? The greatest of them,
Wordsworth, retired (in middle-age phrase) into a monas-
tery. I mean, he plunged himself in the inward life,
he voluntarily cut himself off from the modern spirit.
Coleridge took to opium. Scott became the historio-
grapher royal of feudalism. Keats passionately gave
himself up to a sensuous genius, to his faculty for
interpreting nature; and he died of consumption at
twenty-five. Wordsworth, Scott, and Keats have left
admirable works; far more solid and complete works
than those which Byron and Shelley have left. But
their works have this defect - they do not belong to
that which is the main current of the literature of
modern epochs, they do not apply modern ideas to life;
they constitute, therefore, *minor currents*, and all
other literary work of our day, however popular, which
has the same defect, also constitutes but a minor
current....

Now, apart from the objection that the above sketch does
does not attempt to value what Coleridge did as a prose
writer - it may be a sufficient account of his inspiration
as a poet to say that he 'took to opium' - we can see no
reason to dispute its correctness and adequacy. Such a
history as it unfolds is in truth a melancholy record of
the highest faculties, not indeed quite wasted, but turned
to an unworthy purpose, unworthy of their century, unworthy of themselves. But the account of our losses will
be incomplete unless we add to the above the name, too, of
Tennyson. He seems to us to have a genuine wish, indeed,
to apply the modern spirit to literature, but to have

failed because he has no proper conception of the modern
spirit, no true sense of what that spirit really is. And
he has suffered from the same cause, from 'the want of
intelligent sympathy to guide and uphold' him. And it is
from this that he has erred, we believe, as to the real
tendency of modern thought, that he has mistaken a minor
current for the main stream itself, and has surrendered
himself as far as he has idealized anything modern, to the
idealization of an abortive and unphilosophical criticism.
Tennyson is a modern, indeed, but he is only a modern
Englishman. We cannot pronounce his work a failure; it is
a success, indeed; but a success of little value. He is no
Philistine: but he has sadly blundered on his way to the
land of promise.

Further, we may see from the above examples that the
modern spirit, critical though it is, is scarcely less
truly creative. We cannot doubt that for a time its
merely critical tendency is likely to predominate, but it
has none the less a creative energy of its own. It is at
present a spirit as it were without a body; moving, indeed,
upon the face of the waters, but with its work not yet
accomplished; finding the earth still without form and
void. It cannot, then, idealize, except by anticipation,
a state of society which does not yet exist; and its work
in literature is therefore mainly critical. The shifting
phases of modern life cannot as yet furnish it with its
proper stimulus. A revolution, though it has extended
over five eventful centuries, is no proper subject for
noble poetry. The modern spirit has not indeed lost faith
in ideas: it is of its very essence that it has not; its
life and being are bound up with them. But it has been
taught that some ideas, which it once supposed final, are
not final – are not even properly its own. They were sufficient in their day to furnish matter for the genius of a
Shakspeare; but if we compare Shakspeare with Goethe, we
may see how vastly the course of time and experience has
changed the direction of the spirit of modern Europe. It
is not in the difference of their personal characters that
we can find an explanation of their essential difference
as poets. We must seek it rather in the difference of
their circumstances, or, to borrow a word from the French,
of their *environment*. We have ceased more completely than
ever to believe in the permanence of the present, or in
the possibility of containing new wine in the tatters of
old bottles; but we have not therefore surrendered one
particle of our confidence about the future. When the reconstruction which we are seeking has been brought about,
when the work of creation is over, the time will then
come to celebrate with songs of triumph the destinies of

a new-born world. We may be content at present that the
modern spirit in literature should display itself chiefly
as critical.

Notes

1 'criticism'.
2 'grocer'.
3 'high morality' or 'virtuous behaviour'.

6. FITZJAMES STEPHEN, MATTHEW ARNOLD AND HIS COUNTRYMEN,
'SATURDAY REVIEW'

3 December 1864, 683-5

Stephen (see No. 3) returned to his debate with Arnold in
this famous review. Arnold, he says, writes with brilliance. He is good-natured and entertaining - 'even
instructive'. But he is nevertheless 'fundamentally
wrong'. Stephen says that Arnold's 'transcendentalism',
his illogicality and lack of system, and his woeful lack
of practical sense, make him insensitive to English
strengths and therefore untrustworthy as a critic. It
was largely Stephen's review that elicited Arnold's controversial My Countrymen.

Mr. Matthew Arnold has contributed to the first number of
the new series of the 'National Review' a paper on the
functions of criticism at the present time, which is an
excellent specimen of that peculiar turn, both of style
and thought, with which of late years he has so often
amused and rather surprised his readers. Few readers of
the better class of periodical literature need to be told
that Mr. Arnold is a very clever man, possessed in an
unusual degree of some very uncommon gifts. He is always
brilliant, good-natured, entertaining, and even instructive. There is generally a certain degree of truth in
what he says, and, whatever its nature may be, there can
never be any doubt about its good faith. Mr. Arnold's
utterances may not be the result of any profound medita-
tion, but they at least represent genuine likes and

dislikes. He does really work himself, at any rate for
the time being, into an esoteric enthusiasm for the particular point which he enforces. It is also to be noticed
that his points are always of the same kind. His self-
imposed mission is to give good advice to the English
people as to their manifold faults, especially as to their
one great fault of being altogether inferior, in an intellectual and artistic point of view, to the French. He is
so warm upon this subject that he has taught himself to
write a dialect as like French as pure English can be.
Indeed, it is a painful duty to admit that his turn for
French is so strong that the undefiled well is sometimes
very near defilement. Take such a sentence, for instance,
as the following: - 'But Burke is so great because, almost
alone in England, he brings thought to bear upon politics,
he saturates politics with thought; it is his accident that
his ideas were at the service of an epoch of concentration,
not of an epoch of expansion.' We can almost hear the
head-voice, with its sharp nasal ring, and see the eloquent hands gracefully turned outwards, as if to point
first to the epoch of concentration and then to the epoch
of expansion, with which a French lecturer would hand us
this neat little sentence. The exquisite French-English
in which Mr. Thackeray so much delighted is only a very
little more of a caricature.

    Mr. Arnold's present object is to make English criti-
cism ashamed of itself and conscious of its own contemptible character. Like all that he writes, his article is
very pretty reading, but from first to last it appears to
us to be fundamentally wrong, and, in particular, it
totally fails to apprehend that against which it is directed. The truth is that, like his French models, Mr.
Arnold has quick sympathies and a great gift of making
telling remarks; but, also like them, he has hardly any
power of argument. At least, if he has, he rarely shows
it. His general object in the paper before us is to
defend some observations which he had made elsewhere on
the functions of criticism; but the greater part of it is
composed of illustrations of the poverty and vulgarity of
the modern English mind, with an attempt to explain the
cause and the remedy. The cause of our unfortunate condition is, he says, our constant anxiety about immediate
practical results. The remedy is that criticism, and
thought in general, ought to be disinterested. 'And how
is it to be disinterested? By keeping aloof from practice;
by resolutely following the law of its own nature, which
is to be a free play of the mind on all subjects which it
touches; by steadily refusing to lend itself to any of
those ulterior political practical considerations about

ideas which plenty of people will be sure to attach to
them, which perhaps ought to be attached to them, which,
in this country at any rate, are certain to be attached
to them quite sufficiently, but which criticism has really
nothing to do with. Its business is simply to know the
best that is known and thought in the world, and, by in
its turn making this known, to supply a current of new and
fresh ideas.'
    In illustration of his meaning, he tells us that the
French live by ideas. Speaking of the French Revolution,
he says, 'That a whole nation should have been penetrated
with an enthusiasm for pure reason' (can Mr. Cobden have
been looking at the 'National Review'?), 'and with an
ardent zeal for making its prescriptions triumph, is a
very remarkable thing... The French Revolution derives
from the force, truth, and universality of the ideas which
it took for its law, and from the passion with which it
could inspire a multitude for those ideas, an unique and
still living power.' It failed in practice by attempting
to give an immediate practical application to those 'fine
ideas of the reason;' but we English, who are great in
practice, never ascend to ideas at all. A member of Parliament blasphemously said to Mr. Arnold, 'That a thing is
an anomaly I consider to be no objection to it whatever.'
We think ourselves a wonderful people - teste Mr. Adderley, who made a speech to that effect to the Warwickshire
farmers, and Mr. Roebuck, who said so to the Sheffield
cutlers; but criticism ought to see how short we fall of
anything like ideal beauty. Mr. Roebuck spoke of the
'unrivalled happiness' of England. Mr. Adderley spoke of
'the Anglo-Saxon race ... the best breed in the whole
world.' Mr. Arnold, representing the higher criticism,
read in a newspaper that a woman named Wragg was in custody at Nottingham for child murder. Of this the higher
criticism says: - 'Wragg! If we are to talk of ideal perfection, has any one reflected what a touch of grossness
in our race, what an original shortcoming in the most delicate spiritual perceptions, is shown by the natural
growth amongst us of such hideous names - Higginbottom,
Stiggins, Bugg ... and the final touch, Wragg is in custody? The sex lost in the confusion of our unrivalled
happiness.' Criticism ought to show that Wragg should
have been called (say) Fairfax; and that, instead of
saying 'Wragg is in custody,' the brutal journalist
should have said, 'And so, on that cold November night,
the door of Nottingham gaol was shut behind our sinful
sister.' To the general public this way of putting it
may not seem to make much difference, but Mr. Arnold
thinks otherwise: - 'Mr. Roebuck will have a poor opinion

of an adversary who replies to his defiant songs of triumph only by murmuring under his breath, "Wragg is in
custody," but in no other way will these songs of triumph
be gradually induced to moderate themselves.' We do not
envy the higher criticism if it has to go about 'murmuring
Wragg is in custody,' till all afterdinner speeches rise
to the level of ideal beauty.

More serious functions, however, do present themselves
for criticism in the other illustrations given by Mr.
Arnold. He tells us, for instance, that 'the British
Constitution, seen from the speculative side, sometimes
looks a colossal machine for the manufacture of Philistines.' Then criticism, looking at the Divorce Court, 'in
which the gross, unregenerate British Philistine has
indeed stamped an image of himself' ... 'may be permitted
to find the marriage theory of Catholicism refreshing and
elevating.' Some parts of the marriage theory of Catholicism, as expressed in Suarez' 'De Matrimonio,' would, by
the way, form an appropriate appendix to 'The Times''
report of the Codrington case. Dr. Colenso is a mere
Philistine of rather a contemptible kind, though M. Renan
(with whom Mr. Arnold by no means agrees) is quite the
reverse: - 'Bishop Colenso's book reposes on a total misconception of the essential elements of the religious
problem as that problem is now presented for solution.
To criticism, therefore ... it is, however well meant, of
no importance whatever. Mr. Renan's book attempts a new
synthesis of the elements furnished to us by the four
Gospels,' and such a synthesis 'is the very essence of
the religious problem as now presented.' The higher criticism, of course, knows what the religious problem is,
and how it is presented, and therefore it treats M. Renan
with respect, and Bishop Colenso with the most curious
kind of contempt - the contempt of a benevolent elder
sister for the little girl who thinks that the world is a
sham because she has discovered that her doll is stuffed
with straw.

Mr. Arnold's theory, diffused over more than twenty
pages, may be shortly expressed thus, for the most part
in his own words: -

'The prescriptions of reason are absolute, unchanging,
of universal validity.'

It is the function of the higher criticism to discover
and state these prescriptions of reason, leaving to others
the inferior task of adapting them to practice.

English criticism is deficient in caring only for
immediate practical results, putting on one side the prescriptions of reason.

Unless by some means this is remedied, the nation's

spirit 'must in the long run die of inanition.'
Let us now consider what this theory is worth. Mr.
Arnold overlooks two considerations which dispose of his
whole argument about the present state of English criticism.
These are, first, that there is in England a school of
philosophy which thoroughly understands, and on theoretical
grounds deliberately rejects, the philosophical theory
which Mr. Arnold accuses the English nation of neglecting,
and that the practical efforts of the English people,
especially their practical efforts in the way of literary
criticism, are for the most part strictly in accordance
with the principles of that philosophy. Secondly, that
whereas, according to his own system, practice and theory
form different spheres – practice to be regulated by a
view to immediate results, theory by a view to pure reason
(whatever that may be) – and whereas practical objections
only ought to be applied by him to practical inquiries,
and objections drawn from pure reason to theoretical inquiries, yet again and again he objects to specific practical measures on theoretical grounds.

First, there is in England a school of philosophy which
perfectly understands, and on theoretical grounds deliberately rejects, the philosophical theory which Mr. Arnold
accuses the English of neglecting. Mr. Arnold's whole
essay assumes the truth of the transcendental theory of
philosophy. Englishmen are merely practical; they have no
philosophy in them at all, because they set on one side
'prescriptions of reason, absolute, unchanging, and of
universal validity.' This is just like saying a man has
no religion because he is not a Roman Catholic. Mr.
Arnold surely cannot be ignorant of the fact that, from
the days of Hobbes and Locke to those of Mr. Mill and Mr.
Bain, the most influential of English thinkers have
utterly denied the truth of transcendentalism, and have
constantly affirmed that all knowledge is based upon experience and sensation. This may be true, or it may be false,
but it is just as much entitled to be called philosophy as
anything else. Now the commonest acquaintance with this
view of things will show that in principle, though of
course not in detail, it justifies the common run of English criticism – that is, of the remarks which English
people make on passing events for practical or literary
purposes. Take, for instance, Mr. Arnold's member of
Parliament who did not object to anomalies. What Mr.
Arnold viewed as his blasphemy really amounts to this: –
Political institutions exist for the purpose of producing
a maximum of happiness, in the wide sense of the word.
Experience alone can show what institutions, in a given
case, will produce that result. Experience is either in

the inductive or in the deductive stage. It is in the
inductive stage until its results have fallen into the
shape of general principles, like those of mathematics,
which can be applied at once to particular cases. When
they have, it is in the deductive stage. Our political
experience has not yet reached the deductive stage. It is
still inductive. But, in considering institutions induc-
tively, it can be no objection to them that they are anomalies - *i.e.* that they vary from some principle asserted to
be true, for induction considers them only as facts, and
does not, and by its very nature cannot, recognise the
truth of the principles which they are said to contradict.
Before Mr. Arnold lectures the English nation on their
want of logic, he ought to understand that a man may deny
his major without denying the force of syllogisms in
general. The member of Parliament meant, 'Your general
principles being false, it is no objection to any institution that, judged by them, it is anomalous.' No man out of
a madhouse ever says, Admitting the truth of your premisses
and the form of your syllogism, I deny the truth of the
conclusion.

In fact, no nation in the world is so logical as the
English nation. Once get it well convinced of the truth
of a general principle - which is, as it ought to be, considering how hard it is to state general principles cor-
rectly, a very hard task - and it will do anything. For
instance, the English nation believes in political economy,
and the consequence is that it is the only nation in the
world which has established free trade. The new Poor Law
and the Bank Charter Act were based upon the principles of
the same science. Bentham persuaded the English nation
that the greatest happiness of the greatest number was the
true rule for legislation, and every part of the law has
been reformed by degrees by the application, more or less
skilful and complete, of that abstract principle. Newton
persuaded the English nation that the force of gravity
varies inversely as the square of the distance, and this
doctrine, with its consequences, was accepted and worked
out to its practical results by the English nation before
any other people fully took it in. Mr. Mill has persuaded
the English nation that men ought to argue, not from uni-
versals to particulars, but from particulars to particulars, and the practical influence of this highly abstract
principle is seen in that state of criticism to which Mr.
Arnold objects. Our modern Indian policy has been governed by the abstract principle that the natives ought to
be civilized on the English pattern. When abstract principles like these are embraced by and do influence the
English people most deeply, is it just, or even decent, to

talk about 'British Philistines' because we English do not
choose to recognise as eternal truths a set of platitudes
which may be proved to be false? And is it better than
sophistry to try to bolster up the credit of these platitudes, in the face of their notorious failure, by saying
that they are true in the sphere of absolute reason, and
that, in order to purge our grossness, we ought to go and
live in that sphere, murmuring under our breaths 'Wragg is
in custody'? Our English notion is, that the only test by
which you can judge of the truth of a general principle is
its application to facts. If it will not open the lock,
it may be a very pretty key, but it is certainly not the
true one. It is from facts only that principles can be
got, and it is by facts only that their truth, when they
are got at, can be tested. Mr. Arnold is like a man who
says to a painter or a sculptor, 'What a gross Philistine
you are to pass your time in chipping at that hideous
stone, dabbling with that nasty clay, or fiddling about
with oil-paints and canvas! Why do you not at once rise
to the sphere of pure reason, and produce, as I do in my
dreams, statues and pictures of eternal and absolute
beauty?'

Mr. Arnold, like other transcendentalists, is very shy
of giving us an eternal truth to look at. He does, however, try his hand at one, and a better illustration of
that great maxim, 'I never heard of an eternal truth without thinking of an infernal lie,' has seldom been seen: -
'The prescriptions of reason are absolute, unchanging, of
universal validity. *To count by tens is the simplest way
of counting.* That is a proposition of which every one
from here to the antipodes feels the force; at least, I
should say so if we did not live in a country where it is
not impossible that any morning we may find a letter in
"The Times" declaring that a decimal coinage is an absurdity.' This is a marvellous passage. The Decimal Coinage
Commissioners declared against the scheme. One of them
was Lord Overstone. Imagine Mr. Matthew Arnold asserting
that Lord Overstone is incapable of abstract thought on
his own subjects! Apart from this, Mr. Arnold is not only
wrong, but so clearly wrong that there is probably little
hope of convincing him of it. What he calls a self-
evident proposition is, in the first place, not abstract;
in the second place, it is not true; and in the third
place, if it were both abstract and true, it would not
prove the consequence connected with it. First, it is
not abstract. The abstract proposition is that, if any
system of notation whatever be given, there will be some
convenience in making the base of that system the unit of
tables of weights, measures, and coinage. This is, no

doubt, true. But some other abstract propositions are
also true, one of which is that to be a multiple of many
factors is a convenience to which regard should be had in
choosing a base of notation. Now, the number ten has but
two factors, two and five, both of which are prime numbers, and ten is therefore a very inconvenient base for a
system of any kind. Twelve, on the other hand, is highly
convenient, being divisible by four factors, of which two
only are primes. Hence there is a balance of advantages.
To count by tens has the advantage of taking as your unit
the base of an established system of notation. To count
by twelves has the advantage of taking as your unit a
number in itself far more convenient for that purpose.
The advantage of counting by twelve is principally felt in
small calculations done in the head. The advantage of
counting by ten is principally felt in large calculations
done on paper, and is not felt till you get past twenty.
Hence a system of pounds reckoned on the decimal basis,
and shillings and pence reckoned on the duodecimal basis,
combines two sets of advantages. On the other hand, the
decimal system is notoriously inconvenient for small
transactions.

     To sum up - our transcendentalist supposes himself to
be stating an abstract proposition when he is stating a
concrete one. Instead of saying 'to count by tens,' he
should say, 'to take as your unit an established base of
notation.' He supposes himself to be stating a true proposition when he is stating a false one. It is not true
that to count by tens is the simplest way of counting, or
that it is the most convenient, unless you add the very
material clauses - 'ten being given as the base of notation,' and 'except for numbers under twenty.' Lastly, he
supposes himself to be stating a complete proposition
when he is stating one which is incomplete; for it does
not follow that, because a particular way of counting is
the simplest, any special system of coinage ought to be
adopted. To count by ones, to have a separate name for
each number, would no doubt be simpler than to count by
tens, but no one advocates such a system. Let it be
observed that each of these objections is theoretical.
Mr. Arnold may call his countrymen gross Philistines as
much as ever he pleases, but they will always be able to
reply - We object to what you call your theories, not
because they are theories, but because they are not true
theories, but arbitrary generalities, which we can show to
be rash, false, or at best incomplete.

     The second objection to Mr. Arnold's theory is that,
according to his own view, theory and practice form different spheres - practice to be regulated by a view to

immediate results, theory by pure reason. Yet he constantly objects to practical measures on theoretical
grounds. Thus, he says that the Divorce Court is a
hideous institution, and that it is refreshing to turn
from it to the Catholic marriage theory. What relation,
on his principles, is there between the two things? By
his own rule, he cannot inquire into, and has no right to
notice, the hideousness of the Divorce Court. That is a
practical question, a matter of business to be decided on
common earthly grounds. The Catholic marriage theory, we
suppose, is a matter of pure reason. Let each have its
sphere, but unless and until pure reason can work out its
marriage theory in a sufficiently definite shape to solve
every practical question connected with the marriage law,
those who hold it have no other right to call the Divorce
Court hideous than the authors of the Divorce Act have to
call them visionary. If theorists are not sure enough of
the truth of their theories to take the responsibility of
putting them in practice, they have no right to depreciate
the rule of thumb. When Don Quixote refused to try his
sword on the second edition of his helmet, he surely
renounced the right to sneer at less romantic wares. When
Mr. Arnold has got a theory which will fully explain all
the duties of the legislator on the matter of marriage, he
will have a right to abuse the Divorce Court.
    Much the same may be said of Mr. Arnold's criticism on
Dr. Colenso. His book, he says, is 'of no importance
whatever' to criticism. It 'reposes on a fundamental misconception of the essential elements of the religious
problem.' M. Renan's book, on the other hand, deals with
the very essence of the religious problem. 'For saying
this' (in 'Macmillan's Magazine'), says Mr. Arnold, 'I was
greatly blamed, because I was told that I was a liberal
attacking a liberal; yet surely I had a right to say that
a man in pursuit of truth had taken a false method.' Certainly some of Mr. Arnold's readers thought, and still
think, that, considering how desperately hard the lower
criticism was of Dr. Colenso, the higher criticism might
have chosen some other victim, or some other time for
scourging that particular victim. It was not, however,
for this alone that Mr. Arnold was blamed, but for something very different. It was for the way in which he
argued that it was a crime against literary criticism and
the higher culture to attempt to inform the ignorant. He
was blamed for saying much which was summed up in these
words, 'Knowledge and truth, in the full sense of the
words, are not attainable by the great mass of the human
race at all.' In reference to the matter in hand, this
meant, 'Ordinary English people have no business to have

any opinion on the question whether or not the whole of
the Pentateuch is true. The higher minds have, but the
great bulk of the nation ought to leave such matters to M.
Renan and a few others, and it is bad taste, a low vulgar
thing, to address them on the question.' This was very
different from saying that Dr. Colenso's method was false.
It said that his object was bad. Granting the goodness of
the object and the truth of the assertions, it was simply
absurd to deny their relevancy. Indeed, Mr. Arnold did
not deny it. His point was, that the book ought not to
have been written. This is altogether inconsistent with
his present view, which is, that practice and theory ought
to be divorced. Theory ought to sit on a hill retired,
and argue high about a new synthesis of the four Gospels,
and care nothing for practice. Let it, then, care nothing
for practice, but do not let it attack practical men for
making practical remarks. Dr. Colenso wrote *ad populum*.
(1) Mr. Arnold denied his right to do so, but it is very
hard now to change the charge, and to blame him for having
addressed the higher culture of Europe in a popular way.
Dr. Colenso's book may or may not repose on a false conception of the religious problem, though it is a strong
thing to assert that a critical inquiry into the Old
Testament must, under all circumstances, be simply worth-
less; but Mr. Arnold's criticism certainly reposes on a
false conception of Dr. Colenso's book. Indeed, his two
criticisms 'repose' on conflicting conceptions, and, as
in the case of other attempts to sit on two stools at
once, the result is grotesque.
    The way in which Mr. Arnold treats Dr. Colenso is an
excellent illustration of the fundamental weakness which
affects all that he writes. With all his ability, he
sometimes gives himself the airs of the distinguished
courtier who shone so bright and smelt so sweet when he
had occasion to talk with Hotspur about the prisoners.
He is always using a moral smelling-bottle, like those
beloved countrymen, who, at foreign *tables d'hôte*, (2)
delight to hold forth on the vulgarity of 'those English.'
Dr. Colenso condescended to do a sum about the '800 and
odd pigeons.' Mr. Arnold is almost ready to faint, till
he is consoled by the thought of M. Renan and his sublime
synthesis. He reads or looks at the Codrington case
(which certainly had a strong scent about it), and, murmuring under his breath, 'Gross unregenerate British Philistines,' flies in despair to the Catholic marriage
theory, which purifies the country of Rabelais, Diderot,
Faublas, Montépin, and M. Dumas *fils*. (3)

Notes

1 'to the people'.
2 'hotel restaurants'.
3 'son'.

7. R. H. HUTTON, UNSIGNED REVIEW, 'SPECTATOR'

25 February 1865, xxxviii, 214-15

Richard Holt Hutton (1826-97) was a theologian and a
journalist. He edited the 'National Review' with Walter
Bagehot, and from 1861 to the time of his death he was
joint editor and proprietor of the 'Spectator'. His respect for Arnold probably determined the 'Spectator's'
generally favourable response to Arnold's works; indeed,
Hutton himself wrote many of the reviews. Evidently
Arnold did not entirely return Hutton's respect: he complains of Hutton seeing 'very far into a millstone'.
Hutton was in fact an able critic. In this review of
'Essays in Criticism' he makes a comparison that continued to interest him between Arnold and Newman. And while
finding fault with several of Arnold's specific judgments,
he concludes with the opinion that these 'are essays that
will live'.

Mr. Arnold has few equals amongst the living writers of
English prose; - perhaps but one, whose style he has
himself taken occasion to appreciate with his usual delicate insight, and no doubt without any suspicion that in
pronouncing his eulogy upon it he was in reality also
pronouncing the eulogy of his own, - we mean Dr. Newman.
Yet the likeness is too striking to be overlooked by any
who feel keenly the impression which the form, apart from
the substance, of thought makes upon the mind of a reader.
It may be thought that the resemblance is only such as
deep draughts of the culture of Oxford received into
sensitive and poetical natures would be sure to produce.
But there is more resemblance than this would explain.
The light and flexible precision of thought, the luminous
line which every sentence seems to present without any use
of high colour, the dislike of eccentricity and, as Mr.

Arnold well terms it in relation to Dr. Newman, the
'urbanity' *lenis minimeque pertinax* (1) of their most
trenchant judgments, the happy power of striking a clear
key-note for every separate essay or lecture in which
there is neither obscurity nor exaggeration, the easy
play of the preparing intelligence, the severe edge of
imperturbable dogma beneath, all mark a closer approach
in the manner of presenting thought to the public than
any community of culture could account for. True, there
is in Mr. Arnold a slight tinge of consciousness, a faint
intellectual elation which is entirely absent from Dr.
Newman, and this for the very good reason that Mr.
Arnold's dogmatic intellectualism is self-evolved, while
Dr. Newman's dogmatic theology is taken up in the humility
of self-abegnation. The leader of the intellectual ranks
against the Philistinism of our century, must feel, and
does feel, a deeper self-reliance than the leader who goes
back to the Past almost expressly to avoid the semblance
of setting up for himself, and whose deepest current of
thought is disgust with nineteenth-century enlightenment
and religious 'progress.' There is a deeper and wider
nature - a more *liberal* nature - in spite of his reactionary creed, at the source of Dr. Newman's powers of expression than of Mr. Arnold's equally beautiful, equally delicate, but much thinner genius; but the resemblance is not
to be mistaken for a moment. Take, for example, the
following sentence, which, till we disclose its predecessor, would be instantly identified by any critic familiar
with modern literature as belonging to some one of Dr.
Newman's numerous comments on the victory of divine weakness over human strength. 'Of this quality the world is
impatient; it chafes against it, rails at it, insults it,
hates it; it ends by receiving its influence and undergoing its law.' What is this quality? When we come to
understand the passage, we see at once what is the difference in root between Dr. Newman's mind and Mr. Arnold's,
and why there is so much of resemblance between their
styles with such a world of thought between their principles. The passage from which we took the sentence is
one of Mr. Arnold's key-note passages, describing the
characteristic powers of the new double star which has
been recently discovered in the sky of French literature,
Maurice and Eugénie de Guérin:-

> She was very different from her brother; but she too,
> like him, had that in her which preserves a reputa-
> tion. Her soul has the same characteristic quality as
> his talent, - *distinction*. Of this quality the world
> is impatient; it chafes against it, rails at it,

insults it, hates it; it ends by receiving its influence, and by undergoing its law.... To the circle of
spirits marked by this rare quality, Maurice and
Eugénie de Guérin belong; they will take their place
in the sky which these inhabit, and shine close to one
another, *lucida sidera*. (2)

The last two words have more than critical felicity,
they are the happy application of a poet to express the
essence of such minds as those of Maurice and Eugénie de
Guérin. 'Lucida sidera' describe them as nothing else
would, and reiterate, too, without repeating Mr. Arnold's
key-note - the idea of 'distinction.' But that he should
apply such language as this to purely intellectual 'distinction,' is, to use another of Dr. Newman's expressions,
the characteristic 'note' of his thought, - which aims
consistently and permanently at establishing what we may
call a school of intellectual conscience, - at answering
the question 'what *ought* we to prefer in intellectual
things?' - and not only at answering this question, but
almost at trying to show that the intellectual discriminations of high culture are more certain, more capable of
demonstration, more worthy of dogmatic elaboration, than
even the moral discriminations. Thus in one of his
essays, where he is contrasting the French width with the
English limitation of mind, he says: -

1789 asked of a thing, Is it rational? 1642 asked of
a thing, Is it legal? or, when it went furthest, Is
it according to conscience? This is the English
fashion; a fashion to be treated, within its own
sphere, with the highest respect; for its success,
within its own sphere, has been prodigious. But what
is law in one place, is not law in another; what is
law here to-day, is not law even here to-morrow; and
as for conscience, what is binding on one man's conscience is not binding on another's; the old woman who
threw her stool at the head of the surpliced minister
in St. Giles's Church at Edinburgh obeyed an impulse
to which millions of the human race may be permitted
to remain strangers. But the prescriptions of reason
are absolute, unchanging, of universal validity.

If we were *discussing* Mr. Arnold's doctrine we might
point out the unfairness of contrasting the dictate of an
uncultivated conscience with the dictate of a cultivated
reason, - but we are not discussing it, only trying to
show the root of Mr. Arnold's dogmatism, and the point at
which that finest expression of literary character, his

prose style, diverges from the prose style of Dr. Newman.
But there is another resemblance not quite so close as
that of the luminous, urbane, delicately expressed dogmatism, but still remarkable, in the style of Mr. Arnold's
and Dr. Newman's irony, both of which tend to run into
caricature. Mr. Arnold, laughing at spick and span
'religions of the future,' says, not without real
humour, -

> These works often have much ability; they often spring
> out of sincere convictions, and a sincere wish to do
> good; and they sometimes, perhaps, do good. Their
> fault is (if I may be permitted to say so) one which
> they have in common with the British College of Health,
> in the New Road. Every one knows the British College
> of Health; it is that building with the lion and the
> statue of the Goddess Hygeia before it; at least, I
> am sure about the lion, though I am not absolutely
> certain about the Goddess Hygeia. This building does
> credit, perhaps, to the resources of Dr. Morrison and
> his disciples; but it falls a good deal short of one's
> idea of what a British College of Health ought to
> be....

Which reminds one strongly of many of the ironical
passages in Dr. Newman's lectures to Anglicans; - take
this, for example, almost at random: -

> The idea, then, of the so-called Anglo-Catholic div-
> ines was simply and absolutely submission to an exter-
> nal authority; to it they appealed, to it they betook
> themselves; there they found a haven of rest; thence
> they looked out upon the troubled surge of human
> opinion, and upon the crazy vessels which were labour-
> ing, without chart or compass, upon it. Judge, then,
> of their dismay when, according to the Arabian tale,
> on their striking their anchors into the supposed
> soil, lighting their fires on it, and fixing in it the
> poles of their tents, suddenly their island began to
> move, to heave, to splash, to frisk to and fro, to
> dive, and at last to swim away, spouting out inhos-
> pitable jets of water upon the credulous mariners who
> had made it their home.

And from both writers we could produce passages in
which the reins, always kept upon their *thought*, are
abandoned to their sense of the ludicrous, and the usual
dignity of their style is lost in the extravagance of
their caricature. Of such passages there are two or

three not without some fun in the amusing preface to this
little volume, as, for example, the following ironical
criticism on the Philistines of the press: -

> Yes, the world will soon be the Philistines'; and then,
> with every voice not of thunder silenced, and the whole
> earth filled and ennobled every morning by the magnifi-
> cent roaring of the young lions of the 'Daily Tele-
> graph,' we shall all yawn in one another's faces with
> the dismallest, the most unimpeachable gravity....

Is there not, as Mr. Arnold says of a great contemporary
writer, just a grain of fatuity - 'of that failure in
good sense which comes from too warm a self-satisfaction,'
- in this? It reminds us of some of the passages in Dr.
Newman's lectures on Catholicism, where the great theologian's contempt for the prejudices of the limited Protestant Philistine, bursts the bounds of irony and passes
into broad farce. This tendency to lose hold of the
reins where they are delineating not what they think
worthy of answer, but what they think worthy only of
scorn, is an incident of the dogmatic temper when it
attempts to dramatize imbecility. As Mr. Arnold's dogmatism is based less on deep conviction and more upon
taste and insight than Dr. Newman's, the resulting style
has in it more flavour of personality, more that is
arbitrary and despotic, more that seems to rest on the
mood, less that rests upon the unalterable conviction
of the writer. Hence it chafes its victims more with a
false semblance of superciliousness, though it is
not more caustic in itself.
     The point where Mr. Arnold's prose style branches off
from Dr. Newman's is the point where a purely intellectual imagination branches off from a moral and spiritual
imagination. Mr. Arnold quotes from Goethe that to *act*
is so easy, while it is so hard /to *think* truly, and the
whole colour of his style transmits, if we may so to
speak, the impulse or effort to think apart from the
disturbing influence of action. This thins the whole
imaginative sphere of his mind, and even his poetry is
written in the intellectual plane, and strives to crystal-
lize its thought wholly in that plane, without permitting
the perturbations of practical life to influence it there.
This is manifest everywhere on the very surface of Mr.
Arnold's writings, both in prose and verse, and we take
it to exercise, on the whole, whether it be due to original genius or to deliberate purpose, a clarifying, but
not an enlarging influence on his criticism. What he
does see is exquisitely distinctly defined, but he

excludes so much of which he cannot clearly define the
influence, that many of his criticisms are thin. Dr.
Newman's secret axiom that those thoughts must be true
which are necessary for the highest actions, is the root
no doubt of much that is strained in his dogma, but is
also the incitement to a far broader imaginative school of
thought. He tries to enter into the whole nature of man
first, and to deduce thence the highest intellectual
dogma that is adequate to guide him. Mr. Arnold stands
apart observing serenely on the intellectual plane all
that goes on outside it, and exaggerating rather than
attempting to bridge over the chasm between life and
thought. Hence his imaginative criticism, always clear,
almost always true, very generally striking, gives us too
often the sense of something thin and superficial. His
essay on Heine, for instance, almost limits itself to the
relation between Heine and Philistinism, – an important
element no doubt in the life of the man, but by no means
the key-note of the poet's greatness. Hence, too, Mr.
Arnold's curious preference of the more perfect but
shallow and slightly weak relaxed beauty of Maurice de
Guérin to the deeper weight of poetic profundity and
humour in his sister. Hence, again, his strong preference
for the poetry of Keats, with its soft, wax-like impressi-
bility to external nature, to the far more various and far
stronger flight of Shelley's idealism. Mr. Arnold dilates
on two kinds of poetry which he calls the poetry of
'natural magic' and the poetry of 'moral profundity,' and
says, with what seems to us a strangely narrow judgment:-

> In Shelley there is not a balance of the two gifts, nor
> even a coexistence of them, but there is a passionate
> straining after them both, and this is what makes
> Shelley as a man so interesting. I will not now
> inquire how much Shelley achieves as a poet, but
> whatever he achieves, he in general fails to achieve
> natural magic in his expression.... I will not deny,
> however, that Shelley has natural magic in his rhythm;
> what I deny is that he has it in his language. It
> always seems to me that the right sphere for Shelley's
> genius was the sphere of music, not of poetry; the
> medium of sounds he can master, but to master the more
> difficult medium of words he has neither intellectual
> force enough nor sanity enough.

Here Mr. Arnold seems to us to have carefully prepared
a general definition of poetical excellence expressly in
order to exclude a particular poet to whom his own somewhat special intellectual tastes does not incline him to

do justice. We should not claim for Shelley to excel
either in 'natural magic' or in 'moral profundity,' but
we should claim for him to have given the most perfect
poetical expression to the yearnings of unsatisfied desire,
to the sense of the 'vide et néant' (3) underlying all
absorbing emotions, which has ever been given by an English poet. It seems to us simply false criticism to say
that the lines on the Euganean hills 'try to render nature' at all. The whole drift of the poem is missed in
such an expression to the transient relief which beauty of
scenery and beauty of association will sometimes give to
minds pierced, like his own, by an agony of thirst for
beauty and truth.

> Many a green isle needs must be
> In the deep wide sea of misery,

are his first words, and that key-note is struck again and
again throughout the poem. If by 'natural magic' Mr.
Arnold means magical power in delineating external nature,
we think he is right in refusing to attribute it to
Shelley. But if he means magic of expression for whatever essence of want, or yearning, or pain he sought to
express, we doubt if any one ever possessed it in equal
force. What does Mr. Arnold say of the lines concerning
Venice in this very poem, - concerning Venice as Shelley
then imagined her, desolate and a prey to the encroaching
sea? -

> A less drear ruin then than now,
> With thy conquest-branded brow,
> Stooping to the slave of slaves
> From the throne amongst the waves,
> Wilt thou be when the sea mew
> Flies, as once before he flew,
> O'er thine isles depopulate;
> And all is in its ancient state
> *Save where many a palace gate,*
> *With green sea flowers overgrown,*
> *Like a rock of Ocean's own*
> *Topples o'er the abandoned sea*
> *As the tides change sullenly.*

Those last few lines do not show, - perhaps nothing that
Shelley ever wrote did show, - what Mr. Arnold means by
sanity, - the command of a clear intellect over its own
thoughts. But the agony of desire and the rapture of
emotion do not specially require 'sanity' for their most
perfect expression, and Mr. Arnold's intellectual

criticism ignores a large part of the most perfect lyrical
poetry when it excludes such poetry as this from a rank
far higher than that of Keats, though not so high as that
of Wordsworth. The clear, intellectual medium by which,
in Mr. Arnold's estimate, all poets should work, is in
truth the medium of a few.

We can feel what it is that Mr. Arnold is repelled by
in Shelley. Everywhere he loves *measure* in literature.
He cannot bear that rampancy of insatiable, unmeasured
longing with which the intellect stands on no terms. He
worships Goethe for that steady and constant recognition
of limitation which was the intellectual rather than the
poetical side of his mind. He has no pity for that 'true
English narrowness of view' (*die ächt Britische
Beschränktheit*) which arises from some *arrière pensée* (4)
of practical prejudice; but he *is* a little inclined to a
'true French narrowness of view' of his own, - the limitation which arises from no prejudice, but from a deficiency
in sympathies lying beyond the intellectual sphere. His
favourites in literature are men whose intellects or perceptive powers are fully commensurable with their genius,
- whose 'unction,' where they have it, is shed upon us
through clear, bright understandings. What Goethe called
the 'daemonic' in himself, - which was even deeper in
Heine than in Goethe, - he prefers to ignore, - yet it is
often (as in Shelley) the essence of poetry.

Still these essays are full of brilliant and keen
truth, like this, for instance, from the essay on Joubert
in relation to the power poetry may have of exciting
tears: - 'True tears are those which are called forth by
the *beauty* of poetry; they must have as much admiration
in them as sorrow.' Of such exquisite criticisms as this
there are not few in Mr. Arnold's essays. They are the
expressions of a fine, if of a somewhat too fastidiously
intellectual criticism. They are essays that will live.

Notes

1 'lightly and least pertinent'.
2 'glittering stars'.
3 'emptiness and nullity'.
4 'ulterior motive'.

8.   J. M. LUDLOW (?), UNSIGNED REVIEW, 'READER'

8 April 1865, v, 391-93

John Malcolm Ludlow (1821-1911), a Christian Socialist,
reformer, and prolific reviewer, was the apparent writer
of this piece in the 'Reader'. Ludlow finds a unity in
'Essays in Criticism': each essay, he says, 'helps to
interpret the rest'. He agrees with Arnold's sense of
the importance of criticism and thinks Arnold its ablest
practitioner. But Ludlow goes even further than Arnold,
insisting that 'the critics must account themselves the
real lords and dictators of the world'. This is Shelley's
dictum about poets in a new and odd guise.

This volume contains various articles which Mr. Arnold has
contributed to our magazines. The subjects have no obvious connexion with each other. Yet the book leaves on the
reader's mind an impression of completeness and unity
which is equally rare and delightful. The opening essay
in part explains the secret. Mr. Arnold desires to reform
English criticism. Every one of his articles has been
written to illustrate his conception of its true nature.
Each one, therefore helps to interpret the rest; the
greater the diversity of topics, the more they conduce to
the general object. And every essay being written with
this design, is a far more elaborate composition than it
could be under any other conditions. The workmanship is
too skilful ever to betray itself. Mr. Arnold's style is
so graceful, so perfect, that it has all the appearance
of being the most natural and spontaneous expression of
his thoughts.
    After a preface which must have been meant as a foil to
the beauty of the volume which it introduces, or to illustrate by example the errors of taste which that volume
denounces, Mr. Arnold proceeds at once to his main business. As his essay On the Function of Criticism at the
Present Time is to teach us our own duties, we are bound
to notice it first. In spite of a natural dislike to a
judge, we have every motive to hear this judge. He has
the highest notion of the grandeur of our craft. There
may come a time of creative energy. At present the critics must account themselves the real lords and dictators
of the world. On the way in which they shall use this
tremendous power is dependent the condition of the next

age - what poets, philosophers, theologians shall be hereafter will be decided by the conduct of critics now.

How then ought we to behave? We wish we could answer
the question in Mr. Arnold's language. But the passage to
which we would refer our readers is too long for extrac-
tion. We can only give its substance in our feeble words.
The English people are given up to facts. They abhor
ideas. They are given up to parties. Criticism has
indulged these habits. It has stooped to facts. It has
been Whig, or Tory, or Radical. It has paid homage to
the habits and tastes of our own race. It must become
'disinterested.' It must hold itself aloof from all
facts. It must simply aim at 'creating a current of true
and fresh ideas.' No application of these ideas, in one
way or another, must be attempted. 'The best' must be
sought everywhere and in every department. There must be
no preference for English writers or thinkers; on the
contrary, a deliberate preference for those whom Englishmen are least likely to care for, are most likely to overlook or despise. Mr. Arnold remarks:

> It is because criticism has so little kept in the pure
> intellectual sphere, has so little detached itself
> from practice, has been so directly polemical and con-
> troversial, that it has so ill-accomplished, in this
> country, its best spiritual work, which is to keep man
> from a self-satisfaction which is retarding and vul-
> garising, to lead him towards perfection, by making
> his mind dwell upon what is excellent in itself, and
> the absolute beauty and fitness of things.

This 'retarding and vulgarising' self-satisfaction is
illustrated by extracts from speeches of Mr. Adderley and
Mr. Roebuck, in which the English are eulogised 'as the
best breed in the world.' Their statements are confronted
by the case of a girl who murdered her illegitimate child
at Nottingham, and whose name was Wragg. 'In Ionia and
Attica,' exclaims our critic, 'they were luckier in this
respect than the best race in the world; by the Ilissus
there was no Wragg.'

Now it seems to us that self-satisfaction of the kind
which Mr. Arnold denounces, or of any kind, is very
odious; that British orators, like the orators in Athens,
are tempted to flatter Demus, panegyrizing their own race
as the best in the world, and denouncing other races from
which they might learn much; that critics may confirm,
and have confirmed, this evil habit; that they ought to
fight against it; that we should be most thankful to any
person like Mr. Arnold, who raises his voice against it;

still more to any person who, like Mr. Arnold, teaches us
to know and admire men not of our race. We admit all that
tendency to worship facts and scorn ideas which he attributes to Englishmen; we admit that the party spirit of our
journals is connected with that tendency; we admit that
there should be a strenuous effort to counteract both the
effect and the cause. But we are as strongly convinced
that the remedy which Mr. Arnold proposes would not cure
or alleviate the disease, but would strengthen it; that
all remedies against it which have been effectual have
been exactly of the opposite character; that what he calls
'a current of true and fresh ideas' has been most created
by those Englishmen who have most stooped, even against
their inclination, to their countrymen's love of facts;
that the wisest teachers and critics - those whom Mr.
Arnold himself reverences most - have sought for ideas in
the facts, instead of bringing them from their own minds
to the facts, or letting them stand aloof from the facts;
that our history, our science, our literature, all alike
prove this to be the method which we must follow if we
would work any reform in the English faith or the English
practice.

Take one signal instance. Mr. Arnold is a sincere, even
a passionate admirer of Burke. He owns that this great
man lived 'in the world of ideas, not the world of catch-
words and party habits.' No sentence can be more just or
more happily expressed. But Burke was emphatically, from
the beginning of his life to the end of it, from the
publication of his thoughts on the Sublime and Beautiful,
to the publication of his Letters on a Regicide Peace, a
man who sought for the idea in the fact, a man who was
impatient of all ideas that were not deduced from the
study of facts. This is what reconciles his earliest
political treatises with those which are supposed to
contradict them; this is what vindicates him from Goldsmith's charge, which Mr. Arnold so justly repudiates.
He did not like the pedantry of those who opposed the
American war, merely by talking about the necessary connexion of representation with taxation, any more than the
pedantry of those who talked about the rights of man.
Both seemed to him doctors who idealised out of their own
minds, instead of seeking a far deeper, larger, grander
idea in history - God's idea, not their own. He pleaded
for actual relations between the mother country and her
colonies, for duties which she owed to them, apart from
all formulas. And when in a passage which Mr. Arnold
has quoted with great honour, but which he pronounces
quite 'un-English,' Burke confesses that hereafter some
of the ideas of the French Revolution against which he

protested, might establish themselves, it was precisely
because he believed that facts might come to light of
which he had not taken account.

What, again, is all experimental science but the
search for the idea in the fact, in the particular
instance? Against what did Bacon protest, but against the
school habit of bringing forth ideas either to control the
facts, or to exist apart from them?...

To this law, we believe, English criticism, the criticism of this day, must conform itself. If it does not –
if a set of men called critics, or men of letters, or
children of light, form themselves into a caste, and try
to spread certain ideas through society, looking down upon
facts, and resigning them to the custody of an inferior
Sudra caste, whom they call hodmen or Philistines – we believe that the ordinary Englishman will wrap himself more
and more closely in his hatred of all ideas – of all that
is graceful and beautiful – and that the so-called ideal-
ists, differing from them in all things else, will be like
them in that self-satisfaction which Mr. Arnold feels to
be so retarding and vulgarising....

The able article following the one on which we have
commented, On the Literary Influence of Academies, is in
the strictest harmony with it. That Mr. Arnold has
alleged many ingenious arguments against our chartered
libertinism, – in favour of an organised opinion to control the taste and promote the urbanity of authors – no
one will deny. The real weight of his argument, however,
depends on our admission of his suppressed premiss, that
it is desirable to have a caste of writers and critics who
shall keep up a certain tone and habit of thought and
feeling distinct from that of general society, and shall
hold itself aloof from the common movements of the world.
As we do not wish to see such a caste, as we think the
nearest approximation ever made to it was in that body of
highly-accomplished men whom the world has called the
sophists, whom Mr. Grote perhaps more rightly calls the
professors of Greece, who might bear the name of Critics
more properly than either; as we hold that these men, who
diffused ideas upon all possible subjects among the young
men of the finest race in the world, were, most happily
for those young men, resisted and defeated by a man who
had an Anglo-Saxon love for facts, who put all propound-
ers of theories to a horrible torture: as we believe that
out of this pursuit of facts, this persecution of theorists, was developed the most lofty and effectual idealism which the world has ever seen, and a style even more
exquisite (can we say more?) than Mr. Arnold's – we may
doubt whether an Academy, which all admit must have had a

number of inconveniences, can be desirable merely for the
creation and support of a literary guild, probably much
inferior to its Greek prototype. Since its main function
would be to cultivate prose - poetry being in Mr. Arnold's
judgment better without such an influence - we may venture
to ask whether the prose of Bossuet was not formed to meet
the necessities of the pulpit, and of ecclesiastical controversy; whether the prose of Pascal was not forged
amidst hard mathematical and theological studies, because
a very sharp weapon was needed to cut through the webs of
the Jesuit fathers; whether the prose of Rousseau was not
fashioned admist the hills about the Lake of Geneva, and
developed by political controversies; whether Voltaire's
prose was not sharpened and perfected by continual attri-
tion with the debates, serious and trifling, of the eighteenth century; whether the Academy can be really credited
with the strength, or delicacy, of fervour, or wit, of any
one of the four.

An admirable essay on 'Maurice de Guérin' is far more
likely than this to cultivate our affection for Frenchmen,
and to abate our Anglo-Saxon conceit. It is pleasant to
observe that Mr. Arnold can sympathise heartily with a man
who had no ambition to be a critic, who loved nature more
than a book; who had an unsatisfied yearning for spiritual
treasures, who, if he could have followed Lamennais, would
willingly have shared his best thoughts with the people.
The biography of such a man, illuminated by translations
which are a study in English as well as in French, is a
real gift to us all. There, indeed, Mr. Arnold shows us
the true function of a critic. Through a special instance
he unfolds ideas which Englishmen and Frenchmen may prize
equally.

Eugénie de Guérin, the sister of Maurice, presents us
with another, also a very striking, type of character. We
grudge no admiration which Mr. Arnold bestows on the graceful saint in the Château of Languedoc. But was he not
aware that he was spoiling the effect of his portrait, and
disclosing too evidently his purpose in painting it, when
he introduced an unknown lady of Margate, whose biography
he had happened to meet with, because she seemed to him a
very ordinary and vulgar person, as the parallel representative of English female devotion? We ask him, as an
honest critic, with a high sense of his functions and
responsibility, whether he sincerely believed that this
lady was the best specimen he could find for such a comparison - whether he did not know from personal experience
and from reading that she was not? If so, may there not
be something 'vulgarising and retarding' in the wish to
discover and expose whatever is weakest and least

attractive in his own land, as well as in the wish to
glorify it at the expense of every other?

That question we will repeat in reference to the next
and very different subject of the next sketch. We pass
from France to Germany, from Eugénie de Guérin to Heinrich
Heine. The leap, we need not say, is prodigious; the contrast serves to display the comprehensiveness of Mr.
Arnold's taste. Of Heine himself and his genius we would
gladly have heard more. Mr. Arnold regards him merely as
par excellence (1) the antagonist of Philistines or idea-
less men. His three qualifications for the task are
apparently these: 1. He disliked his own country. 2. He
hated England. 3. He considered France the holy land of
Europe. We should have listened willingly to some apology
for Heine's want of patriotism and his incapacity for sympathy with a country which has produced Shakespeare and
one or two eminent men besides. If we had been reminded
of his Jewish birth - his want of a proper home in any
European country - we should have felt we had no right to
treat him harshly for these intellectual infirmities, even
though they had some relation to that immorality in act
and word which Mr. Arnold deplores. But if they are produced as signs of a vocation, proofs of his right to take
place among the liberators of humanity, we must pause.
The liberators would, it strikes us, turn out to be the
haughtiest and most mischievous tyrants the world has yet
seen.

The entire freedom of Joubert from such disagreeable
characteristics makes the sketch of him one of the most
satisfactory in the volume. Mr. Arnold does not merely
use him to expose the pretensions of the best breed in
the world. He compares Joubert with Coleridge, treating
his own countryman, on the whole with much respect and
appreciation. To us the suggestion of a likeness between
the two men is most instructive and edifying. Coleridge
was always in danger of becoming a mere idealist. He was
kept, in spite of himself, in perpetual contact with the
facts of life, being a vehement politician in youth -
still busy with politics, though under a new phase, when
he had returned from Germany, and was writing his
'Friend,' - compelled in later days by contrition and the
consciousness of moral weakness to seek for a practical
faith. Mr. Arnold shows us that Joubert had more of this
useful counteraction to the natural habit of his mind than
Coleridge; that he had a healthy dislike of scholastic
phraseology, for which our philosopher had a dangerous
affection; that he submitted more to the ordinary demands
of duty and of social life. Surely he was a greater enemy
of Philistines than Heine, because he did not confront

their arrogance with a worse kind of arrogance.

Spinoza, to whom Mr. Arnold has devoted an inadequate
and superficial, but of course, graceful essay, is another
specimen of a man who lived in a world of ideas, and was
cut off from the world of facts; but who was always
exhibiting his discontent with those who regarded ideas as
products of their own intellects, who reverenced them as
substantial and divine. Mr. Arnold is satisfied, and
thinks Goethe was satisfied, with considering Spinoza as
an enemy of final causes. A true, possibly, but a most
feeble estimate of a noble man, who was ever struggling
after light - of a man who fell into ten thousand confus-
ions, which we fall into without knowing it, because he
could not find the God in whom he was sure that he was
living, and moving, and having his being. Mr. Arnold
treats with lofty superiority certain Christians who have
thought that Spinoza meant by love of God what they mean
by it, and a Hegelian critic who boasted of him as one
that banished God altogether, and substituted an idea in
His place. Might he not have been nearer the truth if he
had done justice to both the Christian and the Hegelian
critic; if he had believed that Spinoza intended love when
he spoke of love, and not at all less because he speaks as
St. Paul does, of knowing love, and that he was never able
to find, much as he often tried to find, how the idea
passes into reality?

Was it otherwise with the greatest heathen emperor,
who is the subject of a more satisfactory essay than that
on the excommunicated Jew? The worth of Marcus Aurelius
as the pursuer of an ideal, Mr. Arnold has perceived and
not exaggerated; his intense conviction that the idea
must have fact to dwell in and sustain it, he has not
understood nearly as well. If he had, he would have
found a far better apology than he has found for his
conduct to the Christian Church. Unless this Church proclaims that the highest ideal is embodied in fact, it is
nothing. Had Marcus Aurelius accepted the Cross as the
reconciliation of Idea and Fact, he would have been what
Mr. Mill wishes he had been, the precursor of Constantine,
who merely saw that the Cross was stronger than the Eagle.
As he did not, he was obliged by the devoutness of his
mind to take the old fictions as attempts to embody some
conception of the divinity; his duty as the head of the
Roman State obliged him to persecute a rival kingdom.

The praises of Philistines cannot be acceptable to Mr.
Arnold. But for the sake of our readers, and for the
satisfaction of our own consciences, we must say that he
has given us a remarkable book, which ought to benefit
all its readers, specially those who reject as cordially
as we do its fundamental maxim.

Note

1 'an excellent example of'.

9. HENRY JAMES, UNSIGNED REVIEW, 'NORTH AMERICAN REVIEW'

July 1865, ci, 206-13

James (1843-1916), who later looked back on the summer of
1865 as a golden time, a time 'for the play of young
intelligence and young friendship [and] the reading of
Matthew Arnold and Browning', was already at the writing
of this review something of a disciple of Arnold's. He
finds fault with Arnold's style and his reasoning - he
later retracted both criticisms - but Arnold takes 'high
ground': he has the sensibility, the seriousness, the
sense of true and disinterested criticism, and he is an
important foe of the Philistine on both sides of the
Atlantic. James was to write another, much more laudatory
essay on Arnold (see 'Matthew Arnold, The Poetry' 276-86),
but the basis of his devotion to Arnold can be seen in
this early review.

Mr. Arnold's 'Essays in Criticism' come to American readers with a reputation already made, - the reputation of a
charming style, a great deal of excellent feeling, and an
almost equal amount of questionable reasoning. It is for
us either to confirm the verdict passed in the author's
own country, or to judge his work afresh. It is often the
fortune of English writers to find mitigation of sentence
in the United States.
    The Essays contained in this volume are on purely
literary subjects; which is for us, by itself, a strong
recommendation. English literature, especially contemporary literature, is, compared with that of France and Germany, very poor in collections of this sort. A great deal
of criticism is written, but little of it is kept; little
of it is deemed to contain any permanent application. Mr.
Arnold will doubtless find in this fact - if indeed he has
not already signalized it - but another proof of the
inferiority of the English to the Continental school of
criticism, and point to it as a baleful effect of the

narrow practical spirit which animates, or, as he would
probably say, paralyzes, the former. But not only is his
book attractive as a whole, from its exclusive literary
character; the subject of each essay is moreover particularly interesting. The first paper is on the function of
Criticism at the present time; a question, if not more
important, perhaps more directly pertinent here than in
England. The second, discussing the literary influence
of Academies, contains a great deal of valuable observation and reflection in a small compass and under an inadequate title. The other essays are upon the two De
Guérins, Heinrich Heine, Pagan and Mediaeval Religious
Sentiment, Joubert, Spinoza, and Marcus Aurelius. The
first two articles are, to our mind, much the best; the
next in order of excellence is the paper on Joubert;
while the others, with the exception, perhaps, of that
on Spinoza, are of about equal merit.

Mr. Arnold's style has been praised at once too much
and too little. Its resources are decidedly limited; but
if the word had not become so cheap, we should nevertheless call it fascinating. This quality implies no
especial force; it rests in this case on the fact that,
whether or not you agree with the matter beneath it, the
manner inspires you with a personal affection for the
author. It expresses great sensibility and at the same
time great good-nature; it indicates a mind both susceptible and healthy. With the former element alone it would
savor of affectation; with the latter, it would be coarse.
As it stands, it represents a spirit both sensitive and
generous. We can best describe it, perhaps, by the word
sympathetic. It exhibits frankly, and without detriment
to its national character, a decided French influence.
Mr. Arnold is too wise to attempt to write French English;
he probably knows that a language can only be indirectly
enriched; but as nationality is eminently a matter of
form, he knows too that he can really violate nothing so
long as he adheres to the English letter.

His Preface is a striking example of the intelligent
amiability which animates his style. His two leading
Essays were, on their first appearance, made the subject
of much violent contention, their moral being deemed
little else than a wholesale schooling of the English
press by the French programme. Nothing could have better
proved the justice of Mr. Arnold's remarks upon the 'provincial' character of the English critical method, than
the reception which they provoked. He now acknowledges
this reception in a short introduction, which admirably
reconciles smoothness of temper with sharpness of wit.
The taste of this performance has been questioned; but

wherever it may err, it is assuredly not in being provincial; it is essentially civil. Mr. Arnold's amiability
is, in our eye, a strong proof of his wisdom. If he were
a few degrees more short-sighted, he might have less equanimity at his command. Those who sympathize with him
warmly will probably like him best as he is; but with such
as are only half his friends, this freedom from party passion, from what is after all but a lawful professional
emotion, will argue against his sincerity. For ourselves,
we doubt not that Mr. Arnold possesses thoroughly what the
French call the courage of his opinions. When you lay
down a proposition which is forthwith controverted, it is
of course optional with you to take up the cudgels in its
defence. If you are deeply convinced of its truth, you
will perhaps be content to leave it to take care of
itself; or, at all events, you will not go out of your
way to push its fortunes; for you will reflect that in the
long run an opinion often borrows credit from the forbearance of its patrons. In the long run, we say; it will
meanwhile cost you an occasional pang to see your cherished theory turned into a football by the critics. A
football is not, as such, a very respectable object, and
the more numerous the players, the more ridiculous it becomes. Unless, therefore, you are very confident of your
ability to rescue it from the chaos of kicks, you will
best consult its interest by not mingling in the game.
Such has been Mr. Arnold's choice. His opponents say that
he is too much of a poet to be a critic; he is certainly
too much of a poet to be a disputant. In the Preface in
question he has abstained from reiterating any of the
views put forth in the two offensive Essays; he has simply
taken a delicate literary vengeance upon his adversaries.
    For Mr. Arnold's critical feeling and observation, used
independently of his judgment, we profess a keen relish.
He has these qualities, at any rate, of a good critic,
whether or not he have the others, - the science and the
logic. It is hard to say whether the literary critic is
more called upon to understand or to feel. It is certain
that he will accomplish little unless he can feel acutely;
although it is perhaps equally certain that he will become
weak the moment that he begins to 'work,' as we may say,
his natural sensibilities. The best critic is probably he
who leaves his feelings out of account, and relies upon
reason for success. If he actually possesses delicacy of
feeling, his work will be delicate without detriment to
its solidity. The complaint of Mr. Arnold's critics is
that his arguments are too sentimental. Whether this complaint is well founded, we shall hereafter inquire; let us
determine first what sentiment has done for him. It has

given him, in our opinion, his greatest charm and his
greatest worth. Hundreds of other critics have stronger
heads; few, in England at least, have more delicate perceptions. We regret that we have not the space to confirm
this assertion by extracts. We must refer the reader to
the book itself, where he will find on every page an
illustration of our meaning. He will find one, first of
all, in the apostrophe to the University of Oxford, at the
close of the Preface, - 'home of lost causes and forsaken
beliefs and unpopular names and impossible loyalties.'
This is doubtless nothing but sentiment, but it seizes a
shade of truth, and conveys it with a directness which is
not at the command of logical demonstration. Such a process might readily prove, with the aid of a host of facts,
that the University is actually the abode of much retarding conservatism; a fine critical instinct alone, and the
measure of audacity which accompanies such an instinct,
could succeed in placing her on the side of progress by
boldly saluting her as the Queen of Romance: romance being
the deadly enemy of the commonplace; the commonplace being
the fast ally of Philistinism, and Philistinism the heavi-
est drag upon the march of civilization. Mr. Arnold is
very fond of quoting Goethe's eulogy upon Schiller, to the
effect that his friend's greatest glory was to have left
so far behind him *was uns alle bändigt, das Gemeine,* that
bane of mankind, the common. Exactly how much the inscru-
table Goethe made of this fact, it is hard at this day to
determine; but it will seem to many readers that Mr. Arnold
makes too much of it. Perhaps he does, for himself; but
for the public in general he decidedly does not. One of
the chief duties of criticism is to exalt the importance
of the ideal; and Goethe's speech has a long career in
prospect before we can say with the vulgar that it is
'played out.' Its repeated occurrence in Mr. Arnold's
pages is but another instance of poetic feeling subserving
the ends of criticism. The famous comment upon the girl
Wragg over which the author's opponents made so merry, we
likewise owe - we do not hesitate to declare it - to this
same poetic feeling. Why cast discredit upon so valuable
an instrument of truth? Why not wait at least until it
is used in the service of error? The worst that can be
said of the paragraph in question is, that it is a great
ado about nothing. All thanks, say we, to the critic who
will pick up such nothings as these; for if he neglects
them, they are blindly trodden under foot. They may not
be especially valuable, but they are for that very reason
the critic's particular care. Great truths take care of
themselves; great truths are carried aloft by philosophers and poets; the critic deals in contributions to
truth. Another illustration of the nicety of Mr. Arnold's

feeling is furnished by his remarks upon the quality of
distinction as exhibited in Maurice and Eugénie de Guérin,
'that quality which at last inexorably corrects the
world's blunders and fixes the world's ideals, [which]
procures that the popular poet shall not pass for a Pindar,
the popular historian for a Tacitus, nor the popular preacher for a Bossuet.'   Another is offered by his incidental
remarks upon Coleridge, in the article on Joubert; another,
by the remarkable felicity with which he has translated
Maurice de Guérin's 'Centaur'; and another, by the whole
body of citations with which, in his second Essay, he for-
tifies his proposition that the establishment in England
of an authority answering to the French Academy would have
arrested certain evil tendencies of English literature, -
for to nothing more offensive than this, as far as we can
see, does his argument amount.

In the first and most important of his Essays Mr.
Arnold puts forth his views upon the actual duty of criticism. They may be summed up as follows. Criticism has
no concern with the practical; its function is simply to
get at the best thought which is current, - to see things
in themselves as they are, - to be disinterested. Criticism can be disinterested, says Mr. Arnold,

> by keeping from practice; by resolutely following the
> law of its own nature, which is to be a free play of
> the mind on all subjects which it touches, by steadily
> refusing to lend itself to any of those ulterior poli-
> tical, practical considerations about ideas which
> plenty of people will be sure to attach to them, which
> perhaps ought often to be attached to them, which in
> this country, at any rate, are certain to be attached
> to them, but which criticism has really nothing to do
> with. Its business is simply to know the best that is
> known and thought in the world, and, by in its turn
> making this known, to create a current of true and
> fresh ideas. Its business is to do this with inflex-
> ible honesty, with due ability; but its business is to
> do no more, and to leave alone all questions of practi-
> cal consequences and applications, - questions which
> will never fail to have due prominence given to them.

We used just now a word of which Mr. Arnold is very
fond, - a word of which the general ruler may require an
explanation, but which, when explained, he will be likely
to find indispensable; we mean the word *Philistine*. The
term is of German origin, and has no English synonyme.
'At Soli,' remarks Mr. Arnold, 'I imagined they did not
talk of solecisms; and here, at the very head-quarters of

Goliath, nobody talks of Philistinism.' The word *epicier*,
(1) used by Mr. Arnold as a French synonyme, is not so
good as *bourgeois*, and to those who know that *bourgeois*
means a citizen, and who reflect that a citizen is a
person seriously interested in the maintenance of order,
the German term may now assume a more special significance. An English review briefly defines it by saying
that 'it applies to the fat-headed respectable public in
general.' This definition must satisfy us here. The
Philistine portion of the English press, by which we mean
the considerably larger portion, received Mr. Arnold's
novel programme of criticism with the uncompromising dis-
approbation which was to be expected from a literary body,
the principle of whose influence, or indeed of whose
being, is its subservience, through its various members,
to certain political and religious interests. Mr.
Arnold's general theory was offensive enough; but the
conclusions drawn by him from the fact that English practice has been so long and so directly at variance with it,
were such as to excite the strongest animosity. Chief
among these was the conclusion that this fact has retarded
the development and vulgarized the character of the English mind, as compared with the French and the German
mind. This rational inference may be nothing but a poet's
flight; but for ourselves, we assent to it. It reaches us
too. The facts collected by Mr. Arnold on this point have
long wanted a voice. It has long seemed to us that, as a
nation, the English are singularly incapable of large, of
high, of general views. They are indifferent to pure
truth, to *la verité vraie* (2). Their views are almost exclusively practical, and it is in the nature of practical
views to be narrow. They seldom indeed admit a fact but
on compulsion; they demand of an idea some better recommendation, some longer pedigree, than that it is true.
That this lack of spontaneity in the English intellect is
caused by the tendency of English criticism, or that it is
to be corrected by a diversion, or even by a complete reversion, of this tendency, neither Mr. Arnold nor ourselves suppose, nor do we look upon such a result as desirable. The part which Mr. Arnold assigns to his reformed
method of criticism is a purely tributary part. Its indirect result will be to quicken the naturally irrational
action of the English mind; its direct result will be to
furnish that mind with a larger stock of ideas than it has
enjoyed under the time-honored *régime* of Whig and Tory,
High-Church and Low-Church organs.
    We may here remark, that Mr. Arnold's statement of his
principles is open to some misinterpretation, - an accident against which he has, perhaps, not sufficiently

guarded it. For many persons the word *practical* is almost
identical with the word *useful*, against which, on the
other hand, they erect the word *ornamental*. Persons who
are fond of regarding these two terms as irreconcilable,
will have little patience with Mr. Arnold's scheme of
criticism. They will look upon it as an organized preference of unprofitable speculation to common sense. But
the great beauty of the critical movement advocated by Mr.
Arnold is that in either direction its range of action is
unlimited. It deals with plain facts as well as with the
most exalted fancies; but it deals with them only for the
sake of the truth which is in them, and not for *your* sake,
reader, and that of your party. It takes *high ground*,
which is the ground of theory. It does not busy itself
with consequences, which are all in all to you. Do not
suppose that it for this reason pretends to ignore or to
undervalue consequences; on the contrary, it is because
it knows that consequences are inevitable that it leaves
them alone. It cannot do two things at once; it cannot
serve two masters. Its business is to make truth generally accessible, and not to apply it. It is only on condition of having its hands free, that it can make truth
generally accessible. We said just now that its duty was,
among other things, to exalt, if possible, the importance
of the ideal. We should perhaps have said the intellectual; that is, of the principle of understanding things.
Its business is to urge the claims of all things to be
understood. If this is its function in England, as Mr.
Arnold represents, it seems to us that it is doubly its
function in this country. Here is no lack of votaries of
the practical, of experimentalists, of empirics. The tendencies of our civilization are certainly not such as
foster a preponderance of morbid speculation. Our national genius inclines yearly more and more to resolve
itself into a vast machine for sifting, in all things,
the wheat from the chaff. American society is so shrewd,
that we may safely allow it to make application of the
truths of the study. Only let us keep it supplied with
the truths of the study, and not with the half-truths of
the forum. Let criticism take the stream of truth at its
source, and then practice can take it half-way down.
When criticism takes it half-way down, practice will come
poorly off.

   If we have not touched upon the faults of Mr. Arnold's
volume, it is because they are faults of detail, and because, when, as a whole, a book commands our assent, we
do not incline to quarrel with its parts. Some of the
parts in these Essays are weak, others are strong; but the
impression which they all combine to leave is one of such

beauty as to make us forget, not only their particular
faults, but their particular merits. If we were asked
what is the particular merit of a given essay, we should
reply that it is a merit much less common at the present
day than is generally supposed, - the merit which pre-
eminently characterizes Mr. Arnold's poems, the merit,
namely of having a *subject*. Each essay is *about* something.
If a literary work now-a-days start with a certain topic,
that is all that is required of it; and yet it is a work
of art only on condition of ending with that topic, on
condition of being written, not from it, but to it. If
the average modern essay or poem were to wear its title at
the close, and not at the beginning, we wonder in how many
cases the reader would fail to be surprised by it. A book
or an article is looked upon as a kind of Staubbach water-
fall, discharging itself into infinite space. If we were
questioned as to the merit of Mr. Arnold's book as a whole,
we should say that it lay in the fact that the author
takes high ground. The manner of his Essays is a model of
what criticisms should be. The foremost English critical
journal, the 'Saturday Review,' recently disposed of a
famous writer by saying, in a parenthesis, that he had
done nothing but write nonsense all his life. Mr. Arnold
does not pass judgment in parenthesis. He is too much of
an artist to use leading propositions for merely literary
purposes. The consequence is, that he says a few things
in such a way as that almost in spite of ourselves we
remember them, instead of a number of things which we
cannot for the life of us remember. There are many things
which we wish he had said better. It is to be regreteed,
for instance, that, when Heine is for once in a way seriously spoken of, he should not be spoken of more as the
great poet which he is, and which even in New England he
will one day be admitted to be, than with reference to the
great moralist which he is not, and which he never claimed
to be. But here, as in other places, Mr. Arnold's excellent spirit reconciles us with his short-comings. If
he has not spoken of Heine exhaustively, he has at all
events spoken of him seriously, which for an Englishman is
a good deal. Mr. Arnold's supreme virtue is that he
speaks of all things seriously, or, in other words, that
he is not offensively clever. The writers who are willing
to resign themselves to this obscure distinction are in
our opinion the only writers who understand their time.
That Mr. Arnold thoroughly understands his time we do not
mean to say, for this is the privilege of a very select
few; but he is, at any rate, profoundly conscious of his
time. This fact was clearly apparent in his poems, and
it is even more apparent in these Essays. It gives them a

a peculiar character of melancholy, - that melancholy
which arises from the spectacle of the old-fashioned
instinct of enthusiasm in conflict (or at all events in
contact) with the modern desire to be fair, - the melancholy of an age which not only has lost its *naïveté*, but
which knows it has lost it.

The American publishers have enriched this volume with
the author's Lectures on Homer, and with his 'French Eton.'
The Lectures demand a notice apart; we can only say here
that they possess all the habitual charm of Mr. Arnold's
style. This same charm will also lend an interest to his
discussion of a question which bears but remotely upon the
subject of education in this country.

Notes

1 'grocer'.
2 'the absolute truth'.

10. E. S. DALLAS ON ARNOLD THE CRITIC, 'THE GAY SCIENCE'

1866, i, 65-8

Eneas Sweetland Dallas (1824-79) gained little fame from
his ambitious attempts to systematize criticism. Neither
'Poetics' (1852) nor 'The Gay Science' attracted much
attention, although both made important contributions to
critical theory. Perhaps Dallas's books were, as the
'D.N.B.' biographer says, 'too abstruse for the general
reader'. Dallas's views often parallel Arnold's (he may
have influenced the 1853 preface), but he considers Arnold
something of a misguided amateur. The following passage
is one of two brief discussions of Arnold in a long and
sober treatise. Dallas belittles Arnold's concept of criticism and his high estimate of Sainte-Beuve.

He who is in our day the most hearty in denouncing the
weakness of our criticism, Mr. Matthew Arnold, is also the
most imperious in vaunting the office of the critic; and
there is a danger lest from his unguarded expressions it
should be supposed that criticism promises more than it

can perform. Mr. Arnold, for example, tells us that the
the main intellectual effort of Europe has for many years
past been a critical one; and that what Europe now desires
most is criticism. What he means by this it is not easy
to make out. For on the one hand, he assures us that Homer,
Dante, and Shakespeare, are to be regarded as critics, and
that everything done in literature is at root criticism;
from which it would appear that there can be nothing specially critical in the intellectual movement which is now
in progress. On the other hand, we stumble once and
again upon the statement that the first of living critics
is M. Sainte-Beuve. Now, we know M. Sainte-Beuve as an
indefatigable, a clever, and well-informed writer - a man
of good judgment, and in France of great literary influence. But when we are told in succession that the great
intellectual movement of our age is critical, and that the
first of living critics - therefore, the leader of this
intellectual movement, is M. Sainte-Beuve, who is not
greatly puzzled to know what so dainty a writer as Mr.
Arnold can possible mean? Is it a proof of our English
want of insight that with all the vivacity of his Monday
chats, we on this side of the water fail to see in M.
Sainte-Beuve the prophet of the age - a great leader of
thinking - the enlightener of Europe? He is a brilliant
essayist, a man of great knowledge; his taste is unim-
peachable; and he dashes off historic sketches with wonderful neatness. But for criticism in the highest sense
of the word - for criticism in the sense in which Mr.
Arnold seems to understand it - for criticism as the mastery of dominant ideas and the key to modern thought - as
that one thing which Europe most desires - we should
scarcely go to the feuilletons of M. Sainte-Beuve.
    Once more we return to another form of the statement
that the intellectual movement of our time is critical.
Mr. Arnold identifies criticism with the modern spirit;
and then he tells us that the modern spirit arises in a
sense of contrast between the dictates of reason and of
custom, the world of idea and the world of fact. We live
amid prescriptions and customs that have been crusted upon
us from ages. When we become alive to the fact that the
forms and institutions of our daily life - the life individual and the life national, are prescribed to us not by
reason but only by custom, that, says Mr. Arnold, is the
awakening of the modern spirit. The truth is, however,
that what he describes as the peculiar spirit of modern
thought - that is, nineteenth-century thought - is the
spirit of every reforming age. It was, for example, the
spirit of Christianity as it showed itself at first in
the midst of surrounding Judaism. It was the spirit that

actuated the protest against the mummeries of Romanism in
the sixteenth century.

From these and other illustrations of what he understands by criticism, it would seem that Mr. Arnold has
allowed himself, in the graceful eagerness of a poetical
nature, to be carried headlong into generalizations that
are illusive. But the general effect of his expressions
is to spread abroad an inflated idea of criticism - what
it is, what it can do, what is its position in the world.
People will not stay to examine patiently whether Mr.
Arnold makes out his case or not. They will but carry
away the general impression, that here is a man of genius
and of strong conviction, who speaks of criticism as just
now the greatest power upon earth. They will, therefore,
expect from it the mightiest effects; and grievous will
be their disappointment at the modesty of its actual exploits.

On the Study of Celtic Literature (1867)

11. LORD STRANGFORD (PERCY ELLEN SMYTHE), MR. ARNOLD ON
CELTIC LITERATURE, 'PALL MALL GAZETTE'

19 March 1866, no. 346, 3-4

Lord Strangford (1826-69), a friend of Arnold and a noted
philologist and ethnologist, contributed regularly to the
'Saturday Review' and the 'Pall Mall Gazette'. The
'Gazette', in which Arnold published several important
articles, had been founded in the previous year by George
Smith, the prominent mid-century publisher, who had taken
the title from Thackeray's satiric magazine in 'Penden-
nis'. In this article, Strangford finds the first essay
of 'Celtic Literature' both 'original and striking', a
seminal discussion in the field. But he calls 'dangerous'
some of Arnold's speculations and suggests that, valuable
as it is, Arnold's study is based upon too much misinform-
ation and upon linguistic inadequacy. Strangford was to
write a short, complementary piece (22 September 1866), in
which he speculated about the difficulties of finding a
Professor of Celtic Studies.

We have been waiting for a week or two in hopes that some
adequate notice of Mr. Matthew Arnold's remarkable paper
on Celtic Literature might have been taken by an authority
competent to deal with the subject as a master. There is
doubtless no great novelty in the view that the English
nation is destined to be affected beneficially by some
considerable infusion of the artistic and imaginative
faculty through a more complete incorporation of the

various Celtic fragments, existing within its bosom, which
it has been absorbing and has yet to absorb. But this has
always been put in a merely rhetorical and suggestive way,
or in a bare dry ethnological way, and without the remot-
est reference to the actual nature and extent of that
faculty as possessed and manifested in detail by the Celts.
It has been reserved for Mr. Arnold to deduce this conclusion legitimately from a true knowledge of the Celtic
ideals obtained by a direct study of the highest and most
standard works on Celtic literature. And there is the
greatest novelty in boldly challenging public attention
and admiration on behalf of these ideals from an independ-
dent point of view. Mr. Arnold's style needs no laudation
at our hands, nor do his special opinions require any exposition. It is not difficult to construct his argument
out of his previous writings, nor to imagine the contrast
between the Celtic children of light and the Saxon Philistines which may be assumed to pervade the present essay,
without even taking the trouble of cutting the leaves.
We presume everybody has read it; otherwise we might say
that anybody might thus write its main argument for himself. We may further say that, even if he did that alone,
he would be very much the better for so doing; so entirely
do we concur in the conclusions to which Mr. Arnold is led,
in some measure no doubt by the spirit of antipathy, but
in a far greater measure by the keen instinct of a just
and long-withheld sympathy. But Mr. Arnold, so far from
meeting with the criticism of appreciation or depreciation, has hardly met with any notice at all. His subject
is new and just now appropriate, and it is represented in
a way both original and striking. We consider that it
requires some notice, and that any notice is better than
no notice. We are but proselytes of the gate ourselves in
Celtic matters, with no authoritative knowledge of Celtic
details, yet we feel moved to hazard a brief remark or two
in the present case, more with the intention of assisting
Mr. Arnold than of criticising him. Celtic literature,
indeed, and the study of the Celtic past - we may as well
say all Celtic questions, past, present, and to come -
bear much resemblance to the face of nature in a Celtic
landscape. There is fair display of cultivated ground, in
which it is the fertility of the soil which strikes the
eye rather than the art of the cultivation or the bounty
of the crop; there is the wild alternation of mountain and
lake and sea, and there are the dreariest stretches of bog
and moor and swamp, impracticable and interminable. It is
given to very few to traverse with impunity, or even to
set foot upon, the quaking bogs of Celtic archaeology.
We own that we gazed with no small trembling as we found

Mr. Arnold, who knows no literary fear any more than his
French friends know physical fear, venturing boldly upon
this dangerous surface; and we cannot but admire the great
skill with which he has as yet managed to plant his foot
upon firm ground, or extricate himself from the quagmire
before sinking more than knee-deep at most. We would fain
lend him such assistance as lies in our power, by placard-
ing the unsafe portions of his course, and writing
'danger' in very large letters over Gomer and the Cimmerians, over the attribution of antiquity to any Celtic
language as we have it, and over everything connected
with the Scotch Highlanders, whom he has fortunately left
alone for the present.

If Mr. Arnold means seriously to insist upon his classification of writers upon Celtic literature and antiqui-
ties, wherein he divides them into Celt-lovers and Celt-
haters, and to uphold it as an exact or exhaustive one, or
as one which is at all justifiable in the present day, we
must beg him to change his mind forthwith, and shall do
our best to convert him as fast as we can. It is not a
just one now, and it was not a just one in the days of
Edward Lhuyd at the beginning of the last century. It is
only just when applied to the intervening period when
chaotic nonsense reigned supreme, when the Celtomaniacs
had it all their own way in Wales and Ireland, their
absurdities being incorporated into the national self-
love, and when these extravagant pretensions called into
existence the reactionary extravagances of Pinkerton and
his school. This state of things is all past and gone
now, or, if it lingers at all, it abides with the body of
the people as a matter of vulgar prejudice, not with
their leaders as a matter of enlightened belief. It is
only found among Welsh and Irish Philistines on one hand,
among Gothic Philistines on the other hand, and we would
fain warn Mr. Arnold of the danger of falling among these.
The dawn of the neutral and scientific spirit, first manifested in Dr. Prichard's excellent little book, became as
the meridian light of full noon after the publication of
Zeuss's immortal 'Grammatica Celtica.' The great German,
dying, founded a school of Celtic philology which is one
of the most conspicuous and flourishing branches of the
new and irreversible science for which the world is
indebted to Professor Francis Bopp. This school works
upon language alone as its subject-matter; but it has been
able thus to construct a firm basis of general scientific
investigation upon all other points. Celtic archaeology
is now only trustworthy when in harmony with the teaching
of the Zeussian school. If their doctrines are not accepted in England, it is not for want of any inculcation of

them, for they have been presented over and over again to
the public, notably so in certain articles which are to be
found in the earlier numbers of the 'Saturday Review.'
Upon the anonymous authorship of these we care not to in-
trude, further than to advert to the fact of our having
recently cited their writer under his own name, as being
emphatically a man of genius, and the ablest philologist
of the new school who is native to these isles. The real
name of 'Mac dá Cherda,' the gifted 'Son of two Arts,' is
better known in Germany than in England, and we take shame
for this. These topics in England are left to grow wild
and to run adrift; nor do we admit them into the canon of
science until they have undergone what is called public
discussion, or have been sanctioned by those who have got
the right of affirming and denying things, and who act as
our bell-wethers. On the Continent it is the common consent of an authoritative and competent body which admits
truth at sight in such points, and which then proceeds to
work on further by means of the principles thus obtained.
Here, when such a theory is started for the first time,
all persons, docti indoctique, (1) have a voice in discussing it, without any ascertained principles of discussion; it has to be read a second time, and the Ethnological Society has to go into committee about it, and it
has to be read a third time, and then it is sent to our
recognised hereditary legislators in philology, such as
Mr. Crawfurd and Mr. Farrar, and the new cuneiform man
who made an exhibition of himself in the 'Fraser' of last
November, and then it has to be sent up to the Sir Corne-
wall Lewis of the period to receive his royal assent,
before it can pass among us as law. This is well in politics and Reform Bills; but it is anything but well for
questions such as that whether Welsh is in the category of
Basque or in the category of modern French to pass through
the hands of unqualified vestrymen and jurymen, with
nothing but common sense and the coarser Minerva to help
them. Yet thus it comes to pass that in England there are
real living men who doubt the mutual affinity of the Indo-
European languages, who know nothing of the details of
their comparative grammar, and who listen to Mr. Crawfurd
quite as seriously as to that Professor Bopp whom the
universal academic world of the Continent at this moment
is uniting to honour. But the Irish Academicians have
identified themselves actively with the new learning; and
the leading Welsh scholars, such men as Mr. Basil Jones,
or Mr. Longueville Jones, or Mr. Williams of Rhydycroesau,
fully adopt its principles, and would be ashamed to repeat
any of the weary and ridiculous outbursts of national
self-love in which their forefathers gloried. Mr. Nash,

an Englishman, who has honestly studied the subject from
the beginning, and who has received unqualified praise
from the Celtic Saturday Reviewer alluded to above, has,
we think, been most unfairly classified by Mr. Arnold
among Celt-haters. Mr. Nash undertook to expose, and
succeeded in exposing, the 'dishonesty and blundering,'
the 'scandalous suppressions, mistranslations, and forger-
ies,' with which the old school of writings on Welsh
literature teemed, which alienated Englishman from the
study of that literature, and which misled even such men
as Sir F. Palgrave and Bunsen. This is not hatred of
Celts; it is destroying the tares planted by Celts in the
field of science, and Mr. Arnold is hardly right or just
in attributing to Mr. Nash, a conscientious and valuable
workman of the new school, a preconceived anti-Celtic
animosity. The words in inverted commas are not ours,
they are the words of the Celt who is the first authority
on the subject. The classification should stand, not as
Celt-lovers and Celt-haters, but as science-lovers and
party-lovers - those who are urged by the partisan's
Philistine spirit, and those whose path is lighted up by
the scientific spirit. We must do Mr. Arnold the justice
to say that he hesitates before committing himself. Mr.
Nash does not hate the Welsh; he chastises them. His
position towards them is, in fact, precisely Mr. Finlay's
position towards the modern Greeks.

One word more. There is a touch here and there in Mr.
Arnold's delightful picture of the chattering French maid,
moving among her Celtic cousins, who speak her own ances-
tral language about her unconscious ears, which affects us
with a pang of dreadful misgiving. How comes the French
maid to be a daughter of Gomer, and how come the Welshmen
or Cymry to be his sons? What was 'the common dwelling-
place in the heart of Asia'? Who were the Cimmerians of
the Euxine who 'came in on their Western kinsmen'? and by
what kinship are they kinsmen? When the Welshman calls
white and red and rock and field and church and lord,
gwyn and *goch* (lege *coch*) and *craig* and *maes* and *llan* and
arglwydd, in the genuine tongue of his ancestors, how old
does Mr. Arnold suppose that tongue to be? This last
point had better be settled at once. Till thirty years
ago it was usual to attribute a mysterious and unfathomable antiquity to the two Celtic main languages. Their
history was uninvestigated; nobody knew or thought of
asking whether or not they had any recorded stages of
development; on their surface they were utterly unlike
anything else in the world; and this halo of age and
mystery pleased their speakers and compensated them for
the loss of political power. But the result of recent

inquiry, which has admitted them into the fullest and most
equal right of brotherhood in the great Aryan confrater-
nity of speech, has, in so doing, broken down the charmed
circle and dissipated the obscuring and magnifying halo.
These languages are no granitic or protozoic formation of
the elder world; they are, broadly speaking, the mere
detritus of an older speech, just as French or English is
a detritus. It redounds to the credit of the leading
Welsh and Irish scholars that they can look at this
honestly in the face without blinking, accept it as a
definite principle, and embody it in their teaching.
These words, old as they may be for a modern language, as
these go, are not in their old form; they are phonetically
corrupt; they have lost their case-endings; and two of
them are simply Latin of the later Empire. *Llan* is *plana*,
an enclosed level ground; *coch* is *coccinus*, red, in modern
Greek κόκκινος. Strangely enough, the later Latin words
for yellow and red, *melinus* and *coccinus*, survive nowhere
- the Greek excepted - but in Welsh, and in that queer
little tongue, the Rumonsch of the Grisons, where they
appear as *mellen* and *cotschen*. The first work of the
Zeussian school was to restore conjecturally, by means of
comparison of all existing or recorded forms found in the
Celtic languages, the older speech from which they were
held to have been derived. Now it cannot be too often
repeated that these conjectural forms, restored with such
wonderful acuteness, have since been literally verified by
their actual discovery in inscriptions written in the old
Gaulish language which have recently come to light. These
are inadequate as regards the verb, but are simply identical as regards the noun. Next to the resurrection of the
ancient language of Persia, this is surely the greatest
triumph of comparative philology yet achieved. The old
Proto-Celtic language may be defined, in a word, as having
Welsh or Irish roots - the primitive difference being but
small - inflected with terminations after the Latin fashion, all but identical with the Latin ones themselves.
The word Cymry has nothing whatever to do with Cimmerians,
nor with Cimbri. It is later than the Romans; it was once
written with two *m*'s, and its oldest form was demonstrably
Combroges, meaning a united or confederate people, as
opposed to Allobroges, or alien people. All this, since
Zeuss's proof, has been accepted without a dissentient
word, except where dissent signifies nothing. As for
Gomer, he belongs to Dr. Cumming by vested right, and Mr.
Arnold had better leave him to the patentee. We conclude
by hoping that Mr. Arnold will not be long in perceiving
that the one man who has done more irretrievable harm to
the proper appreciation of the imaginative literature of

the Gael than ten thousand Pinkertons is James Macpherson,
the fabricator of one of the greatest delusions upon earth,
and the incarnation of literary injustice to Ireland.

Note

1 'the learned and the ignorant'.

12. UNSIGNED ARTICLE IN 'THE TIMES'

8 September 1866, 8

'The Times' can be taken as a fair indicator of what
Arnold considered Philistine tastes and attitudes, and
though they sometimes found praise for Arnold, they more
usually treated him as an enemy. The occasion for the
present attack was partly Arnold's lectures on Celtic
Literature, published in the 'Cornhill' from March to
July 1866; more immediately it was a letter that Arnold
had written to Sir Hugh Owen, declining an invitation to
speak at the annual Eisteddfod (the revived Congress of
Welsh Bards). Arnold's letter had appeared in both 'The
Times' and the 'Pall Mall Gazette'. 'The Times' attacks
Arnold for 'one of the most mischievous and selfish pieces
of sentimentalism which could possibly be perpetrated'.
Arnold's 'penchant' for the Welsh is seen as a sign of
weakness that verges on cultural treason.

'In the year one thousand eight hundred and sixty-six, the
sun approaching the autumnal equinox, at the hour of noon
on the fourth day of September, after due proclamation,
this Gorsedd is opened in Chester, with invitation to all
who may assemble here, where no weapon is unsheathed
against them, and judgment will be pronounced upon all
works of genius submitted for adjudication in the face of
the sun - the eye of light.' This extraordinary announcement for the year 1866 was proclaimed at Chester, on the
Rhoodee, by a personage styled 'Talhaiarn,' at a monument
'supposed to be of great antiquity, consisting of 12
stones in a circle, with a large one in the middle for an
altar;' and after this solemnity the 'National Eisteddfod'

of Wales was declared open.

This is an age of Exhibitions, and so far as it affords
any pleasure to Welshmen to make this exhibition of themselves and their antiquated customs we have nothing to say
against it. If it gives a number of people any satisfaction to pay a visit to a dozen stones in order to be informed by 'Talhaiarn' that a Gorsedd is opened in which no
weapons will be unsheathed, to contemplate a Red Dragon on
a green field, to wear the leek, and to listen to barbaric
music, it may seem unreasonable to grudge them the satisfaction. It is an amusement which we fail to appreciate,
but if it were only an amusement, like dancing Highland
reels, we should certainly have nothing to say about it.
But this 'National Eisteddfod' assumes to be something
more than an amusement, and professes to have a definite
object. According to Mr. Matthew Arnold, a letter from
whom, read at the meeting, appeared in our columns on
Thursday, it is supposed to help to 'preserve and honour
the Welsh language and literature,' and it is even encouraged by this gentleman to undertake a still more magnificent task.
    The Welsh, he informs us, in their culture, their
morals, and their intelligence, possess the same superiority over their conquerors, the English, as the Greeks in
former times over the Romans, and he exhorts 'the descendants of Taliesin and Ossian' to repeat 'the famous feat of
the Greeks,' and to 'conquer their conquerors.' We are to
be invaded by the Welsh language and literature, by Welsh
harps and bards, and Mr. Arnold even recommends a deputa-
tion from the Eisteddfod to the University of Oxford, to
urge the importance of establishing a chair of Celtic,
with the view of imbuing our 'vulgar,' 'coarse,' and
'unintelligent' youth with Welsh taste, morals, and intelligence. Now, we are quite willing to believe that this
effusion from the Professor of Poetry at Oxford may have
been too absurd even for the bards and other enthusiasts
who assembled under the banner of the Red Dragon, and
indeed 'Talhaiarn' condescended to disclaim any sinister
designs upon England. Nevertheless, to put it in the
mildest form, these Eisteddfods are intended to preserve
not only the memory of old Welsh customs, but the Welsh
language and Welsh literature. They are intended to
assist, and they do assist, in inducing the Welsh people
to cherish their ancient tongue, and to believe that it
will still be understood and 'honoured' in this country.
    Now, from this point of view we must protest against
such proceedings as one of the most mischievous and

selfish pieces of sentimentalism which could possibly be
perpetrated. The Welsh language is the curse of Wales.
Its prevalence and the ignorance of English have excluded,
and even now exclude, the Welsh people from the civilization, the improvement, and the material prosperity of their
English neighbours. It is, perhaps, little known to what
an extent this unknown tongue still keeps its hold upon
the Welsh population. There are villages in Wales where
there are not more than two or three persons, including
the parson, who habitually speak English. The Government
have done all they can by providing that English shall be
taught in the schools, but as it is not spoken in the
cottages it is soon forgotten. The result has been that
the Welsh have remained in Wales, unable to mix with their
fellow-subjects, shut out from all literature except what
is translated into their own language and incapable of
progress. A Welsh boy or girl cannot seek employment in
Chester or Gloucester because they are ignorant of the
language which would be spoken around them. It is a more
mischievous consequence that practices and customs which
would greatly shock Mr. Matthew Arnold's refined notions
of 'delicacy and spirituality' have been perpetuated among
the people. The gentry, moreover, must necessarily speak
English; and the use of different language among the peasantry creates a most injurious division between classes.
The poor are wholly separated from the rich; they have
their own thoughts, their own objects, and can pursue them
in the very hearing of their superiors. Their antiquated
and semibarbarous language, in short, shrouds them in
darkness. It both prevents them from finding their own
way into the world, and excludes the light of day from
themselves. And all this cruel incapacity and social dis-
organization must needs be fostered and encouraged for the
gratification of a mere antiquarian conceit, and is actually made a subject of gratulation by sentimentalists who
talk nonsense about 'the children of Taliesin and Ossian,'
and whose dainty taste requires something more flimsy than
the strong sense and sturdy morality of their fellow
Englishmen.
     It ought to be obvious even to these sentimentalists
that this persistent prevalence of the Welsh language is
one of the greatest misfortunes of their countrymen.
Mr. Matthew Arnold himself, who appears more Welsh than
the Welsh, professes a desire 'to avoid the danger of
giving offence to practical men by retarding the spread of
the English language in the Principality.' But he believes that 'to preserve and honour the Welsh language and
literature is quite compatible with not thwarting for a
single hour the introduction so undeniably useful of a

knowledge of English throughout all classes in Wales.'
We must be permitted to say plainly that this is arrant
nonsense. It will be observed that even in this concession to 'practical men,' Mr. Arnold takes care to reserve
the very point we are protesting against. He would 'preserve the Welsh language' as the first thing, but would
have 'a knowledge of English' introduced. Can he possibly
suppose that the peasantry of a whole district will continue the knowledge of another and an alien language for
'practical' purposes? One language is quite sufficient
for the mass, and the common people of Wales will either
speak Welsh or English. If measures are taken to 'preserve' Welsh, the knowledge of English will decay; and
such, we believe, has already been the effect of these
Welsh demonstrations. The native language was giving way,
but has since taken another false start, and the people,
therefore, have been so far thrown back in their civilization. If Wales and the Welsh are ever thoroughly to share
in the material prosperity, and, in spite of Mr. Arnold,
we will add the culture and the morality, of England, they
must forget their isolated language, and learn to speak
English, and nothing else. As for Welsh literature, it
may be left to antiquaries and historians, and to critics
who have nothing more solid to occupy them. The literature is curious, no doubt, and interesting in its way,
but it is rather too absurd to send us to Ossian and Tal-
iesen for mental culture. All that is valuable in the
language belongs to the past; and the Welsh literature of
the present day is about as original and valuable as the
Latin verses of the public school. For all practical purposes Welsh is a dead language. If these Eisteddfodau
were mere shows and amusements, they would be deserving
of no attention whatever, but if they cannot be held
without assisting to perpetuate the mischievous delusions
we have denounced, the sooner they come to an end the
better. They are simply a foolish interference with the
natural progress of civilization and prosperity. If the
Red Dragon wants to become a useful animal, he must change
his motto and cease 'to lead the way.'

13.   JAMES MACDONELL, UNSIGNED ARTICLE, 'DAILY TELEGRAPH'

8 September 1866, 4-5

James Macdonell (1842-79) was a young and successful journalist when he wrote this piece. The 'Telegraph', biggest
of the daily papers and one of Arnold's constant targets,
had hired him away from an Edinburgh paper because of his
trenchant prose. He attacks Arnold as a 'kid-glove'
Jeremiah (several of his phrases became standard) whose
philosophy is effete and whose views are dangerous. Macdonell later admitted that Arnold was England's best
critic, but he insisted that the 'Telegraph' review was
justifiable as a response to Arnold's egoism.

We have entertained a vast respect for the Celtic race
ever since we heard M. Renan's charming explanation of a
seemingly naughty practice of the Bretons. Those people
are not quite so temperate as their French brethren; to
tell the truth, their potations are, for those of Conti-
nentals, both deep and strong. But the race is not to be
condemned on that account. On the contrary, it is to be
honoured. For with all the weight of his great critical
authority, M. Renan assures us that the Bretons get drunk,
not because they are like other people, but because they
have such a passion for the ideal, such a longing for com-
munion with the unseen world, that nothing can bring
peace to their troubled spirits save strong brandy. They
go to the bottle for the same reason that other people
go to church. They are most devotional when least able to
stand; and they are in a state of religious ecstasy when
afflicted with *delirium tremens*. The explanation is of
incalculable value. It sets in a completely new light the
Highlander's passion for pure Glenlivat, and it brings us
to the proceedings of the Eisteddfod with a fresh eye.
Not that for one moment we mean to insinuate that the
great Welsh gathering stands in need of a rebuke from the
Total Abstinence Society. Not that we think its *raison
d'etre* the same as that of the famous convivial club in
St. Andrews, which was composed exclusively of clergymen
who, after the tenth tumbler, could distinctly articulate
the words 'biblical criticism.' But it is possible to
become intoxicated in more ways than one. Patriotism will
effect the object as surely as strong drink. A man may
reel home with his head full of ballads as easily as if it

were full of punch. And, after a debauch of songs and
legends, he may see visions - nay, see double visions -
as distinctly as if he had been carousing in Brittany or
Strathdon. We say nothing worse of the Eisteddfod, therefore, than that it is a grand national debauch, conducted
with the strictest propriety, resulting in no headaches,
and producing no worse delusions than that it is worth a
man's while to learn Welsh. The coarse, brutal, money-
making, city-loving, idea-hating, soulless Englishman
may sneer at the sight of people leaving their shops for
a week to recite songs, and sing ballads, and read essays,
and talk patriotism, and eat leeks. But if he reads
Renan he will be less contemptuous; and if he glances at
Mr. Matthew Arnold's letter on the grand services to be
achieved by the Eisteddfod, he will send in his guinea to
the secretary, buy a Welsh grammar, and forthwith open his
mouth to catch the accent and get 'Geist.' (1)
   In fact, Mr. Arnold has done it at last. He has long
been telling us that we are a nation of vulgar, illiterate
boors. There is no sin in the decalogue of culture that
we do not commit every hour of the day. We, who think
ourselves the first among civilised peoples, are in reality a horde of coarse, bullying shopkeepers, with minds
bounded by our counters, with an ultimate belief in nothing but digestion, with no souls and no 'Geist.' But
when, crest-fallen at such a torrent of invective, we have
asked the elegant Jeremiah what he would have us do to get
souls and get 'Geist,' he has contented himself with a few
Delphic utterances, in which our darkened understandings
have failed to see a glimmer of meaning. At last, however, he has spoken out with a distinctness that admits
of no mistake. The Eisteddfod is to be our deliverer from
the Egyptian bondage in which we have been held for ever
so many centuries. Our aristocracy can do nothing for us;
it has no 'ideas,' and besides its 'day is fast coming to
an end.' Nor can the lower class; for it is still in a
state of 'rawness,' and its 'day is only beginning.'
Least of all can the middle class, which for beauty and
taste has vulgarity; for morals and feeling, coarseness;
for mind and spirit, unintelligence; and for everything
it should have, 'Philistinism.' But all that is to be
changed. The Eisteddfod - the greater delicacy and
spirituality of the Celtic people - the children of
TALIESIN and OSSIAN - the founding of a Celtic chair at
Oxford - and the singing of bits of ballads, are all to
combine towards one beneficent end; so that the garden of
British Philistinism shall yet blossom as the rose with
culture, and 'Geist', and MATTHEW ARNOLDS. Very well; we
shall greet the day with fervent gratitude when it comes.

Meantime, Philistines as we are, we may be permitted to
ask a sight of the prophet's credentials. From what place
does he hail? What has he done that he should put on
airs, and proclaim himself so immensely holier than other
men! The answer is simple: he is the high-priest of the
kid-gloved persuasion. He has what used to be called a
'mission;' that is, he has come to this earth to preach
the gospel of urbanity and to wage war against emphasis.
You musn't hold any opinion very tightly, - that is
provincialism. You musn't show that you are in earnest
about anything, - that is vulgarity. You musn't make a
fuss because you have no vote, - that is vulgarity too.
You musn't hold big meetings to agitate for Reform Bills
and to repeal Corn Laws, - that is the very height of vulgarity. Least of all may you hint that Great Britain can
spin better cotton, or that she has better machines,
better horses, and better men than some other countries:
for that is the cardinal sin against the new gospel. What
must we do, then? In the first place, we must fall into
no raptures; but, taking Sir CHARLES COLDSTREAM for our
patron saint, we must exclaim, with a yawn of indifference, that there is nothing in anything. Then, when we
have learned to make no fuss either about the heaven
above, the earth beneath, or the waters under the earth,
we are to cross the Channel and take lessons from Germany
and France. It is true that we have done some things in
literature and in science that even those nations are
ready to applaud; and it is true that in political matters we have beaten them both. None the less are we to
be the humble pupils of a people which cannot govern
itself, which cannot advance without revolutions, and
which has borrowed more thoughts from us than it has ever
repayed. None the less must we imitate another people
which is all theory and no practice; which is passive to
tyranny and vigorous only by spurts; which has wasted the
profoundest intellects in Europe in weaving intellectual
wind; and which, with all its culture, is still so barbaric in its tastes as to place the soldier in the front
rank of professions. That is a portion of our curriculum.
Next, when the urbane atmosphere of France and Germany has
softened our native rudeness, we must come home and regularly buy two-penny worth of second-hand culture. Our
education will then be so far complete that we shall be
able to recognise Mr. Matthew Arnold as an apostle. And
at last we shall, as the crown of our reward, have the
satisfaction of seeing our own immeasurable superiority
to the millions of our countrymen who clamour for votes,
and who think it worth while to discuss the difference
between a Liberal and a Tory without yawning.

That, no doubt, is a mighty result. Still, such is our
unregenerate state, that we question whether the game is
worth the candle. When 'Geist' is a little more common in
these islands, a nation of Matthew Arnolds may be toler-
able. Till that day, we may be permitted to offer up a
reverent prayer for deliverance from such a visitation.
Vulgarity, we agree with our superfine friend, is far from
pleasant; but vulgarity, we may be permitted to add, can
assume more forms than one. It can speak the language of
the study as well as of the street; it is none the less
repulsive because it employs the words of culture; and
sometimes - even in the case of Professors of Poetry - it
can take the form of self-conceit. Airs may be put on in
a fashionable magazine as well as in a fashionable park.
A literary coxcomb is quite as offensive to a cultured
taste as the kind of coxcomb who is more common. Nor, we
would add, is it surprising that personal vanity should
sometimes find vent in rebuking the vanity of nations. A
little arrogance is no doubt pardonable in a Jeremiah denouncing the sins of a people; but the assurance must
first of all be given that the Jeremiah is real. The time
has not come for recognising as a Jeremiah the man who can
pen pretty verses, turn pretty sentences, and express
pretty sentiments. There is no analogy, we would remind
Mr. Arnold, between a prophet and a fop.

Note

1 'spirit' or 'soul'.

14. ROBERT GIFFEN, ON 'CELTIC LITERATURE', 'FORTNIGHTLY
REVIEW'

1 July 1867, vii, n.s., 124-6.

Robert (later Sir Robert) Giffen (1837-1910) was a Scot-
tish-born economist and statistician, who served for many
years on the Board of Trade. His official work scarcely
interrupted a journalistic career, begun in 1860. Giffen
wrote mainly on economic matters and contributed to the
'Globe', 'The Economist', the 'Spectator', and the 'Fortnightly'.
    He accuses Arnold of 'engaging in doubtful controversy'

on a number of matters, and in fact he finds Arnold a
'doubtful' ethnologist. Recognizing, however, the need
for Arnold's book, even if he questions its ultimate
effect on the politicians, Giffen says 'the chief value of
the book will consist in its tendency [to popularize] the
Celtic case'.

This book is substantially a reprint of four articles
which appeared last year in the 'Cornhill Magazine'.
Hardly any alterations have been made in the text. A preface has been added, in which Mr. Arnold reproduces a
letter of advice to the Celts, replies to some strictures
which 'The Times' passed upon him, vindicates his criticism of Mr. Nash, one of the Celt haters he comments on in
the book, and once more takes up his parable against the
Philistines. A more important addition consists of a few
notes by Lord Strangford, which Mr. Arnold has been candid
enough to print, although they are destructive of a good
deal of the philological matter he had originally ventured
to use. Thus, at the very beginning, a little fine writing, based on the supposed contrast between English departure from and Welsh adherence to the tongue of their
ancestors, is spoiled by Lord Strangford's information
that the Welshman no more speaks the tongue of his ancestors than the Englishman; modern Welsh being a thoroughly
Romanised language. It is as well that the philology
should be rectified; but it is just to add that the notes
do not touch the soundest part of Mr. Arnold's plea for
Celtic studies, which is based on the undoubted importance of Celtic language and literature in all researches
into the early history of the Indo-European race. That
plea will probably have in its favour the unanimous suf-
frages of the literary world. The great difficulty is to
create such a movement of opinion beyond that world as
will be sufficient to disturb the slumbers of politicians
who care for none of these things, though they are indispensable agents in endowing professorships and appointing
commissions to catalogue and publish old MSS, and other
remains of primaeval literature. Accordingly, the chief
value of the book will consist in its tendency to produce
such a movement by popularising the Celtic case. It is
still necessary, in order to overcome unreasonable prejudice, to insist on the connection of Teuton and Celt,
high up in the family tree though it be, while the facts
as to Celtic literature extant, its originality and
possible value, are certainly not well known. It would,
perhaps, have been well had Mr. Arnold devoted even more

space to the latter questions – the originality and
value of Celtic literature – instead of entering on the
more doubtful question as to what Celtic fibre there is
in Englishmen. Instead of engaging in a doubtful controversy, he might have settled the question decisively in
favour of Celtic literature by a few more specimens,
demonstrating by their evident novelty and beauty the
value of the unexplored region from which they had been
gathered. As it is, he does enough to whet curiosity and
to make it less safe for any future Lord Macaulay to declare confidently the valuelessness of a mass of Celtic
MSS. before pains have been taken to sift their contents;
but there he leaves us. So far as it goes, however, the
positive value of the book is very great.

So much has been said of late on the question of our
Celtic origin, that Mr. Arnold's contribution to the controversy, which is of historical interest, though of
little practical moment, is worth looking at. Leaving
physiology and philology alone, he argues that certain
features in the Celtic character and literature not to be
found generally in the Teutonic race must, when they
exist in the English, be due to the admixture of Celtic
blood. This is assuming too much. The similarity of
certain features may be due to similarities of history,
and would argue simply that the Teutonic race had a latent
power, like the Celtic, which was only developed in the
English branch. But assuming that the argument is logically constructed, the premises are faulty. A wrong type
for the Teutonic – the High German – has been taken, so
that the whole process is vitiated. Admitting that the
English have as large an admixture of the Celtic as Mr.
Arnold supposes, they would still be as pure a Teutonic
type as the High Germans with their Slavonic admixture.
As Lord Strangford points out, instead of going to our
most distant cousins in the Teutonic family for the type,
he ought to have taken an intermediate branch, such as the
Dutch or Scandinavians. Farther, if we have certain
qualities by virtue of our Celtic fibre, the inquiry, to
be complete, should have embraced other nations, if any,
possessing the same fibre. The French, for instance, are
as much Celts as we are said to be, and the qualities seen
in us should have their analogues in the French. This is
a point altogether overlooked by Mr. Arnold, though it
might have led him to withhold some of his illustrations.
He instances a certain deficiency of the Celts in the
arts. They write good verse, but do not construct a
poem; they make excellent small ornaments, but do not
paint pictures or excel in architecture. In these qualities, on the other hand, the Germans excel, the English

race showing its mixture by excelling the pure Celtic and
falling short of the pure Teutonic. How then does it
happen that 'composition' is the very quality of art which
the French - our brother Celts - pretend to ? It is in
our poetry Mr. Arnold finds most distinct traces of the
Celtic element. We get from the Celts 'style,' a 'chord
of penetrating passion and melancholy,' and a power to
reproduce the magic of nature. But as to the first
quality, style, he is very doubtful, and the judgment may
go against him. He admits the presence of style in the
Icelandic eddas, and the only fact he adduces to show that
the Norsemen may also have got style from the Celts - the
contact of Norsemen with the Irish in Iceland - is demo-
lished by Lord Strangford, who points out that the Irish
had left Iceland long before the Norsemen came. As to the
'chord of penetrating passion and melancholy' in English
and Celtic poetry, the quality is almost too intangible
for disputation, but a venture may be made. Mr. Arnold
associates with it or ascribes it to the Titanism in
Celtic nature, rebelling against the despotism of fact;
yet the only Celtic specimen of this Titanism given
('Lywarch Hen's Address to his Crutch') is simply the
querulous complaint of an old man - not a tone of rebel-
lion or protest in the whole. Again, the Titanism cited
in English poetry is that of Byron, who is certainly *sui
generis*, (1) if he does not owe his Titanism rather to
Ossian and 'Werther' than directly to his own Celtic
fibre. Only one other instance is given, that of Milton's
Satan, four or five lines being quoted, beginning - 'What
though the field be lost, all is not lost.' But there is
fair reason to doubt whether Milton was exhibiting in
Satan a Titan impatient with a higher power and necessity.
The character is rather that of an old Norse sea-king -
fighting on to the last with unyielding stubbornness, but,
instead of rebelling against the despotism of fact, keeping his conflict within real conditions. Satan boasts of
having waged 'dubious battle,' of the immortal nature of
his essence, of hoping to profit by experience of the
past dire event in waging eternal war, and finally, of
holding, by means of evil, 'divided empire with heaven's
king.' Where there are so few illustrations, and so much
doubt in those given, the area of observation must obviously be widened. As for the Celtic turn for natural
magic, it is sufficient to say that the instances are
again too few. There are quotations enough from the
Celtic, but the only citations from English poetry, with
the exception of a stray passage from Keats, are from
Shakespeare, who might easily be a rare instance, possessing more than an average share of Celtic blood, or

developing, through singular force of genius, inspired by
the novel energy and romance of his age, a comparatively
new quality of poetic power. There is no attempt to show
that the Celtic gift is manifested by many of our poets.
Again, we might have expected traces, which we do not
find, of a careful comparison with the poetry of our
neighbours, to show that the absence of these gifts in
them, and their exclusive possession by Celts and English,
can fairly be affirmed. Mr. Arnold's mere opinion on a
question of this sort is no doubt sufficient to obtain
attention for it, but to carry conviction he must give the
subject a more elaborate treatment. Fortunately the
grounds for studying Celtic literature are quite independent of this line of argument.

Note

1   'unique'.

Schools and Universities on the Continent (1868)

15. F. W. FARRAR, 'SCHOOLS AND UNIVERSITIES ON THE
CONTINENT', 'FORTNIGHTLY REVIEW'

June 1868, ix, 709-11

Frederick William Farrar (1831-1903), a broad-church
clergyman, novelist, critic, and author of a 'Life of
Christ', studied at London University and Cambridge,
where he joined 'The Apostles'. His diverse and outspoken career culminated in his becoming Dean of Canterbury. Farrar's religious views were influenced by
F. D. Maurice, his scientific views by Darwin. On many
issues he was in substantial agreement with Arnold, and
his short, laudatory review in the 'Fortnightly' is one
of few unstinting contemporary assessments of Arnold's
educational ideas.

Education is a subject on which every one asserts his
right to speak, and the consequence is a multiplication
of theories and of treatises so rapid that it far out-
strips the reading capacities even of those who are most
interested in educational questions. But the study of one
really authoritative book spares us the necessity of reading many others, and we cannot be too grateful for a work
like the present, written as it is by a man of high genius,
who, to his hereditary interest in education, adds a long,
ripe, and varied experience, and who describes his facts
and states his conclusions in a singularly pure and winning style. In 1865 Mr. Arnold was appointed by the
Schools Inquiry Commission to investigate the educational

system of the upper and middle classes in France, Italy,
Germany, and Switzerland; and the work now before us is a
handsome and convenient reprint of the report which he has
drawn up, divested of details in which the general reader
would take little interest. It is a narrative of observations continued during seven months in the four countries
named; and although Mr. Arnold's facts and inferences must
carry with them very great weight in settling problems
which have long been under dispute, they are not stated
with the heat of a partisan, but in the calmest and most
judicial manner. The dignified and persuasive tone which
Mr. Arnold has adopted will give him even more weight than
if he had entered as a formidable gladiator into the arena
of controversy, armed with those keen and polished weapons
of wit and satire which no man knows how to wield more
effectively than himself. In his short and weighty preface Mr. Arnold points out the entire fallacy involved in
the assumption of Lord John Manners and others, that 'our
primary education is ahead of all countries in the world
except Prussia.' He shows that the tables from which this
conclusion was deduced are wholly untrustworthy; that the
sense in which the word 'scholar' is used by the Educational Commissioners is widely different from that in
which it is used in France and Germany, and implies in
most cases an amount of attainment immeasurably inferior;
that whereas in England Mr. Fraser 'thinks it vain to talk
of keeping in school the mass of our children after their
tenth year,' Swiss and German children, on the other hand,
are obliged to be under teaching from their sixth to their
fifteenth year; that our schoolmasters are socially and
ungenerously discouraged, as though their influence were
regarded with positive jealousy; that since the Revised
Code, and its payment for results, our education has
dwindled more and more into a matter of 'the three R's,'
and that, in national education, prosperity and compul-
soriness have generally gone together. So that, on the
whole, Mr. Arnold evidently inclines to the judgment of a
foreign report, which he contrasts with our own too self-
complacent imaginations, that 'l'Angleterre, proprement
dite, est le pays d'Europe où l'instruction est le moins
répandue.' (1) These reasonings are so important that it
seems desirable to draw special attention to them; but the
main part of Mr. Arnold's book is devoted, not to the primary, but to the *secondary* education of the Continent; and
with respect to this also he endeavours to prove that in
England, as compared with France and Prussia, the middle
class in general is brought up on the *second* rather than
on the *first* plane; that technical and special education
ought not to be an isolated matter, but 'the crown of a

long co-ordered series, designed and graduated by the best
heads in the country;' and that, partly from our crude
jealousy of State interference, partly from our high opinion of our own energy and wealth, we settle the most important matters (such as competitive examinations and
other questions connected with schools) without any appeal
to the best educational opinion in the country.

Into Mr. Arnold's most interesting account of the various continental systems which he examined it is, of course,
impossible for us in this brief space to follow him; but
if we are ever to have any legislation on the subject
which is worth the name, it is the plain duty of all who
take part in it to consider carefully the facts which Mr.
Arnold has had such exceptional opportunities for observing. No unprejudiced man will, I think, rise from the
perusal of his report without a saddening conviction - a
conviction possibly deepened by personal experience - that
the intellectual training afforded to boys in France and
Germany is far more rich and valuable than that enjoyed by
the great majority of English boys. That there is another
and more encouraging aspect of the matter no one will
deny; for no one in his senses would exchange the brightness, the freedom, the self-government, the healthy and
happy elasticity, which prevail in our best English
schools for that moping listlessness which we have sometimes observed in German play-grounds, or for the surveillance, the confinement, in a word, the *vie de caserne*,
(2) which so unhappily characterises the *lycées* (3) of
France. But to assume that we cannot improve our teaching without injuring the physique and high spirits of our
boys, - and that all who advocate a wider and more fruitful system of instruction must necessarily desire the
evils, due to other causes, which in some cases accompany
it, - is to adopt a style of argument so shallow that its
prevalence would surprise us if we did not know that it
originated in the very deficiencies which some of us are
trying to remove.

We are glad to claim Mr. Arnold's high authority for
many of the views which have recently been pressed upon
public attention by school-reformers. Thus he is opposed
to our present 'half-disgusting, half-ridiculous' method
of flogging, a relic of barbarism which will probably have
disappeared before ten years are over; he draws a just
distinction between the elementary facts and the philosophic rationale of grammar; he points out that England
alone is still content to make Euclid her text-book of
geometry; he calls attention to the volume and irresist-
ibility of the disbelief in a solely classical culture,
and the demand for a scientific training; he quotes the

eminent name of Mr. Marsh in favour of the view that a
mere polyglot familiarity with spoken languages 'tends to
make the thoughts thin and shallow, and so far from in
itself carrying us to vital knowledge, needs a compensat-
ing force to prevent its carrying us away from it'; he
shows that Greek and Latin, when not taught in a wooden
and pedantic manner, but with a real reference to the
literature which they enshrine, may be transformed from a
dull mechanical discipline into a valuable and formative
knowledge; and, lastly, he tells us how much we lose by
our present aimlessness, and how necessary it is to fix a
centre of responsibility in an educational minister, aided
by a high council of education, which shall comprise,
without regard to politics, the persons most entitled to a
hearing on educational questions. Generally speaking, he
regards the present state of things with unconcealed dis-
quietude. Seven years ago he urged upon us an organisation of our secondary instruction. 'That advice passed
perfectly unheeded, the hubbub of our sterile politics
continued, ideas of social reconstruction had not a
thought given them, our secondary instruction is still the
chaos it was; and yet now, so urgent and irresistible is
the impression left upon me by what I have again seen
abroad, I cannot help presenting myself once more to my
countrymen with an increased demand, - *organise your
secondary and your superior instruction.*'
This brief sketch gives no adequate conception of the
extreme value of this book. It is one of the most important contributions to a most important question, and even
'amid the hubbub of our sterile politics,' it is to be
hoped that it may meet with the attention which it so well
deserves.

Notes

1 'England, accurately described, is the European
  country where education is the least widespread.'
2 'barracks life'.
3 'secondary schools'.

16. WALTER BAGEHOT ON ARNOLD AND THE UNIVERSITIES,
'FORTNIGHTLY REVIEW'

June 1868, iii, n.s., 639-47

Bagehot (1826-77), best known for his 'English Constitu-
tion', was a prominent economist and editor (of both the
'National Review' and, towards the end of his life, 'The
Economist'). He was a widely read, influential thinker,
who contributed literary, political, and educational
essays to various periodicals. His response to Arnold's
'Schools and Universities on the Continent' involves a
rare discussion of Arnold on higher education, although
Bagehot's main interest and focus is London University.
Arnold, he says, judges too much from an Oxford point of
view.

Mr. Arnold is not only a very interesting writer, but a
very bold writer. He has the courage to despise points
of form, and to disregard the unconscious expectations
which the title of a book naturally begets. In an official Report, presented to the School Commissioners upon
'Schools and Universities on the Continent,' no one
would have expected to find an able criticism of the
'London University.' But whether in strictness this
criticism be quite in place or not, every one attached
to that University will be most glad to have it, as it is
one of the acutest which has ever appeared, and the most
favourable perhaps that an Oxford man, and attached to
Oxford, has ever written. Oxford breeds people who hate
her, and these have been favourable to London; but Mr.
Arnold loves Oxford, and when he praises a University
utterly unlike it, it is an effect of conviction, not a
freak of ill-temper. Yet I cannot say that I think Mr.
Arnold understands the conditions under which the University of London acts; as is natural, he knows simply nothing of her internal history; he is altogether blind to
the latent causes which stop her action. If I were to
write on Oxford I should doubtless use what the great
Oxford teacher calls 'unreal words' - words which would
show I had not in my mind a vivid image of the facts; I
should not like to say so much of Mr. Arnold, - he has
studied the University of London far too well; still
there are shades and touches which he does not know.
    Mr. Arnold is bolder, too, than a mere critic ever can

be; he proposes or imagines, at least, a scheme of reform.
He sketches a great future of what the University of
London might be, and seems half to wonder that those who
rule it do not at once create that future. I have but a
few pages before me, but I should like shortly to bring
out - what is the great truth which Mr. Arnold so finely
inculcates, and, on the other hand, what are the impedi-
ments to instant action, which those who know the ground
and have tried to move where he directs feel at every
step.
   The charm of Mr. Arnold's language is so exquisite that
it is always painful to translate his meaning into other
words, and happily the following passage puts his conception of the University and his plan for it very plainly.
After speaking of the defects of Oxford and Cambridge,
after calling them *hauts lycées* ('finishing schools for
the upper classes,' as poor Clough used to put it); he
then continues: -
   'The University of London labours under a yet graver
defect as an organ of scientific or superior instruction.
It is a mere *collegium*, or board, of examiners. It gives
no instruction at all, but it examines in the different
lines of study, and gives degrees in them. It has real
University examinations, which Oxford and Cambridge have
not; and these examinations are conducted by an independent board, and not by college tutors. This is excellent;
but nevertheless it falls immensely short of what is
needed. The idea of a University is, as I have already
said, that of an institution not only offering to young
men facilities for graduating in that line of study to
which their aptitudes direct them, but offering to them,
also, *facilities for following that line of study systematically, under first-rate instruction*. This second function is of incalculable importance; of far greater importance, even, than the first. It is impossible to overvalue the importance to a young man of being brought into
contact with a first-rate teacher of his matter of study,
and of getting from him a clear notion of what the systematic study of it means. Such instruction is so far
from being yet organised in this country, that it even
requires a gifted student to feel the want of it; and such
a student must go to Paris, or Heidelberg, or Berlin,
because England cannot give him what he wants. Some do
go; an admirable English mathematician who did not, told
me that he should never recover the loss of the two years
which after his degree he wasted without fit instruction
at an English University, when he ought to have been under
superior instruction, for which the present University
course in England makes no provision. I dare say he *will*

recover it, for a man of genius counts no worthy effort
too hard; but who can estimate the loss to the mental
training and intellectual habits of the country, from an
absence, - so complete that it needs genius to be sensible
of it, and costs genius an effort to repair it, - of all
regular public provision for the scientific study and
teaching of any branch of knowledge?'
   And again, a little farther on: - 'The University of
London should be re-cast and faculties formed in connection with it, in order to give some public voice and place
to superior instruction in the richest capital of the
world; and for this purpose the strangely devised and
anomalous organisations of King's College and University
College should be turned to account, and *co-ordered*, as
the French say, with the University of London. Contributions from Oxford and Cambridge, and new appointments,
might supply what was wanting to fill the faculties, which
in London, the capital of the country, should, as at Paris
or Berlin, be very strong. London would then really have,
what it has not at present, a University.' No one can
deny that this is a noble conception; if half of it only
could be once accomplished, the University of London would
be not only one of the first, but by far the first University in Great Britain. By virtue of its position it could
effect more, and secure that what it did should be seen
better, than any other. London, skilfully picked, would
yield a set of professors that no English city would rival;
and their teaching would fall on an audience that cannot
be equalled in the whole world for number, variety, and,
if I may so say, curiously-*invested* intelligence. But
yet I could find plenty of men, and those the best friends
of the London University, and those to whom she is indebted most, who would discard at once this plan of Mr.
Arnold's as Utopian, visionary, and absurd; who would say
'the University of London *is* only an examining body, *can*
be only an examining body, *shall* be only an examining
body.'
   Every generation is unjust to the preceding generation;
it respects its distant ancestors, but it thinks its
fathers were 'quite wrong.' And this revolt of nature is
a principal propelling force, and a power in civilisation;
for, without it, some set of strong men, consistently
acting for a few generations, would soon stereotype the
world. Yet this tendency is as unamiable as it is unfair,
or even more unamiable. We enter into the fresh riches
our fathers made for us, and at once we begin to say they
are not the right sort; we enjoy and we grumble. We live
in the house, and we say, 'If *I* had been the builder, that
corner would not have stood out; if I could have had my

way, the stairs would have been of oak; and how very
obstinate my father always was about the smoke in the kit-
chen!' But we forget very likely that we are of a weaker
force and more inefficient mind, and that, if we had had
to build, probably there would have been no house at all.
Just so with the London University. We, who were educated
at it, grumble at much of it. I at least have often done
so, and have often heard others. But yet I know well how
much the founders of the University have done; how difficult in their case was every sort of success; how easy
every sort of failure. If some of us who criticise had
had the founding of the University, I fear it would not
have lasted till this time.

Thirty years ago it was a great step to establish an
independent and examining University. That improvement
was a purely English idea, but like so many English ideas,
it existed only in solution; it was there, but it was
hidden. Just as the English are the inventors of Cabinet
government - of government by a committee of Parliament
which can dissolve Parliament, and just as we have hidden
away this masterpiece of polity under an historical growth
of King, Lords, and Commons, and a pompous theory of three
branches - just so we invented a *testing* University - a
University distinct from the studies whose effects it
verified. I fancy we came upon the idea by chance. The
University of Oxford, for example, had ceased either to
examine or to instruct. Adam Smith, a Scotch Balliol
scholar, tells us that when he was there the University
had given up even 'the pretence of teaching'. The examination at Oxford,' said Lord Eldon, 'was a farce in *my*
time. I was only asked who founded University College,
and I said - though, by the way, the fact is very doubtful - King Alfred.' Possibly the Tory Chancellor exaggerated a little, but still he is an excellent witness
against Oxford. At the Nadir of that University, it neither examined nor taught. Then some strong men revived
the College teaching. When the Scotch reviewers attacked
Oxford, Coppleston was able to show that Oriel College
taught better than any school in Scotland. Then improvers
tried to amend the University, but there was no longer any
room for its tuition; there was better tuition already; so
they revived the examining function, and suggested the new
idea of a central verifying body surrounded and aided by
many instructing bodies. Historical nations, I apprehend,
mostly come upon their improvements in some such way as
this. A miscellaneous *débris* of old things has come down
to them, and, without much thinking, they pick out of the
heap the particular bit that looks best for the particular
matter in hand. The inestimable gain of historical

nations is, that they inherit this mixed mass of materials;
and their countervailing disadvantage is that the accumu-
lation of old débris hides the shape of the work, and that
they have no plain intelligible theory to bequeath to
common nations which must build de novo.

At any rate, when the London University started, the
notion of a University which did not teach those whom it
tested, was very strange. Even when I was a student, some
years later, the outer world did not understand it; there
are many to whom the knowledge has not penetrated yet.
Even Mr. Arnold, though he recognises the full value of
the idea - though he sees that the London University carries it into practice more thoroughly than Oxford or Cambridge, (where, though the colleges as such, do not regulate the examination, yet members of the colleges -
college tutors - do regulate it, because they are the
examiners); - even Mr. Arnold has a vestige of puzzle on
the matter. He knows that the foreign Professors, from
whom he is fresh, do not understand a University without
tuition, and he dares not tell them that a graduating
machine, as Lord Brougham used to say, not preparing for
degrees, and therefore conferring them without favour and
without the suspicion of favour, is an English creation of
the first magnitude.

I acknowledge that there is an excuse for him. He says
that a University should 'provide facilities for following
that line of study systematically, and under first-rate
instruction.' I should rather say a perfect University
would possess an attendant apparatus for such instruction
- would be surrounded by sufficient colleges. You cannot
'have it both ways;' you cannot obtain an article without
paying its price. If you want a University which is trusted without suspicion to decide on the results of tuition,
because it has no share in tuition, you must not let it
begin to interfere in tuition. But it might retain effectual satellites - those 'anomalous bodies, University College and King's College,' which give, and were affiliated
because they give, appropriate instruction. Years ago
many of us contended that no degree should be given by the
University of London save to persons trained in, and so to
say, vouched for by such colleges; and I still maintain
that for 'Plato's Republic' such would be the ideal conception. There is no falser notion than Carlyle's that
the true University of the present day is a 'great collection of books.' No University can be perfect which does
not set a young man face to face with great teachers.
Mathematics in part may teach themselves, may be learned
at least by a person of great aptitude and at great cost
of toil from written treatises; but true literature is

still largely a tradition, it does not go straight on like
mathematics, and if a learner is to find it for himself in
a big library, he will be grey-headed before his work is
nearly over. And besides 'character forms itself in the
stream of the world' - by the impact of mind on mind.
There are few impacts so effectual as that of ardent
student upon ardent student, or as that of mature teacher
upon immature student. I concede to Mr. Arnold that a
perfect University would be attended by appropriate colleges for teaching its students, and would grant its full
degrees to no one not so educated. But in the London
University we could not attain this, though we tried.
Some of the very strongest among its founders thought the
collegiate system an English superstition, and believed
that examinations were enough alone. And also there was
the great difficulty that good colleges cannot be found
all over England; that it would have long retarded the
work of the University to confine its examinations to the
very few colleges that would be worthy the name; that
almost at the outset many bodies that were only high
schools had been affiliated, - that many others quite
equal were asking to be recognised, and could not be
refused except by an invidious and unjust distinction.
In the London University the collegiate system had not a
chance, for there were far too few good colleges, much
too many schools claiming to be colleges which were not,
and a senate which did not believe in colleges.
  But though Mr. Arnold would do harm if he persuaded
the University of London to descend into the arena and
become one of the trainers of the students it examines,
though he could not find suitable colleges scattered over
England to give effectual instruction, yet I think he has
hold of a great idea, which ought to be separated from
the less valuable elements with which he has mixed it.
I believe that it is a misconception to regard a University as having but two possible duties, that of examining
students, and that of instructing those students; I believe it has a third duty - a duty to the world. Mr.
Arnold gives some outline of the history of the French
Universities; he goes back to times when France was the
metropolis of European learning in the same sense that
Germany has been lately- he tells us of the great times
of the University of Paris. 'Hither,' he says, 'repaired
the students of other countries and other universities,
as to the main centre of mediaeval science, and the most
authoritative school of mediaeval teaching. It received
names expressing the most enthusiastic devotion: the
fountain of knowledge, the *tree of life*, the *candle-stick
of the house of the Lord*. "The most famous University of

Paris, the place at this time and long before whither the
English, and mostly the Oxonians, resorted," says Wood.
*Tandem fiat hic velut Parisiis . . . . . ad instar Parisi-
ensis studii . . . . . quemadmodum in Parisiensi studio
. . . .* (1) say the rules of the University of Vienna,
founded in 1365.   Here came Roger Bacon, Saint Thomas
Aquinas, and Dante; here studied the founder of the first
university of the Empire, Charles IV., Emperor of Germany
and King of Bohemia, founder of the University of Prague;
here Henry II. in the twelfth century proposed to refer
his dispute with Becket; here, in the fourteenth, the
schism in the papacy and the claims of the rival Popes
were brought for judgment.'   And this account implies what
everything confirms, that Universities in their first age
not only taught and examined young students, but influenced society at large, gave lectures which broke up adult
thought, diffused ideas which interfered with fixed
creeds, and which were felt as powers even by those who
disagreed with them.   The Universities in that age had a
social function as well as a national function; they influenced the whole grown up society besides teaching particular young students.

This is what I understand certain reformers to mean
when they ask that the University of London should be made
a seat of learning.   Professor Seeley, one of the most
skilful of living writers, says: - 'With our present
habits of thought, it is not very easy for us to conceive
a real University.   We understand competition; that means
fighting.   We understand trying for fellowships; that
means money-making.   But the University proper has no connection with either of these intelligible things; it is
neither an almshouse of pensioners, nor a cockpit of competition, but a seat of learning.'   If I interpret aright,
Mr. Seeley means that a University ought to have about it
a set of men who live in the still air of science and
learning, who are to influence their age, who are to make,
if they can, some kind of impression, not upon 'the
masses,' for that would be absurd, but the augmenting
number of cultivated and half-cultivated people.

I believe that there never was a time in English history when there was such an appetite for knowledge.   The
visible success of physical science has awakened a sort of
craving to know about nature which nothing before ever
resembled.   That sort of knowledge has been tested by
'results,' and no one can impugn the answer which they
give.   Railways, telegraphs, steamships, are so many
'marks,' which count for much in the perpetual examination
of knowledge by the world.   Years ago, when Lord Bacon
wrote the 'Advancement of Learning,' it was not very easy

to find a sharp conclusive proof that any difficult knowledge was good. The obvious pursuits, as contemporary
languages, reading, writing, speak for themselves, and
want no advocate. But when the claim of any hard, settled
study came to be set forth, the case was laboured, and the
effect of its exposition, though conclusive to the best
minds, was very dubious upon all others. But now there
is, at least, one kind of very hard knowledge which works
its own way, needs no pushing, makes every one admit that
some one ought to know it, and makes most people wish that
they themselves knew it. And the definite fame of this so
to say advertised knowledge extends into other and distant
regions. All other modern sciences, such as geology or
ethnology, which have no plain influence on visible
machines, nor plapable effect on indisputable results,
share the repute of the more effectual sciences. The
method is the same; the evidence, to those who knew it,
of like character. And to the world at large 'science' is
one entity; it is the force which sends quick messages,
which makes fast trains, which helps ships to sail safely.
All the world wants to know about science; there is an
irritable accumulated curiosity in us and about us, such
as history never saw equalled.
    All branches of knowledge share in this curiosity more
or less. There is a sort of feeling that we do not know
where we stand in things, and that we ought to know; that
the 'modern spirit' rules or questions most things without
knowing how far it denies them and how far it confirms
them - at least without knowing it broadly. Modern science is indisputably developing a new temper of mind;
something which as a diffused mental habit the ancients
had not, the Middle Ages had not, till now modern times
had not. An instinct of revision is felt to be abroad in
human opinion, of which thinking men want to know the
direction, and wish, if they could, to see the end. There
is a dissatisfaction with old beliefs, and a difficulty in
finding satisfying new beliefs, which engenders a passion
for true teaching.
    There is another co-operating force. Now-a-days man-
kind are thrown into big cities where they have little to
do; where they are loosely connected with, and see very
little of each other; where they want something on which
to employ their minds. Formerly people lived in country
towns, where there was a sort of impact of mind on mind -
a perpetual contention and reaction - a formative process,
though often a violent and barbarous one. In a small
town with a few streets and a common life, every one knew
every one, and every one acted upon every one. But among
the ninety families who live in the ninety similar houses

in New Street, Hyde Park, not five know one another. And
most of them know no one else well; a certain dull distance pervades everything; occupied men know that they
have a 'visiting list,' but they would come to grief if
Mr. Lowe examined them on its contents. A new vacancy of
mind is created by new habits which seeks for occupation,
and would be very grateful for good occupation. The sort
of success which such lectures as those of the Royal
Institution at present have show the wonderful appetite
there is for such teaching. If the London University
could give anything like it, it would give it with greater
prestige, greater authority, and, I think, greater
attractiveness. People would be attracted by the very
authority; they would come there because they knew that
the teaching in its kind was first-rate, (whatever, which
might often be arguable, was the intrinsic and ineradic-
able defect of that kind). And a University would be
free from the sort of taint which every other lecturing
body must have. It would have no wish, it need be thought
to have no wish, to be overpopular; it would choose really
learned professors, really sound professors, and would
wish them to teach thorough thought.
    I suppose the Oxford professoriat has now something
like the function I mean. Its functions are not to the
students *before* examination, but to grown-up men *after*
examination. I apprehend that Mr. Arnold's lectures on
poetry had no part or share in the studies of Oxford
undergraduates; they prepared men for no examinations;
they competed with no college which did prepare them.
They were careful 'studies' addressed to thoughtful men
already educated; they would have been fit for no other
audience. I could not find an instance to describe my
notion more exactly. I wish to see at the London University many accomplished men addressing high-class lectures
to high-class hearers.
    But though I have exceeded my limits, I must point out
(or I should be unfair) two practical difficulties which
Mr. Arnold cannot be expected to divine, but which those
nearer well know. Several 'movements' have in truth been
made in this direction, though no substantial result has
been attained - no actual lecture has ever been given;
but by means of this experience the dangers in the path
are known.
    First. There is a great dread of losing the place
which the University has gained. It is now admitted to
be an impartial judge of teaching, because it does not
itself teach, - but if it began to teach, even though the
teaching were of a different species, and were addressed
to the 'after-degree' world, the University might begin

184 Arnold, Prose Writings: The Critical Heritage

to be suspected. On paper this danger may not seem so
extreme as it is; but in practice the difficulty of distinguishing the teachings is great, and those who created
the University dislike, as by an apprehensive instinct,
everything which might undo their work or impair it. I
doubt if the present Senate would be willing administra-
tors of a professorial plan, and the conception is so
delicate that it would fail if those who were entrusted
with it did not believe in it.

Secondly. There is the most dangerous of all difficulties - a religious difficulty. The University of London
is now supported by all religious bodies ; by orthodox
Dissenters, by Unitarians, by Roman Catholics, by English
Churchmen. The *dryness* and limitation of its work is a
great help in gaining that support; it lessens the number
of disputable decisions - it precludes a theatrical prominence in any decision. But yet this combined support
by antagonistic bodies has not been gained easily. Years
of cautious and conscientious management have been necessary to gain it - so delicate is education, and so scrupulous men's temper. But if impressive lectures were delivered at the University by conspicuous lecturers, the
difficulty would be enhanced tenfold. There might be much
in many lectures which many would object to; very often
there would be something which some would object to.
Gradually it might, and no doubt would, come to be comprehended that the contents of these lectures were not certi-
fied to be true by the University; that the University
only put forward the lecturer as a man of eminence in
science or learning who was worth attention. And in time
it would be seen too, that these superior lectures had
nothing to do with the common University work; that the
examination system went on apart from and independently of
them; that all persons might derive exactly all the advantages they now derive from the examinations, after these
lectures were established, and though they might disapprove of some of the lectures. But the task would be nice,
success hard, failure easy, and infinite caution would be
wanted in the beginning.

Those brief remarks on a great subject will explain, I
think, why I cannot accept for the London University, Mr.
Arnold's plan exactly as he puts it and conceives it, but
why, also, I believe there is an analogous work which some
one must soon undertake in London, which ought at once to
be undertaken, and which the University would have singular, and perhaps unequalled, advantages for doing well.

Note

1 'Thus is it done in Paris', etc.

17.   OSCAR BROWNING, UNSIGNED REVIEW ON ARNOLD AND
EDUCATION, 'QUARTERLY REVIEW'

October 1868, cxxv, 473-90

Oscar Browning (1837-1923), fellow of King's College,
Cambridge, where he was a friend of Henry Sidgwick,
became a master at Eton and an eminently successful, if
controversial, teacher. At both Cambridge and Eton,
Browning devoted himself to educational reform. He cared
about teaching and about schools, and his review of Arnold
is a reasonable defence of some aspects of English education against Arnold's sweeping censure. Omitted from the
selection are a few technical discussions and a comparison
with a French educational reformer, a M. Demogeot, whom
Browning says he finds more accurate than Arnold.

We do not propose to accompany Mr. Arnold through the
whole of his Report. The greater part of it is occupied
with a statement of facts from official sources, very
neatly and clearly put, about which no difference of
opinion can exist. Twenty-seven pages are devoted to
Italy, only fifteen to Switzerland. For this we are very
sorry; we believe that there is no country where education
attains so completely the end it aims at, and where the
problem of giving a cheap, useful, and at the same time a
free and manly education to large numbers is so successfully solved. Mr. Arnold is of course loud in its praise,
but he confines himself almost entirely to the means by
which schools are governed and maintained, and to knowledge which can be derived from books. Of the life of the
pupils and the professors, and the relations between them,
as of the full cost of an education in Switzerland –
matters which he was especially instructed to examine – he
tells us nothing. Switzerland is preeminently a country
of schoolmasters. A history of Pestalozzi and Fellenberg
would have been as valuable and as much to the point as
Mr. Arnold's history of the University of Paris; and we

think that Geneva and Lausanne deserve more than the passing allusion which Mr. Arnold has vouchsafed to them.
Germany has sixty pages given to her, and this is the most
valuable and trustworthy portion of the whole. But here
we must complain of excessive meagreness. We get from
Mr. Arnold's account no idea of the life of a German
school. Schulpforte is dismissed in a page and a half.
It is a school about which all Englishmen must feel a
strong curiosity, as the boasted meeting-place of foreign
systems with our own. If Mr. Arnold had spent a week at
Schulpforte, and given us a picture of the living action
of the school, it would have been of the highest value.
We believe that an article by M. Esquiros, in the 'Revue
des Deux Mondes,' describing a week spent in the summer
half at Eton or Rugby, would do more to spread abroad a
knowledge of English education than any number of statistics. If Mr. Arnold had done this for us, he would find
more readers. Mr. Arnold was instructed to inquire into
the books and apparatus used in schools. A full report on
the German school-books would be of great service.
Instead of this, we have a statement which, although tech-
nically true, is misleading, and a tirade against English
school-books which is unfounded and uncalled for. Mr.
Arnold says that all German school-books must be approved
by the Educational Council. But practically there is the
most perfect freedom in the choice of school-books and
editions. Every gymnasium uses its own, and there is a
lively competition between rival publishers. In England,
he tells us, 'most schools make a trade of book-dealing,'
which we imagine is quite untrue of all public schools.
'Half, at least, of our school-books are rubbish,' which
is again untrue. Mr. Arnold will find, if he inquires,
that the books used throughout our classical schools have
nothing to equal them in France; that Dr. Smith's dictionaries and manuals have no rival in Europe or America.
These hasty statements can only be explained by Mr.
Arnold's ignorance of the present state of English
schools, and are drawn from his hazy recollections of
thirty years since.

But the portion of Mr. Arnold's Report which is most
characteristic is that which relates to France. The
French schools received the first fruits of his attention
and enthusiasm when he had not as yet lost any portion of
interest in his subject. It is here, also, that the comparison with England is drawn in the deepest shadow. We
have ourselves seen something of French education, and we
differ very widely from the conclusions to which he would
lead us. The public mind seems already to have been
influenced by this account of our neighbours' institutions.

M. Duruy is the model of a Minister of Education; and his
extreme activity, backed by the strong personal interest
of the Emperor, is likely to invite us to a similar course.
There is a symmetry and preciseness about French arrangements which is tempting and alluring to the official mind.
We are destined, we hope, soon to have a Minister of Education in England; and he will in all probability borrow
some ideas from across the Channel. It is for this reason
most important that we should get a clear conception of
what French education really is. We propose, therefore,
to examine Mr. Arnold's account at some length in those
particulars where we dissent from him.

After a long history of education in France, and an
account of the organisation of the Ministry of Instruction,
Mr. Arnold gives us a description of the École Normale,
the *pépinière* (1) ,of professors, and of the professors
themselves. The École Normale is undoubtedly one of the
glories of France; it provides the very best instruction
which the country can give to 110 young men entirely free
of charge; and the admissions to it are granted solely by
competition, without favour or patronage. Mr. Arnold
thinks that the establishment of such a school in England
should be the first step to the improvement of our teaching staff. But we must remember that the École Normale
stands in place of both our Universities. The real
representatives of these 110 *bourses* (2) of 40*l*. a year
each are our Balliol and King's Scholarships, our Oriel
and Trinity Fellowships. At Oxford alone, 90,000*l*. a
year are given away in prizes for learning. The 12,300*l*.
of the École Normale are very poor in comparison. The
professors of the École Normale, distinguished as they are,
are not superior to the teachers of Oxford and Cambridge;
whereas the moral education of the two places cannot be
for a moment compared. The young men of the Normal School,
whose ages vary from eighteen to twenty-eight, are under
the very same surveillance as the schoolboys of the
Lycées. The place of *pion* (3) is supplied by men a few
years older, who wish to prosecute their studies farther,
and who answer to the young fellows of our colleges who
stay up for the purpose of reading. When we visited the
École Normale we saw the pupils in the playground, some
swinging, some playing leapfrog or prisoner's-base, with
a fair sprinkling of *maîtres d'études* (4) watching them
from the windows. This surveillance is continued at night.
It is true that the beds in the dormitories are screened
by partitions, but at the end sleeps the *maître d'étude*,
with a window which rakes them all; and our cicerone told
us that it was his duty to come out whenever they made a
noise, which was not seldom. Does Mr. Arnold really

prefer this to the freedom and manliness of our college
life? The intelligent young man who showed us round
stared in surprise at what we told him of our English
liberty, he exclaimed, 'Voilà le self-government appliqué
à l'éducation.' (5) In this matter we certainly prefer
anarchy to authority. But after all, the Normal School is
chiefly a political engine; the lectures, the conferences,
the studies, are narrowly guarded by the Minister; and if
the pupils applaud the teaching of a too liberal professor the school is summarily broken up, and the career of
so many men is ruined. We can imagine that a despot in
England would be glad to collect under one roof all the
holders of scholarships in Oxford and Cambridge, and to
teach them contemporary history according to the interests
of his dynasty.
From this school proceed the body of French professors,
and there follows in Mr. Arnold's pages a comparison of
French with English teachers, which is anything but com-
plimentary to the latter, and which in our opinion is
extremely unfair. He says 'the service of public instruction in France attracts a far greater proportion of the
intellectual force of the country than in England,' and
quotes as examples MM. Nisard, Pasteur, and others who are
professors in the Normal School, and have nothing whatever
to do with the Lycées. The Professors of Oxford and
Cambridge, of University College, and King's College,
London, and of Owens College, Manchester, could furnish as
illustrious names as those he has enumerated, and would in
France be all under the Minister of Education, whereas
MM. Taine and Prévost Paradol have no more to do with
public teaching than Mr. Gladstone or Sir Roundell Palmer.
But the masters of our chief public schools are, we should
say, in ability, education, and social position decidedly
superior to the similar class in France. They have gained
greatly by being brought up to a late age with those who
are to follow other careers, instead of being confined to
a special place of education. Many of our bishops have
been schoolmasters. The late Archbishop of Canterbury was
a master at Eton. The Rugby masters of the last twenty
years have given a distinct impress to English education
by filling nearly all head-masterships of newly-
established schools. It is well-known that the colleges
of our Universities cannot restrain some of their best
tutors from taking places in schools which give them a
reasonable income and enable them to marry. We could
quote the authority of a high official of the University
of Cambridge, that during a long experience he had seen
a larger number of the ablest University men devote themselves to teaching than to any other profession. Which

does Mr. Arnold suppose is the most distinguished body of
men, the masters of public schools or the school inspec-
tors? And in France both one and the other would form
part of the Public Instruction. Mr. Arnold says, 'a
French professor has his three, four, or five hours' work
a day in lessons and conferences, and then he is free, he
has nothing to do with the discipline or the religious
teaching of the Lycée, he has not to live in its pre-
cincts, he finishes his teaching and then he leaves the
Lycée and its cares behind him altogether.' This goes to
the root of the matter; that such is the life of a French
Professor is the great blot on all French teaching, which
it is impossible to improve until this blot is removed.
A French teacher knows nothing of his pupils except their
names, he is never brought face to face with them in
friendly and familiar intercourse. They spend a dull and
cheerless life under the eye of a common drudge whom they
hate and despise, and from week to week they have not a
human soul with whom they can take counsel or from whom
they can ask advice. Of the Proviseur they know nothing.
The Censeur knows only the best and the worst boys, whom
he is called upon to punish or to praise. They sleep,
dress, dine, under the *pion's* eye, and are drummed into
class in single file where the Professor whom they never
see but then doles out the history or the geography of
the hour and the day from which he may not depart a hairs-
breadth, after which they march back to their dreary studies to prepare for the mechanical teaching of another
professor. This Mr. Arnold prefers to the free and affectionate intercourse of English tutor and pupil, and an
education based on those principles which his father
sacrificed his life to propagate and diffuse. A proba-
tionary master at a public school is in the position of a
French professor. He receives a certain salary to teach
in class without the care of a house or pupils. But if
he is at all fit for his profession he looks anxiously
for the time when he will be brought into nearer and
closer union with those of whom he is obliged to see so
little. Winchester, Wellington College, and Marlborough,
are adopting the system of boarding-houses which was
before confined to Eton, Harrow, and Rugby.

Mr. Arnold gives a glowing account of the Lycée St. Louis.
As he had previously admired the leisure and freedom from
care of the French professors as compared with their
English brethren, so now he is delighted with the activity of the *proviseur*. (6) 'Constantly appealed to with
a rain of letters, messages, meetings, applicants,

visitors, perpetually beating upon him, he seemed to suffice to all claims, and to suffice not only industriously
but smoothly; but he began his work, he told me, at five
in the morning.' These posts are the prizes of the pro-
fessoriate, so that the teacher who would rise must cultivate those habits of business which Mr. Arnold has represented as the special bane of our own schoolmasters. But
as Mr. Arnold remarks with exquisite *naïveté*, 'every one
who has had opportunities of observing, must have been
struck to see how much work Frenchmen seem able to do,
and to do with spirit and energy.' The various arrangements of the Lycée are recounted with undeviating praise.
We are only requested to make allowances for the difference of habits and nationality. Our own impressions of
the Lycée St. Louis were not so favourable. The long
dormitories seemed to us uncomfortable, the small lava-
tories in the middle of the room insufficient, the refec-
tories overcrowded, filled with little tables with marble
tops, but no tablecloths. We went to the top of the house
to see the prisons, of which Mr. Arnold makes no mention;
they are like the *piombi* (7) of Venice. In one of them
was a bed; and the servants told us that the boys were
sometimes condemned for four or five days, and had to
sleep in the solitary confinement which is the French
substitute for an English flogging. The ordinary offence
for which boys are imprisoned is disorder in class. The
rooms for study are commodious, but they are the boys'
only sitting-rooms. Each boy has a cupboard behind his
sitting place. The *maître d'étude* was in each case sitting at a desk reading a newspaper, but not helping or
answering questions. The whole arrangements reminded us
of some of the more recently-founded English schools, and
the advantage of the comparison was not on the side of the
French. The cleanliness and order of English Catholic
schools, such as that attached to the Oratory at Birmingham, are far superior to anything we have seen in France.

Mr. Arnold admits, with some reluctance, that the
French boy is probably overworked, with ten or eleven
hours given to study and only two to meals and recreation;
but he enters into a defence of gymnastics which is to us
entirely incomprehensible. He apparently believed the
statement of the master of a *pension,* (8) who told him
that when he took his boys on long excursions, 'the
English boys, vigorous at first, knocked up sooner than
his French boys.' This, Mr. Arnold remarks, is the old
reproach of the Latin races against the northern barbarian, that 'he is lusty, and melts and gives way in the
sun.' We would suggest that the Frenchmen are not a
Latin race at all, but are the descendants of those very

Gauls to whom this taunt was applied by the Romans. But
whatever superiority exists in boyhood certainly dis-
appears in after life. If it were not so, the Alpine
Club would long ago have dissolved into non-existence, and
we should see Frenchmen scaling Monte Rosa and the Matter-
horn, and Englishmen riding with parasols up the Montan-
vert. We are told further, that gymnastics do not flourish in our schools because they are too much of a drill
and a lesson, and that the 'young English *pensionnaire* (9)
is easily damped in exercise by a sense of constraint or
rule. The truth is, that gymnastics do flourish where
they have been introduced, but merely as a *pis aller*. (10)
The English boy has so much to do that is better for him.
But what can show more complete subjection to rule than
the training of a Harrow boy for the Eleven, or of an Eton
boy for the Eight? They both require a perseverance,
industry, and a surrender of individual will to corporate
action far more than in gymnastics. Mr. Arnold, we suppose, would reply that it is the 'Celtic element' in a
school that secures the victory at Henley or at Lord's.
He says 'that long school-hours are inevitable results of
placing large boarding-schools in the hearts of large
cities,' as if the boys of Westminster and Charterhouse
were not full partakers of our English games, and that 'a
body of professors, such as the Lycées of Paris are proud,
and justly proud of possessing, is hardly to be obtained
out of a large city,' a statement which, with the example
of Göttingen, Tübingen, Bonn and Leyden before our eyes,
appears the culmination of absurdity. Is the standard of
Charterhouse masters likely to be lowered when the school
is moved into the country? Mr. Arnold blinks the real
reason why the recreations of a French school are like
everything else, arranged by rule and programme. It is
the necessity of never-ending surveillance. The fundamental theory of a French Lycée is, that a boy is never
to be left unwatched for a single instant day or night;
and this, we are bound to admit, is most faithfully and
completely carried out. This is of itself destructive of
any free and manly exercise, and it is useless to search
about for any more subtle or recondite reason. The
French boy when he is come to manhood envies and tries to
emulate the pursuits of Englishmen. But he copies that
which is worst in them, the glittering form and the
extravagant dissipation of sport, instead of the vigorous
core which underlies the evil. In Italy the summer is
too hot, and in Russia the winter too cold, to adopt the
bracing practice of English games. France has no such
excuse, and we are happy to think that all M. Duruy's
reforms are tending gradually to implant a spirit of

self-reliance and self-government in French schoolboys.
There follows in Mr. Arnold's pages a statement so
entirely without foundation, and so opposed to what we
believe to be the truth, that we cannot imagine the
authority on which he makes it: -

> The French Lycées, however, are guiltless of one pre-
> posterous violation of the laws of life and health
> committed by our own great schools, which have of late
> years thrown open to competitive examination all the
> places on their foundations. The French have plenty
> of examinations, but they put them almost entirely at
> the right age for examinations - between the years of
> fifteen and twenty-five, when the candidate is neither
> too old nor too young to be examined with advantage.
> To put upon little boys of nine or ten the pressure of
> a competitive examination for an object of the greatest
> value to their parents, is to offer a premium for the
> violation of Nature's elementary laws, and to sacri-
> fice, as in the poor geese fatted for Strasburg pies,
> the due development of all the organs of life to the
> premature hypertrophy of one....

If any proof were wanting, this paragraph would be
enough to show Mr. Arnold's entire unfitness for the task
to which he has been set. It misstates the practice of
the English schools, it entirely misconceives the results
of that practice, and it shows a complete ignorance of
the kind of pressure by which French boys are made to
work. As the foundation scholarships of Charterhouse and
Christ's Hospital are still supplied by private patronage,
Mr. Arnold can only refer to the practice of Eton and
Winchester. Thirty years ago these great foundations
were nearly useless. Admission was granted by nomination.
A boy, entered a colleger at Eton at nine years old,
would go of due course to King's College without examination, would obtain his fellowship after three years' pro-
bation, and be provided for for life. Even these advantages were not enough to attract candidates. The seventy
scholarships at Eton remained unfilled, and King's College occupied one of the lowest places in the University.
Now there is a keen competition for every scholarship at
Eton: there are eighty candidates for ten vacancies, and
the honours gained by King's men in the schools surpasses
in number those of any other college in the University.
This has been entirely the result of throwing open the
scholarships to public competition.

Mr. Arnold goes on to say that the bursarships in Lycées
are given on the ground of poverty; and he wishes the
commission to remark how we suffer from the 'feudal and
incoherent organisation of our society,' and how we
gratify 'an ignorant public's love of claptrap' by throwing everything open to competition. Such a public ought
to be gratified with Mr. Arnold's Blue Book. We would
only answer that at Eton College very valuable exhibitions
and scholarships are given in precisely the manner of
which Mr. Arnold approves; but that the Public School Commissioners, who have at least as much 'special acquaintance with educational matters' as Mr. Arnold, recommend
strongly that they should all be awarded by competitive
examinations.

After a description of Vanves, which is situated in the
country, and which is, we hope, the type of the Lycées of
the future, we have a statement of the expense of French
education. This, if not carefully read, is apt to mis-
lead. There is no doubt that for boys who board at home
France, Germany, and Switzerland offer a very admirable
education at a very low rate. It is a disgrace that England does not do the same, and her first effort in educational reform should be directed to this end. But, for
boarders who live at the schools, French education is at
least as expensive as our own.

Mr. Arnold passes by Sainte Barbe with a slight mention,
as if it were merely a boarding-house for the supply of
the Lycée Louis le Grand. It is in fact the school which
best deserves the name of a 'French Eton.' It was founded in the middle of the fifteenth century, and its history, which has been written by M. Quicherat, is the history of secondary education in France. It has a distinguished set of professors: *esprit de corps* among old
Barbistes is stronger than at any other French College,
and the firmness of its *proviseur* saved the cause of
classical studies during the first Empire. As a private
institution it is a formidable rival to the establishments for education provided by the State.

Then follows a description of the communal college at
Boulogne. At the end of it we are told that the degree
of Licentiate means more than an Oxford or Cambridge
degree of Master of Arts, for which there is no examination; which is only true if we admit that the inferior
degree of Bachelier is equal to our Bachelor of Arts.
The degree of Bachelier is given to boys when they leave
the Lycée, and is merely a certificate of proficiency in
school studies. A Master of Arts must have matriculated

at a college, and have submitted to a full course of college and university teaching. 'But I should like to see,'
says Mr. Arnold, 'in any one of our considerable towns
over against Boulogne - Dover, Ramsgate, Canterbury - a
public school with a staff of thirteen functionaries holding degrees, literary or scientific, from the Universities
of Oxford, Cambridge, or London.' We do not as a rule
place public schools in considerable towns, but Mr. Arnold
may see what he wishes at Canterbury or at Brighton, Lan-
cing and Hurstpierpoint. After an account of the Jesuit
school at Vaugirard, which is one of the best and most
interesting in the neighbourhood of Paris, Mr. Arnold
remarks that the 'cosmopolitan character of France is well
shown by the number of boys from different parts of the
world whom one finds getting their education in her
schools.' Mr. Arnold would find just the same in England.
There is a considerable American colony at Rugby. Our
public schools do not receive Roman Catholics, but Oscott,
Birmingham, and Salt Hill, have pupils from every nation
in Europe. We have found that French education is generally distrusted and disliked upon the Continent, although,
from its method and regularity, it is very easy to imitate.

We are next informed that the 'modern spirit,' whatever
that may be, has 'irrevocably doomed flogging as a school
punishment.' We are not told whether the same spirit
tolerates imprisonment, which is the *dernier ressort* (11)
in French schools. 'The employment of punishments is
however certainly less than with us.' It would be difficult to collect statistics, but we should very much doubt
the truth of this assertion; and the greater number of
school hours must tend rather to increase than diminish
the occasions of punishment. Mr. Arnold remarks on the
waste of time in class. This is the necessary result of
French disciplinary arrangements. The boys must all be in
class at the same time, and there can be no repetition and
looking over exercises, as with us, while the rest of the
class is otherwise employed.

At the end of a short lecture on the rationale of
teaching grammar, in which, as usual, the French are shown
to be right and the English wrong, we are told that 'with
all the faults of the old Latin grammar twenty years ago,
boys of twelve and thirteen did their grammar work a
thousand times better than they do it now.' How can Mr.
Arnold know anything about it? The old Eton grammars
were full of mistakes and absurdities, which a boy learned
by heart that he might avoid them in practice. Ὅποταν,
(12) we learnt in our youth, 'gaudet optativo:' (13) a
remarkable instance of self-denial, our master pointed out
to us, because, although it delighted in the society of

that word, it was never by any chance seen in its company.
   Mr. Arnold concludes his account of French education by
a description of the *instruction supérieure*, (14) into
which we will not follow him. We would ask those who do,
to read as a corrective the articles of M. Renan on the
same subject, which have lately been republished in a
separate volume. We are very glad to have come to the
end of our criticisms, because with a great deal which is
contained in the rest of Mr. Arnold's Report we cordially
agree. His concluding advice is well worth reading. He
points out with justice that the countries he visited –
France, Italy, Germany, Switzerland, and he might have
added Austria – consider National Education as an important duty of the State, and that England apparently does
not. A better time seems to be approaching. The addresses of candidates for the new Parliament are full of Education, and the appointment of a Minister for that service
will be the work of any party that comes into power. But
there are two principles on which National Education may
be based. The one pays especial regard to the individual;
it considers its great aim the development of character;
it rejoices in diversity, and cheerfully sacrifices
method and order to the vigour of spontaneous enterprise
and devotion. We imagined that this policy has been advocated by all the friends of culture from Goethe and W. von
Humboldt down to Mr. Arnold himself. The other makes discipline and obedience the test of efficiency; it surren-
ders the individual to the majority. Instead of following
and interrogating Nature in the hidden processes by which
she developes the mind of man, it establishes an undeviating rule by which all intellects are supposed to grow.
It delights in programmes, and is great on paper; it can
be worked by any one, and is capable of indefinite extension. It is naturally a favourite with those Governments
who fear the force of free intellect, or who are anxious
that all the splendour of the national mind should appear
to radiate from their thrones. The one method is English,
and the other is French; liberty is just as impossible
with the one as it is certain to spring up and grow out of
the other.
   It is most important that we should examine carefully
these travellers' tales of foreign education. Is it,
after all, desirable that the literature and science of a
country should be placed in professors' chairs which are
under the command of a Minister of State? Are not Darwin
and Mill and Grote more entirely free to speculate and to
publish than if they could be dismissed, like Renan, from
the College de France, or like the famous Seven from
Göttingen? 'Professors and mistresses,' said our English

Ernest on that occasion, 'are always to be had for money.'
The multiplicity of German States has secured a freedom to
teaching which will not exist when Germany is one.
Several of the most distinguished German professors have,
to our knowledge, sighed for chairs at Cambridge or Oxford,
where they would be members of a self-governing and independent body.

Education in England wants the help of Parliament, not
to enact courses of uniform study or to establish some
great central and national examination, but to revise sta-
tutes which were drawn up for other times, and to set free
enormous sums of money for legitimate and fruitful uses.
The revenues of Oxford and Cambridge, and the school revenues of every county, would supply an efficient secondary
and superior education for the whole country with no other
contribution from the State. But in this case self-reform
is impossible. The ties and restraints of law can only be
broken by Acts of Parliament; and Parliament, if it acted
blindly or hastily, would do more harm than good. We
arrive, therefore, at the necessity of some responsible
person in Parliament who is to organise and direct its
action in these matters. The Public School Bill - which
is a very small instalment of educational reform - dragged
its slow length along for five years, and was at last de-
spatched with indecent haste because it was nobody's precise business to watch over its passage. To redistribute
the revenues of our Universities, or to pass a series of
measures such as are recommended by the Report to which
Mr. Arnold's volume is an appendix, would at this rate,
take at least a hundred years. Let us hope to see a Minister of Education, with just enough power and just a
sufficient staff, to take care that the property of
schools is on the whole fairly and honestly applied. But
we hope we may never see a Minister à la Française. (15)
We would rather remain barbarians than purchase civilization at such a price. But, whether any action is taken or
none, it is most desirable that we should get a true
notion of our neighbours' institutions; and we caution
everybody from attempting to do so from Mr. Arnold's book.
A Commissioner appointed for this purpose should have a
thorough knowledge of English education with industry and
perseverance enough to penetrate below the surface of
plausible arrangements, and should confine himself to
describing exactly what he sees. But men gifted with the
insight and veracity of De Tocqueville are rare. Perhaps
the best plan is to publish translations of foreigners'
reports upon their own institutions, and to correct them
by examining Englishmen who have been long resident in the
country. Dr. Perry's account of the German universities,

given before Mr. Ewart's Committee, is worth any number of
Commissioners' Reports. Of this we are sure, that any one
who is intimately acquainted with the education of France,
Switzerland, and Germany, and with the best phases of our
public schools, will, without hesitation, award the palm
to England.

Notes

1   'professional preparatory school'.
2   'scholarships'.
3   'proctor'.
4   'teachers'.
5   'There is self-discipline applied to education.'
6   'headmaster'.
7   'Doge's prison'.
8   'boarding-school'.
9   'boarder'.
10   'last resource'.
11   'ultimate motivation'.
12   'Whenever'.
13   'rejoices in the optative'.
14   'higher education'.
15   'French style'.

Culture and Anarchy (1869)

18. FITZJAMES STEPHEN, MR. ARNOLD ON THE MIDDLE CLASSES,
'SATURDAY REVIEW'

10 February 1866, xxi, 161-3

Stephen (see Nos 3 and 6), who was partly responsible for
Arnold's writing My Countrymen, takes his old adversary
to task in this almost Xenophobic review for ignoring
England's strengths and overestimating those of her
rivals. From the time of his review of 'England and the
Italian Question' (1859) Stephen had been appalled by
what he thought was Arnold's political blindness. Here,
without his usual pretence of courtesy, he joins 'The
Times' and 'The Telegraph' in attack. We have omitted a
long middle part of Stephen's article, which deals in more
detail with Arnold's specific points.

The last number of the 'Cornhill Magazine' contains one
of those odd articles which Mr. Matthew Arnold so much
delights in writing. It is called My Countrymen, and is
written apparently in order to teach that degraded part
of creation, the British middle classes, what the intelligent foreigners think about them. The article begins
by referring to some advice which we had the honour of
tendering to Mr. Arnold about a year ago, on the impropriety of describing the whole English nation as a parcel
of miserable Philistines, destitute of all the higher
mental gifts, and especially of a certain quasi-divine
power of understanding and believing in ideas which it
appears belongs exclusively to the French. Mr. Arnold

was struck, he tells us, by this article. It made him
'make a serious return on himself,' and he resolved never
to call his countrymen Philistines again till he had
thought more about it. In the course of his meditations,
he found that other people besides the 'Saturday Review'
were opposed to him. In the face of Mr. Bazley, the member for Manchester, the 'Nonconformist,' the 'Daily News,'
and the 'Daily Telegraph,' by all of which authorities he
was contradicted, he found it impossible to persist in his
old accusations. He decided that he would never call his
countrymen Philistines any more, and he recorded his resolution in a beautiful and appropriate Scriptural quota-
tion. 'He that is unjust let him be unjust still, and he
that is filthy let him be filthy still, and he that is
righteous let him be righteous still, and he that is holy
let him be holy still.' We should be sorry to suggest
that Mr. Arnold has broken his good resolutions by describing the unfortunate Philistines as unjust and filthy,
but it appears to us that he thinks there are few just
men, and not many clean beasts, on this side of the British Channel. His way of conveying his impression as to
the 'filthiness' of the unclean animals who ought to rush
violently down the cliffs at Dover and Brighton is by
repeating the views taken by (possibly ideal) foreigners
of our national character, and communicated to him during
a foreign tour of some months which he lately made upon
public business. He shows us what a terrible opinion our
foreign friends have formed of us, and he tells us by
implication that we may or may not be Philistines, but
that foreigners consider us as such, and that, in his own
opinion, they have much the best of the argument. It is
worth while to state the arguments of his foreign friends,
and to say just a few words on them. It may be true that
we care too little what foreigners think about us, and,
whatever else may be said of Mr. Arnold, no one will deny
that few people can be better qualified to repeat in a
pleasant half-foreign style the commonplaces about England
and things English which happen to be current for the
moment amongst literary foreigners.

It is hardly worth while to write seriously upon such a
subject, and yet the greatness of the nation to which we
belong is a topic on which the coldest of cold Englishmen
can hardly write merely in the tone of banter, however
trifling may be the occasion which leads him to treat it.
Amongst thirty millions of men and women there will of
course be found a vast mass of dull, commonplace, stupid
people, whose lives must look to bystanders, whether

countrymen or not, drearier than they really are. If such
persons are free, and accustomed as such to speak their
minds on all sorts of subjects with perfect openness, they
will no doubt talk a vast deal of nonsense, and lay themselves open to any quantity of criticism. There are,
moreover, real faults in the English character, and some
of them are in a rough way caricatured by Mr. Arnold's
foreign friends; but if any one seriously doubts whether
England is a great nation and is doing a great work in
the world, let him look, not at the position which our
country may hold for the time being in the opinion of
foreign diplomatists, or at the phrases which happen to
be fashionable in French or German society about our
middle class (of which they know considerably less than
they know about the feelings of polar bears and walruses),
but at a few broad facts.

England is the only great European country which enjoys
political freedom to its full extent, and has succeeded in
reducing it to a practical shape. The prospects of political freedom all over Europe depend largely on its success and permanence in England.

England is the only great country in which the religious controversies of the day, controversies deeper and
more important than those which caused the Reformation,
have taken a practical form, and are likely to lead to
definite practical results. What in France and Germany
is confined to a small class of learned men is coming to
be preached on the housetops in England to a people slow
to be convinced, but apt to be much in earnest in acting
on their convictions.

England governs with absolute power 150,000,000 of
people in India. The English Government there is labour-
ing honestly and vigorously to use its power for the good
of those millions, and to lead them on to changes, political, moral, and religious, hardly exemplified before in
the history of any part of the world.

England exercises a qualified and ill-defined supremacy
over Canada, South Africa, Australia, New Zealand, and
various other places of less importance. These regions
will be the homes of many millions of English people in
another century and their fortunes may be influenced most
deeply, for good or evil, by English legislation and
English thought.

Look well at these four facts, think what they mean,
try for a moment to take their measure, and then ask
whether it is worth while to give even a passing thought
to the opinion which the Prussians may form of our attitude in the Danish question. Think, too, for a moment of
the intense and varied energy with which millions of men

are working out different bits of one or more of these
vast problems. Remember that every ship loaded by the
despised shopkeeper, every order taken by the vulgarest
traveller, every article written in a penny paper, every
vote given by a 10*l.* householder, goes to make up the
vast whole which constitutes the action of England on the
world; and if you still sneer at the general result, and
still fail to see the lines of greatness and majesty
through the dust and sweat and noise and turmoil which
obscure what they develop, you despise human life itself.
There are those who think otherwise, and who would prefer
to grind in such a mill, ever so roughly, ever so
coarsely, ever so meanly, all the days of their life, to
the most aesthetic form of dawdling that could be invented by a joint committee from all the *cafés* and theatres
between the Mediterranean and the Baltic.

19. UNSIGNED ARTICLE, 'MORNING STAR'

28 June 1867, 4

The 'Star', which drew so many of Arnold's ironic barbs
(and gave as much as it took), was the organ of John
Bright and the Manchester School. Samuel Lucas (1811-65)
was its first editor (1856). Before being incorporated
into the 'Daily News' in 1869, the 'Star' rivalled the
'Daily Telegraph' as one of the most popular daily papers.
This review of Culture and its Enemies begins mildly, but
in its defence of Bright and its impatience with Arnold,
its language becomes stronger. 'To be a man of culture
... is to be a small, pedantic Tory prig....'

Mr. Matthew Arnold is a writer for whom we must all have a
high respect. Few of us there are who have not derived
pleasure and profit from his works. He is one of the few
living Englishmen who can properly be called critics in
the broader and truer sense which other countries give to
that word. He is an original and a penetrating thinker -
one who knows realities generally, and can distinguish
them from mere names or shadow or shams. Were it but as
the satirist and denouncer of Philistinism, he deserves
the gratitude of all rational Englishmen of our day. We

are the more sorry, therefore, to see Mr. ARNOLD lately
allowing himself to be ruled and ridden by one of his
intellectual weaknesses - especially sorry when this leads
him, as it appears to have done, into giving indirectly
his endorsement and authority to one of the silliest and
most contemptible cants of our day. The 'Cornhill Magazine,' just published, contains an essay by Mr. ARNOLD,
entitled Culture and its Enemies. This essay, it appears,
was originally delivered 'as Mr. ARNOLD's last lecture in
the Poetry Chair at Oxford,' and the readers of the 'Cornhill' are informed that 'it has been thought advisable,
under the circumstances, to print it as it was delivered.'

     The lecture, or essay, is in substance a vindication of
what Mr. ARNOLD very properly calls 'culture' against persons whom he accuses of being the enemies of it. Now, the
enemies of culture, according to Mr. ARNOLD, are first and
foremost Mr. BRIGHT, and Mr. FREDERIC HARRISON, and indirectly 'men like COMTE, or the 'late Mr. BUCKLE, or Mr.
MILL;' and judging by one passage in which Mr. ARNOLD is
very severe on a certain famous line adopted as the motto
of a London newspaper, even EDMUND BURKE as well. Perhaps, having thus summed up the enemies of culture, one
might, perhaps, safely leave Mr. ARNOLD's complaints to
answer themselves. If these be culture's enemies, most
people will naturally exclaim, tell us who on earth are
its friends - or tell us what sort of thing you define
the culture to be to which such men are hostile? But it
is fair to say that Mr. ARNOLD accuses MILL and COMTE of
being enemies of culture only inasmuch as they are 'men
of a system, disciples of a school,' and leaves us to
infer that all such persons are naturally and inevitably
opposed to culture, and to infer of course likewise that
ARISTOTLE and PLATO stood in a similar position. It is
right to say, too, that when Mr. ARNOLD falls foul of
some words of BURKE's, he does not appear to know, or at
least to remember, that the words are BURKE's; and he,
therefore, is not to be understood as deliberately ranking
the best educated man of his age as a deadly foe to culture. The great enemies to culture are, in Mr. ARNOLD's
eyes, Mr. BRIGHT and Mr. FREDERIC HARRISON; and it is
about these gentlemen and their supposed opinions that he
has talked and written an essay which is founded from
beginning to end on the most absurd and obvious misconception, and which echoes here and there some nonsensical
sneers which we had supposed until yesterday were always
regarded by thinking men as the exclusive property of
blockheads, the distinguishing mark of cads, and consequently the peculiar delight of small Tory scribblers.

     Mr. ARNOLD begins his dissertation by stating that 'in

203 Arnold, Prose Writings: The Critical Heritage

one of his speeches last year, or the year before last,
that famous Liberal, Mr. BRIGHT, took occasion to have a
fling at the friends and preachers of culture.' Mr.
BRIGHT, according to Mr. ARNOLD, spoke contemptuously of
'people who talk about what they call culture - by which
they mean a smattering of the two dead languages of Greek
and Latin.' On this sentence, which may be taken as the
keynote of Mr. ARNOLD's whole essay, is founded a long
elaborate argumentation, the object of which is to show
that culture is a good thing and that Mr. BRIGHT is wrong
in disparaging it. Now we should just like to ask, is
there to be found any educated Englishman alive who would
not speak contemptuously of people whose sole notion of
culture is a smattering of Greek and Latin? Does Mr.
ARNOLD mean to tell us that he does not feel a contempt
for all such persons? Does he mean to say that he seriously thinks a smattering of Greek and Latin constitutes
culture? Of course he does not; and, indeed, one leading
purpose of his essay is to show that nothing less than an
absolute striving after perfection constitutes culture.
Mr. ARNOLD, in fact, understands culture to be exactly
what GOETHE would have described it, and his intellectual
peculiarities being (of course, in a very small way)
somewhat like those of GOETHE, he falls into the mistake
which was the great German's chief error, of supposing
that robust political energy has something in it which is
naturally rather hostile to culture. Of course, nobody
objects to Mr. ARNOLD's developing any such philosophical
theory if it attracts him; but it is a very serious error
indeed, when such a man chooses to put on the words of a
great orator and statesman a meaning which they obviously
and avowedly do not bear, and out of this absurd misconception creates opportunities for the exhibition of a very
small, sneering, and unworthy style of criticism. We do
not know what speech of Mr. BRIGHT Mr. ARNOLD alludes to -
indeed, our anti-Philistine philosopher does not appear to
know himself, but we venture to assert that in no speech
made last year, or the year before last, or any other year,
has Mr. BRIGHT ever said one single word in disparagement
of true 'culture.'
    Doubtless Mr. BRIGHT is, as Mr. FREDERIC HARRISON
acknowledges himself to be, and as we think all sensible
and educated men are, sick of the cant about culture in
politics. Has Mr. ARNOLD lived so much out of the world
of political literature that he does not know what culture
means when the word is used as the slang phrase of those
who have lately made it odious and contemptible to all
intelligent ears? He would never, we think, have prepared
this long essay if he had known what sort of thing that

was which, misnamed 'culture,' is the boast of small
Tories, and which provokes the just contempt of thinking
men. To be a man of culture, then, in the modern and
slangy sense - we explain for Mr. ARNOLD's instruction -
is to be a small, pedantic Tory prig who, knowing very
little Latin and less Greek, is proud of declaring that
he knows and wants to know nothing else. Among these
self-styled men of culture we do not believe there is one
single scholar, even in their own narrow sense of the
word, which avowedly restricts scholarship to a knowledge
of Greek and Latin and ostentatiously repudiates all concern with the treasures of modern discovery, the development of science, the literature of modern languages. A
man of culture in this sense is to a scholar what an
Elizabethan Euphuist was to one who spoke the English of
SHAKSPEARE; what the vapid jargon of the *precieuses* was to
the nervous, noble style of MOLIERE; what a shallow,
self-conceited pedant, in fact, always is to a man of true
education and thought. Does Mr. ARNOLD mean to tell us
that he is for that sort of culture? If he is, then
indeed him have Mr. BRIGHT and Mr. HARRISON offended. If
he is not, then his philosophy and his invective have in
this instance gone for nothing; he has been speaking, and
writing, and publishing on a preposterous misconception,
and his attack on Mr. BRIGHT only reminds one of the
famous story of 'Capers, not Anchovies,' which THACKERAY
told so well. We cannot but be sorry to see Mr. ARNOLD
even for the moment in the society of the pedants and the
prigs, and we cannot but blame him for the thoughtless-
ness with which he allowed himself to blunder into such
uncongenial and humiliating companionship.

20. EDWARD MIALL (?) UNSIGNED ARTICLE, 'NONCONFORMIST'

10 July 1867, xxviii, 557-8

Edward Miall (1809-81), who gave his name to Arnold's
'Mialism' (as John Stuart Mill gave his to 'Millism'),
was a prominent Dissenter, a Member of Parliament, and
the editor of the 'Nonconformist'. Arnold was right
about the narrowness of Miall's views: 'Apart from the
question of disestablishment', writes the 'D.N.B.' biographer, 'Miall had few interests, and sought few distractions.' Miall's tone in this piece begins with a

kind of reserve and moderation, but it becomes shrill
towards the end. Understandably, Miall (like many
writers) wonders how Arnold's critical canons allow him
the unremitting attacks on his adversaries - especially
the Dissenters. Miall also points to Arnold's favourite,
Burke, as the source of the 'Nonconformist's' motto:
'the Dissidence of Dissent and the Protestantism of the
Protestant Religion'.

In the July number of the 'Cornhill Magazine' there is a
paper by Mr. Matthew Arnold, headed Culture and its
Enemies, his last lecture, as he informs us in a foot-
note, in the Poetry Chair at Oxford. Like most of Mr.
Arnold's writings, it is well worth reading. The idea it
is intended to set forth is not, indeed, a new one. It
is but an expansion and adaptation of the lines of Ovid
which the Eton Latin Grammar has pushed into the popularity of a proverb -

Ingenuas didicisse fideliter artes,
Emollit mores, nec sinit [esse] feros, (1)

the last word of which the late Professor of Poetry would,
no doubt, translate, 'Philistines.' Culture, he tells us,
in his own vivacious style, implies not 'a frivolous and
unedifying activity' of the intellectual powers, 'not
solely the scientific passion.' It 'consists in being
something rather than having something, in an inward condition of the mind and spirit, not in an outward set of
circumstances,' and produces, in the language of Swift,
'the two noblest things, *sweetness and light.*' Mr.
Arnold, in working out this idea, aims a severe blow at
our unworthy selves. We cannot give our readers an adequate impression of its force without extracting the
whole paragraph.

The impulse of the English race towards moral
development and self-conquest has nowhere so
powerfully manifested itself as in Puritanism;
nowhere has Puritanism found so adequate an
expression as in the religious organisation of
the Independents. The modern Independents have
a newspaper, the 'Nonconformist,' written with
great sincerity and ability, which serves as
their organ, the motto, the standard, the
profession of faith which this organ of theirs
carries aloft, is: 'The dissidence of Dissent

and the Protestantism of the Protestant religion.'
There is sweetness and light, and an ideal of
complete harmonious human perfection! One need
not go to culture and poetry to find language
to judge it. Religion, with its instinct for
perfection, supplies language to judge it:
'Finally, be of one mind, united in feeling.'
says St. Peter. There is an ideal which judges
the Puritan ideal!

Now, we are not about to contest Mr. Arnold's theory of
culture, which, however, as he uses it, is just another
word for true Christianity. He is quite right in deplor-
ing the one-sided culture of Puritanism; there is some
truth - more than we can take pleasure in confessing - in
what he says about modern religious organisations. Nor
are we about to claim for the 'Nonconformist' higher
credit than it may be found to deserve, but we submit
that the sentence passed upon us is unfair, and that it
expresses a judgment based upon a very hasty examination,
if not upon a contemptuous refusal of any examination at
all, of the evidence upon which it should have been
founded. We do not blame Mr. Arnold for not including
this paper among those which he reads, but we cannot hold
him justified, in the absence of all knowledge respecting
it, in jumping to extreme conclusions on what it suits
his purpose to hold up to scorn.
    We feel it our duty to relieve the Independents of all
responsibility for the shortcomings of this journal. Mr.
Arnold, speaking to his class at Oxford, and through the
'Cornhill Magazine' to the literary world, has been content to make his statement on hearsay. The 'Nonconformist' never was an organ of the Independents - never was
an organ of any religious organisation whatever - never
displayed any great concern to uphold any of them as
such, or their theological tenets, or their ecclesiastical discipline, or their modes of perpetuating themselves.
It has always been free. It never knew any committee of
management, and its editor alone is answerable to the
public for what may appear in its columns. It is unjust
to saddle the community of Independents with faults which
are exclusively ours. It is an illustration neither of
'sweetness' nor of 'light,' to brand them with the mark
of reprobation which, if deserved at all, is deserved
only by a single individual whose course has never very
closely identified him with the denominational specialities of any religious body.
    But out 'motto,' our 'standard,' our 'profession of
faith' - 'the dissidence of Dissent, and the Protestantism

of the Protestant religion.' Well, this sentence from
Burke, selected about twenty-six years ago, expressed
then, as it now expresses, not the totality of our faith,
described not the range of our sympathies, but exhibited
in as few words as could be choosen, the heart of our
purpose. That purpose was twofold - to deliver religious
life as embodied in the churches from the overruling and
corrupting influence of Civil Governments, and to uphold
the rights of private judgment against sacerdotal tyranny
- to replace religious thought, feeling, and action, upon
the law of love, and to free the mind from the domination
of usurped authority - in fact, to secure the conditions
which are indispensable to 'sweetness and light.' We commenced this journal with no other object in view, and at a
time when compromise of principle in regard to both Erast-
ianism and priestism was far more common than it is now.
Our motto was intended to 'hold aloft' our intention that
our enterprise should be grounded, not on minor or sectarian differences, but on broad, fundamental, and catholic
truths, and upon these, not in their accidental forms, but
in their spiritual essence. If Mr. Arnold had been well
acquainted with this paper, he would not have character-
ised it as he has done, nor would he have held up to the
contempt of men utterly ignorant of its general tenour,
the life imaged by it, as 'a life of jealousy of the
Establishment, disputes, tea-meetings, sermons.' He has
not done justice to his assumed office - there is neither
'culture nor poetry' in magnifying trivial blemishes, if
so he regards them, into a full-sized portrait of the
kind of intellectual and religious life reflected in this
paper, especially as in doing us this wrong, hap-hazard,
in quarters where he knew it could never be set right by
us, but where it could stamp us at once as wholly unworthy
of exercising the smallest influence.

'A life of jealousy of the Establishment'! Why of *jealousy*? Why find for us, and for those whom he incorrectly
supposes us to represent, the meanest motive which can
prompt public effort? Why not rather say a life of undying hostility to what in its very nature and purpose is
destructive of 'sweetness and light,' and 'the ideal of
human perfection complete on all sides'? Does Mr. Arnold
mean to imply that the State organisation of religious
life is such an example of beauty and harmony and all-
sidedness, as renders enmity to it a proof in itself of
a narrow and inadequate ideal? What have we battled
against for this last quarter of a century? Against
'doing unto others as we would they should do to us'?
Against religious liberality, zeal, generosity, magnanimity, gentleness, charity? Against culture and the means

of it, free inquiry of thought, of utterance, of combination, of action? What have we battled *for*? Exclusiveness, intolerance, monopoly, or priestly assumption? No -
we challenge the verdict of our readers on this head. We
have not asked to shut any one of the Universities, not
insisted upon sectarian education, nor desired to compel
others to support our religious organisations, nor been
jealous of the intrusion of other than our own clergy
into parochial burying places, nor cast contempt upon
other's right to teach Christianity, nor advocated tests,
nor infringed upon the sacredness of social life. We have
left these things to the Establishment, and to its hierarchy, clergy, and abettors. We have set our faces
against these things, and against the enlisting of the
civil power to do these things - and it is all set down
to 'jealousy of the Establishment,' by criticism 'speaking a language not to be sophisticated.' 'Sweetness and
light,' forsooth - we should like to be informed how they
can be diffused under a system which is professedly jealous of all others, and which is so insinuating in its
influence as to pervert even 'men of culture and poetry'
into winking at its selfish sectarianism, and into
attributing to it those whose heart's desire is to put an
end to it?

If Nonconformists are narrow and inadequate in their
ideal of human perfection - if they do not attach sufficient importance to culture and poetry - it ill becomes
an Oxford Professor, lecturing at Oxford, to tax them with
their deficiency. For two hundred years they have been
shut out from that University by the exclusive and jealous
spirit of the Establishment, and from whatever sweetness
and light it is supposed to diffuse. Why select the victims of its meanness and intolerance as an illustration of
one-sidedness, when the cruel monopolist to whose injustice it should be attributed is suffered to escape? Why
ridicule the stunted proportions and deformities which
have been the result of hard usage, and not rather de-
nounce the narrow and inadequate ideals of the Establishment which deliberately and persistently inflicted them?
Man of culture and poetry as Mr. Matthew Arnold is, he has
not showed himself free from the vice of the system in
connection with which he was trained. His sympathies are
with the oppressor, not the oppressed, or, if it be otherwise, he is so infected with the spirit of the place that
he refrains from 'speaking a language not to be sophisticated.' Seizing upon our motto, misinterpreting our design, caricaturing the scope and drift of our labours, he
stands up in the very presence, as it were, of a religious
life organised on a basis of intolerant sectarianism, and

smites not it, but those who have suffered from it. And
he cannot understand their hostility to it, nor enter
into their indignation, but sets it down to jealousy.
May we not use his own contemptuous sarcasm, and exclaim
in astonishment, 'There is sweetness and light and an
ideal of complete harmonious human perfection'? This is
what men of letters bred up under the perverting influence
of the Establishment are too apt to do. They seldom
rebuke the strong tyrant - they make their sport of the
weak and suffering victim. There is no magnanimity in
hunting down caged animals. Why do they not strike at a
more formidable quarry? They ought at least to know that
a legalised monopoly of intellectual and spiritual advantage and offices is the fiercest enemy of the sweetness
and light which they deem it their special function to
promote, and they ought not to strike down the hand which
is armed to assail it. At any rate, we should have
expected nobler things from Mr. Matthew Arnold.

Note

1 'Faithful study of the liberal arts
   Softens the character and does not allow it to be
      bestial.'

21. HENRY SIDGWICK, THE PROPHET OF CULTURE, 'MACMILLAN'S
MAGAZINE'

August 1867, xvi, 271-80

Henry Sidgwick (1838-1900), the Cambridge philosopher,
was still a young man in his twenties when he wrote this
astute, if overly critical, essay on Arnold. Sidgwick's
critique is a sort of highbrow equivalent of the strictures in the daily press, the difference being that Sidgwick has a trained mind. He discusses the current trend
of signing articles ('We did not ... foresee a Matthew
Arnold') and goes on to discuss what he feels is an
important but dangerous phenomenon, this 'Prophet of
Culture'. For Sidgwick distrusts Arnold as shallow and
elitist, too ready to speak out, too much the intellectual
Pharisee. Arnold was aware of Sidgwick's article and

replied in later essays, though some of Sidgwick's charges
were difficult to counter.

The movement against anonymous writing, in which this
journal some years ago took a part, has received, I think,
an undeniable accession of strength from the development
(then unexpected) of Mr. Matthew Arnold. Some persons
who sympathised on the whole with that movement yet felt
that the case was balanced, and that if it succeeded we
should have sacrificed something that we could not sacrifice without regret. One felt the evils that 'irrespon-
sible reviewers' were continually inflicting on the progress of thought and society: and yet one felt that, in
form and expression, anonymous writing tended to be good
writing. The buoyant confidence of youth was invigorated
and yet sobered by having to sustain the *prestige* of a
well-earned reputation: while the practised weapon of age,
relieved from the restraints of responsibility, was wielded with almost the elasticity of youth. It was thought
we should miss the freedom, the boldness, the reckless
vivacity with which one talented writer after another had
discharged his missiles from behind the common shield of
a coterie of unknown extent, or at least half veiled by a
pseudonym. It was thought that periodical literature
would gain in carefulness, in earnestness, in sincerity,
in real moral influence: but that possibly it might
become just a trifle dull. We did not foresee that the
dashing insolences of 'we-dom' that we should lose would
be more than compensated by the delicate impertinences
of egotism that we should gain. We did not imagine the
new and exquisite literary enjoyment that would be created when a man of genius and ripe thought, perhaps even
elevated by a position of academic dignity, should deliver
profound truths and subtle observations with all the dogmatic authority and self-confidence of a prophet: at
the same time titillating the public by something like the
airs and graces, the playful affectations of a favourite
comedian. We did not, in short, foresee a Matthew Arnold:
and I think it must be allowed that our apprehensions have
been much removed, and our cause much strengthened, by
this new phenomenon.

I have called Mr. Arnold the prophet of culture: I will
not call him an 'elegant Jeremiah,' because he seems to
have been a little annoyed (he who is never annoyed) by
that phrase of the 'Daily Telegraph.' 'Jeremiah!' he exclaims, 'the very Hebrew prophet whose style I admire the
least.' I confess I thought the phrase tolerably

felicitous for a Philistine, from whom one would not expect any very subtle discrimination of the differentiae of
prophets. Nor can I quite determine which Hebrew prophet
Mr. Arnold does most resemble. But it is certainly hard to
compare him to Jeremiah, for Jeremiah is our type of the
lugubrious; whereas there is nothing more striking than
the imperturbable cheerfulness with which Mr. Arnold seems
to sustain himself on the fragment of culture that is left
him, amid the deluge of Philistinism that he sees submerg-
ing our age and country. A prophet however, I gather, Mr.
Arnold does not object to be called; as such I wish to
consider and weigh him; and thus I am led to examine the
lecture with which he has closed his connexion with
Oxford, - the most full, distinct, and complete of the
various utterances in which he has set forth the Gospel of
Culture.

As it will clearly appear in the course of this
article, how highly I admire Mr. Arnold as a writer, I
may say at once, without reserve or qualification, that
this utterance has disappointed me very much. It is not
even so good in style as former essays; it has more of the
mannerism of repeating his own phrases, which, though very
effective up to a certain point, may be carried too far.
But this is a small point: and Mr. Arnold's style, when
most faulty, is very charming. My complaint is, that
though there is much in it beautifully and subtly said,
and many fine glimpses of great truths, it is, as a whole,
ambitious, vague, and perverse. It seems to me over-
ambitious, because it treats of the most profound and
difficult problems of individual and social life with an
airy dogmatism that ignores their depth and difficulty.
And though dogmatic, Mr. Arnold is yet vague; because
when he employs indefinite terms he does not attempt to
limit their indefiniteness, but rather avails himself of
it. Thus he speaks of the relation of culture and religion, and sums it up by saying, that the idea of culture
is destined to 'transform and govern' the idea of religion. Now I do not wish to be pedantic; and I think that
we may discuss culture and religion, and feel that we are
talking about the same social and intellectual facts,
without attempting any rigorous definition of our terms.
But there is one indefiniteness that ought to be avoided.
When we speak of culture and religion in common conversation, we sometimes refer to an ideal state of things and
sometimes to an actual. But if we are appraising, weighing, as it were, these two, one with the other, it is
necessary to know whether it is the ideal or the actual
that we are weighing. When I say ideal, I do not mean
something that is not realized at all by individuals

at present, but something not realized sufficiently to be
much called to mind by the term denoting the general
social fact. I think it clear that Mr. Arnold, when he
speaks of culture, is speaking sometimes of an ideal,
sometimes of an actual culture, and does not always know
which. He describes it in one page as 'a study of perfection, moving by the force, not merely or primarily of the
scientific passion for pure knowledge, but of the moral
and social passion for doing good.' A study of this vast
aim, moving with the impetus of this double passion, is
something that does, I hope, exist among us, but to a
limited extent: it is hardly that which has got itself
stamped and recognised as culture. And Mr. Arnold afterwards admits as much. For we might have thought, from
the words I have quoted, that we had in culture, thus
possessed by the passion of doing good, a mighty social
power, continually tending to make 'reason and the will
of God prevail.' But we find that this power only acts
in fine weather. 'It needs times of faith and ardour to
flourish in.' Exactly; it is not itself a spring and
source of faith and ardour. Culture 'believes' in making
reason and the will of God prevail, and will even 'endeavour' to make them prevail, but it must be under very
favourable circumstances. This is rather a languid form
of the passion of doing good; and we feel that we have
passed from the ideal culture, towards which Mr. Arnold
aspires, to the actual culture in which he lives and
moves.

Mr. Arnold afterwards explains to us a little further
how much of the passion for doing good culture involves,
and how it involves it. 'Men are all members of one
great whole, and the sympathy which is in human nature
will not allow one member to be indifferent to the rest,
or to have a perfect welfare independent of the rest.....
The individual is obliged, under pain of being stunted
and enfeebled in his own development if he disobeys, to
carry others along with him in his march towards perfection.' These phrases are true of culture as we know it.
In using them Mr. Arnold assumes implicitly what, perhaps, should have been expressly avowed - that the study
of perfection, as it forms itself in members of the human
race, is naturally and primarily a study of the individual's perfection, and only incidentally and secondarily
a study of the general perfection of humanity. It is so
incidentally and secondarily for the two reasons Mr.
Arnold gives, one internal, and the other external:
first, because it finds sympathy as one element of the
human nature that it desires harmoniously to develop; and
secondly, because the development of one individual is

bound up by the laws of the universe with the development
of at least some other individuals. Still the root of
culture, when examined ethically, is found to be a refined
eudaemonism: in it the social impulse springs out of and
re-enters into the self-regarding, which remains predominant. That is, I think, the way in which the love of
culture is generally developed: an exquisite pleasure is
experienced in refined states of thought and feeling, and
a desire for this pleasure is generated, which may amount
to a passion, and lead to the utmost intellectual and
moral effort. Mr. Arnold may, perhaps, urge (and I would
allow it true in certain cases) that the direct impulse
towards perfection, whether realized in a man's self or
in the world around, may inspire and impassion some minds,
without any consideration of the enjoyment connected with
it. In any case, it must be admitted that the impulse
towards perfection in a man of culture is not practically
limited to himself, but tends to expand in infinitely
increasing circles. It is the wish of culture, taking
ever wider and wider sweeps, to carry the whole race, the
whole universe, harmoniously towards perfection.

   And, if it were possible that all men, under all circumstances, should feel what some men, in some fortunate
spheres, may truly feel - that there is no conflict, no
antagonism, between the full development of the individual and the progress of the world - I should be loth to
hint at any jar or discord in this harmonious movement.
But this paradisaical state of culture is rare. We
dwell in it a little space, and then it vanishes into
the ideal. Life shows us the conflict and the discord:
on one side are the claims of harmonious self-development,
on the other the cries of struggling humanity: we have
hitherto let our sympathies expand along with our other
refined instincts, but now they threaten to sweep us into
regions from which those refined instincts shrink. Not
that harmonious self-development calls on us to *crush* our
sympathies; it asks only that they should be a little re-
pressed, a little kept under: we may become (as Mr. Arnold
delicately words it) philanthropists 'tempered by
renouncement.' There is much useful and important work to
be done, which may be done harmoniously: still we cannot
honestly say that this seems to us the most useful, the
most important work, or what in the interests of the world
is most pressingly entreated and demanded. This latter,
if done at all, must be done as self-sacrifice, not as
self-development. And so we are brought face to face with
the most momentous and profound problem of ethics.

   It is at this point, I think, that the relation of
culture and religion is clearly tested and defined.

Culture (if I have understood and analysed it rightly)
inevitably takes one course. It recognises with a sigh
the limits of self-development, and its first enthusiasm
becomes 'tempered by renouncement.' Religion, of which
the essence is self-sacrifice, inevitably takes the other
course. We see this daily realized in practice: we see
those we know and love, we see the *élite* of humanity in
history and literature, coming to this question, and after
a struggle answering it: going, if they are strong clear
souls, some one way and some the other; if they are
irresolute, vacillating and 'moving in a strange diagonal'
between the two. It is because he ignores this antagonism, which seems to me so clear and undeniable if stated
without the needless and perilous exaggerations which
preachers have used about it, that I have called Mr.
Arnold perverse. A philosopher [Hegel] with whom he is
more familiar than I am speaks, I think, of 'the reconciliation of antagonisms' as the essential feature of the
most important steps in the progress of humanity. I seem
to see profound truth in this conception, and perhaps Mr.
Arnold has intended to realize it. But, in order to reconcile antagonisms, it is needful to probe them to the
bottom; whereas Mr. Arnold skims over them with a lightly-
worn tranquillity that irritates instead of soothing.

Of course we are all continually trying to reconcile
this and other antagonisms, and many persuade themselves
that they have found a reconciliation. The religious man
tells himself that in obeying the instinct of self-
sacrifice he has chosen true culture, and the man of
culture tells himself that by seeking self-development he
is really taking the best course to 'make reason and the
will of God prevail.' But I do not think either is quite
convinced. I think each dimly feels that it is necessary
for the world that the other line of life should be chosen
by some, and each and all look forward with yearning to a
time when circumstances shall have become kinder and more
pliable to our desires, and when the complex impulses of
humanity that we share shall have been chastened and puri-
fied into something more easy to harmonize. And sometimes the human race seems to the eye of enthusiasm so
very near this consummation: it seems that if just a few
simple things were done it would reach it. But these
simple things prove mountains of difficulty; and the end
is far off. I remember saying to a friend once - a man
of deep culture - that his was a 'fair-weather theory of
life.' He answered with much earnestness, 'We mean it to
be fair weather henceforth.' And I hope the skies are
growing clearer every century; but meanwhile there is
much storm and darkness yet, and we want - the world

wants - all the self-sacrifice that religion can stimulate. Culture diffuses 'sweetness and light;' I do not
undervalue these blessings; but religion gives fire and
strength, and the world wants fire and strength even more
than sweetness and light. Mr. Arnold feels this when he
says that culture must 'borrow a devout energy' from
religion; but devout energy, as Dr. Newman somewhere says,
is not to be borrowed. At the same time, I trust that
the ideal of culture and the ideal of religion will continually approach one another: that culture will keep
developing its sympathy, and gain in fire and strength:
that religion will teach that unnecessary self-sacrifice
is folly, and that whatever tends to make life harsh and
gloomy cometh of evil. And if we may allow that the progress of culture is clearly in this direction, surely we
may say the same of religion. Indeed the exegetic arti-
fices by which the Hellenic view of life is introduced
and allowed a place in Christian preaching would sometimes
be almost ludicrous, if they were not touching, and if
they were not, on the whole, such a sign of a hopeful
progress; of progress not as yet, perhaps, very great or
very satisfactory, but still very distinct. I wish Mr.
Arnold had recognised this. I do not think he would then
have said that culture would transform and absorb religion, any more than religion transform and absorb culture.
To me the ultimate and ideal relation of culture and religion is imaged like the union of the golden and silver
sides of the famous shield - each leading to the same
'orbed perfection' of actions and results, but shining
with a diverse splendour in the light of its different
principle.
    Into the difficulties of this question I have barely
entered; but I hope I have shown the inadequacy of Mr.
Arnold's treatment of it. I think we shall be more persuaded of this inadequacy when we have considered how he
conceives of actual religion in the various forms in
which it exists among us. He has but one distinct thing
to say of them, - that they subdue the obvious faults of
our animality. They form a sort of spiritual police:
that is all. He says nothing of the emotional side of
religion; of the infinite and infinitely varied vent which
it gives, in its various forms, for the deepest fountains
of feeling. He says nothing of its intellectual side: of
the indefinite but inevitable questions about the world
and human destiny into which the eternal metaphysical
problems form themselves in minds of rudimentary development; questions needing confident answers, nay, impera-
tively demanding, it seems, from age to age, different
answers: of the actual facts of psychological experience,

216 Arnold, Prose Writings: The Critical Heritage

so strangely mixed up with and expressed in the mere conventional 'jargon' of religion (which he characterizes
with appropriate contempt) - how the moral growth of men
and nations, while profoundly influenced and controlled
by the formulae of traditional religions, is yet obedient
to laws of its own, and in its turn reacts upon and modi-
fies these formulae: of all this Mr. Arnold does not give
a hint. He may say that he is not treating of religions,
but of culture. But it may be replied that he is treating
of the relation of culture to religions; and that a man
ought not to touch cursorily upon such a question, much
less to dogmatize placidly upon it, without showing us
that he has mastered the elements of the problem.

I may, perhaps, illustrate my meaning by referring to
another essayist - one of the very few whom I consider
superior to Mr. Arnold - one who is as strongly attached
to culture as Mr. Arnold himself, and perhaps more passionately, - M. Renan. It will be seen that I am not
going to quote a partisan. From 'my countryman's' judgment of our Protestant organizations I appeal boldly to a
Frenchman and an infidel. Let any one turn to M. Renan's
delicate, tender, sympathetic studies of religious phenomena - I do not refer to the 'Vie de Jésus,' but to a
much superior work, the 'Essais d'Histoire religieuse,' -
he will feel, I think, how coarse, shallow, unapprecia-
tive, is Mr. Arnold's summing up, 'they conquer the more
obvious faults of our animality.' To take one special
point. When Mr. Arnold is harping on the 'dissidence of
Dissent,' I recall the little phrase which M. Renan
throws at the magnificent fabric of Bossuet's attack upon
Protestantism. 'En France,' he says, 'on ne comprend pas
qu'on se divise pour si peu de chose.' (1) M. Renan
knows that ever since the reviving intellect of Europe
was turned upon theology, religious dissidence and varia-
tion has meant religious life and force. Mr. Arnold, of
course, can find texts inculcating unity: how should
unity not be included in the ideal of a religion claiming
to be universal? But Mr. Arnold, as a cultivated man,
has read the New Testament records with the light of
German erudition, and knows how much unity was attained
by the Church in its fresh and fervent youth. Still,
unity is a part of the ideal even of the religion that
came not to send peace, but a sword: let us be grateful
to any one who keeps that in view, who keeps reminding us
of that. But it may be done without sneers. Mr. Arnold
might know (if he would only study them a little more
closely and tenderly) the passionate longing for unity
that may be cherished within small dissident organizations. I am not defending them. I am not saying a word

for separatism against multitudinism. But those who feel
that worship ought to be the true expression of the convictions on which it is based, and out of which it grows,
and that in the present fragmentary state of truth it is
supremely difficult to reconcile unity of worship with
sincerity of conviction; those who know that the struggle
to realize in combination the ideals of truth and peace
in many minds reaches the pitch of agony; will hardly
think that Mr. Arnold's taunt is the less cruel because
it is pointed with a text.

I wish it to be distinctly understood that it is as
judged by his own rules and principles that I venture to
condemn Mr. Arnold's treatment of our actual religions.
He has said that culture in its most limited phase is
curiosity, and I quite sympathise in his effort to vindi-
cate for this word the more exalted meaning that the
French give to it. Even of the ideal culture he considers curiosity (if I understand him rightly) to be the
most essential, though not the noblest, element. Well,
then, I complain that in regard to some of the most
important elements of social life he has so little curiosity; and therefore so thin and superficial an appreciation of them. I do not mean that every cultivated man
ought to have formed for himself a theory of religion.
'Non omnia possumus omnes,' (2) and a man must to some
extent, select the subjects that suit his special faculties. But every man of deep culture ought to have a conception of the importance and intricacy of the religious
problem, a sense of the kind and amount of study that is
required for it, a tact to discriminate worthy and unworthy treatment of it, an instinct which, if he has to
touch on it, will guide him round the lacunae of apprehension that the limits of his nature and leisure have
rendered inevitable. Now this cultivated tact, sense,
instinct (Mr. Arnold could express my meaning for me much
more felicitously than I can for myself) he seems to me
altogether to want on this topic. He seems to me (if so
humble a simile may be pardoned) to judge of religious
organizations as a dog judges of human beings, chiefly by
the scent. One admires in either case the exquisite
development of the organ, but feels that the use of it
for this particular object implies a curious, an almost
ludicrous, limitation of sympathy. When these popular
religions are brought before Mr. Arnold, he is content to
detect their strong odours of Philistinism and vulgarity;
he will not stoop down and look into them; he is not sufficiently interested in their dynamical importance; he
does not care to penetrate the secret of their fire and
strength, and learn the sources and effects of these;

much less does he consider how sweetness and light may be
added without any loss of fire and strength.

This limitation of view in Mr. Arnold seems to me the
more extraordinary, when I compare it with the fervent
language he uses with respect to what is called, *par
excellence*, (3) the Oxford movement. He even half associates himself with the movement - or rather he half associates the movement with himself.

It was directed, he rightly says, against 'Liberalism
as Dr. Newman saw it.' What was this? 'It was,' he
explains, 'the great middle class Liberalism, which had
for the cardinal points of its belief the Reform Bill of
1832 and local self-government in politics; in the social
sphere free trade, unrestricted competition, and the
making of large industrial fortunes; in the religious
sphere the dissidence of Dissent and the Protestantism of
the Protestant religion.' Liberalism to Dr. Newman may
have meant something of all this; but what (as I infer
from the 'Apology') it more especially meant to him was
a much more intelligent force than all these, which Mr.
Arnold omits; and *pour cause*; (4) for it was precisely
that view of the functions of religion and its place in
the social organism in which Mr. Arnold seems at least
complacently to acquiesce. Liberalism, Dr. Newman thought
(and it seems to me true of one phase or side of Liberalism), wished to extend just the languid patronage to religion that Mr. Arnold does. What priesthoods were good for
in the eyes of Liberalism were the functions as I have
said, of spiritual police; and that is all Mr. Arnold
thinks they are good for at present; and even in the
future (unless I misunderstand him), if we want more, he
would have us come to culture. But Dr. Newman knew that
even the existing religions, far as they fell below his
ideal, were good for much more than this; this view of
them seemed to him not only shallow and untrue, but perilous, deadly, soul-destroying; and inasmuch as it commen-
ded itself to intellectual men, and was an intelligent
force, he fought against it, not, I think, with much
sweetness or light, but with a blind, eager, glowing
asperity which, tempered always by humility and candour,
was and is very impressive. Dr. Newman fought for a point
of view which it required culture to appreciate, and
therefore he fought in some sense with culture; but he did
not fight for culture, and to conceive him combating side
by side with Mr. Matthew Arnold is almost comical.

I think, then, that without saying more about religion,
Mr. Arnold might have said truer things about it; and I
think also that without saying less about culture - we
have a strong need of all he can say to recommend it - he

might have shown that he was alive to one or two of its
besetting faults. And some notice of these might have
strengthened his case; for he might have shown that the
faults of culture really arise from lack of culture; and
that more culture, deeper and truer culture, removes them.
I have ventured to hint this in speaking of Mr. Arnold's
tone about religion. What I dislike in it seems to me,
when examined, to be exactly what he calls Philistinism;
just as when he commences his last lecture before a great
university by referring to his petty literary squabbles,
he seems to me guilty of what he calls 'provincialism.' -
And so, again, the attitude that culture often assumes
towards enthusiasm in general seems to spring from narrowness, from imperfection of culture. The fostering care of
culture, and a soft application of sweetness and light,
might do so much for enthusiasm - enthusiasm does so much
want it. Enthusiasm is often a turbid issue of smoke and
sparks. Culture might refine this to a steady glow. It
is melancholy when, instead, it takes to pouring cold
water on it. The worst result is not the natural hissing
and sputtering that ensues, though that cannot be pleasing
to culture or to anything else, but the waste of power
that is the inevitable consequence.

It is wrong to exaggerate the antagonism between enthusiasm and culture; because, in the first place, culture
has an enthusiasm of its own, by virtue of which indeed,
as Mr. Arnold contemplates, it is presently to transcend
and absorb religion. But at present this enthusiasm, so
far from being adequate to this, is hardly sufficient -
is often insufficient - to prevent culture degenerating
into dilettantism. In the second place, culture has an
appreciation of enthusiasm (with the source of which it
has nothing to do), when that enthusiasm is beautiful and
picturesque, or thrilling and sublime, as it often is.
But the enthusiasm must be very picturesque, very sublime;
upon some completed excellence of form culture will rigorously insist. May it not be that culture is short-sighted
and pedantic in the rigour of these demands, and thus
really defeats its own ends, just as it is often liable to
do by purely artistic pedantry and conventionality? If it
had larger and healthier sympathies, it might see beauty in
the stage of becoming (if I may use a German phrase), in
much rough and violent work at which it now shudders. In
pure art culture is always erring on the side of antiquity
- much more in its sympathy with the actual life of men
and society. In some of the most beautiful lines he has
written, Owen Meredith expresses a truth that deserves to
be set in beautiful language:

> I know that all acted time
> By that which succeeds it is ever received
> As calmer, completer, and more sublime,
> Only because it is finished; because
> We only behold the thing it achieved.
> We behold not the thing that it was.
> For while it stands whole and immutable
> In the marble of memory, how can we tell
> What the men that have hewn at the block may have been?
> Their passion is merged in its passionlessness;
> Their strife in its stillness closed for ever;
> Their change upon change in its changelessness;
> In its final achievement their feverish endeavour.

Passion, strife, feverish endeavour - surely in the midst
of these have been produced not only the rough blocks with
which the common world builds, but the jewels with which
culture is adorned. Culture the other day thought Mr.
Garrison a very prosy and uninteresting person, and did
not see why so much fuss should be made about him; but I
should not be surprised if in a hundred years or so he
were found to be poetical and picturesque.

And I will go farther, and plead for interests duller
and vulgarer than any fanaticism.

If any culture really has what Mr. Arnold in his finest
mood calls its noblest element, the passion for propagat-
ing itself, for making itself prevail, then let it learn
'to call nothing common or unclean.' It can only propagate
itself by shedding the light of its sympathy liberally; by
learning to love common people and common things, to feel
common interests. Make people feel that their own poor
life is ever so little beautiful and poetical; then they
will begin to turn and seek after the treasures of beauty
and poetry outside and above it. Pictorial culture is a
little vexed at the success of Mr. Frith's pictures, at
the thousands of pounds he gets, and the thousands of
people that crowd to see them. Now I do not myself admire
Mr. Frith's pictures; but I think he diffuses culture more
than some of his acid critics, and I should like to think
that he got twice as many pounds and spectators. If any
one of these grows eagerly fond of a picture of Mr.
Frith's, then, it seems to me, the infinite path of culture is open to him; I do not see why he should not go on
till he can conscientiously praise the works of Pietro
Perugino. But leaving Mr. Frith (and other painters and
novelists that might be ranked with him), let us consider
a much greater man, Macaulay. Culture has turned up its
nose a little at our latest English classic, and would, I
think, have done so more, but that it is touched and awed

by his wonderful devotion to literature. But Macaulay,
though he loved literature, loved also common people and
common things, and therefore he can make the common people
who live among common things love literature. How Philistinish it is of him to be stirred to eloquence by the
thought of 'the opulent and enlightened states of Italy,
the vast and magnificent cities, the ports, the arsenals,
the villas, the museums, the libraries, the marts filled
with every article of comfort and luxury, the factories
swarming with artizans, the Apennines covered with rich
cultivation up to their very summits, the Po wafting the
harvest of Lombardy to the granaries of Venice, and carrying back the silks of Bengal and the furs of Siberia to
the palaces of Milan.' But the Philistine's heart is
opened by these images; through his heart a way is found to
his taste; he learns how delightful a melodious current of
stirring words may be; and then, when Macaulay asks him to
mourn for 'the wit and the learning and the genius' of
Florence, he does not refuse faintly to mourn; and so Philistinism and culture kiss each other.
   Again, when our greatest living poet 'dips into the
future,' what does he see?

   The heavens fill with commerce, argosies of magic
      sails,
   Pilots of the purple twilight, dropping down with
      costly bales.

Why, it might be the vision of a young general merchant.
I doubt whether anything similar could be found in a
French or German poet (I might except Victor Hugo to
prove the rule): he would not feel the image poetical, and
perhaps if he did, would not dare to say so. The Germans
have in their way immense honesty and breadth of sympathy,
and I like them for it. I like to be made to sympathize
with their middle-class enthusiasm for domestic life and
bread-and-butter. Let us be bold, and make them sympathize with our middle-class affection for commerce and
bustle.
   Ah, I wish I could believe that Mr. Arnold was describing the ideal and not the actual, when he dwells on the
educational, the missionary, function of culture, and says
that its greatest passion is for making sweetness and light
prevail. For I think we might soon be agreed as to how
they may be made to prevail. Religions have been propagated by the sword: but culture cannot be propagated by the
sword, nor by the pen sharpened and wielded like an offensive weapon. Culture, like all spiritual gifts, can only
be propagated by enthusiasm: and by enthusiasm that has got

rid of asperity, that has become sympathetic; that has got
rid of Pharisaism, and become humble. I suppose Mr.
Arnold would hardly deny that in the attitude in which he
shows himself, contemplating the wealthy Philistine
through his eyeglass, he has at least a superficial resemblance to a Pharisee. Let us not be too hard on Pharisaism
of any kind. It is better that religion should be self-
asserting than that it should be crushed and stifled by
rampant worldliness; and where the worship of wealth is
predominant it is perhaps a necessary antagonism that
intellect should be self-asserting. But I cannot see that
intellectual Pharisaism is any less injurious to true culture than religious Pharisaism to true worship; and when a
poet keeps congratulating himself that he is not a Philistine, and pointing out (even exaggerating) all the differences between himself and a Philistine, I ask myself, Where
is the sweetness of culture. For the moment it seems to
have turned sour.

Perhaps what is most disappointing in our culture is
its want of appreciation of the 'sap of progress,' the
creative and active element of things. We all remember
the profound epigram of Agassiz, that the world in dealing
with a new truth passes through three stages: it first
says that it is not true, then that it is contrary to
religion, and finally, that we knew it before. Culture is
raised above the first two stages, but it is apt to dis-
port itself complacently in the third. 'Culture,' we are
told, 'is always assigning to the system-maker and his
system a smaller share in the bent of human destiny than
their friends like.' Quite so: a most useful function:
but culture does this with so much zest that it is continually overdoing it. The system-maker may be compared to a
man who sees that mankind want a house built. He erects a
scaffolding with much unassisted labour, and begins to
build. The scaffolding is often unnecessarily large and
clumsy, and the system-maker is apt to keep it up much
longer than it is needed. Culture looks at the unsightly
structure with contempt, and from time to time kicks over
some useless piece of timber. The house however gets built,
is seen to be serviceable, and culture is soon found bene-
volently diffusing sweetness and light through the apart-
ments. For culture perceives the need of houses; and is
even ready to say in its royal way, 'Let suitable mansions
be prepared; only without this eternal hammering, these
obtrusive stones and timber.' We must not forget, however,
that construction and destruction are treated with equal
impartiality. When a miserable fanatic has knocked down
some social abuse with much peril of life and limb, culture
is good enough to point out to him that he need not have

taken so much trouble: culture had seen the thing was falling; it would soon have fallen of its own accord; the
crash has been unpleasant, and raised a good deal of disagreeable dust.

All this criticism of action is very valuable; but it is
usually given in excess, just because, I think, culture is
a little sore in conscience, is uncomfortably eager to
excuse its own evident incapacity for action. Culture is
always hinting at a convenient season, that rarely seems
to arrive. It is always suggesting one decisive blow that
is to be gracefully given; but it is so difficult to strike
quite harmoniously, and without some derangement of attitude. Hence an instinctive, and, I think, irrational,
discouragement of the action upon which less cultivated
people are meanwhile spending themselves. For what does
action, social action, really mean? It means losing oneself in a mass of disagreeable, hard, mechanical details,
and trying to influence many dull or careless or bigoted
people for the sake of ends that were at first of doubtful
brilliancy, and are continually being dimmed and dwarfed by
the clouds of conflict. Is this the kind of thing to which
human nature is desperately prone, and into which it is
continually rushing with perilous avidity? Mr. Arnold may
say that he does not discourage action, but only asks for
delay, in order that we may act with sufficient knowledge.
This is the eternal excuse of indolence - insufficient
knowledge: still, taken cautiously, the warning is valuable, and we may thank Mr. Arnold for it: we cannot be too
much stimulated to study the laws of the social phenomena
that we wish to modify, in order that 'reason the card' may
be as complete and accurate as possible. But we remember
that we have heard all this before at much length from a
very different sort of prophet. It has been preached to us
by a school small, but energetic (energetic to a degree
that causes Mr. Arnold to scream 'Jacobinism!'): and the
preaching has been not in the name of culture, but in the
name of religion and self-sacrifice.

I do not ask much sympathy for the people of action
from the people of culture: I will show by an example how
much. Paley somewhere, in one of his optimistic expositions of the comfortableness of things, remarks, that if he
is ever inclined to grumble at his taxes, when he gets his
newspaper he feels repaid; he feels that he could not lay
out the money better than in purchasing the spectacle of
all this varied life and bustle. There are more taxes now,
but there are more and bigger newspapers: let us hope that
Paley would still consider the account balanced. Now,
might not Mr. Arnold imbibe a little of this pleasant
spirit? As it is, no one who is doing anything can feel

that Mr. Arnold hearing of it is the least bit more
content to pay his taxes - that is, unless he is doing it
in some supremely graceful and harmonious way.

One cannot think on this subject without recalling the
great man who recommended to philosophy a position very
similar to that now claimed for culture. I wish to give
Mr. Arnold the full benefit of his resemblance to Plato.
But when we look closer at the two positions, the dis-
similarity comes out: they have a very different effect
on our feelings and imagination; and I confess I feel more
sympathy with the melancholy philosopher looking out with
hopeless placidity 'from beneath the shelter of some wall'
on the storms and dust-clouds of blind and selfish conflict, than with a cheerful modern liberal, tempered by
renouncement, shuddering aloof from the rank exhalations
of vulgar enthusiasn, and holding up the pouncet-box of
culture betwixt the wind and his nobility.

To prolong this fault-finding would be neither pleasant
nor profitable. But perhaps many who love culture much -
and respect the enthusiasm of those who love it more - may
be sorry when it is brought into antagonism with things
that are more dear to them even than culture. I think Mr.
Arnold wishes for the reconciliation of antagonisms: I
think that in many respects, with his subtle eloquence,
his breadth of view, and above all his admirable temper,
he is excellently fitted to reconcile antagonisms; and
therefore I am vexed when I find him, in an access of
dilettante humour, doing not a little to exasperate and
exacerbate them, and dropping from the prophet of an ideal
culture into a more or less prejudiced advocate of the
actual.

Notes

1 'In France people don't split up over such a little
   thing.'
2 'Everyone can't do everything'.
3 'pre-eminently'.
4 'for good reason'.

22.   FREDERIC HARRISON, CULTURE: A DIALOGUE, 'FORTNIGHTLY
REVIEW'

November 1867, xi, 603-14

Frederic Harrison (1831-1923) was to become well known, in
the course of a long career, as a legal expert, a historian, and a critic, but he is perhaps best remembered for
his advocacy of Positivism. He was later to suggest that
Arnold had himself been a follower of Comte - without
knowing it. In this early and witty piece for the 'Fortnightly', Harrison borrows Arnold's own Arminius to use
against Arnold, pretending himself to be Arnold's inadequate defender. He says of Arnold's notions of culture:
'a master of style like our teacher may put his own sense
on the word, I suppose?' Since Arnold was often charged
with being a self-styled Socrates, Harrison adds to the
irony of his satire simply by using the dialogue form - a
form that Arnold could not or at least did not employ.
Arnold's response to Harrison was: 'I laughed till I
cried.'

GRAND CHAMBERLAIN (*introducing* ROLAND). See, sir! No
buckles to his shoes!
DUMOURIEZ. Ah, sir! All is lost.

        The sovereign'st thing on earth
    Was parmaceti for an inward bruise.

In the course of my autumn ramble on the Continent it was
my fortune to meet a young gentleman from Prussia, in
whose bright and cultured mind I soon recognised one who
is a great favourite with us. Arminius von Thunder-ten-
dronck. We were soon on easy terms, and he spoke often of
his friends in England, and especially of the brilliant
writer who first made the German known to us here. 'Ah!'
said I, with enthusiasm, 'there is a master of our English tongue, spiritual with true Teutonic *geist*, (1)
radiant as the sunniest wit of France. Admit,' I cried,
'that Heines are of every soil, peculiar or confined to
none.'
    'Yes,' said he frankly, 'I am glad we are agreed on
that; a born poet, a consummate critic. He may yet loosen
the yoke of the Philistine from your necks. But they tell
me of late that he is but playing with the sling of David,

and showing boys and girls how prettily he wields it.
Tell me, do you think that in very truth he hates this
Goliath who oppresses you, and in his soul desires to slay
him?'

'Nay,' said I, with a smile, 'these serener natures
desire neither to hate nor to slay, not even evil itself.
It is unmannerly, to say nothing of the Gospel. Thus much
have I learned to cherish of Sweetness and Light.'

'Well,' replied Arminius, 'but in this same discourse
upon Culture with which my friend so gracefully retired
from his academic chair, in which from report there must
have been fine things as finely said, I am told there were
lurking traces of your superlative dandyism, some of your
flabby religious phrases, your hash of metaphysical old
bones. Was it so indeed, or have they wholly misinformed
me?'

'Indeed they have,' I rejoined warmly, hurt to hear our
first living critic so treated, and feeling that the
Teuton would have been the better had he heard it; 'it was
a discourse of a solemn and even of a devotional kind,
subtle in thought and form, with I know not what of
antique courtliness and classic grace - '

'What your fine ladies call an air of distinction,'
cried he abruptly.

'It might have come,' said I, 'straight from some lost
dialogue of Plato, such the ethereal glance of the idea,
such the lyric charm of words.'

'Yes,' muttered he, with one of his learned quips,
'τὸ κομφὸν καὶ τὸ καινοτομὸν καὶ τὸ ζητητικόν.' (2)

'Culture,' said I, not noticing his interruption, of
which I hardly followed the drift, 'culture is the moral
and social passion for doing good; it is the study and
pursuit of perfection, and this perfection is the growth
and predominance of our humanity proper, as distinguished from our animality. It teaches us to conceive of
perfection as that in which the characters of beauty and
intelligence are both present; which unites the two noblest of things, Sweetness and Light.'

'Good,' said the German, smiling as I warmed over these
beautiful words. 'Well said, and truly said: now you are
coming to the point.'

'Ah,' I replied, 'I thought you would see it aright
before long.'

'Yes,' said he, 'a truth which our great Goethe taught
all his life, and which the small parasitic fry who follow
him have carried abroad far and near. But stay,' cried
he, as if doubting; 'why is all this called culture? I
had not so understood the word in your most mysterious
insular tongue.'

'Well,' said I, rather at a loss, 'because he tells us
it is so.'

'Nay,' said the German, in his arrogant way instructing
me in my own mother tongue. 'I thought your word culture
implied simply the amenities of education, the training of
the taste - *belles lettres*, and aesthetics, in short?'

'True,' I answered, a little piqued by his pertinacity,
'so it does in dictionaries, in common writing, and in
ordinary speech; but a master of style like our teacher
may put his own sense on the word, I suppose?'

'Eh!' said Arminius in his biting way, 'and carp at
those who take it in its usual sense?'

'My friend,' I replied in a deprecating tone, 'you are
in this unjust, and exaggerate the nature of his attack.
He a little misconceived the meaning of his opponents.
Were it not so there would have been no trace of the
slightest irritation.'

'Misconception, attack, irritation!' shouted Arminius,
with his reckless laugh, 'this of your Ithuriel and Ariel
in one! His spear-point dipped in aromatic vinegar, I
suppose! Well, go on,' said he, seeing that I was really
hurt by his rough humour; 'go on with your account of
Sweetness and Light; we seem to be rather wandering from
it at present.'

'Go on?' I replied seriously; 'with what am I to go
on?'

'Why, go on,' retorted the trenchant German, 'and
explain to me, as you have undertaken to do, how this
perfection, this harmonious expression of all the powers
which make the beauty and worth of human nature (to adopt
your own words), how, in short, this same sweetness and
light is to be attained. You have excellently described,
in a vein which indeed recalls to me many a fine bit from
Goethe, and even from Plato, a very noble condition or
state of the soul. We can all describe this state in
words, though not in words so fine as you have chosen.
Let me now ask you to describe the process by which it is
attained.'

'Attained? got at?' said I drearily, for I felt stunned
by this unexpected question.

'Yes,' rejoined he in a resolute tone; 'how is it
got at?' and he waited for my answer.

'I suppose it comes,' said I vaguely.

'But if it does not come,' he retorted.

'Nay,' I rejoined gently, for I was now conscious of my
advantage, 'forgive me, but you are asking too much. We
began by describing (adequately, as you admit) a lofty
state of the soul, the goodness and delights of which
every tunable spirit is in itself apt to understand.

There is no question here of some crabbed system, - it is
no mechanical method, no ambitious philosophy, no syllabus
of universal education, we are revealing. Culture, my
friend, is an inspiration, a glow, an afflatus which
steals into the attuned soul, and into no other. O that
you had heard him dwell on it himself with that well-bred
ardour and in that simple unsystematic way which best
suits his tastes and his powers! You ask too much if you
look to us for a system of philosophy. 'Tis ours but to
cull the finer flowers, to scent out the hidden perfumes,
along the by-paths in the garden of truth;' and I uttered
this with some conscious humility, for I confess that I
was thinking of Montaigne.

'Ah!' said the German brusquely, 'so poodles scent out
truffles. But tell me how to find the truffles without
myself becoming a poodle.'

'Train your soul, then,' I cried with spirit, 'to feel
sweetness and light. Be the καλοκἀγαθός, (3) or if you
are not, listen to one who is! Ah! had you but heard with
what light keen hand he touched the gross hide of our English Philistinism, as it sat squat like a toad beside our
poor dazed countrymen; had you but heard the Olympian
scorn with which he lashed our machinery, our wealth, our
formalism, the hideous and grotesque illusions of our
middle-class liberalism, and Protestantism, and industri-
alism! Is it not something to have one amongst us before
whose touch these creatures cower? Come, tell me, do you
then maintain, love, defend these things?' I said, pushing the German by this home-thrust.

'Softly,' he replied, steadily enough. 'Do you ask if
I, Arminius, love these things? Do I love Philistines or
the friends of Philistines? Come, we are at one after
all. Is not this your Admirable Crichton, my own fast
friend and brother in arms? Do I not admire and follow
him when he girds on his sword, and grieve to see him
lounging with the ineffable haw-haw air of your Rotten
Row? But are we not of one bone, or am I then a Philistine?'

'Forgive me,' I cried - and as I looked into the clear
eyes of the young Teuton I felt that I was doing him a
wrong - 'but you do now see how noble this love of perfection, this culture is; that it is a state of spiritual
health, an equipoise of the living soul, a harmony of its
intellectual and moral faculties?'

'Yes,' he replied, 'admirably put. Plato has not drawn
it better. And now, then, how do you get it? It is very
good to tell me how beautiful this is; but if a physician
tells me only what a beautiful thing health is, how happy
and strong it makes those who possess it, and omits to

tell me how I can gain health, or says only, Be healthy,
desire, seek after health, I call him no physician, but a
quack. So, if I describe in words a very admirable state
of the soul, it matters little what I call it. I might
say this beautiful and god-like state is such and such,
and I call it fiddlestick or sauerkraut, or the like; but
what am I profited unless I learn how this same fiddlestick, or sauerkraut, or culture (call it as you please),
comes to a man? Men of sense care little for names, so
long as they get the thing.'

'Now, are you serious, my friend?' I rejoined, 'that
one who can describe culture and its gifts in words like
those can have left us no clue how to get culture?'

'Well, what is it, then?' said the downright German.

'Why,' replied I earnestly, 'temper your soul to feel
those impulses towards action, help, and beneficence, the
desire for stopping human error, clearing human confusion,
and diminishing the sum of human misery, the noble aspiration to leave the world better and happier than we found
it. Call for more light, more sweetness - '

'Call!' he broke in with his sardonic way; 'call
spirits from the vasty deep; but will they come when thou
dost call them?'

'And then,' I went on, without noticing his jest,
'attune the soul to a state of harmony; let not the least
breath of vulgarity, restlessness, or vehemence disturb
its self-possession; temper it to that spirit of inexhaustible indulgence towards all things good or evil, to
that repose - '

'Which marks the caste of Vere de Vere,' laughed the
incorrigible Prussian.

'Lieber Herr,' said I, determined to be unruffled,
'this is hardly fair. Culture, as I am explaining, is
all this, and more than I have said or can say; and that
because the moral and social passion for doing good, the
noble aspiration to leave the world better, the social
idea, I may say, comes in as part of the grounds of culture, and the main and primary part. So culture, you
must see, includes all these things, and harmonises them.
They are but the raw materials, the elements of culture.'

'The passion for doing good, then,' he said, 'is permitted to come into your conception of culture?'

'Certainly,' I rejoined; 'a most charming ingredient of
it, properly subdued and sweetened.'

'The butter in your omelette!' cried he, with one of
his shocking peals of laughter. 'You have read, I suppose,' he went on presently, 'the letters of your Lord
Chesterfield to his son?'

'Yes,' I replied; 'there was a fine gentleman indeed,

with an inexhaustible indulgence both towards himself and
towards others!'

'Good!' said the Prussian. 'And you remember the passage in which, in the course of a panegyric on breeding,
he breaks forth, or (in fairness to him and to you) I will
say glows forth, into the saying that a Frenchman, who
possesses the cultivated matter habitual to his countrymen, *and at the same time has a fund* of virtue, education,
and good sense, is the first of the human race. Do you
see no risk, now, that the *fund* of virtue, education, and
good sense may become rather an extra in your finishing
academy, and the science of mental deportment may be
unduly developed?'

'I really fail to follow you,' I answered, for I hardly
knew what he would say next. 'Culture, as I am showing
you, includes in itself those valuable gifts and faculties.'

'Good,' said he; 'this talisman, then, this something,
this culture, if that word please you, is a gift yet
better than active beneficence?'

'Surely,' said I; 'for it includes this, and chastens
its sallies by good taste.'

'And it is yet better,' he went on, 'than a passionate
desire for truth?'

'True!' I replied, with some pathos; 'for it belongs to
the heart as much as to the head.'

'And it is yet better than any social philosophy?' said
he.

'Oh!' I answered as humbly as I could say it, 'culture
sits in judgment on all philosophies, social as well as
natural. This is, indeed, its peculiar function and privilege.'

'And it is yet better than religion?' he asked.

'Yes!' I replied, quite boldly; 'it coincides with it,
and passes beyond it. Only, whereas religion is the
voice of the deepest human experience, so culture combines all the voices of human experience, - art, science,
poetry, philosophy, history, as well as religion. Culture,' said I, with enthusiasm, 'is perfection in all
things; in everything it fixes standards of perfection,
and standards which are real. Perfection in all things!
In all things perfection! Ambrosial grace, immortal
calm!'

'And your Seraphic Doctor is willing to teach you all
this?' cried Arminius, almost fiercely.

'Yes,' I replied, suffused with pride as I thought on
my teacher.

'And he knows all this?' shouted the excitable German.

'It would indeed appear so,' said I calmly, enjoying

his manifest confusion.

'Gott im Himmel!' murmured my ungovernable friend; and he was silent, as if musing.

'Ah!' he went on after a long pause, 'I had never yet done justice then wholly to my friend. What a range of gifts - what a mastery of knowledge!' It was now my turn to triumph. 'I have much,' he went on, humbly enough, 'to learn from you. Tell me, now, in this noble aim of diminishing the sum of human misery, you do not rest until you see the sources of the poison subtly pervading our social system? You put trust in your diagnosis of its morbid symtoms?'

'Your language savours of the mechanical,' I replied, with quiet pride; 'but it is surely not we who are content with unintelligent benevolence.'

'Right!' he said; 'then how do you describe the basis of your social philosophy?'

'Remember, my friend,' I rejoined, with a confident smile, 'culture knows nothing so finite as a system.'

'No!' he answered; 'not any system, but you have prin ciples? These principles are of course coherent; they are independent, subordinate, and derivative, I presume?'

I was still silent, and smiled as blandly as was courteous.

'They are derived,' he went on, 'through some definite logical process surely, either from history, or from con- sciousness, or from experiment, or the life? They agree in part or in whole, or they disagree, with the stated principles of known moralists and thinkers? They can be harmonised with other branches of philosophy as a whole, they can be grasped by the student and imparted to the disciple. Your principles are of this sort, I suppose?' said he, puzzled by my continued silence.

'My friend,' I replied, laughing aloud, though, I trust, always within the limits of the courteous and the graceful, 'has Dagon stricken thee, too? Why so, too, say the mere uncircumcised, the creatures of systems and methods. Away with them, my friend, and their abstrac- tions, their limitations, their immaturities. Learn how culture - with that flexibility which sweetness and light give, with that exquisite sensibility to truth which is its note - has no need of these leading-strings and finger-posts. It is possessed ever by its own intelli- gent eagerness after the things of the mind. It is eter- nally passing onwards and seeking - seeking and passing onwards eternally. Where the bee sucks, there suck I,' I murmured cheerily, as I observed the increasing bewil- derment of my philosophical friend.

'Well!' said he, after a long pause for reflection,

for, as I expected, this was something undreamt of in his
philosophy - if, indeed, it be not in any man's philosophy;
'you search and probe and test the schemes of the great
thinkers of mankind, making known what therein is best and
most fruitful?'

'Certainly!' I replied. 'Culture, as I have said, is
nourished on the best ideas of the time. It diffuses
these ideas, it clarifies them, it attunes them. As I have
told you, its function is to humanise *all* knowledge.'

'Then you have a clear and intense grasp,' he went on,
'upon definite doctrines in philosophy?'

'Clear,' I replied, with rather a sly touch, 'if you
please, but sweetness knows nothing *intense*, my friend.'

'Well!' he cried impatiently, 'but you grasp great doctrines of thought?'

'I trust that we do,' said I mildly.

'What are they, then?' replied he. But I only smiled,
not less softly than before. 'Are they, as one may say,
à *priori* or à *posteriori*, metaphysical or positive, experimental or intuitional?'

'My dear Arminius,' I said, after a pause, 'so also ask
the Sadducees and publicans. What, again, I say, has culture to do with all these finalities, rigidities, inade-
quacies, and immaturities? Where be their quiddits, and
their quillits, now? Do you ask of culture what are its
principles and ideas? The *best* principles, the *best* ideas,
the *best* knowledge: - the perfect! the ideal! the complete!'

'But how does it recognise these,' he asked helplessly,
evidently now striking at random, 'if it has neither system, method, nor logic?'

'By Insight,' I replied triumphantly; 'by its own
inborn sensibility to beauty, truth, and life.'

'But if a man is born without it?' he asked.

'God help him then,' I rejoined, 'for I cannot;' and as
Arminius was still silent, I hummed gaily to myself,
'Sordid, unfeeling, reprobate, degraded, spiritless out-
cast;' and indeed there are but too many in that plight.

'Tell me,' said Arminius, at length recovering himself
for a last effort, 'are you then of the intuitional
school?'

'School!' I replied, as contemptuously as was consistent
with perfect politeness, 'no! nor are we anything intuitional at all. Culture, I say, questions, studies, pon-
ders. But as in other views study follows set methods, in
this view study is guided only by perennial curiosity and
an innate sense of refinement. There is thus harmony, but
no system; instinct, but no logic; eternal growth, and no
maturity; everlasting movement, and nothing acquiesced in;

perpetual opening of all questions, and answering of none;
infinite possibilities of everything; the becoming of all
things, the being nothing.'
    'I am confounded,' sighed Arminius, as indeed was but
too obvious.
    'And now,' said he, after a long pause, 'your passion
for doing good moves you to distinguish the noxious and
the vile?'
    'Yes,' I replied quietly, 'but what language about the
poor lower intelligences!'
    'And it stirs you to abolish them?' he asked.
    'No,' I answered decisively. 'Above all things, let us
abolish nothing. To desire to abolish is to be fierce, to
be fierce is to be unideal, to be unideal is to be sanguin-
ary. It begins in want of tone, and it ends with the
guillotine!'
    'And your passion for doing good works - ' he said.
    'By diffusing an atmosphere of sweetness and light; by
broadening the basis of life and intelligence; by the
children of Thy spirit making their light shine upon the
earth,' said I, with some unction, easily gliding into my
old chant when the college service was intoned, and rever-
entially repeating some beautiful words I had once heard
there.
    This, however, was too much for my poor friend, whose
privilege it had never been to know the bent of the old
Oxford nature for sweetness.
    'Soul of my namesake!' he burst forth with sad, sad
vehemence of manner, 'must I hear more? Here are we, in
this generation, face to face with the passions of fierce
men; parties, sects, races glare in each other's eyes
before they spring; death, sin, cruelty stalk amongst us,
filling their maws with innocence and youth; humanity
passes onwards shuddering through the ranging crowd of
foul and hungry monsters, bearing the destiny of the race
like a close-veiled babe in her arms, and over all sits
Culture high aloft with a pouncet-box to spare her senses
aught unpleasant, holding no form of creed, but contemplating all with infinite serenity, sweetly chanting snat-
ches from graceful sages and ecstatic monks, crying out
the most pretty shame upon the vulgarity, the provinciality, the impropriety of it all. Most improper, quotha,
most terrible, most maddening. Judge philosophies, but by
no fuller philosophy! Social action, without a social
faith! Religion, without a doctrine or a creed! A sense
of the eternal fitness of things, the eternal judge of all
things! Intelligence, curiosity, right reason! Abailard,
Montaigne, say you? Abailard of Magazines, Common-room
Montaigne! Doctor Subtilissimus! Or Coleridge is it, with

his pilfered rags about the reason and the understanding?
"Ideal of perfection," "inexhaustible indulgence," "intelligent eagerness," "passion of doing good,"' he kept on
repeating in a mincing tone, which I summoned all my
sweetness to endure without laughing.

'Arminius,' I said gravely, after waiting till this
absurd ebullition was spent (all emotion is absurd to the
eye of true taste), 'if you think that Culture is a simple
matter of refinement, or that its principles are formed on
aesthetic grounds entirely, you were never more thoroughly
mistaken. I have shrunk very naturally from pressing into
a general discussion the higher spiritual ideas, but it
now becomes a duty to tell you that the true and esoteric
mission of Culture is this - that "reason and the will of
God prevail," and this, I may say, is in the very words of
no less a person than a mitred bishop of our Church!'

'Culture deals with religion, does it?' he asked carelessly, and not much affected by the authority I had cited.

'Yes,' I said; 'as religion is but one sphere of human
experience, one side of our manifold activity, Culture
turns the light of its guiding beacon calmly in due turn
upon that.'

'And what may be its function in religion?' he asked,
still suffering from his last outburst.

'Chiefly in this,' I answered, 'that it deprecates any
strain upon the nervous system. It eliminates from the
well-nurtured soul all that savours of the zealot. Here
again it diffuses a chastened atmosphere of sweetness and
light. If one says that this or that is true, Culture
steps in and points out the grossness of untempered belief.
If one says that this or that is untrue, it shows how
little edification consists in opening the eyes of the
herd. It tells us the beauty of picturesque untruth, the
indelicacy of mere raw fact, the gracefulness of well-bred
fervour, the grotesqueness of unmannerly conviction; truth
and error have kissed one another in a sweet serener
sphere; this becomes that, and that is something else. The
harmonious, the suave, the well-bred waft the bright particular being into a peculiar and reserved parterre of
paradise, where bloom at once the graces of pantheism, the
simplicities of Deism, the pathos of Catholicism, the roman-
ticisim of every cult in every age, where he can sip elegan-
cies and spiritualities from the flowerets of every faith'
- I perorated with effusion, thinking of many a transcendental sermon.

'Lieber Gott,' (4) cried the incorrigible German, 'I
know not what this means. In your heathen, sottish, put-
rid critics! (one saw at once the distempered perversity
of the man) 'Have I seen some *petit-maitre* (5) preacher

passing his white hands through his perfumed curls, and
simpering thus about the fringes of a stole. Come,' said
he, with a sort of fierce sadness, 'in the name of human
woe, what Gospel does this offer to poor stricken men?'
   'The will of God, the will of God,' said I, almost
sternly, for the man had called up all the spirit of
devoutness within me.
   'Of God,' said the audacious Teuton, 'but of which God,
for there be many Gods, of little family resemblance; the
God who spoke from Horeb and Sinai, or the God of the
Bull Apis, Moloch, or Juggernaut; the god of Torquemada or
of Fénélon; of Cromwell or of Hume; of which God, for
there be many?' and his eyes flashed with a total want of
self-possession.
   'What if culture could show you, my friend,' said I,
quite gently, for I really pitied his unsophisticated
emotion, 'that all of these were in sooth one and the
same, manifold phases of one idea?'
   'And His will was equally manifest in all?' he asked
impatiently.
   'The kingdom of God is within you,' I said devoutly,
gliding again into my old college-chapel tone, 'and His
will is made manifest - '
   'In good taste!' rang forth the ungovernable man.
   I am a professed lover of free speech, and do not pass
for a literalist, but I confess that my English instincts
were too strong for me, and I looked round with real un-
easiness to see if the scandalous language of my friend
were overheard. I insisted on quitting a topic which he
treated with blunt indecorum; nor will I pain the reader
by relating his other indiscretions of the kind.
   Arminius now felt that he had carried his bluntness
too far, and wishing to conciliate me, and to show the
admiration he feels for his friend, he began in a gentler
tone. 'But I hear that he has done a knight's service in
consigning to public odium a sect of bloodthirsty fana-
tics who were striving to undermine society in your
country, and has crushed the sour French pedant by whose
writings their crimes were inspired.' I felt that this
question was a little perplexing, for it partly concerned
some youthful indiscretion of my own, and indeed was a
phase of Culture which I was hardly prepared to defend.
   'A French sciolist was it not,' he asked, 'who invented
some random formulae from the prejudices current in his
clique?'
   'I suppose they said the same of Bacon and Leibnitz,'
I replied, wishing to escape the subject.
   'A man, I think it was said, full of furious indignation with the past,' he went on.

'Well,' I answered, 'he is usually charged with preposterous veneration for it; but that, like everything else,
is a matter of taste.'

'Who proposed a wholesale system of violent renovation, I believe?' he went on.

'No! pardon me,' said I: 'as I read him, it was just
the reverse.'

'Who hated all thorough cultivation of the human faculties?' he said.

'I had strangely supposed him its principal apostle,'
I rejoined.

'With no spark of any moral or social passion?' he
asked.

'Well,' I replied; 'I used to think that he had something of the sort.'

'And your Jacobins,' said he; 'have the police secured
them?'

'Oh, it is not so bad as that yet,' I answered.

'Well, but I thought,' he rejoined, 'that one of them
had been caught oiling a guillotine in some highly suspicious costume?'

'Oh!' I said, with a smile, 'that was only, I believe,
what is called a sweet and light practical joke. The
truth is, to be frank, my friend,' for I felt the necessity of saying something, 'I must admit that Culture made
some trifling blunder in the matter. Jacobinism, as you
say, denounces the past, seeks violent revolutions, and
disdains all complex cultivation. The school you speak
of, on the contrary, love and take counsel of the past,
discard all violent for moral agencies of progress, and
preach universal and perfect education. You see that
believing in infinite, though peaceful and gradual, progress, to be gained by spiritual methods alone, they
exactly contrast with Jacobinism, which imposes its crude
type by tyrannical force. They occupy, in a word, the
opposite pole of modern politics, except as both dream of
an infinite change.'

'Why,' cried Arminius, whom I had long seen swelling
with a new storm, 'this was rank misrepresentation, then,
on the part of Culture!'

'My friend, my friend,' I urged, pained at this in-
delicate plainness, 'inadequate illumination, partial
observation, misapprehension, hastiness, or rather, say
fleetness - anything you please but that; let us say
airiness.'

'You mean that Culture had not adequately studied the
great French thinker whom it travestied?' said Arminius.

'Perhaps it was so,' I replied; 'but reflect - the bee
touches not the root of any tree. His to suck the

floweret; ours to sip his honey.'
'And yet,' he mused, 'there seems very much in which
the higher Culture may be said to coincide with this
philosopher, just as you say it coincides with religion.'
'Oh!' said I, figuratively, 'of the mighty river of
Egypt whole tribes drink and are refreshed, not knowing
whence those living waters come, and many cast their bread
upon them, and find it after many days!'
'What!' said the German, 'then here, too, Culture was
at fault?'
I was silent.
'And the higher intelligence blundered?' he cried.
'My friend, my friend - ' I entreated.
'And the "instinct" proved about as real as Jack
Falstaff's?' he ran on. 'And this bright being - '
'Hush!' I insisted; 'have you learned no more of
sweetness than this?'
'Why, it is a crucial instance by which to test
Culture,' he cried, 'and this potent and magic gift -
incommunicable as blue blood - the talisman to cure all
evil, the touchstone of falsehood, the beautifier of
life - ' But I refused to hear more, for I saw him
pacing the room and murmuring to himself -

But I remember when the fight was done -

And telling me the sovereign'st thing on earth
Was parmaceti for an inward bruise;

and his blue eyes kindled under his fair hair, as of one
of his Cimbrian sires.
So I left the untunable man, and walked out to air my
soul in the light of a sweet autumn sunset.

Notes

1 'spirit' or 'soul'.
2 'the refined and the innovative and that which is
   devoted to inquiry'.
3 'beautiful and good'.
4 'Dear God'.
5 'dandy'.

23.   UNSIGNED REVIEW OF 'ANARCHY AND AUTHORITY',
'DAILY NEWS'

30 December 1867, 4

The 'Daily News' (a paper founded by Dickens) was rarely
kind to Arnold; it had begun its criticism of his prose
with Harriet Martineau's review of 'England and the
Italian Question' (1859).   (See also 'Matthew Arnold,
The Poetry', 134-6, for her review of the 1853 'Poems'.)
This review is typical in what Arnold would have considered its provincialism.   But it is in fact an articulate,
literate, and suggestive discussion of Arnold's ideas,
especially his ideas about the State.   The reviewer
notes, as Frederic Harrison later noted, the parallels
between Arnold and the philosophy of Comte.

What Dalilah has shorn the locks of the champion of
light, and delivered him up manacled to make sport for
the Philistines?   This question will rise in the mind of
many readers whom Mr. MATTHEW ARNOLD's name and the
graces of his style attract to an article in the current
number of the 'Cornhill Magazine.'   They will scarcely
recognise their hero.   DAVID has laid aside his sling
and his staff, and has put on the armour of SAUL, and he
is borne down by its weight.   Mr. ARNOLD is essentially
a *frondeur,* (1) and is ill at ease with the weapons of
regular warfare.   In the field of political controversy
he is the swan on land, and we sigh for his return to the
softer and more liquid element natural to him.
     Mr. ARNOLD, though with all knightly courtesy and
grace, is an aggressive writer, and in the natural course
of things it is now his turn to stand on the defensive.
More opponents than one, whose shields he has lightly
and playfully touched with the point of his spear, have
responded to the challenge, and it has become his duty to
make good the cause for which he stands.   He is the
champion of Culture, the apostle of Light and Sweetness.
The very words carry a spell with them.   The proclamation
of the doctrine half persuades conversion.   In the heat
and bustle of the present time, exhortations to men to
lift themselves into an ampler ether and a purer air,
above the dust of an age bent too much upon petty and
material objects, are not superfluous; and Mr. ARNOLD
deserves gratitude for the refined criticism with which

he has enforced, and the exquisite poetry in which he has
illustrated his precepts. His writings have been a
refreshment of the spirit to numbers of busy and thought-
taxed men. Culture, in Mr. ARNOLD's vocabulary, is the
search after perfection; its intellectual fruits are
largeness of mind and openness to ideas; its moral result
is expressed in manners attuned to a gentle and graceful
spirit within. As a gospel of human nature, this teaching, perhaps, covers but a limited ground. But, so far
as it goes, who can quarrel with it? Who would not desire
to see the asperities and brutalities of controversy and
of daily life softened, the barbarisms of an uncultivated
taste refined, humane and elevating amusements substituted
for those which are gross or depraving, the mental horizon
of men enlarged, its scenery varied, and a just balance of
interests substituted for the fanaticism of an exclusive
pursuit? So far, Mr. ARNOLD has no gainsayers. But his
practice is not altogether in harmony with his theory.
He has often, and with true aim, launched the shafts of
his satire against the narrowness of mind which is the
besetting danger of practical politicians, who are bound
to act on the emergency of the moment, and cannot think
much beyond it; and against philosophical system-builders,
who are prone to compress all facts into the framework of
a preconceived theory. But there is another sort of
narrowness, of which it behoved him more seriously to
take account, because it forms the danger which lay in
wait for himself. We mean the narrowness which falls
upon the prophet, who, giving himself up to the proclamation of the few truths which, in his view, society most
needs to learn, and which most deeply impress his own
mind, soon becomes absorbed in and mastered by them, and
ends by being unable to see aught beside them. Mr. CAR-
LYLE is an illustrious instance of this conversion of
ill-balanced strength into weakness. There is nothing in
the phrases or in the ideas which they embody to save the
preacher of Culture, Light, Sweetness, and the Grand
Style, from the fate which has befallen the worshipper of
Force, Rhythmic Drill, the Silences, Veracities, and Im-
mensities. Openness to ideas may be insisted on in a
narrow spirit, and a certain tone of peevishness may creep
over the pleader for sweetness.
     Culture, in the sense in which Mr. ARNOLD understands
it, as the quest of perfection, is, one would think, a
purely private and individual thing. Each must develop
his own faculties for himself with the best external aid
he can procure. So long as Mr. ARNOLD's teaching was
positive, no one could quarrel with it. But he presently
began to set up his doctrine in strange rivalry with

various things lying, one would have fancied, wholly in
another plane of thought. Culture, we were told, was
better than Free Trade, or than Reform Bills; and men who
spent their time upon bringing to pass changes of laws and
institutions became the objects, in Mr. ARNOLD's writings,
of a somewhat narrow and fanatical disparagement. So we
are told by the advocates of the Temporal Power that faith
and the saintly virtues are better than manufactures and
railways. Mr. ARNOLD appeared to preach an egotistic
pursuit of personal culture analogous to the spiritual
selfishness which led monks and hermits from the world to
cultivate apart the Christian graces, or to the intellectual Sybaritism which TENNYSON has so finely portrayed in
'The Palace of Art.' Against this imputation he protests
justly, we think, as regards himself, but unreasonably,
we think, as a logical inference from his writings. In
doing so, he brings out another doctrine, not new with
him, but not easily reconcilable with his main ideas.
This is the function of authority, or of the State in
human life. It is his answer to the charge of self-
regarding individualism. On this subject, which brings
him fairly into the field of politics, Mr. ARNOLD's theory
is a medley compounded of the doctrines of COMTE and
CARLYLE, and the practice of French Imperialism and the
ancient democracies.

Mr. ARNOLD's doctrine of the State is justified by an
indictment against modern liberalism consisting of two
counts: the first is its worship of machinery, or of
means without regard to the ends they are to serve; the
second is its worship of liberty, as an end in and for
itself, and not simply as a means to something beyond
itself. The charges seem to us to be contradictory. In
the first, there is no doubt some truth. A great deal of
activity is spent upon objects very far remote from the
highest or from any real wants of human nature. Any one
who should direct human energy into nobler channels would
be a public benefactor. Morally and intellectually,
roads are made which lead no whither, and vehicles pass
up and down them which carry nothing that human nature
needs. But when Mr. ARNOLD says that the liberty to do
what a man likes is the object of popular idolatry, and
that no one cares to inquire what it is reasonable that a
man should like to do, he is guilty of a common but inex-
cusable representation. The alternative is between a
man's doing, under safeguards and checks which reserve
the same liberty for others, what he likes, and his doing
what some one else, probably not one whit wiser than himself, likes. In the interest of that culture which
absorbs Mr. ARNOLD's worship, it is better that there

should be an infinite variety of experiments in human
action; first, because as the explorers multiply the
true track is more likely to be discovered, and secondly,
because the diversity of individual character requires
for its highest culture specialities of treatment, No
doubt, the common reason of society ought to check the
aberrations of individual eccentricity. It can only do so
by its action on the individual reason, and it will do so
in the main sufficiently if left to this natural operation. Mr. ARNOLD will make the State the organ of the
common reason. He may make it an organ of something or
other, but how can he be certain that reason will be the
quality which will be embodied in it? Here, again we
have a sort of parody of the Roman catholic doctrine and
practice. An orthodoxy of culture and manners is to be
supported and enforced by the secular arm. Mr. ARNOLD
would apparently leave it to the Executive to decide what
demonstrations and meetings and processions are in accordance with right reason and shall be allowed, and what conflict with it and must be suppressed. The meetings of the
Reform League and the Fenian processions would have been
put down in 1867; but so certainly would those of the
Anti-Corn Law League and the Catholic Association and the
Anti-Slavery Society in past times. Right reason, acting
through the organism of the State, would have suppressed
Free Trade and maintained the Penal Laws and Negro
Slavery. While the Executive represented only a class,
Mr. ARNOLD seems inclined to reply, such a power would
have been dangerous in its hands; but in so far as it
represents society as a whole, there is no objection to
the exercise of spiritual authority. In other words, the
tyranny of majorities and oppression of minorities is the
last issue of the doctrine of culture. We doubt whether
the Executive Government of the day, consisting necessarily of men engaged in the routine of business, are the
best organs of the pure reason of society. Perhaps Mr.
ARNOLD would create special departments for this function
- a President of the Board of Light and a Secretary of
State for Sweetness. But the scheme of political organisation and of State management come strangely from the
vituperator of mechanism. The truth seems to be that,
though Mr. ARNOLD, in the 'Cornhill Magazine,' is largely
occupied in attacking the school of COMTE, he has adopted
unconsciously their views of the function of the State,
and is on the high way to their doctrine of an Intellectual Priesthood and a Supreme Pontiff of Humanity. Mr.
FREDERIC HARRISON, to whose wit and logic his antagonist
pays a graceful tribute, is likely to add to his conquest
of ARMINIUS the conquest of the creator and inspirer of

ARMINIUS. Mr. ARNOLD's argument for authority has, however, a non-intellectual root. Like many other eminent
men, he is afraid of the effects of Tory democracy. He
believes in the prevalence of a spirit of anarchy and
rowdyism, which is rapidly growing in English society;
apparently because a period of excitement has succeeded
one of apathy. If, however, he will contrast the turbulence of 1867, not with the stagnation of 1865, but with
the turbulence of 1824 or 1832, he may modify his opinions. As in the natural, so in the social world, light,
sweetness, and order must be the result of a balance of
forces, attained not by artificial suppression, but by
freedom of development, and, it may be, occasional storm
and conflict.

Note

1 'uses a slingshot'.

24. UNSIGNED REVIEW OF 'CULTURE AND ANARCHY', 'SPECTATOR'

6 March 1869, xlii, 295-6

When the Anarchy and Authority essays appeared in book
form there was little excitement among the reviewers. As
the 'Saturday' put it, referring to Arnold's ideas about
society, 'We all of us know pretty well by this time what
to think of Matthew Arnold.' The following review from
the 'Spectator' is typical of this tepid reception.
Arnold can hardly have been pleased. He had become in
the eyes of many educated Englishmen something of an
effete Carlyle - with whom he was often, as here, compared.

Mr. Arnold complains very properly of a critic who called
one of his essays an elegant _jeremiad_, - the composition
of Jeremiah being those among the Hewbrew prophets to
which he is least attracted, which are in truth most
antipathetic to his nature. Probably the critic was only
thinking of the complaints about his age and time which
are to be found in Mr. Arnold's essays, and it would seem

sarcastic to liken him to the writer of Lamentations,
without much thought of whether they had anything else
in common or not. But there may be very different types
of complainers, and the comparison of him with Jeremiah,
harsh, and crabbed, and always at the highest pitch, with
little sweetness or melody, was perhaps as unapt a one as
could have been taken up. This could hardly have been
said if Mr. Arnold had been compared to a prophet, using
that word in its most general sense. Of course, he is
not the least like the men who came up out of the wilderness nursed into fanaticism by solitary musing, unkempt,
rugged, and fierce, and who denounced woe and doom upon
idolatrous nations; but he resembles the prophet race in
one of his intellectual attitudes, that of a teacher of
disagreeable doctrine, separating himself from popular
illusions, and standing by the wayside to tell people of
the wrong paths they are following, beseeching and en-
treating in a variety of tones, and never weary of remonstrances. The latter characteristic is very marked in
the present essay. It is not an analysis of any topic,
not an *inquiry,* which was the old-fashioned idea of a
book called by that name, but an effusion or series of
effusions in which the author's mind is poured out without much order, and one or two principal ideas are itera-
ted and reiterated with manifold illustration and choice
of expression. It has almost all the characteristics of
prophecy except the rapture and enthusiasm and fiery zeal
which have come to be associated with the name, though
Mr. Arnold's example may itself prove how much there may
be of the essence of prophecy without the usual accompani-
ments. Our own day has not been without a prophet of the
rugged sort in Thomas Carlyle, who always appears at
least to be moved to utterance by heat of spirit, though
he cannot be so natural and unconscious as the type he
imitates; but Mr. Arnold is in every way more modern, and
his milder and more refined utterances should tell better
in an age when strong stimulants, of other descriptions
as well as the alcoholic, are very much out of favour.
    The principal besetting thought of Mr. Arnold is one
which we discussed at the time when the first of these
effusions was published in the 'Cornhill Magazine,' and
we are inclined to think it the most valuable contribution of the book to the main current of thinking on political subjects at the present time. That in the history
of mankind there has been an alternative progress - at
times in the direction of Hellenism, the culture and perfection of the whole man, at other times in the direction
of Hebraism, the strengthening of the moral fibre or
sense of duty; that each alternative is imperfect and

incomplete, and the endeavour should be to combine both;
and that at the present time in this country, and among
English-speaking communities, it is Hellenism which is
neglected, and which should therefore be preached up by
those who wish to see progress in the right direction:
such is the central notion which has taken possession of
the writer, and which, notwithstanding misapprehensions
and one-sided statements, with which it is buttressed, is
of no little validity. If it is a conspicuous defect of
many people, and the largest masses of people among us at
the present time, that they believe in the notion of duty
almost to the exclusion of a belief of the importance and
difficulty of knowing what duty is, of seeking out the
'intelligible law of things,' and striving not to lose
life itself in the means of living, then a preacher may
be forgiven much who recalls the forgotten idea. Much
the same may be said of the subsidiary leading notions
which find vent in these pages, for instance, the worship
of machinery, which Mr. Arnold considers to be an outcome
of the unchecked Hebraizing element. In the excessive
anxiety to do what is right, an easy and obvious notion
of what right is is taken up, so that action may at once
begin, and the monitions of an inquiring spirit which
starts doubts as to the worth of the action itself, or
its complete suitability to always changing circumstances,
are summarily dismissed. People thus get into their heads
certain half-notions which they follow mechanically, and
to the hurt of their own natures and society. Whether the
Englishman's notions of personal liberty, or of free
trade, and the like, are altogether of this character, or
even largely so, as Mr. Arnold assumes, is of less consequence than the fact that all the notions of uncultured
men are too apt to become of this fixed stamp; every
motive grows mechanical; so that a book which batters at
the habit, and insists on a better way, can hardly err
on the side of excess. It is no objection to some of the
ideas which are preached that they have no very distinct
connection with the other notions insisted on, although
this is the reason of their introduction. It is thus very
dubious whether there is much warrant for the association
of the two notions of anarchy and culture; the one is not
necessarily the special opposite of the other, at least
not that anarchy which appears to be in Mr. Arnold's mind,
judging of the instances he gives. It is rather a long
step to argue from the Hyde Park riots, or a certain in-
security in London streets which arose from a deficiency
of police, that the English people are not Hellenistic
enough - that their exclusive devotion to Hebraistic and
mechanical notions has brought them to this pass.

Hebraistic nations have not failed in establishing the
outward order of society and supremacy of law, whatever
else they have failed in. This is precisely one of those
notions which may be taken up and pursued mechanically,
and in which a Hebraistic people was therefore likely to
succeed. But we may thoroughly sympathize for all that
with Mr. Arnold's dislike of anarchy or the least appearance of social disorder, though we should be more inclined
to ascribe the facts of which he complains to much more
partial and temporary causes, coupled with an absence of
timidity about them, derived from an inward assurance in
most men's minds that they would not be allowed to go far.
It is somewhat of a mistake to discover a tendency to
social anarchy in the mistakes of a chief of police, who
was very good at one time, but had grown somewhat *passé*;
and in the errors of a Home Secretary, weak and vacillating, and representing a government which was rather
invidiously placed. Still it is good to have the supremacy of law vigilantly watched, and the least appearance
of evil tracked out and condemned. But for such writing
as Mr. Arnold's, events that need not have indicated any
rooted mischief might have finished by teaching a lesson
of lawlessness that would have cost us much to unteach.
     The same remark might be made of another idea which
seems to have much weight with Mr. Arnold, - the value of
great institutions, and most of all the State and minor
institutions which it can establish, as a means of stimulating the better self in men, setting up an external
standard of excellence, and giving weight to the notion of
a right reason superior to the interest of classes, however numerous and strong. It is not a vital part of his
preaching of culture, nor is it necessary to correct
anarchy, especially anarchy in that narrow sense in which
he has sometimes used the word, and it is introduced somewhat incidentally in the application of his sermon to a
criticism of liberal action in the matter of the Irish
Church, but nothing could be better as a good text for a
new series of prophecies. Thus the book is rich in
pieces of thinking, if not as a whole, and although it
may be full of errors and false impressions and exaggerations. But no more can be expected in a prophet than
great emphasis upon one or two ideas into which he has
got insight, and which he manages to impress upon people
by happy repetition and the intellectual energy which has
no end to its repertory of words and illustrations for
dressing out the old thought. What is peculiar to Mr.
Arnold is the exceeding suggestiveness of his most occasional glances at men and things, and an exquisiteness of
style for which any writer might envy him, and which

never grows stale. We are always coming upon something
fresh and bright, whether it be the discovery of Jacobinism in the thinking and advocacy of the adherents of positivism, or a discrimination between St. Paul and theologians who blunderingly quote his words and miss his meaning; or a comparison between England of the present day
and the England of Elizabeth in respect of real greatness
as distinguished from mere bulk of riches or material
power; of the classification of English Philistines into
Barbarians, Philistines proper, and the Populace – the
former being the Philistines of the aristocracy, self-
contained and with governing instincts, possessing external gifts and sweetness, but deficient in light; the
Philistines proper being the middle-classes generally and
the majority of the working-classes, who, as Mr. Arnold
rightly notes, closely resemble the middle-classes; and
the populace being what the rest of the world means by
the 'residuum.' Mr. Arnold's phrases are themselves a
possession. He has all Mr. Disraeli's knack *plus* a sincerity which Mr. Disraeli has not, and grafted on a
poetic and intellectual temperament of a transcendently
higher stamp.
      Very unnecessarily Mr. Arnold enters into a defence of
his abstinence from taking a part in the Liberal political movement of the time. His function being to pro-
phesy, to call people's attention to forgotten things,
and make them uncomfortable about their omissions, there
is nothing for him but to communicate his thought. There
are plenty of other people to do the active work of the
world. But unfortunately in justifying his abstention,
which did not need any defence, he has done not a little
to spoil the effect of his prophecy by showing an ignorance on certain points of 'the intelligible law of things'
which will cause his authority to be distrusted. Thus,
in a criticism of the Liberal movement of the Irish question, which he is quite right in assailing blind volunt-
aryism and other influences which cause the remedy for
the Irish Church grievance to be levelling-down and not
levelling-up, he is wrong in concluding that the idea of
National Church Establishments is *relatively* so valuable
that the process of levelling-down is not worth having.
He forgets that the Irish difficulty will not wait – that
English Philistines have been guilty of other sins
besides Nonconformity, and of unjust dealing with Ireland
among others; that the Philistines being convinced of the
latter, though not of the former, it is expedient for the
safety of the Empire to take advantage of their best convictions. Besides, as all moralists agree that the
quickest way to become just and perfect is to do the duty

that lies nearest, the reflex effect of a right action
being so great, it is plain that by being wrought up to
an act of just dealing to Ireland, English Philistines
are being educated in the most effective way for acting on
just aspirations in politics, - are being brought into
the temper, in short, when teaching about establishments
could be listened to. We are not disputing that Mr.
Arnold is himself right in keeping aloof, but a little
more discrimination would give his utterances more weight.
In political economy he is absolutely at sea. He has a
vague impression that the blind pursuit of free trade produces an accumulating pauperism along with the wealth it
also produces; that the stock notions encourage over-
population; and that the thing to be taught is apparently
Malthusianism. No doubt the generation which legislated
free trade was most imperfect, and there is a world of
work before us in far more important matters, like education; but what is certain is that free trade is not bad,
and is not responsible for pauperism, which, taking the
whole free-trade period into account, has *not* accumulated.
Its necessary tendency in the conditions of modern life
is to diminish pauperism, as Mr. Arnold will see it has
done, if he only reads the accounts of popular distress
which was so appalling before the free-trade time. On
the other hand, pauperism will be little affected one way
or the other by Mr. Arnold's own remedy - changing the
popular belief about large families. A diminishing population may just as well have an accumulating pauperism as
a growing one. This is the 'law of things' in the matter.
The true remedy is education, to make people better workers and make the workers more thrifty; and unless you get
these, putting on the screw to repress population will not
give us a less proportion of poor.

25. WILLIAM KIRKUS ON 'CULTURE AND ANARCHY', 'FORTNIGHTLY
REVIEW'

March 1869, v, n.s., 371-3

William Kirkus (1830-1907) was a clergyman and a periodical writer. His review of 'Culture and Anarchy' reflects
the ambivalence of the 'Fortnightly' towards Arnold's
works. Founded in 1865, the 'Fortnightly' was a vigorous
and outspoken magazine, which pioneered the practice of

signed articles. Although reviewers like Swinburne
praised Arnold's poetry, Kirkus is typical of the 'Fortnightly's' censure of Arnold's social philosophy. He
begins by complimenting Arnold for his view of culture but
promptly suggests that 'Mr. Arnold's Culture could
scarcely fail to produce Anarchy'. And by the time he
concludes, Kirkus is calling Arnold 'an exquisite result of
infinite mistakes'. The self-contradictory views, though
rarely so obvious as here, reflect the difficulties of the
liberal press when they discussed the 'liberal of the
future'.

There is so much truth, and of just now the most necessary
kind for us, in what Mr. Matthew Arnold has written -
moreover, his style has so severe a grace, his satire is
so quiet and yet so incisive - that his readers can
scarcely fail to be either fascinated or enraged by him.
That we are far enough from 'sweetness and light,' even
'the editor of the "Daily Telegraph"' would scarcely deny;
and it is an evil omen that we can even boast of our
Philistinism. There may possibly enough be something
better for mankind than culture, but that something
better is assuredly not the contempt of culture. For
when we allow Mr. Matthew Arnold, as he may fairly expect
from us, to define his own terms, we find that *the culture
in which he believes* is not 'a smattering of Greek and
Latin,' much less 'a turn for small fault-finding,' or the
faculty of criticising new books. It has for its object
on the intellectual side, 'to render an intelligent being
yet more intelligent;' and on the practical side, 'to make
reason and the will of God *prevail.*' It aims at the perfection of the individual and the perfection also of
society, and at a perfection of the individual which is
impossible without the perfection of society. Hence the
objection that 'the man of culture is in politics one of
the poorest mortals alive,' is no more than a contradiction in terms when urged against Mr. Matthew Arnold's
culture. For his culture *includes* politics. On this
point nothing can be plainer than Mr. Arnold's own words:-

> Culture, or the study of perfection, leads us to con-
> ceive of no perfection as being real which is not a
> *general* perfection, embracing all our fellow-men with
> whom we have to do....Individual perfection is impos-
> sible so long as the rest of mankind are not perfected
> along with us.... So all our fellow-men, in the east
> of London and elsewhere, we must take along with us in

the progress towards perfection, if we ourselves
really, as we profess, want to be perfect.

Nor can anybody reasonably complain that Mr. Matthew
Arnold desires that 'reason and the will of God should
prevail' instead of selfishness and ignorance. Neither
an individual nor a nation can afford to take many 'leaps
in the dark;' nor, again, are admitted evils to be removed on such principles as would themselves produce a
pestilent swarm of new and perhaps more fatal evils.
Few politicians, even devoid of culture, would disestab-
lish the Irish Church by an Act of Parliament affirming
in its preamble that the Christian religion itself was an
impudent delusion; or render legal the marriage of a
decreased wife's sister by an Act affirming the right of
every Englishman to cohabit in whatever manner he might
think fit with whomsoever he might choose.
    It may be admitted, too, that if Mr. M. Arnold's
teachings and warnings be somewhat one-sided and extravagant - therein furnishing a melancholy proof of an almost
universal degeneracy, in that he himself has not attained
to a perfect εὐφυΐα (1) - he warns us with excessive
vehemence against the dangers which are most pressing to
that enormous majority of Englishmen who are not yet the
loyal servants of culture. There is scarcely a single
department of public life in which action is not terribly
in advance of knowledge. What satisfactory basis of
legislation is there as yet in knowledge and science in a
matter where, nevertheless, legislation is imminent and
perhaps inevitable - the settlement of the long-standing
and mischievous quarrel between employers and employed?
Even state education is scarcely better than guess-work -
a series of doubtful experiments where failure may not
only waste the present generation, but corrupt the next.
    Nevertheless, Mr. Arnold's Culture could scarcely fail
to produce Anarchy; because it not only aims at perfection, which is good, but seems incapable of acting at all,
even for the removal of admitted wrongs, until perfection
is attained, which is mischievous and anarchic. Until we
are quite certain not only that we have light - be it
only such glimmer as may lead us on to the perfect day -
but that we have the very noon flooding every path, we
may not stir a single step. The very examples which Mr.
Arnold gives us of great movements which he, for his part,
must keep aloof from until the noon of culture shall have
come, are exactly of a kind to convince us that his culture, as a practical force, making reason and the will of
God prevail, is little better than the mocking prophet of
an impossible perfection. Even the examples themselves

are far better illustrations of his incisive sarcasm than
of his political sagacity. To represent the endeavour to
obtain a repeal of the law forbidding marriage with a
deceased wife's sister as a great liberal movement at all
closely resembling the movements for free trade and the
disestablishment of the Irish Church is - at least I
should think so if the misrepresentation were not Mr.
Arnold's - so exceedingly silly as to be scarcely honest.
Yet even against this poor attempt to obtain a very
paltry power Mr. Arnold has very little to urge: -

> 'I was lucky enough,' he says, 'to be present when Mr.
> Chambers, I think, brought forward in the House of
> Commons his Bill for enabling a man to marry his
> deceased wife's sister, and I heard the speech which
> Mr. Chambers then made in support of his Bill. His
> first point was that God's law - the name he always
> gave to the book of Leviticus - did not really forbid
> a man to marry his deceased wife's sister. God's law
> not forbidding it, the Liberal maxim that a man's
> prime right and happiness is do as he likes, ought at
> once to come into force, and to annul any such check
> upon the assertion of personal liberty as the prohibi-
> tion to marry one's deceased wife's sister.... And
> this exactly falls in with what Mr. Hepworth Dixon,
> who may almost be called the Colenso of love and mar-
> riage, - such a revolution does he make in our ideas
> on these matters, just as Dr. Colenso does in our
> ideas on religion, - tells us of the notions and pro-
> ceedings of our kinsmen in America.'

This is surely a very remarkable piece of writing for
an apostle of culture. What revolution has Dr. Colenso
made in our ideas on religion? He has *affirmed* precisely
what Mr. Arnold *means* by his rather unfair sarcasm, when
he says of Mr. Chambers, 'he always gave the name, God's
law, to the Book of Leviticus.' Dr. Colenso, like Mr.
Arnold, protests against 'Hebraising' to the extent of
regarding the Old Testament as for all peoples and times,
the law of God, the whole of that law, and nothing but
that law. And why were the English people shocked that
Dr. Colenso could so far 'Hellenize'? Precisely because
he is a bishop of the Established Church. Dr. Pusey was
horrified, indeed, but not surprised, by Dr. Davidson's
'Introduction to the Old Testament,' because Dr. Davidson
was a Dissenter. Mr. Arnold ridicules the notion of
taking our law of marriage from a people whose wisest
king had seven hundred wives and three hundred concu-
bines; but when Dr. Colenso does the same thing, in a much

better way, he is the Hepworth Dixon, I suppose, of
religion; and, nevertheless, the Church which, apart from
dissent, would long since have burnt Colenso for being so
like Mr. Arnold, is the great focus and instrument of
culture. On what principle did, and do, the clergy
oppose the law of divorce? Because the clergy of the
Established Church, unlike the 'provincial' Dissenters,
are exactly like Mr. Chambers in the estimate of Leviticus
and the Bible.

Having been taught *by the Established Church* that Leviticus is the law of God, Mr. Chambers was bound to obey
it, and to take good heed that no Bill he introduced into
Parliament should be in opposition to this Divine law.
But no such opposition being apparent to him in the
matter of deceased wives' sisters, why should not 'the
right and happiness of a man to do as he likes' come into
play? Unhappiness is in itself an evil. The natural
desires are never wholly misleading, and the burden of
justifying itself rests not upon indulgence, but upon
restraint. Possibly Adam may have been εὐφυής, but a
horrid chasm yawns between such an Adam and all the rest
of mankind. Within the whole space of history men have
had to seek culture by the rough road of 'liberty.'
What a man ought to like can only be ascertained by a
vast multitude of experiments, whereof the most will be
foolish. Mr. Arnold sees clearly enough that for free
intercourse and for culture a good high road is needful;
and that to set out on a long journey without so much as
seeing your road is idiotic. Therefore, before anything
else can be done a road must be made; and for this purpose there must be fitting tools and waggons for the con-
veyance of material and construction of the road. With
due 'play of consciousness' Mr. Arnold gets ready his
tools and waggons, and - waits till somebody else makes a
road for his road-constructing waggons to travel alone.
Mr. Arnold is himself an exquisite result of infinite
mistakes, and looks down with a half-divine contempt upon
the very elements of which he himself is constructed.

Note

1 'fine, cultured nature'.

Friendship's Garland (1871)

26. MARGARET OLIPHANT, UNSIGNED REVIEW, 'BLACKWOOD'S
MAGAZINE'

April 1871, cix, 440-64

Margaret Oliphant (1828-97), who supported her family
through long years of writing, was a novelist, biographer
(and friend and biographer of the publisher Blackwood),
as well as a prolific reviewer and literary historian.
Her criticism of Arnold is less severe here than elsewhere (see 'Matthew Arnold, The Poetry', 391-4), since
she acknowledges the justice of Arnold's charges against
the Philistines. But with an eye to the reading public,
which she presumably knew well, Mrs Oliphant says that
Arnold's overly 'ponderous' wit and his creaking jokes
will have little impact on the 'obtuse British intelligence'. Arnold in effect does not understand and therefore cannot hope to reach his audience.

And what shall we say of 'Friendship's Garland'? Is it
amusement - is it instruction - which Mr. Matthew Arnold
is minded to convey to us in this quaint publication, by
which, we have no doubt, many honest brains will be bewildered? Perhaps his name is sufficient to warrant the
supposition that the latter is what is chiefly intended;
and we cannot but in all humility venture a doubt whether
Mr. Matthew Arnold - whose literary powers we admire, if
not as much as he does himself (for that is a very high
standard), at least as much as a defective education
permits - has been adapted by nature to afford any vivid

amusement to his fellow-creatures. When he does so to
any high degree, we fear it will not be wittingly or
willingly, but in his own despite. The disquisitions of
Baron Arminius von Thunder-Ten-Tronkh whose lamentable
death was mournfully celebrated not very long ago in the
'Pall Mall Gazette,' contain, we believe, a great many
true as well as many caustic sayings. But the fun is
very ponderous, to say the least of it, and has a heavy
German roll, which no doubt is true to the character, but
which has the terrible defect, worse than any other
viciousness, of not being in the very least funny. Fun
is not the forte of the editor of this interesting collection of papers; the play is elephantine, the jokes
creak on their hinges like doors hard to open, and the
central figure, which is Mr. Matthew Arnold himself, is
distressingly prominent and deeply self-conscious. He
was always so, to be sure, in or out of masquerade, and
so are all the personages in this little drama. We have
great doubt, indeed, whether the effect of the volume
upon the obtuse British intelligence to which it is
meant to be so very cutting, will be at all commensurate
with the trouble taken; for, oddly enough, Mr. Arnold
does not seem to take into consideration the important,
and we should say essential, matter of reaching the
special audience to which he preaches. His discussion of
the shortcomings of the British Philistine, which are
uttered in a voice much too finely pitched ever to reach
that culprit's veritable ear, remind us somewhat of the
awakening sermons aimed at brutal vice which evangelical
clergymen often thunder at a meek score of innocent
women, guilty of no enormity greater than a bit of scan-
dal. Does Mr. Arnold suppose that his shadowy Bottles,
for instance, who 'is one of our self-made middle-class
men - a radical of the purest water, quite one of the
Manchester school; who was one of the earliest of Free
Traders; who has always gone as straight as an arrow about
Reform; who is an ardent voluntary in every possible line
- opposed the Ten Hours' Bill, was one of the leaders of
the Dissenting opposition out of Parliament which smashed
up the education clauses of Sir James Graham's Factory
Act; who paid the whole expenses of a most important
church-rate contest out of his own pocket; and, finally,
who looks forward to marrying his deceased wife's sister;'
- does Mr. Arnold, we repeat, believe for a moment that
this attack of his will ever reach Bottles? Our satirist
stands and mocks at the pit in a highly-refined small
voice which never reaches beyond the orchestra stalls;
some of the people there, it is true, are much entertained by the abuse of their neighbours; but still it is

wasted zeal. Neither will Lord Lumpington, nor the sport-
ing parson whom Mr. Arnold sets forth as another genuine
type of the uninstructed Briton (though we thought the
species was nearly extinct), be likely to benefit much by
the onslaught made upon him.

But yet they are all very fair game; and we wish Mr.
Arnold a great deal better luck than he is likely to have
in persuading the British public that it is not in reality
the very fine thing it supposes itself to be. There is
enough of truth in his description of the strange changes
English sentiment has undergone on many matters, and
enough that is alarming in the national aspect both at
home and abroad, to make us grieve greatly when any competent critic, who might be of real service to his country, chooses to put on the mountebank's cap and bells
instead. We, for one, do not in the least undervalue the
importance of such subjects, nor the serious use and
advantage to a country of hearing the truth about the
opinions its neighbours entertain of it. The gift of
seeing ourselves as others see us is of as much importance
to a community as to an individual; and all the curious
discussions of recent days - that about national honour,
for example, which our publicists never venture to discuss without a certain shrinking alarm for the consequences of a decided conclusion - are very remarkable
signs of the times; as is also that universal outburst
of brag and boast over our charities, which, did any private individual do it, would sink that individual to the
lowest depths of contempt. What is bad for the character
of a man cannot be very noble in the character of a
nation; and we confess that it is with a sickening sense
of shame that we have read the over-and-over-again
repeated paeans of self-applause into which the British
press has burst over the recent liberalities of England
to France. Could we individually ever look our neighbour in the face again after thus boasting of our alms to
him? if that neighbour were our washerwoman instead of our
equal, we know very well that we dare not do it, except at
the risk of universal scorn. But we do it nationally,
without a doubt or hesitation. This is such a proof of
the surging upwards of all that is ignoble and petty in
the public as opposed to the private mind, that its
importance as a symptom is very grave indeed. And accordingly, of all things in the world that the British public
want, we believe there is nothing half so important as
sound and unexaggerated public criticism. And here is
what we get for it. Mr. Matthew Arnold astride upon the
British Philistine, whipping and spurring over hedges and
ditches - alas! as Philistinish, as intent upon his own

beautiful qualities, as deliciously unconscious of his
weakness, as his steed.

   In those, however, who take a cynical pleasure in
seeing a man make himself look ridiculous, there will be
good sport in this little volume. Never was there more
loving banter, more affectionate abuse, more tender
snubbing, than is apportioned to Mr. Matthew Arnold in
every page of 'Friendship's Garland.' The editor of that
volume cannot think enough or say enough of him. With a
hundred pretty tricks of love, such as an English Sevigné
might employ in order to bring in the beloved recollection
of her idol, this little book returns and again returns,
to the one adored name. He is pelted with delirious
gibes, such as a bridegroom employs when he jeers fondly
at his bride; in short, we are obliged to exhaust the
fondest and dearest relationships in order to express,
and that imperfectly, the tender devotion of this book
to its author, and its sense of the supreme thought,
cleverness, wit, genius, and universal superiority which
are embodied in that name of Matthew Arnold and breathe
forth in it the very music of the spheres.

27. R. H. HUTTON (?), UNSIGNED REVIEW, 'SPECTATOR'

8 July 1871, xliv, 616

Hutton's review is, in the first place, one of few notices of 'Friendships' Garland'. It is also an excep-
tionally sympathetic response, just the response Arnold
must have wanted, but not, at this period, what usually
awaited his publications. 'There is no danger', Hutton
writes, 'that such prophets [as Arnold] will ever be too
much listened to.' Both senses of 'too much' would seem
to apply to 'Friendship's Garland'. Hutton himself
remained an advocate for Arnold's poetry and criticism,
but he became impatient with the religious writings of
the 1870s.

What is this book, with its appearance of elegant sorrow,
recalling to such readers as may be old enough to appreciate the suggestion as 'annual' in mourning? It is the
tribute which Mr. Matthew Arnold pays to his departed

friend, Arminius, Baron von Thunder-ten-Tronkh, whose
signature our readers may remember to have seen from time
to time in the 'Pall Mall Gazette.' Why 'departed'? He
is gone, presumably from the the same cause that hurried
Don Quixote and Sir Roger de Coverley to their graves,
that his literary friend would not or could not keep him
alive. He fell, we learn, at the siege of Paris, not
altogether without honour, as 'three English members of
Parliament, celebrated for their ardent charity and
advanced civilization,' whom Adolescens Leo, Esq., of the
'Daily Telegraph,' the teller of the sad story, had discovered sitting at breakfast, 'adorned with a red cross
and eating a Strasburg pie,' officiated at his funeral.
Here we have his 'conversation, letters, and opinions.'
Of course the book is a delightful one to read. Mr.
Arnold wields his weapon of satire with rare skill, and
has especially the admirable gift of being personal without being rude. Once or twice he steps beyond the line,
and makes an allusion which can hardly fail to be painful; but for the most part, his raillery is of a kindly,
pleasant kind, not positively pleasant, perhaps, to the
person struck, for the smoothest and keenest rapiers do
really *hurt*, but as far as possible removed from brut-
ality. But the blows are hard enough. So to his friend
boasting of the Atlantic Telegraph says Arminius,
'Pshaw! that great rope with a Philistine at each end of
it talking inutilities!' So the great philosopher,
again, describes German constitutionalism: 'It comes up
to the throne, "With fullest heart-devotion we approach
Prussia's King, reverently beseeching him to turn away
his unconstitutional ministers." Prussia's gracious
King gives a grunt, and administers a sound kick to his
petitioners' behind, who then depart, singing in fervent
tones, "Hoch for King and Fatherland."' So, again, Mr.
Arnold apologizes for his countrymen, when Arminius, who
has been hearing Lord Lumpington, Mr. Bottles, and the
Reverend Esau Hittall administer justice, remarks, 'To
administer at all, even at the lowest stage of public
administration, a man needs instruction.' 'We have never
found it so, said I.' We need not, however, spend time
in proving that Mr. Matthew Arnold can say very good
things very well. But the question rather is, - what is
the upshot of it all? That he gives an impression of a
certain pride and exclusiveness of culture and cleverness
is clear enough; the charge has been made over and over
again, and is not without some foundation. Yet the evident sincerity and integrity of this belief in culture,
its entire freedom from all association with class and
party interests and prejudices, must be held, on the

whole, we think, to absolve it from all serious blame.
That all our national life, our government, our education, even our business, is done without discipline and
training, without fitness and special preparation in those
who do them, without even the sense that these are good
things, that in these days, when other nations are organ-
izing their material and intellectual resources, this
neglect and defect are constantly becoming more dangerous,
that we are actually losing or have lost our *prestige*,
that our superiority in some things is gone, and in others
endangered, is what Mr. Arnold preaches to his countrymen.
There is no danger that such prophets will ever be too
much listened to.

St. Paul and Protestantism (1870)

28. T. H. HUXLEY IN A LETTER TO ARNOLD

10 May 1870

W. H. G. Armytage notes that it was in 1869, just as
Arnold embarked on his efforts to reform theology in
accordance with what he took to be the modern, scientific
mind, that a close and intimate friendship developed between him and 'the foremost protagonist of the scientific
school', T. H. Huxley (1825-95). This letter is part of
a ten-year correspondence on books and ideas between
these two leading Victorians. They came, of course, to
represent antithetical positions on the question of educational curricula, and even in this letter Huxley hints
at wider disagreements.

My dear Arnold - Many thanks for your book ['St. Paul']
which I have been diving into at odd times as leisure
served, and picking up many good things.
    One of the best is what you say near the end about
science gradually conquering the materialism of popular
religion.
    It will startle the Puritans who always coolly put the
matter the other way; but it is profoundly true.
    These people are for the most part mere idolaters with
a Bible-fetish, who urgently stand in need of conversion
by Extra-christian Missionaries.
    It takes all one's practical experience of the import-
ance of Puritan ways of thinking to overcome one's feeling of the unreality of their beliefs. I had pretty well

forgotten how real to them 'the man in the next street'
is, till your citation of their horribly absurd dogmas
reminded me of it. If you can persuade them that Paul is
fairly interpretable in your sense, it may be the beginning of better things, but I have my doubts if Paul would
own you, if he could return to expound his own epistles.
    I am glad you like my Descartes article. My business
with my scientific friends is something like yours with
the Puritans, nature being *our* Paul. - Ever yours very
faithfully, ...

29. JOHN MORLEY, UNSIGNED NOTE IN CRITICAL NOTICES,
'FORTNIGHTLY REVIEW'

June 1870, vii, 752

A year after this note appeared, Arnold was to write to
his mother about his antagonist, John Morley (1838-1923):
'the editor of the "Fortnightly", who has several times
attacked my things severely, but who has certainly learnt
something from me, and knows it. But more than half the
world can never frankly accept the person of whom they
learn, but kick at the same time that they learn' ('Letters', ii, 51). The reasons for Arnold's confidence are
not clear. Yet in spite of this damning notice, Morley
himself did later admit to having learned from Arnold.
In a review of Arnold's letters (1895), he spoke respectfully of him as a wise and influential contemporary. Like
many others, however, he could not tolerate the theological books.

A valuable contribution to the formation of a Rosa-
Matilda school of theology, prefaced by an exhortation to
the Dissenters to submit with a sweet reasonableness to
the pretensions of the Anglican sect. Theological rose-
pink would have a better chance if there were less
science in the air, for one thing, and if Mr. Arnold
could, for another, blot out from men's minds all that
half of New Testament teaching which is dead against
rose-pink. And the Dissenters would be more likely to be
impressed by the exhortation, if it had shown any faintest appreciation of the ignoble attitude, morally,

intellectually, socially, of the other side. If truth
were a thing of minor consequence, and justice an open
question, Mr. Arnold's essay and its preface would be
extremely important.

30. UNSIGNED REVIEW OF 'ST. PAUL AND PROTESTANTISM',
'BRITISH QUARTERLY REVIEW'

July 1870, lii, 170-99

The 'British Quarterly Review' was founded in 1845 as an
organ of what Arnold called 'political Dissent'. It was
not an extremist journal, and it sought to maintain fairly
high intellectual standards. In 1865 Arnold wrote to the
'Quarterly's' editor that this journal had 'the function
of forming a public whose intellectual growth is going on
or is just beginning'. The reviewer here is not Arnold's
typical philistine gargoyle, neither Mr Murphy nor the
Rev. Cattle. Though irate and at times boastful, the
comments on Arnold's book are sharp, accurate, and telling. Due to its length, we reprint only parts of the
first half of the review, dealing with the question of
church unity. The second half, not reprinted here, considers several of Arnold's major assertions about theology
and tends to reassert conventional Nonconformist positions.

Mr. Matthew Arnold, in his two recent books, has taken
upon himself to expound St. Paul and to rebuke Puritanism.
There can be no possible reason connected with either for
any regret that he has done so. Men and things, human
things and divine, must ever be submitted to fresh judgments, and be increasingly elucidated by the light of new
thought. If the Apostle Paul has hitherto been misunderstood in the true scope and full breadth of his teaching,
we are thankful to any one who can contribute to the
better comprehension of it. If Puritanism has been defective in the 'sweetness' of its life and the 'light' of its
thought, it must in every way be good for Puritanism to
have its failures pointed out, and remedies for them suggested.
     Certainly it has not hitherto met with one who has

acted towards it the part of the 'candid friend' with such
strong professions of respect, and with such a sinister
enjoyment of the process of rebuke. 'It is all for your
good, my dear;' and the merciless pedagogue searches carefully for another abrasion of the skin, and eagerly lays
on in the name of Culture and the Church of England, carefully rubbing in his preparation of Hellenic sulphur,
ecclesiastical nitre, and anti-dogmatic charcoal. The
process is not an agreeable one, but it may not on that
account be less wholesome. Had it been an enemy who had
done this, we might have borne it, as we have often done
before; but from Mr. Arnold, who 'knows something' of 'the
best of the Nonconformist ministers,' who addresses them
'out of no sort of malice or ill-will, but from esteem for
their fine qualities, and from desire for their help,' it
is very hard. The only peril is to him who adventures
themes so high as the reconstruction of Paul's theology
and the reversal of Puritan history; for while high admiration and praise must be awarded to the great faculties
which prove themselves adequate to such achievements, the
proverbial fate of rash presumption and ignorant conceit
awaits the man who fails.

If, aspiring to teach others, he only exposes his own
incompetence, he deservedly provokes the derision which a
juster self-estimate would have avoided. Success alone
can discriminate just daring from foolhardiness. He,
especially, who vaunts or complacently assumes his own
sufficiency, really exhibits the credentials of his unfitness. Even in the ablest men there is no ingredient
of character or qualification more perilous than conceit.
It works like a subtle poison, and from the faintest
taint rapidly innoculates the whole blood.

Whether Mr. Arnold possesses the qualifications needful
for the task he has undertaken, or whether he has permitted this fatal quality to impair his judgment and deterio-
rate his intellectual nature, as his successive books seem
to intimate, and as with portentous accord his countrymen
are assuming, may appear in the sequel; it is quite certain that, from some cause or other, he has lamentably
misconceived St. Paul and grossly misrepresented Puritanism.

Mr. Arnold devotes a preface and an introduction, which
occupy nearly the half of his book, to Puritanism and
Nonconformity. With this, therefore, we must first deal,
although it imposes upon us a very ungrateful necessity.
His misrepresentations and virulence in all that relates
to both, compel us to speak with a plainness of denial and
a severity of rebuke, that we would fain avoid towards one
bearing his name, endowed with his gifts, and in many

qualities so estimable. He has, however, left us no
alternative. He has thought fit to assail us with an unfairness and an invective that compel us to speak plainly
and to characterize strongly.

Mr. Arnold's parentage, and many associations of his
life, might well be supposed to have conferred some fitness for the task that he has undertaken. His intellectual genius, accomplished scholarship, and a certain liberal habit of thought in relation to dogmas and Churches,
are additional qualifications. Two or three things, however, have marred his competence. First, his rash and
self-confident assumption of the character of 'prophet of
culture' in general, and of the vocation in that capacity
to reprobate as Philistinism all forms of intellectual
life that have not upon them the mint-mark of the national
universities. His state of feeling is like that of the
University Don whose arithmetical acquisitions convinced
him that there were many well-to-do people who had not
been educated at the national universities; 'And yet,'
said he, in a sublime perplexity concerning the ways of
God to man, 'they are God Almighty's creatures.'

Next, in Mr. Arnold's culture, perhaps in his nature, the
Hellenic element is too exclusive; the Hebraic has scarcely any place. In all that he writes, the purely intellectual predominates over the emotional and spiritual.
Where, in his speculations, reason fails, and can give no
answer to the demand for solution which the great mysteries of being make, there is no voice of faith to supply
the lack, as is painfully exemplified in the cold, blank
negations of his last volume of poems. Thus the intellectual becomes too exclusively the test and measure of the
religious. Instincts that cannot be formulated are re-
pressed; the mute, mysterious yearnings and sympathies of
Hebraic souls are disallowed, if not scorned. The depths
are covered over if not filled up; and of the mystic sense
of God, and of the things of God, which constituted so
profound and predominant a part of the nature and life of
men like David, and Isaiah, and Paul, Mr. Arnold has
apparently no sense. In his determination to infuse Hellenic intelligence and refinement into the Hebraic inspirations of the religious life, he has gone so far, and
with such absorption of purpose, that the inspirations
themselves are evaporated into mere forms. Thus theology
is to him merely a system of ethical ideas, and the Church
merely a machinery for their culture - a national organization for the comprehension and good order of citizens of
all varieties of theological belief.

Another thing that neutralises the force of Mr. Arnold's rebuke is, that while, as an avowed and even vehement Churchman, he has taken upon himself to lecture Nonconformists upon the defectiveness of their Christian spirit, he does not, even by implication, admit any such shortcomings in his own Church, or acknowledge the great provocation to Nonconformists that it has given. It, poor innocent, has simply suffered from the gratuitous provocation of perverse Nonconformists.

If the spirit of dissent be evil, this does not of course diminish its intrinsic sin.   As Mr. Arnold justly says, it is no sufficient answer for a Christian man, 'We are to defer giving up our ordinary self until our neighbour shall have given up his; that is, we are never to give it up at all.' No doubt it is our imperative duty to repent of any sin proven against us, and to forsake it, irrespective of the sin of others. But we submit that in this case Mr. Arnold's partial accusations must impair the essential value of his lecture, inasmuch as he virtually assumes to adjudicate between Episcopalians and Nonconformists, and to apportion to each their respective praise or blame. In this, an adjudication differs from a simple indictment. In assigning blame, therefore, only to Nonconformists, contrary to notorious and acknowledged facts, he is guilty of a *primâ facie* (1) injustice so palpable, that the sense of it cannot fail to neutralise the effect of whatever rebuke they may deserve; whereas from a more equitable censor they might thankfully have received it. Where one of the two parties in a dispute is in the acknowledged position of an oppressor, no injustice can be more flagrant or insulting than to dwell only upon the evil temper of the oppressed, and to justify the homily by the general Christian principle that all evil temper is naughty.

Is it, forsooth, a 'fractious mixture' of politics and religion, to protest against the accumulated wrong of which the English State Church has been the embodiment; to seek the removal of the unjust disabilities which it has imposed; to claim for the religious conscience and life freedom to worship and serve God according to honest conviction? If Mr. Arnold can point to a single instance in which Nonconformists have taken political action for any other purpose, or in any other form, than simply to struggle for liberty, we will plead guilty to his accusation. And why are they, because religious men, to be debarred the right of seeking the reversal of unjust legislation, or even of that which they think unjust? Is there

a page of English history, save the short period of the
Commonwealth - which, although not without its excesses,
we must ever exult in as the glorious uprising of an outraged people against ecclesiastical and civil tyranny -
in which the Episcopal Church does not appear as employing
the strong arm of the civil power for its own aggressive
purposes? A more amazing exemplification of the fable of
the wolf and the lamb, than this accusation of political
religiousness, has surely never been gravely presented to
intelligent men.

In the contest for that perfect religious liberty and
equality before the civil law, which is every man's
inherent and sacred right, and which, though largely won,
is not crowned yet, we trust that Nonconformists will
maintain a Christian spirit of patience, gentleness, and
magnanimity, and 'as much as lieth in them, live peaceably
with all men;' and if in the stress and heat of contention
they fail of this difficult grace, let them be rebuked,
only with due consideration and gentleness; but let no
man forbid the contention itself. If to resist every un-
warrantable usurpation over the religious conscience and
life; if to demand the removal of all civil disabilities
on account of religious opinions or habits; if to strive
earnestly and by Christian and lawful means so to influence public opinion, and through it the Legislature, as
to procure the repeal of any law or prerogative which
places Nonconformists at a disadvantage; if this be what
Mr. Arnold means by a 'fractious mixture of religion and
politics,' we can give him no hope of forbearance from
it. This we hold to be both a patriotic and a religious
duty; and if this be to be 'vile' in his eyes, we must,
we fear, be 'viler still.' For if one thing be more certain than another, it is, that whether the struggle be
long or short, against enormous odds or on equal terms,
to end in utter discomfiture or complete success, the
Nonconformists of Great Britain are determined not to
rest until every vestige of religious disability and civil
inequality be removed. That this can be achieved by a
common establishment, even Mr. Arnold must, we think, now
see to be impossible; the only alternative is a common
disestablishment, and for this Nonconformists contend.
If Mr. Arnold has exactly shaped his thought, he can mean
only to scold or cajole some of the larger bodies of Nonconformists, who would thus be guilty of the meanness of
leaving the rest to their enfeebled fate, into inclusion
in the Establishment. Can he think us capable of this
meanness? Hardly are Nonconformists likely to repent and

recant, now that their day of obloquy has nearly gone,
their arduous and much-enduring battle well-nigh won, and
when the involuntary verdict of a great and even increasing number of those who, by tradition and sympathy and
ecclesiastical position, are the farthest removed from
them, is pronouncing their justification. Men learn to
love the cause for which they suffer, and do not ordinarily lay down their arms when the advantage is with them
in the fight; especially at the summons of one who mocks
their convictions, and pours cold contempt upon their
earnestness.

The more general and subtle ground of Mr. Arnold's repugnance to Nonconformity is, that it is vulgar. It characteristically lacks 'sweetness and light,' and is therefore obnoxious to the Hellenic soul -

Odi profanum vulgus et arceo:
Favete linguis. (2)

Will it be any satisfaction to him if we frankly plead
guilty to the accusation? The upper classes of English
society, who are supposed to exhibit the supreme results
of Hellenic culture, do not attend Nonconformist chapels
nor are many Nonconformist ministers younger sons of noble
or wealthy houses; nor, whatever their comparative
scholarship, have many of them received that last exquisite touch of gentlemanliness which is supposed to distinguish Oxford and Cambridge. They are not, however, the
blundering ignoramuses that, by the invidious emphasis
which he gives to the supposed exceptions, Mr. Arnold
seems to assume. Doubtless, we too have our literates,
but we would show Mr. Arnold, even in small villages, aged
and honoured scholars and thinkers, and younger men who
have won the B.A. and M.A. degrees of the London University - the comparative value of which he should know.
Nonconformity has never been without its great scholars,
and a history of the comparative contributions of such
to English theology and Biblical science would not, we
suspect, be to their disadvantage. The great bulk of Nonconformist ministers, however, have been chosen simply for
their ability to do the work of the ministry, and are not
superlatively educated.
    But the accusation suggests one or two curious quest-
ions concerning Episcopal Church-life. Are its congregations so predominantly cultured, that the presence in them
of the vulgar element in English life is not felt? If so,
what becomes of the 'Church of the poor?' As a simple

matter of fact, vast classes of our English people, as of
all people, are vulgar, in the sense intended by Mr.
Arnold. Either, therefore, these vulgar people are not
found at all in Episcopal congregations, or they are so
dominated by the cultured classes and the cultured clergymen, that their real life finds no expression. This is,
we know, the ideal of Church-and-Stateism. To 'fear God,
honour the king, and be regular and obsequious at Church,'
is the whole duty of the working man and his children.
But is this subdued, negative life either natural or
desirable? Does not such tame, deferential obsequiousness
far exceed all legitimate and healthy recognition of superior rank and culture? Is there in it any true manliness, any wholesome educational influence? Is it the
highest ideal of Christian Church-fellowship? There may
be 'sweetness and light' in such services of worship ex-
ternally regarded, but in their intrinsic character they
are repressive and indurating, rather than communicative
and educational; the real life of the people finds no expression in such Church life. And we are not aware that
in other respects it produces a general intelligence, or
social refinement, which makes the Episcopal tradesman,
or artizan, or peasant, superior to his Nonconformist
neighbour. In Nonconformist Churches, whatever the real
character and life of its members, it finds free and
natural expression. No section of the congregation is
subdued to an implicit submission of its thought to a
Sunday rubric of prayer and preaching; all are called to
an active participation in the things in which all have
an interest. The humblest pauper may not unfrequently be
heard controverting the judgment of the wealthiest and
most aristocratic. Neither cultured minister mor wealthy
deacon has his unquestioned way. While culture and
wealth do not fail of their due influence, they are not
permitted to be substitutes for intelligence and just
reason. The fundamental principle of Free Church life is,
that in the Church of Christ there is 'neither bond nor
free,' that each must respect the equal rights of all, and
prevail only by superior intelligence and goodness. And
with more or less of success. Free Churches are ever
striving after a perfect realization of their principle.

Notes

1 'self-evident'.
2   'I despise the common crowd and avoid them:
      Keep holy silence.'

31. EDITH SIMCOX, PSEUDONYMOUS REVIEW, 'ACADEMY'

13 August 1870, i, 282-3

The 'Academy', less than a year old when the following
review appeared, had been initiated by Charles Edward
Appleton to provide a critical paper, 'in which' - as Mark
Pattison put it - '"review writing" as understood and
practised in England should not be permitted, but in which
experts should report upon new publications each in his
own province'. Edith Simcox, writing under the pseudonym
of H. Lawrenny, approaches 'St. Paul and Protestantism'
with a cool, sceptical logic unusual for the reviewer of
the period, observing at once that there is no necessary
connection between Arnold's revision of Pauline theology
and his call for church unity. This is the keynote of a
review that finds Arnold illogical, confused, and self-
deceiving. His work is 'a favourable example of the literary chaos in which we shall be plunged when everybody
has all his faculties cultivated at once'.

This volume has the disadvantage of having been written,
so to speak, backwards, with the argument, that is to say,
at the end, and the application at the beginning, and
moreover with an argument and an application that have
very little to do with each other. Mr. Arnold's appeal
to Dissenters to rejoin the Established Church misses its
aim from his inability to see that there are two ways of
disagreeing, and that one is as final as the other. Let
us say, for instance, that the original difference between
Anglicans and Puritans was concerning the question whether
A was black or white; Mr. Arnold suddenly maintains on
behalf of the Establishment that it doesn't matter whether
A is black or white: but if, as is natural, the Nonconformists retort, it does matter whether A is black or white,
the dispute is at least one degree further from settlement
than it was to begin with. Mr. Arnold then shifts the
ground of his appeal to the domain of quasi-history: if
the English Puritans separated for the sake of doctrines
more important than Christian unity, which he denies,
these doctrines have now, he maintains, had their angles
so efficiently rubbed off on both sides by the spirit of a
latitudinarian time that the schism can only be kept up by
the artificial help of rival church machinery. But, in
the first place, no doctrine is of less than absolute

importance to the theologian; in the second place, it is
well to let sleeping dogs lie, and the experience of
Germany shows how easy it is to revive the ashes of an
apparently extinct controversy; and, in the third place,
it is a perfectly tenable view that a particular theory
and form of church organization is part of the essential
idea of Puritan Protestantism.

It is curious to find, side by side with references to
a decidedly unbelieving _Zeitgeist_, (1) an argument for
amity which was perfectly satisfactory to the Church of
England fifty years or more ago, but which is seldom met
with now except in tracts for village use. The Dissenters
are supposed to ask (very naturally) why they are more
blamed than the Church for the strife arising out of their
rival existences. 'Because,' returns Mr. Arnold, 'the
Church cannot help existing, and you can! Because the
Church is there, the clergyman is there: a national offi-
cer with an appointed function' - and you voluntary per-
formers needn't be there unless you like, and in fact the
established authorities would much rather that you weren't.
But surely if there is one thing about which the _Zeitgeist_
is quite positive it is this, that the fact that a thing
is, is no reason why it should continue to be: churches
which were established by law can be disestablished by
law; what was once a national persuasion may become the
badge of a sect; and an unauthorized dogma may make the
conquest of a whole people. This obvious argument for
liberty of conscience, as understood by Protestant sects,
can only have been overlooked by Mr. Arnold by reason of
the many incongruous positions which he tries to occupy at
once; he Erastianizes too much to be serious in vindicating the authority of the Church as such; he rationalizes
too much to be a competent judge between parties which,
whatever their faults of temper, their errors of judgment,
agree in staking their hopes of present and future happiness upon one solution or another of questions which Mr.
Arnold contentedly refers to an impossible 'happy moment'
of future illumination. He is, in fact, the victim of his
own 'totality;' he imports into the domain of theology the
brilliant perspicacity of an essayist, whose utterances
are in no danger of being rigorously followed up, and his
inconsistencies are therefore so transparent that the
reader is almost persuaded that the fault is his own, and
that he has somehow missed one step in the argument. The
genuine irritation which Mr. Arnold betrays when one set
of people, who differ from him on every conceivable point
of doctrine, decline to oblige him by pretending to agree
with another set of people - who differ as much in an
opposite direction - can only be explained as an

expression of the critic's 'ordinary self,' a result, not
of a real theological bias, but of the sum total of his
tastes for order, for intellectual peace, for literary
harmony, and for the mixture of absolutism and liberty
which a regime of popular authors might administer. It is
a matter of course for zealots to enforce renunciation of
the ordinary self by their converts, and if Mr. Arnold
were to recommend, in the interests of culture, that those
who hold religious convictions should be as if they held
them not, he might preach to deaf ears, but his sermon and
his text would not be evidently self-contradictory. The
belief of those who consider the Christian Church to be a
living and miraculous entity is equally clear and respectable: but the notion of schism as a sin depends upon this
belief, which has nothing in itself to make it the natural
and lawful rallying point for the friends of peace. Mr.
Arnold's patronage of a church, whose claims he mistakes
and whose position he misrepresents, would be a harmless
whim if he did not provoke his antagonists to borrow his
own weapons. 'This fatal self-righteousness,' he says,
'grounded on a false conceit of knowledge, makes comprehension impossible, because it takes for granted the
possession of the truth, and the power of deciding how
others violate it; and this is a position of superiority,
and suits conquest rather than comprehension.' The sentiment would admit of application to a writer who is authoritative without being really precise, and even without
being practically liberal.
     The positive element in the dissertation on Puritanism
and the Church of England is not much more felicitous than
the negative panacea of a 'sweet reasonableness.' The
doctrine of development which was invented to explain the
volte-faces (2) of an inspired corporation, loses its
significance when applied to merely secular changes of
intellectual fashion: besides, it is an abuse of language
to give the name of development to the natural progress of
scepticism, and to talk of the growth of a religious body,
that has just been described as laying aside, one by one,
its most peculiar and essential doctrines. If it was
development for Constantine to transfer his state patronage from the religion of Jupiter to that of Christ, if it
was development for Lutheran and Calvinistic churches to
succeed to mediaeval endowments, then the hazy universalism which is, we admit, one outcome of the spirit of the
age, might claim to be the Christianity of the future;
but even so it is not clear what it has to gain by claiming solidarity of inheritance with intervening views, very
likely as chimerical as its own, of - for instance - St.
Paul's theory of salvation. The ground of Mr. Arnold's

quarrel with the Protestant sects is, that they not only
believe certain things which he prefers to explain away,
but believe them as a matter of duty binding on all men,
and furnishing the real warrant for all moral precepts.
In making righteousness an end in itself and St. Paul
before everything a moralist, the import of two religious
tendencies, both based ostensibly on the Epistle to the
Romans, is ignored. Puritanism, according to its critic,
'finds its starting point either in the desire to flee
from eternal wrath or in the desire to obtain eternal
bliss;' its doctrines rest on the witness of our hopes and
fears. But hopes and fears however natural, cannot be
mistaken for proofs, they have a much more important function; the sanctions of Paleyism supply the readiest arguments to bring to bear on outsiders, but the true mystic
or ascetic is not convinced by them, he is created by
their possibility. Puritanism at its best - and it is not
fair to criticise the abuse or degeneracy of a system as
the system itself - is pre-eminently spiritual; its truths
are subjective, and, in one sense, matter of experience,
though not of the universal experience from which science
is derived. Approaching the subject from without, Mr.
Arnold writes, 'Paul's starting point, it cannot be too
often repeated, is the idea of righteousness; and his concern with Christ is as the clue to righteousness, not as
the clue to transcendental ontology.' Transcendental
psychology would be a truer phrase for Puritan and Pauline
religion.
     It would be unprofitable to follow Mr. Arnold through
his analysis of St. Paul's doctrinal system. Science is
wronged, art is wronged, and religious faith would be
wronged, if it had any concern in the matter, when serious
questions are arbitrarily dismissed, or discussed by
canons taken at haphazard as the argument proceeds. It is
enough to say that Mr. Arnold's softened explanation of
the doctrines, 'calling,' 'justification,' 'sanctifica-
tion,' as a not too literally understood 'dying with
Christ,' 'resurrection from the dead,' and 'growing into
Christ,' contains nothing which has not been said, in one
contest or another by orthodox Puritan divines, and little
which has not been anticipated by the rationalizers of
Christian dogma. At the same time the book contains much
common sense, many acute remarks, and enough eloquence to
make it a favourable example of the literary chaos in
which we shall be plunged when everybody has all his
faculties cultivated at once. Every man has his theological proclivities, and Mr. Arnold writes a paper on St.
Paul to air his own, because the perfect man can write a
clear and creditable paper about anything: but the

perfection of the man and of the theologian are two, and
not the least curious point about the present volume is
the gradual triumph of the latter. The perfect man is
too tolerant to condemn those who merely disagree from
him, but the moral precepts he lays down as to *how* discordant views shall be held, are inevitably deduced from
his own tenets, and if he allows himself to enforce them
with some acrimony, because morality is common ground, he
departs not the less surely from the sweet reasonableness
of the artist, who sees 'beauty' in sharp outlines; the
humane culture of the poet, whose imagination knows neither true nor false while feeling the 'charm' of contrast
and conflict amongst excellencies, and the miscellaneous
perfection of the critic who has no time to believe anything himself till he had done justice to the innumerable
arguments for and against any possible thesis.

Notes

1   'vision of an era'.
2   'reversal of opinion'.

32. R. W. CHURCH, THE CHURCH AND NONCONFORMITY,
'QUARTERLY REVIEW'

April 1871, cxxx, 432-61

Richard William Church (1815-90) was Dean of St Paul's
for the last years of his life and a prominent High Church
spokesman. He had roots in both the Evangelical and High
Church traditions. His boyhood schooling was strongly
Evangelical, and he entered Wadham College, Oxford (1833),
in order to work with tutors of that persuasion. But in
1835 he met Keble and Newman, with whom he became closely
involved, renouncing a fellowship during the uproar over
Tract XC. When Newman finally joined the Church of Rome,
Church broke off their relationship. From the 1840s
Church published many works on religious and literary
topics, among them his history of the Oxford Movement. He
wrote this review just a few months before his friend
Gladstone had him appointed dean. Although we have cut
Church's article, his line of argument remains clear.

It may be said to be one of the open secrets of our time
that great religious changes are impending in England.

To all minds which feel the interest of religion the momentous question is presenting itself, - What is to be the
future of religion in England, as far as religion is
affected by the outward framework and visible form under
which it lives and acts? These outward conditions in
England have been very peculiar. Nothing exactly like it
has been known in Christendom. Religion has been organized simultaneously on two different and antagonistic
principles, and on both of them organized naturally,
strongly, and popularly. The Church principle and system,
and the Nonconformist principle and system, have long been,
like two nations and two manner of people, struggling in
the womb of English Christianity.

They are essentially separated by a great gulf. The basis
on which one rests is a public one, that on which the
other rests is a private one.

Whether these two great roads are still to remain open for
the religion of Englishmen, or whether one of them is to
be closed, and closed for ever, is becoming one of the
serious questions of the time. From the earliest days of
English history, with one short interruption, there has
been a public Church, a public religion. We do not call
it national, for it has not always been such; but it has
always been public, open to the public, and for the public; public in its aims, public in its management. Whatever its origin, it was not private; whatever its changes,
they have been brought about by great public influences,
and they have been fixed by the acts of public authority.
Whether there shall be such a thing any longer, is what
the present generation will have to decide for themselves
and those who come after them.

The general direction of Liberal thought in politics and
religion is in favour of reducing all religious organization to a private matter: that is to say, to giving to the
Nonconformist principle and system a complete and final
triumph over the older principle and system. And this is
natural; for the Nonconformists claim to have been in all
periods of English history the staunch supporters of
Liberal principles; and, as regards the embodiment of

these principles in definite political changes and acts of
legislation, the claim is well-founded. Whether the vaun-
ted Nonconformist support of Liberal ideas has always been
accompanied with what gives them their value - breadth and
accuracy of knowledge, clearness and enlightenment of
view, largeness of purpose and ends, and the moral qualities of nobleness, single-mindedness, and generosity - is
fairly open to question. But the Liberal party owes them
much, and is with reason expected to listen to their
claims. But their claims are not paramount, and must be
open to re-examination and scrutiny.

Parties, political and religious, go on, repeating more
and more emphatically their assumptions and watchwords;
till at last, wearied out, perhaps, or rendered suspicious
by confident and unqualified assertion and by the increasing disproportion of assertion to proof, the cross-
examiner appears. He asks the reason why, of things which
are taken for granted without misgiving, and are glibly
and easily reiterated; and the difficulty and trouble
which the answer gives are the measure of the usefulness
of his function even to his own side. The oscillations
and development of religious and philosophical thought
exemplify this law at all times, and it has not been without its remarkable and significant instances in our own.
This office, with respect to the current assumption among
Liberal thinkers and talkers that the Nonconformist principle of religious organization is the true and right one,
and that it ought to be made, at the cost of great organic
changes, the only one, has been undertaken by Mr. Matthew
Arnold; and there are few men who, from their position,
the character of their mind, and their special gifts, are
better qualified to discharge it with keenness and force,
and, what is more important still, with unflinching
straightforwardness and honesty.
    Mr. Arnold has come forward to challenge the ordinary
Liberal assumption that the victory of Dissent, which to
so many people seems imminent, will be the victory of
religious freedom, religious right, and religious improvement. He disputes the favourite Nonconformist thesis that
levelling down, the equalization in external conditions of
all religious societies, is the exclusively true theory of
religious organization in a free country, and its right
and wholesome state. As a Liberal he has endeavoured to
put before Liberals, as a religious man he has endeavoured
to put before religious men, what is likely to be the
effect on human progress and on religion in England, of
the extinction, in the name of equality, of that ancient

public characteristic form in which Englishmen have up to
this time known and practised religion; and of the suppression and obliteration, it may be said on mere grounds
of theory, of one of the two great spheres of religious
interest and religious activity in England.

Mr. Arnold's claim to be listened to with attention, as
an original and independent thinker, certainly not biassed
in favour of ecclesiastical theology or ecclesiastical
exclusiveness, no one would affect to question. But there
are two things which are likely to prejudice him with many
of those whom he addresses, especially among the Nonconformists. One of them is his manner as a writer; the
other is the view of doctrine which he professes. As to
the first, it is one for which Mr. Arnold, ever since he
began to write, has been severely dealt with. He has been
accused of not being in earnest; of playing with what is
serious, and amusing himself with his own ingenuity and
caprices of taste and prepossession; of being too delicate
and fastidious in dealing with the pressing questions of a
bold and energetic age, which require ready and broad, and
perhaps rough answers, rather than far-fetched and refined
ones. People take up his phrases, and expect on producing
them to call up a smile: they except to his classifications
and terminology, *Hebraizing* and *Hellenizing, Mialism* and
Millism, as unreal, impertinent, and fantastic; they
resent being ticketed as *Barbarians* or *Philistines* by the
preacher of culture. These are tricks of writing, and
belong to a man's manner and favourite ways of expressing
himself; and all of us have a right to our likes and dislikes in such matters of taste. But there never was a
greater mistake than that of supposing from this that Mr.
Arnold had not thought deeply and really on what he writes
about, or that he is anything short of being in the most
anxious and often sorrowful earnest.

The other point is more important. Nonconformists, whose
theology Mr. Arnold criticises so severely, have certainly
some reason to except to the theology of their critic.
Mr. Arnold's interpretation of St. Paul, if it is the true
and the adequate one, makes a clean sweep of a good deal
more than Puritan divinity and tradition; and it certainly
seems to us that in his anxiety to bring out in its due
importance the moral basis and moral significance of
religion, which he does with great beauty and truth, he
overlooks two things, - the inextricable connection with
even the moral side of Christianity of real outward facts
of history, which if they fall, must bring down Christianity with them, and which is intelligible to deny, but

idle to ignore; and next, the value of those efforts after
a philosophy of religion - efforts, often, doubtless, misdirected and barren, yet also, as certainly, involving
deep and true work of the human mind, close scrutiny of
its ideas, and patient and skilful use of the materials of
knowing, which have gone on without interruption during
the most progressive ages of man, and which we call theology. Mr. Arnold, for instance, is so deeply impressed
and so amply satisfied with St. Paul's moral use of the
idea of resurrection, that he does not seem to want for
himself or further to care to see in St. Paul, any great
stress laid on the historical fact of our Lord's resurrection. But to leave out the capital and supreme significance of that actual rising from actual death in the
belief and teaching of St. Paul, is surely as arbitrary
and hopeless a suppression as any that can be laid to the
charge of those Puritan interpreters who have been blind
to St. Paul's morality, and have dropped it out of his
doctrine. It is vain to say that St. Paul did not want
it as a real fact and step in the history and development
of human destiny, as well as a great figure and suggestion
of moral progress. It is in vain to attempt to expound
St. Paul on the supposition that though he believed the
resurrection as a fact, he put it, as an historical event,
in the background as secondary: it is in vain to explain
the meaning of Christianity on the supposition that it may
be left aside, to succumb to or to wait for the decision
of science. The great alternative which the question
about it offers ought never to be absent from the mind of
any one who speaks of Christianity. If it cannot be, then
Christianity cannot be; and then it is waste of time to
write about churches and sects, and to compare their
merits.

33.   J. C. SHAIRP, THE LITERARY THEORY OF CULTURE, FROM
'CULTURE AND RELIGION'

1871

_____

John Campbell Shairp (1819-85) lived the life of a conventional, mildly productive, reasonable mid-Victorian
academician. After some training at Edinburgh and Glasgow
he went to Balliol College, Oxford (1840), where he be-
friended Clough and John Duke Coleridge. After some years

of study and teaching, he became Latin professor at St
Andrew's (1861) and later Principal of United College
(1868).   During all this time he contributed poems and
reviews to periodicals.   'Culture and Religion' (1871),
a series of five lectures delivered at United College in
the winter of 1870, was a popular book in its day, running
into several editions.   The following selection represents
only those passages dealing with Arnold.

Mr. Arnold sets before us a lofty aim, - he has bid us
seek our good in something unseen, in a spiritual energy.
In doing this he has done well.   But I must hold that he
has erred in his estimate of what that spiritual energy
is, and he has missed, I think, the true source from which
it is to be mainly derived.   For in his account of it he
has placed that as primary which is secondary and subordinate, and made that secondary which by right ought to
be supreme.

You will remember that when describing his idea of the
perfection to be aimed at, he makes religion one factor
in it, - an important and powerful factor no doubt, still
but one element out of several, and that not necessarily
the ruling element, but a means towards an end, higher,
more supreme, more all-embracing than itself.   The end
was a many-sided, harmonious development of human nature,
and to this end religion was only an important means.

In thus assigning to religion a secondary, however
important, place, this theory, as I conceive, if consistently acted on, would annihilate religion.   There are
things which are either ends in themselves or they are
nothing; and such, I conceive, religion is.   It either is
supreme, a good in itself and for its own sake, or it is
not at all.   The first and great commandment must either
be so set before us as to be obeyed, entered into, in and
for itself, without any ulterior view, or it cannot be
obeyed at all.   It cannot be made subservient to any
ulterior purpose.   And herein is instanced 'a remarkable
law of ethics, which is well known to all who have given
their minds to the subject.'   I shall give it in the words
of one who has expressed it so well in his own unequaled
language that it has been proposed to name it after him,
Dr. Newman's law: - 'All virtue and goodness tend to make
men powerful in this world; but they who aim at the power
have not the virtue.   Again: Virtue is its own reward, and
brings with it the truest and highest pleasures; but they
who cultivate it for the pleasure-sake are selfish, not

religious, and will never gain the pleasure, because they
never can have the virtue.'
   Apply this to the present subject. They who seek religion for culture-sake are aesthetic, not religious, and
will never gain that grace which religion adds to culture,
because they never can have the religion. To seek religion for the personal elevation or even for the social
improvement it brings, is really to fall from faith which
rests in God and the knowledge of Him as the ultimate
good, and has no by-ends to serve. And what do we see in
actual life? There shall be two men, one of whom has
started on the road of self-improvement from a mainly
intellectual interest, from the love of art, literature,
science, or from the delight these give, but has not been
actuated by a sense of responsibility to a Higher than
himself. The other has begun with some sense of God, and
of his relation to Him, and starting from this centre has
gone on to add to it all the moral and mental improvement
within his reach, feeling that, beside the pleasure these
things give in themselves, he will thus best fulfill the
purpose of Him who gave them, thus best promote the good
of his fellow-men, and attain the end of his own existence. Which of these two will be the highest man, in
which will be gathered up the most excellent graces of
character, the truest nobility of soul? You cannot doubt
it. The sense that a man is serving a Higher than himself, with a service which will become ever more and more
perfect freedom, evokes more profound, more humbling, more
exalted emotions than anything else in the world can do.
The spirit of man is an instrument which cannot give out
its deepest, finest tones, except under the immediate hand
of the Divine Harmonist. That is, before it can educe the
highest capacities of which human nature is susceptible,
culture must cease to be merely culture, and pass over
into religion. And here we see another aspect of that
great ethical law already noticed as compassing all human
action, whereby 'the abandoning of some lower object in
obedience to a higher aim is made the very condition of
securing the said lower object.' According to this law
it comes that he will approach nearer to perfection, or
(since to speak of perfection in such as we are sounds
like presumption) rather let us say, he will reach further, will attain to a truer, deeper, more lovely humanity,
who makes not culture, but oneness with the will of God,
his ultimate aim. The ends of culture, truly conceived,
are best attained by forgetting culture, and aiming higher.
And what is this but translating into modern and less forcible language the old words, whose meaning is often greatly
misunderstood, 'Seek ye first the kingdom of God, and all
other things will be added unto you?' But by seeking the

other things first, as we naturally do, we miss not only
the kingdom of God, but those other things also which are
only truly attained by aiming beyond them.

Another objection to the theory we have been considering remains to be noted. Its starting-point is the idea
of perfecting self; and though, as it gradually evolves,
it tries to forget self, and to include quite other elements, yet it never succeeds in getting clear of the taint
of self-reference with which it set out. While making
this objection, I do not forget that Mr. Arnold, in drawing out his view, proposes as the end of culture to make
reason and the kingdom of God prevail; that he sees
clearly, and insists strongly, that an isolated self-
culture is impossible, that we cannot make progress towards perfection ourselves, unless we strive earnestly to
carry our fellow-men along with us. Still may it not with
justice be said that these unselfish elements - the desire
for others' good, the desire to advance God's kingdom on
earth - are in this theory awakened, not simply for their
own sakes, not chiefly because they are good in themselves, but because they are clearly discerned to be necessary to our self-perfection, - elements apart from which
this cannot exist? And so it comes that culture, though
made our end never so earnestly, cannot shelter a man from
thoughts about himself, cannot free him from that which
all must feel to be fatal to high character, - continual
self-consciousness. The only forces strong enough to do
this are great truths which carry him out of and beyond
himself, the things of the spiritual world sought, not
mainly because of their reflex actions on us, but for
their own sakes, because of their own inherent worthiness.
There is perhaps no truer sign that a man is really
advancing than that he is learning to forget himself, that
he is losing the natural thoughts about self in the thought
of One higher than himself, to whose guidance he can commit
himself and all men. This is no doubt a lesson not quickly
learnt; but there is no help to learning it in theories of
self-culture which exalt man's natural self-seeking into a
specious and refined philosophy of life.

Again, it would seem that in a world made like ours,
Culture, as Mr. Arnold conceives it, instead of becoming an
all-embracing bond of brotherhood, is likely to be rather
a principle of exclusion and isolation. Culture such as he
pictures is at present confessedly the possession of a very
small circle. Consider, then, the average powers of men,
the circumstances in which the majority must live, the
physical wants that must always be uppermost in their
thoughts, and say if we can conceive that, even in the most
advanced state of education and civilization possible, high

culture can become the common portion of the multitude.
And with the few on a high level of cultivation, the many,
to take the best, on a much lower, what is the natural
result.. Fastidious exclusiveness on the part of the former, which is hardly human, certainly not Christian. Take
any concourse of men, from the House of Commons down to
the humblest conventicle, how will the majority of them
appear to eyes refined by elaborate culture, but not hum-
anized by any deeper sentiment? To such an onlooker will
not the countenances of most seem unlovely, their manners
repulsive, their modes of thought commonplace, - it may
be, sordid? By any such concourse the man of mere culture
will, I think, feel himself repelled, not attracted. So
it must be, because Culture, being mainly a literary and
aesthetic product, finds little in the unlettered multitude that is akin to itself. It is, after all, a dainty
and divisive quality, and cannot reach to the depths of
humanity. To do this takes some deeper, broader, more
brotherly impulse, one which shall touch the universal
ground on which men are one, not that in which they
differ, - their common nature, common destiny, the needs
that poor and rich alike share. For this we must look
elsewhere than to Culture, however enlarged.

As perfection is put forward in the theory I have been
examining, one cannot but feel that there is a very inadequate notion of the evil in the human heart that is to
be cured, and of the nature of the powers that are needed
to cope with it. And in this respect we cannot but be
struck with how greatly Christianity differs from Culture,
and differs only to surpass it: its estimate of the disease is so much deeper, and the remedy to which it turns
so far transcends all human nostrums. Christianity, too,
holds out perfection as the goal. But in doing so its
view is not confined to time, but contemplates an endless
progression in far-on ages. The perfection the Culturists
speak of, if it does not wholly exclude the other life,
seems to fix the eye mainly on what can be done here, and
not to take much account of what is beyond. That was a
higher and truer idea of perfection which Leighton had:
'It is an union with a Higher Good by love, that alone is
endless perfection. The only sufficient object for man
must be something that adds to and perfects his nature,
to which he must be united in love; somewhat higher than
himself, yea, the highest of all, the Father of spirits.
That alone completes a spirit and blesses it, - to love
Him, the spring of spirits.'
     To sum up all that has been said, the defect in Mr.
Arnold's theory is this: It places in the second and

subordinate place that which should be supreme, and ele-
vates to the position of command a power which, rightly
understood, should be subordinate and ministrant to a
higher than itself. The relation to God is first, this
relation is last, and Culture should fill up the inter-
space, - Culture, that is, the endeavour to know and use
aright the nature which He has given us, and the world
in which He has placed us. Used in such a way, Culture
is transmuted into something far higher, more beneficent,
than it ever could become if set up for itself and claimed
the chief place....

Literature and Dogma (1873)

34. UNSIGNED REVIEW OF 'LITERATURE AND DOGMA', 'SATURDAY REVIEW'

1 March 1873, xxxv, 284-6

Sceptical as ever about Arnold's ideas, the 'Saturday' typifies in this article much of the contemporary dissatisfaction with Arnold the amateur theologian. The reviewer offers the usual damning faint praise of Arnold as a man of literature and culture, but only to suggest that his ideas may be determined by his charming style and that his religious writing is a 'capricious and illegitimate ... exercise of his power'. Arnold's *Zeitgeist* is turned upon himself, since it is Arnold, the reviewer says, who may be out of date.

Mr. Arnold is happier than many of his contemporaries; he has clear views on religious subjects, and is able to give them ingenious and lucid expression. But even this happiness has its limits, and Mr. Arnold may possibly be disappointed on finding a disposition prevalent to deny that approval to his matter which is freely granted to his manner. Such a distinction, of course, should in his case be drawn with caution, and not insisted on too much; for Mr. Arnold is a man of genius, and with him, however it may be with the herd of common men, matter and manner are intimately connected. But there is reason to think that he allows manner to overrule matter; so that his opinions are insensibly determined, to no inconsiderable extent, by their fitness to be put into transparent, elegant, and

occasionally sarcastic language. Culture is his special
province; and by culture he means, knowing the best that
has been thought and said in the world. To gain this
knowledge, he tells us, we must read a great deal, and
read on system; we shall then acquire the power of estim-
ating the proportion and relation of what we read, and
shall attain the tact which comes in a fair and clear mind
from a wide experience. Of specialists, as such, he has a
low opinion; they are apt to be deficient in culture, and
therefore to lack that delicacy of perception which is
perhaps more necessary than any other quality for drawing
a right conclusion from facts. Mr. Arnold thus seems to
be of opinion that, if we are to discover the truth on any
subject, we have more need to know a good deal about many
things than to be thoroughly acquainted with the subject
in hand. Whether this opinion is right or wrong, it is
evidently liable to frequent and tempting abuse. How
delightful it is to the instinctive vanity and idleness of
human nature to be assured that the discursive and flighty
intellect which looks at the world from above, and takes
habitually bird's eye views of things, is a nobler and
more successful instrument than powers devoted to patient
and prolonged inquiry. What pleasure it would give many
of us to think that, if we read with a view of picking out
the best things that have been thought and said, and write
in such a manner as to supply inferior minds with neat
ideas and nice quotations in abundance, we shall be model
students, wise thinkers, and edifying authors. Mr. Arnold
is himself superior to any such delusion, but his unskil-
ful disciples must be in great danger of it. Woe to them
if, without being masters of his almost inimitable grace,
they take, as he does, a phrase of Goethe, or a text of
the Bible, or some bright original conception, play with
it as a juggler does with a gilded ball, and leave off at
last, apparently with the impression that they have proved
something.

So far as we can see, Mr. Arnold has not arrived at any
valuable results by distrusting special studies and trusting the Zeit-Geist. Culture and literature are admirable
things, and give, no doubt, to the minds in which they are
naturalized a peculiar breadth of view, a delicacy and
grace of conception, a sense of fitness, harmony, and proportion. But somehow, when free and unfettered genius has
glanced over the universe, there is plenty left to reward
the research of a quiet plodding little man in spectacles;
and perhaps, if there had not been many previous generations of plodders, even Mr. Arnold would not have found

so wide a field open to his view, and might have been in
actual danger of originating speculations akin to those
which he is now forward to condemn. The limits of inquiry
on most subjects are more likely to be ultimately ascertained by students who approach them from within than by
the most ingenious lookers-on; and the man who comes, worn
and wearied, and perhaps with little definite result, from
a painful search for what he thinks the highest truth, may
still be the best authority attainable as to its general
outline. Mr. Arnold would have owed more respect to theology and theologians than he has shown, even if his speculations had landed him on anything which could be fairly
accepted as a body of reasoned truth; but, as we have
seen, his literary method conducts him a little way, and
then fails him utterly. He soon reaches a point at which
he can see nothing distinctly, and then he stands still,
and distributes freely his censures on ignorance and
blindness.

We must not, however, forget the Zeit-Geist, the spirit
of the day, the prophetic soul of the wide world dreaming
on things to come. Mr. Arnold thinks that the Pope is,
in idea, this very Zeit-Geist, only unhappily the interpretations of the Vatican are far less true than its
instincts. He also speculates on what effects time and
its familiar spirit might possibly have wrought on the
opinions of a distinguished Romanist among ourselves. He
suggests that, if Dr. Newman had been born into the world
twenty years later, and been touched with the delicate
breath of the Zeit-Geist, that exquisite and delicate
genius would himself have been the first to feel the unsoundness of his views about the Bible, and would have
inclined to Mr. Arnold's literary method of interpretation. We are tempted to catch at the idea, and, by parity
of argument, to speculate in our turn whether, if Mr.
Arnold had been born twenty years earlier, his exquisite
and delicate genius might not have been likewise retrospective, and have sympathized dogmatically with Dr.
Newman. Time stays for no man; and to gather the evanes-
cent bloom of its opinions and sentiments requires a
rapid as well as a dexterous hand. Even Mr. Arnold perhaps, is in danger of falling behind. He is impartial in
his suspicion of specialists, and is prepared to defend
the claims of literature not only against theologians,
but against the advocates of physical science. It is
painful to think of the consequences which may ensue in a
few years if Mr. Arnold, with his delicate intellectual
organization, is forced into rude contact with those un-
sparing inquirers who put such direct questions both to
matter and men. He may be asked what he means by saying

that spirit is influence; whether he holds mind to be a
function of matter, or matter a function of mind; what
reason he has for maintaining that 'righteousness leadeth
to life,' or any similar formula, is a synthetical proposition conveying a moral truth, and not a physical statement in disguise, embodying a piece of pure utilitarianism. It is to be feared that the merely literary faculty
will prove itself incapable of dealing with the fundamental questions thus suggested, and that Mr. Arnold may find
his relations as awkward to the disciples of Mr. Herbert
Spencer and Mr. Huxley, if not to those gentlemen themselves, as they now are, by his own confession, to the
Bishops of Winchester and Gloucester.

The mention of these distinguished prelates reminds us
of the last thing that need here be said about Mr.
Arnold's book. In it he shows himself as usual a master
of literary style. He writes the best of all prose, the
prose of a poet. His sentences follow with the utmost
freedom the mould of his thought; he repeats himself continually, but with variations like those of a skilful
musician on a familiar air, and he avoids dulness with
instinctive felicity. But he fails occasionally when his
work is tried by the high moral, or, as he will have it,
religious standard which he has freely proposed to his
readers. No one but himself can tell how far in the process of composition he exemplified the 'method' and the
'secret' on which he insists; to what self-examination he
submitted himself as a writer; what self-renunciation he
practised sooner than say a trivial or superficial thing;
what pleasure, peace, and happiness he derived from hitting his mark. It is with regard to the 'element' that
he is sometimes obviously at fault; his *epieikeia*, (1) his
mildness, his sweet reasonableness, are liable to serious
interruption. Not being a theologian, he can claim immu-
nity from the *odium theologicum*; (2) but he indulges in a
strain of mocking personality which is unworthy of any
serious subject whatever. Early in his book he quotes
remarks of the Bishops of Winchester and Gloucester which
imply that those Bishops have some esteem for dogmatic
theology. After that, he makes fun of them freely and
repeatedly, as if they had lost the character of sensible
men. They are described, one or both, as particularly
strong in metaphysics, as men with more metaphysics than
literary tact, as meditating on personality, or in lighter
moments on political economy, as given to clever learned
trifling, as having lost the sense that religion begins
and ends in righteousness, while capable of deducing
properties with success and brilliant logical play. The
Bishops in question, we all know, are not specially

remarkable as metaphysicians. The Bishop of Winchester,
though quite capable of handling abstractions, generally
takes things in the concrete, and is never so felicitous
as when dealing directly with men. The Bishop of Gloucester is best known to students as an exact and patient
verbal critic, who is particularly slow to sacrifice the
literal meaning of the text to generalizations of any kind
whatever. Mr. Arnold would be obliged to respect these
prelates if he described them as they are; but he describes them as they are not, and laughs at them. Another
instance of ill-placed facetiousness is still more to be
regretted. From what has been said above, it will be
easily understood that Mr. Arnold does not accept the
doctrine of the Trinity. In order that he may deal with
it more freely, he puts forward as a parallel what he is
pleased to call the fairy tale of three Lord Shaftesburys - there being supposed to be one Lord Shaftesbury
with a race of vile offenders to deal with, whom natural
goodness would incline him to let off, but justice will
not allow it; a younger Lord Shaftesbury, on the scale of
his father and very like him, who consents to live among
the offenders and be put to an ignominious death, on condition that his merits shall be counted against their de-
merits; and, finally, a third Lord Shaftesbury, still on
the same high scale, who works in a very occult manner,
and is busy in applying everywhere the benefits of the
son's satisfaction and the father's goodness. Surely
there is something very different from sweet reasonableness in a parody such as this, not just hinted at as if
by accident, but told at greater length than we have ventured to tell it, and referred to again and again. The
gratuitous introduction in such a context of a living
man whose character and opinions are evidence beforehand
that he will feel the proceeding as something worse than
a personal insult, is such a violation of good taste as
happily is seldom met with. If a master of the literary
faculty is betrayed into so capricious and illegitimate
an exercise of his power as this within his natural province of allegory and illustration, he must expect his
words and opinions to go for very little when, on the
strength of the same faculty, he ventures freely upon
subjects which good men hold sacred, and on which wise
men, before they speak, think twice at the very least.

Notes

1   'mildness', 'reasonableness'.
2   'theological odium'.

35. JOHN TULLOCH, AMATEUR THEOLOGY, 'BLACKWOOD'S MAGAZINE'

June 1873, cxiii, 678-92

John Tulloch (1823-86) became, upon his appointment as Chief Clerk of the General Assembly (in 1875), the most prominent churchman in Scotland. He began writing for periodicals in 1848 and contributed to the 'Scotsman', 'North British Reivew', 'British Quarterly Review', 'Contemporary', 'Nineteenth Century', 'Fraser's', the 'Edinburgh' and 'Blackwood's'. In 1854 Tulloch became Principal of St Mary's College, St Andrew's, and its Professor of Theology. A professional theologian, Tulloch had little time for Arnold's efforts in the field, as his title to this review of 'Literature and Dogma' indicates. Arnold was later to turn to Tulloch for information, reading his 'Rational Theology and Christian Philosophy in England in the Seventeenth Century' (1872) before writing Falkland in 1877.

Ours is said to be an age of great religious thoughtfulness. 'Thinkers' are rife in all departments of knowledge, but especially in that which used to be supposed the highest and most difficult of all, and in which men only ventured to speculate who had trained themselves by long and laborious culture. We have changed all that. Our most notable religious teachers are no longer men who have spent their days and nights in the study of Holy Scripture, and in calm and grave reflection on the great subjects which its study suggests, but 'able' editors, 'advanced' dukes, and 'literary' men with no function for 'dogma,' and who despise it accordingly. If it were said that our age was one of great religious restlessness and excitement, there could be no doubt of the truth of the saying. For the very air around us is resonant with theological disturbance.

Our complaint is, not that theology is undergoing, as it must undergo, great modifications of its accumulated opinions and traditions, but that its old opinions are frequently set aside as valueless by those who have never studied them, and that its accumulated treasures are held to be so much waste-paper by many who know nothing of

them, and have never tried to estimate them. There may be
progress in theology as in other things, and the old
phrases and forms of doctrine cannot be expected to hold
their place permanently here any more than elsewhere. But
true advance is not to be sought in any branch of knowledge by merely turning our back on what is old and welcoming all manner of novelties. We may have to unlearn
much that our forefathers believed; but it is only a
shallow philosophy that does not recognise what was true
and good, as well as defective and false, in the grounds
of their belief. With all our increased knowledge and
more exact canons of verification, the capacity of human
thought varies but slightly from age to age. It may be
fairly questioned, indeed, whether the power of brain,
in individual cases, retains its old level with the wider
diffusion of intellectual culture. The attitude of the
student, therefore, towards past forms of opinion, ought
always to be an attitude of respectful criticism. If no
doctrines, however venerable, are entitled to acceptance
merely because they are old, it is yet the business of the
student to trace and acknowledge the true conditions of
thought or faith out of which they grew, and the genuine
elements of knowledge which they embrace, or were supposed to embrace, against the errors of their time. The
study of dogma, pursued in this manner, becomes a study
which at once illuminates the past and guides the present.
It is the best corrective of extravagant theory and self-
confidence. The student learns how varied, subtle, and
multiplied have been the relations of religious thought in
all ages of intellectual excitement - how constantly these
relations repeat themselves under modified forms - and how
little essential novelty there frequently is in the most
'modern' theories. He acquires an instinct of appreciation and balance of judgment that enables him to estimate
the real constituents of progress in any movement, and to
guide possibly the course of the movement in a useful or
beneficial direction.
     It is one of our most serious objections to the work
before us that it betrays so inadequate an estimate of the
true meaning and value of dogma, and of the high uses
which may come from its intelligent study to the advance
of religious thought. We take this objection the more
freely, because the author is evidently not without serious aims in this and other publications which he has
devoted to religious questions, however easy it may be
for many readers to doubt this. We credit Mr. Arnold,
after a careful perusal of these writings, with a desire
upon the whole to help religious inquiry, and to bring the
claims of the Christian Church before a certain class of

minds disposed to set them aside altogether. There are
passages here and there so admirably expressed, and even
lines of thought at times so finely worked out, that we
are bound to accept them as fruits of a genuine religious
interest. We have felt inclined to say to ourselves,
this author is not a mere amateur - one who writes upon
theology because it is the fashion of the day to do so.
  This, we are sorry to confess, is not the impression
left by Dr. Arnold's latest and apparently most mature
work. It has, upon the whole, fewer traces of earnest
intelligence, while the faults of the author appear in
their most aggravated form. Especially, it has all those
characteristics which stamp the mere amateur writer in
theology or in anything else. Although in the form of a
book 'Literature and Dogma' is really only a large pamphlet directed in great part against the bishops of the
Church of England, particularly the Bishops of Winchester
and Gloucester. The same continuous vein of flippant
personality, designed as pleasantry, which marked 'St
Paul and Protestantism' towards the Dissenters, pervades
this volume towards the bishops. And here it is more
offensive, because at once more obtrusive and less
directly connected with the subject. The previous volume
was, after all, in form little more than a pamphlet. It
was of the nature of a special appeal to the Nonconformists; but the present volume is meant to be 'An Essay
towards a better apprehension of the Bible.' It seems to
have grown out of a natural wish of the author to work
out in a larger and more consistent form, with reference
to Scripture as a whole, the threads of thought which he
had previously started in relation to St Paul. No object
could well be more grave or elevated. It was surely un-
desirable to mix up with such an object any grievances the
author may have with the Bishops of Gloucester or Winchester, or the Archbishop of York, or the Dean of Norwich.
Evidently, these ecclesiastical authorities have not
judged highly of Mr. Arnold's efforts to expound St Paul
or to minimise religious dogma. It was not to be expected
that they would. But this is no reason why they should
be made to play the part - not of chorus, but, we might
say, of scullion; in his present volume. Appearing in the
introduction as the representatives of dogmatic theology,
they reappear in the background of his argument, whenever
it is convenient for him to discharge some of that irre-
pressible scorn with which his style is constantly mant-
ling. There may be, to certain readers, something of
entertainment in their first or second appearance, and the
'chaff' which he levels at them; but even the reader in
search of amusement gets heartily tired of them. The

'chaff' becomes very dreary, indeed; and Mr Arnold's
taste, if not his sense, should have made him avoid this.

In one instance, indeed - an illustration of what he calls
'the Protestant story of Justification' - he has allowed
his love of personal allusion to hurry him into a parallel
of such merely vulgar profanity as to shock every true and
right instinct. No Philistine who had never heard of
'sweetness and light' could have further transgressed.
Our author would do well to remember that there may be a
Philistinism of thought as well as of manner, and that the
true British character of that name may appear all the
more offensively when clothed with a certain external
polish. It is a deeper outrage to drag the sacred
thoughts of your fellow-creatures into that aspect of
caricature to which the highest subjects often lend themselves most easily, than to cherish honestly even the most
imperfect and debased notions of such subjects. It cannot
advance the conception of religion to have any of its doctrines, and especially one which has so powerfully swayed
many devout minds, presented under images of ludicrous
inaptitude.
   The great object of Mr Arnold's present volume, as it
was in a more limited degree of his previous essay on St
Paul, is to draw out the distinction betwixt dogma, or
what he frequently calls 'metaphysics' in religion, and
religion itself.
   Now of course it is needless to say, and it was hardly
necessary for Mr Arnold to announce with such repetitory
emphasis, that there is a distinction betwixt religion
and dogma. The distinction lies obviously in the respective nature of the things. 'Religion is conduct,' as the
author says, or touches conduct. It is practical, and
may and frequently does exist where there is little or no
knowledge of dogma. Dogma, again, is in form at least
intellectual. It represents our conception of religious
truth, and, like all other intellectual products, it may
be clearly apprehended without any practical result. But
surely the fact that opinion does not necessarily influence conduct, by no means destroys the value of 'right
opinions' in religion any more than in other things.
Because dogma is something quite distinct from conduct,
and the one may exist without the other, this is no reason
for disparaging dogma, or for putting it aside as of no
account. For what are dogmas, after all, but men's highest thoughts about religion - the thoughts of the Church
formulated and set down in order respecting those Divine
relations out of which all religion comes, and into which

when we make it a subject of reflection, it always runs?
Man, as our author quotes, 'is a being of a large discourse looking before and after,' and he cannot help
thinking out what appears to him the conditions of right
conduct. It is of the essence of religion that these conditions are felt largely to be beyond ourselves. Of this
very fact Mr Arnold makes much. 'The *not ourselves*,'
which is in us and around us, and exercises constantly so
much influence over us, in his own phrase to express the
religious side of life. Or again, more definitely, '*The
not ourselves which makes for righteousness*;' or, more
definitely still, 'the *enduring power, not ourselves,
which makes for righteousness*.' These are the forms
under which he conceives the Divine, or that which is
more than we are, and in conformity with which religion
arises. Even he cannot get quit of dogma so far. God is
for him - not a person or a cause (this is to anthro-
pomorphise) - but the 'Eternal,' or 'enduring Power not
ourselves which makes for righteousness.' To talk of God
as a person, still more as a 'personal First Cause, the
moral and intelligent Governor of the universe,' is to
talk what appears to him unverifiable nonsense. But to
talk of God as 'the stream of tendency by which all things
fulfil the law of their being,' or as the 'Eternal' -
the 'enduring Power not ourselves which makes for righteousness' - this is to talk in one case the language of
science, and in the other case the language of religious
experience. We say nothing in the mean time of the value
of these definitions, or whether they have any claim to
stand for what our author makes them stand; we point
merely to the obvious fact that in both cases they are
generalisations of the nature of dogma. They are the
intellectual forms in which the Divine seems true to him,
or the opinions regarding it which he would wish us to receive for our mental peace and our practical good.

But to most minds - may we not say to a catholic *con-
sensus* of minds? - the Divine is far more truly conceived
as a 'great intelligent First Cause, or moral Governor of
the universe.' Does Mr Arnold suppose that the Bishops
of Winchester or Gloucester, or even the Archbishop of
York, have invented 'the idea of God as a person,' that
this idea is a mere product of their metaphysics, or of
anybody's metaphysics? Even the more formal Christian
dogmas are in no sense metaphysical inventions. Who has
invented them or given them their dominances in the
sphere of religion? Powerful as bishops and archbishops
are, they are hardly equal to any such task as this.
Surely they are only there, the most abstruse of them,
because they were in their day real growths of Christian

thought and experience - as real as any products of
modern thought, to say the least of it. If Christian
theology teaches that 'God is a person,' it is not merely
that any bishops have thought or reasoned so, but because
all the revelations of the Divine, 'the not ourselves,' in
history and in human life, have pointed towards this conclusion. When men were athirst for the Divine, and could
not find it in such mere stoical conceptions of order and
righteous power as Mr Arnold once more tenders for our
acceptance, then the words of Christ revealed to them a
living Father - not merely a Power making for righteousness, but a divine Person loving righteousness and hating
evil.

If we are to take the language of Scripture as expressive
of religious truth at all, on what ground can we accept
its witness to the Divine righteousness and exclude its
witness to the Divine personality? The 'idea of God as a
person' may seem ridiculous to Mr Arnold, but it was
plainly a very real and true idea, and no mere poetical
imagination to the mind of Hebrew Psalmist and Prophet.

The idea of *righteousness* was no doubt a very vital and
fruitful growth of the Hebrew mind, but it was of later,
and, at the end, of more imperfect development than the
idea of personality. God was a conscious Will or Provi-
dence - a personal Power to help and guide and punish,
before He was seen to be in all things a righteous Power,
demanding not merely sacrifice and burnt-offering, but
clean hands and a pure heart. Looking, therefore, merely
at the religious consciousness of the Hebrew, how can we
reject its primary and accept its secondary revelation?
on what principle can we pronounce the one to be poetry
and the other experience or fact? Certainly Israel felt
Jehovah to be more truly a person - one who cared for,
and loved, and protected them - than anything else.
    And who can doubt, in reading the Gospels, that this
element of personality, sublimed into the perfect conception of fatherhood, is the conception of God which is
everywhere present to the mind of Jesus?

God as a *power not ourselves making for righteousness*, is
not only something less, as indeed Mr Arnold admits, than
the 'God and Father of our Lord and Saviour Jesus Christ,'
but something else - something outside the genuine Christian conception, and quite different from it. Not that

there is any question of righteousness being an element
of this conception. It is so invariably. The very glory
of the Christian idea of God is that it blends in undis-
tinguishable union the elements of righteousness and
fatherhood or personality.

Father - *my* God and Father - is what the Christian heart
means by God - what it knows as God - what it has verified
to be God, although not in Mr Arnold's sense of verification.
    It is surprising that Mr Arnold did not feel that his
own notion of verification takes him quite outside the
Christian, or indeed the religious, sphere.

Now, if Mr Arnold means ... that religious truth is to be
tested by experiments of the same nature as that by which
we prove that fire burns, and that no religion has claim
upon us which cannot stand this test - it is surely evident, first of all, that this is not the order of religious certitude. Men do not *find* religion in this way.
It finds them. It seizes them not as a law of being, or
conduct, to which they must conform, but as a living awe,
a conscious presence haunting them. God is not a power
outside of them which they seek to verify after Mr
Arnold's manner, but a power within them which their whole
life confesses. He *is*, they feel: and their spirits witness with His Spirit the *fact*. God, in short, is a revelation to the human heart and conscience, and not a mere
law or order which we verify, as we verify the properties
of fire or water, or any other natural substance. Whether
His righteous power is not also verifiable in this manner
is another question. We believe it is. All Christian
thinkers, no less than Mr Arnold, hold that righteousness
is the only law of happiness in individuals or states,
and that the course of every life and of every national
history more or less proves this. Nothing can be finer
or truer than much that he says on this subject. But the
sphere of experimental verification in individual conduct
- in history - is not the inner religious sphere. It is
not properly this sphere at all. This is within the
spirit alone. It is the life of the soul abiding in God;
and finding all its strength and righteousness and rest
in Him. To such a spirit and life there is no doubt of
God; and of God as a Father, and not merely a Power - as
a Personal Love dealing with us, and not a mere Force
binding us.

Is all the accumulated experience of the Christian ages
to pass for nothing, or less than nothing - 'a huge mistake,' 'an enormous blunder'? With so much talk of
experience, is nothing to be allowed for what Christian
men have felt and thought from the beginning? It is
surely an egregious misreading of human history - to say
nothing else - to suppose that the deepest and most sacred
convictions of the human heart have been nothing but mis-
applied metaphysics. Nor is it less an astounding affectation to suppose that it has remained to Mr Arnold to
point out this, and to recall men from the region of
'abstruse reasoning' to the region of 'fact and experience' in religion. It is not he indeed, but the 'Zeit-
Geist' - he says, in a concluding passage of banter -
that has discovered this. But the 'Zeit-Geist,' powerful
as it is, is nothing but a transitory phase in the evolution of human experience. It will take its place and
leave its result in the onward course of history. It has
no claims to do anything more, and least of all to dis-
possess us of our old treasures till it has provided for
us something better than 'a Power not ourselves making
for righteousness.' Moreover, it has other prophets than
Mr Arnold; some of whom will not even allow us so much as
this - will have nothing to do with righteousness, or
with the Bible as the great lesson-book of righteousness.
    This is the second point of weakness, as it appears to
us, in our author's plan of verification. Try conduct,
he says, and you will find that *righteousness is salvation, life, happiness*. So far Mr Arnold is at one with
the ordinary Christian; and we observe that there are
those in these 'thoughtful' weekly and monthly organs of
opinion, which report to us every 'advance' of the 'Zeit-
Geist' in religion, and in other things, who are full of
gratitude to our author for this acknowledgment as to
righteousness. Almost, they feel and say, he is persuaded
to be a Christian; and although they cannot approve of his
flippancies towards the Bishops of Winchester and Gloucester, and 'the Council of Nicaea,' they are disposed to
pardon them for the sake of this admission. But there are
many others, we need not say, who look upon Mr Arnold as
unfaithful to the 'Zeit-Geist' just in so far as he is
weak enough to talk about *righteousness* at all - or a
Power not ourselves making for righteousness. And these
are the 'men of science,' *par excellence*, in our day -
the men who are given to verification, and will allow of
nothing that we cannot verify, as we verify the fact that
fire burns. Righteousness, they will say, - what has
science to do with righteousness? Such an idea is just as
much a product of metaphysics as personality - the one as
untangible, as unverifiable as the other.

There are many things, evidently, that do not make for
righteousness, *so far as we can see*. The wicked are seen
to flourish 'like a green bay-tree,' and the pure and
humble and good to live and die in misery. If there is a
rapture in righteousness, this does not come from any outside view of its effects, or because righteousness (as Mr
Arnold so often quotes) 'tendeth to life,' but from the
undying faith *within* that there is a living Power above us
that loveth righteousness, and will make it triumph in the
end. It is, in short, that very faith in a personal God,
which Mr Arnold ridicules, which alone sustains the idea
of righteousness, and makes it a passion to any poor,
weak, human soul.

And so, as it appears to us, Mr Arnold's verifying test
returns upon himself. We cannot verify righteousness,
still less that there *is a power not ourselves that makes
for righteousness*, as we verify the fact that fire burns.
All that he can verify in this manner is the recurrence
of certain outward conditions to which he chooses to give
this name, and behind which he supposes that there is a
power working or making for them. This is the measure of
his faith; but beyond question it *is faith* and not science
which so far utters itself in Mr Arnold's creed, scanty
as it is, no less than in all other creeds. The idea of
righteousness is as truly a product of conscience, or what
he calls metaphysic, as the idea of personality - born
within, and not gathered from without. Nay, they are twin
ideas - the one lying within the other in the common conscience everywhere - a law or order of conduct (righteousness), and a lawgiver or personal authority from whom the
law comes. This is the voice of *experience*, not in Mr
Arnold's sense, but in a higher and truer sense - the
voice of the righteous heart and religious life everywhere - the voice of Psalmist, and Prophet, and Apostle,
and Fathers, and Saint in all ages. Always they have felt
and realised not only a law of righteousness, but a living
source of righteousness - a power *not* indeed *themselves,*
but conscious, intelligent, *like themselves,* - holding
them not merely by blind force, but loving, guiding, and
educating them as their Shepherd and Father - 'the
Shepherd and Bishop of their souls.'
    And this brings us back to the initial and pervading
absurdity of Mr Arnold's volume - his conception of dogma
as a mere excrescence or disease of religion. All the
creeds are to him mere mistakes; all Christian theology a
mere illusion of metaphysics, or jumble of abstract reasonings. They have come out of a misdirected criticism

of the Bible, and must perish with all other products of
misdirected criticism.

The Apostles' Creed, we are told, is 'the popular science
of Christianity;' the so-called Nicene Creed, 'the learned
science' of the same; and the so-called Athanasian Creed,
also 'learned science like the Nicene creed, but learned
science which has fought and got ruffled by fighting, and
is fiercely dictatorial now that it has won; - learned
science with a strong dash of violent and vindictive
temper.' This is very pretty play on the part of our
theological amateur. We can imagine the smile of satisfaction with which he contemplated this effort of creed-
classification; but it is easy to classify creeds, or do
anything else, when we have a proud confidence in our own
opinion, and know so well how everything has happened.
We have heard of a Professor of Church History who, when
questioned as to the writings of the apostolic fathers and
apologists of the second century, that tempus ἄδηλον, (1)
as Scaliger calls it, replied that he knew nothing of
these writings; but 'what with the Bible on the one hand,
and the human consciousness on the other,' he knew very
well what must have happened in that century! Mr Arnold,
without appeal to these aids, can tell all about the three
great Creeds of Christendom. Not only so, but he can explain with ease the misdirected criticism and futile
metaphysics out of which 'the whole of our so-called
orthodox theology' has grown.
     It is hardly necessary to make any reply to such
light-headed confidence. Dogmatic Theology will survive
Mr Arnold's witticisms, and even the touch of that
'Ithuriel spear of the Zeit-Geist' which he evidently
thinks he wields with no little effect. But apart from
any higher considerations, we may surely urge again the
absurdity of conceiving the development of religious
thought, or any other mode of thought, after such a
manner. In every age men have thought more or less deeply
of religion. From the beginning of the Church, the wisest
and most humble no less than the most daring and speculative minds, have been busy with its great facts and questions. If they lacked, as no doubt they did, the aids of
modern criticism, they yet knew profoundly the necessities of our spiritual nature, and the realities of Revelation were living and present to them without the help of
this criticism. The Creeds of Christendom have been the
fruit of all this study and experience. The labours of
dogmatic theologians have sought to organise the highest
ideas of the Church from age to age. They may have some-

times passed beyond the range of permanent Christian
thought, and corrections may await the extravagances of
theology as of other subjects. But the great articles of
the Christian faith have sprung from the very depths of
the Christian consciousness; they are its living utterance; and to this day they continue living in thousands of
Christian hearts. Do they not still witness to a far
grander spirit than this 'Zeit-Geist,' or modern spirit
of which we hear so much, but whose main ambition seems to
be to insult or disparage all that has gone before it?
  Can anything be more unscientific than such a spirit?
It is the very apotheosis of self-opinion intoxicated by
its own pride, and flaunting its dogmatisms with a crude
audacity in the face of preceding dogmas. As a student
of the Bible our author should have learned better than
this. To his expostulatory and clever friends who knew
so much in their time, the patriarchs, Job says, 'No
doubt ye are the people, and wisdom will die with you;
but I have understanding as well as you.' Other ages
besides ours have known something of the Bible; the doctors and theologians of the Church have not quite mistaken
its meaning. Literary critics like Mr Arnold, with their
'wide experience,' and the 'Zeit-Geist favouring,' may
haply add something to our knowledge. But it is neither
modest nor consistent with the progress of truth that they
should claim to do anything more.

Note

1 'a time without distinction'.

36. H. W. PRESTON, REVIEW IN 'ATLANTIC MONTHLY'

July 1873, xxxii, 102-17

Harriet Waters Preston (1836-1911) was born into a
Massachusetts family that had been in the New World since
1635. Educated at home, she supplemented her schooling
by extended trips to Europe, which gave her fluency in
several languages. She worked diligently at a literary
career, translating works from Latin and French and writing encyclopedia articles, novels, and periodical criticism. Her judgment on the coherence and unity of Arnold's

work was both apt and prescient, but Preston is untypical
in her high estimate of the significance of Arnold's
theology.

Mr. Matthew Arnold's new volume comes to us with the old
modest aspect and opens in the subdued and polished tones
to which his previous writings had used us. But before
the attentive reader has proceeded many pages, he becomes
fully aware of a change in his author, - hardly of manner,
certainly not in the crystalline style whose clearness
and symmetry we can only despairingly admire, but rather
of attitude and function. The man who has hitherto seemed
content to roam a little idly over questions of literary,
social, and religious interest, alighting now here and now
there, glorying, as it were, in dilettantism, chanting the
praises of pure art, and setting the Greek, for the time
being, far above the Jew; teasing, with the light lash of
his exquisite satire, now the unsuccessful translators of
Homer, now Mr. Spurgeon, now Mr. Bradlaugh, and now Mr.
Robert Buchanan with his unfortunate 'story of the fig-
leaf time'; the man who, despite his literary grace, his
critical acumen, and his always interesting vivacity, has
fairly laid himself open sometimes to the charge of being
incoherent, inconsistent, and ineffective, appears before
us now in the character of a professed teacher and an
extremely serious one. During a momentary pause in the
noisy debate between science and faith, reason and revelation, or whatever you may choose to call the opposing
parties, this refined voice is lifted proposing an adjustment, and, if possible, a reconciliation. Its delicacy,
in contrast with the ruder tones of the disputants, will
attract attention. Its decision and the pregnancy of its
utterances will be sure to rivet it. Still, as in former
times, Mr. Arnold gracefully calls his work an 'essay,' -
An Essay toward a better Apprehension of the Bible; but
we speedily see that this time the 'essay' has engaged
all the author's powers, and will at least engage all ours
in a right appreciation of it.
     In his Introduction, Mr. Arnold explains the title,
'Literature and Dogma', to mean a plea for a literary
treatment of the Bible records as opposed to the dogmatic
treatment of the professors of scientific theology,
represented by the Bishops of Winchester and Gloucester,
who resolved in convocation 'to *do something* for the honor
of our Lord's Godhead,' and the 'blessed truth that the
God of the Universe is a PERSON,' and by other divines
whom he holds responsible for having strained and

distorted the simplicity of Scripture to suit their own
metaphysical conceptions. 'The valuable thing in letters, that is, the acquainting one's self with the best
which has been thought and said in the world,' he affirms
to be 'the judgment which forms itself insensibly in a
fair mind along with fresh knowledge..... Far more of
our mistakes,' he truly adds, 'come from want of fresh
knowledge than from want of correct reasoning..... So
that minds with small aptitude for abstract reasoning may
yet, through letters, gain some hold on sound judgment
and useful knowledge, and may even clear up blunders committed, out of their very excess of talent, by the
athletes of logic.'

Mr. Arnold's bearing toward the dignitaries whom he
defies is fairly foreshadowed in the last sentence. If
it be thought at times a trifle too sarcastic, and the
homage he scrupulously pays to the ability of his opponents more ironical than is always needful, it should be
remembered that he comes to us now as the earnest advocate of a very positive, however unorthodox, system of
faith in the Bible and in Jesus Crhist, and that the
resistance he has most to apprehend is, of course, not
that of the irreligious, but of those who are eminent in
the Church that now is. To these, his summary work with
the elaborate doctrinal structure of the ages will be the
wildest iconoclasm, and his new-fangled 'righteousness'
the 'filthiest' of 'rags'; and of these, like an adroit
fighter, he never loses sight throughout the volume....

[After a summary of Arnold's arguments, Preston continues:]

It is easy to see, even from the bold outline and the
scant extracts given above, how clean a sweep Mr. Arnold
makes of the principal *tenets* of orthodoxy. What we have
far less adequately illustrated is the deep earnestness
of the book, its quiet confidence and winning clearness,
and the unswerving loyalty it shows to the Bible as the
author reads it, and to its central figure. We think
that many will read 'Literature and Dogma' with a sense
of profound if unspoken relief, that so much may be conceded to the aggressive and seemingly irresistible spirit
of modern inquiry, and yet so much that is reverend and
sacred remain inviolate. It would, of course, be presump-
tuous to attempt to assign the final place of a volume
which, for all its finish and *repose*, must rank among the
controversial literature of its day; but we are ourselves
inclined to think that it embodies more fully than

anything which has yet appeared the purest faith of the
time immediately to come. Mr. Arnold's work allies itself
with many contemporary efforts, but more closely than with
any others, we think, with the work of our own earlier and
more devout Unitarians and with that of the author of
'Ecce Homo'. We place it clearly beyond both.

'Literature and Dogma' is also deeply interesting as
completing and giving consistency to the whole series of
Mr. Arnold's previous works. Whatever in these may have
appeared idle, discursive, or simply tentative seems now
properly regulated and subordinated, as part of a great
plan and necessary to its general fulfilment. This is
especially true of the ardent defence of Hellenism against
Hebraism in 'Culture and Anarchy', the balance of which is
fully restored (if not more than restored) by the devout
tribute paid by Mr. Arnold in the present volume to the
Hebraic spirit. It seems to us also not a little significant that this book should have been written by Dr.
Arnold's son. If to any of those who have felt the personal magnetism of the great head-master of Rugby - and
who that has read Stanley's Memoir or the writings of
Thomas Hughes has not? - it has seemed strange and a little
sad, that from the loins of that fiery, positive, and
apostolic spirit there should have sprung precisely the
pensive and fastidious amateur whom Matthew Arnold has at
times appeared to be, we think they will find, in the
crowning work of the latter's ripened life, the wisdom of
the more heroic father justified of the serener son....

37. UNSIGNED REVIEW, THE BIBLE AS INTERPRETED BY MR.
ARNOLD, 'WESTMINSTER REVIEW'

April 1874, xlv, n.s., 309-23

The 'Westminster', as the organ of the philosophical radicals, spoke for Liberalism in politics, utilitarianism in
governmental theory and ethics, and freethinking in religion. The tradition of Bentham and the Mills, father and
son, lives on, albeit with a somewhat diminished splendour,
in the following review. The point of view is rationalistic, the method strictly logical. Isolating what he takes
to be the four primary arguments in Arnold's book, the
reviewer then tests them, one by one. He finds Arnold's
attempt to yoke 'Bible Religion' together with a rejection

of 'supernaturalism' an 'impossible task'. Arnold considered the objections in this review formidable and devoted
a large part of Chapter III of 'God and the Bible' to
refuting them (see Super, vii, 203-22).

Among the many books which have appeared of late years,
bearing directly or indirectly upon the subject of Religion, all shades of opinion have had their exponents -
from what is called 'Bible Religion' on the one hand, to
the rejection of all supernaturalism on the other; but it
remained for Mr. Matthew Arnold, in his recent work, to
unite these two extremes. The object of the present Essay
is to inquire how far he has been successful in this
apparently impossible task. But before we criticise Mr.
Arnold's opinions, we must endeavour to define them. We
must lay before our readers, as clearly and concisely as we
can, what he affirms and what he rejects. To begin with
the latter, as by far the more easy to grapple with, he
rejects all Church Dogma; not alone the dogmas of any one
Church, but the dogmas which all Christian Churches hold in
common, - nay, more, he strikes at the root of 'Natural
Religion' also, for he rejects the idea of 'a Personal
God, the moral and intelligent Governor of the Universe,'
as an 'unverifiable assumption.'
  Let us now turn to what Mr. Arnold affirms. His fundamental axiom is, 'that there is a power, which is not
ourselves, which makes for righteousness.' For this he
claims that it can be verified by experience, in the same
way that we can verify that 'Fire burns, or bread nour-
ishes.'
  Before we go further we must try to arrive at a right
understanding of this axiom; for on it is based the whole
of Mr. Arnold's system. The first error to guard against
is the idea that this 'Not ourselves which makes for
righteousness' is to be taken as the great central Law of
the Universe, as the Divine Idea, in short, under a new
name. No! Mr. Arnold expressly tells us that there are
many aspects of the 'Not Ourselves,' and that 'the sight
and mention of all of them would tend to raise immoral
thoughts.' The 'not ourselves,' then, means the laws of
nature, as opposed to laws, or rules, which man makes for
himself. Laws which we discover, in contradistinction to
those which we invent. Of these natural laws, that which
concerns righteousness, or conduct, is one. This aspect
of the 'not ourselves,' Mr. Arnold goes on to say, was the
one upon which 'Israel' fixed his regard exclusively.
This moral aspect of the 'not ourselves' was Israel's God -

Jehovah - The Lord, or, as Mr. Arnold prefers to render
it, 'The Eternal.'

Mr. Arnold defines Religion as 'morality touched by emotion,' and, moreover, tells us that this is, essentially
and pre-eminently, the religion of the Bible. We have now
four distinct propositions before us - first, that 'there
is a power, which is not ourselves, which makes for
righteousness;' second, that this Power was what Israel
worshipped under the name of Jehovah; third, that the true
meaning of Religion is 'morality touched by emotion;'
fourth, that this religion is set forth in the Bible as in
no other book - is, pre-eminently, the religion of the
Bible. This series of propositions forms the chain of
argument by which, *if each link be sound*, we are irresistibly led to Mr. Arnold's conclusion - viz., that, though
prophecy, miracle - in a word, all supernaturalism - be
accounted fable, yet the Bible must remain indispensable
as the great inspirer of righteousness or conduct, which,
Mr. Arnold tells us, is three-fourths of life. Besides
the proof by argument above attempted, we are also recommended to make experimental proof of the superior power of
the Bible to create in us an enthusiasm for righteousness,
by taking a course of the Bible first, and then a course of
Benjamin Franklin, Horace Greeley, Jeremy Bentham, and Mr.
Herbert Spencer, and then seeking which has the most
effect. Our readers may, if they feel disposed, try this
experiment. For ourselves, our present concern is with
the proof by argument. We will proceed to discuss Mr.
Arnold's propositions, one by one. To the first, which we
have called Mr. Arnold's fundamental axiom, we have nothing
to object - that is, if the definition of it which we have
given is correct, - viz., that there is, amongst the many
laws of Nature, one which enforces morality. From the
second (viz., that this power, which makes for righteousness, is what Israel worshipped, under the name of Jehovah), we dissent on two counts. First, we believe that
Israel's God was no 'law,' or 'power,' or 'principle,' but
a purely personal God. By a 'person' we mean no metaphysical idea, such as Mr. Arnold attributes to the Archbishop
of York, but the 'magnified and non-natural man of popular
theology,' who, in fact, is, in one form or other, at the
bottom of all Theology. Such a conception implies no
acquaintance with metaphysics. Every savage fashions his
God in his own image; but, on the other hand, such a negative abstraction as 'the not ourselves' is a speciality of
our own race, and our own time. It is, *a priori*, (1) an
improbability almost amounting to an impossibility, that a
barbarous or semi-barbarous people should conceive the

idea of an impersonal God - the embodiment of a law; for
the idea of a law at all is beyond them. It is essentially an abstract thought, and abstract thought has no
existence in the childhood of nations. Mr. Arnold tells
us that Israel had no turn for metaphysics, that he had
not the talent for abstract thought which belongs to the
Aryan races. But Israel must have had a faculty for
abstract thought quite unparalleled, if his conception of
a God came to pass as Mr. Arnold describes it. A people in
a very early stage of civilization is so deeply absorbed
in the study and practice of morality, that they discover
that there is a law, which is not themselves, that makes
for it, which law they proceed to worship! Can improbability go further? Surely such an argument needs only to
be stated, to refute itself. Everything we know of the
history of religions goes to prove that the conception of
a God, of some sort, is the first stage in the process;
while the conception of morality, as a part of his service,
is one of the most advanced.

Having put forward at some length the *a priori* arguments against the opinion that Israel's God was not a
person, but the deification of a natural law, we will next
examine what Israel's own records tell us on the subject.
If we there discover clear and unmistakeable evidence for
Mr. Arnold's opinion, of course, objections founded on its
improbability fall to the ground; but for such evidence we
look in vain. The dealings of Jehovah, as there set forth,
are characterized by none of the blind necessity, none of
the remorseless impassibility of a law. On the contrary,
'The Lord repenteth him of the evil.' He allows himself
to be entreated. 'He is long-suffering, abundant in goodness and mercy.' Intercession, prayer, and sacrifice
avail to change or modify his purposes. He loves his
friends, and hates his enemies, after a thoroughly personal and human fashion. In short, one cannot help seeing
in Israel's God, 'the magnified and non-natural man in
Heaven.' Indeed, the text, 'As for our God He is in
Heaven: He hath done whatsoever hath pleased Him,' seems
to be the same conception in other words.

Our second ground of objection to the proposition that
'the power not ourselves, which makes for righteousness,'
was what Israel worshipped, is that though righteousness
entered largely into Israel's conception of the Eternal,
still that conception contained much which conflicts with
righteousness. But, to reproduce at all a faithful image
of the God of Israel, we must consult the whole of the
documents. We must not rely solely on selections from the
Prophets, on the most spiritual utterances of the most
spiritual writers, but must let the narrative portions,

and those which treat of religious ceremonial, have their
due weight.

[Following this line of inquiry the reviewer discovers
many instances of immoral conduct which the God of the Old
Testament condoned and at times suggested. He concludes
that the Jews worshipped, not the principle of righteousness, but a personal God. He then continues:]

Of the four propositions which we extracted, as embodying
the outline of Mr. Arnold's argument, two still remain to
be considered, viz., that Religion is morality touched
with emotion, and that this is pre-eminently the religion
of the Bible. In support of the former proposition, Mr.
Arnold tells us that 'Religion means either a binding to
Righteousness, or else a serious attending to righteousness and dwelling upon it; which of these two it most
nearly means, depends upon the view we take of the word's
derivation, but it means one of them, and they are really
much the same.' Now we readily admit that, according to
which derivation we prefer, religion means a 'binding to'
or a 'dwelling on,' - but as to any allusion to righteousness, in either derivation, we 'cannot find it, 'tis not in
the bond.' If we take the word in the sense in which it is
generally used religion means a system of belief and worship, not necessarily including morality, for many religions have been, and some are, utterly immoral. But if we
abandon the accepted meaning of the word, and frame definitions, each man according to his own fancy, many could
be found, perhaps, not less true, though differing widely
from Mr. Arnold's. Thus religion might be defined as the
'Aberglaube' which has in all ages obscured and disguised
morality, as mists enshroud a mountain, concealing its
real outlines, and lending to it, at one time a glory and
effulgence not its own, at another investing it with adven-
titious gloom and terrors. Or, religion might be defined
as bearing the same relation to morality as alchemy to
chemistry - astrology to astronomy. To the proposition,
that 'morality touched by emotion is the religion of the
Bible,' we have already had occasion to take exception
when giving our reasons for rejecting Mr. Arnold's theory
of the God of the Bible. We have endeavoured to prove
that Israel's first conception of a God was that of an
unseen but powerful foe, whose enmity might be turned
aside and his wrath assuaged by the death of victims. But
this first and lowest stage of religious thought belongs
essentially to a pre-historic age. When Israel's history
opens with the call of Abraham, already a higher phase had

been reached. The custom of sacrifice was still in force,
but the victims now offered were chosen from the flocks
and herds. The spirit, too, in which the offering was
made, was greatly changed: belief, obedience, and even
love, were elements of worship, and had modified, though
not cast out, the abject fear in which worship had its
origin. From this point no substantial progress was ever
made. The chasm which separates a religion chiefly consisting of worship, with an imperfect morality as a subsidiary element, from Mr. Arnold's ideal religion, in
which morality is all in all - was never bridged over by
Israel. We have already admitted that many utterances may
be found in the Prophets exalting righteousness above
ceremonial observances; but whether we regard these expressions of enthusiasm for righteousness, and of delight in
the law of the Lord, as embodying the national sentiment,
or as expressing the more spiritual thought of a chosen
few, the truth which they illustrate, if read with the
commentary afforded by Israel's history, is the same. It
is that the connexion between lip-righteousness, and
righteous living is small indeed, and that the praises of
virtue, however ecstatically sung, are powerless to create
in men's hearts an effectual love for it. Yet, Mr. Arnold
thinks that the words which failed to turn the hearts of
those to whom they were originally addressed, have an
efficacy beyond all other words for the regeneration of
our 'masses.' The formula which Mr. Arnold employs to
bring the Bible into harmony with his theory is, that,
'the language of the Bible is literary, not scientific;'
and he tells us in his Preface, that the power to read it
aright is only attained by culture. Only by help of the
literary experience which culture implies, can we know
what to insist upon, and what to pass over lightly. With
this we entirely concur, but if we venture to take exception to Mr. Arnold's exegesis of the Hebrew Scriptures,
it is not on the ground that he attaches less importance
to some portions of them than to others, but because he
imports into them his own ideas - ideas purely modern,
and inconceivable as the product of the age and race to
which Mr. Arnold attributes them. So powerfully does his
theory possess him, that in some cases he refuses to see
the obvious sense of a passage - preferring to find in it
an esoteric meaning having reference to 'The Eternal Power
which makes for righteousness.'

We must now turn to Mr. Arnold's theory respecting the New
Testament writings, which, though occupying by far the
larger portion of the volume, may yet be summed up in

comparatively few words. First - he asserts that Jesus
was the Son of God, *i.e.*, of course, of 'the Power, which
is not ourselves, which makes for Righteousness;' 'that
he is the offspring of this power is verifiable from
experience.' Second, that the 'Mission' of Jesus was to
'renew the Intuition' formerly possessed by Israel, of the
eternal power which makes for righteousness. Third, that
Jesus fulfilled this mission by giving to mankind his
'Method' (inwardness), and his 'Secret' (self-renunciation). These are the cardinal points in Mr. Arnold's
Theory of Christianity; but, in considering them, we shall
have to notice many minor points, subsidiary to these. In
the consideration of these points, we are stopped on the
very threshold, by the difficulty of comprehending the
assertion, that Jesus was the offspring of the Power which
makes for Righteousness. When we are told that Jesus is
the Son of a Personal God, we may dissent from the proposition, - it certainly, as Mr. Arnold observes, is unverifiable. But, at least, we know what it means. But, that
Jesus was the offspring of an abstract Principle, conveys
no meaning to our mind.

In the first place, the existence of 'the power, not
ourselves, which makes for righteousness' is utterly unverifiable, except in the sense we have assigned to it,
viz.: a natural law, which enforces a certain line of
conduct, by affixing good consequences to its performance, and bad consequences to its non-performance. But
even this law is not an objective reality - all that we
can predicate is, that certain consequences are found to
follow upon certain courses of conduct. The law which we
deduce from the observation of this external fact, is
purely subjective - has no existence except in our minds;
consequently, to say that any man is the son of a natural
law is (with all deference to Mr. Arnold) absurd. Even
waiving for the moment that a natural law is not an external reality, still, it can do nothing but perform its
peculiar function. The law which makes oxygen and hydro-
gen unite in fixed proportions to form water, cannot send
men into the world to teach its action; still less can any
man be said to be the son of such a law. Yet this is precisely a parallel case. It follows that, though the teaching of Jesus may contain truths essential to morality,
neither this, nor anything else, could prove him to be, in
any real sense, the Son of 'the Power which makes for
righteousness.' But, perhaps, in interpreting Mr.
Arnold's words, as really meaning what they say, we are
sinning in the same way as those who put a literal

interpretation on biblical language. Perhaps Mr. Arnold's
language, on this point, is, like that of the Bible, 'not
scientific, but literary;' '*thrown out* at a not fully
grasped object of consciousness.' We should, undoubtedly,
have so taken it, from the sheer impossibility of giving
it any scientific meaning, which should be, at the same
time, reasonable, were it not that Mr. Arnold puts forward
the statement that Jesus is the Son of the Power which
makes for Righteousness, in the form of a logical demonstration, and claims for it an experimental basis; thereby
taking it out of the province of literature into that of
science. Nevertheless, considering Mr. Arnold's abandonment of supernaturalism, it is probable that he speaks of
Jesus as the Son of God only by a violent metaphor,
inspired by the hope of retaining the revered names
('familiar in his mouth as household words'), while changing the entire basis of religion, by new definitions of
them.

A striking instance of this union in Mr. Arnold, of
liberal thought and conservative feeling, is his new definition of Faith. 'Faith is the being able to cleave to a
power of goodness appealing to our higher and real self,
not to our lower and apparent self.' The old watchword of
Religion is retained with a meaning not its own indeed,
but better calculated than its own to conciliate modern
thought, which revolts from the idea that belief without
evidence is to be regarded as a virtue. But if we are to
follow Mr. Arnold's recommendation, and 'use words as
mankind generally use them', we cannot perceive that the
reconciliation of faith with science is one whit the
nearer for his reformed definition; for, though it contains nothing repugnant to science, it does not touch
upon faith, but describes a power of steadfast adherence
to virtue, against which science has not a word to say.
From these passages and another we gather that some
scheme of revolutionizing the Spirit of Religion, while
retaining its ancient Language, has recommended itself to
Mr. Arnold; but we feel sure that such a scheme would have
no success in actual working. A considerable proportion
of mankind would never perceive that any change had been
wrought, and, even among those who comprehended the change,
it would soon be lost sight of; for two great forces would
tend continually to reproduce the old order of things –
the power of words to mould ideas, and man's inveterate
tendency to anthropomorphism.

The idea of the 'mission of Jesus' is open to the same
objections that we have already advanced against the
opinion that he was the offspring of the Power that makes
for righteousness. Before a man can have a 'mission,' it

must be entrusted to him by some one, and a law cannot, of
course, communicate a mission. But neither can a man
receive a mission from any but a human source: for this at
once implies supernaturalism, or non-naturalism, as Mr.
Arnold philosophically prefers to term it. As regards the
object of the 'mission,' viz., 'to restore the intuition,'
we have already endeavoured to prove that Israel never had
this 'intuition.' Of the proposition that Jesus 'fulfilled this mission by giving to mankind his method (inwardness, or change of heart), and his secret (self-
renouncement),' we must treat at some length. Setting
aside the idea of a 'mission,' which seems to us to be
quite unnecessary to the main conception, we think that in
singling out these two important principles of morality as
the great gift of Jesus to mankind, Mr. Arnold has shown a
fineness of perception, and power of generalization, of
the highest order. No doubt these principles have always
been recognised as characteristic precepts of Christianity, but Mr. Arnold has been the first, so far as we know,
to assign to them their true relative value. There may
perhaps be something of hyperbole, something more emotional than philosophic, in his way of regarding them; but
then Mr. Arnold is the avowed advocate of 'morality
touched by emotion.' In truth, in his treatment of the
New Testament, and of Jesus its great central figure, as
in his treatment of the Bible and Israel's God, Mr. Arnold
is an advocate, and herein, in our opinion, lies his
inferiority to Dr. Strauss, whose criticism derives added
weight from its judicial character. Now, one cannot help
feeling that Mr. Arnold, having once discovered the
'method,' and the 'secret,' desires to find them pervading
every word ascribed to Jesus by the Evangelists, and,
accordingly, he does find them in many passages where they
are not visible to an ordinary observer, and in others
concerning which the only certainty that we can reach is,
that Jesus never uttered them.

In attempting to define with any degree of precision, Mr.
Arnold's views on the main topics of the New Testament
writings, we are constantly baffled by what seems like an
unwillingness to accept the necessary consequences of his
own admissions. Thus, he admits that the record contained in our Gospels 'passed through half a century or
more of oral tradition, and through more than one written
account' before reaching its present form; yet, he accepts
from our Gospels, as really uttered by Jesus, many things
which, on that view, are wholly inexplicable, but which
on the supposition that they were ascribed to Him after

the dogmas which they assert had come into existence,
require no explanation. The most remarkable instance of
this is to be found in Mr. Arnold's treatment of the
passage (John ix. 58), 'Jesus said unto them, before
Abraham was, I am' - in which Jesus clearly asserts his
identity with Jehovah, who revealed himself to Moses under
the name, 'I am that I am' (Exodus iii. 14). Mr. Arnold
endeavours to explain away this obvious meaning, by a
process which he has stigmatized elsewhere in the words
of Bishop Butler, as one by which 'anything may be made to
mean anything,' rather than reject the whole passage as
an 'effort to do something for the honour of our Lord's
Godhead,' of which dogma the author of the fourth Gospel
was as zealous of a champion as ever were Mr. Arnold's
'twin bishops.'

In the same spirit, though attempting no defence of
miracles, and confessing that, if he could turn his pen
into a penwiper, he should not, thereby, make what he
wrote more true, or more convincing - by far the most
humorous passage in the book - yet, Mr. Arnold would fain
imagine in Jesus a power of healing, and, especially, of
casting out unclean spirits, not granted to mere men. He
pronounces, ex cathedra, that 'the action of Jesus in
these cases, however it may be amplified in the reports,
was real;' but it 'is not thaumaturgy.' Mr. Arnold
ascribes it to 'moral therapeutics;' but this power was
not supposed to be possessed exclusively by Jesus, witness
the question, 'If I by Beelzebub cast out devils, by whom
do your sons cast them out?' Then, did the Jews, too,
cast out devils by 'moral therapeutics'?

Finally, though Mr. Arnold heaps scorn on the doctrine
of 'the Godhead of the Eternal Son,' he yet invests Jesus
with attributes which we can only characterize as Divine.
As examples, we may adduce - first, Prescience, as shown
in predictions of his death and the manner of it, as to
the credibility of which predictions Mr. Arnold seems to
have no misgivings; and second, an intuitive and unerring
knowledge, little short of Omniscience, shown in his
entire superiority to all error, Jewish or Christian, in
the interpretation of the Scriptures - a superiority which
Mr. Arnold is so bent on maintaining that when Jesus, in
argument with the Jews, uses the passage, 'The Lord said
unto my Lord,' &c., in the sense in which it was understood by them and has been understood by all Christendom
ever since, Mr. Arnold would rather believe that Jesus
used an argument which he knew to be fallacious (which
amounts, as we think, to imputing *mala fides*), (2) than
allow that he participated in an error of interpretation
which was universal in his day, and was not discovered to

be an error until more than eighteen centuries after his
death.

Regarding this remarkable work as a whole, we think it
a most ingenious and original attempt to place Religion on
a scientific basis. Its great blemish, in our eyes, is
its tone of uncompromising advocacy, which begets inconsistent and conflicting utterances. Of Jesus it reflects
no clear mental image, for we are equally forbidden to
think him human, or divine. The old proverb tells us
that 'we cannot eat our cake and have it;' but this seems
to us to be exactly what Mr. Arnold attempts to do. He
would gladly be rid of supernaturalism, yet he clings to
the Bible, of which supernaturalism is the key-note.

At the commencement of this Essay we stated that its
object was to inquire how far Mr. Arnold had succeeded in
the apparently impossible task of reconciling Bible religion with the rejection of supernaturalism. We are now
convinced that the impossibility of the task was not only
apparent, but real; since Mr. Arnold, with all his known
ability, has, in our judgment, failed to accomplish it.

Notes

1 'presumptively'.
2 'bad faith'.

God and the Bible (1875) and
Last Essays on Church and Religion (1877)

38. ALBERT RÉVILLE, REVIEW OF 'GOD AND THE BIBLE', 'ACADEMY'

18 December 1875, viii, 618-19

Réville (1826-1906), French Protestant clergyman and theologian, accepted the job of pastor at the Walloon church in Rotterdam in 1851. His 'Essais de critique religieuse' were published in 1861. In 1873 he wrote a review of 'Literature and Dogma' which so pleased Arnold that he wrote to the editor of the 'Academy' saying, 'I think so highly of Réville and his opinion that I should have read with interest even the most hostile judgment from him; how much more a judgment which is in many respects so favourable!' However, Réville's enthusiasm for Arnold's theology had visibly waned by the time he wrote his review of 'God and the Bible' for the 'Academy'. He consumes a great deal of space in a lacklustre summary of Arnold's ideas, most of which he dislikes. Here we omit the summary, reprinting only the first two paragraphs, which adequately characterize his response.

The reading of a new work by Mr. Matthew Arnold is always an intellectual feast. We may differ from him ever so widely, and even feel slightly irritated by his decided taste for paradox. Yet his manner, with its combination of seriousness and humour, the originality of his views, his novel and unforeseen modes of presenting things, cause us to read him to the end with an interest very like that

which we feel in a fascinating novel. He abhors the
'vigorous and rigorous' theories of certain German critics, and it must be owned that rigour is not precisely
the distinctive quality of his own. But his personal
theory is undeniably vigorous; he must have in truth a
vigour peculiarly British to maintain that theory with
such imperturbable serenity against the objections of
every kind which, from the most opposite camps, crash in
upon it like converging artillery fires. There is a moral
grandeur in this isolation, so proudly accepted and defended so stoutly, to which it would be unjust to refuse
recognition. I know not whether Mr. Matthew Arnold will
ever see allies rally round him to assist in repelling
the onslaughts directed against him. But while reading
his works of religious criticism the student is tempted
to inscribe on his escutcheon the words of the Medea of
the poet, 'Moi, moi, dis-je, et c'est assez.' (1)
  We have here to deal with a thinker who has broken
theoretically with all the theologies and all the metaphysics of the past, who has saturated himself with all
the results of independent criticism, who absolutely
rejects the supernatural, who has adopted the idea that
God may be nothing but an impersonal force, an unconscious
influence, in a word a thing rather than a person: and who
at the same time is an ardent supporter of the Christian
tradition, who shows himself every moment more severe
towards its assailants than its defenders, who feels all
the enthusiasm of a mystic for the Jahveh of the Jews and
the Saviour of the Christians, and who above all professes
a reverence for the Bible which scarcely yields to that of
the most decided partisans of verbal inspiration. And
with what resources of wit and knowledge, with what subtle
and caustic *persiflage* (2) against opponents on right and
left, with what assurance of the truth and legitimacy of
his singular position, only a perusal of his work will
show. What a pity that so much ability and science, so
much literary art and moral vigour, should be utterly
wasted - as I fear it is - and should finally produce
only one of those curious fruits which we examine atten-
tively for their strangeness but never so much as wish to
taste, so clear is it that we cannot even pierce the rind
with our teeth....

Notes

1 'I talk about myself, and that's enough.'
2 'banter'.

39.   UNSIGNED REVIEW IN THE 'WESTMINSTER REVIEW'

January 1876, xlix, n.s., 221-3

The 'Westminster', which had devoted a long and complex
article to 'Literature and Dogma' (No. 37), granted 'God
and the Bible' just a few pages of its regular section on
recent books in theology. The remarks typify a growing
impatience with Arnold's rhetorical manner and a conviction that he speaks with dubious authority. The reviewer
recommends some 'elementary knowledge' of Hebrew.

As far as we can understand Mr. Arnold's mental attitude,
it is this: - The world is divided into two elements, -
those who have read (and appreciated) 'Literature and
Dogma,' and those who have not. The latter class is (at
present) numerous, but is intrinsically insignificant, and
tends in the nature of things constantly to reduce itself
towards a vanishing-point. We will therefore ignore it.
The former class, having read 'Literature and Dogma,'
proceeded to read the Bible, and had just begun to enjoy
it, when it was disturbed by certain bishops, metaphysicians, and critics, who - each in his sort - endeavoured
to show that 'Literature and Dogma,' was not entirely to
be trusted. Upon this the readers of 'Literature and
Dogma' turn anxiously to Mr. Arnold: 'they want to know
what they are to think of these things,' and of course
their prophet is equal to the occasion. Hence these
'Answers' - addressed, like the Hampshire farmer's ora-
tion, to 'most thinking people,' i.e., to admirers of
'Literature and Dogma.' This unparalleled self-assertion
is aggravating to a high degree; but Mr Arnold's delicious
freshness and raciness can carry off anything, and with
whatever feelings we take up and read this book, it is
impossible long to resist its fascination, or to lay it
down again until absolutely compelled to do so. But as to
whether this intense enjoyment in any way 'makes for
righteousness,' we must confess to having grave doubts.
We fear it is the carnal, and not the spiritual, man that
is refreshed. Considered as sport, what can be finer than
to watch Mr Arnold 'baiting' a bishop! The unhappy
ecclesiastic is chained by his position and his antecedents, and the brilliant litterateur, (1) unrestrained
and reckless, darts round and round his victim, dodges in
and out to dig him in the ribs or pinch him black and

blue, skips behind him to twitch his hair, and is all the
while bubbling over with half-repressed yet wholly irre-
pressible laughter! And when the miserable victim, who
has to retain his dignity (!) under all this, turns round
at last and hits out wildly, his assailant suddenly assumes an aspect of grave expostulation, and standing well
out of his reach, tells him he wonders how he can be so
frivolous! Then we leave the bishops for a moment, and
turn upon the metaphysicians. Here we encounter once more
that peculiar species of satirical mock-humility in which
Mr. Arnold is altogether inimitable. 'This is the best
fooling, when all is done!' but if it is even indirectly
to serve any further purpose than that of amusement, the
author had better continue his researches in 'Walton's
noble Polyglott Bible,' or gain some elementary knowledge
(a very little will do) of Hebrew.

Note

1   'man of letters'.

40.   EDWARD DOWDEN, REVIEW IN THE 'ACADEMY'

19 May 1877, xi, 430-1

Edward Dowden (1843-1913) was, at the time he wrote this
notice, Professor of English literature at Trinity
College, Dublin, and the author of two major books on
Shakespeare, 'Shakespeare, His Mind and Art' (1875) and
'A Shakespeare Primer' (1877). His review of 'Last
Essays' opens with the hope that Arnold's announced return
to literary criticism will begin a fuitful new period in
his life. Dowden is not too happy with Arnold's past
theologizing, or with the present book. After these remarks, which we reprint, Dowden goes on to a detailed examination of one chapter from 'Last Essays', Bishop Butler
and the Zeit-Geist. 'In the main what is true in Mr.
Arnold's criticism of Butler's "Analogy" is not new, and
what is new is erroneous.' This section, because of its
length, we omit.

With this volume closes a period in Mr. Arnold's career as
author. There was first his work in the field of pure
literature, work which proceeded from a state of moral
incertitude and indecision. Next came the period now
closing, in which a faith was found, and delivered as by a
teacher who had himself attained. And henceforward to the
end, as he announces, Mr. Arnold's work is to be again
literature strictly so called, to which he returns forti-
fied by the possession of a doctrine respecting life.
Perhaps the most characteristic quality in those early
volumes was the faithfulness with which the troubles of a
divided intellect, divided emotions, and a divided will
were set forth. There was in Mr. Arnold's nature a moral
truthfulness, a sense of fact, which preserved him from
any temptation to hurry forward to a factitious certitude,
favourable to the purposes of poetical rhetoric, and of
fervour prepense, but lacking reality. Now, when he
returns to literature – and I ardently hope that word is
meant to include poetry as well as criticism – he will
return as one who by patience and honest dealing with himself has attained a vantage-ground. His poetry, if poetry
be written, will speak less of a foiled desire to simplify
life by bringing it under one dominant set of motives,
less of the restlessness and fever of a will attracted on
this side by the world and on that by the desire for recollection and calm. We may with confidence predict that
in his future literary work there will be a harmony, a
continuity, a sane energy, and adult power which we vainly
look for in the work of earlier years.
     But while Mr. Arnold's certitude is sincere, it must be
confessed now, when his work directly concerned with religion is complete, that such work leaves upon the mind of
the thoughtful student of religion a feeling of dissatisfaction. Its essential merit is that it is vital, not
mechanical, of a real, not a notional, kind; but Mr.
Arnold, with his literary talent and fluent sympathy, has
suffered through want of those checks under which an accurate and logical thinker always consciously or unconsciously works. Breathing the atmosphere of our time, he
has come to attach a measureless importance to the words
'verified,' 'scientific,' 'experience;' but Mr. Arnold
ordinarily gets at his 'science,' his 'verification,' by
the facile literary method of assuming them. We must
believe that his results are scientific, as we are bound
to believe that the heroes of second-rate novels are persons of extraordinary genius, because we are told that
they are such. One who comes with no party passion to his
writings, but with a disposition to use them honestly for
his own advantage, though he is quickened and animated,

can hardly be satisfied. Mr. Arnold's religious conservatism consists in part in detaining the devout imagination
as near as may be to the things of the past, while he bids
the enquiring intellect go forward. The old landmarks are
to be moved, but we are to speak as far as possible on the
supposition that they are not. We are orphans, and made
wards in Chancery, but let us call the Court of Chancery
'Our Father,' and the filial emotion will accept the tran-
sition more easily. No; if we are orphans we feel the
fact so acutely that it only adds to our pain to be mocked
with words. If our wine is new, it is the part of pru-
dence to put it in new bottles. Our endeavour must be to
keep intellect, emotions, and imagination as near to one
another as possible in a mutually quickening activity....

Arnold in the 1870s

41. W. J. COURTHOPE, MODERN CULTURE, 'QUARTERLY REVIEW'

October 1874, cxxxvii, 389-415

Educated at Harrow and Corpus Christi, William John Courthope (1842-1917) had just recently (1869) come to London
to serve in the Education Office when he wrote this ambitious survey of the modern 'Girondins', Goethe, Carlyle,
and Arnold. Following a long discussion of their ideas -
see our introduction for a summary - Courthope here con-
centrates on modern criticism and its reliance on 'tact'.

It is curious to note how closely, and perhaps unconsciously, the modern Sophists tread in the steps of Protagoras, and how, by denying all positive distinctions
between what is true and false, by maintaining that what
appears true to any man is true to *him*, they press to
their logical conclusion that criticism should be a matter
of feeling not of judgment. The quality that is most in
favour with our modern critics is 'tact.' 'Perhaps,' says
Mr. Arnold, 'the quality specially needed for drawing the
right conclusion from the facts, when one has got them,
is best called *perception*, delicacy of perception.' Now
criticism, in the old and honest acceptation of the word,
can only mean the act of judging from evidence, and the
judgments formed, as well as the premises from which they
are drawn, must be plain and palpable to common sense.
We are as much bound to apply this method to problems of
taste, as to questions of science or of practical conduct, though as the subject-matter of the former is more

obscure and debatable, no doubt the conclusion arrived at
will always have a smaller degree of certainty. The critic who forms a judgment on a matter of taste and feeling
is simply required to lay his premise before his audience
in the clearest possible shape, leaving the jury to
consider whether his conclusion is just. But 'tact' is
evidently considered by Mr. Arnold to be a peculiar gift,
a spiritual insight, which enables its possessor to see
farther through a stone wall than is permitted to the
common reason. In point of fact, we find it to be a
quality chiefly cultivated by French writers, and consisting in the ability to draw vast conclusions from almost
invisible premises. This mode of judging has the advantage of being easy. Given a quick perception, a lively
fancy, a wide knowledge of books, and a faculty for
skipping over awkward negative facts, it is plain that a
bold dogmatic affirmation is certain to impress the mind
bewildered in the region of the uncertain or the unknown.
It was by a remarkable exercise of 'tact' that Dr. Ken-
ealy constructed the character of Roger Tichborne out of
his own imagination. Fortunately the 'insight' of the
learned counsel was unequal to contend with the weight of
overwhelming evidence, marshalled against him with unrivalled clearness and precise arrangement. But when a
critic, adopting the same principle, assures his readers
in the most persuasive style that his 'perception' con-
vinces him St. Paul did not understand the meaning of his
own theology, the assertion is attractive, because it is
a paradox, and safe, because it is beyond the region of
proof.
   Now, how do the modern critics seek to strengthen the
sophistry of their position? In the first place, like
their Greek prototypes, they have invented an art of
rhetoric. If we once concede the position of Protagoras
that all truth is relative to the individual, it follows,
as a matter of course, that the prime-object of education
should be to cultivate individual perception. And this is
just what Mr. Arnold wants. The great secret of life, in
his eyes, is to give an air of philosophy to commonplace,
'to let,' as he says, our 'consciousness play freely round
our present operations and the stock notions on which they
are founded, so as to show what these are like, and how
related to the intelligible law of things, and auxiliary
to true human perfection.' Of course this *modus operandi*
(1) results in a science of style. All Mr. Arnold's skill
is expended on giving an apparently general character to
his own personal perceptions by crystallising them in
precise forms of expression. Men naturally suppose that
words represent things, and just as Gorgias caught the

Athenians by his antithetical sentences and curious com-
pounds, so are the cultivated world persuaded that Mr.
Arnold's literary shibboleths, numerous as those of a
religious sect, have a positive novel significance. Yet
it is plainly a mere device of rhetoric when he ascribes
the impression which he himself derives from the New
Testament to the inspiration of the 'Zeit-Geist,' or
'Time-Spirit;' and rhetoric again teaches him to conceal
the purely esoteric nature of such criticisms, as that
Byron was a 'Philistine,' and Pope 'provincial,' under the
piquant dogmatism of his language.

     This art of spiritualising language has received a
curious development. As culture has turned poetry into
criticism so does it transform criticism into poetry.
Aristotle blamed the Sophists for making prose poetical,
observing acutely that those who wrote in this manner
sought to conceal the poverty of their thought by the
showiness of their style. Poetical prose, however,
introduced by Mr. Ruskin and Mr. Carlyle, has made rapid
advances in England. The following extract from Mr.
Pater's criticism on Leonardo da Vinci's picture 'La
Gioconda' is a good specimen of this epicene style: -

     The presence that so strangely rose beside the waters
     is expressive of what in the ways of a thousand years
     man had come to desire. Hers is the head upon which
     all the ends of the world are come, and the eyelids
     are a little weary. It is a beauty wrought out from
     within upon the flesh, the deposit, little cell by
     cell, of strange thoughts, and fantastic reveries,
     and exquisite passions. Set it for a moment beside
     one of those white Greek goddesses or beautiful women
     of antiquity, and how would they be troubled by this
     beauty into which the soul, with all its maladies, has
     passed!

     Now all this is plain, downright, unmistakable poetry.
The picture is made the thesis which serves to display
the writer's extensive reading and the finery of his
style. Of reasoning in the ordinary sense there is positively none. 'The eyelids are a little weary,' therefore
it is quite plain that 'all the ends of the earth are
come upon her head.' The beauty is different from the
Greek type. What then can be more obvious than that this
particular face expresses the whole experience of mankind
between the age of Phidias and Leonardo? The lady appears
to Mr. Pater to have a somewhat sensual expression. A
fact which fully warrants a critical rhetorician in concluding that she is an unconscious incarnation of all the

vices which he has found preserved in the literature of
the Renaissance. Judgments of this kind, we are told,
are the result of 'penetrative sympathy' of 'perceptive
insight.' It may be so; we cannot say that the qualities
Mr. Pater discovers in this picture are not to be found
there. What we can say is that, as the reasoning in the
above passage assumes a knowledge in the critic of motives which are beyond the reach of evidence, there is no
justification for calling that criticism which is in fact
pure romance. In some cases we may go farther, and show
that the freemasonry acquired by perpetual reading,
uncorrected by actual observation, is really of a kind to
weaken that acute sagacity which is necessary for a judge.
For instance, by an error precisely resembling Winckel-
mann's absurd overestimate of Raphael Mengs, a critic of
such natural good sense and sound judgment as Mr. Symonds,
whose book we have classed with Mr. Pater's at the head
of our article, has been induced to assert that an exec-
rable American scribbler, one Walt Whitman, is the true
representative of Greek life in the nineteenth century.
A hundred other instances might be quoted to prove how
critics who reject the natural standards of common sense
in favour of private perceptions derived from books are
made the dupes of quackery and imposture.

Note

1 'way of operating'.

42. F. H. BRADLEY, CONCLUDING REMARKS, 'ETHICAL STUDIES'

1876

Francis Herbert Bradley (1846-1924) studied at University
College, Oxford, and obtained a fellowship at Merton
College in 1870. Along with numerous journal essays he
wrote three major philosophical works, 'Ethical Studies'
(1876), 'Principles of Logic' (1883), and 'Appearance and
Reality' (1893). A highly polemical writer, Bradley
chose, in the conclusion to his 'Ethical Studies', to
attack Arnold's theological ideas. Bradley's own conclusion about human morality is that it is a never-ending
process in which the individual desiring righteousness

will, no matter how virtuous, still feel the 'impulse to
transcend ... existing reality'. Bradley goes on to
assert that 'there is some connection between true religion and morality', and this leads him to consider
Arnold's position, where, to a great extent, religion has
become morality.

Are we to say then that morality is religion? Most certainly not. In morality the ideal is not: it forever
remains a 'to be.' The reality in us or the world is
partial and inadequate; and no one could say that it
answers to the ideal, that, morally considered, both we
and the world are all we ought to be, and ought to be
just what we are. We have at furthest the belief in an
ideal which in its pure completeness is never real-
which, as an ideal, is a mere 'should be.' And the question is, Will that do for religion? No knower of religion, who was not led away by a theory, would answer Yes.
Nor does it help us to say that religion is 'morality
touched by emotion'; for loose phrases of this sort may
suggest to the reader what he knows already without their
help, but, properly speaking, they *say* nothing. *All* morality is, in one sense or another, 'touched by emotion.'
Most emotions, high or low, can go with and 'touch'
morality; and the moment we leave our phrase-making, and
begin to reflect, we see all that is meant is that morality 'touched' by *religious* emotion is religious; and
so, as answer to the question What is religion? all that
we have said is 'It is religion when with morality you
have - religion.' I do not think we learn a very great
deal from this.
     Religion is more than morality. In the religious con-
sciousness we find the belief, however vague and indis-
tinct, in an object, a not-myself; an object, further,
which is real. An ideal which is not real, which is
only in our heads, cannot be the object of religion; and
in particular the ideal self, as the 'is to be' which is
real only so far as we put it forth by our wills, and
which, as an ideal, we cannot put forth, is not a real
object, and so not the object for religion. Hence, because it is unreal, the ideal of personal morality is not
enough for religion. And we have seen before that the
ideal is not realized in the objective world of the state;
so that, apart from other objections, here again we cannot
find the religious object. For the religious consciousness that object is real; and it is not to be found in the
mere moral sphere.

But here once more 'culture' has come to our aid, and
has shown us how here, as everywhere, the study of polite
literature, which makes for meekness, makes needless also
all further education; and we felt already as if the
clouds that metaphysic had wrapped about the matter were
dissolving in the light of a fresh and sweet intelligence. And, as we turned toward the dawn, we sighed over
poor Hegel, who had read neither Goethe nor Homer, nor the
Old and New Testaments, nor any of the literature which
has gone to form 'culture,' but, knowing no facts, and
reading no books, nor ever asking himself 'such a tyro's
question as what being really was,' sat spinning out of
his head those foolish logomachies, which impose on no
person of refinement.

Well, culture has told us what God *was* for the Jews;
and we learn that 'I am that I am' means much the same as
'I blow and grow, that I do,' or 'I shall breathe, that I
shall'; and this, if surprising, was at all events definite, not to say tangible. However, to those of us who do
not think that Christianity is called upon to wrap itself
any longer in 'Hebrew old clothes,' all this is entirely a
matter for the historian. But when 'culture' went on to
tell us what God *is* for science, we heard words we did not
understand about 'streams,' and 'tendencies,' and 'the
Eternal'; and, had it been anyone else that we were reading, we should have said that, in some literary excursion,
they had picked up a metaphysical theory, now out of date,
and putting it in phrases the meaning of which they had
never asked themselves, had then served it up to the
public as the last result of speculation, or of that
'flexible common sense' which is so much better. And as
this in the case of 'culture' and 'criticism' was of
course not possible, we concluded that for us once again
the light had shone in darkness. But the 'stream' and the
'tendency' having served their turn, like last week's pla-
cards, now fall into the background, and we learn at last
that 'the Eternal' is not eternal at all, unless we give
that name to whatever a generation sees happen, and believes both has happened and will happen - just as the
habit of washing ourselves might be termed 'the Eternal
not ourselves that makes for cleanliness,' or 'Early to
bed and early to rise' the 'Eternal not ourselves that
makes for longevity,' and so on - that 'the Eternal,' in
short, is nothing in the world but a piece of literary
clap-trap. The consequence is that all we are left with
is the assertion that 'righteousness' is 'salvation' or
'welfare,' and that there is a 'law' and a 'Power' which
has something to do with this fact; and here again we
must not be ashamed to say that we fail to understand

what any one of these phrases mean, and suspect ourselves
once more to be on the scent of clap-trap.

If what is meant be this, that what is ordinarily
called virtue does always lead to and go with what is
ordinarily called happiness, then so far is this from
being 'verifiable'* in everyday experience, that its opposite is so; it is not a fact, either that to be virtuous
is always to be happy or that happiness must always come
from virtue. Everybody knows this, Mr. Arnold 'must know
this, and yet he gives it, because it suits his purpose,
or because the public, or a large body of the public,
desire it; and this is clap-trap.'

It is not a fact that to be virtuous is always, and
for that reason, to be happy; and, even were it so, yet
such a fact cannot be the object of the religious consciousness. The reality, which answers to the phrases of
culture, is, we suppose, the real existence of the phrases
as such in books or in our heads; or again a number of
events in time, past, present, and future (*i.e.*, conjunc-
tions of virtue and happiness). We have an abstract term
to stand for the abstraction of this or that quality; or
again we have a series or collection of particular occur-
rences. When the literary varnish is removed, is there
anything more?† But the object of the religious
consciousness must be a great deal more. It must be what
is real, not only in the heads of this person or set of
persons, nor again as this or that finite something or set
of somethings. It is in short very different from either
those thin abstractions or coarse 'verifiable' facts, between which and over which there is for our 'culture' no
higher third sphere, save that of the literary groping
which is helpless as soon as it ceases to be blind.

Notes

*   We hear the word 'verifiable' from Mr. Arnold pretty
    often. What is to verify? Has Mr. Arnold put 'such
    a tyro's question' to himself? If to verify means to
    find in outward experience, then the object of true
    religion cannot be found as this or that outward thing
    or quality, and so cannot be verified. It is of its
    essence that in this sense it should be unverifiable
    [Bradley's note].
†   'Is there a God?' asks the reader. 'Oh yes,' replies
    Mr. Arnold, 'and I can verify him in experience.'
    'And what is he then?' cries the reader. 'Be virtuous,
    and as a rule you will he happy,' is the answer.
    'Well, and God?' 'That is God'; says Mr. Arnold,

'There is no deception, and what more do you want?'
I suppose we do want a good deal more. Most of us,
certainly the public which Mr. Arnold addresses, want
something they can worship; and they will not find
that in an hypostasized copy-book heading, which is
not much more adorable than 'Honesty is the best
policy,' or 'Handsome is that handsome does,' or various other edifying maxims which have not yet come to
an apotheosis [Bradley's note].

43. GEORGE SAINTSBURY, FROM MODERN ENGLISH PROSE,
'FORTNIGHTLY REVIEW'

February 1876, xix, n.s., 243-59

In 1876, when George Saintsbury (1845-1933) wrote the
following piece, he was not yet a famous, widely
published literary critic. Rather, a young man of thirty-
one years, with little writing experience, he had just
arrived in London to try to live by his pen. Modern English Prose is a bold undertaking. Saintsbury opens with
the sweeping assumption that during the past forty to
fifty years most English writers have ceased to take
pains with their prose, and as a consequence modern style
is characterized by: 'Diffuseness; sacrifice of literary
proportion to real or apparent clearness of statement;
indulgence in cut-and-dried phrases; undue aiming at pictorial effect' and so on. Having examined the causes for
this degeneration, Saintsbury turns to a quick survey of
the few authors, including Arnold, 'free from these defects or [having] vigour enough to excuse or transform
them'.

'We do not,' says an author with whom I am surprised to
find myself in even partial and temporary agreement, 'we
do not get angry so much with what Mr. Matthew Arnold
says as with his insufferable manner of saying it.' In
other words, there is no fear of omitting to notice a
deliberate command and peculiarity of manner in Mr.
Arnold, whether that manner be considered 'insufferable'
or no. For myself I must confess, that though I have
very rarely felt the least inclincation to get angry with

anything which the author of 'Culture and Anarchy' may
have chosen to say, and though I have in common with all
the youth of Zion an immense debt to acknowledge to his
vindication of our faith and freedom from the chains of
Philistia, yet I could very frequently find it in my heart
to wish that Mr. Arnold had chosen any other style than
that which appears to afford him such extreme delight.
Irony is an admirable thing, but it must be grave and
not grimacing. Innocence is an admirable thing, but it
should not be affected. To have a manner of one's own is
an admirable thing, but to have a mannerism of one's own
is perhaps not quite so admirable. It is curious that
his unfortunately successful pursuit of this latter possession should have led Mr. Arnold to adopt a style which
has more than any other the fault he justly censured
twenty years ago as the special vice of modern art - the
fault of the *fantastic*. No doubt the great masters of
style have each a *cachet* (1) which is easily decipherable
by a competent student; no doubt, in spite of Lord Macaulay, Arbuthnot is to be distinguished from Swift, and the
cunningest imitators of Voltaire from Voltaire himself.
But to simulate this distinction by the deliberate adop-
tion of mere tricks and manners is what no true master of
style ever yet attempted, because for no true master of
style was it ever yet necessary. Mr. Ruskin, to use the
old Platonic simile, has not his horses sufficiently well
in hand; at times the heavenly steed, with a strong and
sudden flight, will lift the car amid the empyrean, at
times the earth-born yoke-fellow will drag it down, with
scarcely the assistance and scarcely the impediment of
the charioteer. But even this is better than the driving
of one who has broken his horses, indeed, but has broken
them to little but the mincing graces of the Lady's Mile.

Note

1   'mark'.

44.   SAMUEL BUTLER, 'NOTEBOOKS'

Entry from 1883

Samuel Butler (1835-1902), the archtype of the rebellious

Victorian son, after enduring the domineering influence
of his father as long as he could, fled to New Zealand and
became a sheep-herder in order to find himself. What he
found was a writer with a taste for the iconoclastic. His
fortune doubled, he returned to England to write a series
of books, among them 'The Way of All Flesh', which sought
to invert received opinions. Here he takes Arnold to task
for misunderstanding 'righteousness'.

According to Mr. Matthew Arnold, as we find the highest
traditions of grace, beauty, and the heroic virtues among
the Greeks and Romans, so we derive our highest ideal of
righteousness from Jewish sources. Righteousness was to
the Jew what strength and beauty were to the Greek or
fortitude to the Roman.

This sounds well, but can we think that the Jews taken
as a nation were really more righteous than the Greeks and
and Romans? Could they indeed be so if they were less
strong, graceful, and enduring? In some respects they
may have been - every nation has its strong points - but
surely there has been a nearly unanimous verdict for many
generations that the typical Greek or Roman is a higher,
nobler person that the typical Jew - and this referring
not to the modern Jew, who may perhaps be held to have
been injured by centuries of oppression, but to the
Hebrew of the time of the old prophets and of the most
prosperous eras in the history of the nation. If three
men could be set before us as the most perfect Greek,
Roman, and Jew respectively, and if we could choose which
we would have our only son most resemble, is it not
likely we should find ourselves preferring the Greek or
Roman to the Jew? And does not this involve that we hold
the two former to be the more righteous in a broad sense
of the word?

I dare not say that we owe no benefits to the Jewish
nation, I do not feel sure whether we do or do not, but I
can see no good thing that I can point to as a notoriously Hebrew contribution to our moral and intellectual
well-being as I can point to our law and say that it is
Roman, or to our fine arts and say that they are based on
what the Greeks and Italians taught us. On the contrary, if asked what feature of post-Christian life we
had derived most distinctly from Hebrew sources I should
say at once 'intolerance' - the desire to dogmatize about
matters whereon the Greek and Roman held certainty to be
at once unimportant and unattainable. This, with all its
train of bloodshed and family disunion, is chargeable to

the Jewish rather than to any other account.

There is yet another vice which occurs readily to any
one who reckons up the characteristics which we derive
mainly from the Jews; it is one that we call, after a
Jewish sect, 'Pharisaism.' I do not mean to say that no
Greek or Roman was ever a sanctimonious hypocrite, still,
sanctimoniousness does not readily enter into our notions
of Greeks and Romans and it does so enter into our notions
of the old Hebrews. Of course, we are all of us sanctimonious sometimes; Horace himself is so when he talks
about *aurum irrepertum et sic melius situm*, (1) and as for
Virgil he was a prig, pure and simple; still, on the
whole, sanctimoniousness was not a Greek and Roman vice
and it was a Hebrew one. True, they stoned their prophets
freely; but these are not the Hebrews to whom Mr. Arnold
is referring, they are the ones whom it is the custom to
leave out of sight and out of mind as far as possible, so
that they should hardly count as Hebrews at all, and none
of our characteristics should be ascribed to them.

Taking their literature I cannot see that it deserves
the praises that have been lavished upon it. The Song of
Solomon and the book of Esther are the most interesting in
the Old Testament, but these are the very ones that make
the smallest pretensions to holiness, and even these are
neither of them of very transcendent merit. They would
stand no chance of being accepted by Messrs. Cassell and
Co. or by any biblical publisher of the present day.
Chatto and Windus might take the Song of Solomon, but,
with this exception, I doubt if there is a publisher in
London who would give a guinea for the pair. Ecclesiastes
contains some fine things but is strongly tinged with
pessimism, cynicism, and affectation. Some of the Pro-
verbs are good, but not many of them are in common use.
Job contains some fine passages, and so do some of the
Psalms; but the Psalms generally are poor and, for the
most part, querulous, spiteful, and introspective into the
bargain. Mudie would not take thirteen copies of the lot
if they were to appear now for the first time - unless
indeed their royal authorship were to arouse an adventi-
tious interest in them, or unless the author were a rich
man who played his cards judiciously with the reviewers.
As for the prophets - we know what appears to have been
the opinion formed concerning them by those who should
have been best acquainted with them; I am no judge as to
the merits of the controversy between them and their
fellow-countrymen, but I have read their words and am of
opinion that they will not hold their own against such
masterpieces of modern literature as, we will say, 'The
Pilgrim's Progress,' 'Robinson Crusoe,' 'Gulliver's

Travels,' or 'Tom Jones.' 'Whether there be prophecies,'
exclaims the Apostle, 'they shall fail.' On the whole I
should say that Isaiah and Jeremiah must be held to have
failed.

I would join issue with Mr. Matthew Arnold on yet
another point. I understand him to imply that righteousness should be a man's highest aim in life. I do not like
setting up righteousness, nor yet anything else, as the
highest aim in life; a man should have any number of
little aims about which he should be conscious and for
which he should have names, but he should have neither
name for, nor consciousness concerning the main aim of
his life. Whatever we do we must try and do it rightly -
this is obvious - but righteousness implies something
much more than this: it conveys to our minds not only the
desire to get whatever we have taken in hand as nearly
right as possible, but also the general reference of our
lives to the supposed will of an unseen but supreme
power. Granted that there is such a power, and granted
that we should obey its will, we are the more likely to
do this the less we concern ourselves about the matter
and the more we confine our attention to the things
immediately round about us which seem, so to speak,
entrusted to us as the natural and legitimate sphere of
our activity. I believe a man will get the most useful
information on these matters from modern European sources;
next to these he will get most from Athens and ancient
Rome. Mr. Matthew Arnold notwithstanding, I do not think
he will get anything from Jerusalen which he will not find
better and more easily elsewhere.

Note

1 'gold undiscovered and thus better placed'.

45. MARK PATTISON, REVIEW IN THE 'ACADEMY'

17 May 1879, xv, 425-6

Mark Pattison (1813-84), educator and reviewer, endured a
life of depressing failures. A morbidly shy and sensitive
boy, he did not do well at school, flirted with Newmanism,
became a priest and college tutor in 1843, and finally

surprised everyone by being appointed college examiner
for Lincoln College in 1848. He did his job too well.
A cabal of conservative academics drove him out in 1851,
and by the time a grateful school elected him rector in
1861 he was no longer interested. In the interim he had
turned to scholarship, working for thirty years on a biography of Scaliger he never finished and writing articles
for most of the major Victorian periodicals. His response
to 'Mixed Essays' is comprehensive in scope and warm in
appreciation. Arnold himself was delighted with the
review.

When twenty, or more, years ago Mr. Matthew Arnold first
named the name of Ste.-Beuve, 'the master of us all,'
there were probably not twenty people in England who had
ever heard that name, or who, if they knew the name, knew
what it signified. Arnold did not adopt Ste.-Beuve as
his master and exemplar, but his instinct led him at once
to the French critic as the one judge in whom he found
any perception of that quality in books in virtue of which
they are brought within the range of 'literature.'
Arnold has never practised the profession of reviewer;
his reviews of books have been quite occasional and exceptional. Yet his influence upon the style of periodical
criticism in England has been very valuable.
    The traditional tone of reviewing in this country was
that of Warburton in the last century, and Christopher
North in this. If you disliked a man, you abused, de-
famed, libelled him, and called him all the scurrilous
names you could muster. If you were his friend, you
puffed his book with magniloquent epithets of praise.
The Irish ferocity of the bludgeon-and-tomahawk school
was, indeed, somewhat toned down by 1850, before Matthew
Arnold came upon the scene. But the notion which the
professional reviewer still entertained of his business
was that he was either to demolish a book or to recommend
it. The most brilliant reviewer of that period was Macaulay, and the barbarous manners of the time are stereo-
typed for us in the two essays in which he threw himself
upon Milton with laudatory rhetoric, and upon Croker with
withering scorn.
    In the innumerable host of amateur critics in the pre-
sent day are still to be found some surviving practi-
tioners of the stick-and-horsewhip system, by whom we are
treated to occasional exhibitions of the rampant onslaught of the days of Jeffrey and Blackwood. But a
better tone undoubtedly prevails in the best class of

periodical, and among the influences which have contributed to this improvement not the least has been the better
way pointed out by Matthew Arnold, and his incessant inculcation of it by precept or by example.

Critics required to be taught two things. One, that
when a man undertakes to pronounce a judgment upon a
writer's treatment of any subject, the critic ought to
have, to begin with, a knowledge of the subject at least
equal to that of the author under review. This obvious
principle, so long unknown in this country, English
reviewers learnt from Germany. The 'Academy' may justly
claim the credit of having naturalised and established it
among us. The other lesson we might have learnt from
France, but we did not. That we are learning it at all
is due to Matthew Arnold. There is such a thing, in the
management of written speech, as 'style, taste, elegance -
in a word, form. Of the existence of such a thing as
style no German of this day has any idea. Hence German
books, valuable as they are in point of matter, resemble
the Mosaic chaos - a *tohu* and *bohu*, 'without form and
void.' In the materialistic age of England through which
we have passed, if it can be said to be past, the tendency
of our books has been to neglect form. Some of our most
accredited doctors still maintain the German doctrine of
'say it anyhow.' Only the other day Mr. Frederic Harrison told a London audience, with great applause, that
provided what you said was good, it was matter of indifference how it was worded. I may observe, by the way,
that Frederic Harrison is far too knowing to act upon his
own advice. He has taken care to provide himself with,
and to keep for his own exclusive use, one of the most
careful, trenchant, lucid styles now written: a style,
which if it does not always satisfy the perceptions of
taste, exemplifies the most elaborate art of composition.

What Matthew Arnold has made us begin to attend to is
something which reaches beyond mere style, beyond the
syntax or wording of our sentences. There is an urbane
quality, a play of mind for the play's sake, a quality
the possession of which raised the Athenians to the pre-
eminence they hold in the annals of ancient civilisation,
and their hold upon which still keeps the French nation
at the head of civilised Europe. Of this mental quality,
manners, social intercourse, art, are severally expressive. Literature is also an expression of the same quality, and one which is become far more important than it
used to be, through the diffusion of the opportunities
of reading. Many things we may have learnt from Matthew
Arnold, but this, I think, especially: that a book is not
merely a vehicle of information, but a work of art. It

should please by its form. It should not merely instruct,
it should appeal to the cultivated humanity which education brings out in the reading classes.

I have said that Matthew Arnold has had a large share
in the reform of our criticism. He has taught the professional reviewer that neither praise nor blame, nor yet
an impartial mixture of the two, is a sufficient discharge
of his function. For science a critic should have knowledge, and this the Germans have taught us. Matthew
Arnold teaches us that the critic of literature must have
soul: in the words of Cleveland's epitaph on Ben Jonson -

> The soul which answer'd best to all well said
> By others, and which most requital made.

Arnold's influence on the critic has gone much beyond the
negative influence of restraining him from hitting out.
The spread of civilisation tends to confine club-law in
criticism to the Bohemian newspapers. Arnold has endeavoured to inspire our critics with a new perception, that
of refinement as a quality which should pervade writing
as well as speech.

But Arnold's ambition as a social reformer goes much
beyond a desire to improve the tone of the critical
journals. He desires to purify and elevate, not only the
writers of criticism, but the readers. He does not, in
these essays, appear in the character of a national
reformer. He does not propound ultimate social problems
and offer a remedial reorganisation of society from top
to bottom. He assumes society to go on as now constituted, and the relation of classes, of capital and labour,
either to be what it now is, or to be somehow arranged by
economic law. This as it may be. In any case there will
be people - large classes of shopkeeping and business
men, and all the women - who have not to work, and who
have leisure. To these perishing souls, destitute of all
share in the most precious outcome of the ages of preparation, is Arnold's mission. He sees the herds of the
English middle class as they look to a foreign looker-on,
one of whom wrote in a French paper: -

> To understand the success of Messrs. Moody and Sankey
> one must be familiar with English manners; one must
> know the mind-deadening influence of a narrow Biblism;
> one must have experienced the sense of *ennui* which the
> aspect and the frequentation of this great division of
> English society produce in others, the want of elasti-
> city and the chronic *ennui* which characterise this
> class itself, petrified in a narrow Protestantism, and
> in a perpetual reading of the Bible.

This class, the great middle-class, a class which
comprehends the whole English nation between the highest
aristocracy on the one hand and the peasant and artisan on
the other, the class by which we are known on the Continent as 'the vulgar nation,' 'in the beginning of the
seventeenth century entered the prison of Puritanism, and
had the key turned upon its spirit there for two hundred
years.' The power of intellect, the power of beauty, the
power of social life and manners, amenity, accomplishment,
gentleness, docility, attractive behaviour, the desire for
elegance, for grace of life and surroundings, the effort
to please - all these things are unknown to our great
vulgarian herd. Instead of averting his face from the
unpleasing spectacle, Arnold is smitten with a profound
pity for this weltering mass of prosperous, well-to-do
barbarism, and would fain raise them out of the slough of
materialism in which they lie, self-pleasing, well content
to be where they are.

How is this sordid and unintellectual mass to be
reached? How is an apostle of 'things of the mind' to
find access for a new idea to those whose minds are closed
to all ideas, as such? If by preaching, Arnold will
preach, and does so most eloquently. But we all know that
preaching is in vain till the soul is first awakened to a
sense of its want. And it is characteristic of the trad-
ing, thriving, calculating class in question to be
entirely satisfied with itself and its form of existence.
Its only want is more income, and to attire itself with
the fashions and designations which have become associated
with aristocracy. Its ambitions are wholly material;
moral or religious aspiration is unknown to it. Its
strong, self-reliant, self-asserting quality, the very
quality which gives it its wealth and material comfort,
excludes from it any suspicion of its own moral deficiencies. It cannot have refinement; for refinement is not a
possession, but an endeavour, and this class knows of no
endeavour except after more prosperity.

As far as I see in this volume of 'Mixed Essays',
Matthew Arnold has no very hopeful remedy to offer for a
state of things so deplorable as we all feel this to be.
While he is painting the misery of this moral apathy, this
living death, of our well-to-do classes, he is striking
and stimulating in a way which raises him much above those
of our essayists whose only aim is to weave for us a
tissue of beautiful words. A distinct spiritual aim
inspires this volume, urging to effort, and pointing to
a high ideal. But when we enquire into the means of
attaining this end, I do not find them distinctly marked.
There may be casual indications, but two reforms only are

definitely stated as means to the desired end. These are
'equality' and a good system of secondary schools.
    Of these two engines of moral renovation 'equality' is,
as Arnold himself points out, a result of refinement
rather than a cause. Or, rather, 'equality' may come in
two very different ways: it may result from the middle
class coming within the scope of the ideal of character
which the refined class proposes to itself; or 'equality'
may come in a democracy, as it has in America, by the
obliteration of any moral ideal, a social state in which
the notion we attach to the terms 'gentleman,' conduct
'becoming a gentleman,' is wanting.
    We have, then, only the other proposal to fall back
upon - that of a system of secondary schools erected and
supported by the State. Matthew Arnold, who knows officially more about schools than most of us, is certainly
not less aware than the rest of us of the cramping nature
of the education given in our classical and commercial
academies, in our colleges for the sons of licensed vic-
tuallers, for the sons of medical men, and other boarding-
schools of private adventure, which owe their existence
and adapt their instruction to the spirit of commercial
enterprise. He thinks that the establishment over the
face of England of a system of high schools of the calibre
of the French Lycées, administered by the State, would of
itself elevate the tone of the middle classes. He says: -

    By giving to these schools a public character, the
    State can bring instruction in them under a criticism
    which the stock of judgment in our middle classes is
    not itself able to supply. By giving to them a
    national character, it can confer on them a greatness
    and a noble spirit which the tone of these classes is
    not of itself at present adequate to impart.

The French Lycée, then, seems to be the one only and sufficient antidote on which Matthew Arnold relies for the
cure of the manifold distempers in mind, manners, and
moral bearing which he has pointed out and described with
so much force and humour. I confess myself unable to feel
as much confidence in Matthew Arnold's prescription as he
seems to do himself. It is a fashion just now, whenever
we encounter a social evil, to invoke 'education' as the
omnipotent force which can remove mountains and cure all
diseases. But between 'education' and 'school' there is
a wide difference. School is only a very small part of a
man's education. Will a few years' schooling, I wonder,
turn a Philistine into a child of 'light and sweetness'?
How is it that Philistinism is rampant among the French

bourgeois who have the run of these wonder-working Lycées?
Where are the teachers to be found who are to communicate
to so many thousand stagnant pools of municipal and provincial ditchwater, the sweetness of the fountain of life?
In vain are the liberal arts and sciences professed in a
school or college if they are not taught liberally, and
by liberally-bred teachers. The study of all the humanities extant could not make an Ultramontane college anything but a machine for turning out Ultramontanes, where
the humanities are manipulated by Catholic teachers for
Catholic ends. Will Arnold's new State middle-schools
follow in the wake of the public grammar-schools, and forsake liberal education for education sake, and go in for
a mechanical grind yielding much fruit in prizes, pecuni-
ary and honorary, but crushing out of the young spirit all
free delight and genial play with the 'things of the
mind'? Before we invite the middle class to enter a
system of schools, modelled after the schools used by the
gentry and aristocracy, we ought to be sure that we preserve in our own schools and universities the lamp of
science, the condition of humane culture, the key to all
the arts, which is only to be found in a teacher animated
himself by a lofty ideal and a disinterested love for the
things he teaches to others.

Thus it appears to me that these essays are most successful in bringing before us, in all its unloveliness,
the dismal blank of the domestic interior of the English
middle-class family. They are not equally distinct on the
methods of prevention and cure. But it would be a very
imperfect account of a charming volume to leave the impression that this one topic is a complete summary of its
contents. It is rich in suggestion up and down the field
of pure literature. It is in his feeling for pure literature, as such, that Matthew Arnold stands alone among the
writers of our day. When he descends into the arena of
social debate his opinions are but the opinions of one
among many thoughtful men. When he takes an historical
view he is open to be challenged by many. I cannot, for
instance, allow his dictum on Cromwell's foreign policy
to pass without a protest. He says it was Cromwell's
foreign policy which gave Europe 'the Grand Monarch and
all that he denoted.' The Protector's foreign policy was
directed to forming a strong Protestant party, which would
have made the Grand Monarch and his conquests in the Low
Countries impossible. It was the Stuart foreign policy,
which abetted the French Crown in crushing the Protestants in France, that produced the Grand Monach.

While Arnold's historical view is often imperfect, his
literary perception is never at fault, and his verdict

all but infallible. I leave this little loophole for
dissent, in order that I may challenge something he has
said of Cowper in this volume. Stopford Brooke had said
that in the retired poet's thought is to be found the new
thought upon the subject of mankind, which was soon to
take so fierce a form in Paris! Arnold contradicts this.
It appears to me a true and happy *rapprochement*. (1) The
mild parochial philanthropy of Cowper is Rousseau taken in
the shape adapted to the English village-green. I must
here side with Stopford Brooke rather than with his
critic. But these are rare occasions. In this very
essay, the review of the 'Primer of English Literature,'
Matthew Arnold is more than once content with barely rev-
ersing Stopford Brooke's proposition, and leaving things
so. For instance, 'It is not true to say that Milton
"summed up in himself all the higher influences of the
Renascence."' There is probably no other living critic
who could be permitted, and whom we should all recognise
as being entitled, to deal with books in this style of
summary jurisdiction. Such is our confidence in Arnold's
judgment and discernment in literary things, that no one
would think of appealing from a ruling of his, even when
delivered without its reasons.

Note

1 'comparison'.

46. W. C. BROWNELL (?), ANONYMOUS REVIEW, 'NATION'

23 October 1879, xxix, 276-7

William Crary Brownell (1851-1928), editor at Scribner's
from 1888 to 1928 and author of a series of influential
books of criticism, was working on the staff of the
'Nation' when this review, typical of his conceptual
approach and literary style, appeared. Brownell became,
in John Raleigh's words, perhaps 'the most thoroughgoing
Arnoldian of all American critics'. Here, however,
Brownell argues that Arnold has taken a wrong turn in his
recent concern for the 'practical', which 'takes the place
of something else, something upon the whole, better'.

Under this title Mr. Arnold has collected nine essays;
one, that on Democracy, published nearly twenty years ago,
but the others so recently that they must be familiar to
readers of the prominent English reviews. They are as
follows: Equality, Irish Catholicism and British Liberalism, Porro Unum est Necessarium, A Guide to English
Literature, Falkland, A French Critic on Milton, A French
Critic on Goethe, and George Sand. Collection of them in
one volume has been esteemed a mere piece of book-making
by some of the large class of critics permanently hostile
to Mr. Arnold, we believe, but what he says in his preface, that they have 'a unity of tendency,' is true,
though, since we gain a preface thereby, we are none the
less obliged to him for pointing it out. Literature, he
says, is a great force of civilization, but it cannot do
everything to secure it, and is indeed only a part of it.
Civilization is really the humanization of man in society.
This is in great measure the goal of man's endeavour, and
the means of attaining it are various. 'First and foremost of the necessary means toward man's civilization we
must name *expansion*,' says Mr. Arnold. The need for expansion is as genuine an instinct as the need for right
conduct. Railroads and the telegraph, and 'all the con-
veniences of life by which man has enlarged and secured
his existence,' are manifestations of this instinct; but
that which 'we English know best and prize most' is the
love of liberty. 'The love of liberty is simply the instinct in man for expansion,' and the fatal objection to
Prince Bismarck's ideal of a benevolent despotism, for
example, is that it is 'against nature.' Besides liberty
the love of equality is a manifestation of the instinct of
expansion; of this, however, 'we English,' have little,
but it is just as real a tendency as the other, and
'inequality, like absolutism, thwarts a vital instinct.'
The instinct of expansion, in short, manifested by the
love of liberty and of equality, is 'the basis which man's
whole effort to civilize himself presupposes.' The basis
given, Mr. Arnold sums up the powers which contribute to
build up civilization as 'the power of conduct, the power
of intellect and knowledge, the power of beauty, the
power of social life and manners.' And he goes on: 'That
the aim for all of us is to make civilization pervasive
and general; that the requisites for civilization are
substantially what have been here enumerated; that they
all of them hang together, that they must all have their
development, that the development of one does not compen-
sate for the failure of others; that one nation suffers
by failing in this requisite, and another by failing in
that - such is the line of thought which the essays in

the present volume follow and represent. They represent
it in their variety of subject, their so frequent insistence on defects in the present actual life of our nation,
their unity of final aim.'
    This is excellent constructive criticism of his volume.
But it is also a substantially accurate statement of 'the
unity of final aim' of all of Mr. Arnold's writings, and
there is perhaps nothing in this last volume to indicate
a revision in any important respect of one's former notion
of its author, of his sentiments, and of the value of
them. Another way of putting this is to say that Mr.
Arnold is still harping on the same string, and there is
nothing new to report of him. And doubtless there are
many persons of distinguished culture who think of Thackeray's wish that Carlyle would 'hang up his damned old
fiddle' when they read another essay insisting in the
same way and in almost the same phraseology upon the
'sweet reasonableness' of another than 'the Puritan
ideal,' and upon 'our old remedy, culture,' for the cure
of all present ills. Nevertheless, several of these
essays have an air of practicality that is perhaps a
little more distinct and emphatic than heretofore it has
been - a definiteness and particularity of statement
which many persons may hitherto have missed in Mr. Arnold.
The charge of vagueness has been one of the principal
charges against the 'religion of culture,' as it is
derisively termed, and of which its promulgator wrote
some eight or ten years ago: 'It is said to be a religion
proposing parmaceti, or some scented salve or other, as a
cure for human miseries; a religion breathing a spirit of
cultivated inaction, making its believer refuse to lend a
hand at uprooting the definite evils on all sides of us,
and filling him with antipathy against the reforms and
reformers which try to extirpate them. In general, it is
summed up as being not practical, or - as some critics
familiarly put it - all moonshine.' We should say that
the criticism which this so happily and vivaciously epi-
tomizes had been gradually decreasing in volume and intensity since 'Culture and Anarchy' was printed, and that
it had been to some extent replaced by a recognition on
the part of 'my countrymen' that 'our urgent want now is,
not to act at any price, but rather to lay in a stock of
light for our difficulties'; or, at least, that such a
position was a tenable one.
    To several of these essays, at all events, it would
not be necessary to apply it. They are none of them, to
be sure, essays in practical politics, but they certainly
are, as Mr. Arnold says in that on Equality, 'for the
thoughts of those who think.' The first is a plea for

regarding state-action as something which may be right or
wrong as circumstances indicate, but which in itself contains no fundamental error or tyranny. 'If I were a
Frenchmen I should never be weary of admiring the independent, individual, local habits of action in England, of
directing attention to the evils occasioned in France by
the excessive action of the state. Being an Englishman,
I see nothing but good in freely recognizing the coherence, rationality, and effectiveness which characterize
the strong state-action of France.' The second is a plea
for Equality, by which is meant social equality, and is
perhaps the most elaborate and the most substantial in
the volume. 'Equality before the law,' says Mr. Arnold,
' we all take as a matter of course: that is not the
equality which we mean when we talk of equality. When we
talk of equality we understand social equality; and for
equality in this Frenchified sense of the term almost
everybody in England has a hard word' - Lord Beaconsfield,
Sir Erskine May in his 'History of Democracy,' Mr.
Froude, Mr. Lowe, and Mr. Gladstone had lately been stig-
matizing it each in his own way. Mr. Arnold makes an
examination of contemporary national opinion upon the
subject, and regards freedom of bequest as a bulwark of
inequality, since the constitution of property with which
the feudal Middle Age left the societies of Europe was
full of inequality and tends thus to preserve itself. And
after showing his country to be in a minority of one in
the matter, he accuses her social inequality of 'material-
izing our upper class, vulgarizing our middle class, and
brutalizing our lower class. And this is to fail in
civilization,' he dryly adds, proceeding to support his
accusation in his familiar manner. Irish Catholicism and
British Liberalism is a plea for an Irish Catholic university, for recognizing that hostility to Catholicism as
such tends to increase its dogmatism and its Ultramontanism, which are its worst side and are already conspicuous
in Irish Catholicism, and for transforming the English
middle class, if Ireland is still to be governed in deference to its prejudices. The next essay is in behalf of
better secondary schools in England, and the next a suggestive review of Mr. Stopford Brooke's 'Primer of English
Literature.' That on Falkland - 'our martyr of sweetness
and light, of lucidity of mind and largeness of temper' -
is too familiar to need further mention, and the remain-
ing three contain much delicate and just literary criticism, besides representing the tendency which gives them
a place in this volume.
   This is not vague or impractical. It is, on the contrary, all very simple and plain. It is, most of it,

directed to Mr. Arnold's own countrymen, to one class of
them, to one fault of that class: it is, all of it, English, local and personal. This, indeed, we take to be
the essential mistake of Mr. Arnold's later writings –
their distinctly practical tendency, namely; whether or
no they be considered to have any really practical value,
is another matter. A writer may merely be 'holding out
his pouncet-box in the midst of the general tribulation,'
as Mr. Arnold says he is accused of doing, or he may indicate with precision and power one great source of the
evils in question, and advocate with luminous persuasive-
ness one plain but very widely negelected remedy for them,
and yet it may be that his true function is not to be continually concerned with the general tribulation at all.
Few Anglo-Saxons probably sympathize with the regret of
M. Taine that in Thackeray the gain of morals was the loss
of art. But few of Mr. Arnold's sincerest admirers, we
imagine, are reconciled to the exclusiveness with which
of late years he has devoted himself to his missionary
work. It is possible to go along with him completely and
still regret this. One may be fully convinced of the
provinciality and faith in machinery of 'our English
race,' of the worth of ideas and of knowing the best that
has been thought and said in the world, of the nobility
of sweetness and the necessity of light, of the just
demands of intellect as well as the claims of morals, may
even accept the theology and theory of 'Literature and
Dogma,' and still regret that pure literature does not
more completely absorb his attention. To feel this one
need be neither ungrateful for nor tired of Mr. Arnold's
advocacy of culture. It is so good a thing that it
cannot be too much insisted upon, and few people we
imagine, easily tire of witnessing the way in which he
exhibits the inadequacy of Puritan and 'progressive'
ideals. There is always an intimate pleasure to be
obtained by the disinterested observer when the process
of flaying somebody is going on, and no one has reached
the perfection in this art which belongs to Mr. Arnold.
The spectator need fear no remorse accompanying his enjoyment, since it generally happens that· the victim is
both as unconscious as is consistent with squirming, and
guilty as well. And if Mr. Arnold's power and dignity
were less than they are it would be possible to go over
the list of those whom he has delicately castigated, from
Bishop Colenso to that school 'whose mission is to bring
into order and system that body of truth with which the
earlier Liberals merely fumbled,' with positive satisfaction. But controversy cannot be said to lose all its
evil by losing all its grossness; no one has shown its

weakness, and the contrasted strength of statement not
deliberately persuasive, better than Mr. Arnold; and,
however delightful and instructive it may be, it has at
least one serious defect - it takes the place of something else, something, upon the whole, better. 'The
general public carries away little from discussions of
this kind,' said Mr. Arnold long ago, 'except some vague
notion that one advocates English hexameters, or that one
has attacked Mr. Newman. On the mind of an adversary one
never makes the faintest impression.' And later: 'Only
think of all the nonsense which you now hold quite firmly,
which you would never have held if you had not been contradicting your adversary in it all these years.' And
evangelization necessitates controversy. It is true that
writing about literature and contending for nothing, for
no principle underlying literary phenomena, so to speak,
is only dilettanteism, but there is a level which Mr.
Arnold sometimes reaches, upon which he writes in such
wise as to show that he is perfectly at home there, upon
which we always find him when he gives us joy instead of
pleasure, as he says of Joubert, and upon which he seems
to evince almost no concern for the transformations of
the British Puritan. At such times he brings to literature - to the 'criticism of life' - a union of intelligence, culture, divination, and seriousness of thought
which many who admire the vivacity that his tact brings
to the conduct of controversy never suspect in him. At
such times few other writers so well satisfy one's reason,
who so effectively stir one's susceptibility. 'Freedom
of speech may be necessary for the society of the future,
but the young lions of the "Daily Telegraph" in the meanwhile are sacrificed,' said Mr. Arnold once, and we may
say in the same way that the British Puritan certainly
needs transformation, but that in the meanwhile Mr. Arnold
sacrifices himself. In the meanwhile he is in a measure
lost to letters.

The Last Decade

47. J. A. SYMONDS, MATTHEW ARNOLD'S SELECTIONS FROM
WORDSWORTH, 'FORTNIGHTLY REVIEW'

November 1879, xxvi, n.s., 686-701

John Addington Symonds (1840-93), the able and influential
writer, was for a long time hindered in his literary work
by a severe case of tuberculosis. Throughout the 1860s
he oscillated between fits of hard work (for example, the
first three volumes of the 'History of the Renaissance in
Italy', 1875, 1877) and therapeutic rest. Symonds's
response to Arnold's 'Wordsworth' is a fascinating commentary by a man of a younger generation on Arnold the
mid-Victorian. Symonds wants to agree with Arnold's
emphasis on 'criticism of life', but he fears its didactic overtones. In trying to strike a balance between the
demands of content and style, Symonds seems to forget
Arnold's own, careful qualification of his idea. In fact,
the two men are in fairly close agreement.

It is both interesting and instructive to hear what masters of a craft may choose to say upon the subject of
their art. The interest is rather increased than diminished by the limitation of the imperfection of their view,
inseparable from personal inclination, idiosyncrasy of
genius, or absorbing previous course of study. When Heinrich exclaims, 'There's no lust like to poetry;' when
Goethe asserts, 'Die Kunst ist nur Gestaltung;' (1) when
Shelley writes 'Poetry is the record of the best and
happiest moments of the happiest and best minds,' we feel

in each of these utterances - too partial to express an
universal truth, too profound to be regarded as a merely
casual remark - the dominating bias and instinctive lean-
ings of a lifetime. If, then, we remember that Mr.
Matthew Arnold is equally eminent as a critic and a poet,
we shall not be too much surprised to read the following
account of poetry given in the preface to his Selections
from Wordsworth: 'It is important, therefore, to hold fast
to this: that poetry is at bottom a criticism of life;
that the greatness of a poet lies in his powerful and
beautiful application of ideas to life - to the question:
How to live.'
   At first sight this definition will strike most people
as a paradox. It would be scarcely less startling to
hear, as indeed we might perhaps hear from a new school of
writers upon art, that 'Criticism is at bottom the poetry
of things,' inasmuch as it is the critic's function to
select the quintessential element of all he touches, and
to present that only in choice form to the public he professes to instruct. Yet, when we return to Mr. Arnold,
and compare the passage above quoted with the fuller expression of the same view upon a preceding page, the apparent paradox is reduced to the proportions of a sound and
valuable generalization: 'Long ago, in speaking of Homer,
I said that the noble and profound application of ideas to
life is the most essential part of poetic greatness. I
said that a great poet receives his distinctive character
of superiority from his application, under the conditions
immutably fixed by the laws of poetic beauty and poetic
truth, from his application, I say, whatever it may be,
of the ideas -

   On man, on nature, and on human life,

which he has acquired for himself.' An important element
in this description of poetic greatness is the further
determination of the ideas in question as moral: 'It is
said that to call these ideas *moral* ideas is to introduce
a strong and injurious limitation. I answer that it is
to do nothing of the kind, because moral ideas are really
so main a part of human life. The question, *how to live*,
is itself a moral idea; and it is the question which most
interests every man, and with which, in some way or other,
he is perpetually occupied.'
   With the substance of these passages there are few who,
after mature reflection on the nature of poetry, will not
agree. That the weight of Mr. Arnold's authority should
be unhesitatingly given against what he calls the poetry
of revolt and the poetry of indifference to morals, is a

matter for rejoicing to all who think the dissemination of
sound views on literature important. It is good to be
reminded at the present moment that Omar Kayam failed of
true greatness because he was a reactionary, and that
Théophile Gautier took up his abode in what can never be
more than a wayside halting-place. From time to time critics arise who attempt to persuade us that it does not so
much matter what a poet says as how he says it, and that
the highest poetical achievements are those which combine
a certain vagueness of meaning with sensuous melody and
colour of verbal composition. Yet, if one thing is proved
with certainty by the whole of history of literature to
our time, it is that the self-preservative instinct of
humanity rejects such art as does not contribute to its
intellectual nutrition and moral sustenance. It cannot
afford to continue long in contact with ideas that run
counter to the principles of its own progress. It cannot
bestow more than passing notice upon trifles, however
exquisitely finished. Poetry will not, indeed, live
without style or its equivalent. But style alone will
never confer enduring and cosmopolitan fame upon a poet.
He must have placed himself in accord with the permanent
emotions, the conservative forces of the race; he must
have uttered what contributes to the building up of vital
structure in the social organism, in order to gain more
than a temporary or a partial hearing. Though style is an
indispensable condition of success in poetry, it is by
matter, and not by form, that a poet has to take his final
rank.

Of the two less perfect kinds of poetry, the poetry of
revolt and the poetry of indifference, the latter has by
far the slighter chance of survival. Powerful negation
implies that which it rebels against. The energy of the
rebellious spirit is itself a kind of moral greatness.
We are braced and hardened by contact with impassioned
revolutionaries, with Lucretius, Voltaire, Leopardi.
Something necessary to the onward progress of humanity -
the vigour of antagonism, the operative force of the
antithesis - is communicated by them. They are in a high
sense ethical by the exhibition of hardihood, self-
reliance, hatred of hypocrisy. Even Omar's secession from
the mosque to the tavern symbolizes a necessary and recurring moment of experience. It is, moreover, dignified by
the pathos of the poet's view of life. Meleager's sensu-
ality is condoned by the delicacy of his sentiment. Tone
counts for much in this poetry of revolt against morals.
It is only the Stratons, the Beccadellis, the Baudelaires,
who, in spite of their consummate form, are consigned to
poetical perdition by vulgarity, perversity, obliquity of

vision. But the carving of cherry-stones in verse, the
turning of triolets and rondeaux, the seeking after sound
or colour without heed for sense, is all foredoomed to
final failure.

While substantially agreeing with Mr. Arnold, it may be
possible to take exception to the form of his definition.
He lays too great stress, perhaps, on the phrases, *application* of ideas, and *criticism*. The first might be qualified as misleading, because it seems to attribute an
ulterior purpose to the poet; the second as tending to
confound two separate faculties, the creative and the
judicial. Plato's conception of poetry as an inspiration,
a divine instinct, may be nearer to the truth. The application of ideas should not be too conscious, else the poet
sinks into the preacher. The criticism of life should not
be too much his object, else the poet might as well have
written essays. What is wanted is that, however spontaneous his utterance may be, however he may aim at only
beauty in his work, or 'sing but as the linnet sings,' his
message should be adequate to healthy and mature humanity.
His intelligence of what is noble and enduring, his expression of a full harmonious personality, is enough to
moralise his work. It is even better that he should not
turn aside to comment. That is the function of the homi-
list. We must learn how to live from him less by his precepts, than by his examples and by being in his company.
It would no doubt be misunderstanding Mr. Arnold to suppose that he estimates poetry by the gnomic sentences con-
veyed in it, or that he intends to say that the greatest
poets have deliberately used their art as the vehicle of
moral teaching. Yet there is a double danger in the wording of his definitions. On the one hand, if we accept
them too literally, we run the risk of encouraging that
false view of poetry which led the Byzantines to prefer
Euripides to Sophocles, because he contained a greater
number of quotable maxims; which brought the humanists of
the sixteenth century to the incomprehensible conclusion
that Seneca had improved upon the Greek drama by infusing
greater gravity into his speeches; which caused Tasso to
invent an *ex post facto* (2) allegory for the *Gerusalemme*,
and Spenser to describe Ariosto's mad Orlando, the triumphant climax of that poet's irony, as 'a good governor and
a virtuous man.' On the other hand, there is the peril of
forgetting that the prime aim of all art is at bottom only
presentation. That, and that alone, distinguishes the
arts, including poetry, from every other operation of the
intellect, and justifies Hegel's general definition of Art

as 'Die sinnliche Erscheinung der Idee.' (3) Poetry is
not so much a criticism of life as a revelation of life,
a presentment of life according to the poet's capacity for
observing and displaying it in forms that reproduce it for
his readers.

The main thing to keep in mind is this, that the world
will very willingly let die in poetry what does not contribute to its intellectual strength and moral vigour. In
the long run, therefore, poetry full of matter and moral-
ised wins the day. But it must, before all else, be
poetry. The application of the soundest moral ideas, the
finest criticism of life, will not save it from oblivion,
if it fails in the essential qualities that constitute a
work of art.   Imagination, or the power to see clearly
and to project forcibly; fancy, or the power to flash new
light on things familiar, and by their combination to
delight the mind with novelty; creative genius, or the
power of giving form and substance, life and beauty to the
figments of the brain; style, or the power to sustain a
flawless and unwavering distinction of utterance; dramatic
energy, or the power to make men and women move before us
with self-evident reality in fiction; passion, sympathy,
enthusiasm, or the power of feeling and communicating
feeling, of understanding and arousing emotion; lyrical
inspiration, or the power of spontaneous singing; - these
are among the many elements that go to make up poetry.
These, no doubt, are alluded to by Mr. Arnold in the
clause referring to 'poetic beauty and poetic truth.' But
it is needful to insist upon them, after having dwelt so
long upon the matter and the moral tone of poetry. No
sane critic can deny that the possession of one or more of
these qualities in any very eminent degree will save a
poet from the neglect to which moral revolt or indifference might otherwise condemn him. Ariosto's vulgarity of
feeling, Shelley's crude and discordant opinions, Leopardi's overwhelming pessimism, Heine's morbid sentimental-
ity, Byron's superficiality and cynicism, sink to nothing
beneath the saving virtues of imagination, lyrical inspiration, poetic style, humour, intensity and sweep of passion. The very greatest poets of the world have combined
all these qualities, together with that grand humanity
which confers upon them immortal freshness. Of Homer,
Pindar, Sophocles, Aeschylus, Dante, Virgil, Shakspere,
Molière, Goethe, it is only possible to say that one or
other element of poetic achievement has been displayed
more eminently than the rest, that one or other has been
held more obviously in abeyance, when we come to

distinguish each great master from his peers. But lesser
men may rest their claims to immortality upon slighter
merits; and among these merits it will be found impossible
to exclude what we call form, style, and the several
poetic qualities above enumerated. To borrow a burlesque
metaphor from the Oxford schools, a poet may win his
second-class on his moral philosophy papers, if the others
do not drag him down below the level of recognition; or he
may win upon his taste papers, if he has not been plucked
in divinity. It is only the supreme few whom we expect to
be equally good all round. Shelley and Leopardi have,
perhaps, the same prospect of survival on their artistic
merits, as Wordsworth on the strength of his moral ideas.
    It will be seen that we have now arrived at Mr.
Arnold's attempt to place Wordsworth among the European
poets of the last two centuries. Omitting Goethe and
living men, it seems, to Mr. Arnold, indubitable that to
Wordsworth belongs the palm. This distinction of being
the second greatest modern poet since the death of Molière
is awarded to Wordsworth on his moral philosophy paper.
'Where, then, is Wordsworth's superiority? It is here: he
deals with more of *life* than they do; he deals with *life*,
as a whole, more powerfully.' There is some occult fascination in the game of marking competitors for glory, and
publishing class-lists of poets, artists, and other eminent persons. For myself, I confess that it seems about
as reasonable to enter Wordsworth, Dryden, Voltaire, Leopardi, Klopstock, and the rest of them for the stakes of
poetical primacy, and to announce with a flourish of critical trumpets that Wordsworth is the winner, as to run
the moss-rose against the jessamine, carnation, clematis,
crown imperial, double daisy, and other favourites of the
flower garden. Lovers of poets and of flowers will have
their partialities; and those who have best cultivated
powers of reflection and expression will most plausibly
support their preference with arguments. There the
matter ends; for, both in the case of the poets and the
flowers, the qualities which stimulate our several admira-
tions are too various in kind to be compared. Mr. Arnold
has undoubtedly given excellent reasons for the place he
assigns to Wordsworth. But it is dangerous for Wordsworth's advocate to prove too much. He has already gained
a firm, a permanent, an honourable place upon the muster-
roll of English poets. Why undertake the task of proving
him the greatest? Parnassus is a sort of heaven, and we
know what answer was given to the sons of Zebedee.

Wordsworth's fame will rest upon his lyrics, if we extend

the term to include his odes, sonnets, and some narrative
poems in stanzas - on these, and on a few of his medita-
tive pieces in blank verse. His long philosophical experiments - the 'Prelude,' the 'Excursion' - will be read for
the light they cast upon the poet's mind, and for occasional passages of authentic inspiration. Taken as a
whole, they are too unequal in execution, too imperfectly
penetrated with the vital spirit of true poetry, to stand
the test of time or wake the enthusiasm of centuries of
students. Those, then, who love and reverence Wordsworth,
for whom from earliest boyhood he has been a name of worship, will thank the delicate and sympathetic critic who
has here collected Wordsworth's masterpieces in the compass
of three hundred pages. They will also thank him for the
preface in which he has pointed out the sterling qualities
of Wordsworth's poetry.

At the same time Mr. Arnold recognises the poet's inequali-
ties, and the critical importance of his essay consists
mainly in the broad and clear distinction he has made
between what is more and less valuable in his work. 'In
Wordsworth's case, the accident, for so it may almost be
called, of inspiration is of peculiar importance. No
poet, perhaps, is so evidently filled with a new and
sacred energy when the inspiration is upon him; no poet,
when it fails him, is so left "weak as is a breaking
wave."' The object, therefore, of Mr. Arnold is 'to dis-
engage the poems which show his power, and to present them
to the English-speaking public and to the world.' He
thinks that the volume 'contains everything, or nearly
everything, which may best serve him with the majority of
lovers of poetry, nothing which may disserve him.' Tastes
will differ considerably about both clauses of this sentence; for while Wordsworthians may complain that too much
has been omitted, others, who are anxious that our great
and beloved poet should appear before the world with only
his best singing robes around him, may desire an even
stricter censorship than Mr. Arnold's.

Notes

1 'Art is only form'.
2 'after the work was finished'.
3 'The material embodiment of the Ideal'.

48.   T. H. HUXLEY, FROM 'SCIENCE AND CULTURE, AND OTHER
ESSAYS'

1880

Huxley (see No. 28) expresses here as elsewhere his respect for 'our chief apostle of culture'. He nevertheless
associates Arnold with traditional apologists for 'liberal
education' and opposes his own theories of education to
what he thinks implicit in Arnold's narrower notions of
culture. While aware that Arnold was no enemy of science,
Huxley finds him a useful target, and for his own rhetorical distinctions, he relies on some of the common distortions of Arnold's views. We reprint here only a part of
Huxley's argument.

How often have we not been told that the study of physical
science is incompetent to confer culture; that it touches
none of the higher problems of life; and, what is worse,
that the continual devotion to scientific studies tends to
generate a narrow and bigoted belief in the applicability
of scientific methods to the search after truth of all
kinds? How frequently one has reason to observe that no
reply to a troublesome argument tells so well as calling
its author a 'mere scientific specialist.' And, as I am
afraid it is not permissible to speak of this form of
opposition to scientific education in the past tense; may
we not expect to be told that this, not only omission, but
prohibition, of 'mere literary instruction and education'
is a patent example of scientific narrow-mindedness?

I hold very strongly by two convictions - the first is,
that neither the discipline nor the subject-matter of
classical education is of such direct value to the student
of physical science as to justify the expenditure of valuable time upon either; and the second is, that for the
purpose of attaining real culture, an exclusively scientific education is at least as effectual as an exclusively
literary education.
    I need hardly point out to you that these opinions,
especially the latter, are diametrically opposed to those
of the great majority of educated Englishmen, influenced
as they are by school and university traditions. In their
belief, culture is obtainable only by a liberal education;

and a liberal education is synonymous, not merely with
education and instruction in literature, but in one particular form of literature, namely, that of Greek and
Roman antiquity.   They hold that the man who has learned
Latin and Greek, however little, is educated; while he who
is versed in other branches of knowledge, however deeply,
is a more or less respectable specialist, not admissible
into the cultured caste. The stamp of the educated man,
the University degree, is not for him.

I am too well acquainted with the generous catholicity
of spirit, the true sympathy with scientific thought,
which pervades the writings of our chief apostle of culture to identify him with these opinions; and yet one may
cull from one and another of those epistles to the Philistines, which so much delight all who do not answer to that
name, sentences which lend them some support.

Mr. Arnold tells us that the meaning of culture is 'to
know the best that has been thought and said in the world.'
It is the criticism of life contained in literature. That
criticism regards 'Europe has being, for intellectual and
spiritual purposes, one great confederation, bound to a
joint action and working to a common result; and whose
members have, for their common outfit, a knowledge of
Greek, Roman, and Eastern antiquity, and of one another.
Special, local, and temporary advantages being put out of
account, that modern nation will in the intellectual and
spiritual sphere make most progress, which most thoroughly
carries out this programme. And what is that but saying
that we too, all of us, as individuals, the more thoroughly we carry it out, shall make the more progress?'

We have here to deal with two distinct propositions.
The first, that a criticism of life is the essence of culture; the second, that literature contains the materials
which suffice for the construction of such a criticism.

I think that we must all assent to the first proposition. For culture certainly means something quite different from learning or technical skill. It implies the
possession of an ideal, and the habit of critically esti-
mating the value of things by comparison with a theoretic
standard. Perfect culture should supply a complete theory
of life, based upon a clear knowledge alike of its possibilities and of its limitations.

But we may agree to all this, and yet strongly dissent
from the assumption that literature alone is competent to
supply this knowledge. After having learnt all that
Greek, Roman, and Eastern antiquity have thought and said,
and all that modern literatures have to tell us, it is not
self-evident that we have laid a sufficiently broad and
deep foundation for that criticism of life, which constitutes culture.

Indeed, to any one acquainted with the scope of physical science, it is not at all evident. Considering progress only in the 'intellectual and spiritual sphere,' I find myself wholly unable to admit that either nations or individuals will really advance, if their common outfit draws nothing from the stores of physical science. I should say that an army, without weapons of precision and with no particular base of operations, might more hopefully enter upon a campaign on the Rhine, than a man, devoid of a knowledge of what physical science has done in the last century, upon a criticism of life.

49. W. E. HENLEY, UNSIGNED REVIEW OF 'POETRY OF BYRON', 'ATHENAEUM'

25 June 1881, 839-40

From the age of twelve William Ernest Henley (1849-1903) was crippled by a disease which would have incapacitated a man of less energy. Instead, Henley studied in bed, endured twenty months in an Edinburgh hospital to save a leg from amputation, and transformed the experience into a series of lyric poems that helped to make his fame. When his health mended he settled in London (1877) editing periodicals ('London', 'Magazine of Art'), writing reviews, and publishing several volumes of poetry. In this review of Arnold's 'Byron', he admits to disappointment. Arnold writes at his 'pellucid' best, but he is in fact blind to Byron's powers and shares the Philistine judgments of his countrymen. We have omitted Henley's opening account of Byron's reputation.

A reaction [to the English neglect of Byron] was inevitable; and of late years - in the face of what Mr. Symonds has called 'our neo-Alexandrian taste,' our liking for exquisite workmanship and daintiness and subtlety of thought, and melody of metre, and minor chords of colour and sentiment - such a reaction has set in strongly. One of the earliest signs of it was the striking critical essay prefixed by Mr. Swinburne to his anthology from Byron in Moxon's 'Miniature Poets.' Another, not less remarkable in its way, was the extremely pertinent and

just comparison between Byron and Wordsworth made some
months back by Mr. Ruskin in the pages of the 'Nineteenth
Century.' A third was the excellent article on Byron contributed to Mr. Ward's 'English Poets' by Mr. J. A. Symonds. A fourth is the volume at present under consideration. It is scarcely satisfactory in itself, but it is,
perhaps, the most important sign of all those that have
appeared, inasmuch as it proves that Byron's place and
function in art and morals are deemed so worthy of serious
consideration as to make an edition of him desirable for
family reading.

Mr. Matthew Arnold was moved to make this selection,
he says, by the desire of seeing beside his own anthology
from Wordsworth, 'as a companion volume, a like collection
of the best poetry of Byron.' To his selections Mr.
Arnold has prefixed an interesting critical preface.
Still, like the collection itself, it is to some extent a
disappointment, especially to those who remember Mr.
Arnold's own verses: -

> With shivering heart the strife we saw
> Of passion with eternal law;
> And yet with reverential awe
> We watch'd the fount of fiery life
> Which served for that Titanic strife.

The essay cannot be called one of this admirable critic's
happiest efforts. It is written in Mr. Arnold's neatest
vein and in Mr. Arnold's most pellucid manner, but it
somehow fails to convey a definite impression of Byron.
The fact is, we take it, that Mr. Arnold is not altogether
in sympathy with his subject. Byron, though he had his
share in the work of making Mr. Arnold possible, is the
antipodes of those men of culture and contemplation -
those artists pensive and curious and sedately self-
contained - whom Mr. Arnold best loves, and of whom the
nearest to our hand is Wordsworth. Byron and Wordsworth
are like the Lucifer and the Michael of the 'Vision of
Judgment.' Byron's was the genius of revolt, as Wordsworth's was the genius of dignified and useful submission;
Byron preached the dogma of private revolution, as Wordsworth the dogma of private apotheosis; Byron's theory of
life was one of liberty and self-sacrifice, Wordsworth's
one of self-restraint and self-improvement; Byron's practice was dictated by a generous and voluptuous egoism,
Wordsworth's by a benign and lofty selfishness; Byron was,
in Mr. Arnold's phrase, the 'passionate and dauntless
soldier of a forlorn hope,' Wordsworth a kind of inspired
clergyman. Both were influences for good, and both are

likely to be influences for good for some time to come.
Which is the better and stronger, is a question that can
hardly be determined at this time. It is certain that
Byron's star has waned, and that Wordsworth's has waxed;
but it also certain that there are moments in life when
the 'Ode to Venice' is almost as graceful and as precious
as the ode on the 'Intimations,' and when the epic mockery
of 'Don Juan' is to the full as beneficial as the chaste
philosophy of the 'Excursion' and the 'Ode to Duty.'
Meanwhile it is evident that Mr. Arnold is with the
Michael of our comparison heart and soul, and is only
interested in the Lucifer. He approaches his subject with
too much of deprecation. He thinks it necessary to quote
M. Edmond Scherer's opinion that Byron is but a coxcomb
and a rhetorician: partly, it would appear, for the pleasure of seeming to agree with it in a kind of way, and
partly to have the satisfaction of distinguishing, and of
showing, as he does most conclusively, that it is a mistake. Then he cannot quote Goethe without apologizing
for the warmth of that consummate artist's expressions,
and explaining some of them away. Again, he is pitiful
or disdainful, or both, of Scott's estimate; and he does
not care to discuss the sentiment which made that great
and good man think 'Cain' and the 'Giaour' fit stuff for
reading aloud to his family on Sunday after prayers,
though, as Mr. Ruskin has pointed out, in one of the
wisest and subtlest bits of criticism written of late
years, the sentiment is both natural and beautiful, and
should assist us not a little in the task of judging
Byron, and of knowing him for what he was. That Mr.
Arnold should institute a comparison between Leopardi and
Byron was perhaps inevitable. Leopardi had culture and
the philosophic mind, which Byron had not; he is incapable of influencing the general heart, as Byron can; he
is, and must ever remain, a critics' poet, which Byron
can never be; he was always an artist in words, which
Byron was not. But it was hardly worth while to institute the comparison seriously. Byron was not interested
in words and phrases, but in the greater truths of destiny and emotion. His empire is over the passions and
the imagination. His personality was large and varied
enough to make his egoism representatively human. And as
mankind is wont to feel first and to think afterwards,
it seems certain that a single one of his heart-cries may
prove to the world of greater value as a moral agency
than all the intellectual reflections that Leopardi con-
trived to utter. It must be added that, after examining
this and that opinion and doubting over and deprecating
them all, Mr. Arnold finds firm ground at last in a dictum

of Mr. Swinburne's - the most pertinent and profound since those of Goethe - to the effect that in Byron there is a 'splendid and imperishable excellence which covers all his offences and outweighs all his defects: the excellence of sincerity and strength.' With this 'noble praise,' as Mr. Arnold rightly calls it - and it is not less just than noble - the critic agrees absolutely, and it becomes the key-note in the latter part of his essay. Here Mr. Arnold speaks out to excellent purpose, and at the close it is not a surprise to find him declaring Byron the equal of Wordsworth, and asserting of this 'glorious pair' that 'when the year 1000 is turned, and the nation comes to recount her poetic glories in the century which has just then ended, the first names with her will be these.'

The essay contains some literary criticism that is worth noting. For instance, Mr. Arnold quotes, as exampling Wordsworth at his highest, the single line,

Will no one tell me what she sings?

which, divided from its context, seems insignificant enough, but which has evidently mysterious qualities and virtues not apparent to the uncultured eye and ear. Also, Mr. Arnold's method of proving Byron a bad workman is peculiar enough to be remarkable. Just as he demonstrated the inferiority of the 'Chanson de Roland' to the 'Iliad' by confronting a poor passage from the one poem with a gem from the other, so does he demonstrate Byron's innate untunefulness by the comparison of neat and appropriate selections from his worst work with quotations from the best of Milton and Shakspeare. Such a master chord of imagination made rhythmical as

In the dark backward and abysm of time

is shown in triumphant apposition with slip-shod doggerel like

Which now is painful to these eyes,
Which have not seen the sun to rise;

while the gorgeous romance and suggestiveness of

Presenting Thebes of Pelops' line,
Or the tale of Troy divine,

are presented in competition with twaddle like

All shall be void -
Destroyed!

It is superfluous to add that, in comparing Byron with
Leopardi, Mr. Arnold is careful to oppose one of the most
childish lapses in 'Cain' with one of the best-wrought
stanzas in 'La Ginestra.' Some years back Mr. Swinburne
felt constrained to admonish a writer who had judged between Byron and the Laureate as Mr. Arnold judges between
Shakspeare and Byron. With all respect for a great
critic, we must say that there is no apparent reason why
what was held unfair in Mr. Alfred Austin should be held
just in Mr. Arnold.

The anthology, we regret to say, cannot be called
representative, and compares unfavourably not only with
Mr. Swinburne's, but even with that one made of late by
Mr. Symonds for the 'English Poets' of Mr. Ward, brief
and incomplete as of necessity that was. Mr. Arnold does
not include 'Prometheus,' nor the 'Ode to Venice,' nor the
well-known 'Fare thee well, and if for ever,' one of the
high water marks of Byron's achievement; and there are
other notable absences. On the other hand, there is much
that might as well have been away; as, for instance, the
comic versicles to Murray, the 'Epistle from Mr. Murray to
Dr. Polidori,' the affected opening stanzas of 'Childe
Harold,' 'Napoleon's Farewell,' and so forth. Most of the
extracts from the tales have been severely edited. In
those from 'Mazeppa' Mr. Arnold prints stanzas ix.-xiii.
as Byron left them; he omits five lines from the beginning of stanza xiv.; he cuts two lines from the end of the
first half of xvii., and fills their room with four lines
from the second half, all the rest of which, some forty-
one lines, together with the first twenty lines of xviii.,
he omits, as he does the last twenty-two lines of xx.
Upon his specimens from the 'Siege of Corinth' he has
operated still more vigorously, and, for some mysterious
reason or other, he omits, to the great detriment of the
general effect, the last three stanzas of the tremendous
'Incantation' in 'Manfred.' As he is as sparing of notes
and asterisks as he is liberal of changes and suppressions, and leaves his readers to find out his action for
themselves, his theory of editing is as peculiar as his
theory of demonstration by comparisons. The great fault
of his selection, however, is its scrappiness. Mr. Swinburne, who holds that Byron 'can only be judged or
appreciated in the mass,' quoted the 'Vision of Judgment'
in its entirety, and did wisely and well; Mr. Arnold
quotes but seven stanzas of it. 'Don Juan' is represented, not by an episode - not by the dedication, nor the
shipwreck, nor the slave market, nor the death of Haidée,
nor Donna Julia's letter nor the immortal love scene between Juan and Haidée - but by detached and independent

morsels, consisting of one or three or five stanzas: apos-
trophes to Fry and Wilberforce, descriptions of costume,
short general reflections, odds and ends of scenery, and
so forth. Mr. Arnold deals with 'Beppo' very sparingly,
and with 'Childe Harold' in like wise. The effect produced by his collection, therefore, is really curious.
Byron is Byron no more. 'The daring, dash, and grandio-
sity' which Goethe found in him have dwindled; the 'splendid and puissant personality,' 'in eminence such as has
never been yet, and is not likely to come again,' has
been chipped up into insignificant fragments; the fiery
energy, the incomparable brightness, and swiftness, and
strength, have faded. The poet of Haidée and Lucifer has
been toned down to the level of Mr. Arnold's enemies the
Philistines. In his new guise Byron appears as a very
pleasing poet, often capable of short flights of passion
and excellent at the composition of *vers de société*. (1)

Note

1 'social verse'; i.e. trivial.

50. ANDREW LANG ON MATTHEW ARNOLD, 'CENTURY MAGAZINE'

April 1882, xxiii, 849-64

Andrew Lang (1844-1912) was a prolific writer of periodical essays, a charming and innovative poet, a successful translator of Homer, and an anthropologist of international repute. While still a fellow at Merton College
he published his first collection of poetry ('Ballads
and Lyrics of Old France', 1872), and by 1875 he had
already published some of the papers that were to become
his 'Custom and Myth' (1884) and was deep into his col-
laborative translation of the 'Odyssey'. In 1882 Lang did
a survey of Matthew Arnold's works, including the following estimate of his prose. Lang is sympathetic to
Arnold's poetry, but he thinks that 'in prose [Arnold] has
been able to say, more definitely, what he thinks as a
critic of life, literature, and society'.

His poetry, on the whole, to use his own words about
Greek tragedy, aims at producing a sentiment of sublime
acquiescence in the course of fate and in the dispensa-
tions of human life. In prose he has been able to say,
more definitely, what he thinks as a critic of life,
literature, and society. Not long since, in a preface to
Mr. Ward's 'Anthology of English Poets,' Mr. Arnold spoke
of poetry as if it might become a substitute for religion.
Now, if we allow the word religion to include authoritative speaking on the interests of man's spirit and on the
conduct of his life, Mr. Arnold's own experience bears
hardly upon his argument. As long as he wrote poetry
alone, the great public did not much mark him. I doubt if
the Lord Mayors (our official patrons of literature) ever
heard of Mr. Arnold, or asked him to dine with Mr. Sala,
in the days when he was only a poet. But as soon as he
began to talk about religion, morality, education, and
literature in prose, the great public heard him, though
not very gladly. As soon as he began to criticise the
middle classes and their teachers - the newspapers - the
middle classes and the newspapers pricked up their ears
and listened, with many interruptions and remonstrances,
to what he had to tell them. He spoke to them in a new
voice to which they were not accustomed. He did not
merely glorify England and everything English. He looked
outside our country and our literature, to France, Germany, Italy. He employed a strain of humor and sarcasm,
which has an extraordinary power of irritating his victims.

    I believe Mr. Arnold has done us a great deal of good.
The self-sufficiency of this country, our belief in our
enterprise, trade, intelligent middle classes, jealous
dissent, right of free speech, and so forth, were, fifteen years ago, perfectly incredible and intolerable.
Events have since taken a good deal of our conceit out of
us. Sadowa, Sedan, Isandhlana, and Majuba have opened the
eyes of many of us. Ireland and the East have taught us a
few lessons of self-distrust. But Mr. Arnold has kept on
enforcing the lessons. He will not let us rest for an
hour in the delusion that our newspapers utter the voice
of unmitigated wisdom; that our free speech is necessarily true or instructed speech; that our middle classes,
or lower classes, or upper classes, are educated on sound
principles; that our dissenters are living and working in
a pure spirit of generous and liberal and genial Christianity. All our Dagons he has blasphemed. Our popular
writers, our popular theologians, our popular philosophers, our popular philanthropists, he has touched with
his irreverent wit. 'These be thy Gods, O Israel!' he

has cried, and the idols look as decrepit as 'that twice-battered god of Palestine,' or the superannuated Olympians in Bruno's satirical tract. In this pious and universal crusade, I do not mean that Mr. Arnold has always had right on his side. He has said things that seemed cruel, or otherwise indefensible. He has made the dissenters writhe with impotent desire to smite, controversially, this cool and agile opponent. Many people, doubtless, have quite shut their senses against him - like the adder who, says St. Augustine, thrusts the tip of his tail into one of his ears and lays the other in the dust. But even these deaf ones know and feel that the bubbles of British optimism are being pricked. They are less comfortable than of old among their idols. They may never repent and be converted, but their children and their kinsmen are beginning to listen to Mr. Arnold, and to try to winnow the wheat from the, perhaps, too copious 'chaff' which he offers the public.

Mr. Arnold's first appearance as a critic was in the field of literature. We have already spoken of his interesting prefaces to 'Merope' and a volume of poems. In 1857, his University recognized his merits by giving him almost the only official position in criticism which England has to offer. He was appointed to the Chair of Poetry in Oxford. The chair has been filled by Warton and Keble, in times when the lectures were delivered in Latin. Now the lecturer addresses his audience in English. He is appointed for a period of five years, generally extended to ten. Since Mr. Arnold's day the chair has been held by Sir Francis Doyle and Principal Shairp. The position, with its chance of influencing young men, seems an enviable one. But there are so many compulsory lectures at Oxford, and attendance thereon is such a weariness, that many, even of the undergraduates who care for literature, seldom go. I never, I am ashamed to say, availed myself cf the opportunity of listening to Mr. Arnold, because his lectures were delivered in the afternoon, when cricket or the river seemed more attractive than Apollo's lute. The first fruits of his appointment were two sets of 'Lectures on Translating Homer' (Longmans, 1861, 1862). These are full of just and penetrating criticism. They also have the marks of Mr. Arnold's critical manner. He takes a few points, such as the nobility, simplicity, and speed of the Homeric manner; to these he constantly returns, enforcing his text by repetition. Again, he frequently uses ridicule and irony. Professor Francis Newman had just published a translation of the 'Iliad', stuffed with odd criticisms, and written in the meter of 'Yankee Doodle.' This unlucky translation was Mr. Arnold's butt, and he

kept provoking his audience to mirth as inextinguishable
as that of the Homeric gods, by reference to Mr. Newman.
That poet spoke of 'dapper-greav'd Achaeans,' of 'Hector
of the motley helm,' and his heroes were 'sly of foot and
nimble'; while Helen was made to call herself 'a mischief-
working vixen'! These served Mr. Arnold as examples of
the individualism, the whimsical eccentricity, of the
English literary character, nor was he ill-pleased if he
found Mr. Newman calling 'a fine calf' a 'bragly bulkin.'
The natural result was that Mr. Newman thought Mr.
Arnold's judgment effeminate. But, on the whole, the
genius of English literature has sided with Mr. Arnold,
and Mr. Newman's is not the standard translation of Homer.
As to Mr. Arnold's own theories on a point which it were
out of place to discuss here, I agree with his premises,
but cannot accept his conclusions. He admirably characterizes the genius of Homer, and then he tells us that
English hexameters are the proper meter for the English
translator. But it is rarely possible to scan Mr.
Arnold's own English hexameters with certainty, nor is
one's opinion altered by those of Mr. Longfellow, Mr.
Clough, or Mr. Stedman. Hexameters seem foreign to the
genius of English verse.

A large familiarity with foreign literature and Continental criticism has enabled Mr. Arnold to widen the
scope of contemporary English literature. The judgments
of French and German authors are now tolerably well known
to the British reviewer; there is a free trade in ideas.
Many Englishmen keep us acquainted with foreign opinion,
while M. Scherer, M. Taine, and others enable France to
understand what is being done and said in England. When
Mr. Arnold published his 'Essays in Criticism' (1865)
this free trade was much more restricted. French, especially, was comparatively neglected. One of the recurring
periods in which the French reacts on the English intelligence was just beginning, and Mr. Arnold helped the new
movement. He tried to raise criticism from its low
estate – described by Wordsworth as 'an inglorious employment.' It can hardly be denied that his efforts have been
successful, and that we have now a more studious, learned,
disinterested, and careful sort of reviewers than of old.
Mr. Arnold tried his best to make critics feel that their
duty is to see things as they are. A poet is now rarely
reviled because his opinions, as a private citizen, are
Radical, or Tory; because he lives at Hampstead, or in
Westmoreland; because he goes to church, or stays away.
A somewhat higher standard has been set, even for journey-
man-work, and, as far as an English looker-on can judge,
American literature, too, has benefited by this increased

earnestness of purpose, and this growing desire for
wider and clearer knowledge. Our affection for ridiculous whims - about the Christian theology concealed in
Homer, about the Jewish origin of our race, or its Egyptian affinities - is not extinct by any means; but Mr.
Arnold's ridicule has helped to diminish this national
failing in literature, in politics, in religion; he has
succeeded in making many converts to the belief that,
after all, we are not a 'chosen people,' that all our
prejudices are not inspirations. He had the audacity to
say that our 'atmosphere' tells unfavorably even on men
of genius, and 'may make even a man of great ability
either a Mr. Carlyle or else a Lord Macaulay.' This was
flat blasphemy fifteen years ago; but now there are but
few readers but will acknowledge that the pleasure and
instruction they derive from Mr. Carlyle's and Lord Macaulay's works are marred by their want of repose, by
their obtrusion of eccentricities and personal peculiarities of style. Nay, we may go further and hint that our
'atmosphere' of insular eccentricity has harmed Mr. Arnold
himself. 'Physician, heal thyself,' we might say, and
regret some escapades of flippancy and, one might almost
say, irreverence, which mar certain passages of Mr.
Arnold's theological writings. But we are looking at the
good his literary criticism has done, - at his wide
appreciation of excellence, at his honest determination to
state his own opinion, and not to be misled by a blind
admiration even of Shakespere, even of Burke, even of
Shelley, even of Keats. After much reading, for example,
of Mr. Ruskin, nothing can be more salutory than a return
to Mr. Arnold's clearer and colder intellect, - not incapable of freaks, but occasionally indulging in them
with an ironical knowledge of their true nature - not
with a belief that they are 'supremely' precious inspirations.

To any reader whose time for study is scanty, and who
wishes to secure an adequate impression of Mr. Arnold as
a critic, one would especially recommend the volume of
'Essays in Criticism'. It contains the germs of all his
later critical work, and his ideas and manner are there
presented in the most engaging way. In purely literary
matter there are the studies of Heine, Joubert, and the
two Guérins. Mr. Arnold has never excelled these productions; in charm of style, in novelty of idea, in the
attraction of a pleasant personality, they are matchless
among his works and in the English literature of his time.
In the papers on the Guérins, too, we have the earnest
expression of his sympathy with the Celtic element in
literature, with that 'magical,' sweet, and melancholy

mood which perhaps the modern world owes to an ancient
race, that has lost its lands, and almost lost its language, but never lost its rare, incommunicable gift of
poetry. A fuller study of this topic is presented in Mr.
Arnold's 'Celtic Literature,' a remarkable addition to
what the world, as apart from specialists, knows about
this topic. In the paper on Maurice and Eugénie de
Guérin, he sufficiently indicated the nature of what we
might call 'the Celtic mood.' It has a strange melancholy brightness and beauty, like that of a golden autumn
day among the hills and lochs and birch-woods of Western
Scotland.

And the Celtic mood has a singular nearness to nature.
Any one can feel its charm who has listened to the plead-
ing accents of a Gaelic song. That music is the music of
a natural people - a *natur volk*. I have heard such a
song, in Scotland, from a Gaelic poet; and shortly after-
ward have listened to another chant - a song of the wild
folk of the Melanesian Islands. The two were strangely
alike, and seemed to move one with the pathos of a people
whose day is passed, whose glories are little more than a
myth, but who have never lost their intimate sense of
nature, and never been corrupted by the world. Mr.
Arnold's Celtic studies, and his essays on the two French
poets, brother and sister, have in their prose a touch of
this old melody, and a sweetness derived from an elder
day. In his essay on Spinoza and the Bible, again, we
seem to see the germ of his later and voluminous writings
on religion, of his attempt to take theology and the Bible
out of the range of a hard and too conjectural scientific
criticism, and to bring them into the softer and more sympathetic air of literature. That attempt may not be
wholly successful; something different seems to me to be
needed both by the scientific and the ordinary reader. In
spite of his sympathy with humanity, humanity still
appears to be out of sympathy with Mr. Arnold's effort to
purify its religion. Lastly, in the preface, and in other
parts of the 'Essays in Criticism,' we find the first of
Mr. Arnold's humorous attacks on what he calls the 'Philistinism' of his countrymen - or their arrogance, ignorance, and habit of mistaking mechanical means for ends.

He has a poet's love of England, and he sees England
making herself ridiculous in the eyes of the world. He
sees her policy shift with every alternation of popular
sentiment, and he knows that popular sentiment, with all
its good intentions, is ignorant, unsteady - now hot,
now cold. These defects, and the conceit which

accompanies them, make up what Mr. Arnold chooses to call
Philistinism. This is how he defined Philistinism: 'On
the side of beauty and taste, vulgarity; on the side of
morality and feeling, coarseness; on the side of mind and
spirit, unintelligence.' In literature, politics, religion, Mr. Arnold has made it his business to war against
Philistinism, and especially against the Philistinism of
these 'great sophists,' as Plato would have called them,
the newspapers. A newspaperman myself, - a 'pressman,' as
Mr. Swinburne would scornfully say, - I cannot but
acknowledge the errors of our profession, and wince beneath the birch of the son of Dr. Arnold. Let us conclude
this survey of Mr. Arnold's performance by looking at one
or two of his pitched battles with the armies of the
Philistines who fight under the banners of the British
press.

There was a literary contest even over that harmless
thing, Celtic literature. A large number of our countrymen in Wales, and a smaller number in the West and North
of Scotland, still speak Celtic dialects, and still preserve poetical traditions about the past of the Celtic
race. In Scotland, these traditions have dwindled to
tales told around the turf-fire, in the winter nights.
The stories have been collected and published by Mr. Campbell, of Islay, and are most interesting to read, and most
important materials for the student of human history. In
Wales the Celtic language is preserved with more of pomp
and dignity. Great meetings called Eisteddfods are held,
in which poems are recited, prizes given, and the popular
interest in the legendary past is thereby kept alive. As
a professor of poetry Mr. Arnold was invited to attend one
of these assemblies of the bards, and he expressed his
friendly interest and sympathy, as surely no man of letters could fail to do. Almost all the old popular lore of
song, and customs, and legend has been crushed out of our
English laborers, whose lives, like Sir Tor's shield in
the 'Idylls of the King,' are 'blank enough.' Mr. Arnold
recognized the happier effect which their traditions of
the past exercise on the Welsh. For this 'The Times' fell
foul of him with clumsy ferocity. 'An Eisteddfod is one
of the most mischievous and selfish pieces of sentimentalism which could possibly be perpetrated.' 'It is monstrous folly to encourage the Welsh in a loving fondness
for their old language.' Mr. Arnold was described as 'a
sentimentalist who talks nonsense, and whose dainty taste
requires something more flimsy than the strong sense and
sturdy morality of his fellow Englishmen.' These are
beautiful blatant expressions of the Philistinism against
which Mr. Arnold did battle. That eternal bluster about

'strong sense and sturdy morality' is one of the most
provoking weapons of the 'robustious' writer who is perpetually fingering his moral biceps in public. Well, the
robust sense and sturdy morality of 'The Times' has been
wasted. English science has recognized the need of serious study of the Celtic literature, and professorships of
Celtic have actually been founded in Oxford and Edinburgh.
But, in 'The Times's' Pumblechookian vein, when it blus-
ters like the swaggering, stupid moralist of 'Great Expectations,' Mr. Arnold rightly recognizes one of England's
difficulties in governing Ireland.

This brings us to the political warfare against Philistinism. It is impossible here to go into details about
the burial of dissenters, the endowment of the Irish
Church, the marriage with a deceased wife's sister, and
other causes of battle. These things must be unintelligible in America; even here I do not quite understand the
interest which Mr. Arnold feels in them. His general
charges against his countrymen in politics are to be
studied in a queer little book, 'Friendship's Garland'
(Smith and Elder, 1871) - the pretended memoirs of a
German guide, philosopher, and friend of the author's.
Arminius, the philosopher in question, does not spare us.
He goes to Eton and sees young Plantagenet hit 'that beast
Bottles,' full on the nose. He finds the spirit which delights in getting up a fight rampant in our newspapers.
He finds our gentry, middle class, and populace almost
equally underrated. He finds that we worship 'mere
liberty' as a fetich. We are so certain that free speech
deserves all the praise Herodotus gave it long ago, that
we think it does not matter what we say, with our famous
freedom of expression. 'There are many lessons,' says
Arminius, 'to be learned from the present war: I will tell
you what is for *you* the great lesson to be learned from
it - *obedience*. That, instead of every man airing his
self-consequence, thinking it bliss to talk at random
about things, and to put his finger in every pie, you
should seriously understand there is a *right* way of doing
things, and that the bliss is, without thinking of one's
self-consequence, to do them in that way, or to forward
their being done. This is the great lesson your British
public, as you call it, has to learn, and may learn, in
some degree, from the Germans in this war.' Well, we have
not learned the lesson. As I write, the 'Standard' and
'The Times,' and other prints, are gravely lecturing all
Europe: lecturing France for her 'madness' in imitating in
Africa our seizure of Cyrpus; lecturing the Prince of Bul-
garia; lecturing every one, insulting many, putting 'a
finger in every pie,' - and all this though we can no more

back our words by deeds than we can move mountains.
Pretty words, like 'lie' and 'liar,' are being exchanged
by the French and English press; and what resolute purpose
have we at the back of all this show of words? Arminius
said, ten years ago: 'Lord Granville has behind him, when
he speaks to Europe, your Philistines, or middle class,
and how should the world know, or much care what your
middle class mean, for they do not know it themselves?'
In 1879, they were, or seemed to be, all for Lord Beaconsfield and advance. In 1880, they were all for Mr. Gladstone and retreat. A melancholy impression do the words
of Arminius make upon Englishmen who love their famous
ancient land, and can only hope that, when the evil day
comes, England may at last read clearly in her own mind,
and not lack her old force in action. Mr. Arnold's business is to insist on the paramount necessity of knowledge
- of what he calls *culture*. Unfortunately, while his
matter is so sound, a public accustomed to the pulpit and
the press is repelled by the daintiness of his manner.
One who jests is supposed to be incapable of speaking
truth. And the stumbling-block of his manner trips up
the public most when Mr. Arnold is writing about religion.
    I do not propose to examine minutely Mr. Arnold's reli-
gious teaching. The subject cannot here be properly
handled. His design is to retain the morality of the Old
and New Testament, without retaining what he thinks superstitious excrescences - the miracles, the promises of a
physical life after death, and the like. In his view, it
was in righteousness, in 'conduct,' that the prophets and
our Lord placed the kingdom of heaven. He, too, holds
that happiness depends on morality, and that the Bible is
the great teacher and inspirer of morality. On the Continent, it is being rejected because of its want of conformity to physical science. In England and America, where
religion is still so strong, Mr. Arnold hopes to anticipate and weaken the crude skepticism which rejects what is
true and divine, because it is mixed up with what is human
and erroneous. One can scarcely expect very wide and
satisfactory results from Mr. Arnold's efforts. He de-
prives his disciples of precisely those hopes (superstitions, in his view) which have always been offered by
every successful religion. It is natural to fear that, if
Christianity be robbed of her heaven, the unhappy people
who find this world so hard will demand a new heaven from
some fantastic new revelation - like that of spiritualism,
for example. Again, Mr. Arnold's own hypothesis of the
development of religion seems inconsistent with facts -
a topic on which one could, with personal satisfaction,
write a volume. Lastly, a trace of flippancy and scorn in

his manner repels, and is likely to repel, many devout
readers who are, at heart, in agreement with him on the
essential topic of righteousness. Mr. Arnold, in his
'Last Essays on Church and Religion,' closes this chapter
of his life's work. What he wished to say has been said.
He has tried to import into popular religion the flexibility of mind and balance of judgment which are (or,
rather, which ought to be) the fruits of literary training. But let us take the case of a hard-working and convinced dissenter, or ardent ritualist, who lives in a
parish where life, for the people, is either unbroken toil
or semi-starvation; where the summer nights are a swelter-
ing misery; where winter means cold, hunger, and death.
How is he to comfort his people with Mr. Arnold's doctrine? In this grievous battle of life, he will think of
the author of 'Literature and Dogma' as Hotspur, at Holme-
don fight, thought of 'a certain lord, neat and trimly
dressed *** and still he smiled and talk'd.' That judgment would be unjust, but it would not be unnatural, and
as long as it is general, Mr. Arnold's religious writings
will prove of but little avail. It is pleasant to think
that he has returned to his own province - to literature,
though he still hankers after politics, and still finds
that we govern Ireland ill, because men like Dickens's
'Mr. Creakle' educate our middle classes. Let us hope
that Mr. Arnold will return, not only to literature but
to verse, and add to that scanty golden store, that
'eternal possession,' his poetry. For whether Mr. Arnold
is revealing to us our national faults, or criticising,
our earthly conception of religion, we hear a voice murmur
his own lines addressed to the spirit of Heine:

> Ah, to help us forget
> Such barren knowledge awhile,
> God gave the poet his song.

We gladly acknowledge his clear sight, his cheerful
patience, his skilled satire, and the 'educated insolence'
of the wit with which he plagues a whole Dunciad of 'dissenters,' journalists, bishops, and Parliament men. But
he was born for other and better things. Sense and noble
satire, though rare, are still not so rare as poetry. It
is poetry that is scarce, and it is poetry that works on
men's minds like a spell....

51.   A. C. SWINBURNE ON WORDSWORTH AND BYRON, 'NINETEENTH
CENTURY'

April 1884, xv, 583-609; May 1884, 764-90

When Algernon Charles Swinburne (1837-1909) wrote the
following essay the period of his greatest successes as a
poet had passed, and he was producing a good deal of literary criticism. His response to Arnold's editions of Wordsworth and Byron is really a rambling essay on Romantic
poetry generally, since it deals as well with Coleridge,
Keats, and Shelley. Swinburne is intent on asserting his
own evaluations of these poets, evaluations widely different from Arnold's, and it is from this point of view that
he judges Arnold's critical ability. This essay was originally fifty-two pages long. We have been forced to cut
a good deal but have tried to preserve the outline and
tone of Swinburne's argument.

Among the more eminent or prominent names of famous men,
and perhaps especially of famous poets, some must inevitably be longer than others in finding their ultimate level
of comparative account in critical no less than in popular
repute. But it is singular enough at first sight that
among all the many memorable names of our countrymen
which ennoble for the retrospect of all time the first
quarter of this century, two alone should still remain
objects of so much debate as are those of the two poets
who have recently supplied one of their most eminent suc-
cessors with subject-matter for the exercise of his ability in discussion and the display of his daring in paradox. For although it has ever been my desire, in the expressive words of the Church Catechism, to order myself
lowly and reverently to all my betters; and although I
hope never to write a word incompatible with deep gratitude and cordial admiration for all the gifts of poetry
and prose - to say nothing just now of admonition and
castigation - which his too frequently offending countrymen owe to the just and liberal hand of Mr. Matthew
Arnold; yet I cannot but feel that in his recent utterances or expositions regarding Wordsworth and Byron he
has now and then spread a wider sail before a stronger
wind of sheer paradox than ever has any critic of anything
like equal or comparable reputation. We might almost
imagine, on consideration of the task here undertaken,

365 Arnold, Prose Writings: The Critical Heritage

that his aim had been to show how not gold only, but also
the higher criticism, may solder close impossibilities,
and make them kiss.

Let me repeat, at the risk of appearing impertinently
superfluous in protestation, that I have never written
and never mean to write an irreverent word of Mr. Arnold's
own claims to all due deference and all reasonable regard,
whether as poet or as critic: but I must confess, borrow-
ing two favourite terms of his own, that 'lucidity' does
not appear to me by any means to be the distinguishing
'note' of his later criticisms. His first critical confession of faith - the famous and admirable if not exhaustive or conclusive preface of October 1st, 1853 - was a
model of the quality which now, it should seem, appears to
him rather commendable than practicable, - a matter of
pious opinion or devout imagination. When we are told
that the distinguishing merit of such poetry as we find in
Keats's 'Ode on a Grecian Urn' is that it gives us, of all
gifts in the world, the expression of a moral idea comparable with the gravest and the deepest utterances of
Shakespeare and of Milton, we begin to perceive, or at all
events we begin to suspect, that Mr. Arnold's excursive
studies in theology have somewhat infected him with the
theologian's habit of using words and phrases in a special
and extranatural sense which renders their message imper-
vious, their meaning impenetrable, to all but the esoteric
adept. 'A criticism of life' becomes such another term or
form of speech as 'prevenient grace,' or 'the real presence,' or 'the double procession of the Holy Ghost:' if,
Hamlet-like, we consider too curiously what it may mean,
the reverent reader may haply find himself on the high
road to distraction, the irreverent will too probably find
himself on the verge of laughter. A certain criticism of
life, a certain method or scheme of contemplation, a devotion to certain points of view and certain tones of
thought, may unquestionably be discerned in the highest
work of such poets as Milton, Wordsworth, and Shelley, in
the past; in our own days, of such poets as Lord Tennyson,
Mr. Browning, and Mr. Arnold himself. But how this fact
can possibly be shown to imply that it is this quality
which gives them rank as poets; and how the definition of
this quality can possibly be strained so as to cover the
case of Keats, the most exclusively aesthetic and the most
absolutely non-moral of all serious writers on record;
these are two questions to which the propounder of such
postulates may surely be expected to vouchsafe at least
some gleam of a solution, some shadow of a reply.

Mr. Arnold has at once a passion and a genius for definitions. It is doubtless good to have such a genius, but it
is surely dangerous to have such a passion. All sane men
must be willing to concede the truth of an assertion which
he seems to fling down as a challenge from the ethical
critic to the aesthetic - that a school of poetry divorced
from any moral idea is a school of poetry divorced from
life. Even John Keats himself, except in his most hectic
moments of sensuous or spiritual debility, would hardly, I
should imagine, have undertaken to deny this. What may
reasonably be maintained is a thesis very different from
such a denial; namely, that a school of poetry subordinated to any school of doctrine, subjugated and shaped and
utilized by any moral idea to the exclusion of native impulse and spiritual instinct, will produce work fit to
live when the noblest specimens of humanity are produced
by artifical incubation. However, when we come to consider the case of Byron, we must allow it to be wholly
undeniable that some sort of claim to some other kind of
merit than that of a gift for writing poetry must be discovered or devised for him, if any place among memorable
men is to be reserved for him at all.

'That man *never* wrote from his heart,' says Thackeray,
sweepingly and fiercely: 'he got up rapture and enthusiasm with an eye to the public.' The only answer to this
is that on one single point, but that one a point of un-
surpassed importance and significance, the imputation is
insupportable and unjust. He wrote from his heart when he
wrote of politics - using that sometimes ambiguous term in
its widest and most accurate significance. A just and
contemptuous hatred of Georgian government, combined with
a fitful and theatrical admiration of the first Bonaparte,
made him too often write and speak like a vilely bad
Englishman - 'the friend of every country but his own':
but his sympathy with the cause of justice during the
blackest years of dynastic reaction on the continent makes
him worthy even yet of a sympathy and respect which no
other quality of his character or his work could now by
any possibility command from any quarter worth a moment's
consideration or regard. On the day when it shall become
accepted as a canon of criticism that the political work
and the political opinions of a poet are to weigh nothing
in the balance which suspends his reputation - on that day
the best part of the fame of Byron will fly up and vanish
into air. Setting aside mere instances of passionately
cynical burlesque, and perhaps one or two exceptional
examples of apparently sincere though vehemently

demonstrative personal feeling, we find little really
living or really praiseworthy work of Byron's which has
not in it some direct or indirect touch of political emotion.

But, without wishing to detract from the just honour
which has been paid to him on this score, and paid at
least in full if not with over-measure, we must not overlook, in common justice, the seamy side of his unique
success among readers who did not read him in English.
It is something, undoubtedly, to be set down to a man's
credit, that his work - if his work be other than poetic -
should lose nothing by translation: always assuming that
it has anything to lose. But what shall be said of a poet
whose work not only does not lose, but gains, by translation into foreign prose? and gains so greatly and indefi-
nitely by that process as to assume a virtue which it has
not? On taking up a fairly good version of 'Childe
Harold's Prilgrimage' in French or Italian prose, a reader
whose eyes and ears are not hopelessly sealed against
all distinction of good from bad in rhythm or in style
will infallibly be struck by the vast improvement which
the text has undergone in the course of translation. The
blundering, floundering, lumbering and stumbling stanzas,
transmuted into prose and transfigured into grammar,
reveal the real and latent force of rhetorical energy that
is in them: the gasping, ranting, wheezing, broken-winded
verse has been transformed into really effective and
fluent oratory.

And this is the author placed almost at the head of modern
poets by the eminent poet and critic who has so long, so
loudly, and so justly preached to the world of letters the
supreme necessity of 'distinction' as the note of genuine
style which alone enables any sort of literary work to
survive! Shakespeare and Hugo are not good enough for
him: in 'Macbeth' and in 'Hernani' he finds damning faults
of style, and a plentiful lack of distinction: the text of
the latter he garbles and falsifies as Voltaire garbled
and falsified the text of Shakespeare, and apparently for
the same purpose - as unworthy of the one philosopher as
of the other. But in Byron - of all remembered poets the
most wanting in distinction of any kind, the most dependent for his effects on the most vulgar and violent
resources of rant and cant and glare and splash and splut-
ter - in Byron the apostle of culture, and the author of
such nobly beautiful and blameless work as 'Thyrsis' and
the songs of Callicles, finds a seed of immortality more
promising than in Coleridge or Shelley, the two coequal
kings of English lyric poetry.

Mr. Arnold has spoken with exemplary contempt of Lord
Jeffrey's style and principles of criticism: but whenever
he speaks of Shelley he borrows from the old Edinburgh
fencing-school the rusty foil of that once eminent reviewer, to show off against his object of attack the very
same tricks of fence which Jeffrey made use of, with a
skill and strength of hand at least equal to his pupil's,
against the struggling reputation of Wordsworth. This can
do no manner of harm to Shelley, but it must of necessity
affect our estimate of the value of his assailant's
opinion on the subject of other men's poetry. Wordsworth,
to Lord Jeffrey, was merely the poet of idiot boys,
preaching pedlars, bibulous waggoners, and the mendicant
class in general: his poetry was typified in Alice Fell's
torn cloak - 'a wretched, wretched rag indeed.' But Lord
Jeffrey did not add that 'those who extol him as the poet
of rags, the poet of clothes-tubs, are only saying that
he did not, in fact, lay hold upon the poet's right
subject-matter.' He would have known that outside 'the
all-miscreative brain' of a critical jester these erroneous persons had and could have no existence: that those
who extolled Wordsworth, though the scope of their admiration might or might not include the poems which dealt with
such matters, extolled him as the poet of things very different from these. And Jeffrey's imitator in this trick
of criticism cannot surely affect to imagine that 'those
who extol him as the poet of clouds, the poet of sunsets,'
- if any there be whose estimate of his poetry is based
exclusively or mainly on their value for such attributes
of his genius - are in any truer or fitter sense to be
accepted as representatives of Shelley's real admirers,
than are those sickly drivellers over the name of another
great poet, the fulsome worshippers of weakness whose
nauseous adoration Mr. Arnold has so justly rebuked, to
be fairly accepted as representatives of those who share
his admiration for the genius of Keats. These, I must be
allowed to say, are the sort of critical tricks which
recoil upon the critic who makes use of them for a showy
and hazardous instant. Those to whom, as to the humble
writer at present engaged in rash controversy with 'the
most distinguished Englishman of his time,' the name of
Shelley seems to be indisputably the third - if not the
second - on the list of our greatest poets, no more extol
him as exclusively or principally the poet of clouds and
sunsets than Mr. Arnold extols Wordsworth as the poet of
rags and tatters or Keats as the poet of underbred and
weakly sensuousness. Not that we do not prefer the nebu-
losity of Shelley at his cloudiest to the raggedness of
Wordsworth at his raggedest or the sickliness of Keats at

his sickliest: but this is a point quite beside the main
question. Averting our faces from the clouds and sunsets
whose admirers give so much offence to Mr. Arnold, what
we see in his own judgment on Shelley and Byron might be
symbolically described as a sunset of critical judgment
in a cloud of hazy paradox. It is a singular certainty
that on the subject of Shelley this noble poet and brilliant critic has never got beyond what may be called the
'Johnny Keats' stage of criticism. The Shelley of his
imagination has exactly as much in common with the author
of the 'Ode to Liberty' as the Keats of Gifford's or
Wilson's had in common with the author of the 'Ode to a
Nightingale.' The main features of the phantom's character are apparently these: enthusiastic puerility of mind,
incurable unsoundness of judgment, resistless excitability
of emotion and helpless inability of intelligence, con-
sumptive wakefulness of fancy and feverish impotence of
reason, a dreamily amiable uselessness and a sweetly fantastic imbecility: in a word, the qualities of a silly
angel. I venture, in the face of a very general opinion,
to doubt whether such a poet as this ever existed: but I
do not doubt at all that none was ever further from any
resemblance to such a type than Percy Bysse Shelley.

In politics, Shelley looked steadfastly forward to the
peaceful and irreversible advance of republican principle,
the gradual and general prevalence of democratic spirit
throughout Europe, till the then omnipotent and omni-
present forces of universal reaction should be gently but
thoroughly superseded and absorbed. Wordsworth could
apparently see nothing between existing Georgian or Bour-
bonian society and a recrudescence of revolutionary chaos
but the maintenance of such divine institutions as rotten
boroughs and capital punishment. I do not ask which poet
held the nobler and the more inspiriting views of the
immediate future: I ask which of the two showed himself
the befogged, befooled, self-deluded, unpractical dreamer
among the clouds and sunsets of his chosen solitude and
his chosen faith, and which approved himself the man of
insight and foresight, the more practical and the more
rational student of contemporary history, alike in its
actual pageant of passing phenomena and in its moral
substance of enduring principles and lessons? I know
nothing more amusing and amazing than the placid imperturbable persistency with which the conservative of reactionary class is prone to claim and assume - or all things
in the world - the credit of being at any rate the practical party, as opposed to the dreamy and visionary herd

of hot-brained young poets and crack-brained old enthusiasts.

Mr. Arnold has chosen as a subject for special praise -
indeed, as the crowning and redeeming point of interest
in an otherwise commonplace if not unworthy character -
Byron's aspirations after a republic, his expressed conviction that 'the king-times are fast finishing,' his
full and whole-hearted acceptance of the assured prospect
that 'there will be blood shed like water and tears like
mist, but the peoples will conquer in the end.' Mr.
Arnold can scarcely, I should imagine, be readier than I
to give all due credit and all possible sympathy to the
writer of these wise and noble words: but he seems to
overlook the fact that if this feature in Byron's character is deserving of such credit and such sympathy, in
Shelley's, whose whole nature was pervaded and harmonized
by the inspiration of this faith, it is tenfold more
worthy of reverence and regard.

But Mr. Arnold, in a passage which if the argument would
allow me to pass it over I should really be reluctant to
transcribe, affirms that 'Byron threw himself upon poetry
as his organ; and in poetry his topics were not Queen Mab,
and the Witch of Atlas, and the Sensitive Plant, they were
the upholders of the old order, George the Third, and Lord
Castlereagh, and the Duke of Wellington, and Southey, and
they were the canters and tramplers of the great world,
and they were his enemies and himself.' If I wanted an
instance of provincial and barbarian criticism, of criticism inspired by a spirit of sour unreasonableness, a
spirit of bitterness and darkness, I should certainly
never dream of seeking further than this sentence for the
illustration required. It is almost too contemptibly
easy to retort in kind by observing that when Shelley
threw himself upon poetry as his organ, his topics were
not Hours of Idleness, and Hints from Horace, and the
Waltz, they were the redemption of the world by the martyrdom of righteousness, and the regeneration of mankind
through 'Gentleness, Virtue, Wisdom, and Endurance'; and
they were the heroism of Beatrice and the ascension of
Adonais, and they were the resurrection of Italy and of
Greece, and they were the divinest things of nature,
made more divine through the interpretation of love
infallible and the mastery of insuperable song. But so
to retort, though the reply would be as perfectly legitimate as the parody is exactly accurate, were to answer a

perverse man of genius according to his perversity; and I
will rather content myself with a serious indication of
this astonishing criticism as matter for serious regret -
not, assuredly, on Shelley's account; nor even, perhaps,
on Byron's.

But if Mr. Arnold is somewhat erratic and eccentric in the
display of his preference for Byron as a poet, how may we
decorously characterize the insular or individual eccentricity of his preference for Shelley as an essayist and
correspondent?

Shelley - or Shakespeare, for that matter - is hardly more
superior to Byron in poetry than in prose is Byron to
Shelley. Shelley's letters are in general very 'nice,' as
women say - very ingenuous, and rather ladylike; the letters of a candid and amiable young person who tries steadily to see for himself, without any great faculty of insight or capacity for getting away from his own subjective
line of vision. Byron's are full of violence, insolence,
bluster, affectation, hypocrisy, pretention, bullying egotism and swaggering nonsense: but no less certainly and
unmistakably are they the letters of a man with a great
gift for writing, a man of commanding genius, of indisputable and insuppressible powers. There are no doubt
passages in them which are merely foolish or feeble or
vulgar, as in Shelley's there are passages and touches of
exquisite truth and felicity, of admirable feeling and
good sense and delicacy; but the general characteristics
of either correspondence are such as have just been indicated. Byron's letters would be worth reading, had they
been written by the obscurest of dilettante dabblers in
politics or literature: if at every turn there is something to provoke irritation or repulsion, at every other
turn there is at the same time something to excite admiration or amusement. Nobody, I should have thought, or at
least only a very few specialists who have almost a craze
for the literature of 'Elegant Epistles,' would dream of
reading Shelley's if they had not been written by the hand
which wrote his poems.
    The fact is - and it is a fact which for some time past
has been growing only too perceptible to some of Mr.
Arnold's most cordial and earliest admirers - that to him,
in spite of all Wordsworth's guidance, years have brought
the unphilosophic mind. Like Philip van Artevelde, he was
'very philosophic in his youth' - I will not add, with Sir
Henry Taylor's self-contemplative hero - 'and twilight of

philosophy.' It is now just thirty years since he began
to rebuke his generation for its irregularity and waywardness and undisciplined bewilderment of taste. Eccentricity, whimsicality, caprice - the mood of mind in which a
man would rather say a new thing that is not true than a
true thing that is not new - such were the subjects of his
fervent and strenuous remonstrance: and such are now, in
more instances than one, the dominant notes or the distinctive qualities of his literary criticism. At all
events, at all hazards, at any price, he is bent upon
startling the reader with some vehement and wayward affirmation of his insurgent and rebellious originality. Because his countrymen accept Shakespeare, Milton, and
Shelley as poets of the first order, he is impelled to
insist that an Athenian - that a countryman of Aeschylus -
would have been simply disgusted or diverted by 'Hamlet,'
'Othello,' or 'King Lear'; to present for the respectful
consideration of Englishmen the shallow, narrow, captious,
pointless and irrelevant animadversions of M. Scherer upon
'Paradise Lost' - remarks in which if there are haply some
grains of truth and reason, they are as stale and rancid
as the critic's general conclusion is untenable and worth-
less; and to write himself down an eccentric too rampant
and extravagant in his dogmatism for the atmosphere of
Crotchet Castle, by advancing an opinion that the first of
English lyric poets deserves remembrance chiefly as a
writer of occasional prose. Let me have leave, as a loyal
and lifelong admirer of Mr. Arnold, to remark that no critical reputation can possibly survive much more of this
sort of thing; that it is annually becoming more and more
difficult for the most devoted and sincere goodwill to
regard him as a serious judge or authority on questions of
literature, or to answer those who think it impossible
for him to be considered by steady-going and rational students as other than the most brilliant and the most hare-
brained of all eccentric dealers in self-willed and intem-
perate paradox; and that surely no scholar, and still more
surely no poet, can regard with equanimity such a risk of
being confounded with the Carlyles and Emersons of his
day as must inevitably be incurred by a writer whose estimate of Shelley is such as hitherto has found utterance
only from Craigenputtock or from Bedlam, from Concord or
from Earlswood. For not only does he lack the excuse
which may be pleaded alike for the transatlantic and the
cisatlantic pseudosopher, that each had failed as a poetaster before he began to yelp at the heels of poets: he
is, with the single exception of Mr. Aubrey de Vere, the
only man who has ever written a poem so exactly after the
manner of Shelley that both in style and spirit it is not

unworthy of the honour to be mistaken for a genuine lyric
of the second order among the minor poems of our greatest
lyric poet.

52.   JOSEPH JACOBS, UNSIGNED REVIEW OF 'DISCOURSES IN
AMERICA', 'ATHENAEUM'

27 June 1885, 817-18

Joseph Jacobs (1854-1916), Jewish scholar and folklorist,
was born in Australia, moved to England, and later made
his home in the USA. A prolific writer, he published five
books on Jewish studies between 1888 and 1894. He also
wrote literary criticism and was a regular contributor to
the 'Athenaeum'. A number of his 'Athenaeum' reviews,
including this on Arnold, were collected in his 'George
Eliot, Matthew Arnold, Browning, and Newman' (1891).
Jacobs is an acute and sympathetic critic. Arnold alone,
he says, 'possesses the lightness of touch, width of view,
sanity of criticism, and individuality of style which are
needed to give permanent value to what seems at first
sight to be merely a form of the higher journalism'.

Every one will welcome another volume of *causeries* from
the hand of our only English master in this branch of
literature, Mr. Matthew Arnold. Notwithstanding the
attempts of many would-be imitators, he alone possesses
the lightness of touch, width of view, sanity of criticism, and individuality of style which are needed to give
permanent value to what seems at first sight to be merely
a form of the higher journalism. The combination of these
qualities is rare enough to account for the influence
possessed by the men in whom they occur. Mr. Matthew
Arnold in England, M. Renan and M. Scherer in France, and
Mr. Lowell in America, almost exhaust the list; and of all
the masters of the *causerie* (1) Mr. Matthew Arnold is in
some respects the most influential in England, for reasons which may well engage our attention after we have
made a few remarks on the present instalment of his work.
   This consists of only three discourses - the Rede
Lecture adapted to American audiences and the specially
American lectures on Numbers and Emerson. With the aid of

wide margins and a liberal amount of 'fat,' as the prin-
ters call it, the text is doled out in pages of but nine-
teen lines each, and thus the three articles are successfully expanded into a booklet of over two hundred pages.
Small as it is, the volume differs favourably from some of
the recent republications of Mr. Arnold's utterances in
that it contains only specimens of his best work, and we
may perhaps add that in it he dismounts from his over-
ridden hobby - State schools for the middle classes. Each
of the three essays attracted attention when first delivered - readers will remember the ludicrous blunders made
by the American reporters with the goddess Lubricity in
'Numbers' - and they were as eagerly read when republished
in magazines. Now collected in a volume, they will be as
popular as any in the series in which they are published,
and have a good chance of being revived in the far distant
day when their copyright shall have run out - the most
practical test that occurs to us to determine whether a
book really belongs to English literature.

Much comment on essays so much commented on at the time
of their appearance were perhaps needless. We may remark,
however, that the lecture on literature and science has
lost somewhat in its passage across the Atlantic. There
was a peculiar aptitude in its delivery in the Senate
House at Cambridge, where everything seems to be telling
for science rather than literature. And there was a
specially interesting passage in the original, now omitted, which dealt with the difference of the two universities - Oxford the home of great movements, Cambridge of
great men. On the general merits of the great question -
literature or science as training for life - Mr. Arnold is
clearly on the right side, and even Professor Huxley
scarcely attempts to deny this. But it is curious that
Mr. Arnold omits to notice that there is a side of literary work which tends to give all, or nearly all, the educational advantages claimed for science. A work like
Munro's 'Lucretius' is in reality as scientific as Roscoe
and Schorlemmer's 'Chemistry.' In Germany both would be
included under the comprehensive 'Wissenschaft.' Observation, induction, hypothesis, verification, quantitative
analysis, and even to some extent experiment, are all
applicable to Homer or the 'Nibelungenlied' as to the tri-
assic strata. Indeed, a good case might be made out for
showing that Mr. Arnold, in his discourse on Numbers, is
simply applying the ordinary scientific law of error - the
principle of deivations from an average so admirably
applied in Mr. Galton's 'Hereditary Genius.' His comfortable doctrine of the remnant is in reality based on a
similar assumption, and much of it is seen to be

untrustworthy when one remembers that the curve of error
may take different forms, and the remnant be smaller
though the numbers be larger. As a matter of fact, is it
not the universal experience that the saving remnant, even
in America, is small in proportion to the mass of self-
seeking Philistinism? And if we turn to China or India,
the doctrine of the remnant has very little comfort left
for us. Opinions, too, might differ as to the extent to
which the worship of the goddess Aselgeia is corrupting
French culture. The success of a mediocre master like M.
Ohnet, simply because he does not bow to the ruling goddess, is sufficient to show the strength of the protest
against the worship of Lubricity.

Here, probably, Mr. Matthew Arnold would agree with us,
the only difference of opinion being as to the extent of
the evil. On this it may be remarked that it has been
long existent without producing any widely apparent ill
effects, and that it is in large measure counteracted by
the intense family love of the Frenchman and the more
robust life of the provinces. But we prefer not to parade
differences where there is so much with which we can agree
and from which we can learn. The analysis of the French
character and its threefold strain - Gallic, Latin, and
Germanic - recalls some of the best parts of the 'Celtic
Literature.' The admirable quotations from Newman, Carlyle, Goethe, and Emerson, in the opening passage of the
essay on the last, together with the remarks on each
author - often but a word, but what an instructive word!
- exhibit Mr. Arnold at one of his best moments; as,
indeed, the whole discourse on Emerson shows him to us in
one of his happiest hours of inspiration, and might be
selected as giving an admirable specimen of his peculiar
qualities as a critic of letters and of life; or, as Mr.
Arnold would say, it gives us his method and his secret.

There is an apt phrase - we believe, of Professor
Huxley's - which exactly expresses the *differentia* (2)
of Mr. Arnold's studies: they are lay sermons. The object
of the sermon may be assumed to be the moral regeneration
of the hearers. This is clearly and avowedly the object
of most of Mr. Arnold's utterances. Notice how he invariably picks out the favourite sin of his audience. At the
Royal Institution, in the midst of the London season, he
lectures on equality. At Cambridge he avers that with the
majority of mankind a little of mathematics goes a long
way, and that science cannot satisfy the soul of man. He
crosses to America, and there he chooses as his special
topic Numbers, preaching to the text, 'The majority are
bad.' For every one will recognise that Mr. Arnold's
lectures have the note of the sermon method in this at

least, that they start from a text - it may be from the
Bible, it may be from Menander - to which the discourse
returns time after time, with a reiteration which some may
find wearisome, but which clearly effects the purpose of
impressing itself on the method.

His method, then, is that of the lay sermon. Would
that clerical sermons were ever as good! His secret is
his subacid reasonableness and his serious levity or
frivolous seriousness. What strikes one in his criticisms
of life even more than their penetration is their sanity
and completeness. Many a controversial victory he has won
in discussions about letters or life, or sometimes even in
politics, by attending to the one question, What are the
actual and complete facts of the case? He takes human
nature all round, and sees how far a proposed remedy
answers to all its needs. Herein he is really penetrated
by the scientific spirit in its best aspect, and he has
been no insufficient teacher of the higher anthropology.
That in part is the secret of his influence. Men see that
what he says tallies in the main with what they know, and
at the same time they are half attracted half repelled by
the tone in which he says it. If we may so put it, he
pretends not to be serious, and by the very pretence con-
vinces one of his seriousness. It is, in fact, this seriousness, the conviction his words convey that his deepest
concern is with the things of moral import, that gives
such authority to his word among Englishmen. The things
of conduct are, after all, what both he and they have most
at heart, and they listen to him as he discourses on
things of sweetness and light - now, alas! becoming rarer
and rarer with him - because they know that in his hands
they have intimate bearing on conduct. Hence Mr. Matthew
Arnold may say things in a tone which would be censured
in another. There is a passage in these discourses about
M. Blowitz and the Eternal which, even in Mr. Arnold, is
as near want of taste as it is possible to go. But one
knows that Mr. Arnold, after all, is not really lacking in
reverence, and so the lapse is overlooked. Reflecting on
this, one cannot help thinking what a force Mr. Arnold
would be if he dropped his cloak of levity. He has given
a clever sermon on Gray; text: 'He never spoke out.' One
feels that Mr. Arnold has never spoken out the faith that
is in him. He began life as an Hellene of the Hellenes,
and was as one of those who are at ease in Zion. He has
gradually become more Hebraic than the Hebrews, but yet
retains the easy manner of the sons of light. What a
motive force he might be if he adapted his style to his
matter! Mr. Arnold has some admirable words on Carlyle
here in the pages before us. Carlyle is weighed in the

balance and found wanting; but if we may deplore the want of sweetness in Carlyle, might we not regret its over-abundance in Mr. Arnold's nature? His best friends might wish to see him - they would certainly be curious to see him - lose his temper for once in a way over some subject that deserves to rouse his ire.

Notes

1 'chat'.
2 'specific character'.

53. ALFRED AUSTIN, MR. MATTHEW ARNOLD ON THE LOVES OF THE POETS, 'NATIONAL REVIEW'

February 1888, x, 768-78

Alfred Austin's life (1835-1913) was littered with fail-ures, none of which ever prevented him from considering himself a great man. After a Roman Catholic education Austin was called to the bar in 1857 but turned from law to literature in 1858, certain that he was a poet. His verse received an indifferent response from the critics, and from 1862 to 1871 he published no more. Instead, he turned to periodical writing, attacking Hugo, Tennyson, Browning, Arnold, Morris, Clough, and Swinburne as femi-nine and childish poets because they failed to write epics or dramatic romances dealing with love, patriotism, and religion. Between 1871 and 1908 in twenty published vol-umes of poetry Austin tried to fill this gap in Victorian literature, and though he was awarded the laureateship in 1896, few critics ever thought that he had succeeded at his self-appointed task. In this review Austin belittles Arnold for his criticism of Edward Dowden's life of Shelley. The ironic title, with its allusion to Samuel Johnson's more elastic approach towards artists' lives, sets the tone for an exercise in mockery.

Mr. Matthew Arnold is the most airy and nimble of all our prose wits. In France he would be called *très spirituel*; (1) and very few English writers would be called that, in

the classic land of *esprit*. (2) He is the dainty Ariel of
exegetical criticism, who shows us, difficult though it
be, how

> To run upon the sharp wind of the North.

Children of darkness have sometimes dubbed him a pedagogue,
and Philistines in their wrath have even taxed him with
'literary conceit.' If the reproach be just, I wish literary conceit were more common, for it is a most agreeable
quality. Whether gracefully patronizing the New Testament,
or exhorting us, in the name of true Culture, to send our
children to school with those of the butcher, the baker,
and the candlestick maker, though Mr. Arnold may not quite
succeed in convincing us, still he never fails to please.
He has been picking his way among naked swords for many
years; and, till within a month ago, he had never once
wounded himself. How priceless is such dexterity, such
tact, among a clumsy and stumbling race.
   But call no writer happy till he has done writing; and,
alas! Mr. Arnold has tripped at last. There must be joy
in Philistia over that article on Shelley which appeared
in the January number of the 'Nineteenth Century,' joy
over the sinner that repenteth. In that portion of the
Elysian Fields allotted to good Englishmen, 'where congregations never part, and sermons never end,' the ghost of
the late Mr. Miall must be thoroughly happy. Mr. Matthew
Arnold has taken a brief from the Philistines; he has sate
down to bread and salt with the Ten-Pound Householder, and
is found perfectly at home in the severe company of the
advocates of the Deceased Wife's Sister.
   Mr. Arnold cites a passage from one of Shelley's
letters to his first wife, and says it is *bête*. (3) It is
a marvellous letter, truly, but I should not myself describe it by that term. Neither do I think M. Renan, M.
Taine, or M. Cherbuliez would do so. Indeed I am not sure
that, in a land honeycombed, as Mr. Arnold assures us,
with lubricity, it would not be regarded as a specimen of
ethical catholicity somewhat refreshing in an Englishman.
It is rather concerning Mr. Arnold's own article on Shelley, and what the *spirituel* race on the other side of the
silver sea will think of it, that one is anxious. I
greatly fear they will pronounce *it* a *bêtise*. 'It is not
for nothing,' I think I can hear a French critic saying,
'that one is an Englishman. One is not born in that land
of fogs, religions, and *le shocking*, without partaking in
some degree of its insatiable appetite for propriety.
Blood is thicker than water, and the blood in Mr. Arnold
has spoken at last. He requires even the poets to be

proper and well-behaved. We have done our utmost to teach
him better, and he has done his utmost to learn. But *il
chasse de race*. (4) His last word upon Shelley, Byron,
and their friends and companions, male and female, is
'What a set! what a world!' *Et ego in Philistiâ*. (5) Our
only English convert to French *esprit* turns out to be but
a *Bourgeois Gentilhomme* (6) after all.'

Mr. Arnold regrets that Professor Dowden has written a
'Life of Shelley.' Moreover he laments that Mr. Dowden
has written it with 'a certain poetic quality of fervour
and picturesqueness,' and himself proceeds to correct this
defect in the narrative, by re-stating the leading facts
of Shelley's life in a style of deliberate and purposed
triteness, compared with which the manner of the 'Annual
Register' would have to be pronounced poetic and picturesque. Certainly, since one of Charles Lever's Irish
heroes 'took the Popery out of the tomb-stone,' there has
been no such instance of terse yet sweeping revision.

But does Mr. Arnold verily believe that he thereby
introduces us more accurately to the facts of Shelley's
life, and presents us with a more real Shelley than that
of Professor Dowden?

'What a set! what a world! is the exclamation that breaks
from us as we come to an end of this history of the occur-
rences of Shelley's private life.... And Lord Byron, with
his deep grain of coarseness and commonness, his affectation, his brutal selfishness - what a set! The history
carries us to Oxford, and I think of the clerical and
respectable Oxford of those old times, the Oxford of
Copleston and the Kebles, and Hawkins, and a hundred
more.' So writes Mr. Arnold in his new vein. Verily,
great is the chaste Diana of the Philistines!

'What a set! what a world!' Surely there is ground for
surprise when a man who has lived so long, and so wisely,
who has honestly cultivated so much sweetness, and really
absorbed and radiated so much light, has withal not discovered that it is bootless work bringing men of genius,
and poets most of all, before the tribunal of 'clerical
and respectable Oxford'! It is most unfair, most wrong,
most wicked, most anything you like, that one cannot.
But what if it is so, and it cannot be helped? It is a
wicked world, and, most of all, an unfair world. Mr.
Arnold says Shelley's school-fellows were right to call
him 'mad Shelley.' Well, it is moreover 'a mad world, my
masters.' It never did act fairly to the people who charm

380 Arnold, Prose Writings: The Critical Heritage

it, any more than it does to the people who bore it; and
it never will. We see proof of this every day. A duchess
- a handsome and self-confident duchess, that is, - may
do with security, indeed with advantage, what a dairy-maid
had better not think of. A popular actor or actress can
with impunity ignore all the Ten Commandments. *You* must
not do it; neither can I. But that is different. Even
if you have a supreme soprano or tenor voice, you can do
pretty much as you wish, let 'clerical and respectable
Oxford' think or say what it will.

We are all 'respectable' in these days, even those of us
who cannot get rid of the bad habit of writing verses;
and the result is the world takes very little interest in
us. Men who, in external circumstances, closely resemble
their neighbours, must not expect to be taken seriously as
poets by a frivolous and superficially judging world.
Let us hope, when the day comes for reminiscences and
revelations concerning them, that our living bards will
turn out to have been more romantic and less respectable
than they seem to be. Otherwise it is to be feared Orcus
will devour both them and their works.
     For, in truth, whatever the beloved Children of the
Muse may fondly think, the world cares very little for
poetry, however much interest it may show in certain
poets. It is interested in poets the incidents of whose
life resemble those of a first-rate novel, or whose biography can be made to resemble a prose romance, with
the aid of 'a certain poetic quality of fervour and picturesqueness' in the biographer. In this respect, Shelley and Byron were the most fortunate of men, and could
not have done better for their fame, had they deliberately
set to work to conduct themselves, and to induce other
people to conduct themselves, for the one sole purpose of
ministering to that end.

I hope it will not be supposed I want to extend the borders of morality in order to suit the disposition of men
of genius. I am only calling attention to facts, patent
facts, which I am surprised Mr. Arnold should have overlooked. Were we all children of sweetness and light, all
cultured, all imbued with the proper amount of high seriousness, in a word, were we all Hawkinses and Coplestons,
and fit company for clerical and respectable Oxford, then,
no doubt, Shelley would horrify, and Byron would appal us.
But Mr. Arnold's conceptions of human nature, and even his
criteria of taste, are, in this article of his, too

narrow. There is such a thing as *le diable dans le corps*;
(7) and so many people have it, more or less, that they
have a fellow-feeling for those who have it egregiously
and extravagantly, which makes them wondrous kind. When
these exceptional 'devils of fellows' write 'Manfred,'
or 'An Ode to the West Wind,' the fellow-feeling waxes
into monstrous partiality and complete forgiveness. Can
we not all read or talk of Shelley and Byron through a
long summer afternoon with unflagging interest, and return
to the subject on the morrow with curiosity unslaked and
sympathy unabated? How long would Mr. Arnold engage to
rivet our attention if the subject consisted of that
blameless set, the aged Wordsworth, his excellent cousin
and wife, Mary Hutchinson, and his superlatively good
sister Dorothy? I fear some of us would be caught glanc-
ing round to see if Coleridge, like a stray dog of doubtful character, were coming in to interrupt 'that d——d
monologue which old gentlemen call conversation.'...

'Do not throw a stone,' says an Eastern proverb, 'into the
well out of which you have drunk.' We all drink of the
fresh well-spring of these men's poetry; and if sometimes
haply an *amari aliquid* (8) bubbles up to the surface, and
leaves for the moment a bitter taste in the mouth, -
well, let us say nothing about it, but drink again, and
this time deeper. Moreover, it is useless, nay, it is at
your peril you revile them. When Genius reaches a certain
height, it carries itself somewhat cavalierly, as though
it should say, *Nemo me impune lacessit*.... (9)

Notes

1 'spirited'.
2 'spirit'.
3 'crude'.
4 'he is true to his nationality'.
5 'And I too [have been] in Philistia!'
6 'bourgeois gentleman'.
7 'a bit of the devil in each of us'.
8 'a little bitterness'.
9 'No one strikes me with impunity.'

1888–1900: Arnold as Man of Letters

54. F. W. H. MYERS, OBITUARY, 'FORTNIGHTLY REVIEW'

May 1888, xliii, n.s., 719-28

Frederick William Henry Myers (1843-1901), after a brilliant career at Trinity College, Cambridge, worked like
Arnold as a school inspector for the balance of his life.
While still a student Myers began to entertain doubts
about Christianity, and later in life he turned to the
study of extra-material phenomena, becoming (in 1882) one
of the founders of the Society for Psychical Research. In
this obituary he is especially interested in Arnold's
theological studies, studies which Myers thinks were not a
'caprice' but an honest response to 'the profound incoherence of current opinion'. However, Myers finds
Arnold's attempts to reconcile Christianity with the new
Stoicism 'incredible'. He considers Arnold to be, not the
'flippant and illusory Christian' that many people think,
but rather a 'devout and conservative agnostic'.

The portions of this essay dealing with Arnold's poetry
will be found in 'Matthew Arnold, The Poetry' (No. 31).

Few men, if any, whom death could have taken from us would
have been more perceptibly missed by a wider range of
friends and readers than Mr. Matthew Arnold. Other men
survive who command a more eager enthusiasm, or who are
more actively important to the work of the world. But
hardly any man was present in so many cultivated minds as
an element of interest in life, an abiding possibility of
stimulating and fruitful thought. His criticism of books

and of life found wider acceptance in the English-speaking
world than that offered by any other writer; and even the
slight affectations or idiosyncrasies of his pellucid
style had become so associated with the sense of intellectual enjoyment that few readers wished them away. And for
those of us who were privileged to know him (and few men
were more widely known) the keen interest, the sometimes
half-smiling admiration of the general reader, was reinforced on its best and deepest side by our perception of
his upright, manly, kindly soul. We saw that his manner
was saved from any real arrogance by its tinge of self-
mockery; that his playful superciliousness changed at once
to grave attentive sympathy on any real appeal. And in
his talk yet more strongly than in his books we felt the
charm of that alert and open spirit, of that ready disinterested concern in almost every department of the
thoughts and acts of men.

His businesses and achievements, indeed, were widely
spread. He was an inspector of schools, a literary,
social, and political essayist, a religious reformer, and
a poet. To the *first* of these pursuits, widening into the
study of state education generally, he probably gave the
largest proportion of his time, and he became one of the
most accomplished specialists in that direction whom England possessed; in the *second* pursuit he was the most
brilliantly successful; to the *third*, as I believe, he
devoted the most anxious and persistent thought; and by
the *fourth* pursuit, as a poet, he will, we cannot doubt,
be the longest remembered. We must not, however, speak as
though these various activities were scattered or separate
things. Rather they formed stages in a life-long endeavour - the endeavour to diffuse, in his favourite words,
'sweetness and light,' by the application to our pressing
problems of his own special gifts, namely, the tact and
flexibility which spring from culture, and the insight
gained by a wide miscellaneous acquaintance with men and
things. His educational work was valuable to him as furnishing a backbone of accurate knowledge of one great
branch of administration with which his discursive social
criticisms might be solidly connected. And it aided, too,
in bringing him into close contact with groups of persons
and modes of thought which the mere man of letters is
tempted to ignore. Matthew Arnold knew much of *all*
classes of English society; his mind contained a picture
of its whole fabric, rich in humorous juxtapositions and
significant detail. As this conception of our society
and its needs took shape within him, his hereditary impulse to teach and to reform grew ever stronger; and the
early essays in stylistic analysis gradually took more and

more of practical purpose, till, even before he touched
the subject of religion, he had become rather a critic of
life and morals, with a special literary gift, than a pure
student of letters. He was thus more truly analogous to
J. S. Mill or to Mr. Morley than (say) to Lamb or Hazlitt,
to Sainte-Beuve or Mr. Swinburne. And since the appearance of 'Culture and Anarchy' in 1869 his literary papers
have been merely incidental. The main current of his production has treated either of definite political measures
of the day, or of national progress in a wider sense, or
of morals and religion. And although his literary papers
have been those most enjoyed by cultivated men, yet there
is a very large public which knows him mainly by his graver
treatises; and a kind of _plébiscite_ recently taken by a
democratic newspaper brought out 'Literature and Dogma' as
his most valued work.

And since space and time press narrowly upon this present paper, I do not propose here to re-discuss Mr.
Arnold's subtle and delicate literary criticisms, or to
recapitulate the pleas for sweetness and light, for more
education, more moderation, and a more lucid and dis-
engaged intelligence in public matters, which have
assuredly played their part in the rapid civilising process which has run through English life in this last
quarter of a century. Rather I shall pass on to the line
of work on which he would himself, I believe, have wished
us to dwell; a work, however, in which he was often misunderstood, nay, which even produced for the most part an
effect quite unlike the effect intended.

In the first place it must be observed that it was no
mere caprice, no wanton divergence into a province not his
own, which led Matthew Arnold to treat of religion. To a
man dealing, as he habitually dealt, with the dominant
ideas, the springs of conduct of various classes of men
around him, a sense of the profound incoherence of current
opinion on the deepest matters must need be ever present.
And the moral earnestness which, beneath all his flippancy
of expression, was the strongest instinct that heredity
had implanted within him, must have led to constant cross
currents of sympathy as he watched the blind literalism,
the deafness to the dicta of critic or historian, which
still possess the inheritors of the Puritan faith. At
first the points on which he dwelt were comparatively external - points as to the relation of the Church and Dissent, which every year, in face of the profounder clouds
that are gathering over both alike, are dwindling to an
interest of a merely practical or political kind. But
gradually he got into deeper water; gradually he was
obliged to think the matter out thoroughly and to speak it

plainly, and he adopted the position which is becoming
perhaps commoner than any other among our leading minds,
namely, the simple resolve to live up to the best light
that conscience gives, without hope of any save this ter-
rene life, of any other reign or continuance of virtue.
Now most of those who adopt this plain resolution as the
only anchor of man find both in Judaism and in Christianity more to offend than to attract them. Old Testament
Judaism, with its tribal ferocities, with its crude
belief in prosperity and length of days as the Lord's re-
compense to His worshippers; Christianity, with its miracles, its resurrection, its doctrine of future rewards
and punishments; both of these seem remote from provable
truth and from disinterested virtue; they seem a fond creation of fabled paradises – an earthly paradise which has
long ceased to flow for Israel with milk and honey, a
heavenly paradise to which no man has found the way. But
Matthew Arnold was himself linked by insuperable attach-
ment to the ancient faiths. Living the life, too, not of
an isolated philosopher, but of the companion and friend
of all conditions of men, he perceived the absolute moral
need that their religion should be transformed and not
destroyed; that it should retain authority and loveliness;
that it should not shrink into the Stoic's bare exhortation to heroic virtue. And feeling how large a part of
all religion is morality, and how deeply the best morali-
ties of Jew, Christian, Stoic coincide, he conceived the
bold idea of carrying over the prestige and beauty of both
Old and New Testament into the Stoic camp, and still nur-
turing a generation with no hope beyond the tomb on the
righteousness of prophet and psalmist, on the spiritual
inwardness of Christ. With the Old Testament it may be
said that he in part succeeded. There was no doubt among
the early Jews a gross interpretation of divine favour –
as it were a lowing of herds in the background of the
sacrifice – which can in no way be conciliated with a
purer ideal. But this was not all. Prophets and psalmists rose high above the grosser expectations of the mass
of their people. They did in truth experience – they
first, as we may say, of mortal men – the full strength,
the full delight of adherence to a moral law. They trusted in an Eternal Power that made for righteousness,
resting that belief upon the experience of their own history, upon the inspiration that spoke within their hearts,
and overriding all curious inquiry into man's destiny by
their imperious summons to virtue.

   Thus far forth they seem as close to the Stoic as to
the Christian, and Matthew Arnold has insisted with justice that for all men in any age who care for

righteousness those ancient songs still keep their solemn
meaning; that the spirit of a Cleanthes or of a Spinoza,
as truly as the spirit of a John or a Paul, lives in that
primal cry, 'I have stuck unto thy testimonies: O Lord,
confound me not!'

But alas! from the Hebrew, from the Christian, from the
modern scientific point of view alike, it is manifest that
the high belief of prophet and psalmist could not close
the fundamental problem, nor give a lasting strength to
Israel. In Job, in Ecclesiastes, in some of the later
Psalms themselves, the very questions of to-day are discussed without a solution. Then as now men could not
refrain from doubting whether there really was a 'not-
ourselves' which made for righteousness; whether behind
the fire, the tempest, and the earthquake, there was
verily a still small voice. We know the sequel. Jesus
Christ appeared; he taught that man had a Father in
heaven; he promised eternal life; he justified (as was
believed) that daring promise by appearing to his disciples after his body had been laid with the dead. So
stating the case, it might have seemed incredible that any
one should attempt to absorb the religion of Christ into
the religion of Marcus Aurelius Antoninus. Yet this is in
effect what Matthew Arnold tries to do. Trusting to the
moral analogy between the creeds of all lofty souls,
pointing to the renunciation of the baser self which
Christ did indeed inculcate with an inwardness, a spirituality far deeper than that of Marcus himself, Matthew
Arnold would have us believe that this is virtually *all*
that Christ meant to teach us; that the religion which came
into the world as a religion of glorious intoxicating hope
was but a vivid restatement of that old religion of
courageous resignation which was still to guide, in the
Danubian marshes, the solitary Emperor's pen.

I have dwelt longer on Mr. Arnold's religious attitude
because, as already stated, he seems to me to have been
misunderstood in a way which does injustice, not indeed to
his arguments, but to his purpose and temper. He has been
treated as a flippant and illusory Christian, instead of
as a specially devout and conservative Agnostic. This was
the consequence of his well-meant efforts to minimise two
points of difference which were in fact fundamental, of
the benevolent juggleries of language by which he strove
to lead his followers dry-shod across Jordan, though this
time out of, and not into, the Land of Promise. Yet by no
arts, no flexibility, could he pour Christian wine into
Stoic bottles; by no unction, no optimist temper, could he

identify the religion of renunciation with the religion
of hope....

55. H. D. TRAILL, OBITUARY, 'CONTEMPORARY REVIEW'

June 1888, liii, 868-81

Henry Duff Traill (1842-1900) was a prolific and respected
writer. He worked on the staffs of the 'Pall Mall' and
'St James' gazettes, wrote leaders and reviews for the
'Saturday', and from 1882 to 1897 was chief political
leader-writer for the 'Daily Telegraph'. In addition he
wrote books on Sterne, Coleridge, Shaftsbury, William III,
Strafford, the Marquis of Salisbury, and Sir John Franklin, as well as two books of his own verse. Traill has
enormous respect for Arnold's literary criticism - which,
he thinks, will give him 'a permanent place in the history
of English letters'. But Arnold's theology is a mistake,
'a hopelessly unpractical and almost visionary attempt',
and the social criticism, though 'more successful', is
lamed by Arnold's inability to offer practical suggestions for improvement.
    The sections of this review dealing with Arnold's
verse will be found in 'Matthew Arnold, The Poetry' (No.
32).

Much has been said since his death of the 'Essays in Criticism' as an 'epoch-making book,' and, with a little care
in defining the precise nature of the epoch which it did
make, the phrase may be defended. It would be too much to
say that the principles of criticism for which Mr. Arnold
contended were new and original - or rather it would be
the reverse of a compliment to say so, since it is literally certain that any fundamentally novel discovery on
this ancient subject would turn out another Invention of
the Mare's-nest. There is no critical canon in the Essays
which has not been observed in and might not be illustrated from the practice of some critics for long before
the Essays appeared. But it is quite true that these
principles were at that time undergoing what from time to
time in our literary history they have frequently undergone, a phase of neglect; and it is equally true that Mr.

Arnold's lucid exposition of these principles, and the
singularly fascinating style of the series of papers in
which he illustrated them, gave a healthy stimulus and a
true direction to English literary criticism, which during
the twenty years now completed since the publication of
the Essays it has on the whole preserved. And to credit
any writer with such an achievement as this is undoubtedly
to concede his claim to a permanent place in the history
of English letters.

In may be that Mr. Arnold would not have made that
place higher or more assured by steadily pursuing his
studies as a literary critic; but the virtual abandonment
of these studies, so far at least as publication is concerned, during his later years, must always remain a
matter of keen regret to all lovers of literature. There
were so many subjects which he had touched so admirably
and yet had only touched; so many on which he had said his
word, but not his last word. To take only one instance of
our loss: it is now five-and-thirty years since, in the
preface to the first collected edition of his poems, he
instituted that subtle and penetrating comparison between
the dramatic methods of Shakespeare and of the Greek tra-
gedians. Nothing could be more striking and suggestive,
nothing more excellently put than that criticism. Yet so
far from exhausting the subject, which indeed is probably
inexhaustible, it seemed merely to open the way into a
wide and fruitful field of critical inquiry, which no one
could have explored with so sure a foot as he. Yet from
this exploration, as from so much other work for which he
was uniquely fitted, Mr. Arnold, for the last ten years of
his life, turned almost wholly away. And he turned away
from it to devote himself, save for occasional and for the
most part singularly ineffectual excursions into the
domain of contemporary politics, to a hopelessly unpractical and almost visionary attempt to put the old wine of
dogmatic Christianity into the new bottles of modern
scientific thought!

Some years ago, on the occasion of the issue of a cheap
reprint of 'Literature and Dogma,' I endeavoured in the
pages of this REVIEW to investigate the validity of Mr.
Arnold's theories of Scriptural interpretation, and to
estimate the amount of acceptance which they were likely
to obtain from those whom it was his avowed desire, and
whom he so strangely conceived it to be his special mission, to instruct. On the former of these two questions I
find nothing now to add to the observations which I then
made. I thought then, and I still think, and, what is
more, I believe it to be the well-nigh universal opinion,
that the critical canons by which Mr. Arnold sought to

refine away what he regarded as the materialistic accretions on the creed of Christianity (but what are really of
its essence as a definite system of doctrines derived from
a supernatural origin and possessing a supernatural sanc-
tion), were valueless for any practical purpose. I
thought, and still think, that the whole of his teachings
on this subject were in part futile and in part superfluous; superfluous, because unneeded by those who have
accepted with him the conclusions of modern science, and
who, if they retain their belief in Christianity at all,
are quite competent to devise their own 'accommodations'
for themselves; and futile, because assured of rejection
by those who, through ignorance of or repugnance to the
scientific conclusions which are tending to destroy its
supernatural element, still cling to their religion,
'superstitions' and all. The assumption that there any-
where exists any considerable class of Christians in so
curiously 'mixed' a mental condition as to be at once
anxious to reconcile the dogmas of their faith with the
informations of their reason, unable to do it for themselves, and willing to allow others to attempt it for
them, was in itself an assumption of a highly doubtful
kind; but the idea that if there were such persons they
would find anything specially persuasive in Mr. Arnold's
method of reasoning with them, or even in his manner of
approaching them, appears to me to have been a positively
monumental instance of self-deception.
 Our spiritual physician reversed the Scriptural precedent, and addressed himself not to the sick, but to the
whole. The style, the argument, and, above all, the
illustrations of a treatise avowedly addressed to persons
still in the bond of servitude to a narrow and superstitious literalism, appeared, nevertheless, to presuppose
the completest 'emancipation' on the part of its readers.
The babes and sucklings who were to be weaned from their
superstition were fed with the strongest of strong meats
by their instructor, and that too, apparently, in perfect
good faith and with no sign of any suspicion of the weakness of their stomachs. An amusing illustration of this
unconsciousness is to be found in the preface to the new
edition of 'Literature and Dogma,' in connection with its
author's astounding figure of 'the three Lord Shaftesburys.' 'Many of those,' observes Mr. Arnold, ' who have
most ardently protested against the illustration, resent
it, no doubt, because it directs attention to that extreme
licence of affirmation about God which prevails in our
popular religion, and one is not the easier forgiven for
directing attention to error because one marks it as an
object for indulgence. To protesters of this sort I owe

no deference, and make no concessions. But the illustration has given pain, I am told, in a quarter where only
deference, and the deference of all who can appreciate one
of the purest careers and noblest characters of our time,
is indeed due; and finding that in that quarter pain has
been given by the illustration, I do not hesitate to expunge it.' In other words, Mr. Arnold, finding that he
has given offence by comparing the Trinity to 'three Lord
Shaftesburys,' apologizes - to Lord Shaftesbury. To the
'protesters,' who were certainly not thinking of Lord
Shaftesbury when they resented the comparison, he thinks
he 'owes no deference,' and will therefore 'make no concessions.' One is left wondering whether Mr. Arnold was
really unaware of the susceptibilities and the persons he
had wounded, or whether he purposely treated them with
contempt. And in either case one wonders still more vehemently whether he was aware that the persons to whom he
owned no deference and would make no concessions were, in
fact, the very persons whom, if his teachings were to bear
any fruit at all, he was bound, before all others, to conciliate. But either of the two explanations will equally
entitle us to say that Mr. Arnold could have formed no
adequate estimate of the fundamental conditions of
success in the task which he proposed to himself.

As a critic of our social life and institutions, Mr.
Arnold was doubtless more successful. No one can say that
his delightful raillery was altogether thrown away upon
its objects. Our 'Barbarians' are probably a little less
barbarous, our 'Philistines' a little more enlightened,
for his pleasant satire. And those who could appreciate
the temper of his literary weapon, and his matchless skill
in using it, were able to watch the periodical perform-
ances for many years with almost undiminished pleasure.
But it must be admitted, I think, that even as a social
instructor he somewhat outstayed his welcome, and that
even his most ardent admirers occasionally found their
patience a little tried by him. His incessant iteration
of his favourite phrases was, no doubt, a tactical expedient deliberately adopted for controversial purposes at the
perceived expense of artistic effect. Mr. Arnold was well
aware that to provoke, to irritate, is better for a disputant than to fail to impress, and he had no doubt persuaded himself that to get our social defects acknowledged
and the proper remedies applied, it was necessary to be as
importunate as the widow suitor of the unjust judge. It
is true he does not tell us, in the admirable lines on
Goethe which adorn the memorial verses to Wordsworth,
that that 'physician of the iron age' was *always* 'striking
his finger on the place,' and saying, 'Thou ailest here
and here;' but Mr. Arnold had abandoned the methods and

the vehicle of the poet - who speaks once for all with a
voice whose echoes are undying - before he started in
business as a reformer of his countrymen's manners and
modes of thought. As a prose physician, so to speak, he
may have thought that his prescriptions needed to be
dinned into the ears of the patient until he actually
consented to try them. But a recognition of that fact
only sets us inquiring what the value of the prescription
is; and when we find ourselves assured that all the
defects of the various classes of our society are to be
corrected, and that all the unsatisfied 'claims' upon
them - the 'claim of beauty,' the 'claim of manners,' and
all the rest of it - are to obtain their due satisfaction
through a reform of our system of secondary education, we
are irresistibly reminded of a homely apologue anent the
superstitious value attached by a certain practitioner of
a very ancient and respectable handicraft to the raw
material of his industry. In this as in other matters we
see how Mr. Arnold's persistent determination to play the
constructive reformer - a part for which he had no natural
aptitude - enticed him beyond the limits of that critical
function in which his true strength lay.

But much as we may regret the perversity, if that be
not too harsh a word, which directed so large a portion of
Mr. Arnold's intellectual energies in later years away
from the natural bent of his genius, it would be ungrac-
ious not to acknowledge the indirect benefit which arose
from this very dispersion of the rays of that penetrating
intelligence. He could not touch any subject without
throwing some light upon it. Everything that he wrote
was suggestive, if too little of it was satisfying; and
though his determination to avoid the commonplace view of
every subject was undoubtedly a snare - since the commonplace, and even what he would have called the Philistine
view, is more often the true view than he was at all prepared to admit - it was also, and as undoubtedly, in many
instances a source of strength. A deliverance of Mr.
Arnold's on any question, social, moral, or political, as
well as literary - was always the most admirable touchstone of received opinions. None of us could be quite
sure of our reason for the faith that is in us on any
matter till it had stood the test of his refined and
searching criticism. More of us have been compelled by
him than by any other writer of our age and country to
review and revise our judgments upon most subjects of
human interest; and not only the world of literature, but
the infinitely larger world of unexpressed thought and
feeling and unembodied imagination, is sensibly the
poorer for his loss.

56. JOHN BURROUGHS, MATTHEW ARNOLD'S CRITICISM, 'CENTURY
MAGAZINE'

June 1888, xxxvi, 185-94

John Burroughs (1837-1921) came from an old New England
family. As a young man he was strongly influenced by
Emerson, and in 1863 he met Walt Whitman, who was to be
a life-long friend as well as the subject of Burroughs's
first book (1867). Burroughs heard Arnold lecture during
his first American tour and wrote to Whitman: 'Arnold
looked hearty and strong, and spoke in a foggy, misty
English voice, that left the outlines of his sentences
pretty obscure....' The following essay is an overview of
Arnold's collected works, just then published in the USA.
Burroughs sees Arnold as a Hellene, always testing ideas
and institutions against a cultural ideal. Arnold may not
be 'a man to build upon', but he is 'a critical force, a
force of pure reason', and therefore of great value on both
sides of the Atlantic.

Readers who know Matthew Arnold only as an occasional contributor to British periodical literature, or as a lecturer
during his brief tour in this country, in the fall and
winter of 1883-84, will do well, before they make up their
minds about him, to give him a hearing as he appears in his
collected works, recently published by Macmillan & Co. A
writer who has a distinct and well-defined point of view of
his own, like Arnold, suffers by being read fragmentarily,
or by the single essay or discourse. His effect is cumu-
lative; he hits a good many times in the same place, and
his work as a whole makes a deeper impression than any
single essay of his would seem to warrant. He is not in
any sense one of those random and capricious minds that
often cut such a brilliant figure in periodical literature,
but the distinguishing thing about him is that he stands
for a definite and well-grounded idea or principle, an idea
which gives a certain unity and simplicity to his entire
work. The impression that a fragmentary and desultory
reading of Arnold is apt to give one, namely, that he is
one of the scorners, a man of 'a high look, and a proud
heart,' gradually wears away as one grows familiar with the
main currents of his teachings. He does not indeed turn
out to be a large, hearty, magnetic man, but he proves to
be a thoroughly serious and noble one, whose calmness and

elevation are of great value. His writings, as now published, in a uniform edition, embrace ten volumes.... Of
this body of work the eight volumes of prose are pure criticism, and by criticism, when applied to Arnold, we must
mean the scientific passion for pure truth, the passion for
seeing the thing exactly as it is carried into all fields.
'I wish to decide nothing as of my own authority,' he says
in one of his earlier essays; 'the great art of criticism
is to get one's self out of the way and to let humanity
decide.' 'A free play of mind' is a frequent phrase with
him, and well describes much of his own criticism. He
would play the rôle of a disinterested observer. Apropos
of his political and social criticisms, he says:

> I do not profess to be a politician, but simply one of
> a disinterested class of observers, who, with no organ-
> ized and embodied set of supporters to please, set
> themselves to observe honestly and to report faithfully
> the state and prospects of our civilization.

He urges that criticism in England has been too
'directly polemical and controversial'; that it has been
made to subserve interests not its own; the interest of
party, of a sect, of a theory, or of some practical and
secondary consideration. His own effort has been to
restore it to its 'pure intellectual sphere' and to keep
its high aim constantly before him, 'which is to keep man
from a self-satisfaction which is retarding and vulgarizing; to lead him towards perfection, by making his mind
dwell upon what is excellent in itself, and the absolute
beauty and fitness of things.'

Arnold is preëminently a critical force, a force of clear
reason and of steady discernment. He is not an author
whom we read for the man's sake or for the flavor of his
personality, for this is not always agreeable, but for his
unfailing intelligence and critical acumen; and because,
to borrow a sentence of Goethe, he helps us to 'attain
certainty and security in the appreciation of things
exactly as they are.' Everywhere in his books we are
brought under the influence of a mind which indeed does not
fill and dilate us, but which clears our vision, which sets
going a process of crystallization in our thoughts, and
brings our knowledge, on a certain range of subjects, to a
higher state of clearness and purity.
     Let us admit that he is not a man to build upon; he is
in no sense a founder; he lacks the broad, paternal, sympathetic human element that the first order of men possess.

He lays the emphasis upon the more select, high-bred
qualities. All his sympathies are with the influences
which make for correctness, for discipline, for taste,
for perfection, rather than those that favor power, freedom, originality, individuality, and the more heroic and
primary qualities. The more vital and active forces of
English literature of our century have been mainly forces
of expansion and revolution, or Protestant forces; our
most puissant voices have been voices of dissent, and have
been a stimulus to individuality, separatism, and to
independence. But here is a voice of another order; a
voice closely allied to the best spirit of Catholicism;
one from which we will not learn hero-worship, or Puritanism, or non-conformity, or catch the spark of enthusiasm, or revolution, but from which we learn the beauty of
urbanity, and the value of clear and fresh ideas.

It is not difficult to get at Arnold's point of view;
it is stated or implied in nearly every page of his works.
It is the point of view of Greek culture and Greek civilization. From this ground the whole body of his critical
work, religious, political, and literary, is launched.
His appeal is constantly made to the classic type of mind
and character.

He divides the forces that move the world into two
grand divisions - Hellenism and Hebraism, the Greek idea
and the Jewish idea, the power of intellect and the power
of conscience. 'The uppermost idea with Hellenism is to
see things as they really are; the uppermost idea with
Hebraism is conduct and obedience. Nothing can do away
with this ineffaceable difference. The Greek quarrel with
the body and its desires is that they hinder right thinking; the Hebrew quarrel with them is that they hinder
right acting.' 'An unclouded clearness of mind, an un-
impeded play of thought,' is the aim of the one; 'strictness of conscience,' fidelity to principle, is the main-
spring of the other. As, in this classification, Carlyle
would stand for unmitigated Hebraism, so Arnold himself
stands for pure Hellenism; as the former's Hebraism upon
principle was backed up by the Hebraic type of mind, its
grandeur, its stress of conscience, its opulent imagination, its cry for judgment and justice, etc., so Arnold's
conviction of the superiority of Hellenism as a remedy for
modern ills is backed up by the Hellenic type of mind, its
calmness, its lucidity, its sense of form and measure.
Indeed, Arnold is probably the purest classic writer that
English literature, as yet, has to show; classic not
merely in the repose and purity of his style, but in the
unity and simplicity of his mind. What primarily distinguishes the antique mind from the modern mind is its

more fundamental singleness and wholeness. It is not
marked by the same specialization and development on particular lines. Our highly artificial and complex modern
life leads to separatism; to not only a division of labor,
but almost to a division of man himself. With the
ancients, religion and politics, literature and sciences,
poetry and prophecy, were one. These things had not yet
been set apart from each other and differentiated. When
to this we add vital unity and simplicity, the love of
beauty, and the sense of measure and proportion, we have
the classic mind of Greece and the secret of the power and
charm of those productions which have so long ruled supreme in the world of literature and art. Arnold's mind
has this classic unity and wholeness. With him religion,
politics, literature, and science are one, and that one is
comprehended under the name of culture. Culture means the
perfect and equal development of man on all sides.

From the point of view of Greek culture and the ideal of
Greek life, there is perhaps very little in the achievements of the English race, or in the ideals which it
cherishes, that would not be pronounced the work of barbarians. From the Apollonarian standpoint Christianity
itself, with its war upon our natural instincts, is a
barbarous religion. But no born Hellene from the age of
Pericles could pronounce a severer judgment upon the
England of to-day than Arnold has in his famous classification of his countrymen into Barbarians, Philistines, and
Populace, an upper class materialized, a middle class vulgarized, and a lower class brutalized. Arnold has not the
Hellenic joyousness, youthfulness, and spontaneity. His
is a 'sad lucidity of soul,' whereas the Greek had a joy-
ous lucidity of soul. 'O Solon, Solon!' said the priest of
Egypt, 'you Greeks are always children.' But the Englishman has the Greek passion for symmetry, totality, and the
Hellenic abhorrence of the strained, the fantastic, the
obscure. His are not merely the classical taste and pre-
dilections of a scholar, but of an alert, fearless, and
thorough-going critic of life; a man who dare lay his
hands on the British constitution itself and declare that
'with its compromises, its love of facts, its horror of
theory, its studied avoidance of clear thought, it sometimes looks a colossal machine for the manufacture of
Philistines.' Milton was swayed by the Greek ideals in
his poetry, but they took no vital hold of his life; his
Puritanism and his temper in his controversial writings
are the furthest possible remove from the serenity and
equipoise of the classic standards. But Arnold, a much

less poetic force certainly than Milton, is animated by
the spirit of Hellenism on all occasions; it is the shap-
ing and inspiring spirit of his life. It is not a dictum
with him, but a force. Yet his books are thoroughly of
to-day, thoroughly occupied with current men and measures,
and covered with current names and allusions.

Another form which Arnold's Hellenism takes is that it
begets in him what we may call the spirit of institutionalism, as opposed to the spirit of individualism. Greek
culture centers in institutions, and the high character
of their literary and artistic productions was the expression of qualities which did not merely belong to individuals here and there, but were current in the nation as a
whole. With the Greek the state was supreme. He lived
and died for the state. He had no private, separate life
and occupation, as has the modern man. The arts, architecture, sculpture, existed mainly for public uses. There
was probably no domestic life, no country life, no individual enterprises, as we know them. The individual was
subordinated. Their greatest men were banished or poi-
soned from a sort of jealousy of the state. The state
could not endure such rivals. Their games, their pas-
times, were national institutions. Public sentiment on
all matters was clear and strong. There was a common
standard, an unwritten law of taste, to which poets,
artists, orators, appealed. Not till Athens began to
decay did great men appear, who, like Socrates, had no
influence in the state. This spirit of institutionalism
is strong in Matthew Arnold; and it is not merely an idea
which he has picked up from the Greek, but is the inevitable outcropping of his inborn Hellenism. This alone
places him in opposition to his countrymen, who are suspicious of the state and of state action, and who give
full swing to the spirit of individualism. It even places
him in hostility to Protestantism, or to the spirit which
begat it, to say nothing of the dissenting churches. It
makes him indifferent to the element of personalism, the
flavor of character, the quality of unique individual
genius, wherever found in art, literature, or religion.
It is one secret of his preference of the establishment
over the dissenting churches. The dissenter stands for
personal religion, religion as a private and individual
experience; the established churches stand for institu-
tional religion, or religion as a public and organized
system of worship; and when the issue is between the two,
Arnold will always be found on the side of institutionalism. He always takes up for the state against the

individual, for public and established forms against private and personal dissent and caprice. 'It was by no
means in accordance with the nature of the Hellenes,' says
Dr. Curtius, 'mentally to separate and view in the light
of contrast such institutions as the state and religion,
which, in reality, everywhere most intimately pervaded one
another.'...

Arnold always distrusts the individual; he sees in him
mainly a bundle of whims and caprices. The individual is
one-sided, fantastical, headstrong, narrow. He distrusts
all individual enterprises in the way of schools, colleges, churches, charities; and, like his teacher, Aristotle, pleads for state action in all these matters.
'Culture,' he says (and by culture he means Hellenism),
'will not let us rivet our attention upon any one man and
his doing'; it directs our attention rather to the
'natural current there is in human affairs,' and assigns
'to systems and to system makers a smaller share in the
bent of human destiny than their friends like.'

The modern movement seems to me peculiarly a movement of
individualism, a movement favoring the greater freedom and
and growth of the individual, as opposed to outward
authority and its lodgment in institutions. It is this
movement which has given a distinctive character to the
literature of our century, a movement in letters which
Goethe did more to forward than any other man – Goethe,
who said that in art and poetry personal genius is everything, and that 'in the great work the great person is
always present as the great factor.' Arnold seems not to
share this feeling; he does not belong to this movement.
His books give currency to another order of ideas. He
subordinates the individual, and lays the emphasis on culture and the claims of the higher standards. He says the
individual has no natural rights, but only duties. We
never find him insisting upon originality, self-reliance,
character, independence, but quite the contrary, on conformity and obedience. He says that at the bottom of the
trouble of all the English people lies the notion of its
being the prime right and happiness for each of us to
affirm himself and to be doing as he likes. One of his
earliest and most effective essays was to show the value
of academies, of a central and authoritative standard of
taste to a national literature; and in all his subsequent
writings the academic note has been struck and adhered to.
With him right reason and the authority of the state are
one. 'In our eyes,' he says, 'the very framework and
exterior order of the state, whoever may administer the

state, is sacred.' 'Every one of us,' he again says, 'has
the idea of country, as a sentiment; hardly any one of us
has the idea of *the state*, as a working power. And why?
Because we habitually live in our ordinary selves, which do
not carry us beyond the ideas and wishes of the class to
which we happen to belong.' Which is but saying because we
are wrapped so closely about by our individualism. His
remedy for the democratic tendencies of the times, tendencies he does not regret, is an increase of the dignity and
authority of the state. The danger of English democracy
is, he says, 'that it will have far too much its own way,
and be left far too much to itself.' He adds, with great
force and justness, that 'Nations are not truly great
solely because the individuals composing them are numerous, free, and active, but they are great when these
numbers, this freedom, and this activity are employed in
the service of an ideal higher than that of an ordinary
man, taken by himself.' Or, as Aristotle says, these
things must be in 'obedience to some intelligent principle,
and some right regulation, which has the power of enforcing its decrees.'...

There seems to be nothing in Hellenism that suggests
Catholicism, and yet evidently it is Arnold's classical
feeling for institutions that gives him his marked Catholic
bias. The Catholic Church is a great institution, the
greatest and oldest in the world. It makes and always has
made short work of the individual....

It appeals to Arnold by reason of these things, and it
appeals to him by reason of its great names, its poets,
artists, statesmen, preachers, scholars; its imposing
ritual, its splendid architecture, its culture. It has
been the conserver of letters. For centuries the priests
were the only scholars, and its ceremonial is a kind of
petrified literature. Arnold clearly speaks for himself,
or from his own bias, when he says that 'the man of imagination, nay, and the philosopher too, in spite of her propensity to burn him, will always have a weakness for the
Catholic Church'; 'it is because of the rich treasures of
human life which have been stored within her pale.'
Indeed, there is a distinct flavor of Catholicism about
nearly all of Matthew Arnold's writings. One cannot always
put his finger on it; it is in the air, it is in that cool,
haughty impersonalism, that *ex cathedrâ* tone, that contempt for dissenters, that genius for form, that spirit
of organization. His mental tone and temper ally him to
Cardinal Newman, who seems to have exerted a marked influence upon him, and who is still, he says, a great name to
the imagination. Yet he says Newman 'has adopted, for the
doubts and difficulties which beset men's minds to-day, a

solution, which to speak frankly, is impossible.' What,
therefore, repels Arnold in Catholicism, and keeps him
without its fold, is its 'ultramontanism, sacerdotalism,
and superstition.' Its cast-iron dogmas and its bigotry
are too much for his Hellenic spirit; but no more so than
are the dogmas and bigotry of the Protestant churches. It
is clear enough that he would sooner be a Catholic than a
Presbyterian or a Methodist.

Arnold's Hellenism is the source of both his weakness
and his strength; his strength, because it gives him a
principle that cannot be impeached. In all matters of
taste and culture the Greek standards are the last and
highest court of appeal. In no other race and time has
life been so rounded and full and invested with the same
charm. 'They were freer than other mortal races,' says
Professor Curtius, 'from all that hinders and oppresses
the motions of the mind.'

It is the source of his weakness, or ineffectualness,
because he has to do with an unclassical age and unclassical people. It is interesting and salutary to have the
Greek standards applied to modern politics and religion,
and to the modern man, but the application makes little or
no impression save on the literary classes. Well may
Arnold have said, in his speech at The Authors Club in New
York, that only the literary class had understood and sustained him. The other classes have simply been irritated
or bewildered by him. His tests do not appeal to them.
The standards which the philosopher, or the political economist, or the religious teacher brings, impress them more.

The force and value of the main drift of Arnold's criticism are probably greater in England than in this country,
because, in the first place, the cramped, inflexible,
artificial and congested state of things which prevails in
England does not prevail to anything like the same extent
among us; and because, in the second place, with us the
conscience of the race needs stimulating more than the
reason needs clearing. We are much more hospitable to
ideas than is the British Philistine, but, as a people, we
are by no means correspondingly sensitive and developed on
the side of conduct. We need Hebraizing more than we need
Hellenizing; we need Carlyle more than we need Arnold.
Yet we need Arnold too.

His recent utterances upon us and our civilization
seem to me just and timely. They are in keeping with the
general drift of his teachings, and could not well be
other than they are. That beauty and distinction, that
reverence and truthfulness and humility and good manners

are at a low ebb in this country – who can deny it? and
that our newspaper press partakes of this condition and
is, in a measure, responsible for it – who can deny that?
   Moreover, the questions of culture, of right reason,
and of a just mean and measure in all things, are always
vital questions, and no man of our time has spoken so
clear and forcible a word upon them as has Matthew Arnold.

57. MOWBRAY MORRIS, UNSIGNED ESSAY, 'QUARTERLY REVIEW'

October 1888, clxvii, 398–426

Mowbray Walter Morris (1847–1911) was an established man
of letters, contributor to periodicals, and editor of
'Macmillan's Magazine'. His long essay in the 'Quarterly'
begins with a list of the books he thinks are Arnold's
best: the two volumes of Homer criticism, 'Essays in
Criticism, First Series', and the collected poems. His
bias is obvious. Arnold's reputation would be 'higher' if
he had never written on theology; his social criticism is
largely concerned with 'ephemeral topics'. His true
sphere is literary criticism and he should have stayed
there.
   The portion of this essay on Arnold's verse will be
found in 'Matthew Arnold, The Poetry' (No. 33).

Mr. Arnold was not one of those writers of whom it can be
said that the greatest of his works was his whole work
taken together. Byron, whom he has praised and judged so
finely, is capable, he says, 'when received absolutely,'
of being tiresome. A poet like Byron, and a writer the
bulk of whose production was in prose, and critical
instead of creative, do not of course stand on quite the
same plane of comparison. Nevertheless Mr. Arnold, when
received absolutely, is also in his way capable of being
tiresome. But he is capable of that unpardonable sin not,
as Byron was, from haste or carelessness, not from the
reckless exercise of great powers or from the prodigal
fertility of his production; he is capable of it because
he too often chose to exercise his talent upon subjects
with whose conditions and environment he was but imperfectly acquainted, and which therefore, to use his own

favourite and famous phrase, he was unable to see as they
really were.

Chief among this imperfect work stand his theological
writings. True it is, we know, that for many of his
admirers they give their author his chief distinction and
influence. We have even heard it said that he himself
regarded them with peculiar satisfaction, and believed his
position in English literature to be most securely founded
in them. This may be so. Men, even men in whom the critical faculty is so native and well-trained as it was in
Matthew Arnold, are rarely the best judges of their own
work. It may also be that the opposition which this part
of his writings received, and the strong expressions of
distaste and even anger it so often evoked, may have drawn
them closer to him, partly from the spirit of contradiction, which was not wanting in him, and partly from that
remorseful sense of pity which sometimes moves parents to
lavish their warmest affections on the ugliest and most
wayward of their offspring. Yet not for these reasons can
we change our opinion; and that opinion is that, had every
line of these theological writings remained unwritten,
their author's claim on the gratitude of his own generations and the regard of the next would have stood far
higher than it now stands or is likely to stand.

No one now doubts that Mr. Arnold believed himself to
be influenced only by the purest and most lofty motives.
He has quoted with admiration Buffon's persistent refusal
to answer all attacks made upon him, and declared his
intention of following that great example. 'I never have
replied,' he said, 'I never will reply, to any literary
assailant; in such encounters tempers are lost, the world
laughs, and truth is not served.' It must be owned that
Mr. Arnold kept this resolution more strictly in the
spirit than in the letter. He never lost his temper nor
made the world laugh at him, but he generally found an
opportunity for giving his assailants - and he had his
fair share of them - a shrewd nip or two for their pains.

The tone of certitude with which he seemed to too many of
his hearers to propound his own dogmas, the unguarded
language which he too often used of the dogmas of others,
have undoubtedly been an embarrassment to him. Neither
men's hearts nor their tempers are as a rule made better
by labelling them with contemptuous nicknames, or by holding up to ridicule all they have been taught to hold most
sacred and most dear.

We have not the mind to attempt any discussion of the substance of his theological teaching. It was no new thing he
aimed at. More than a hundred years before him, one of his
predecessors in the Chair of Poetry had led the way to the
contemplation of what Milman calls the great religious
problem, - the possibility of discovering a test for distinguishing the eternal truths of the Bible from their
imaginative framework. Although we have spoken severely of
the lapses from good taste and manners which it led him
into, we are far from denying that the better qualities of
his mind cannot also be found in it. He was often eloquent, acute, and felicitous; many of his rebukes were
just, many of his arguments sound. But as Carlyle was
forced with groaning to confess: 'Wreckage is swift;
rebuilding is slow and distant.' Mr. Arnold has supplied
a good many foolish persons of both sexes with much idle
chatter and many smart catch-words: he has probably also,
which is the inevitable pity of all these processes of dis-
integration, perplexed and set adrift many unstable minds;
but that he has supplied one reasonable being, capable of
thinking for himself, with a substitute for the system
which he wished to abandon, it is impossible seriously to
suppose.

Mr. Arnold's political and social criticism, which must
also be classed in his imperfect work, comes under no such
ban. It was always amusing, often sensible, rarely if
ever ill-natured. But a great part of it was necessarily
concerned with ephemeral topics, with the subjects of the
hour which passed with it, and which, moreover, perhaps
did not even in their hour possess that large and national
importance which their critic seemed to wish them to take.
The Oracles of the Bald-faced Stag, and of that garret in
Grub Street which Arminius used to fill with his tobacco-
smoke, and his diatribes on the freaks of the Marylebone
Vestry and the oratory of that politician whom men in
those day called Mr. Lowe, have long gone very dumb: the
smile their memory now evokes is but faint and transitory.
All this part of Mr. Arnold's work was in truth nothing
more than a superior order of journalism, and each generation will provide its own journalism. The coming generations will be lucky to find any so good and entertaining
as Mr. Arnold often gave to his; but if they cannot, they
will at least take what they can get - they will not turn
back to the files of the past. And it is precisely this
quality of journalism which secured instant recognition
for such books as 'Friendship's Garland' and 'Culture and
Anarchy', while it denies them permanence. Their party-

spirit, - for in this sphere of criticism Mr. Arnold was, in truth, for all his professions of tolerance, as sheer a partizan as any downright politician of the newspapers or the platform, - it was this party-spirit, we say, that gave piquancy and a seeming force to his utterances. The most part of mankind do not care to be reasoned with, to have all the sides of a question presented to them. Few men have now the time to think long and logically on any matter; they have rarely time to think at all. They prefer to have their thinking done for them, and not too severely; they wish to have that part of their minds which they can spare for the things of the intellect, lightly stimulated, as by the Flappers of Laputa, not rudely shaken by too stern and violent a preacher. In a word, Mr. Arnold may be credited with having performed for a large part of his generation the office it pleased him to say that Macaulay performed for his: to hundreds of men he has proved a great civilizer. But man, when civilized, finds wants he was unconscious of in his savage state; and in matters of politics, as in theological matters, it is at least doubtful whether Mr. Arnold has succeeded in supplying those wants.

Even among those who have neglected this part of his work, there is a general understanding that Mr. Arnold's universal panacea for the failures and shortcomings of our nation was something he called *culture*, - no new word indeed, though it seems, like so many other of his catch-words, to have fallen on men's ears with the shock of a surprise.

True culture will avail in the practice of politics as much as in criticizing new books or in lecturing on *belles lettres*; but it will not avail without a practical know-ledge and experience of politics, or without the power, which only that knowledge and experience can give, of applying what has been learned from the study of the best that has been thought and said in the world to the occa-sions of politics as they arise. All the reading in the world, however well diversified, however ready for appli-cation, will not avail without this. And it is because he is as a rule so entirely wanting in this power, that the man of letters is, to borrow Mr. Arnold's own words, in such peculiar danger of talking at random when he moves off his own ground into the field of politics. And really, when one reflects how desperately at random, even on their own ground, nine-tenths of our professed poli-ticians are in the habit of talking, it is not surprising to find a man of letters who lacks this advantage falling

into the same confusion. But what has his culture taught
him, if not the wisdom of abstaining from matters which he
does not clearly understand? True culture should surely
teach the man of letters, as sad experience taught Jona-
than Oldbuck, not to publish his tract till he has
examined the thing to the bottom.

Interesting then as Mr. Arnold often was when discussing political and social, and even theological questions,
acute, just, and eloquent as he often was, it was not in
any of those spheres that the true exercise of his talent
lay. In writing on Amiel's 'Journal Intime' which had
been so extravagantly praised for its philosophy, for its
powers of speculative intuition, its profound psychological interest, he points out that these critics had altogether missed Amiel's true value, and that even Amiel himself had no clear sight of it. Amiel's true vocation, he
says, was that of a literary critic. Matthew Arnold was
something more than this, but who can doubt that the true
sphere for the exercise of his critical faculty lay not in
politics, nor in theology, nor in social life, but in
literature?

It is true that even here he could be, on occasion, a
little whimsical and perverse. 'Our eternal enemy
caprice' got hold of him even here sometimes, earnestly as
he exhorted us to be on our guard against her. In his
anxiety to make his meaning clear, to press his point
home, he sometimes carried his argument a little too far,
or spoiled it by an anticlimax or a paradox, an unjust or
irrelevant illustration. But all these little aberrations
were on what may be called the side issues of criticism.
On the broad general lines he never went wrong. It is not
always necessary to agree with his judgments, to admire the
processes by which he reaches them; all lovers of good
literature, all lovers of poetry especially, will prefer
sometimes to make their own criticisms, will sometimes
feel it impossible to put away the dictates of their heart
for the cooler verdicts of the judgment. But no one, we
think, who has any sense and feeling for good literature,
will doubt how wisely in the main he loved it, how soundly
he judged it, how truly and nobly he praised it.

It was not that he made any new discoveries in criticism, enunciated any fresh theories, or laid down any
fresh laws. That is not to be done. True it is, as he
has warned literary critics in the words of Menander, that
'laws are admirable things, but he who keeps his eye too
closely fixed upon them runs the risk of becoming,' - a
purist, as he has politely paraphrased the Greek word for
this occasion; but none the less has criticism its laws,
and those laws were settled long years before Mr. Arnold

took up his parable. But he recalled the spirit of criticism to its proper functions at a time when it seemed to
have grown rather forgetful of them; he reminded it that
those functions were after all founded on the eternal laws
of truth and beauty, and not on the mere caprice of personal sentiment or the whim of the hour. He diversified
them, and applied them to a variety of occasions to which
their relation had not been suspected; he pointed out
where they had been wrongly applied or too closely
applied; he at once widened and restricted their application, - restricted it, that is to say, by showing where
they needed to be applied with limitations, or with an
enlarged or changed interpretation according to the
altered needs and broader knowledge of the time. And all
this he did in a manner singularly fresh and piquant, and
entirely unlike any other that had gone before it in English literature. The style and the method of the 'Lectures on Translating Homer' and of the 'Essays in Criticism' may truly be said to mark an era in English criticism. Happy indeed was Oxford to have caught the first
notes of this fresh new voice!

As is always the case with good critics, Mr. Arnold
worked more by indirection and suggestion than by sheer
delivery of judgment. There is hardly a page of the Lectures which is not fruitful of suggestions not only to
every translator of Homer, but to every young student of
poetry. All those passages, for example, in which he
dwells on the plainness and naturalness of Homer's
thought, on the directness and nobility of his language,
and on the imperative necessity for the translator to
reproduce these qualities, to avoid whatever is fanciful
and grotesque and therefore not truly noble, even by the
occasional sacrifice of mere verbal fidelity wherever too
much literalness might give an odd and unnatural effect;
in which he illustrates the value of the Bible and Shakespeare as mines of diction for the translator who knows
how to discriminate truly between what will suit him and
what will not; - such passages are not merely inestimable
in their practical value for the translator, but contain
the soundest possible criticism on the essential differences between ancient and modern poetry.

In his later writings his style showed a tendency to become diffuse and fanciful, almost, one is tempted to say,
at times grotesque. This tendency grew out of a partial
failure of ideas; and this failure he sought to conceal,
as Carlyle also sought to conceal it, by embroidering his
style with fantastic words and phrases, by repeating

himself again and again, and especially by a superabundant
use of raillery. Full of grace and playfulness as his
raillery was in its freshness, and when judiciously and
temperately applied, as he applied it in his earlier writings, it latterly grew capable of being tiresome. The
curse he pronounced on Carlyle recoiled on his own head;
'his sallies, as a staple of literary work, become wearisome.' But in his prime he could use it with singular
felicity and effect, and it is not a quality for which
English writers are as a rule conspicuous. Especially did
he excel in the use of the Socratic irony, as it is called,
- in the assumption, as Mr. Grote explains it, of the
character of an ignorant learner asking information from
one who knew better than himself. And this quality, when
sparingly exhibited, was of great use to him; it gave zest
and novelty to his writing, and cleared it, as it cleared
the conversation of its first great master, from didactic
pedantry and the bias of an advocate. But, to quote again
Mr. Grote's words on Socrates, 'after he had acquired
celebrity, this uniform profession of ignorance in debate
was usually construed as mere affectation, and those who
merely heard him occasionally, without penetrating into his
intimacy, often suspected that he was amusing himself with
ingenious paradox.'

His style at its best had indeed a rare and irresistible
charm. A dangerous style for a model, no doubt, easy to
exaggerate into burlesque, as are all mannered styles; but
in the hands of its own master full of grace, ease, and
vivacity, capable of genuine eloquence and tenderness, and
withal, in its prime, as clear and unconfused as Swift's
or Goldsmith's. And then the master of all these graces
deliberately threw them away upon subjects assuredly not in
themselves unworthy of him, but which his partial and
whimsical treatment of them made to seem unworthy of him.
Inexplicable fatuity! A fatuity only to be paralleled by
that of the princess in the Eastern story, who left her
beautiful palace and the lord who loved her, to share the
filthy hovel of her negro paramour, to endure his blows
and curses, and to eat of the scraps off his plate!

58.   A. E. HOUSMAN, INTRODUCTORY LECTURE

1892

Alfred Edward Housman (1859-1936) was in his thirty-
fourth year, a newly arrived Professor of Latin at University College, London, when, according to a university tradition, he was invited to give the opening lecture of the
school year. His topic is learning for its own sake, and,
in this brief comment, he finds Arnold a perfect example
of a non-professional whose observations are worth more
than those of the exact scholar.

Who are the great critics of the classical literatures,
the critics with real insight into the classical spirit,
the critics who teach with authority and not as the
scribes?   They are such men as Lessing or Goethe or
Matthew Arnold, scholars no doubt, but not scholars of
minute or profound learning.   Matthew Arnold went to his
grave under the impression that the proper way to spell
lacrima was to spell it with a *y*, and that the words
ἀνδρὸς παιδοφόνοιο ποτὶ στόμα χεῖπ' ὀρέγεσθαι meant 'to
carry to my lips the hand of him that slew my son'.   We
pedants know better: we spell *lacrima* with an *i*, and we
know that the verse of Homer really means 'to reach forth
my hand to the chin of him that slew my son'.   But when it
comes to literary criticism, heap up in one scale all the
literary criticism that the whole nation of professed
scholars ever wrote, and drop into the other the thin
green volume of Matthew Arnold's 'Lectures on Translating
Homer', which has long been out of print because the
British public does not care to read it, and the first
scale, as Milton says, will straight fly up and kick the
beam.

59. LESLIE STEPHEN ON MATTHEW ARNOLD, 'NATIONAL AND
ENGLISH REVIEW'

22 December 1893, xxii, 458-77

Leslie Stephen (1832-1904) began life as a tutor at Cambridge, and was ordained a priest in 1859 in order to
retain a fellowship. He had been teaching at Cambridge
for over ten years when his reading in theology and
philosophy led him to question Christianity. In 1864 he
gave up his fellowship and the religious life, moving to
London to live by his pen. Through the assistance of his
brother Fitzjames Stephen (see No. 3) he was soon writing
regularly for the 'Saturday', the 'Pall Mall Gazette', the
'Cornhill', and 'Fraser's'. Stephen was often Arnold's
antagonist, attacking his work from the agnostic point of
view. In fact it was Stephen who, as new editor of the
'Cornhill', stopped publication of the papers which were
to become 'Literature and Dogma'. But following Arnold's
death Stephen wrote the following assessment, which in
its combination of witty irony and generous respect is one
of the best late Victorian estimates of Arnold's achievement.

When your Principal asked me to select a topic for a lecture, I replied, in a moment of weakness, that I would
speak of Matthew Arnold. The choice was partly suggested
by an observation made on a recent visit to the United
States. It struck me that Arnold's merits were more fully
recognized there than in his own country; though I hope
that here, too, they do not lack appreciation. American
opinion is probably not infallible. Still, fame on the
other side of the Atlantic establishes a certain presumption of excellence. It proves that a man's influence was
not created by, and may sometimes indicate that it has
been partly obscured by, our local prejudices. At any
rate, the observation suggested some thoughts, which, it
occurred to me, might be worth submitting to an English
audience. Well, I have been ever since repenting my decision. The reasons against my enterprise are indeed so
strong that I am now almost afraid to mention them. In
the first place, I knew Arnold personally, though I cannot
boast of having known him so intimately as to be provided
with reminiscences. At one of my meetings with him,
indeed, I do remember a remark which was made, and which

struck me at the moment as singularly happy. Unfortunately, it was a remark made by me and not by him.
Nothing, therefore, should induce me to report it,
although, if you attend to what I am about to say, you
will perhaps hear it, and, I hope, recognize it by this
description. But, though our acquaintance was not so
close as I could have wished, it left me with a singularly
strong impression of Arnold's personal charm. Though the
objects of my worship were to him mere wooden idols;
though I once satisfactorily confuted him in an article,
now happily forgotten by myself and everybody else; though
I was once even his Editor, and forced in that capacity to
reject certain articles, on grounds, of course, quite
apart from literary merit; yet he was always not only
courteous but cordial, and, I may almost say, affectionate. He had that obvious sweetness of nature, which it is
impossible not to recognize and not to love. Though in
controversy he took and gave many shrewd blows, he always
received them with a courtesy, indicative not of mere
policy or literary tact, but of dislike to inflicting pain
and of incapacity for having any tolerably decent antagonist in flesh and blood. He was on excellent terms with
the classes whose foibles he ridiculed most unsparingly,
and even his own foibles were attractive. He had his
vanity; but vanity is a quality to which moralists have
never done justice. As distinguished from conceit, from
a sullen conviction of your own superiority, it often
implies a craving for sympathy and a confidence in the
sincerity of your fellows, which is in the main, as his
certainly was, an amiable and attractive characteristic.
If it savoured of intellectual coxcombry, it was redeemed
by a simplicity and social amenity which showed that his
nature had resisted the ossifying process which makes most
of us commonplace and prosaic in later life. Now, I dislike criticism of personal acquaintance. 'I love Robertson,' said Johnson, 'and I won't talk of his books.' I
feel the same, in a rather different sense, about Arnold.
But, besides this, I have a difficulty to which I must
refer at the risk of giving an impression of mock-modesty.
I feel, that is, the great difficulty of speaking to purpose of a man whose intellectual type was so different to
my own. Had Arnold been called upon to pronounce judgment
upon me, he must, however reluctantly, have set me down as
a Philistine. It is a word which I dislike; but I cannot
deny that, in his phraseology, it would be indisputably
appropriate. Sometimes, shrinking from a title which certainly is not flattering to one's vanity, I try to regard
the difference between us as somehow corresponding to the
difference between our Universities. Arnold was a typical

Oxford man in the days when Oxford was stirred by the
'movement' of which it is supposed to be proper to speak
respectfully. Now, at Cambridge, we despised 'movements';
we plodded through our Euclid or our Greek grammar,
scorned sentimentalism and aesthetic revivals, and, if we
took any interest in speculative matters, read John Stuart
Mill, and were sound Utilitarians and orthodox Political
Economists. Cambridge, as you are aware, is the right
place, not Oxford; and a hard-headed senior wrangler is a
superior being to a flighty double first-class man. But
perhaps our well-founded knowledge that we were in the
right path made us rather unfitted to judge of our sister
University. We thought her impulsive, ill-balanced, too
easily hurried into the pursuit of all kinds of theological, philosophical, and literary chimeras; and therefore
were unjust to her substantial merits and even to the
intellectual impulse which, with all its vagaries, was yet
better than stagnation. After all, I am probably only
trying to hint at the fundamental difference, not between
Oxford and Cambridge, but between the poetic and the prosaic mind. We - for I may perhaps assume that some of you
belong, like me, to the prosaic faction - feel, when dealing with such a man as Arnold, at a loss. He has intuitions where we have only calculations; he can strike out
vivid pictures where we try laboriously to construct dia-
grams; he shows at once a type where our rough statistical
and analytical tables fail to reveal more than a few tangible facts; he perceives the spirit and finer essence of
an idea where it seems to slip through our coarser
fingers, leaving only a residuum of sophistical paradox.
In the long run, the prosaic weigher and measurer has one
advantage: he is generally in the right. His tests may
be coarser, but they are more decisive and less dependent
upon his own fancies; but, when he tries to understand his
rival; to explain how at a bound the intuitive perception
has reached conclusions after which he can only hobble on
limping feet, he is apt to make a bungle of it: to despise
the power in which he is so deficient: and probably to
suggest unreasonable doubts as to its reality and value.
    Here is, I feel, my real weakness in speaking of
Arnold; for I may certainly say at once that Arnold, whatever else he was, was a genuine poet. I do not dispute
the general opinion of the day that there were only two
poets of the first rank in his generation. Arnold must,
no doubt, take a lower place than Tennyson and Browning.
But, though I cannot avoid falling into the method of comparison, I do not accept with satisfaction the apparently
implied doctrine that poets can be satisfactorily
arranged in order of merit. We cannot give so many marks

for style and so many for pathos or descriptive power. It
is best to look at each poet by himself. We need only distinguish between the sham and the genuine article; and my
own method of distinguishing is a simple one. I believe in
poetry which learns itself by heart. There are poems which
dominate and haunt one; which, once admitted, sting and
cling to one; and whose tune comes up and runs in one's
head at odd moments; which suddenly revive, after years of
forgetfulness, as vigorous and lively as ever. Such
poetry, as Wordsworth told Arnold, has the characteristic
of being 'inevitable.' You feel that the thing had to be
said just as it was said; and that, once so said, nothing
said by anybody else will just hit the same mark. Of
course, this test, being personal, is not conclusive. I
remember, I am ashamed to say it, some poetry which I know
to be trash, merely, I suppose, because it jingles pleasantly; and I forget a great deal which I know to be good,
because I can perceive that it dominates other people; but
then I do my best to keep my tastes on such occasions to
myself. Now, Matthew Arnold's poetry has, in an eminent
degree, the quality - if not of inevitableness - of adhes-
iveness. I don't know whether my experience is peculiar;
but I have never got out of my head, since I read it, the
little poem about the Neckan, who sings his plaintive song
on the Baltic headlands, or the charming verses - the last,
I fancy, which he wrote - about the dachsund Geist, whose
grave at Cobham should be a goal for all poetic pilgrims.
In certain of his more laboured poems, I am conscious
rather that I ought to admire than that I do admire. To my
brutal mind, the recollection of the classical models is a
source of annoyance, as suggesting that the scholar is in
danger of suppressing the man. But there are other poems
which I love, if not because, at any rate in spite of, the
classical propensities which they reveal. 'Sohrab and Rus-
tum' is to me among the most delightful of modern poems,
though in it Arnold indulges, perhaps more than enough, in
the long-tailed Homeric metaphor, which drags in upon principle all the points on which the thing compared does not
resemble the object. I can always read 'Tristan and
Iseult,' and the 'Church of Brou' and 'Empedocles on Etna';
and know that they leave behind them a sense of sweetness
and delicacy and exquisite feeling, if they do not present
those vivid phrases into which the very greatest men - the
Dantes or Shakespeares - can infuse the very life-blood.
In his 'Essays upon Celtic Literature' - perhaps the most
delightful of his books - Arnold says that English poetry
derived three things mainly from Celtic sources: Its turn
for style, its turn for melancholy, and its turn for
natural magic. The distinction is indicated with admirable

fineness; and my perceptions are not quite fine enough to
follow it. Keats, Arnold is able to perceive, is looking
at nature like a Greek, when he asks

> What little town by river or seashore
> Or mountain built with quiet citadel
> Is emptied of its folk this pious morn?

but becomes Celtic when he speaks of

> Magic casements, opening on the foam
> Of perilous seas in fairy-land forlon!

Possibly: but I am shy of endeavouring to discriminate
these exquisite essences, and I will not attempt to say
whether it is the power of style or of magic, whether it
is the presence of a Greek or a Celtic mode of looking at
nature, that charms us in what is perhaps Arnold's masterpiece, the 'Scholar Gipsy.' Whether the exquisite concluding stanzas, for example, be an instance of the Greek
or of the Celtic element, I know not; but I am quite sure
that it is delightful. At his best Arnold reaches a
felicity of style in which Tennyson alone, of all our
modern poets, if Tennyson himself, was his superior. The
comparison, much as I dislike comparisons, may suggest at
least the question why Arnold's popularity is still as I
think it is below his deserts. One answer is obvious. I
cannot doubt that Arnold fully appreciated the greatest of
contemporary artists. But certain references to Tennyson
in his essays are significant. Arnold incidentally quotes
Tennyson's 'great, broad-shouldered, genial Englishman,'
by way of illustrating his favourite proposition that this
broad-shouldered personage was a 'barbarian,' and conspicuous for insensibility to ideas. He refers with a
certain scorn to the self-complacency implied in the phrase
about freedom broadening slowly down from precedent to precedent. Though Arnold does not criticize the poetry, he
evidently felt - what, to say the truth, I think must be
admitted - that Tennyson interpreted the average - shall I
say, the Philistine? or the commonplace English sentiment
a little too faithfully; but it may be inferred - though
Arnold does not draw the inference - that the extraordinary
popularity of Tennyson was partly owing to the fact that he
could express what occurred to everybody in language
that could be approached by nobody. Arnold, on the contrary, is, in all his poems, writing for the cultivated,
and even for a small class of cultivated poeple. The ideas
which he expresses are not only such as do not commend
themselves, but sometimes such as are rather annoying, to

the average reader. The sentiments peculiar to a narrow,
however refined, class are obviously so far less favourable to poetical treatment. Arnold seems to admit this in
his occasional employment of that rhymeless metre which
corresponds to the borderland between prose and poetry. A
characteristic piece is that upon 'Heine's Grave.' We all
remember the description of England, the 'Weary Titan,'
who with deaf

> Ears, and labour-dimmed eyes,
> Regarding neither to right
> Nor left, goes passively by,
> Staggering on to her goal, &c.

and a phrase which tells us how the spirit of the world,
beholding men's absurdity, let a sardonic smile

> For one short moment wander o'er his lips -
> *That smile was Heine.*

That, of course, is rather epigram than poetry. It matters, indeed, very little whether we call it by one name
or another, so long as we allow it to be effective. But
writing of this kind, call it poetry or prose, or a hybrid
genus, in which the critic shows through the poet, is not
likely to suit the popular mind. It presupposes a whole
set of reflections which are the property of a special
class. And the same may be said of the particular mood
which is specially characteristic of Arnold. In the
'Scholar Gipsy' he laments 'the strange disease of modern
life,'

> With its sick hurry, its divided aims;

speaks of us 'light half-believers of our casual creeds';
tells how the wisest of us takes dejectedly 'his seat upon
the intellectual throne,' and lays bare his sad experience
of wretched days, and 'all his hourly varied anodynes';
while we, who are not the wisest, can only pine, wish that
the long, unhappy dream would end, and keep as our only
friend 'sad patience, too near neighbour to despair.'
This note jars upon some people, who prefer, perhaps, the
mild resignation of the 'Christian Year.' I fail of sympathy for the opposite reason. I cannot affect to share
Arnold's discomfort. I have never been able - doubtless
it is a defect - to sympathize with the Obermans and
Amiels whom Arnold admired; excellent but surely effeminate persons, who taste of the fruits of the Tree of Knowledge, and finding the taste bitter, go on making wry

faces over it all their lives; and, admitting with one
party that the old creeds are doomed, assert with the
other that all beauty must die with them. The universe is
open to a great many criticisms; there is plenty of cause
for tears and for melancholy; and great poets in all ages
have, because they were great poets, given utterance to
the sorrows of their race. But I don't feel disposed to
grumble at the abundance of interesting topics or the
advance of scientific knowledge, because some inconveniences result from both. I say all this simply as explaining why the vulgar - including myself - fail to appreciate
these musical moans over spilt milk, which represent
rather a particular eddy in an intellectual revolution
than the deeper and more permanent emotions of human
nature. But I do not mean to depreciate Arnold's power;
only to suggest reasons for the want of a wider recognition. The 'Scholar Gipsy,' for example, expresses in certain passages sentiment which I must call morbid, but for
all that, even for me, it remains one of the most exquisite poems in the language.
     This leads me to another point. In his essay upon Jou-
bert, Arnold spoke of literature as 'a criticism of life.'
Elsewhere (Introduction to Mr. H. Ward's 'Collection of
Poems') he gave the same account of poetry. But to
poetry, he says in the same breath, we shall have to turn
for consolation, and it will replace much mist of 'what
now passes with us for religion and philosophy.' If so,
he obviously cannot mean that poetry and criticism are
really the same thing. The phrase 'criticism of life'
gave great offence, and was much ridiculed by some writers, who were apparently unable to distinguish between an
epigram and a philosophical dogma. To them, indeed,
Arnold's whole position was naturally abhorrent. For it
is not uncommon now to hear denunciations of all attempts
to connect art with morality and philosophy. It is wicked,
we are told, for a poet, or a novelist, or a painter, to
take any moral consideration into account; and therefore
to talk of poetry as destined to do for us much that
philosophy and religion used to do is, of course, manifestly absurd. I will not argue the point at length,
being content to observe that the cry seems to me oddly
superfluous. Of all the dangers to which modern novelists, for example, are exposed, that against which they
are least required to guard is the danger of being too
philosophical. They really may feel at their ease; nor do
I think that they need be much alarmed as to the risk of
being too moral. Meanwhile, it is my belief that nobody
is the better in any department of life or literature for
being a fool or a brute: and least of all in poetry. I

cannot think that a man is disqualified for poetry either
by thinking more deeply than others or by having a keener
perception of (I hope I may join the two words) moral
beauty. A perception of what it is that makes a hero or
saint is, I fancy, as necessary to a great literary artist
as a perception of what it is that constitutes physical
beauty to a painter. The whole doctrine, in short, seems
to me to be a misstatement of the very undeniable and very
ancient truth that it is a poet's business to present
types, for example, and not to give bare psychological
theory: not that he is the worse for being even a deep
philosopher or a subtle logician; on the contrary, he is
so far the better; but that he is the worse if he gives
the abstract reasoning instead of incarnating his thought
in concrete imagery. And so, when Arnold called poetry a
criticism of life, he only meant to express what seems to
me to be an undeniable truth. The Elgin marbles might, in
his sense, be called a criticism of the physique of the
sightseers. To contrast their perfect forms and
unapproachable grace with the knock-kneed, spindle-
shanked, narrow-chested, round shouldered product of
London slums who passes before them, is to criticize the
poor creature's defects of structure in the most effective
way. In a similar sense, when a poet or a novelist presents us with a style, when Addison gives a Sir Roger de
Coverley, or Goldsmith a Vicar of Wakefield, or Scott a
Dandie Dinmont, or Thackeray a Colonel Newcome, or Dickens
a Mr. Creakle (I choose this example of Dickens only because Arnold made use of it himself), they present us with
ideal types which set off - more effectively than any deliberate analysis - the actual human beings known to us,
who more or less represent similar classes. In his essay
upon the Function of Criticism, Arnold explained his lofty
conception of the art, and showed why, in his sense of the
word, it should be the main aim of all modern literature.
'Criticism,' he said, 'is the disinterested endeavour to
learn and propagate the best that is known or thought in
the world.' The difference between poetry and criticism
is that one gives us the ideal and the other explains to
us how it differs from the real. What is latent in the
poet is made explicit in the critic. Arnold, himself,
even when he turned to criticism, was primarily a poet.
His judgments show greater skill in seizing characteristic
aspects than in giving a logical analysis or a convincing
proof. He goes by intuition not by roundabout logical
approaches. No recent English critic, I think, has
approached him in the art of giving delicate portraits of
literary leaders; he has spoken, for example, precisely
the right word about Byron and Wordsworth. Many of us who

cannot rival him may gain, from Arnold's writings a higher
conception of what is our true function. He did, I think,
more than any man to impress upon his countrymen that the
critic should not be a mere combatant in a series of faction fights, puffing friends and saying to an enemy, 'This
will never do.' The weak side, however, of the poetical
criticism is its tendency to be 'subjective,' that is, to
reflect too strongly the personal prejudices of the author.
It must virtually consist in giving the impression made
upon the critic; and, however, delicate his perception and
wide his sympathy, he will be scarcely human if his judgments are not affected by his personal equation. No one
could be more alive to the danger than Arnold, and his most
characteristic teaching turns upon the mode of avoiding it.
There are times, no doubt, when he relies too confidently
upon the fineness of his perception, and then obviously has
a slight spasm of diffidence. I have noticed how, in his
'Essays on Celtic Lierature,' he uses the true poetical or
intuitive method: he recognizes the precise point at which
Shakespeare or Keats passes from the Greek to the Celtic
note; he trusts to the fineness of his ear, like a musician who can detect the slightest discord. And we feel
perhaps that a man who can decide, for example, an ethnological question by such means, who can by simple inspiration determine which are the Celtic and which are the Teutonic and which are the Norman elements in English character, is going a little beyond his tether. Arnold obviously
feels so too. In the same book he speaks most respectfully
of the opposite or prosaic method. Zeuss, the great Celtic
scholar, is praised because he uses a scientific test to
determine the age of documents. This test is that in Welsh
and Irish the letters p and t gradually changed into b or d
(as if the Celts had caught a cold in their head); that *map*
became *mab*, and *coet*, *coed*. This, says Arnold, is a verifiable and scientific test. When Arnold is himself trying
to distinguish the Celtic element in Englishmen, he starts
by remarking that a Frenchmen would speak of German
bêtise, (1) but of English *gaucherie*: (2) the German is
balourd, (3) while the Englishman *empêtré*; (4) and the
German *niais*, (5) while the Englishman is *mélancolique*. (6)
We can hardly say that the difference between *balourd* and
empêtré is as clear as the difference between t and d: and
Arnold is, perhaps, too much inclined to trust to his intuitions, as if they were equivalent to scientific and
measurable statements. The same tendency shows itself in
his curious delight in discoursing catch-words, and
repeating them sometimes to weariness. He uses such
phrases as 'sweetness and light' with a certain air of
laying down a genuine scientific distinction, as clear-cut

and unequivocal as a chemist's analysis. He feels that he
has thoroughly analyzed English characteristics when he
has classified his countrymen as 'Philistines,* Barbarians,
and the Populace.' To fix a certain aspect of things by
an appropriate phrase is the process which corresponded
with him to a scientific analysis. But may not this
method merely lead to the substitution of one sect of prejudices for another; the prejudices, say, of the fastidious don for the prejudices of the coarser tradesman? The
Frenchman who calls the Englishman empêtré may be as
narrow-minded as the Englishman who calls the Frenchman a
frog-eater. Certainly, Arnold would reply. What we need
is to make a stream of fresh thought play freely about our
stock 'notions and habits.' We have to get out of an un-
fruitful and mechanical routine. Or, as he puts it in
another way, his one qualification for teaching his
countrymen is, he says, his belief in the 'primary need-
fulness of seeing things as they really are, and of the
greater importance of ideas than of the machinery which
exists for them.' That is, we want, above all things, to
get rid of prejudices in general, not of any special prejudice; to have our opinions constructed out of pure, impartial, unbiassed thought, free from all baser alloy of
mephitic vapours. The mere self-willed assertion of our
own fancies can never lift us to the higher point of view
which would reveal our narrowness and ignorance. Hence
the vast importance of 'culture': the one thing needful;
which, again, in another view, is equivalent to a frank
submission of ourselves to the Zeitgeist. The Zeitgeist,
indeed, is an entity not quite easy to define. But it at
least supposes that genuine philosophy and scientific
thought is a reality; that there is a real difference between the scholar and the charlatan; that criticism in a
wide sense has achieved some permanent and definite
results; and that, although many antiquated prejudices
still survive and dominate us, especially in England, and
constitute the whole mental furniture of the Philistine,
they are doomed to decay, and those who hold by them
doomed to perish with them. To recognize, therefore, the
deep, underlying currents of thought, to get outside of
the narrow limits of the popular prejudice, to steep our
minds in the best thought of the past, and to be open to
the really great thoughts of the present, is the one salvation for the race and for reasonable men. The English
people, he often said, had entered the prison of Puritanism, and had the key turned upon their spirit for two centuries. To give them the key and to exhort them to use it
was his great aim. Heine had called himself a 'brave soldier in the war of the liberation of humanity,' and Arnold

took service in the same army. Only - and this was the
doctrine upon which he laid emphasis - to fight effectually we must recognize the true leaders, those who really
spoke with authority, and who were the true advanced guard
in the march to the land of promise. Your individualist
would only take off the fetters so as to allow a free
fight among the prisoners. The prophet of culture alone
can enable us to get free from the prison-house itself.
His strong sense of the mischief of literary anarchy
appeared in his once famous essay upon the French Academy.
Though he guarded himself against recommending an English
institution, he was fascinated by the charm of an acknowledged tribunal of good taste, an outward and visible
symbol of right reason, of a body which, by its moral
authority, should restrain men from those excesses and
faults of taste into which even the greatest Englishmen
are apt to fall, and which should keep distinctly before
our minds the conviction that we only obtain worthy intellectual liberty when we recognize the necessity of subord-
ination to the highest minds. To imbibe the teaching of
the Zeitgeist, to know what is the true living thought of
the age and who are its great men, is to accept a higher
rule, and not merely (as he puts it) to exchange the
errors of Miall for the errors of Mill: to become a vulgar
Freethinker instead of a vulgar Dissenter.

The doctrine of culture is, of course, in some sense
the common property of all cultivated men. Carlyle, like
Arnold, wished for an exit from Houndsditch and a relin-
quishment of Hebrew old clothes. But Arnold detested Carlyle's Puritanism, and was alienated by his sulphurous and
volcanic explosiveness. Mill hated the tyranny of the
majority, and, of course, rejected the Puritan theology.
But Mill was a Benthamite, and Benthamism was the natural
doctrine of the Philistine. Mill's theories would lead,
though in spite of himself, to that consummation which
Arnold most dreaded - the general dominion of the Commonplace: to the definitive imposition upon the world of the
code of the Philistine. To define Arnold's point of view,
we should have, I think, to consider what in our modern
slang is called his environment. Anyone who reads the life
of his father will see how profound was the influence upon
the son. 'Somewhere, surely, afar,' as he says in the
lines in Rugby Chapel,

    In the sounding labour-house vast
    Of being, is practised that strength,
    Zealous, beneficent, firm.

Some of the force, may one say? had passed into the younger

man, though he had lost something of the austere strength, and had gained much in delicacy, and certainly in a sense of humour curiously absent in the elder, as it is, I think, in most good men. Dr. Arnold shared the forebodings common at the period of the Reform Bill. The old dogged Conservatism of the George III and Eldon type was doomed. But who was to profit by the victory? The Radicals, led by Bentham and James Mill? That meant confiscation and disestablishment in practice; and in theory, materialism or atheism. This was the 'liberalism' denounced and dreaded by Newman. But then, to Dr. Arnold, the Oxford Movement itself meant a revival of superstition and sacerdotalism. He held that there was a truer liberalism than Benthamism, a liberalism of which Coleridge expounded and suggested the philosophy: a doctrine which could reanimate the old creeds by exposing them to the light, and bring them into harmony with the last modern thought. The Church, neither plundered nor enslaved by superstition, might be lifted to a higher intellectual level, and become once more the great national organ of spiritual influence and development. Matthew Arnold always always held to this aspiration. He hoped that the Church might open its doors to all dissenters - not only to Protestants, but even in course of time to Roman Catholics. He hated disestablishment, and even in the case of the Church of Ireland, condemned a measure which, though it removed an injustice, removed it at the cost of an alliance with the narrow dissenting prejudices. But the views of the young man were also modified by the fascination of the Newman school. Of Oxford he could never speak without enthusiasm, if he could not quite refrain from a touch of irony. 'Adorable dreamer!' he exclaims, 'whose heart has been so romantic! who has given thyself prodigally, given thyself to sides and to heroes not mine, only not to the Philistines! Home of lost causes and forsaken beliefs, and unpopular names and impossible loyalties!' Oxford, as he says elsewhere, had taught the truth that 'beauty and sweetness are essential characters of a complete human perfection.' Bad philosophies, another critic (I think Professor Flint) has said, when they die, go to Oxford. Arnold admitted the badness of the philosophies, but the beauty and sweetness, he would have added, are immortal. The effect, therefore, upon him was not to diminish his loyalty to philosophy; no one more hated all obscurantism: his belief in 'culture,' in the great achievements of scholarship, of science, of historical criticism, was part of his nature. He was not the man to propose to put back the hand of the dial, or to repel the intellectual ocean with the mop of an orthodox Mrs.

Partington. But his keen appreciation of the beauty of
the old ideals governed his thought. He even held that
the Christianity of the future would be Catholicism,
though Catholicism 'purged' and 'opening itself to the
light,' 'conscious of its own poetry, freed from its
sacerdotal despotism, and freed from its pseudo-scientific
apparatus of superannuated dogma.' Meanwhile, his classical training and his delight in the clearness and symmetry
of the great French writers affected his taste. He has
told us how his youthful enthusiasm took him at one time
to Paris, to spend two months in seeing Rachel's perform-
ances on the French stage, and at another, to visit George
Sand in her country retirement. And then came the experience of his official career which made him familiar with
the educational systems of France and Germany, and with
the chaotic set of institutions which represented an educational system in England. The master-thought, he says,
by which his politics were governed was the thought of
the 'bad civilization of the English middle-class.' This
was, in fact, the really serious aim to which his whole
literary activity in later life converged. Condemned to
live and work among the middle-class, while imbued with
the ideas in which they were most defective, loving, as
he did, the beauty and freshness of Oxford, the logical
clearness and belief in ideas of France, the devotion to
scientific truth and philosophical thoroughness in Germany, the sight of the dogged British Philistine became
to him a perpetual grievance. The middle-class, as he
said in one of his favourite formulae, has a 'defective
type of religion, a narrow range of intellect and knowledge, a stinted sense of beauty, and a low type of
manners.' Accordingly, the function which he took for
himself was to be a thorn in the side of the Philistine:
to pierce the animal's thick hide with taunts, delicate
but barbed; to invent nicknames which might reveal to the
creature his own absurdity; to fasten upon expressions
characteristic of the blatant arrogance and complacent
ineffable self-conceit of the vulgar John Bull, and
repeat them till even Bull might be induced to blush.
Somebody's unlucky statement that English was the best
breed in the world; the motto about the 'dissidence of
dissent and the Protestantism of the Protestant religion';
the notice of Wragg - the woman who was taken up for
child-murder; the assertion of the 'Saturday Review' that
we were the most logical people in the world; the roar-
ings of the 'young lions of the "Daily Telegraph,"' and
their like, which covered our impotence in European wars;
the truss-manufactory which ornamented the finest site
in Europe: upon these and other texts he harped - perhaps

with a little too much repetition - in the hope of bringing to us some sense of our defects. I must confess that,
as a good Philistine, I often felt, and hope I profited by
the feeling, that he had pierced me to the quick, and I
submitted to his castigations as I have had to submit to
the probings of a dentist, I knew they were for my good.
And I often wished, I must also confess, that I too had a
little sweetness and light that I might be able to say
such nasty things of my enemies. We who were young radicals in the days when Arminius von Thunder-Ten Tronckh
was writing to the 'Pall Mall Gazette,' tried to retort by
calling him a mere dandy, a kid-gloved Oxford coxcomb, who
was thinking that revolutions could be made with rose-
water. I think now that we did not do justice to the real
seriousness of his purpose. You do not, we said sometimes,
propose any practical measure. He replied fairly enough
that it was not his business, nor the business of philosophers and poets generally to mix in actual politics and
draft Acts of Parliament. They had to modify ideas. He
might have added that in his own sphere, he had made very
practical criticisms upon our educational system; and had,
for example, pointed out the defects of English secondary
education with a clearness which is only now beginning to
have some recognition from practical politicians. But it
was no doubt his conviction that his countrymen required
less a change of machinery than an intellectual change.
What is indispensable, he said, is that we should not only
do to Ireland something different, but that we should *be*
something different. A writer, however great a thinker
and artist, who deliberately proposes to change the character of his countrymen, is undoubtedly undertaking a
superhuman task. If Philistinism be really part of our
character we shall be Philistines to the end, let our Carlyles and Newmans or Mills and Arnolds preach never so
wisely and never so frequently. And yet their preaching
is not the less useful: more useful, perhaps, than that of
the politicians who boast of keeping to the practical and
confine their energies to promoting such measures as are
likely to catch votes at the next election. 'To see
things as they really are': that, he said, was his great
aim; and it is clearly a good one. And what is the great
obstacle to seeing things as they really are? The great
obstacle is, I take it, that we are ourselves part of the
things to be seen; and that there is an ancient and proverbial difficulty about seeing ourselves. When certain
prejudices have become parts of our mental furniture, when
our primary data and our methods of reasoning imply a set
of local narrow assumptions, the task of getting outside
them is almost the task of getting outside of our own

skins. Our pigtails, as the poet observes, persist in
hanging behind us in spite of all our circumgyrations.
The greatness of a thinker is measured by the width of his
intellectual horizon, or by the height to which he can
rise above the plane of ordinary thought. Arnold's free
play of thought implies the process by which he hoped to
achieve liberation for himself. Be yourself cultured, and
your eyes will be opened to the ugliness of the Philistines. To be cultured, widen your intellectual horizon,
and steep yourself in the best thought of all ages and all
civilized men. If Arnold trusted a little too much to the
aesthetic perceptions thus generated, he succeeded, I
think, in reaching a position from which he both discerned
and portrayed most clearly some palpable blots. Such a
service is great, whatever the accuracy of the judgment.
It is good to breathe a new atmosphere if only for a
space. I have more respect than he had for the masculine
common-sense of Macaulay - the great apostle, as Arnold
called him, of the Philistines - but, after reading Macaulay's unhesitating utterances of the old Whig creed,
which to him was an ultimate and infallible gospel, one
feels oneself raised at once to a higher point of view.
When one attempts, under Arnold's guidance, to assign to
the Whig his proper place in European history, and to see
how far he is from fully representing the ultimate verdict of philosophy, whatever our political creed - and
mine is very different from Arnold's, - he really helps us
to cure the mind's eye of the cataract of dogged prejudice, of whose very existence we were unconscious.

    His position was, no doubt, one which we may call im-
practical. He was a democrat in one sense: for aristocracy was unfavourable to ideas, and the Zeitgeist has
condemned the system. Inequality, as he said in a remarkable essay, 'materializes our upper classes, vulgarizes
our middle classes, brutalizes our lower classes.' He
speaks as one shocked, not less in his moral than in his
aesthetic capacity, of the 'hardly human horror, the
abjection and uncivilizedness' of the populace in Glasgow
and the East of London. He held that the French Revolution, by promoting equality, had raised the lower classes
of France to a marked superiority in civilization above
the corresponding class in England. Democracy, he admitted, might get too much its own way in England. The
remedy was to be sought in a stronger action of the central power. We have not, he complains, the notion, so
familiar on the Continent and to antiquity, of the State;
and the English hatred of all authority has tended to make
us drift towards mere anarchy. When Fawcett preached
self-help, Arnold held that to exhort to self-help in

England was to carry coals to Newcastle. It was the
parrot-like repetition of old formulae that made our
liberalism barren. Our danger was all the other way, the
danger of exaggerating the blessings of self-will and
self-assertion. I do not quote Arnold's view to show that
he was right, or to claim foresight for his predictions.
I doubt, for example, whether anyone would say now that we
hear too much of self-help, or that there is no danger on
the opposite side, or whether Arnold himself would have
been attracted by State Socialism. He was, indeed, deliberately in the habit of giving one side of a question
without caring to add even the corrections of which he
himself approved. That is natural in a man who wishes to
stimulate thought, rather than to preach any definite
practical conclusion. I only urge that there was a real
and very rare merit in such a position taken by a man of
so much insight. The effort to see English life in society and thought, as a German professor or a French politician might see it, to get outside of the prejudices which
are part of ourselves is itself a most useful experience.
And when such criticism is carried on with a singular fulness of perception, with pungent flashes of sarcasm, but
with a power of speaking truths as undeniable as they are
unpleasant, and yet with so much true urbanity - in spite
of certain little defects, when he seems to be rather
forcing himself to be humorous, and becomes liable to an
accusation of flippancy - in such a case, I say, that we
ought to be grateful to our critic. His criticism is anything but final, but it is to be taken into account by .
every man who believes in the importance of really civilizing the coming world. How the huge, all-devouring monster which we call Democracy is to be dealt with: how he
is to be coaxed or lectured or preached into taking as
large a dose as possible of culture, of respect for true
science and genuine thought, is really one of the most
pressing of problems. Some look on with despair, doubting
only by whatever particular process we shall be crushed
into a dead level of monotonous mediocrity. I do not suppose that Arnold could give any solution of the great
problems; what he could do, and did, I think, more effectually than anyone, was to wake us out of our dull company
- to help to break through the stolid crust, whatever
seeds may be sown by other hands. Perhaps this explains
why he is read in America, where the Philistine is a very
conspicuous phenomenon and the ugly side of middle-class
mediocrity is more prominent.

   I have judiciously reserved to the last, in order that
I may pass lightly, the point which to Arnold himself
doubtless appeared to be the most important part of his

teaching - I mean, of course, the criticism of religion,
to which he devoted his last writings. In his last books,
Arnold preached a doctrine which will hardly find many
followers. He seemed even to be taking pains to get into
a position scarcely intelligible to people who take things
practically. He poses, one may say, as a literary critic;
he disavows all logical system, and declares almost ostentatiously that he is no metaphysician; but his apparent
conclusion is - not that he is incompetent to speak of
philosophy, but that philosophy is mere pedantry, so far
as it is not poetry in disguise. The organ by which we
are to discover religious truth does not employ the prosaic method of examining evidence, nor the logical method
of *à priori* reasoning; but that free play of thought which
is our guide in letters: the judgment, as he says, which
insensibly forms itself in a fair mind, familiar with the
best thoughts of the world. The prophet is inspired by
the Zeitgeist, and judges by a cultivated instinct, not by
systematic argument. The rather airy mode of treating
great problems which emerges is often bewildering to the
ordinary mind. The orthodox may revolt against the airy
confidence in which the Zeitgeist puts aside 'miracles'
and the supernatural, - not as disproved, but obviously
not worth the trouble of disproving. The agnostic is
amazed to find that Arnold, while treating all theological
dogma as exploded rubbish, expatiates upon the supreme
value of the sublimated essence of theology. God, Arnold
tells us, is not a term of science, but a term of poetry
and eloquence - a term 'thrown out' at a not fully grasped
object of consciousness - a literary term, in short - with
various indefinite meanings for different people. The
'magnified and non-natural man' of whom theologians speak
is to be superseded by the 'stream of tendency' or the
'not ourselves which makes for righteousness'; and, in
expressing his contempt for the vulgar conceptions, he
perhaps sometimes forgot his usual good taste, as in the
famous reference to the three Lord Shaftesburys. Such
phrases might be taken for the scoffing which he condemned
in others. I glanced the other day at a satirical novel,
in which the writer asks whether an old Irishwoman is to
say, instead of 'God bless you!' 'The stream of tendency
bless you.' I then opened the Preface to Arnold's 'God
and the Bible' and found him making a similar criticism
upon Mr. Herbert Spencer. Nobody, he observes, would say,
'The unknowable is our refuge and strength, a very present
help in trouble.'
Arnold's answer to his critic would, in fact, have been
that he never proposed that the old Irishwoman should give
up her form of expression. He professed to be simply

explaining her real meaning. He apparently thought, as I
have said, that a modified form of Catholicism would be
the religion of the future; the modification amounting to
this, that it would only profess to be poetry instead of
science, and giving symbols 'thrown out' at truth, not
dogmas with the validity of theorems in geometry. He
argued that the Hebrew religion itself is not only to be
taken by us in the poetical sense, but that by the prophets themselves it was never understood differently. So
the text which says that 'Man must be born of a spirit'
means only that man must be born of an influence; and
never meant more. This was the original sense of the
first utterance, which was only twisted into pseudo-
science by later dogmatists. It follows that orthodox
theology is an 'immense misunderstanding of the Bible' -
a misunderstanding because it takes poetry for prose. By
clearing away the accretions we see that the Bible is to
be read throughout in this sense; and therefore that, to
restore its true value, we are not to throw it aside, but
to take it as the original authors meant us to take it.
    The weakness of the poetic or imaginative treatment is
the tendency to confound a judgment of beauty with a
judgment of fact. A creed is so charming or so morally
stimulating that it must be true. Arnold did not accept
this way of putting it. He had too genuine a respect for
the daylight of the understanding, too much hearty loyalty
to the Zeitgeist and scientific thought to accept a principle which would lead to simple reaction and recrudescence of superstition. He unequivocally accepts the
results obtained by German critics, heavy-eyed and pedantic as they may sometimes be, for he believes with all his
heart in thorough, unflinching, scholar-like research. He
will not shut his eyes or mistake mere aesthetic pleasure
for logical conviction. But, he argues, the essence of
the creed is precisely its moral beauty; the power with
which it expresses certain ethical truths - its grasp of
the doctrine (to quote his favourite, though I cannot
think, very fortunate, formula) that conduct is three-
fourths of life, that it is the essence of the religion,
or rather, is itself the religion; and that the whole
framework of historical fact and ecclesiastical dogma is
unimportant. We read Homer, he says, for our enjoyment,
and to turn the book to our 'benefit.' We should read the
Bible in the same way. The truth of the Greek or Hebrew
mythology and history is irrelevant. The true lights of
the Christian Church, he says are not Augustine and Luther
or Bossuet, but à Kempis and Tauler and St. Francis of
Sales; not, that is, the legislators or reformers or
systematizers of dogma, but the mystics and pietists and

men who have uttered the religious sentiment in the most
perfect form. It is characteristic that in his book upon
St. Paul, while dwelling enthusiastically upon the
apostle's ethical teaching, he says nothing of the work
which to St. Paul himself, as to most historians, must
surely have seemed important, the freeing of Christian
doctrine from fetters of Judaism; and treats the theological reasons by which St. Paul justified his position as
mere surplusage or concessions to contemporary prejudice.

The problem here suggested is a very wide one. We may
agree that the true value of a religion is in its ethical
force. We may admit that the moral ideals embodied in its
teaching are the only part which is valuable when we cease
to believe in the history or the dogma; and that they
still preserve a very high value. We may still be edified
by Homer or by Aeschylus, or by Socrates and Epictetus,
though we accept not a word of their statements of fact or
philosophy. But can the essence of a religion be thus
preserved intact when its dogma and its historical assertions are denied? Could St. Paul have spread the Church
of the Gentiles without the help of the theories which
Arnold regards as accretions? Would the beautiful spirit
of the mystics have conquered the world as well as touched
the hearts of a few hermits without the rigid framework of
dogmas in which they were set and the great ecclesiastical
organization for which a definite dogmatic system was required? We may love the mystical writers, but, without
the organizers of Churches and creeds, can we believe that
they would even have made a Church for the world? To set
forth a great moral ideal is undoubtedly an enormous service. But the prosaic mind will ask, Is it enough to present us with ideals? Do we not also require statements of
fact? It is all very well to say be good, and to say this
and that is the real meaning of goodness; but to make men
good, you have also got to tell them why they should be
good, and to create a system of discipline and dogma for
effectually stimulating their love of goodness.

The questions I have suggested are the questions which
upon Arnold's method seem to be passed over. It is his
indifference to them which gives sometimes the very erroneous impression of a want of seriousness. Arnold was, I
think, profoundly in earnest, though he seems scarcely to
have realized the degree in which, to ordinary minds, he
seemed to be offering not stones, but mere vapour, when
asked for bread. Nor can I doubt that he was occupied
with the most serious of problems, and saw at least some
of the conditions of successful treatment. On all sides
his loyalty to culture (the word has been a little spoilt
of late), his genuine and hearty appreciation of

scholarship and scientific thought, his longing to set
himself in the great current of intellectual progress, are
always attractive, and are the more marked because of his
appreciation (his excessive appreciation, may I say?) of
the 'sweetness,' if not the light, of the Oxford Movement.
If, indeed, his appreciation was excessive, I am conscious, I hope, of the value of the doctrine which led
him. We ought, he says, to have an 'infinite tenderness'
for the popular science of religion. It is 'the spontaneous work of nature, the travail of the human mind, to
adapt to its grasp and employment great ideas of which it
feels the attraction.' I feel the truth of this teaching
more, I fear, than I have acted upon it. I belong, as I
have said, to the brutal and prosaic class of mankind. We
ought to catch at least something of Arnold's spirit, so
far as to admit, at least, that the great problem is to
reconcile unflinching loyalty to truth with tenderness
'infinite,' if possible, for the errors which are but a
grasping after truth. If Arnold combined the two tendencies in a fashion of his own, he set a most valuable
example, even to those who cannot think his method
successful. He said of a great contemporary that he was
always beating the bush without starting the hare. I am
under the impression that Arnold, if he started the hare,
did not quite catch it. But beating the bushes is an
essential preliminary. He stirred and agitated many
brains which could not be reached by sober argument or by
coarser invective, and he applied good wholesome irri-
tants to our stolid self-satisfaction. When one remarks
how little is left of most philosophers in the way of
positive result, and yet remembers gratefully the service
they have done in the way of stimulus to thought, one may
feel grateful to a man who, while renouncing all claims to
be a philosopher, did more than most philosophers to rouse
us to new perception of our needs and was one of the most
effective agents in breaking up old crusts of prejudice.

Putting on a mask sometimes of levity, sometimes of
mere literary dandyism, with an irony which sometimes is a
little too elaborate, but which often expresses the keenest intelligence trying to pass itself off as simplicity,
he was a skirmisher, but a skirmisher who did more than
most heavily-armed warriors, against the vast oppressive
reign of stupidity and prejudice. He made the old dragon
Philistine (to use his phrase) wince at times, and showed
the ugliness and clumsiness of the creature; and after all
he did it in a spirit as of one who recognized the monster
was after all a most kindly monster at bottom. He may be
enlisted in useful service if you can only apply the goad
successfully, and made effective, in his ponderous way,

like the Carthaginian elephants, if only you can mount his neck and goad him in the right direction. No single arm is sufficient for such a task; the dragon shakes himself and goes to sleep again in a stertorous and rather less complacent fashion, let us hope; and we feel that the struggle will too probably endure till we have ceased to be personally interested.

I cannot, indeed, get it out of my head that we slow-footed and prosaic persons sometimes make our ground surer; and that, for example, poor Bishop Colenso, whom Arnold ridiculed as the typical Philistine critic, did some good service with his prosaic arithmetic. There are cases in which the four rules are better than the finest critical insight. But there is room for poets as well as for arithmeticians; and Arnold, as at once poet and critic, has the special gift - if I may trust my own experience - of making one feel silly and tasteless when one has uttered a narrow-minded, crude, or ungenerous sentiment; and I dip into his writings to receive a shock, unpleasant at times, but excellent in its effects as an intellectual tonic.

Notes

* Arnold popularized this word, which, I think, first appears in the 'Essays in Criticism' (1865), p. 157. He there says that it was what Carlyle meant by 'gigmanity' or 'respectability.' Carlyle had himself introduced the phrase 'Philistine' in his review of Taylor's 'German Poetry' [Stephen's note].
1 'silliness'.
2 'clumsiness'.
3 'doltish'.
4 'clumsy'.
5 'foolish'.
6 'mopish'.

60. JOHN M. ROBERTSON ON MATTHEW ARNOLD, 'MODERN HUMANISTS'

1895, 137-61

John Mackinnon Robertson (1856-1933), without the benefit

of formal education, began life as a journalist writing
for the 'Edinburgh Evening News' (1878) and in 1884 joined
Charles Bradlaugh at the 'National Reformer', editing that
journal from 1891 to 1893. After several years running
his own 'Free Review' he turned, in 1895, to independent
writing and lecturing. 'Modern Humanists', subtitled
'Sociological Studies of Carlyle, Mill, Etc.' (1895),
examines the leading thinkers of the century from a
rationalistic point of view. Out of his long chapter on
Matthew Arnold we excerpt Robertson's discussion of
Arnold as a prose stylist and his central argument, that
by ignoring consecutive reasoning and trusting to his intuition Arnold condemns his criticism to inconsistency
and error.

As a prosist he learned most from the French, acquiring
from them that urbanity and amenity, that ease and
naturalness which, once cultivated in England, had for a
time gone out of fashion with us under the necessary
stress of a development of ideas that could not be contained in Addisonian moulds. Thackeray, about the same
time, with more need, learned as happily to temper his
youthful English crudity by French example, as well as by
reversion to our own Augustan types.

   But in recognising Arnold's debt to French culture, we
must not overlook the distinct influence of his father.

Dr. Arnold shows a plentiful lack of amenity in many of
his letters; but in his Sermons and his Lectures on
History you will find the obvious origins of the style
of his son - the sensitive search for simplicity and temperance and clearness and flow, the crisp diffuseness of
tissue, the balancing of clauses, and the reiteration of
words and phrases in successive relations - characteristics evidently developed in the father by his function as
a preacher to boys. And that combination of dignity with
lucidity, which gave impressiveness to the discourses of
the schoolmaster, lent to the writings of his son, where
the same qualities were tempered with humour, an influence almost out of proportion to their purport. In the
harsh strife of English schools and parties, full of
echoes of Cobbett and 'The Times,' and reminiscences of
the malevolence of Junius and the violent invective of
the later Burke, where even the penetrating criticism of
Coleridge was touched with the *odium theologicum*, (1) as
was that of Macaulay with the heat of politics, and where

430 Arnold, Prose Writings: The Critical Heritage

the grave polemic of John Mill had visibly the dust of
battle about it - in this atmosphere the serene brightness
of Matthew Arnold's treatment of men and manners, of books
and tendencies and movements, has had from the first a
refreshing and exemplary charm. As a controversialist he
is visibly infirm and inconclusive, and it was a sound instinct that led him to play the part lightly and indirectly; but when he does debate, he does it with a good-
humour that makes much amends for loose logic and imperfect
information. He could banter without indecorum and without
bitterness, and scoff without bluster - French accomplishments, which he pressed on his countrymen both by precept
and example. He has thus been more of a civiliser than a
teacher; but such civilisers are rare and precious. And
while his fastidious concern over things secondary, as if
they were primary, has brought scoffing on himself, and
his serene obstinacy has at times provoked impatience, the
notes of grave melancholy as well as of grave fortitude
which sound through so much of his verse have kept his
standing high even for his opponents. Thus he was for his
time one of the leading figures in intellectual England.

On the other hand, these gifts and graces correlate with
intellectual defects which, if never repellent, are finally
serious. Among the things his strenuous father did not bequeath to him was the turn for hard work. Knowledge and
accomplishments had to come easy to him; that is, they had
to chime with his bent, if he was to receive them at all.
In a late writing, commenting on the receptivity of an
American lady critic, who confessed that it pleased her to
think excellence was common and abundant, he says well
that it is not so, and that to attain excellence a man
must well-nigh wear his heart out. But even where he
brought his taste and culture most happily to bear on his
work, namely, in his poetry, he can at times be flat and
uninspired, because he has not enough of the unweariable
passion for perfection which goads the supreme artists.
Lucky for him was his prolonged classic and other useful
training at school and college, for he could not have cultured himself to the same effect. And where his English
school and college training did not in any degree correct
his intellectual defects, his want of logic and thoroughness of thought, he remained decidedly deficient to the
end.

If, a man come to the criticism of life as Arnold did,
with neither a faculty nor a training for logic, but only
a delicate susceptibility and a cultured taste, it is impossible that he should escape frequent error and

inconsistency, and reach sound moral science. He may see
and correct some mental vices in his contemporaries, but
he will inevitably suffer from some grave ones of his own.
'If the righteous is scarcely saved, where shall the un-
godly and sinner appear?' as his father would say. It is
really grotesque, if one will think of it, that men and
women should reckon to reach accurate knowledge in mental
and moral and historical science by the process of eking
out somewhat their intuitions and their schooling and
their prejudices, when in the natural sciences, as we see
every day, an infinity of patience and comparison of evidence is needed to get at durable generalizations.

The real drawback in Arnold's case is that he lacked the
scientific gift in his own department. Even in his special province of literature, on which he has done some
excellent writing and said many admirable things, he is
arbitrary in his tastes, and methodless in his criticism.
Very characteristic is his way of supporting his plea for
an English Literary Academy. In order to show that the
French Academy has fostered temperance and purity in
French style, he sets an admittedly florid passage of
Jeremy Taylor against an admittedly chaste passage from
Bossuet; he picks out some of the coarsest sentences of
Burke; and he compares what he confesses to be an extra
trite sentence from Addison with a telling sentence from
Joubert. Now, that, to use his own phraseology, is the
method of the Barbarian and the Philistine, not the method
of culture, which, in literary matters, is scientifically
comparative. On his plan of selection you could prove any
proposition you pleased, the negative as easily as the
affirmative.
    It is the reverse of surprising that a critic with such
habits should fall into glaring self-contradictions. In
the essay, A Guide to English Literature, he writes that
in Gray we are 'never very far from' the 'false style'
exemplified in the second last stanza of the 'Elegy.' In
his lecture on Emerson he credits Gray with 'a diction
generally pure in an age of impure diction.' Most literary men agreed in the main with Mr. Swinburne in his tra-
versing of Arnold's late dictum that the names of Wordsworth and Byron will stand highest among those of the
English poets of the century when it closes. But, as it
happens, Mr. Swinburne's vigorous depreciation of Byron
can be reinforced by Arnold's earliest explanation of how
'Byron's poetry had so little endurance in it' and is 'so
empty of matter.' And his literary affections were arbitrary as well as inconstant.

With a very different cast of mind from Emerson's,
Arnold was very like Emerson in his reliance on his pre-
possessions; and the result is that even when there is
something to be said for his thesis he leaves a careful
reader scandalised by the levity and laxity with which he
assumes he has proved it when he has only set it forth in
terms of his tastes. When he would contrast the Catholic
Church with Protestantism, to the disadvantage of the
latter, he goes airily and wittily over the British sects,
saying: 'Anglicanism suggests the English episcopate;
Calvin's name suggests Dr. Candlish; Chalmers's, the Duke
of Argyll; Channing's Boston society; but Catholicism
suggests – what shall I say – all the pell-mell of the men
and women of Shakespere's plays.' It is impossible to
make comparisons more capriciously. On the one hand we
have not even the general term Protestantism, but names of
single men put ostentatiously; on the other, a general
term of wide historical associations, which, again, are
carefully selected from. It would be just as fair to say
that Protestantism suggests all the pell-mell of men and
women in Goldsmith, Fielding, Scott, Jane Austen,
Thackeray, Dickens, George Eliot, and Hawthorne; and that
Catholicism suggests the rack, the stake, the Inquisition,
filthy monks, devout Italian assassins, sham miracles,
winking Virgins, profligate popes, and Lucrezia Borgia.

Note

1 'the odium of theology'.

61.   FREDERIC HARRISON ON MATTHEW ARNOLD, 'NINETEENTH
CENTURY'

March 1896, xxxix, 433-47

_____

Decades had passed since Arnold first attacked Harrison in
Anarchy and Authority and 'Friendship's Garland', and
Harrison seems to bear no grudges, looking back on the
period of their antagonism with a kind of pleasure. He
now reviews Arnold's entire career and finds him a literary critic who 'has no superior, indeed no rival', because
he relied upon 'a group of short, lucid, suggestive canons
of judgment'. In philosophy and theology Arnold refused

the use of similar principles and this vitiated his power
to work reforms. Harrison, a disciple of Comte to the
end, finds Arnold frequently, though unconsciously, in his
own camp, the close of 'Culture and Anarchy' 'summing up
up ... the mission of Culture, is entirely and exactly the
mission of Positivism'.

The introduction and poetry section from this essay
will be found in 'Matthew Arnold, The Poetry' (No. 41).

About Matthew Arnold as critic of literature it is needless to enlarge, for the simple reason that we have all
long ago agreed that he has no superior, indeed no rival.
His judgments on our poets have passed into current opinion, and have ceased to be discussed or questioned. It
is, perhaps, a grave loss to English literature that
Arnold was not able, or perhaps never strove, to devote
his whole life to the interpretation of our best poetry
and prose, with the same systematic, laborious, concentrated energy which has placed Sainte-Beuve at the head of
French critics. With his absorbing professional duties,
his far from austere aloofness from the whirlpool of
society, his guerilla warfare with journalism, Radicals,
theologians, and all devotees of Dagon, it was not fated
that Arnold could vie with the vast learning and Hercu-
lean industry of Sainte-Beuve. Neither as theologian,
philosopher, or publicist, was Arnold at all adequately
equipped by genius or by education for the office of
supreme arbiter which he so airily, and perhaps so
humorously, assumed to fill. And as poet, it is doubtful
whether, with his Aurelian temperament and treacherous
ear, he could ever have reached a much higher rank. But
as critic of literature, his exquisite taste, his serene
sense of equity, and that genial magnanimity which prompted him to give just value for every redeeming quality of
those whom he loved the least - this made him a consummate critic of style. Though he has not left us an exhaustive review of our literature, as Sainte-Beuve has
done for France, he has given us a group of short, lucid,
suggestive canons of judgment, which serve as landmarks
to an entire generation of critics.

The function of criticism - though not so high and
mighty as Arnold proclaimed it with superb assurance - is
not so futile an art as the sixty-two minor poets and the
11,000 minor novelists are now wont to think it. Arnold
committed one of the few extravagances of his whole life
when he told us that poetry was the criticism of life,
that the function of criticism was to see all things as

they really are in themselves - the very thing Kant told
us we could never do. On the other hand, too much of what
is now called criticism is the improvised chatter of a raw
lad, portentously ignorant of the matter in hand. It is
not the 'indolent reviewer' that we now suffer under, but
the 'lightning reviewer,' the young man in a hurry with a
Kodak, who finally disposes of a new work on the day of
its publication. One of them naïvely complained the other
morning of having to cut the pages, as if we ever suspected
that he cut the pages of more than the preface and table of
contents.

Criticism, according to Arnold's practice, if not
according to his theory, had as its duty to lay down decisive canons of cultured judgment, to sift the sound from
the vicious, and to maintain the purity of language and of
style. To do all this in any masterly degree requires most
copious knowledge, an almost encyclopaedic training in
literature, a natural genius for form and tone, and above
all a temper of judicial balance. Johnson in the last century, Hallam, and possibly Southey, in this century, had
some such gift: Macaulay and Carlyle had not; for they
wanted genius for form and judicial balance. Now Arnold
had this gift in supreme degree, in a degree superior to
Johnson or to Hallam. He made far fewer mistakes than they
did. He made very few mistakes. The touchstone of the
great critic is to make very few mistakes, and never to be
carried off his balance by any pet aversion or pet affection of his own, not to be biassed so much as a hair's
breadth by any salient merit or any irritating defect, and
always to keep an eye well open to the true proportion of
any single book in the great world of men and of affairs
and in the mighty realm of general literature.

For this reason we have so very few great critics, for
the combination of vast knowledge, keen taste and serene
judgment is rare. It is thus so hard for any young person,
for women, to become great in criticism: the young lack the
wide experience; women lack the cool judicial temper. It
is common enough to find those who are very sensitive to
some rare charm, very acute to detect a subtle quality, or
justly severe on some seductive failure. The rare power is
to be able to apply to a complicated set of qualities the
nicely adjusted compensations, to place a work, an author,
in the right rank, and to do this for all orders of merit,
with a sure, constant, unfailing touch - and without any
real or conspicuous mistake.

This is what Arnold did, at any rate for our later
poetry. He taught us to do it for ourselves, by using the
instruments he brought to bear. He did much to kill a
great deal of flashy writing, and much vulgarity of mind

that once had a curious vogue. I am myself accused of
being *laudator temporis acti,* (1) and an American newspaper
was pleased to speak of me as 'this hopeless old man'; but
I am never weary of saying, that at no epoch of our literature has the bulk of minor poetry been so graceful, so
refined, so pure; the English language in daily use has
never been written in so sound a form by so many writers;
and the current tastes in prose and verse has never been
so just. And this is not a little owing to the criticism
of Arnold, and to the ascendency which his judgment exerted over his time.

To estimate that lucidity and magnanimity of judgment
he possessed, we should note how entirely open-minded he
was to the defects of those whom he most loved, and to the
merits of those whom he chiefly condemned. His ideal in
poetry is essentially Wordsworthian, yet how sternly and
how honestly he marks the *longueurs* (2) of Wordsworth, his
flatness, his mass of inferior work. Arnold's ideal of
poetry was essentially alien to Byron, whose vulgar, slip-
shod, rhetorical manner he detested, whilst he recognised
Byron's Titanic power: 'our *soul* had felt him like the
thunder's roll.' Arnold saw all the blunders made by
Dryden, by Johnson, by Macaulay, by Coleridge, by Carlyle -
but how heartily he can seize their real merits! Though
drawn by all his thoughts and tastes towards such writers
as Sénancour, Amiel, Joubert, Heine, the Guérins, he does
not affect to forget the limitations of their influence,
and the idiosyncrasy of their genius. In these days, when
we are constantly assured that the function of criticism
is to seize on some subtle and yet undetected quality that
happens to have charmed you, and to wonder, in Delphic
oracles, if Milton or Shelley ever quite touched that
mystic circle, how refreshing it is to find Arnold always
cool, always judicial - telling us even that Shakespeare
has let drop some random stuff, and calmly reminding us
that he had not 'the sureness of a perfect style,' as
Milton had. Let us take together Arnold's summing up of
all the qualities of Wordsworth, Byron, Keats, Shelley,
and we shall see with what a just but loving hand he distributes the alternate meed of praise and blame. *Amant
alterna Camaenoe.* (3) But of all the Muses, she of criticism loves most the alternate modulation of *soprano* and
basso.

Not that Arnold was invariably right, or that all his
judgments are unassailable. His canons were always right;
but it is not in mortals to apply them unerringly to men
and to things. He seems somewhat inclined to undervalue
Tennyson, of whom he speaks so little. He has not said
enough for Shelley, perhaps not enough for Spenser, nor

can we find that he loved with the true ardour the glorious romances of Walter Scott. But this is no place, nor
can I pretend to be the man, to criticise our critic. For
my own part, I accept his decisions in the main for all
English poetry, and on general questions of style. Accept
them, that is, so far as it is in human nature to accept
such high matters; - 'errors excepted,' *exceptis excipien-
dis*. (4) The important point on which his judgment is the
most likely to be doubted or reversed by the supreme court
of the twentieth century, lies in the relative places he
has assigned to Wordsworth and to Shelley. He was by
nature akin to Wordsworth, alien to Shelley; and the 'personal equation' may have told in this case. For my own
part, I feel grateful to Arnold for asserting so well the
daemonic power of Byron, and so justly distinguishing the
poet in his hour of inspiration from the peer in his
career of affectation and vice. Arnold's piece on the
Study of Poetry, written as an introduction to the collected 'English Poets,' should be preserved in our literature
as the *norma*, or *canon* of right opinion about poetry, as
we preserve the standard coins in the Pyx, or the standard
yard measure in the old Jewel-house at Westminster.

Matthew Arnold, the philosopher, the politician, the theologian, does not prolonged notice, inasmuch as he was
anxious to disclaim any title to be ranked as any one of
the three. But he entered into many a keen debate on
philosophy, politics, and religion; and, whilst disavowing
for himself any kind of system of belief, he sate in judgment on the beliefs of others, and assured us that the
mission of Culture was to be supreme Court of Appeal for
all brutalities of the vulgar, and all immaturities of the
ignorant. Indeed, since the very definition of Culture
was 'to know the best that had ever been done and said,'
to be 'a study of perfection,' 'to see things as they
really are,' this Delphic priest of Culture was compelled
to give us oracles about all the dark problems that harass
the souls of philosophers, of politicians, and of theologians. He admitted this sacred duty, and manfully he
strove to interpret the inspirations of the God within
him. They were often charged with insight and wisdom;
they were sometimes entirely mysterious; they frequently
became a matter of language rather than of fact. But
these responses of the Deity have found no successor. Nor
does any living Mentor now attempt to guide our halting
steps into the true path of all that should be done or may
be known, with the same sure sense of serene omniscience.
Of Culture - which has so long been a synonym for our

dear lost friend - it can hardly be expected that I should
speak. I said what I had to say nearly thirty years ago,
and I rejoice now to learn from his letters that my little
piece gave him such innocent pleasure. He continued to
rejoin for years; but, having fully considered all his
words, I have nothing to qualify or unsay. We are most of
us trying to get what of Culture we can master, to see
things as they are, to know the best, to attain to some
little measure of Sweetness and Light - and we can only
regret that our great Master in all these things has carried his secret to the grave. The mystery still remains,
what is best, *how* are things really as they are, by *what*
means can we attain to perfection? Alas! the oracles are
dumb. Apollo from his shrine can no more divine.

What we find so perplexing is, that the Master, who, in
judging poetry and literature, had most definite principles, clear-cut canons of judgment, and very strict
tests of good and bad, doctrines which he was always ready
to expound, and always able to teach others, no sooner
passes into philosophy, into politics, into theology, than
he disclaims any system, principles, or doctrines of any
kind. 'Oh!' we hear him cry, 'I am no philosopher, no
politician, no theologian. I am merely telling you, in
my careless, artless way, what you should think and do in
these high matters. Culture whispers it to me, and I tell
you; and only the Philistines, Anarchs, and Obscurantists
object.' Now, it is obvious that no man can honestly dispose of all that lies *inter apices* (5) of Philosophy,
Politics, and Religion, unless he have some scheme of
dominant ideas. If he cannot range himself under any of
the known schemes, if he be neither intuitionist, experi-
mentalist, or eclectic, if he incline neither to authority,
nor to freedom, neither to revelation, nor to scepticism,
nor to any of the ways of thinking that lie between any of
these extremes - then he must have a brand-new, self-
originated, dominant scheme of his own. If he tend towards
no known system of ideas, then he tends to his own system;
and this is usually the narrowest and most capricious system that can be invented.

Not that Matthew Arnold's judgments in these things
were narrow, however personal. It would be easy to show,
if this were the place, what were the schools and orders
of thought under which he ranged himself. The idea that
he was an Ariel, a 'blessed Glendoveer,' or Mahatma of
Light, was a charming bit of playfulness that relieved the
tedium of debate. Whether as much as he fancied was
gained to the cause of Sweetness by presenting the other
side in fantastic costumes and airy caricature, by the
iteration of nicknames, and the fustigation of dummy

opponents, is now rather open to doubt. The public, and
he himself, began to feel that he was carrying a joke too
far when he brought the Trinity into the pantomime. Some
of his playmates, it is said, rather enjoyed seeing themselves on the stage, and positively played up to harle-
quin and his wand. And it was good fun to all of us to
see our friends and acquaintances in motley, capering
about to so droll a measure.

With his refined and varied learning, his natural
acuteness, and his rare gift of poetic insight, Matthew
Arnold made some admirable suggestions in general philosophy. How true, how fruitful are his sayings about
Hebraism and Hellenism, about Greece and Israel, about the
true strength of Catholicism, about Pagan and Mediaeval
religious sentiment, about Spinoza, about Butler, Marcus
Aurelius, and Goethe! All of these, and all he says about
Education, gain much by the pellucid grace and precision
with which they are presented. They are presented, it is
true, rather as the treasure-trove of instinctive taste
than as the laborious conclusions of any profound logic;
for Culture, as we have often said, naturally approached
even the problems of the Universe, not so much from the
side of Metaphysics as from the side of *Belles-Lettres*.
I can remember Matthew Arnold telling us with triumph that
he had sought to exclude from a certain library a work of
Herbert Spencer, by reading to the committee a passage
therefrom which he pronounced to be clumsy in style. He
knew as little about Spencer's 'Synthetic Philosophy' as
he did about Comte's, which he pretended to discuss with
an air of laughable superiority, at which no doubt he was
himself the first to laugh.

Arnold, indeed, like M. Jourdain, was constantly talking Comte without knowing it, and was quite delighted to
find how cleverly he could do it. There is a charming and
really grand passage in which he sums up his *conclusion* at
the close of his 'Culture and Anarchy.' I cannot resist
the pleasure of quoting this fine piece of English, every
word of which I devoutly believe:-

But for us, - who believe in right reason, in the duty
and possibility of extricating and elevating our best
self, in the progress of humanity towards perfection -
for us the framework of society, that theatre on which
this august drama has to unroll itself, is sacred; and
whoever administers it, and however we may seek to
remove them from their tenure of administration, yet
while they administer, we steadily and with undivided
heart support them in repressing anarchy and disorder;
because without order there can be no society, and
without society there can be no human perfection.

It so happens that this, the summing up of the mission of Culture, is entirely and exactly the mission of Positivism, and is even expressed in the very language used by Comte in all his writings, and notably in his 'Appeal to Conservatives' (1855). How pleasantly we can fancy Culture now meeting the Founder of Positivism in some Elysian Fields, and accosting him in that inimitably genial way: 'Ah, well! I see now that we are not so far apart, but I never had patience to read your rather dry French, you know!'

Of his Theology, or his Anti-Theology, even less need be said here. It was most interesting and pregnant, and was certainly the source of his great popularity and vogue. Here indeed he touched to the quick the Hebraism of our middle classes, the thought of our cultured classes, the insurgent instincts of the People. It was a singular mixture – Anglican divinity adjusted to the Pantheism of Spinoza – to parody a famous definition of Huxley's, it was Anglicanism *minus* Christianity, and even Theism. It is difficult for the poor Philistine to grasp the notion that all this devotional sympathy with the Psalmists, Prophets, and Evangelists, this beautiful enthusiasm for 'the secret of Jesus' and the 'profound originality' of Paul, were possible to a man whose intellect rejected the belief that there was even any probable evidence for the personality of God, or for the celestial immortality of the soul, who flatly denied the existence of miracle, and treated the entire fabric of dogmatic theology as a figment. Yet this is the truth: and what is more, this startling, and somewhat paradoxical, transformation scene of the Anglican creeds and formularies sank deep into the reflective minds of many thinking men and women, who could neither abandon the spiritual poetry of the Bible nor resist the demonstrations of science. The combination, amongst many combinations, is one that, in a different form, was taught by Comte, which has earned for Positivism the title of Catholicism *plus* Science. Matthew Arnold, who but for his father's too early death might have been the son of a bishop, and who, in the last century, would himself have been a classical Dean, made an analogous and somewhat restricted combination that is properly described as Anglicanism *plus* Pantheism.

Let us think no more of his philosophy – the philosophy of an ardent reader of Plato, Spinoza, and Goethe: of his politics – the politics of an Oxford don who lived much at the Athenaeum Club: nor of his theology – the theology of an English clergyman who had resigned his orders on conscientious grounds. We will think only of the subtle poet, the consummate critic, the generous spirit, the

radiant intelligence, whose over-ambitious fancies are
even now fading into oblivion - whose rare imaginings in
stately verse have yet to find a wider and a more discern-
ing audience.

Notes

1 'a praiser of past times'.
2 'tedious length'.
3 'Camoenoe [Roman muses] love alternate rhythms.'
4 'with due exceptions made'.
5 'between the heights'.

62. GEORGE SAINTSBURY, CONCLUSION TO 'MATTHEW ARNOLD'

1899

Saintsbury (see No. 43) had already distinguished himself
as a critic when he published his 'Matthew Arnold' (in
1899). His study is a breezy life-and-letters, but it
offers an early and acute estimate of Arnold's career.
Most of what Saintsbury has to say is summed up in his
Conclusion, which we reprint here in its entirety.
Saintsbury doubts that 'Prince Posterity' will prove kind
to Arnold's religious books; he praises the criticism,
but mostly, it seems, as the criticism grows out of
Arnold's poetic temperament. For unlike Traill and Coleridge, Saintsbury understands Arnold to have been essentially a poet. He thinks, however, that 'it is as a man
of letters, as a poet, as a critic, and perhaps most of
all as both combined, that [Arnold] ranks for history and
for the world'.

That his prose, admirable as it always is in form and
invaluable as it often is in matter, is on the whole
inferior to his verse, is by no means a common opinion,
though it was expressed by some good judges both during
his life and at the time of his death. As we have seen,
both from a chance indication in his own letters and from
Mr Humphry Ward's statement, he took very great pains
with it; indeed, internal evidence would be sufficient to

establish this if we had no positive external testimony
whatsoever. He came at a fortunate time, when the
stately yet not pompous or over-elaborated model of the
latest Georgian prose, raised from early Georgian 'drab-
ness' by the efforts of Johnson, Gibbon, and Burke, but
not proceeding to the extremes of any of the three, was
still the academic standard; but when a certain freedom
on the one side, and a certain grace and colour on the
other, were being taken from the new experiments of
nineteenth-century prose proper. Whether he or his contemporary Mr Froude was the greatest master of this particular blend is a question which no doubt had best be
answered by the individual taste of the competent. I
should say myself that Mr Froude at certain moments rose
higher than Mr Arnold ever did; nothing of the latter's
can approach that magnificent passage on the passing of
the Middle Ages and on the church-bell sound that memor-
ises it. And Mr Froude was also free from the mannerisms,
at times amounting to very distinct affectation, to which,
in his middle period more especially, Mr Arnold succumbed.
But he did not quite keep his friend's high level of distinction and *tenue*. (1) It was almost impossible for Mr
Arnold to be slipshod - I do not mean in the sense of
the composition-books, which is mostly an unimportant
sense, but in one quite different; and he never, as Mr
Froude sometimes did, contented himself with correct but
ordinary writing. If his defect was mannerism, his
quality was certain manner.

The most noticeable, the most easily imitated, and the
most doubtful of his mannerisms was, of course, the
famous iteration, which was probably at first natural, but
which, as we see from the 'Letters', he afterwards deliberately fostered and accentuated, in order, as he thought,
the better to get his new ideas into the heads of what the
type-writer sometimes calls the 'Brutish' public. That it
became at times extremely teasing is beyond argument, and
I should be rather afraid that Prince Posterity will be
even more teased by it than we are, because to him the
ideas it enforces will be, and will have been ever since
he can remember, obvious and common-place enough. But
when this and some other peccadillos (on which it is unnecessary to dwell, lest we imitate the composition-books
aforesaid) were absent or even moderately present, sometimes even in spite of their intrusion, Mr Arnold's style
was of a curiously fascinating character. I have often
thought that, in the good sense of that unlucky word 'gen-
teel,' this style deserves it far more than the style
either of Shaftesbury or of Temple; while in its different
and nineteenth-century way, it is as much a model of the

'middle' style, neither very plain nor very ornate, but
'elegant,' as Addison's own. Yet it is observable that all
the three writers just mentioned keep their place, except
with deliberate students of the subject, rather by courtesy
or prescription than by actual conviction and relish on the
part of readers: and it is possible that something of the
same kind may happen in Mr Arnold's case also, when his
claims come to be considered by other generations from the
merely formal point of view. Nor can those claims be said
to be very securely based in respect of matter. It is impossible to believe that posterity will trouble itself
about the dreary apologetics of undogmatism on which he
wasted so much precious time and energy; they will have
been arranged by the Prince's governor on the shelves, with
Hobbe's mathematics and Southey's political essays. 'But
the criticism,' it will be said, '*that* ought to endure.'
No doubt from some points of view it ought, but will it?
So long, or as soon, as English literature is intelligently
taught in universities, it is sure of its place in any
decently arranged course of Higher Rhetoric; so long, or as
soon, as critics consider themselves bound to study the
history and documents of their business, it will be read by
them. But what hold does this give it? Certainly not a
stronger hold than that of Dryden's 'Essay of Dramatic
Poesy,' which, though some of us may know it by heart, can
scarcely be said to be a commonly read classic.

The fact is - and no one knew this fact more thoroughly,
or would have acknowledged it more frankly, than Mr. Arnold
himself - that criticism has, of all literature that is
really literature, the most precarious existence. Each
generation likes, and is hardly wrong in liking, to create
for itself in this province, to which creation is so scornfully denied by some; and old critics are to all but
experts (and apparently to some of them) as useless as old
moons. Nor can one help regretting that so long a time
has been lost in putting before the public a cheap, complete, handy, and fairly handsome edition of the whole of
Mr Arnold's prose. There is no doubt at all that the
existence of such an edition, even before his death, was
part cause, and a large part of the cause, of the great and
continued popularity of De Quincey; and it is a thousand
pities that, before a generation arises which knows him
not, Mr Arnold is not allowed the same chance. As it is,
not a little of his work has never been reprinted at all;
some of the rest is difficult of access, and what there is
exists in numerous volumes of different forms, some cheap,
some dear, the whole cumbersome. And if his prose work
seems to me inferior to his poetical in absolute and perennial value, its value is still very great. Not so much

English prose has that character of grace, of elegance,
which has been vindicated for this, that we can afford to
lay aside or to forget such consummate examples of it.
Academic urbanity is not so universal a feature of our
race - the constant endeavour at least to 'live by the
law of the *peras*,' (2) to observe lucidity, to shun exaggeration, is scarcely so endemic. Let it be added, too,
that if not as the sole, yet as the chief, herald and
champion of the new criticism, as a front-fighter in the
revolutions of literary view which have distinguished the
latter half of the nineteenth century in England, Mr
Arnold will be forgotten or neglected at the peril of the
generations and the individuals that forget or neglect
him.

Little need be added about the loss of actual artistic
pleasure which such neglect must bring. Mr Arnold may
never, in prose, be read with quite the same keenness of
delight with which we read him in poetry; but he will
yield delight more surely. His manner, except in his rare
'thorn-crackling' moments, and sometimes even then, will
carry off even the less agreeable matter; with matter at
all agreeable, it has a hardly to be exaggerated charm.

But it is in his general literary position that Mr
Arnold's strongest title to eminence consists. There have
certainly been greater poets in English: I think there
have been greater critics. But as poet and critic combined, no one but Dryden and Coleridge can be for a moment
placed beside him: the fate of the false Florimel must
await all others who dare that adventure. And if he must
yield - yield by a long way - to Dryden in strength and
easy command of whatsoever craft he tried, to Coleridge
in depth and range and philosophical grasp, yet he has his
revenges. Beside his delicacy and his cosmopolitan
accomplishment, Dryden is blunt and unscholarly; beside
his directness of aim, if not always of achievement, his
clearness of vision, his almost business-like adjustment
of effort to result, the vagueness and desultoriness of
Coleridge look looser and, in the literary sense, more
disreputable than ever. Here was a man who could not only
criticise but create; who, though he may sometimes, like
others, have convicted his preaching of falsity by his
practice, and his practice of sin by his preaching, yet
could in the main make practice and preaching fit
together. Here was a critic against whom the foolish
charge, 'You can break, but you cannot make,' was confessedly impossible - a poet who knew not only the rule
of thumb, but the rule of the uttermost art. In him the
corruption of the poet had not been the generation of the
critic, as his great predecessor in the two arts, himself

secure and supreme in both, had scornfully said. Both
faculties had always existed, and did always exist, side by
side in him. He might exercise one more freely at one
time, one at another; but the author of the Preface of 1853
was a critic, and a ripe one, in his heyday of poetry, the
author of 'Westminster Abbey' was a poet in his mellowest
autumn of criticism.

And yet he was something more than both these things,
more than both of these at once. But for that unlucky divagation in the Wilderness, his life would have been the
life of a man of letters only as far as choice went, with
the duties of no dishonourable profession superadded. And
even with the divagation it was mainly and really this. To
find parallels for Mr Arnold in his unflinching devotion to
literature we must, I fear, go elsewhere than to Dryden or
to Coleridge, we must go to Johnson and Southey. And here
again we may find something in him beyond both, in that he
had an even nobler conception of Literature than either.
That he would have put her even too high, would have assigned to her functions which she is unable to discharge, is
true enough; but this is at least no vulgar error. Against
ignoble neglect, against stolid misunderstanding, against
mushroom rivalry, he championed her alike. And it was most
certainly from no base motive. If he wanted an English
Academy, I am quite sure it was not from any desire for a
canary ribbon or a sixteen-pointed star. Yet, after Southey himself in the first half of the century, who has done
so much for letters *quâ* (3) letters as Mr Arnold in the
second? His poems were never popular, and he tried no
other of the popular departments of literature. But he
wrote, and I think he could write, nothing that was not
literature, in and by the fact that he was its writer. It
has been observed of others in other kinds, that somehow or
other, by merely living, by pursuing their own arts or
crafts whatever they were, they raised those arts and
crafts in dignity, they bestowed on them as it were a rank,
a position. A few - a very few - at successive times have
done this for literature in England, and Mr Arnold was perhaps the last who did it notably in ours. One cannot
imagine him writing merely for money, for position, even
for fame - for anything but the *devoir* (4) of the born and
sworn servant of Apollo and Pallas. Such devotion need
not, of course, forbid others of their servants to try his
shield now and then with courteous arms or even at sharps -
as he tried many. But it was so signal, so happy in its
general results, so exactly what was required in and for
England at the time, that recognition of it can never be
frank enough, or cordial enough, or too much admiring.
Whenever I think of Mr Arnold it is in those own words of

his, which I have quoted already, and which I quoted to
myself on the hill by Hinksey as I began this little book
in the time of fritillaries -

 Still nursing the unconquerable hope,
 Still clutching the inviolable shade -

the hope and shade that never desert, even if they flit
before and above, the servants and the lovers of the
humaner literature.

Notes

1 'fine thinness'.
2 'goal', 'accomplishment'.
3 'as'.
4 'duty'.

Bibliography

The following is a brief list of books and articles useful for the study of Arnold's nineteenth-century reputation. *Denotes works of most importance.

*ARNOLD, MATTHEW, 'The Complete Prose Works', ed. R. H. Super (Ann Arbor, Mich., 1960-77). The essential text, with superb notes.

ARNOLD, MATTHEW, 'Culture and Anarchy', ed. Ian Gregor (The Library of Literature) (New York, 1971). Includes a useful introduction and chronology.

ARNOLD, MATTHEW, 'England and the Italian Question', ed. Merle M. Bevington (Durham, N. C., 1953). Includes Fitzjames Stephen's review.

ARNOLD, MATTHEW, 'Essays in Criticism, First Series', ed. Sister Thomas Marion Hoctor (Chicago, 1968).

ARNOLD, MATTHEW, 'Essays, Letters, and Reviews', ed. Fraser Neiman (Cambridge, Mass., 1960).

ARNOLD, MATTHEW, 'The Letters of Matthew Arnold, 1848-1888', ed. George W. E. Russell (London, 1895).

ARNOLD, MATTHEW, 'Letters of Matthew Arnold to Arthur Hugh Clough', ed. H. F. Lowry (Oxford, 1932; repr. 1968).

ARNOLD, MATTHEW, 'Unpublished Letters', ed. Arnold Whitridge (New Haven, Conn., 1923).

BROMWICH, RACHEL, 'Matthew Arnold and Celtic Literature: A Retrospect' (Oxford, 1965).

BROWN, E. K., The French Reputation of Matthew Arnold, 'Studies in English by Members of University College' (Toronto, 1931). A brief, perceptive study.

BROWN, LEONARD, Matthew Arnold's Succession: 1850-1914, 'Sewanee Review' (1934).

BUCKLER, WILLIAM E., 'Matthew Arnold's Books: Toward a Publishing Diary' (Geneva, 1958). Includes many central letters.

CONNELL, W. F., 'The Educational Thought and Influence of Matthew Arnold' (London, 1950). A fine, thorough study.

COULLING, S. M. B., 'Matthew Arnold and His Critics' (New York, 1974). Subsumes Coulling's earlier essays.
DELAURA, DAVID J., 'Hebrew and Hellene in Victorian England: Newman, Arnold and Pater (Austin, Tex., and London, 1969). Excellent on Arnold and Pater.
DELAURA, DAVID J., 'Victorian Prose: A Guide to Research' (New York, 1973). Links twentieth- with nineteenth-century discussions of Arnold.
EHRSAM, T. G., DEILY, R. H., and SMITH, R. M., 'Bibliographies of Twelve Victorian Authors' (New York, 1936). Useful, but not always accurate.
ELIOT, T. S., Matthew Arnold, 'The Use of Poetry and of Criticism' (London, 1933).
ELLEGARD, ALLVAR, 'The Readership of the Periodical Press in Mid-Victorian Britain' (Göteborg, 1957).
*FAVERTY, FREDERIC E., Matthew Arnold, 'The Victorian Poets: A Guide to Research' (Cambridge, Mass., 1968).
FAVERTY, FREDERIC E., 'Matthew Arnold the Ethnologist' (Evanston, Ill., 1951).
*HOUGHTON, WALTER, ed., 'The Wellesley Index to Victorian Periodicals, 1824-1900', i (1966), ii (1972). An invaluable source.
JUMP, JOHN, Matthew Arnold and the 'Spectator', 'Review of English Studies' (1949), xxv, 61-4.
LEFCOWITZ, A. B., Arnold's Other Countrymen: The Reputation of Arnold in America from 1853-1870 (unpublished dissertation, Boston University, 1964).
MADDEN, WILLIAM, 'Matthew Arnold: A Study of the Aesthetic Temperament in Victorian England' (Bloomington, Ind., 1967).
*MAINWARING, MARION, Matthew Arnold's Influence and Reputation as a Literary Critic (unpublished dissertation, Radcliffe College, Cambridge, Mass., 1949). A fine piece of scholarship, with a full bibliography.
RALEIGH, JOHN H., 'Matthew Arnold and American Culture' (Berkeley and Los Angeles, 1957). Emphasizes major figures, such as Henry James.
ROLL-HANSEN, DIDERIK, Matthew Arnold and the 'Academy', 'PMLA' (1953), lxviii, 384-96.
SENGUPTA, SATYAPRASAD, The Reception of Matthew Arnold as Poet and Critic, 1849-1871 (unpublished dissertation, University of London, 1961).
*SMART, THOMAS B., 'The Bibliography of Matthew Arnold' (London, 1892; partly repr. in 'Works', 1904; repr. 1968).
SMITH, PETER, and SUMMERFIELD, GEOFFREY, eds, 'Matthew Arnold and the Education of the New Order' (Cambridge, 1969).
SUPER, R.H., Matthew Arnold, 'Cambridge Bibliography of English Literature' (1969). Lists important criticism.
TRILLING, LIONEL, 'Matthew Arnold' (New York, 1949; first pub. 1939).

VOGELER, MARTHA SALMON, Matthew Arnold and Frederic
Harrison: The Prophet of Culture and the Prophet of Posi-
tivism, 'Studies in English Literature' (autumn 1962), ii,
441-62.
WILKINS, C.T., The English Reputation of Matthew Arnold
(unpublished dissertation, University of Illinois, 1959).
WILLIAMS, RAYMOND, 'Culture and Society, 1780-1950' (New
York, 1958).

Index

The index is divided into three sections: I Arnold's writings; II Arnold: topics and characteristics; III General.

II   ARNOLD: TOPICS AND CHARACTERISTICS

III   GENERAL

THE CRITICAL HERITAGE SERIES

GENERAL EDITOR: B. C. SOUTHAM

Volumes published and forthcoming